4.5

SAFe®
REFERENCE GUIDE

SAFe®

REFERENCE GUIDE

SCALED AGILE FRAMEWORK®
FOR LEAN ENTERPRISES

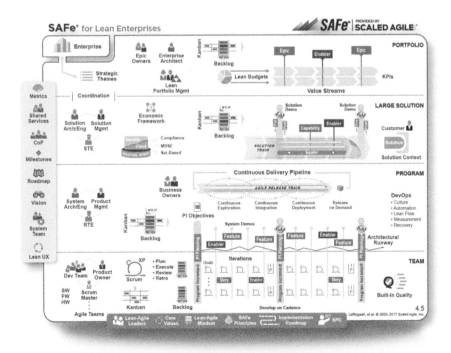

Dean Leffingwell

with Richard Knaster, Inbar Oren,
and Drew Jemilo

For information about buying this title in bulk quantities, or for special sales opportunities (which may include electronic versions; custom cover designs; and content particular to your business, training goals, marketing focus, or branding interests), please contact our corporate sales department at corpsales@pearsoned.com or (800) 382-3419.

For government sales inquiries, please contact governmentsales@pearsoned.com.

For questions about sales outside the U.S., please contact intlcs@pearson.com.

Visit us on the Web: informit.com

Library of Congress Control Number: 2017964126

ISBN-13: 978-0-13-489286-3
ISBN-10: 0-13-489286-0

1   18

Contents

Preface

On behalf of the entire Scaled Agile, Inc., team and the SAFe contributors, it's our personal pleasure to introduce *SAFe® 4.5 Reference Guide: Scaled Agile Framework® for Lean Enterprises.*

SAFe is an online, freely revealed knowledge base of proven success patterns for implementing Lean-Agile development at enterprise scale. It provides comprehensive guidance for work at the Portfolio, Large Solution, Program, and Team levels.

Why SAFe?

The world's economy, and the health and welfare of society as a whole, is increasingly dependent on software and systems. Moreover, these solutions require increasingly complex software and cyber-physical systems of unprecedented scale. The methods used to create these systems must keep pace with this new mandate. However, the assumptive, one-pass, phase-gated, waterfall methods of the past are not scaling to the new challenge. New development methods are needed. Agile shows the greatest promise, but it was developed for small teams and, by itself, does not scale to the needs of larger enterprises and the systems they create. What is truly needed is a new way of working—one that applies the power of Agile, along with the contemporary knowledge found in systems thinking and Lean product development. The Scaled Agile Framework® (SAFe®) is one such approach.

The Framework is developed and provided by Scaled Agile, Inc., where our core belief is simple: Better systems and software make the world a better place. Our mission is to assist those who build these systems through development and publication of the SAFe knowledge base, as well as accompanying certification, training, courseware, and a global network of more than 150 tooling and service partners.

As case studies on the SAFe website (www.scaledagileframework.com) show, many enterprises—large and small—are getting outstanding business results from adopting SAFe.

These results typically include:

- 30–75 percent faster time-to-market
- 25–75 percent increase in productivity
- 20–50 percent improvements in quality
- 10–50 percent increased employee engagement

As you can imagine, with results like those, SAFe is spreading rapidly around the world. The majority of *Fortune* 100 companies have certified SAFe professionals and consultants on site, as do an increasing percentage of the Global 2000.

Why a Book, When You Can Get SAFe Online?

This guide captures the knowledge base from the scaledagileframework.com website, but in book form for easy reference. It's available in paperback and eBook formats (including Kindle) at major book retailers. Like the website, it provides comprehensive guidance for work at the enterprise Portfolio, Large Solution, Program, and Team levels. It also includes the various roles, activities, and artifacts that constitute the Framework, along with the foundational elements of values, mindset, principles, and practices.

We think of *SAFe® 4.5 Reference Guide* as the ideal companion to the website. You can mark it up, scribble in the margins, read it on the plane, add sticky notes, and highlight relevant sections to make it your own. For example, the first night the version 4 book was available, a student from our Denmark SPC class downloaded the eBook to help him study for the certification exam. He came back the next morning raving about it (he passed his exam). Raves aside, we're in the training business, and we know from experience that everyone learns and connects to information in different ways. From that perspective, having SAFe captured in as many forms as possible just makes good sense.

More on SAFe

For more information, please visit scaledagileframework.com, and subscribe to the blog feed, where you can stay up-to-date with the latest developments to SAFe. Also, check out the Resources section, where you can find free posters for the SAFe Big Picture, the House of Lean, and SAFe Lean-Agile Principles. You'll also find links to SAFe videos, recorded webinars, free presentations, and more. Finally, be sure to check out our corporate site, www.scaledagile.com, where you can explore training, certification, and service options, or browse our Partner directory to find an implementation partner. Even better, attend a SAFe course (www.scaledagile.com/which-course-is-right-for-me); perhaps we will meet in person.

Our commitment is to continuously evolve SAFe to provide value to the industry—better systems, better business outcomes, better daily lives for the people who build the world's most important new systems—but only you, the adopters and practitioners, can tell us whether we have accomplished that. As we are fond of saying, "Without you, SAFe is just a website." Stay SAFe!

This book features an accompanying Web Edition. Your free copy of *SAFe® 4.5 Reference Guide, Web Edition* provides convenient access to downloads, updates, and/or corrections as they become available. Access instructions:

1. Go to informit.com/register.
2. Sign in or create a new account.
3. Enter ISBN: 9780134892863.
4. Answer a simple question as proof of purchase.
5. Click on the "Digital Purchases" tab on your Account page to access your free Web Edition.

About the Authors

Dean Leffingwell, Creator of SAFe, Chief Methodologist, Scaled Agile, Inc.
Widely recognized as the one of the world's foremost authorities on Lean-Agile best practices, Dean Leffingwell is an author, serial entrepreneur, and software and systems development methodologist. His two best-selling books, *Agile Software Requirements: Lean Requirements Practices for Teams, Programs, and the Enterprise* and *Scaling Software Agility: Best Practices for Large Enterprises*, form much of the basis of modern thinking on Lean-Agile practices and principles.

Richard Knaster, SAFe Fellow, Methodologist, and Principal Consultant, Scaled Agile, Inc.
Richard has more than 30 years' experience in software and systems development, in roles ranging from developer to executive, and has been leading large-scale Agile transformations for well over 15 years. Richard actively works on advancing SAFe's Lean-Agile methods as a SAFe Fellow and methodologist. As a principal consultant, he is passionate about helping organizations create a better environment to deliver value, improve quality and flow, and be more engaging and fun. Richard is also co-author of *SAFe Distilled: Applying the Scaled Agile Framework for Lean Software and System Engineering*.

Inbar Oren, SAFe Fellow, Methodologist, and Principal Consultant, Scaled Agile, Inc.
Inbar has more than 20 years' experience in the high-tech market. For more than a decade, he has been helping development organizations—in both software and integrated systems—improve their results by adopting Lean-Agile best practices. Previous clients include Cisco, Woolworth, Amdocs, Intel, and NCR. Inbar's current focus is on working with leaders at the Program, Value Stream, and Portfolio levels to help them bring the most out of their organizations and build new processes and culture.

Drew Jemilo, Co-founder and Principal Consultant, Scaled Agile, Inc.
Drew is a principal contributor to the Scaled Agile Framework, a consultant, and an instructor. Drew met Dean Leffingwell in early 2009 when he was developing a scaled Agile methodology for a management consulting company to bridge its strategic business framework with Agile. Since then, they have worked together with global clients to synchronize distributed teams using Agile Release Trains in the United States, Europe, and India.

Acknowledgments

SAFe Community Contributors

We are indebted to those SAFe Fellows, SAFe Program Consultant Trainers (SPCTs), and SAFe Program Consultants (SPCs) who are doing the hard and rewarding work of applying the Framework in enterprises across the globe. Many have contributed indirectly in discussions, certification workshops, LinkedIn forums, and more. More specifically, the following individuals have directly provided content that is included either here or in guidance (advanced topics) articles on the SAFe website (www.scaledagileframework.com).

(In alphabetical order by last name.)

Juha-Markus Aalto – Guidance article: "Six SAFe Practices for 'S-Sized' Teams"

Em Campbell-Pretty (SAFe Fellow) – Release Train Engineer contribution

Gillian Clark (SPCT) – Advanced topic: "Lean Software Development in SAFe"

Charlene Cuenca (SPCT) – Guidance article: "Enterprise Backlog Structure and Management"

Gareth Evans (SPCT) – Guidance article: "Lean Software Development in SAFe"

Fabiola Eyholzer (SPC) – Guidance article: "Agile HR with SAFe: Bringing Lean-Agile People Operations into the 21st Century"

Jennifer Fawcett (SAFe Fellow) – Product Manager and Product Owner contribution and focus

Ken France (SPCT) – Guidance article: "Mixing Agile and Waterfall Development in the Scaled Agile Framework"

Harry Koehnemann (SAFe Fellow) – Lean Systems Engineering and Achieving Regulatory and Industry Standards Compliance with SAFe Whitepaper

Laanti Maarit (SPCT) – "Lean-Agile Budgeting" guidance and white paper

Steven Mather (SPC) – SAFe 2.0 glossary draft

Steve Mayner (SAFe Fellow) – Guidance article: "Achieving Regulatory and Industry Standards Compliance"

Isaac Montgomery (SPCT) – SAFe Toolkits

Colin O'Neill, (SPC) – SAFe 1.0–2.5 contributor

Scott Prugh (SPC) – Guidance article: "Continuous Delivery"

Mark Richards (SAFe Fellow) – Technical and Business Metrics input for SAFe guidance articles and future SAFe releases

Al Shalloway (SPC) – Concept development and community support

Ian Spence (SAFe Fellow) – Guidance article: "Right-Sizing Features for PIs"

Carl Starendal (SPCT) – RTE course product owner

Joe Vallone (SPCT) – SAFe Scrum Master and SAFe Advanced Scrum Master product owner

Eric Willeke (SAFe Fellow) – Guidance articles: "The Role of PI Objectives" and a "Lean Perspective on SAFe Portfolio Limits"

Alex Yakyma (SPC) – SAFe 1.0–4.0 core Framework content development

Yuval Yeret (SPCT) – Guidance article: "Invitation-Based SAFe Implementation"

Additional Acknowledgments

Special Acknowledgment to Production Management and Graphic and Production Designers

We would like to thank our Pearson/Addison-Wesley acquisition editor Greg Doench and production manager Julie Nahil. At Scaled Agile Inc., we are grateful to Regina Cleveland, Director of Communications, and Digital Production Designers Jeff Long and Kade O'Casey.

Contributors to Agile Software Requirements

The initial concepts behind the Scaled Agile Framework were first documented in the 2007 book *Scaling Software Agility: Best Practices for Large Enterprises* by Dean Leffingwell. The Framework itself was first documented in Dean's 2011 book *Agile Software Requirements: Lean Requirements for Teams, Programs, and the Enterprise* (ASR), so it's appropriate to repeat and update the book acknowledgments here.

Thanks to the ASR reviewers, Gabor Gunyho, Robert Bogetti, Sarah Edrie, and Brad Jackson. Don Reinertsen provided permission to use elements of his book, *The Principles of Product Development Flow*. Thanks to the book's Finnish collaborators: Juha-Markus Aalto, Maarit Laanti, Santeri Kangas, Gabor Gunyho, and Kuan Eeik Tan. Alistair Cockburn, Don Widrig, Mauricio Zamora, Pete Behrens, Jennifer Fawcett, and Alex Yakyma contributed directly to book content. Many others—Mike Cottmeyer, Ryan Shriver, Drew Jemilo, Chad Holdorf, Keith Black, John Bartholomew, Chris Chapman, Mike Cohn, Ryan Martens, Matthew Balchin, and Richard Lawrence—contributed words, thoughts, or encouragement.

A Special Acknowledgment to the Agile Thought Leaders

SAFe stands on the shoulders of many who came before us, particularly the Agile thought leaders who created the industry movement. It starts with the signers of the Agile Manifesto and continues with those outspoken thought leaders who have helped move the industry toward the new paradigm. The following people have contributed most directly to our understanding of Agile development: Kent Beck, Alistair Cockburn, Ron Jeffries, Mike Cohn, David Anderson, Jeff Sutherland, Martin Fowler, Craig Larman, Ken Schwaber, Scott Ambler, and Mary and Tom Poppendieck. Still others are acknowledged in the Bibliography.

A Special Acknowledgment to the Lean Leaders

In extending Agile to the enterprise and developing the broader Lean-Agile paradigm, we are fortunate to stand on the shoulders of Lean thought leaders as well, including Don Reinertsen, Jeffrey Liker, Taiichi Ohno, Eli Goldratt, Dr. Alan Ward, Jim Sutton, Michael Kennedy, Dantar Oosterwal, Steve Womack, and Daniel Jones. Still others are acknowledged in the Bibliography.

And to W. Edwards Deming

Finally, where would we be without the seminal works of W. Edwards Deming, to whom we perhaps owe the deepest gratitude of all? He was a visionary and systems thinker, whose tireless quest for the underlying truths and unwavering belief in people and continuous improvement led to a set of transformational theories and teachings that changed the way we think about quality, management, and leadership.

Introduction to the Scaled Agile Framework (SAFe)

The Scaled Agile Framework® (SAFe®) for Lean Enterprises is a freely available knowledge base for people building the world's most important software and systems. This scalable and configurable framework helps organizations deliver new products, services, and solutions in the shortest sustainable lead time, with the best possible quality and value. It synchronizes alignment, collaboration, and delivery for multiple Agile teams.

SAFe combines the power of Agile with Lean product development and systems thinking. An extensive body of knowledge, SAFe is based on Lean-Agile principles and values. It provides guidance for the roles, responsibilities, artifacts, and activities necessary to achieve better business outcomes.

The Big Picture

The SAFe website—scaledagileframework.com—features an interactive 'Big Picture' graphic, which provides an overview of the Framework. Each icon on this graphic is clickable and links to a supporting article and related resources. The site also includes a variety of guidance articles, case studies, downloads, presentations, and videos, as well as a glossary that can be automatically translated into multiple languages.

SAFe allows organizations to adapt the Framework to their business context. It supports smaller-scale solutions employing 50–125 practitioners, as well as complex systems that require thousands of people.

The Configurations

SAFe supports the full range of development environments with four 'out-of-the-box' configurations, as illustrated in Figure 1.

- Essential SAFe

- Large Solution SAFe

- Portfolio SAFe

- Full SAFe

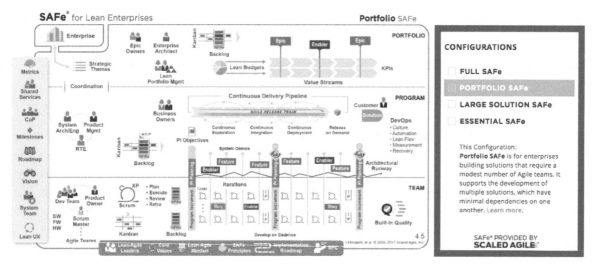

Figure 1. Configurable SAFe

Each configuration is described in the following sections.

Essential SAFe

The Essential SAFe configuration (Figure 2) is the heart of SAFe and is the simplest starting point for implementation. The basic building block for all other SAFe configurations, it describes the most critical elements needed to realize the majority of the Framework's benefits.

Together, the Team and Program levels form an organizational structure called the Agile Release Train (ART), where Agile teams, key stakeholders, and other resources are dedicated to an important, ongoing solution mission.

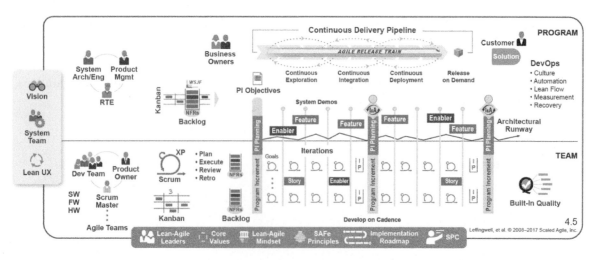

Figure 2. Essential SAFe

Highlights of Essential SAFe

The Essential SAFe configuration provides the fundamental elements of the Framework:

- The ART aligns management, teams, and stakeholders to a common mission through a single vision, roadmap, and program backlog.

- ARTs deliver the features (user functionality), and the enablers (technical infrastructure), needed to provide value on a sustainable basis.

- Team iterations are synchronized and use the same duration and start and end dates.

- Each ART delivers valuable and tested system-level increments every two weeks.

- Program Increments (PIs) provide longer, fixed timebox increments for planning, execution, and inspecting and adapting.

- Solutions can be released on demand, during, or at the end of a PI, based solely on the needs of the business. Frequent or continuous integration of the work from all teams is the ultimate measure of progress.

- ARTs use face-to-face PI planning to assure collaboration, alignment, and rapid adaptation.

- ARTs build and maintain a Continuous Delivery Pipeline used to regularly develop and release small increments of value.

- ARTs provide common and consistent approaches to user experience through Lean UX principles and practices.

- DevOps, which is a mindset, culture, and set of technical practices, provides for communication, integration, automation, and close cooperation among all the people needed to plan, develop, test, deploy, release, and maintain a solution.

The following roles help align multiple teams to a shared mission and vision, with the necessary coordination and governance:

- **System Architect/Engineer** – This individual or small cross-disciplinary team truly applies systems thinking. This role defines the overall architecture of the system, helps distinguish Nonfunctional Requirements (NFRs), determines the primary elements and subsystems, and identifies the interfaces and collaborations among them.

- **Product Management** – The Product Managers provide the internal voice of the customer and work with Product Owners and customers to understand and communicate their needs, define system features, and participate in validation. They are responsible for the program backlog and prioritize features and enablers using an economic approach.

- **Release Train Engineer (RTE)** – The RTE is a servant leader and the chief Scrum Master for the ART. This role helps improve the flow of value in the program using various mechanisms such as the Program Kanban, Inspect and Adapt (I&A) workshop, PI Planning, and more.

- **Business Owners** – This small group of stakeholders has the primary business and technical responsibility for fitness for use, governance, and return on investment for a solution developed by an ART. They are critical ART stakeholders and actively participate in certain ART events.

- **Customer** – The customer is the ultimate decider of value. Customers are an integral part of the Lean-Agile development process and value stream who have specific responsibilities for solution development.

Three primary activities help coordinate the ART:

1. **PI Planning** – A cadence-based, face-to-face planning event, PI planning serves as the heartbeat of the ART, aligning all of its teams to a common mission.

2. **System Demo** – The System Demo provides an integrated view of new features for the most recent iteration delivered by all the teams in the ART. Each demo provides ART stakeholders with an objective measure of progress during a PI.

3. **Inspect and Adapt** – This is a significant event for an ART, in which the current state of the solution is demonstrated and evaluated. Teams then reflect and identify improvement backlog items via a structured problem-solving workshop.

Portfolio SAFe

The Portfolio SAFe configuration (Figure 3) helps align portfolio execution to the enterprise strategy by organizing Agile development around the flow of value through one or more value streams. It provides business agility through the principles and practices of portfolio strategy and investment funding, Agile portfolio operations, and Lean governance.

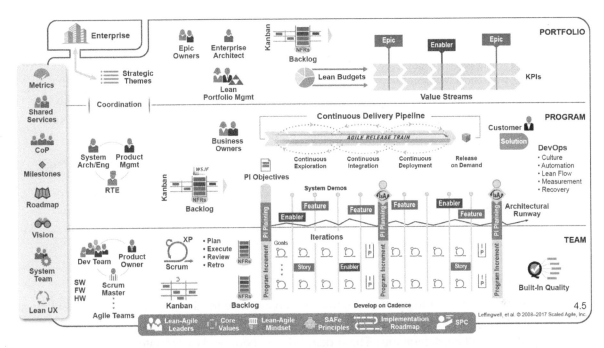

Figure 3. Portfolio SAFe configuration

Organizing the Lean-Agile enterprise around the flow of value through one or more development value streams, the portfolio aligns strategy to execution. Lean budgeting and governance practices help assure that investments will provide the benefits that the enterprise needs to meet its strategic objectives. In the large enterprise, there may be multiple SAFe portfolios.

Portfolio SAFe Highlights

This configuration builds on Essential SAFe by adding the following Portfolio-level concerns:

- **Lean Budgets** – Lean budgeting allows fast and empowered decision-making, with appropriate financial control and accountability.

- **Value Streams** – Every value stream has funding for the people and resources necessary to build solutions that deliver the value to the business or customer. Each is a long-lived series of steps (system definition, development, and deployment) that build and deploy systems that provide a continuous flow of value.

- **Portfolio Kanban** – This element makes the work of the portfolio visible and creates Work-in-Process (WIP) limits to assure that demand matches the actual value stream capacities.

The following roles provide the highest level of accountability and governance, including the coordination of multiple value streams:

- **Lean Portfolio Management (LPM)** – This function represents the individuals with the highest level of decision-making and financial accountability for a SAFe portfolio. This group is responsible for three primary areas: strategy and investment funding, Agile portfolio operations, and Lean governance.

- **Epic Owners** – Epic Owners take responsibility for coordinating portfolio epics through the Portfolio Kanban system.

- **Enterprise Architect** – This person or group of people work across value streams and programs to help provide the strategic technical direction that can optimize portfolio outcomes. The Enterprise Architect often acts as an epic owner for enabler epics.

Large Solution SAFe

The Large Solution SAFe configuration (Figure 4) is appropriate for developing the largest and most complex solutions that typically require multiple Agile Release Trains (ARTs) and suppliers but do not require Portfolio-level considerations. These demands are commonly encountered in industries like aerospace, defense, automotive, and government, where the large solution—not portfolio governance—is the primary concern.

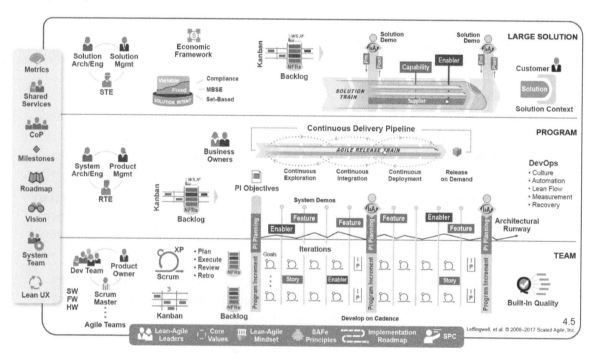

Figure 4. Large Solution configuration

Large Solution Highlights

This configuration builds on Essential SAFe by adding the following Large Solution–level concerns:

- **Solution Train** – The key organizational element of the Large Solution level, the Solution Train aligns the people and the work around a common solution vision, mission, and backlog.

- **System Team** – This internal or external organization develops and delivers components, subsystems, or services that help solution trains offer solutions to their customers.

- **Economic Framework** – This element provides financial boundaries for the Solution Train's decision-making.

- **Solution Intent** – A repository for current and future solution behaviors, the Solution Intent can be used to support verification, validation, and compliance. It is also used to extend built-in quality practices with system engineering disciplines, including Set-Based Design (SBD), Model-Based Systems Engineering (MBSE), Compliance, and Agile architecture.

- **Solution Context** – This element describes how the system will interface and be packaged and deployed in its operating environment.

- **Solution Kanban** – This element facilitates the flow of capabilities and enablers for the solution.

The following roles help align multiple ARTs and suppliers to a common mission and vision, with the necessary coordination and governance:

- **Solution Architect/Engineer** – This individual or small team defines a common technical and architectural vision for the solution under development.

- **Solution Management** – The people filling this role have the content authority for the Large Solution level. They work with customers to understand their needs, create the solution vision and roadmap, define requirements (capabilities and enablers), and guide work through the Solution Kanban.

- **Solution Train Engineer (STE)** – The STE is a servant leader and coach who facilitates and guides the work of all ARTs and suppliers.

Three major activities help coordinate multiple ARTs and suppliers:

1. **Pre- and Post-PI Planning** – These events are used to prepare for, and follow up after, PI Planning for individual ARTs and suppliers in a Solution Train.

2. **Solution Demo** – This demo is where the results of all the development efforts from multiple ARTs—along with the contributions from suppliers—are integrated, evaluated, and made visible to customers and other stakeholders.

3. **Inspect and Adapt (I&A)** – In this significant event, the current state of the value stream's solution is demonstrated and evaluated. Representatives of multiple ARTs and suppliers then reflect and identify improvement backlog items in a structured problem-solving workshop.

Full SAFe

The Full SAFe configuration (Figure 5) is the most comprehensive version of the Framework. It supports enterprises that build and maintain large, integrated solutions that require the efforts of hundreds of people or more and includes all levels of SAFe: Team, Program, Large Solution, and Portfolio. In the largest enterprises, multiple instances of various SAFe configurations may be required.

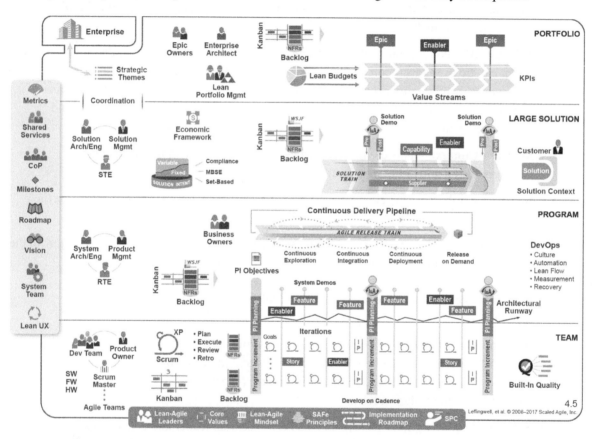

Figure 5. Full SAFe configuration

Full SAFe Highlights

The Full SAFe configuration (Figure 5) builds on Essential SAFe by adding the Portfolio and Large Solution levels. It offers the following benefits:

-   Enables organizations to combine multiple instances of various SAFe configurations
-   Provides the most comprehensive and robust configuration to meet the needs of the largest enterprises

SAFe's configurable framework provides just enough guidance to meet the needs of a product, service, or organization. An enterprise can start simply with Essential SAFe and yet have the ability to grow as its needs evolve over time. Each of these configurations is supported by 'spanning palette' and 'foundation' elements, as shown in Figures 6 and 7, respectively.

The Spanning Palette

The spanning palette contains various roles and artifacts that may be applicable to a specific team, program, large solution, or portfolio context. A key element of SAFe's flexibility and configurability, the spanning palette permits organizations to apply only those elements needed for their configuration.

Figure 6 illustrates two versions of the spanning palette: The one on the left is used for the Essential SAFe configuration, while the one on the right is used for all other configurations. However, since SAFe is a framework, enterprises can apply any of the elements from the larger spanning palette to Essential SAFe.

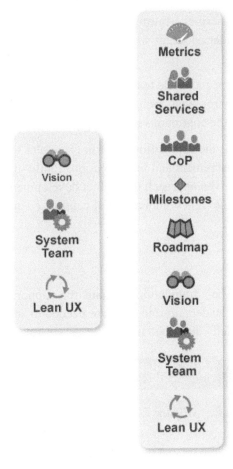

Figure 6. Spanning palette

Following is a brief description of each spanning palette element:

- **Metrics** – The primary measure of progress in SAFe is objective evidence of working solutions. In addition, SAFe defines numerous intermediate and long-term measures that teams, trains, and portfolios can use to evaluate progress.

- **Shared services** – Some specialty roles may be necessary for the success of an ART but may not be dedicated full time to any specific train.

- **Community of Practice (CoP)** – A CoP is an informal group of team members and other experts acting within the context of a program or enterprise who share practical knowledge in one or more relevant domains.

- **Milestones** – Milestones represent planned and specific goals or events. They can include fixed-date milestones, Program Increment milestones, and learning milestones.

- **Roadmap** – The Roadmap communicates the planned deliverables and milestones over a timeline.

- **Vision** – The Vision describes a future view of the solution to be developed, reflecting customer and stakeholder needs, as well as the features and capabilities proposed to address those needs.

- **System Team** – This special Agile team provides assistance in building and using the Agile development environment, including continuous integration and test automation, and other practices of the continuous delivery pipeline.

- **Lean UX** – Lean UX is the application of Lean principles to user experience design. Through constant measurement and learning loops (build–measure–learn), it uses an iterative, hypothesis-driven approach to product development. In SAFe, Lean UX is applied at scale, with the right combination of centralized and decentralized UX design and implementation.

The Foundation

As illustrated in Figure 7, SAFe's foundation contains the supporting principles, values, mindset, implementation guidance, and leadership roles that are needed to successfully deliver value at scale. Each foundation element is briefly described next.

Figure 7. SAFe foundation

- **Lean-Agile leaders** – Management has the ultimate responsibility for business outcomes. As a result, leaders must be trained in, and become trainers of, these leaner ways of thinking and operating. Lean-Agile leaders are lifelong learners and teachers. They understand and embrace Lean and Agile principles and practices.

- **Core values** – Four core values define the belief system of SAFe: alignment, built-in quality, transparency, and program execution. These are described in more detail in the following section.

- **Lean-Agile Mindset** – The Lean-Agile Mindset is the combination of beliefs, assumptions, and actions of SAFe leaders and practitioners who embrace the concepts of the Agile Manifesto and Lean thinking.

- **SAFe Principles** – These nine fundamental truths, beliefs, and economic concepts inspire and inform the roles and practices that make SAFe effective.

- **SAFe Implementation Roadmap** – Implementing the changes necessary to become a Lean enterprise requires a substantial shift in thinking and practices for most companies. SAFe provides an implementation roadmap to guide organizations on this journey.

- **SAFe Program Consultants (SPCs)** – SPCs are change agents who combine their technical knowledge of SAFe with an intrinsic motivation to improve their company's software and systems development processes.

Core Values

SAFe's core values define the ideals and beliefs that are essential to applying the Framework. They act as guides to help people know where to put their focus and how to help companies determine whether they are on the right path to fulfill their business goals. Each core value is briefly described next.

1. **Alignment** – When management and teams are aligned to a common mission, all the energy is directed toward helping the customer. Everyone is on the same team, working toward the same goals. Alignment communicates the intent of the mission and enables teams to focus on how to accomplish it. Alignment occurs when everyone in the portfolio, and every team member on every ART, understand the strategy and the part they play in delivering it.

2. **Built-in quality** – The economic impact of poor quality is much higher at scale. Built-in quality practices increase customer satisfaction and provide faster, more predictable value delivery. They also improve the ability to innovate and take risks. Without built-in quality, the Lean goal of obtaining the maximum value in the shortest sustainable lead time cannot be achieved. Built-in quality practices also ensure that each solution element, at every increment, achieves appropriate quality standards throughout.

3. **Transparency** – "You can't manage a secret." Transparency builds trust. Trust, in turn, is essential for performance, innovation, risk-taking, and relentless improvement. Large-scale solution development is hard: Things don't always work out as planned. Creating an environment where 'the facts are always friendly' (for example, sharing progress and information openly across all organizational levels) is key to building trust and improving performance. It enables fast, decentralized decision-making and higher levels of employee empowerment and engagement.

4. **Program execution** – To achieve broader change, the entire development value stream—from concept to release—must become leaner and more responsive to change. Traditional organizational structures and practices were built for control and stability; they were not specifically designed to support innovation, speed, and agility. Implementing workarounds, such as tiger teams, project-based organizations, and taskforces, cannot overcome these constraints. Simply put, the majority of organizations cannot break through the thick walls of functional silos. Instead, SAFe delivers value by creating stable (long-lived) teams-of-Agile-teams, in the form of an Agile Release Train.

LEARN MORE

[1] http://scaledagileframework.com/about

[2] Kotter, John P. *Accelerate: Building Strategic Agility for a Faster-Moving World.* 2014.

Part 1
The SAFe Foundation

 Lean-Agile Leaders | Core Values | Lean-Agile Mindset | SAFe Principles | Implementation Roadmap | SPC

scaledagileframework.com

Lean-Agile Leaders

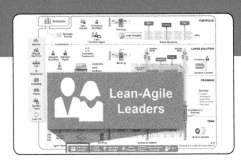

It's not enough that management commit themselves to quality and productivity, they must know what it is they must do.

Such a responsibility cannot be delegated.

　—W. Edwards Deming

Lean-Agile Leaders are lifelong learners who are responsible for the successful adoption of SAFe and the results it delivers. They empower and help teams build better systems by learning, exhibiting, teaching, and coaching SAFe's Lean-Agile principles and practices.

The philosophy of SAFe is simple: As the enablers for the teams, the ultimate responsibility for the adoption, success, and ongoing improvement of Lean-Agile development lies with an organization's managers, leaders, and executives. Only they can change and continuously improve the systems in which everyone operates. Therefore, leaders must be trained in—and become trainers of—these leaner ways of thinking and operating. As Deming notes, "such a responsibility cannot be delegated." Many enterprises that adopt SAFe will need to offer a new style of leadership, one that genuinely teaches, empowers, and engages individuals and teams to reach their highest potential.

Details

SAFe Lean-Agile Leaders are lifelong learners and teachers who help teams build better systems through understanding and exhibiting the Lean-Agile Mindset and SAFe Principles. These leaders take the following actions.

#1 – Lead the Change

The work of steering an organization toward Lean and Agile behavior, habits, and results cannot be delegated. Instead, Lean-Agile leaders exhibit *urgency for change*, communicate that urgency, and build a plan for successful transformation. Leaders must also understand and manage the change process, and address problems quickly as they arise. Adopting Principle #2, Apply systems thinking, is critical to the success of the SAFe Implementation Roadmap.

#2 – Know the Way; Emphasize Lifelong Learning

Create an environment that promotes learning. Encourage team members to build relationships with customers and suppliers and expose them to other worldviews. Strive to learn and understand new developments in Lean, Agile, and contemporary management practices. Create and foster formal and informal groups for learning and improvement. Eagerly read from the recommended reading list and on other topics. Share selected readings with others and sponsor book club events for the most relevant texts.

Allow people to solve their problems. Help them identify a given problem, understand the causes, and build solutions that will be embraced by the organization. Support individuals and teams when they make mistakes—otherwise, learning is not possible.

#3 – Develop People

Employ a Lean leadership style, one that focuses on developing skills and career paths for team members rather than on being a technical expert or a coordinator of tasks. Create a team whose members are jointly responsible for success. Learn how to solve problems together in a way that develops people's capabilities and increases their engagement and commitment. Respect people and culture.

#4 – Inspire and Align with Mission; Minimize Constraints

Provide a mission and vision, with minimum specific work requirements. Eliminate demotivating policies and procedures. Build Agile teams and trains organized around value. Understand the power of self-organizing, self-managing teams. Create a safe environment for learning, growth, and mutual influence. Build an Economic Framework for each Value Stream and teach it to everyone.

#5 – Decentralize Decision-Making

(See Principle #9 for further discussion.)

Establish a decision-making framework. Empower others by setting the mission, developing people, and teaching them to problem-solve. Take responsibility for making and communicating strategic decisions—those that are infrequent, have long-lasting effects, and have significant economies of scale decentralize all others.

#6 – Unlock the Intrinsic Motivation of Knowledge Workers

(See Principle #8 for further discussion.)

Understand the role that compensation plays in motivating knowledge work. Create an environment of mutual influence. Eliminate any and all management by objectives (MBOs) that cause internal competition. Revamp personnel evaluations to support Lean-Agile principles and values. Provide purpose and autonomy; help workers achieve mastery of new and increasing skills. Apply Agile human resources (HR) principles and practices.

Role of the Development Manager

Aligned with the principles of Lean and Agile development, SAFe emphasizes the value of nearly autonomous, self-organizing, cross-functional teams and Agile Release Trains (ARTs). This supports a leaner management infrastructure, with more empowered individuals and teams and faster, local decision-making. In this environment, traditional, day-to-day employee instruction and activity direction are no longer required.

All employees still need someone to assist them with career development, however. Set and manage expectations and compensation, and provide the active coaching they need to advance their technical, functional, individual, and team skills and career goals. Recognize that all employees also have a right to serve as integral members of a high-performing team.

Self-organizing ARTs do not fund themselves or define their mission—that remains a management responsibility since it is an element of implementing the strategy. Much of this traditionally rests with the role of the *development manager*. The adoption of Lean-Agile development does not eliminate the need for sound management. However, in SAFe, the management role is assumed by those who can adapt, thrive, and grow in this new environment.

Responsibilities

The development manager (or engineering manager, for system development) is a manager who exhibits the principles and practices of Lean-Agile leadership as described in the preceding sections. Further, the manager has personal responsibility for the coaching and career development of direct reports, takes responsibility for eliminating impediments, and actively evolves the systems in which all knowledge workers operate. The manager also has final accountability for effective value delivery. These responsibilities are summarized next.

Personnel and Team Development

- Attract, recruit, and retain capable individuals
- Build high-performance teams; establish mission and purpose for individuals and teams
- Perform career counseling and personal development
- Listen and support teams in problem identification, root cause analysis, and decision-making
- Participate in defining and administering compensation, benefits, and promotions
- Eliminate impediments and evolve systems and practices in support of Lean-Agile development
- Take subtle control in assignment of individuals to teams; address issues that teams cannot unblock; make personnel changes where necessary

- Evaluate performance, including team input; provide input, guidance, and corrective actions

- Serve as an Agile coach and advisor to Agile teams

- Remain close enough to the team to add value and to be a competent manager; stay far enough away to let them problem-solve on their own

Program Execution

- Help in building Agile milestones and roadmaps, as well as the building plans that enable them

- Help develop, implement, and communicate the economic framework

- Participate in Inspect and Adapt workshops; support teams by helping them remove systemic impediments and implementing continuous improvement backlog items

- Protect teams from distractions and unrelated or unnecessary work

- Assist the Release Train and Solution Train Engineers with PI Planning readiness and Pre- and Post-PI Planning activities

- Participate in PI planning, System Demo, and Solution Demo

- Build partnerships with suppliers, subcontractors, consultants, partners, and internal and external stakeholders

- Provide other resources as necessary for teams and ARTs to successfully execute their vision and roadmap

- Reinforce the Essential SAFe practices

- Identify delays in the system by facilitating or participating in value stream mapping

Alignment

- Work with Release Train and Solution Train Engineers and stakeholders to help ensure alignment and execution of Strategic Themes

- Work with the System Architect/Engineer, Product Managers, and Product Owners to establish explicit content authority

- Continuously assist in aligning teams to the system mission and vision

- Help ensure the engagement of Business Owners, Shared Services, and other stakeholders

Transparency

- Create an environment where the 'facts are always friendly'

- Provide freedom and safety so individuals and teams are free to innovate, experiment, and even fail on occasion

- Communicate openly and honestly with all stakeholders

- Keep backlogs and information radiators fully visible to all

- Value productivity, quality, transparency, and openness over internal politics

Built-in Quality

- Incrementally adopt the Built-in Quality practices for software, hardware, and firmware

- Understand, teach, or sponsor technical skills development in support of high-quality code, components, systems, and solutions

- Foster Communities of Practice

- Understand, support, and apply Agile architecture and Lean User Experience (UX)

LEARN MORE

[1] Liker, Jeffrey and Gary L. Convis. *The Toyota Way to Lean Leadership: Achieving and Sustaining Excellence through Leadership Development.* McGraw-Hill, 2011.

[2] Manifesto for Agile Software Development. http://agilemanifesto.org/.

[3] Reinertsen, Donald. *The Principles of Product Development Flow: Second Generation Lean Product Development.* Celeritas Publishing, 2009.

[4] Rother, Mike. *Toyota Kata: Managing People for Improvement, Adaptiveness, and Superior Results.* McGraw-Hill, 2009.

Core Values

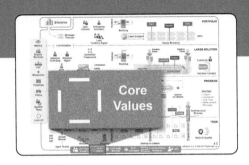

Find people who share your values, and you'll conquer the world together.

   —*John Ratzenberger*

The four *Core Values* of *alignment*, *built-in quality*, *transparency*, and *program execution* are the fundamental beliefs that are key to SAFe's effectiveness. These guiding principles help dictate behavior and action for everyone who participates in a SAFe portfolio.

Details

SAFe is broad and deep and based on both Lean and Agile principles. That's its foundation—but what are its beliefs?

SAFe upholds four Core Values: *alignment*, *built-in quality*, *transparency*, and *program execution*. These values are illustrated in Figure 1 and described in the following sections.

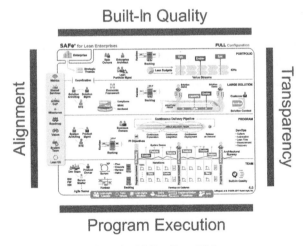

Figure 1. SAFe Core Values

Alignment

Like cars out of alignment, misaligned companies can develop serious problems. They are hard to steer, and they don't respond well to changes in direction [1]. Even if it's clear where everyone thinks they're headed, the vehicle is unlikely to get them there.

Alignment is needed to keep pace with fast change, disruptive competitive forces, and geographically distributed teams. While empowered Agile teams are good (even great), the responsibility for strategy and alignment cannot rest with the combined opinions of the teams, no matter how good they are. Instead, alignment must rely on the enterprise business objectives. Here are some of the ways how SAFe supports alignment:

- It starts with strategy and investment decisions at the portfolio and is reflected in Strategic Themes and the Portfolio Backlog. In turn, this informs the Vision, Roadmap, and backlogs at all level of SAFe. Continuous Exploration gathers the inputs and perspectives from a diverse group of stakeholders and information sources to ensure that the items in the backlogs contain economically prioritized and refined work that is ready for teams to implement. All work is visible, debated, resolved, and transparent.

- SAFe is supported by clear lines of content authority, starting with the portfolio and then resting primarily with the Product and Solution Management roles and extending to the Product Owner role.

- PI Objectives and Iteration Goals are used to communicate expectations and commitments.

- Cadence and synchronization are applied to ensure that things stay in alignment, or that they drift only within reasonable economic and time boundaries.

- Architectures and user experience guidance and governance help ensure that the Solution is technologically sound, robust, and scalable.

- Economic prioritization keeps stakeholders engaged in a continuous, agreed-to, rolling-wave prioritization, based on the current context and evolving facts.

Alignment, however, does not imply or encourage top command and control. Just the opposite, in fact: Alignment enables autonomy and decentralized decision-making, allowing those who implement value to make better local decisions.

Built-in Quality

W. Edwards Deming famously said, "Inspection does not improve the quality, nor guarantee quality. Inspection is too late. The quality, good or bad, is already in the product. Quality cannot be inspected into a product or service; it must be built into it."

Built-in Quality ensures that every increment of the solution reflects quality standards. Quality is not 'added later.' Building quality in is a prerequisite of Lean and flow; without it, the organization will likely operate with large batches of unverified, unvalidated work. Excessive rework and slower velocities are likely to be the unhappy results. There can be no ambiguity about the importance of built-in quality in large-scale systems: It is mandatory.

Software

Put simply, *'you can't scale crappy code.'* The Agile Manifesto certainly focused on quality: "Continuous attention to technical excellence and good design enhances agility" [2]. Addressing software quality in the face of rapid change requires evolving effective practices, and Extreme Programming (XP) inspires much of the framework's guidance:

- Test-First: Test-Driven Development (TDD), Acceptance Test-Driven Development (ATDD), and Behavior-Driven Development (BDD)
- Continuous Integration and Continuous Deployment
- Refactoring
- Pair work
- Collective ownership

Hardware

Coding concerns aside, no one can scale crappy components or systems, either. Hardware elements—electronics, electrical, fluidics, optics, mechanical, packaging, thermal, and many more—are a lot less 'soft.' Errors here can introduce a much higher cost of change and rework. To avoid this, the following practices are recommended:

- Frequent design cycles and integration [3]
- Collaborative design practices
- Model-Based Systems Engineering (MBSE)
- Set-Based Design (SBD)
- Investment in development and test infrastructure

System Integration

Eventually, different components and subsystems—software, firmware, hardware, and everything else—must collaborate to provide effective solution-level behaviors. The following practices support solution-level quality:

- Frequent system- and solution-level integration
- Solution-level testing of functional and Nonfunctional Requirements
- System and Solution Demos

Compliance

Enterprises use SAFe to build some of the world's largest and most important systems, many of which have unacceptable social or economic costs of failure. Protecting the public often requires applying extensive regulatory or customer oversight and rigorous compliance requirements. To that end, SAFe enterprises that build high-assurance systems define their approved practices, policies, and procedures in a *Lean Quality Management System (QMS)*. Such a system is intended to ensure that development activities and outcomes comply with all relevant regulations and quality standards, as well as provide the required documentation to prove it.

In contrast, most Agile development teams typically do not create the same formal artifacts. Instead, they use the team backlog, persistent test cases, and the code itself to document system behavior. However, in the compliance context, it is clear that an organization needs to develop and maintain a Software Requirements Specification (SRS) to support verification and validation without it. The mere fact that an SRS is needed does not necessarily mandate that it be created up-front, in a large batch. That is, the required documentation and artifacts can be incrementally built by Agile teams, as part of the regular flow of work, using Agile tooling and automation, whenever possible. For example, Agile tools can be used to generate an SRS or traceability matrix.

Transparency

Solution development is hard. Things may go wrong or not work out as planned. Without openness, facts can be obscured and result in decisions based on speculative assumptions and lack of data. No one can fix a secret.

For that outcome, *trust* is needed, because without trust no one can build high-performance teams and programs, or build (or rebuild) the confidence needed to make and meet reasonable commitments. Trust exists when one party can confidently rely on another to act with integrity, particularly in times of difficulty. Without trust, working environments are a lot less fun and motivating.

Building trust takes time. Transparency is an enabler of trust, provided through several practices:

- Executives, portfolio managers, and other stakeholders can see the Portfolio Kanban and program backlogs, and they have a clear understanding of the PI objectives for each ART or Solution Train.

- ARTs have visibility into the team's backlogs as well other program backlogs.

- Teams and programs commit to short-term, visible commitments that they routinely meet.

- Inspect and Adapt workshops with all relevant stakeholders create a backlog of improvement items from lessons learned.

- Teams and Agile Release Trains (ARTs) can see portfolio business and enabler epics. They have visibility into new initiatives.

- Progress is based on objective measures of working solutions.

- Everyone can understand the velocity and Work in Progress (WIP) of the teams and programs; strategy and the ability to execute are visibly aligned.

Program Execution

Of course, none of the rest of SAFe matters if teams cannot execute and continuously deliver value. Therefore, SAFe places an intense focus on working systems and business outcomes. History shows us that while many enterprises start the transformation with Agile teams, they often become frustrated as those teams struggle to deliver more substantial amounts of solution value reliably and efficiently.

That is the purpose of the ART, and that is why SAFe focuses implementation initially at the Program Level. In turn, the ability of Value Streams to deliver value depends on the ability of the ARTs and Solution Trains.

Fortunately, with *alignment*, *transparency*, and *built-in quality* on the team's side, they have a little 'wind at their back.' That enables a focus on *execution*. And if they struggle—and they will, because complex solution development is *hard*—they can rely on the Inspect and Adapt workshops to close the loop and execute better and better during each Program Increment.

Of course, program execution cannot just be a team-based, bottom-up thing. Successful Lean-Agile development at scale requires the active support of Lean-Agile Leaders, who couple their leadership with an orientation toward customer results. In turn, that creates a persistent and meaningful context for the teams and their stakeholders.

That's the way the successful teams and programs are doing it, and that's why they are getting the many benefits—employee engagement, productivity, quality, and time-to-market—that Lean-Agile enterprises so enjoy.

LEARN MORE

[1] Labovitz, George H., and Victor Rosansky. *The Power of Alignment: How Great Companies Stay Centered and Accomplish Extraordinary Things.* Wiley, 1997.

[2] Manifesto for Agile Software Development. http://AgileManifesto.org.

[3] Oosterwal, Dantar P. *The Lean Machine: How Harley-Davidson Drove Top-Line Growth and Profitability with Revolutionary Lean Product Development.* Amacom, 2010.

Lean-Agile Mindset

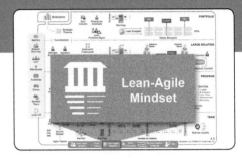

It all starts with a Lean-Agile Mindset.

   —SAFe authors

The *Lean-Agile Mindset* is the combination of beliefs, assumptions, and actions of SAFe leaders and practitioners who embrace the concepts of the Agile Manifesto and Lean thinking. It's the personal, intellectual, and leadership foundation for adopting and applying SAFe principles and practices.

SAFe is based on three bodies of knowledge: Agile development, systems thinking, and Lean product development [1].

Agile development provides the tools needed to empower and engage teams to achieve unprecedented levels of productivity, quality, and engagement. Nevertheless, a broader and deeper Lean-Agile mindset is required to support Lean and Agile development at scale across the entire enterprise. Therefore, there are two primary aspects of a Lean-Agile mindset:

- **Thinking Lean** – Lean thinking is illustrated by the SAFe House of Lean (Figure 1). In this graphical depiction, the roof of the house represents the goal of delivering value. The pillars embody respect for people and culture, flow, innovation, and relentless improvement to support the goal. Lean leadership provides the foundation on which everything stands.

- **Embracing agility** – SAFe is built entirely on the skills, aptitude, and capabilities of Agile teams and their leaders. The Agile Manifesto provides a value system and set of principles that are fundamental to the mindset for successful Agile development.

Understanding and applying this knowledge helps create the Lean-Agile mindset, part of a new management approach and an enhanced company culture. It provides the leadership needed to drive a successful SAFe transformation, helping individuals and businesses achieve their goals.

Details

The SAFe House of Lean

Initially derived from Lean manufacturing, the principles and practices of Lean thinking as applied to software, product, and systems development are now deep and extensive [2]. For example, Ward [3], Reinertsen [4], Poppendieck,[5], Leffingwell [6], and others have described aspects of Lean thinking, placing many of the core principles and practices in a product development context. Along with these, we present the SAFe House of Lean, as illustrated in Figure 1, inspired by the houses of Lean from Toyota and others.

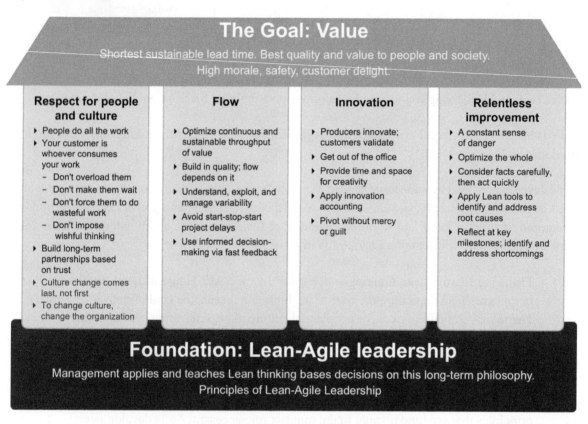

Figure 1. The SAFe House of Lean

The Goal – Value

The goal of Lean is to deliver the maximum customer value in the shortest sustainable lead time while providing the highest possible quality to customers and society as a whole. High morale, safety, and customer delight are additional goals and benefits.

Pillar 1 – Respect for People and Culture

A Lean-Agile approach doesn't implement itself or perform any real work—people do. Respect for people and culture is a basic human need. When they are treated with respect, people are empowered to evolve their practices and improve. Management challenges people to change and may steer them toward better ways of working. However, it's the teams and individuals who learn problem-solving and reflection skills and are accountable for making the appropriate improvements [1].

The driving force behind this new behavior is culture, which requires the enterprise and its leaders to change first. The principle of respect for people and culture should also extend to relationships with suppliers, partners, customers, and the broader community that supports the enterprise.

Where there is an urgency for positive change, improvement of culture is possible. First, understand and implement the SAFe values and principles. Second, deliver winning results. Eventually, the culture will change naturally.

Pillar 2 – Flow

The key to successfully executing SAFe is to establish a continuous flow of work that supports incremental value delivery based on constant feedback and adjustment. Continuous flow enables faster value delivery, effective Built-In Quality practices, relentless improvement, and evidence-based governance.

The principles of flow are an essential part of the Lean-Agile Mindset. They include understanding the full Value Stream, visualizing and limiting Work in Process (WIP), and reducing batch sizes and managing queue lengths. Additionally, Lean focuses on identifying and continuously removing delays and waste (non-value-added activities).

Lean-Agile principles provide a better understanding of the system development process, incorporating new thinking, tools, and techniques that leaders and teams can use to move from a phase-gated approach to DevOps and a Continuous Delivery Pipeline that extends flow to the entire value delivery process.

Pillar 3 – Innovation

Flow builds a solid foundation for value delivery. Without innovation, though, both product and process will steadily decline. To support this critical part of the SAFe House of Lean, Lean-Agile Leaders engage in the following practices:

- Get out of the office and into the actual workplace where the value is produced and products are created and used (known as *gemba*). As Taiichi Ohno put it, "No useful improvement was ever invented at a desk."

- Provide time and space for people to be creative, enabling purposeful innovation, which can rarely occur in the presence of 100 percent utilization and daily firefighting. SAFe's Innovation and Planning Iteration is one such opportunity.

- Apply Continuous Exploration—the process of constantly exploring the market and user needs and defining a Vision, Roadmap, and set of Features that address those needs.

- Apply innovation accounting [7]. Establish nonfinancial, non-vanity Metrics that provide fast feedback for innovation.

- Validate the innovation with customers, then pivot without mercy or guilt when the hypothesis needs to change.

Pillar 4 – Relentless Improvement

The fourth pillar, relentless improvement, encourages learning and growth through continuous reflection and process enhancements. A constant sense of competitive danger drives the company to pursue improvement opportunities aggressively. Leaders and teams do the following:

- Optimize the whole, not the parts, of both the organization and the development process.

- Consider facts carefully, then act quickly.

- Apply Lean tools and techniques to determine the root cause of inefficiencies and apply effective countermeasures rapidly.

- Reflect at key milestones to openly identify and address the shortcomings of the process at all levels.

Foundation – Leadership

The foundation of Lean is leadership, a key enabler for team success. The ultimate responsibility for the successful adoption of the Lean-Agile approach lies with the enterprise's managers, leaders, and executives. According to Deming, "Such a responsibility cannot be delegated" to Lean-Agile champions, working groups, a Program Management Office (PMO), process teams, outside consultants, or any other party [8]. Therefore, leaders must be trained in these new and innovative ways of thinking and exhibit the principles and behaviors of Lean-Agile leadership.

Lean thinking is similar to, but somewhat different than, Agile. It was initially introduced as a team-based process that tended to exclude managers. Unfortunately, that doesn't scale. In Lean-Agile development, by contrast, managers become leaders who embrace the values of Lean, are competent in the basic practices, proactively eliminate impediments, and take an active role in driving organizational change and facilitating unrelenting improvement.

The Agile Manifesto

In the 1990s, responding to the many challenges of waterfall processes, some lighter-weight and more iterative development methods emerged. In 2001, many of the leaders of these frameworks came together in Snowbird, Utah. While there were differences of opinion on the specific merits of one method over another, the attendees agreed that their shared values and beliefs dwarfed the differences. The result was a Manifesto for Agile Software Development—a turning point that clarified the new approach and started to bring the benefits of these innovative methods to the whole development industry [9]. The Manifesto consists of the value statement shown in Figure 2 and the set of principles shown in Figure 3.

The values of the Agile Manifesto

We are uncovering better ways of developing software by doing it and helping others do it.

Through this work we have come to value:

Individuals and interactions over processes and tools

Working software over comprehensive documentation

Customer collaboration over contract negotiation

Responding to change over following a plan

That is, while there is value in the items on the right, we value the items on the left more.

Figure 2. Values of the Agile Manifesto (Source: agilemanifesto.org)

The Principles of the Agile Manifesto

1. Our highest priority is to satisfy the customer through early and continuous delivery of valuable software.

2. Welcome changing requirements, even late in development. Agile processes harness change for the customer's competitive advantage.

3. Deliver working software frequently, from a couple of weeks to a couple of months, with a preference for the shorter timescale.

4. Business people and developers must work together daily throughout the project.

5. Build projects around motivated individuals. Give them the environment and support they need, and trust them to get the job done.

6. The most efficient and effective method of conveying information to and within a development team is face-to-face conversation.

7. Working software is the primary measure of progress.

8. Agile processes promote sustainable development. The sponsors, developers, and users should be able to maintain a constant pace indefinitely.

9. Continuous attention to technical excellence and good design enhances agility.

10. Simplicity—the art of maximizing the amount of work not done—is essential.

11. The best architectures, requirements, and designs emerge from self-organizing teams.

12. At regular intervals, the team reflects on how to become more effective, then tunes and adjusts its behavior accordingly.

Figure 3. Principles of the Agile Manifesto (Source: agilemanifesto.org)

Along with the various practices, the Agile Manifesto provides the foundation for empowered, self-organizing teams. SAFe extends this foundation to teams-of-Agile-teams, applying Lean thinking to understand and relentlessly improve the systems that support their critical work.

LEARN MORE

[1] Knaster, Richard, and Dean Leffingwell. *SAFe Distilled: Applying the Scaled Agile Framework for Lean Software and Systems Engineering.* Addison-Wesley, 2017.

[2] Womack, James P., Daniel T. Jones, and Daniel Roos. *The Machine That Changed the World: The Story of Lean Production—Toyota's Secret Weapon in the Global Car Wars That Is Revolutionizing World Industry.* Free Press, 2007.

[3] Ward, Allen, and Durward Sobeck. *Lean Product and Process Development.* Lean Enterprise Institute, 2014.

[4] Reinertsen, Donald G. *The Principles of Product Development Flow: Second Generation Lean Product Development.* Celeritas, 2009.

[5] Poppendieck, Mary, and Tom Poppendieck. *Implementing Lean Software Development: From Concept to Cash.* Addison-Wesley, 2006.

[6] Leffingwell, Dean. *Agile Software Requirements: Lean Requirements Practices for Teams, Programs, and the Enterprise.* Addison-Wesley, 2011.

[7] Ries, Eric. *The Lean Startup: How Today's Entrepreneurs Use Continuous Innovation to Create Radically Successful Businesses.* Crown Business, 2011.

[8] Deming, W. Edwards. *Out of the Crisis.* MIT Center for Advanced Educational Services, 1982.

[9] Manifesto for Agile Software Development. http://agilemanifesto.org/.

SAFe Principles Overview

The impression that 'our problems are different' is a common disease that afflicts management the world over. They are different, to be sure, but the principles that will help to improve the quality of product and service are universal in nature.

—W. Edwards Deming

SAFe is based on nine immutable, underlying Lean and Agile Principles (Figure 1). These tenets and economic concepts inspire and inform the roles and practices of SAFe.

#1 – Take an economic view

#2 – Apply systems thinking

#3 – Assume variability; preserve options

#4 – Build incrementally with fast, integrated learning cycles

#5 – Base milestones on objective evaluation of working systems

#6 – Visualize and limit WIP, reduce batch sizes, and manage queue lengths

#7 – Apply cadence, synchronize with cross-domain planning

#8 – Unlock the intrinsic motivation of knowledge workers

#9 – Decentralize decision-making

Figure 1. SAFe Lean-Agile Principles

Why the Focus on Principles?

Building enterprise-class software and cyber-physical systems is one of the most complex challenges our industry faces today. For example:

- Building such software and systems requires millions of lines of code
- It combines complex hardware and software interactions
- It crosses multiple concurrent platforms
- It must satisfy demanding and unforgiving Nonfunctional Requirements (NFRs)

And, of course, the enterprises that build these systems are also increasingly sophisticated. They are bigger and more distributed than ever. Mergers and acquisitions, distributed multinational (and multilingual) development, offshoring, and rapid growth are all part of the solution—and part of the problem.

Fortunately, we have an amazing and growing body of knowledge that can help. It includes Agile principles and methods, Lean and systems thinking, product development flow practices, and Lean processes. Thought leaders have traveled this path before us and left a trail of breadcrumbs for us to follow, in the form of hundreds of books and references to draw on.

The goal of SAFe is to synthesize this body of knowledge, along with the lessons learned from hundreds of deployments. This creates a system of integrated, proven practices that can improve employee engagement, time-to-market, solution quality, and team productivity. Given the complexities discussed earlier, however, no off-the-shelf solution can possibly satisfy the unique challenges each enterprise faces. Some tailoring and customization may be required, as not every SAFe recommended practice will apply equally in every circumstance. This is why we work hard to ensure that SAFe practices are grounded in fundamentally stable principles. That way we can be confident they'll apply in most situations.

And when those practices do fall short, the underlying principles can guide the teams to make sure that they are moving continuously on the path to the goal of the House of Lean: "shortest sustainable lead time, with best quality and value to people and society." There is value in that, too.

SAFe practices are based on nine concepts that have evolved from Agile principles and methods, Lean product development, systems thinking, and observation of successful enterprises. Each is described in detail in an article by that principle's name. In addition, the embodiment of the principles appears throughout the Framework. They are summarized in the following sections.

#1 – Take an Economic View

Delivering the best value and quality for people and society in the shortest sustainable lead time requires a fundamental understanding of the economics of building systems. It's critical that everyday decisions are made in a proper economic context. The primary aspects include developing and communicating the strategy for incremental value delivery and creating the Economic Framework. This defines the trade-offs between risk, Cost of Delay (CoD), and operational and development costs, while supporting decentralized decision-making.

#2 – Apply Systems Thinking

Deming observed that the problems faced in the workplace require an understanding of the systems that workers use. Moreover, a system is complex. It has many interrelated components (people and processes) that have defined, shared goals. To improve, everyone must understand and commit to the purpose of the system; that is, optimizing one component does not optimize the whole. In SAFe, systems thinking is applied to the organization that builds the system, as well as to the system under development. Systems thinking also acknowledges how that system operates in its end-user environment.

#3 – Assume Variability; Preserve Options

Traditional design and life cycle practices encourage choosing a single design-and-requirements option early in the development process. Unfortunately, if that starting point proves to be the wrong choice, then future adjustments will take too long and can lead to a suboptimal long-term design. A better approach is to maintain multiple requirements and design options for a longer period in the development cycle. Empirical data is then used to narrow the focus, resulting in a design that creates better economic outcomes.

#4 – Build Incrementally with Fast, Integrated Learning Cycles

Develop solutions incrementally in a series of short iterations. Each iteration results in an integrated increment of a working system, and subsequent iterations build on the previous ones. Increments allow fast customer feedback and risk mitigation. They also may become minimum viable products (MVPs) or prototypes for market testing and validation. In addition, these early, fast feedback points help the organization determine when to 'pivot,' where necessary, to an alternate course of action.

#5 – Base Milestones on Objective Evaluation of Working Systems

Business owners, developers, and customers have a shared responsibility to ensure that investment in new solutions will deliver economic benefit. The sequential, phase-gate development model was designed to meet this challenge, but experience shows that it does not mitigate risk as intended. In Lean-Agile development, integration points provide objective milestones at which to evaluate the solution frequently and throughout the development life cycle. This regular evaluation provides the financial, technical, and fitness-for-purpose governance needed to assure that a continuing investment will produce a commensurate return.

#6 – Visualize and Limit WIP, Reduce Batch Sizes, and Manage Queue Lengths

Lean enterprises strive to achieve a state of continuous flow, in which new system capabilities move quickly and visibly from concept to cash. There are three keys to implementing flow:

1. Visualize and limit the amount of work in process (WIP) to limit demand to actual capacity

2. Reduce the batch sizes of work to facilitate fast and reliable flow through the system

3. Manage queue lengths to reduce the wait times for new capabilities

#7 – Apply Cadence, Synchronize with Cross-Domain Planning

Cadence creates predictability and provides a rhythm for development. Synchronization causes multiple perspectives to be understood, resolved, and integrated at the same time. Applying development cadence and synchronization, coupled with periodic cross-domain planning, provides the tools needed to operate effectively in the presence of uncertainty, inherent in product development.

#8 – Unlock the Intrinsic Motivation of Knowledge Workers

Lean-Agile leaders understand that ideation, innovation, and the engagement of knowledge workers cannot generally be motivated by individual incentive compensation. After all, individual objectives cause internal competition and destroy the cooperation necessary to achieve the larger aim of the system. Providing autonomy and purpose—while minimizing constraints—leads to higher levels of employee engagement, resulting in better outcomes for customers and the enterprise.

#9 – Decentralize Decision-Making

Achieving fast value delivery requires fast, decentralized decision-making. This reduces delays, improves product development flow, enables faster feedback, and creates more innovative solutions by those closest to the local knowledge. However, some decisions are strategic, are global, and have economies of scale that justify centralized decision-making. Since both types of decisions occur, creating a reliable decision-making framework is a critical step in ensuring a fast flow of value.

The nine SAFe principles are discussed in greater detail in Part 3.

LEARN MORE

[1] Leffingwell, Dean. *Agile Software Requirements: Lean Requirements Practices for Teams, Programs, and the Enterprise.* Addison-Wesley, 2011.

SAFe Implementation Roadmap Overview

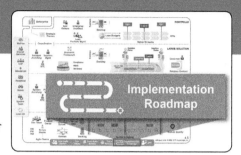

Many leaders pride themselves on setting the high-level direction and staying out of the details. But big picture, hands off leadership isn't likely to work in a change situation, because the hardest part of change—the paralyzing part—is in the details.

Any successful change requires a translation of ambiguous goals into concrete behaviors. To make a switch, you need to script the critical moves.

—Dan and Chip Heath, Switch: How to Change Things When Change Is Hard

The *SAFe Implementation Roadmap* consists of an overview graphic and 12-steps that describe a strategy and an ordered set of activities that have proved effective in successfully implementing SAFe.

Achieving the business benefits of Lean-Agile development at scale is not a trivial effort, so SAFe is not a trivial framework. Before realizing SAFe's rewards, organizations must embrace a Lean-Agile Mindset and understand and apply Lean-Agile principles. They must identify Value Streams and Agile Release Trains (ARTs), implement a Lean-Agile portfolio, build quality in, and establish the mechanisms for continuous value delivery and DevOps. And, of course, the culture must evolve as well.

Based on proven organizational change management strategies, the SAFe Implementation Roadmap graphic and article series describe the steps, or 'critical moves,' an enterprise can take to implement SAFe in an orderly, reliable, and successful fashion.

Details

To achieve the desired organizational change, leadership must "script the critical moves," as described by Dan and Chip Heath [1]. When it comes to identifying those critical moves for adopting SAFe, hundreds of the world's largest enterprises have already gone down this path, and successful adoption patterns have become clear. A fairly standard pattern is shown in Figure 1.

SAFe® Implementation Roadmap

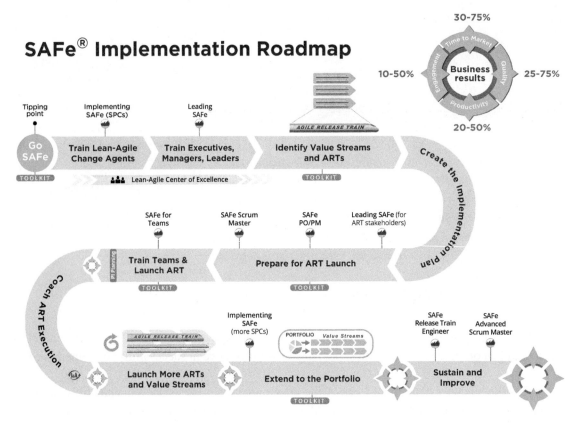

Figure 1. SAFe Implementation Roadmap

While no two adoptions are identical, and there is rarely a perfectly sequential step-by-step implementation in any enterprise, we know that businesses getting the best results typically follow a path similar to that shown in the SAFe Implementation Roadmap. It includes the following 12 steps:

1. Reach the Tipping Point

2. Train Lean-Agile Change Agents

3. Train Executives, Managers, and Leaders

4. Create a Lean-Agile Center of Excellence

5. Identify Value Streams and ARTs

6. Create the Implementation Plan

7. Prepare for ART Launch

8. Train Teams and Launch the ART

9. Coach ART Execution

10. Launch More ARTs and Value Streams

11. Extend to the Portfolio

12. Sustain and Improve

This overview serves as a launching pad for you to explore these steps in detail and understand how to apply them to your own implementation. Each step of the SAFe Implementation Roadmap is described in Part 2 of this book.

LEARN MORE

[1] Heath, Chip, and Dan Heath. *Switch: How to Change Things When Change Is Hard.* Crown Publishing Group, Kindle Edition.

[2] Knaster, Richard, and Dean Leffingwell. *SAFe Distilled: Applying the Scaled Agile Framework for Lean Software and Systems Engineering.* Addison-Wesley, 2017.

SAFe Program Consultant

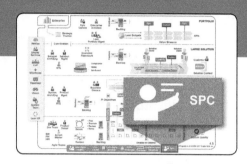

The people who are crazy enough to think they can change the world are the ones who do.

—Apple Computer

SAFe Program Consultants (SPCs) are change agents who combine their technical knowledge of SAFe with an intrinsic motivation to improve the company's software and systems development processes. They play a critical role in successfully implementing SAFe. SPCs come from numerous internal or external roles, including business and technology leaders, portfolio/program/project managers, process leads, architects, analysts, and consultants.

Details

A Critical Role for a Critical Need

As we outlined in the Implementation Roadmap series, changing the development practices and behavior of an enterprise is a significant challenge. To achieve meaningful and lasting change, author John P. Kotter notes that a "sufficiently powerful guiding coalition" of stakeholders is needed [1]. Such a coalition requires:

- Leaders who can set the vision, show the way, and remove impediments
- Practitioners, managers, and change agents who can implement specific process changes
- People with sufficient organizational credibility to be taken seriously
- The expertise needed to make fast, intelligent decisions

In enterprises new to SAFe, many of these attributes rest with trained SPCs.

Responsibilities

As knowledgeable change agents, SPCs participate in most of the activities described in the SAFe Implementation Roadmap. Specifically, they assist with:

- **Reaching the tipping point** – They communicate the business need, urgency, and vision for change.

- **Training executives, managers, and leaders** – They socialize the new concepts and provide orientation and overview training. SPCs teach Leading SAFe to leaders, managers, and stakeholders.

- **Establishing a Lean-Agile Center of Excellence (LACE)** – SPCs assist the LACE with building and executing the transformation backlog.

- **Identifying Value Streams and Agile Release Trains (ARTs)** – Working with stakeholders to understand the flow of value, SPCs identify value streams and ARTs to find those that are the most opportunistic for launch.

- **Creating the implementation plan** – SPCs participate in creating a plan for the rollout, communicate upcoming changes, and establish metrics.

- **Preparing for the ART launch** – SPCs help the LACE plan and prepare for the ART launch. They coach leadership and help facilitate the creation of new Agile Teams. They also train or outsource training of executives, leaders, development teams, and specialty roles—such as Product Owner, Product Manager, Scrum Master, and Release Train Engineer (RTE). They also assess and evolve launch and backlog readiness.

- **Training teams and launching the ART** – SPCs often directly plan and execute the SAFe Quickstart or other rollout strategies. They train or outsource training for teams and participate in initial, critical events such as Program Increment (PI) Planning and Inspect and Adapt (I&A). SPCs help establish the ART launch date and the calendar for ART and team events.

- **Coaching ART execution** – SPCs coach leaders and stakeholders to build and maintain the Vision, Roadmap, and Program Backlogs. They coach teams, Product Owners, Product Managers, Architects, and RTEs. They also participate in Scrum of Scrums and System Demo, facilitate I&A workshops, and follow up on improvement items. Finally, they help teams establish a DevOps culture and mindset, the Continuous Delivery Pipeline, infrastructure, and associated Agile technical practices.

- **Launching more ARTs and value streams** – SPCs work to enable new change agents to increase organizational capacity to support new value streams, start more ARTs, and expand the reach of the LACE. They communicate progress and highlight early accomplishments.

- **Extending to the portfolio** – Once Lean-Agile practices gain momentum, SPCs can socialize and drive portfolio practices to other areas of the company, including Lean budgets, Lean Portfolio Management, leaner approaches to CapEx and OpEx, and Agile contracts. They also communicate the value of Strategic Themes.

- **Sustaining and improving** – An enterprise can never be too Lean. SPCs take a long-term view in advancing quality, fostering a Lean-Agile approach to human resources, supporting enhanced skill development with continuing education, and establishing Communities of Practice (CoPs). They encourage self-assessments (see the discussion of Metrics) and help perform value stream mapping.

How Many SPCs Do You Need?

At first glance, the preceding list seems daunting. No single SPC could accomplish all this alone. Viewed broadly, however, the knowledge and skills of an SPC cannot be limited to a few select people. Instead, many leaders across the emerging Lean-Agile business must master these distinctive new competencies. This means most companies will need to have many SPCs (perhaps as many as 3–5 per 100 development practitioners) to drive and sustain the implementation.

Training SPCs

SPCs must be trained for their new role, acquiring the skills and tools needed to execute their responsibilities as well as to coach and teach others to implement and support the change. The best way to achieve this is to take the Implementing SAFe 4.0 with SPC4 Certification class. This four-day course prepares SPCs to become the change agents who lead the transformation. Attendees learn how to effectively apply the principles and practices of SAFe and organize, train, and coach Agile teams. They also learn how to identify value streams, design and launch ARTs, and help build and manage a Lean portfolio.

Scaling Lean-Agile across the enterprise also requires training all the people who do the work. To make this practical and cost-effective, Scaled Agile, Inc. supports a train-the-trainer, fan-out model, licensing SPCs to teach SAFe courses that support the other key roles in the implementation. This provides an affordable training strategy and supplies the trainers needed to achieve the mission of company-wide change.

I'm an SPC, Now What?

After passing an exam, attendees become certified SPCs, gaining access to a variety of helpful SPC resources (https://www.scaledagile.com/spc-resources/) to facilitate SAFe adoption. They are also licensed to teach a specific set of courses listed here: https://www.scaledagile.com/becoming-an-spc/#TrainingOthers

---

LEARN MORE

[1] Kotter, John P. *Leading Change.* Harvard Business Review Press, 1996.

Part 2

The SAFe Implementation Roadmap

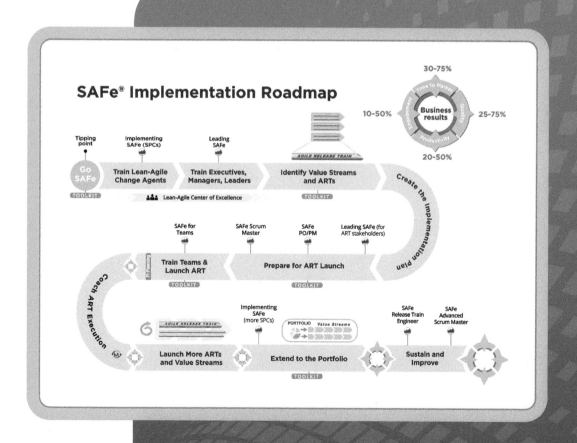

SAFe® Implementation Roadmap

Business results
- Time to Market: 30-75%
- Quality: 25-75%
- Productivity: 20-50%
- Engagement: 10-50%

Tipping point — Go SAFe
TOOLKIT

Implementing SAFe (SPCs) — Train Lean-Agile Change Agents

Leading SAFe — Train Executives, Managers, Leaders

Lean-Agile Center of Excellence

Identify Value Streams and ARTs
TOOLKIT

AGILE RELEASE TRAIN

Create the Implementation Plan

SAFe for Teams — Train Teams & Launch ART
TOOLKIT

SAFe Scrum Master / SAFe PO/PM / Leading SAFe (for ART stakeholders) — Prepare for ART Launch
TOOLKIT

Coach ART Execution

AGILE RELEASE TRAIN

Implementing SAFe (more SPCs)

PORTFOLIO Value Streams

Launch More ARTs and Value Streams

Extend to the Portfolio
TOOLKIT

SAFe Release Train Engineer / SAFe Advanced Scrum Master — Sustain and Improve

scaledagileframework.com/**implementation-roadmap**

Reaching the Tipping Point

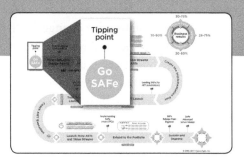

The success of any kind of social epidemic is heavily dependent on the involvement of people with a particular and rare set of social skills.

—*Malcolm Gladwell, The Tipping Point*

Changing the way of working—both the habits and the culture of a large development organization—is hard. Many enterprises report that implementing SAFe was one of the toughest, and at the same time, the most rewarding change initiatives that they had ever undertaken.

People naturally resist change, and you will often hear phrases like "That's the way we've always done it around here" or "That won't work here." Accepting change means accepting the possibility that you are not currently doing things the best way or, even worse, it may challenge a person's long-held beliefs or values.

It's easy for people to keep their old behavior—unless there is an exceptionally good reason to make such a change. A reason so compelling that the status quo becomes simply unacceptable. A reason so strong that change becomes the only reasonable way forward to success.

In other words, the enterprise must reach its 'tipping point'—the point at which the overriding organizational imperative is to achieve the change, rather than resist it [1].

Details

The Need for Change

We've observed two primary reasons that cause an organization to tip to SAFe:

- **A burning platform** – Sometimes the need to change a product or service is obvious. The company is failing to compete, and the existing way of doing business is obviously inadequate to achieve a new solution within a survivable time frame. Jobs are at stake. This is the easier case for change. While there will always be those who are resistant, they are likely to be overcome by the wave of energy that drives mandatory change through the organization.

- **Proactive leadership** – In the absence of a burning platform, leadership must drive change proactively by taking a stand for a better future state. Lean-Agile Leaders must exhibit what Toyota [2] would call "a constant sense of danger"—a never-ending sense of potential crisis that fuels continuous improvement. This is often the less obvious reason to drive change, as the people in the trenches may not see or feel the urgency to do the hard work that comes with change. After all, they are successful now—why should they assume they won't continue to be successful in the future? Isn't change risky? In this case, senior leadership must constantly impress the need for change on all, making it clear that maintaining the status quo is simply unacceptable.

Establish the Vision for Change

In any case, there must be a compelling reason for the change and a vision to go along with it. Kotter notes that establishing a "vision for change" is a primary responsibility of leadership [3]. The vision for change provides three key benefits:

- **Purpose** – It clarifies the purpose and direction for the change and sets the mission for all to follow. It avoids the confusing potential details and focuses everyone on the *why*, not the *how*, of the change.

- **Motivation** – It starts to move people in the right direction. After all, change is hard, and pain is inevitable, especially in the early going. People's jobs will change. The vision helps motivate people by giving them a compelling reason to make the change. Perhaps most importantly, it underlines the fact that there is really no job security in the status quo.

- **Alignment** – It helps start the coordinated action necessary to assure that hundreds, perhaps even thousands, of people work together toward a new—and more personally rewarding—goal. With clarity of vision, people are empowered to take the actions necessary to achieve the vision, without the constant need for management supervision or check-in.

Take an Economic View

Whether reactive or proactive, the primary reason to drive change in an organization is to realize the business and personal benefits that it's intended to deliver. SAFe Principle #1 reminds us to always take an economic view. In this context, leaders should articulate the goal of the change in terms that everyone can understand. Dozens of case studies show that enterprises can expect to see benefits in four major areas, as Figure 1 illustrates.

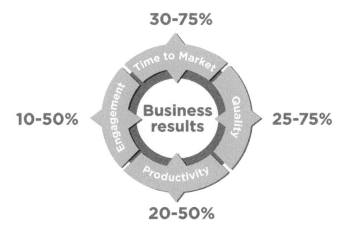

Figure 1. SAFe business benefits: improved time-to-market, quality, productivity, and employee engagement

Change leaders should communicate these intended benefits as part of the vision for the change. In addition, leaders should describe any other specific, tangible objectives they hope to accomplish. Measurable improvement on these key performance indicators will provide the fuel necessary to escape the inertia of the status quo.

Moving Forward

The next critical move is to Train Lean-Agile Change Agents.

LEARN MORE

[1] Gladwell, Malcolm. *The Tipping Point: How Little Things Can Make a Big Difference.* Little, Brown and Company, Kindle Edition.

[2] Cho, Fujio. Chairman of Toyota, 2006–2013.

[3] Kotter, John P. *Leading Change.* Harvard Business Review Press, Kindle Edition.

Train Lean-Agile Change Agents

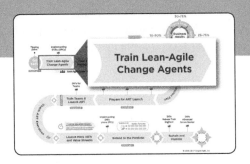

A strong guiding coalition is always needed. One with the right composition, level of trust, and shared objective.

—John Kotter

As we described in Reaching the Tipping Point, the need to adopt new practices for solution development is often driven by a burning platform—that is, a problem too severe to solve using the enterprise's current way of working. It creates the level of urgency needed to inspire significant change.

Even if that is not the case, as the pace of technological and market changes and digital disruption reshapes the modern business model, this sense of urgency has become the new norm. Now, more than ever, the ability to substantially improve development practices is the key to success. Change is at hand. For those following the proven critical moves identified in the SAFe Implementation Roadmap, this chapter describes the second step: Train Lean-Agile change agents.

Details

The Need for a Powerful Coalition

Once an organization reaches its tipping point and the rationale for a significant change becomes obvious, the difficult journey begins. In *Leading Change*, Kotter discusses eight stages of guiding organizational transformation and what it takes to make such a transformation stick [1]:

1. Establishing a sense of urgency
2. Creating the guiding coalition
3. Developing a vision and strategy
4. Communicating the change vision
5. Empowering employees for broad-based action
6. Generating short-term wins
7. Consolidating gains and producing more change
8. Anchoring new approaches in the culture

For step two, a "sufficiently powerful guiding coalition" of stakeholders is needed. As Kotter notes: "In a rapidly moving world, individuals and weak committees rarely have all the information needed to make good non-routine decisions. Nor do they seem to have the credibility or the time required to convince others to make the personal sacrifices called for in implementing changes. Only teams with the right composition and sufficient trust among members can be highly effective under these circumstances." [1]

This guiding coalition requires the following things to be effective:

- Leaders who can set the vision, show the way, and remove impediments to change
- Practitioners, managers, and change agents who can implement specific process changes
- Sufficient organizational credibility to be taken seriously
- The expertise needed to make fast, intelligent decisions

To create a SAFe coalition that is sufficiently powerful to initiate change, our experience shows that the organization must take three critical steps:

1. Train Lean-Agile change agents as SAFe Program Consultants (SPCs). They provide the knowledge and horsepower needed to implement the change.
2. Train executives, managers, and other leaders. They sponsor the change and support the implementation. Leading SAFe is a two-day course designed for this purpose.
3. Charter a Lean-Agile Center of Excellence (LACE). This working group becomes the focal point and continuous source of inspiration and energy for change management activities.

This chapter addresses the first step, which is to introduce a process that develops people who have the knowledge, skills, and resources needed to successfully implement SAFe. (Elements 2 and 3 of the guiding coalition are addressed in the next two chapters, Training Executives, Managers, and Leaders and Creating a Lean-Agile Center of Excellence, respectively.)

Develop SPCs as Change Agents

In most enterprises, the primary SAFe change agents appear on the scene as certified SPCs. Sourced internally and externally, they come from many roles:

- Trusted consulting partners
- Internal business and technology leaders

- Portfolio/program/project managers

- Architects

- Analysts

- Process leads

Their common path to success? The Implementing SAFe with SPC Certification class. This four-day course prepares SPCs to become the change agents who lead the transformation. Attendees learn how to effectively apply the principles and practices of SAFe and organize, train, and coach Agile teams. They also learn how to identify Value Streams and Agile Release Trains (ARTs), launch ARTs, and build and manage an Agile portfolio.

Scaling Lean-Agile practices across the enterprise—or any material change for that matter—requires training all the people who do the work. To make it practical and cost-effective, Scaled Agile, Inc. supports a train-the-trainer fan-out model. It licenses SPCs (either partner personnel or enterprise employees) to teach a number of SAFe courses inside the enterprise. This provides an affordable training strategy and develops the trainers needed to initiate and implement the change.

More on Implementing SAFe with SPC Certification

This intensive four-day course prepares internal change agents and external consultants to take on three rather large challenges:

- Lead an enterprise Lean-Agile transformation

- Implement SAFe

- Train managers and executives in Leading SAFe

The first two days of this class are an intensive version of Leading SAFe. The goal is to prepare certified SPCs to teach Leading SAFe (and other courses in the SAFe role-based curriculum, as described later in this section).

These change agents gain the knowledge needed to lead an enterprise-wide Agile transformation by leveraging SAFe and its underlying principles of Agile development, systems thinking, and Lean product development flow. They leave with an understanding of how the principles and practices of SAFe support Agile teams, Agile programs, Lean Portfolio Management (LPM), and Agile Architecture.

The second two days of the class demonstrate how to identify, plan, and implement SAFe. In addition, attendees learn about the briefings, artifacts, and templates needed to identify value streams, prepare the organization, launch ARTs, plan and execute major events, and implement effective processes and measures to sustain and improve the organizational transformation.

After passing an exam, attendees become certified SPCs, giving them access to a variety of helpful resources to be used in the transformation. They are also licensed to teach Leading SAFe as well as other courses in the role-based curriculum. Currently, there are three other courses:

- SAFe for Teams
- SAFe Scrum Master
- SAFe Product Owner/Product Manager

This curriculum is constantly evolving. For more, check out Implementing SAFe with SPC Certification and review the other courses at ScaledAgile.com.

Making the Next Moves

Once trained, SPCs have the knowledge, skills, and resources needed to educate and train managers, teams, and the other stakeholders necessary to effectively drive the change. They become a critical part of the sufficiently powerful coalition for change needed to drive the next critical moves:

- Training executives, managers, and leaders
- Forming or participating in the LACE
- Identifying value streams and ARTs
- Creating the implementation plan

LEARN MORE

[1] Kotter, John P. *Leading Change.* Harvard Business Review Press, Kindle Edition.

[2] Knaster, Richard, and Leffingwell, Dean. *SAFe Distilled: Applying the Scaled Agile Framework for Lean Software and Systems Engineering.* Addison-Wesley, 2017.

Train Executives, Managers, and Leaders

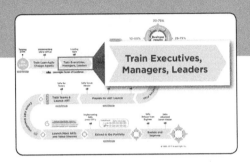

The questions is 'Does the group include enough proven leaders to be able to drive the change process?'

—John Kotter

In the previous chapter, Training Lean-Agile Change Agents, we described the three steps needed to create a guiding coalition:

1. Train a number of Lean-Agile change agents as SAFe Program Consultants (SPCs)

2. Train executives, managers, and other leaders

3. Charter a Lean-Agile Center of Excellence (LACE)

We described how SPCs—acting as change agents—can ignite transformation within an enterprise. But they alone do not constitute a "sufficiently powerful guiding coalition" for change. To create and sustain the necessary momentum, other stakeholders and senior executives must step in, step up, and lead the change.

After all, as Deming noted, "It is not enough that management commit themselves to quality and productivity, they must know what it is they must do." This chapter describes the second part of the coalition—the need and mechanism to train executives, managers, and leaders.

Details

Strong leadership is needed to successfully implement any change in an organization. In the context of SAFe, some of these leaders will provide direct and ongoing sponsorship for the change by participating in the LACE. Others will be directly involved in implementing SAFe, or leading, managing, and influencing the other players in the transformation. Their role could include participating directly in launching Agile Release Trains (ARTs), or it could mean working at higher levels to eliminate impediments that arise in the company's current governance, culture, and practices. *All* of these stakeholders need the knowledge and skills to lead—rather than follow—the implementation.

Exhibit the Lean-Agile Mindset

 To effectively implement SAFe, and to provide the inspiration for relentless improvement, the enterprise's leaders must embrace the Lean-Agile Mindset. This includes:

- **Thinking Lean** – Much of the thinking in Lean is represented in the SAFe House of Lean icon, which is organized around six key constructs. The roof represents the goal of delivering value. The pillars support that goal via respect for people and culture, flow, innovation, and relentless improvement. Lean leadership provides the foundation upon which everything else stands.

- **Embracing agility** – SAFe is built entirely on the skills, aptitude, and capabilities of Agile teams and their leaders. And while there is no one definition of what an Agile method is, the Agile Manifesto provides a unified value system that helped introduce Agile practices into mainstream development.

Putting these concepts into practice has proved to be a powerful recipe for success. Unfortunately, when leaders support the Lean-Agile mindset only through words and not actions, their efforts are quickly recognized as a half-hearted attempt at change. When leaders' actions don't match their words, the discrepancy can produce the exact opposite of the intended effect by hardening people against change. When that happens, the journey will end before it begins, without leading to the personal or economic benefits of SAFe.

Apply Lean-Agile Principles

 For an organization to successfully integrate SAFe, management must understand and reinforce its values. Leaders are expected to embrace and apply the nine principles that underlie SAFe, as highlighted in Figure 1 and in the chapter SAFe Principles.

#1 – Take an economic view

#2 – Apply systems thinking

#3 – Assume variability; preserve options

#4 – Build incrementally with fast, integrated learning cycles

#5 – Base milestones on objective evaluation of working systems

#6 – Visualize and limit WIP, reduce batch sizes, and manage queue lengths

#7 – Apply cadence, synchronize with cross-domain planning

#8 – Unlock the intrinsic motivation of knowledge workers

#9 – Decentralize decision-making

Figure 1. The SAFe Lean-Agile Principles

The Responsibilities of SAFe Lean-Agile Leaders

SAFe suggests seven specific activities, outlined in the Lean-Agile Leaders chapter, that leaders can use to improve business outcomes:

- **Lead the change** – Exhibit and express the urgency for change. Communicate the need and build a plan for successful change. Understand and manage the change process, addressing problems as they arise.

- **Know the way; emphasize lifelong learning** – Create an environment that promotes learning. Strive to learn and understand new developments in Lean, Agile, and contemporary management practices.

- **Develop people** – Employ a Lean leadership style that focuses on developing skills and career paths for team members, rather than on being a technical expert or a coordinator of tasks.

- **Inspire and align with mission; minimize constraints** – Provide the mission and vision with minimum specific work requirements. Eliminate demotivating policies and procedures. Build Agile teams and ARTs organized around Value Streams.

- **Decentralize decision-making** – Take responsibility for making and communicating strategic decisions—those that are infrequent and long-lasting, and have significant economies of scale. Decentralize all other decisions.

- **Establish a decision-making framework** – Empower others by setting the mission, developing people, and teaching problem-solving skills.

- **Unlock the intrinsic motivation of knowledge workers** – Provide purpose and autonomy. Help workers to continually master new skills.

Learning New Skills

These responsibilities raise a question: How do leaders learn these new skills? The two-day class, Leading SAFe: Leading the Lean-Agile Enterprise with the Scaled Agile Framework, is designed for this purpose.

This course teaches leaders the SAFe Lean-Agile mindset, principles and practices, and the most effective leadership values for managing the new generation of knowledge workers. They will also learn how to:

- Execute and release value through ARTs

- Build large systems with the Large Solution Level

- Build an Agile portfolio

- Lead a Lean-Agile transformation at enterprise scale

Of course, this class is just the beginning of the transformational journey. As Bill Gates reminds us, "The moment you stop learning is also the one in which you will stop leading." That's wise advice for anyone wanting the full benefits that are achievable through SAFe. To this end, the class provides a recommended reading list and many other activities and exercises to help emerging Lean-Agile Leaders master their new skills.

To test their knowledge, attendees have the opportunity to take an exam, and upon passing, become certified SAFe Agilists (SAs). This gives them access to the SAFe community platform, which hosts various assets, such as training videos and a dedicated forum for sharing knowledge.

Moving Forward

By making the first three 'critical moves,' in the SAFe Implementation Roadmap—Reaching the Tipping Point, Training Lean-Agile Change Agents, and Training Executives, Managers, and Leaders—the enterprise is launched on the path toward success. There is, however, one more step needed to complete that powerful guiding coalition: Create a Lean-Agile Center of Excellence. That is the topic of the next chapter.

LEARN MORE

[1] Knaster, Richard, and Dean Leffingwell. *SAFe Distilled: Applying the Scaled Agile Framework for Lean Software and Systems Engineering.* Addison-Wesley, 2017.

Create a Lean-Agile Center of Excellence

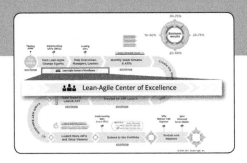

A guiding coalition that operates as an effective team can process more information, more quickly. It can also speed the implementation of new approaches because powerful people are truly informed and committed to key decisions.

—John Kotter

The Lean-Agile Center of Excellence (LACE) is a small team of people dedicated to implementing the SAFe Lean-Agile way of working. It is often one of the key differentiators between companies practicing Agile in name only and those fully committed to adopting Lean-Agile practices and getting the best business outcomes. The LACE is the third element of the "sufficiently powerful guiding coalition" for change, which is made up of three primary ingredients:

- Training a number of Lean-Agile change agents as SAFe Program Consultants (SPCs)
- Training executives, managers, and other leaders
- Creating a LACE

This chapter provides guidance on the size, structure, and operation of the LACE. It is based on our own experience, as well as the experience of others working directly in the field.

Details

In the chapters Training Lean-Agile Change Agents and Training Executives, Managers, and Leaders, we described how the organization can help change agents and leadership gain the knowledge and skills necessary to lead the transformation.

The challenge is that most of the people who are qualified to drive the change have full-time responsibilities in their current roles. While a significant portion of their time can perhaps be devoted to *supporting* the change, a smaller, more dedicated group of people is required to *drive* the transformation throughout the organization. Although these groups go by different names—the Agile Center of Excellence, Agile Working Group, Lean-Agile Transformation Team, Learning and Improvement Center—they are all staffed with people whose primary task is to implement the change.

Team Size

How many dedicated individuals does it take to create an effective LACE team and accomplish the change? In addition to the number of people, one must take into account the organizational and financial impact of assigning talented resources to the new charter. As author John P. Kotter notes: "The size of an effective coalition seems to be related to the size of the organization. Change often starts with just two or three people. The group in successful transformations then grows to half a dozen in relatively small firms or in small units of larger firms."[1]

For perspective, we've observed that in SAFe-practicing companies, small teams of four to six dedicated people can support a few hundred practitioners, while teams of about twice that size support proportionally larger groups. Beyond that, team size gets unwieldy, and a decentralized or hub-and-spoke model is typically more effective.

Responsibilities

No matter its size, a LACE typically has the following responsibilities:

- Communicating the business need, urgency, and vision for change
- Developing the implementation plan and managing the transformation backlog
- Establishing the metrics
- Conducting or sourcing training for executives, managers and leaders, development teams, and specialty roles such as Product Owner, Product Manager, Scrum Master, and Release Train Engineer
- Identifying Value Streams and helping define and launch Agile Release Trains (ARTs)
- Providing coaching and training to ART stakeholders and teams
- Participating in critical, initial events such as Program Increment (PI) Planning and Inspect and Adapt (I&A)
- Fostering SAFe Communities of Practice (CoPs)
- Communicating progress
- Implementing Lean-Agile focus days, with guest speakers, and presenting internal case studies
- Benchmarking and connecting with the external community
- Promoting continuing Lean-Agile education

- Extending Lean-Agile practices to other areas of the company, including Lean Budgets, Lean Portfolio Management, contracts, and human resources

- Helping to establish relentless improvement (see Sustain and Improve in the roadmap)

For a small team, this is a pretty significant list of responsibilities. Luckily, many of them are shared with numerous SPCs, who may or may not be regular members of the LACE.

Organization and Operation

The LACE may be a part of an organization's emerging Lean-Agile Program Management Office (Agile PMO), or it may exist as a stand-alone unit. In either case, it serves as a focal point of activity, a continuous source of energy that can help power the enterprise through the necessary changes. Additionally, since becoming a Lean-Agile enterprise is an ongoing journey, rather than a static destination, the LACE often evolves into a longer-term center for continuous improvement.

Operationally, the LACE typically functions as an Agile team and applies the same iteration and PI cadences. This allows the LACE to plan and inspect and adapt in harmony with the ARTs, serving as an exemplar for Agile team behavior. As a result, similar roles are needed:

- A Product Owner works with stakeholders to prioritize the team's transformation backlog.

- A Scrum Master facilitates the process and helps remove roadblocks.

- The team is cross-functional. Credible people from various functional organizations are integral members of the team. That allows the team as a whole to address backlog items wherever they arise, whether those items are related to organization, culture, development process, or technology.

- A 'C- level' leader typically acts as the team's Product Manager.

Mission

The LACE team needs to align its work with a common mission. An example mission statement is included in Table 1.

Lean-Agile Center of Excellence Mission Statement	
For	EMV Productions, Inc.
who	produces automated guided vehicles and amusement park rides
the	EMV Lean-Agile Center of Excellence
is a	full-time, cross-functional lean-agile change management team
that	is driving the transformation of our enterprise to a Lean-Agile way of working using the Scaled Agile Framework
Unlike	Our traditional ad-hoc transformation efforts
we	provide dedicated practitioners and the committed leadership to implement the training, process, technology, tooling, culture, and governance changes needed to achieve the business benefits of a Lean-Agile way of working

In Scope	Out of Scope	Success Criteria
▸ Communication	▸ Organizational structure changes	▸ % practitioners trained in their new roles
▸ Leadership and team training and coaching	▸ Outsourcing strategy changes	▸ % leaders trained in their new roles
▸ ART launches and coaching	▸ …	▸ # Value streams applying SAFe
▸ Agile tooling		▸ # ARTs stood up
▸ Consultant/supplier coaching and training management		▸ ARTs exhibit relentless self improvement

Table 1. Example LACE mission statement

Team Distribution

As mentioned earlier, the size of the team must be proportional to the size and distribution of the development enterprise. For smaller enterprises, a single, centralized LACE can balance speed with economies of scale. However, in larger enterprises—typically those with more than 500 to 1,000 practitioners—it's useful to consider employing either a decentralized model or a hub-and-spoke model (Figure 1).

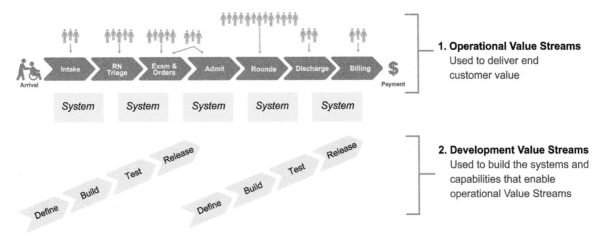

Figure 3. Operational and development value streams

- **Operational value streams** – These are the people and steps used to provide goods or services to a customer. Examples might include manufacturing a medical instrument or ordering and receiving a part from a supplier.

- **Development value streams** – These are the people and steps used to develop new products, systems, solutions, and services sold by the enterprise, or that support internal operational value streams. These value streams constitute a SAFe portfolio.

SAFe concerns itself primarily with development value streams. After all, delivering new solutions in the shortest sustainable lead time is the focus of SAFe, and value streams help us understand how to get there. However, the enterprise's operational value streams must be identified to determine the *development value streams* that support them.

Identify Operational Value Streams

For some organizations, identifying operational value streams is easy. Many are just the products, services, or solutions that the company develops and sells.

In the larger enterprise, however, the task is more complicated. Value flows through various applications, systems, and services—across many parts of the distributed organization—to both *internal* and *external* customers.

In these cases, identifying operational value streams is an essential analytical activity. Figure 4 provides a set of questions that help stakeholders through that process of identification.

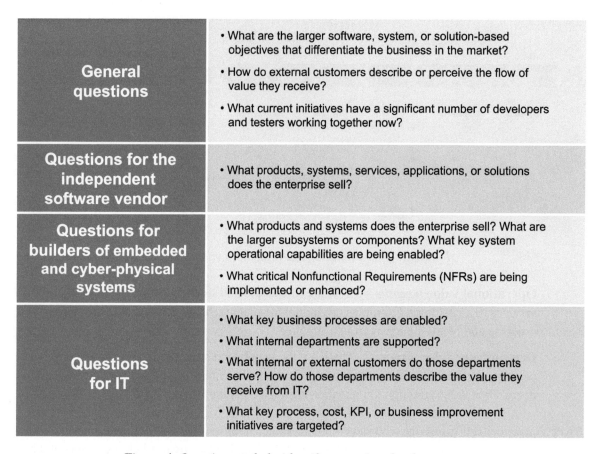

General questions	• What are the larger software, system, or solution-based objectives that differentiate the business in the market? • How do external customers describe or perceive the flow of value they receive? • What current initiatives have a significant number of developers and testers working together now?
Questions for the independent software vendor	• What products, systems, services, applications, or solutions does the enterprise sell?
Questions for builders of embedded and cyber-physical systems	• What products and systems does the enterprise sell? What are the larger subsystems or components? What key system operational capabilities are being enabled? • What critical Nonfunctional Requirements (NFRs) are being implemented or enhanced?
Questions for IT	• What key business processes are enabled? • What internal departments are supported? • What internal or external customers do those departments serve? How do those departments describe the value they receive from IT? • What key process, cost, KPI, or business improvement initiatives are targeted?

Figure 4. Questions to help identify operational value streams

Identifying operational value streams in the large enterprise is not a trivial undertaking. It requires an awareness of the organization's broader purpose and an explicit understanding of how specific elements of value flow to the customer. To assist you, we've illustrated two examples in the sections that follow—one from healthcare, and one from financial services.

Value Stream Definition Template

The *value stream definition template* can be used to further elaborate and understand the characteristics of the identified value stream. Table 1 provides an example.

Name	Consumer Loans
Description	Provides customers with unsecured / secured loans
Customer(s)	Existing retail customer
Triggers	The customer wants to borrow money and approaches the bank through any of the existing channels
Value received to enterprise	Repayment plus interest
Value received to customer	Loan

Table 1. Value stream definition template with an operational value stream example

Healthcare Provider Operational Value Stream Example

Our first operational value stream example is a healthcare network provider, as illustrated in Figure 5 [2].

As part of their further analysis, the teams decided to focus on the hospital. Specifically, they examined the value stream that represents the processes and information systems that support patient treatment—from intake through treatment and billing.

The trigger for this value stream is the arrival of a patient at the hospital. The hospital receives the full value after the patient is treated and payments are made for the services provided, as shown in Figure 6.

The people indicated at the top are the individuals who execute the various steps in the value stream.

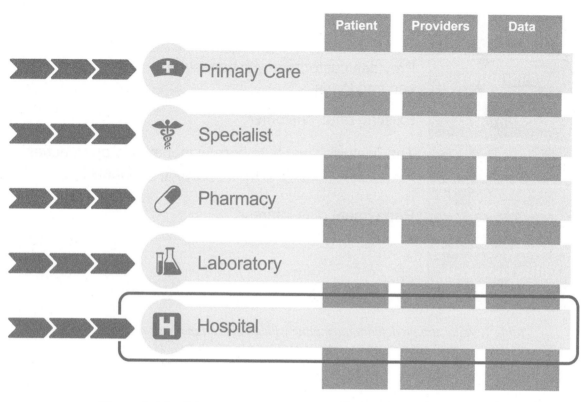

Figure 5. A healthcare network provider's operational value streams

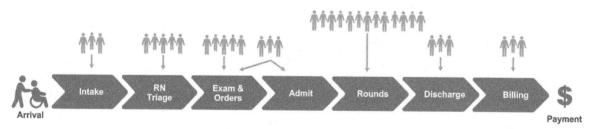

Figure 6. Steps in the patient billing value stream

Financial Services Value Stream Example

The second operational value stream example, which we will develop further, is a banking institution. Upon initial analysis, the teams determined that there were some primary value streams, as indicated in Figure 7.

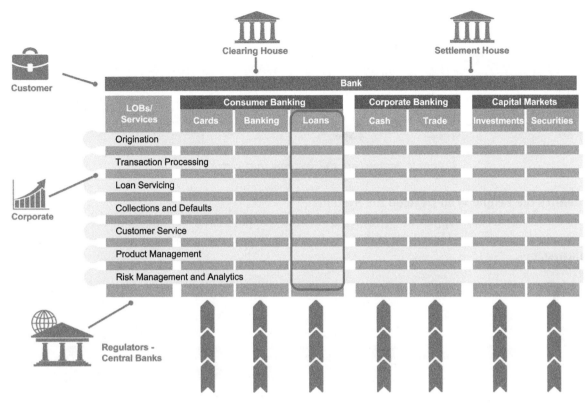

Figure 7. A bank and its operational value streams

For additional analysis, the team selected the 'consumer banking loan' value stream. This flow is triggered by the granting of a loan (origination) and ends when the customer repays the loan with interest. The team identified the steps and the people who perform them, as highlighted in Figure 8. (Note that the customer is also a direct participant in this value stream.)

Figure 8. The consumer loan value stream

Identify the Systems That Support the Value Stream

Once the operational value stream steps are identified, the next activity is to identify the systems that are developed to support the value stream. For larger value streams, it's important to map the connections from the systems to the various steps in the value stream. This creates a deeper understanding of how it all works, as illustrated for our consumer loan example in Figure 9.

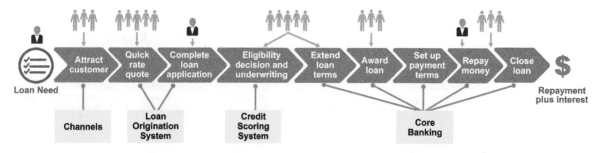

Figure 9. Identifying the systems that support the steps

Identify the People Who Develop the Systems

Once the systems that support the operational value stream have been identified, the next activity is to estimate the number and locations of the people who build and maintain those systems, as Figure 10 illustrates.

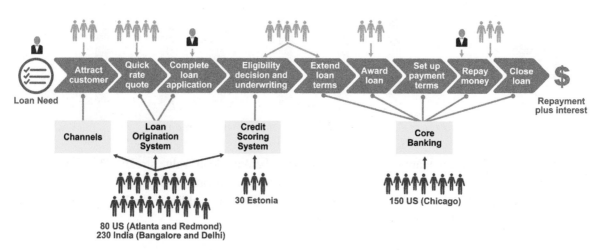

Figure 10. Identifying the people who develop the systems

Define the Development Value Streams

Next, we move to identify the development value streams, which represent the steps needed to develop those systems as well as the people who develop them. Since these are different value streams from the operational ones, we need to identify the trigger and the value. The systems support and enable better operation through the operational value streams; as such, the value comprises the new or amended features in the systems. The triggers, then, are the requirements and ideas that drive these features.

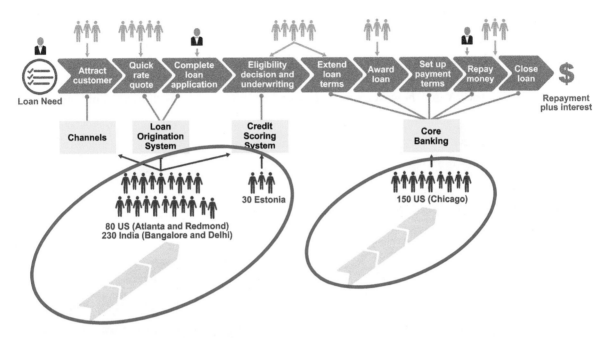

Figure 11. Defining the development value streams

We can use these triggers to identify how many development value streams we have. If most requirements necessitate touching all systems to enable the new functionality, we probably have one development value stream. In contrast, if the systems are decoupled, we might have a few of these value streams. In any case, development value streams should be mostly or wholly independent and able to develop and release by themselves, without too many intra-value stream dependencies. In the example in Figure 11, most requirements touch the first three systems or the last two but rarely touch all of them. In this case, then, we have two development value streams, each capable of developing, integrating, deploying, and releasing independently of the other.

Development Value Streams Cross Boundaries

Once the value streams are identified, the next step is to understand how to form ARTs to realize them. The ARTs contain all the people and other assets needed to enhance the flow of value. We must first understand where in the organization that value is created—because that is where the people, processes, and systems are. When doing so, it becomes obvious that development value streams cross many boundaries. Enterprises are organized the way they are for many reasons: history, functional convenience, the efficiency of centralization, acquisitions, geography, and more. As a result, it's entirely possible that no one understands the complete series of events necessary to continually develop and enhance the systems that help deliver the value. Further, attempts to improve to focus on functional, local improvements may result in optimization of one function or step but sub-optimization of the end-to-end flow.

It is the long-lived nature of value streams that triggers different thinking in the Lean organization. To address this issue, enterprises use Principle #2, Apply systems thinking and come to understand how various parts of the system need to work together to accomplish improved flow. Typically, larger enterprises are organized functionally. In addition, people are distributed across multiple geographies and multiple countries. Value, however, moves *across* these boundaries, as illustrated in Figure 12.

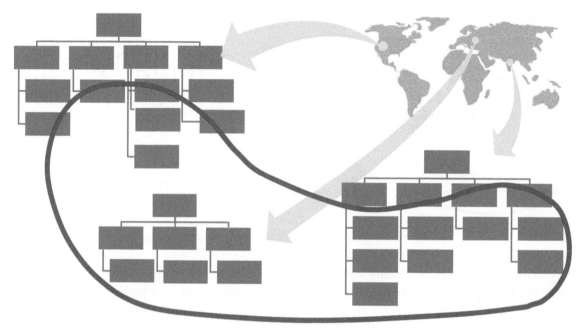

Figure 12. Value flows across functional, organizational, and geographic boundaries

Identify the ARTs

The final activity is to define the ARTs that realize the value. Experience has shown that the most effective ARTs have the following attributes:

- Supported by 50–125 people

- Focused on a holistic system or related set of products or services

- Long-lived, stable teams that consistently deliver value

- Minimal dependencies on other ARTs

- Can release value independent of other ARTs

Depending on how many people do the work, three possible ART scenarios can arise (Figure 13):

- **Multiple development value streams can fit within a single ART** – When several related products or solutions can be produced with a relatively small number of people, a single ART may deliver multiple value streams. In this case, the ART is roughly equivalent to the value stream. Everyone is on that ART!

- **A single development value stream can fit within an ART** – Often, a value stream can be realized with 100 or fewer practitioners. Many development groups are already organized into units of about that size, so this is a common case. Again, everyone is on the ART.

- **Multiple ARTs are required for large development value streams** – When a lot of people are involved, the development value must be split into multiple ARTs, as described in the next section, and form a Solution Train.

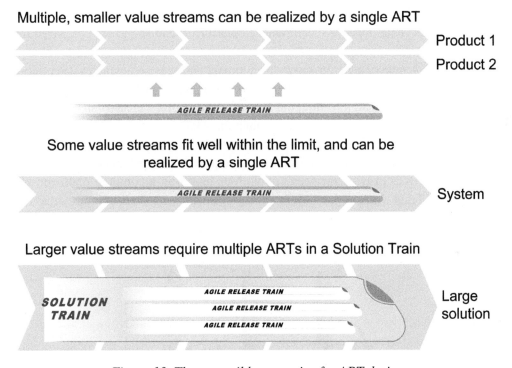

Figure 13. Three possible scenarios for ART design

Splitting Large Value Streams into Multiple ARTs

The last case is very common in large enterprises, and some additional analysis of this model is required. When possible, trains should focus on a single, primary system, or a set of closely related products or services in that value stream. This is a fairly simple design—one ART delivering a well-defined set of valuable things.

Sometimes, however, many people are needed to deliver a single system. In that case, the best approach is for those teams developing features and components that have high degrees of interdependency to work together. This leads us to the fairly common pattern of organizing ARTs around 'feature areas' or subsystems.

- **Feature area ARTs** are optimized for flow and speed. In this case, individual teams on the train, and the entire train itself, can deliver end-to-end features. The benefit is obvious, and that's why these kinds of ARTs are preferred. But pay attention to subsystem governance, or else the system architecture will decay, ultimately reducing velocity. Often, a system architect (one or more individuals, or even a small team) is dedicated to maintaining platform integrity.

- **Subsystem ARTs** (applications, components, platforms, and so on) are optimized for architectural robustness and reuse of subsystems and services. Again, the benefit is obvious, as this approach can increase development and reuse efficiencies. (Service-oriented architectures leverage these benefits.) However, depending on the separation of concerns in the system architecture, the flow of value in this scenario can create more dependencies, and require coordination among the ARTs.

There's no one right solution, and large systems often require both types of ARTs. A typical example is when multiple ARTs provide services or solutions based on a common platform. Figure 14 illustrates a Solution Train that has four ARTs: It is organized with three 'feature area' trains and one 'platform' train.

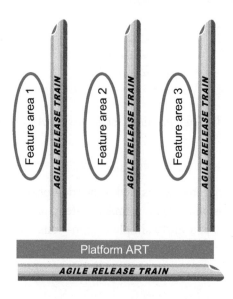

Figure 14. A common feature area ART and platform ART pattern

In another common pattern, ARTs realize specific *segments* in a larger value stream. That may not seem to provide fully end-to-end delivery, but the 'beginning and end' of a value stream are actually relative notions. The types of input, value, and systems may be very different in these segments, creating a logical dividing line.

Of course, combinations of these models often appear in the larger value streams, as our final example in Figure 15 illustrates.

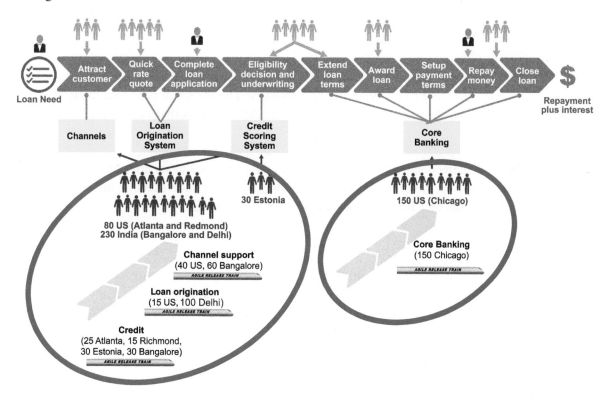

Figure 15. ARTs in the bank loan example

Finally, there are other ART design and optimization factors based on concerns such as geography, spoken language, and cost centers—all of which may influence the ART design. In general, these are far less desirable.

The SAFe Value Stream Workshop Toolkit

As you can see, critical thinking and analysis are required in this process. To help you identify value streams, Scaled Agile, Inc. provides a Value Stream Workshop Toolkit, consisting of a workshop and other artifacts that SAFe Program Consultants (SPCs) can use to guide stakeholders. The workshop provides a structured approach to identifying value streams and to defining ARTs, which can realize the flow of value in the enterprise. This toolkit provides a proven, systematic approach to optimize the design by considering the dependencies, coordination, and constraints.

The Value Stream Workshop is often run directly following a Leading SAFe class with key stakeholders. The objective is to take them through the process of identifying the value streams, designing the ARTs, and perhaps even picking the date for the first ART launch.

Because no design is perfect, enterprises sometimes run this workshop again after learning more, as part of the Sustain and Improve step. This allows them to refine their understanding of value streams and ARTs and incorporate new learnings into the organizational design.

Moving Forward

In this chapter, we've described how teams do the work to identify the value streams and design the ARTs that form the basic organizational structure for the transformation. Now we're ready for the next step, Create the Implementation Plan, which is the subject of the next chapter.

LEARN MORE

[1] Ward, Allen. *Lean Product and Process Development*. Lean Enterprise Institute, 2004.

[2] Contributed by SPCT candidates Jane Tudor, Justine Johnston, Matt Aaron, Steve Mayner, and Thorsten Janning.

[3] Contributed by SPCT candidates Darren Wilmshurst, Murray Ford, Per-Magnus Skoogh, Phillip Manketo, Sam Bunting, and Virpi Rowe.

[4] Knaster, Richard, and Leffingwell, Dean. *SAFe Distilled: Applying the Scaled Agile Framework for Lean Software and Systems Engineering*. Addison-Wesley, 2017.

Create the Implementation Plan

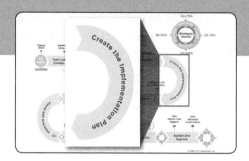

The more detailed we made our plans, the longer our cycle times became.

—Don Reinertsen

In this chapter, we discuss the next 'critical move' in the SAFe Implementation Roadmap: Create the implementation plan.

It's a big deal to implement organizational change of this magnitude, and some strategizing and planning help. But Reinertsen's quote reminds us not to overthink the problem. It's far better to plan a bit, execute a bit, and learn a bit. Then repeat. In other words, we need to take an Agile, incremental approach to implementation—just as we do with solution development.

We'll do that by picking one Value Stream and one Agile Release Train (ART) to serve as the vehicles for our journey.

Details

In the last chapter, Identifying Value Streams and ARTs, we described a process typically executed in one or more workshops, where the key enterprise stakeholders gathered to identify the flow of value through the organization. By 'stakeholders,' we mean SAFe Program Consultants (SPCs), members of the Lean-Agile Center of Excellence (LACE), newly trained Lean-Agile leaders, and other essential team members.

Using their new knowledge from SAFe training, the Lean-Agile mindset and principles, and the value stream workshop, the enterprise stakeholders start to identify strategies for implementing this new way of working. That brings us to the next step, creating the implementation plan. This is where the rubber meets the road in a SAFe implementation.

Until now, it's been all talk. The next move, however, requires real and tangible changes to individual and organizational behavior. Specifically, creating the plan involves three activities:

- Pick the first value stream
- Select the first ART
- Create a preliminary plan for additional ARTs and value streams

Pick the First Value Stream

Each of the development value streams identified in the prior step is a candidate for the new way of working. A large enterprise offers a lot of opportunities for improvement, and while there's no one right way to begin, for many companies the next smart move is to just pick one target. After all, it's likely this significant change is untested in this business's environment. Picking one target allows the newly trained SPCs and leaders to focus their full attention and resources on a specific opportunity.

Once a value stream is selected, some additional analysis is required to further define the development value stream boundaries, people, deliverables, potential ARTs, and other parameters. To assist, we offer Figure 1, a Value Stream Canvas that stakeholders can use to capture their emerging understanding [1].

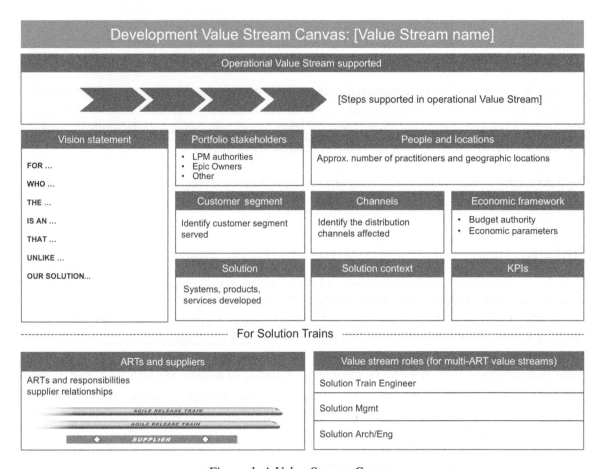

Figure 1. A Value Stream Canvas

Filling in the fields typically requires some homework. It calls for an understanding of how things work now, as well as how they're intended to work in the future. As highlighted in the bottom section of Figure 1, some additional analysis is needed to define prospective ARTs and governance in a Solution Train (multi-ART value stream).

Development Value Streams Cross Boundaries

As the value streams are identified, it becomes obvious that development value streams often cross many boundaries, as illustrated in Figure 2.

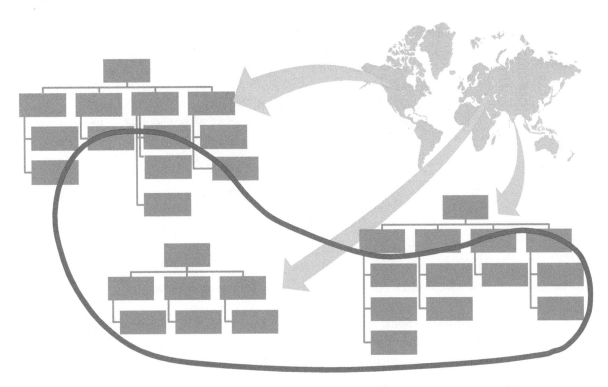

Figure 2. Value flows across functional, organizational, and geographic boundaries

In turn, many of the development value streams—and, as a result, the ARTs—will be geographically distributed rather than collocated. While that might complicate things, it's a reality, and it doesn't change the basic operating model. ARTs use a variety of techniques to mitigate this challenge, including multi-location face-to-face Program Increment (PI) Planning. Although we've observed that a SAFe implementation provides opportunities to advance more geographically collocated development practices, companies simply have to start with their current situation.

Select the First ART in a Large Value Stream

Once the first value stream has been identified, it's time to create the initial 'short-term win' by focusing on the first ART. That will yield institutional knowledge that can be applied to other ARTs. In some cases, the first value stream is also the first ART, and no other decisions are needed. In larger value streams, however, the next step will require the active support of many more leaders and other stakeholders in that value stream. Many organizations decide to look for a first, 'opportunistic' ART, one that can be found at the intersection of the factors illustrated in Figure 3.

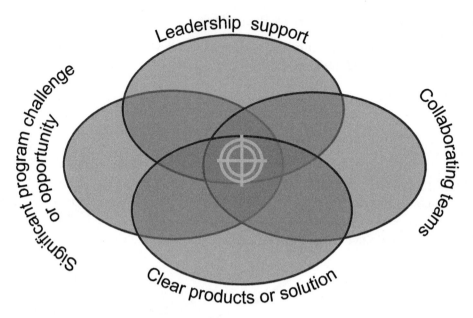

Figure 3. Finding an opportunistic ART

The target for the first ART is often one that best meets the following criteria:

- **Leadership support** – Some senior leaders may have already been trained in SAFe and will be anxious to put their training to work. Moreover, it's likely that many of these leaders have previous experience with Agile development.

- **Clear products or solutions** – SAFe is most easily applied to a clear and tangible solution, something the company sells directly or values highly.

- **Collaborating teams** – Somewhere in the enterprise, there are already teams collaborating on building a larger solution. Some may be Agile, some not. But given the business's current challenges, the teams may be ready to embrace this change.

- **Significant challenge or opportunity** – Change is hard. The smart enterprise selects a subject that is truly worthy of its effort, ideally a large existing challenge or a new opportunity. Creating a short-term win there will produce immediate benefits and facilitate faster and broader adoption.

Once this ART is selected, the enterprise is nearly ready to move forward.

Create a Preliminary Plan for Additional ARTs and Value Streams

Before we move on to launching that first ART, we note that it's likely that a broader implementation plan may already be forming. Although it's still early in the process, strategies for rolling out additional

ARTs and for launching additional value streams may be starting to take shape. In short, change is starting to happen, and the signs are everywhere:

- The new vision is being communicated around the company

- Principal stakeholders are aligning

- Something big is in the air, and people are catching on

As we described in Creating a Lean-Agile Center of Excellence, the LACE and various SPCs and leaders typically guide the transformation using Agile and SAFe as their operating framework. In accordance with SAFe practices, the LACE holds internal PI Planning and invites other stakeholders, such as Business Owners, to help further define the implementation strategy. One natural output would be a PI Roadmap for the implementation, as illustrated in Figure 4. The roadmap further details the plan and a PI cadence for implementation.

Before committing to the roadmap, it's probably a good idea for stakeholders to reflect on the existing culture and the 'how' of the larger implementation strategy. Yes, it's a committed change initiative, and that means it's a largely centralized decision (see the chapter Principle #9: Decentralize decision-making). The change is not optional, but how it is received depends on many factors. Oftentimes, mandated change can be uninspiring to those who are on the receiving end of the decision. In that case, you may want to try the approach described in Yuval Yeret's chapter, Invitation-Based SAFe Implementation, which describes how to create a more collaborative organizational change effort.

Don't be too concerned about getting your strategy perfect right at the start. Any such preliminary plan is only the current hypothesis and will be incrementally improved as your implementation evolves. We'll revisit the larger planning cycle later in Launching More ARTs and Value Streams.

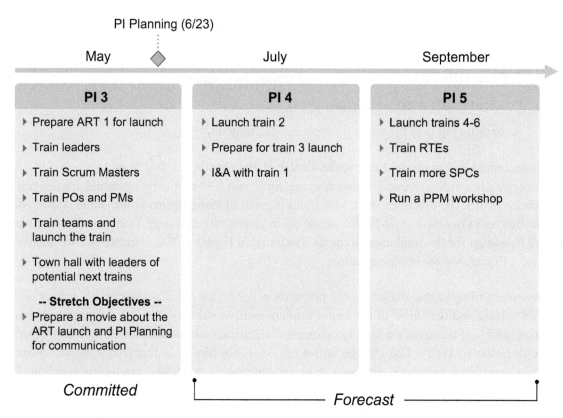

Figure 4. An example PI Roadmap

Moving Forward

In any case, with the first value stream selected and one or more initial ARTs defined, it's time to move on to the practical matter of implementing the first ART. That is the subject of the next chapter, Prepare for ART Launch.

LEARN MORE

[1] Thanks to SPCT Mark Richards for contributing the Value Stream Canvas concept.

[2] Martin, Karen, and Mike Osterling. *Value Stream Mapping.* McGraw-Hill, 2014.

[3] Knaster, Richard, and Dean Leffingwell. *SAFe Distilled: Applying the Scaled Agile Framework for Lean Software and Systems Engineering.* Addison-Wesley, 2017.

Prepare for ART Launch

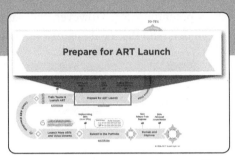

Short-term wins help build necessary momentum.

  —*Kotter*

By now, the enterprise has identified its value streams and established an implementation plan. It will also have loosely defined the first Agile Release Train (ART). This is a pivotal moment, as plans are now moving toward implementation. From a change-management perspective, the first ART is very important, with potentially far-reaching implications. This will be the first material change to the way of working and will generate the initial short-term wins that help the enterprise build momentum.

This chapter describes the activities necessary to prepare for the ART launch.

Details

Now is the time to execute the activities necessary for a successful ART launch. SPCs often lead the implementation of the initial ARTs, supported by SAFe-trained program stakeholders and members of the Lean-Agile Center of Excellence (LACE).

No matter who leads, some larger activities are part of preparing the launch:

- Define the ART
- Set the launch date and cadence for the program calendar
- Train ART leaders and stakeholders
- Establish the Agile teams
- Train Product Managers and Product Owners (POs)
- Train Scrum Masters
- Assess and evolve launch readiness
- Prepare the program backlog

Each of these activities is described in the following sections.

Define the ART

In creating the implementation plan, stakeholders defined a process to identify the first value stream and ART. At that stage of planning, the ART is defined with just enough detail to determine that it's a potential ART. However, the parameters and boundaries of the ART are left to those who better understand the local context, as shown in Figure 1 [1].

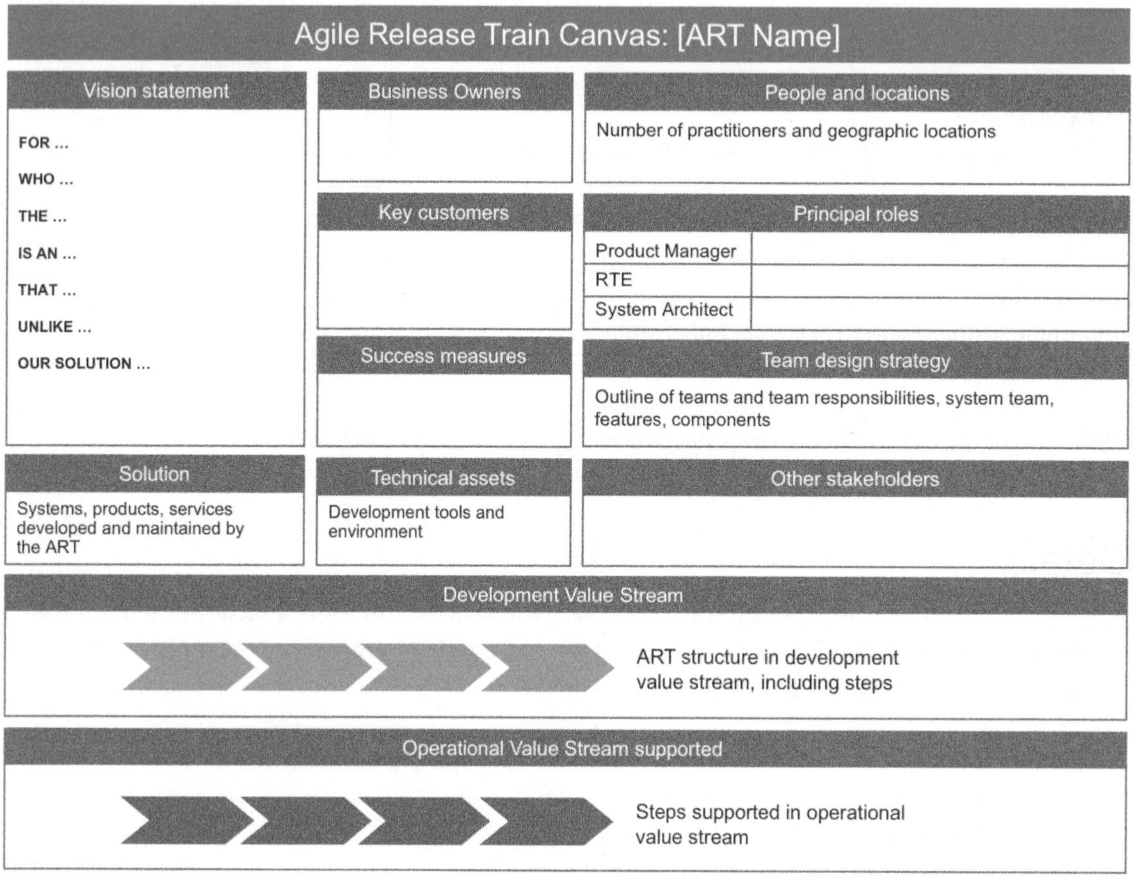

Agile Release Train Canvas: [ART Name]

Vision statement	Business Owners	People and locations
FOR ... WHO ... THE ... IS AN ... THAT ... UNLIKE ... OUR SOLUTION ...		Number of practitioners and geographic locations

Key customers / Principal roles: Product Manager, RTE, System Architect

Success measures / Team design strategy: Outline of teams and team responsibilities, system team, features, components

Solution	Technical assets	Other stakeholders
Systems, products, services developed and maintained by the ART	Development tools and environment	

Development Value Stream
ART structure in development value stream, including steps

Operational Value Stream supported
Steps supported in operational value stream

Figure 1. Agile Release Train Canvas

A key benefit of the ART canvas is that it helps identify the principal ART roles. ARTs work only when the right people are given the right responsibilities. After all, the ART organization is a system. All the necessary responsibilities of solution definition, building, validation, and deployment have to be realized for this system to function properly. Filling in the key roles on the canvas fosters these discussions and highlights the new responsibilities.

To understand who the Business Owners are, special care must be taken. Clearly, they include internal and external customers and/or their Product Management proxies. 'Taking a systems view,' however, means that others should often be included—for example, vice presidents of development/technology, data center managers, enterprise and security architects, and marketing and sales executives. Only the right set of Business Owners can collectively align differing organizational responsibilities and perspectives.

Set the Launch Date and Program Calendar

With the ART definition in hand, the next step is to set the date for the first Program Increment (PI) Planning event. This creates a forcing function, a 'date-certain' deadline for the launch, which will in turn create a starting point and define the planning timeline.

The first step is to establish the cadence for the program, including both the PI and iteration lengths. The SAFe Big Picture shows a 10-week PI, which consists of four regular iterations and one Innovation and Planning (IP) iteration. There is no fixed rule for the PI cadence, nor for how much time should be reserved for the IP iteration. The recommended duration of a PI is between 8 and 12 weeks, with a bias toward the shorter duration (10 weeks, for example). Once the cadence is chosen, it should remain stable and not arbitrarily change from one PI to another. This allows the ART to have a predictable rhythm and velocity. The fixed cadence also allows a full year of program events to be scheduled on people's calendars. The PI calendar usually includes the following activities:

- PI planning
- System Demos
- ART Sync, or individual Scrum of Scrum and PO Sync meetings
- Inspect and Adapt (I&A) workshop

Having such advance notice of upcoming activities reduces travel and facility costs and helps assure that most of the stakeholders will be able to participate. Once the program calendar is set, team events can then be scheduled, with each team defining the time and place for its daily meetings, iteration planning, demos, and retrospectives. All teams on the train should use the same iteration start and end dates, which facilitates synchronization across the ART.

Train the ART Leaders and Stakeholders

Depending on the scope and timing of the rollout, there may be a number of ART stakeholders (e.g., Business Owners, managers, internal suppliers, operations) who have not attended a Leading SAFe training session. They will likely be unfamiliar with SAFe and unclear on expectations, and they may not understand the need for and benefits of their participation. It's important that they understand and support the model, as well as the responsibilities of their role.

To ensure their commitment to the plan, SPCs will often arrange a Leading SAFe class to educate these stakeholders and motivate participation. This is often followed by a one-day implementation workshop, where newly trained stakeholders and SPCs can create the specifics of the launch plan. After all, it's their ART: Only they can plan for the best outcomes. Essentially, this is the handoff of primary responsibility for the change from the change agents to the stakeholders of the newly formed ART.

Organizing Agile Teams

During the implementation workshop, questions will arise as to how to organize the Agile teams with respect to the system architecture and solution purpose. Similar to organizing the ARTs themselves (see Creating the Implementation Plan in Part 2), there are two primary patterns for organizing Agile teams:

- **Features teams** – These teams are focused on user functionality and are optimized for fast value delivery. This is the preferred approach, as each features team is capable of delivering end-to-end user value. They also facilitate the growth of "T-shaped" [2] individual skills.

- **Components teams** – These teams are optimized for system robustness, component reuse, and architectural integrity. It is recommended that their use is limited to when there are significant component reuse opportunities, high technical specialization, and critical Nonfunctional Requirements (NFRs). After a component has matured, the features teams, with some lightweight governance, can take on future development of the component. The original component team can then be reorganized to assume other feature or component work.

Most ARTs have a mix of features and components teams (see Features and Components in Part 9). However, ARTs should generally avoid organizing teams around a technical system infrastructure (e.g., architectural layer, programming language, middleware, user interface), as this creates many dependencies, impedes the flow of new features, and leads to brittle designs.

Forming the Agile Teams

The next step is to form the Agile teams that will be on the train. One innovative solution is to enable the people on the ART to organize themselves into Agile teams with minimal constraints (see Em Campbell-Pretty's blog on self-organization [3]). In other cases, management makes the initial selections based on the managers' objectives, knowledge of individual talents and aspirations, timing, and other factors. In most cases, a bit of back-and-forth between management and the teams will be needed. Teams have a better understanding of their local context and know how they like to work. Managers add perspective based on current individual, organizational, and product development strategies.

Prior to PI planning, all practitioners must be part of a cross-functional Agile team. In addition, the initial roles of Scrum Master and Product Owner must be established.

The team roster template shown in Figure 2 is a simple tool that can help bring clarity and visibility to the organization of each team. The simple act of filling out this kind of roster can be quite informative, as it starts to make the more abstract concepts of Agile development concrete. After all, the structure of an Agile team is fairly well defined; the question of who is on the team, and the nature of the specialty roles, can lead to interesting discussions. Even the seemingly simple act of dedicating an individual to one Agile team can be an eye-opening experience. But there's no going back: These rules of Agile (one person–one team) are fairly clear.

Team #	Team name	Role	Team member name	Geographic location
1	Team A	Scrum Master	LastName, FirstName	City, Country
2	Team A	Product Owner	LastName, FirstName	City, Country
3	Team A	Developer		
4	Team A	Developer		
5	Team A	Developer		
6	Team A	Tester		
7	Team A	Tester		
8	Team A	<role>		
9	Team A	<role>		

Figure 2. An Agile team roster template

The geographic location column of Figure 2 is quite interesting, as it defines the level of collocation and distribution for each team. Collocation is better, of course. In some cases, however, one or more individuals may not be able to be physically collocated with the others. That situation may evolve over time, but at least everyone understands where the current team members reside, so they can start thinking about Daily Stand-up (DSU) times and other team events.

Train Product Owners and Product Managers

Product Owners and Product Managers steer the train together. They have content authority over features and stories, respectively. These two roles are critical to the success of the ART, and the people fulfilling these roles must be well trained to ensure optimal collaboration, learn the new way of working, and understand how to best fulfill their specific responsibilities. In addition, these roles will be largely responsible for building the initial program backlog, which is a key artifact for PI planning.

Scaled Agile, Inc.'s two-day SAFe Product Owner/Product Manager course is designed specifically for this purpose. This course teaches Product Owners and Product (and Solution) Managers how to drive the delivery of value in the SAFe enterprise. Attendees get an overview of SAFe's Lean-Agile Mindset and principles and have the opportunity to engage in an in-depth exploration of role-specific practices. Attendees learn how to write Epics, features, and user Stories; how to establish the Team and

Program Kanban systems to manage the flow of work; and how to manage and prioritize backlogs using Weighted Shortest Job First (WSJF).

Train the Scrum Masters

Effective ARTs, in large part, rely on the servant leadership of their Scrum Masters and their ability to coach Agile Team members and improve the performance of the team. It's a specialty role that includes both traditional Scrum leadership duties and responsibilities relevant to the larger team-of-Agile-teams that constitute the ART. In SAFe, Scrum Masters also play a critical role in PI planning and help coordinate value delivery through Scrum of Scrums meetings. Obviously, it's incredibly helpful if they receive appropriate training prior to the start of the first PI.

Scaled Agile, Inc.'s two-day SAFe Scrum Master course teaches Scrum fundamentals and explores the role of Scrum in the context of SAFe. It prepares Scrum Masters to facilitate team iterations, to successfully plan and execute the PI, to participate in ART events, and to measure and improve the flow of work through the system using Kanban. This course is beneficial for both new and experienced Scrum Masters.

Assess and Evolve Launch Readiness

Training people in their new roles and responsibilities is a key part of ART readiness, but it's only one element of a successful ART launch. Additional activities are required. However, since SAFe is based on the empirical plan–do–check–adjust (PDCA) model, there is no such thing as perfect readiness for a launch. Even attempting to achieve such a state is a fool's errand, as the experience of the first PI will inform future activities. What is more, trying to be too perfect up-front will delay learning, postponing the transformation and realization of its benefits.

That said, a certain degree of readiness will help assure a more successful planning event the first time. Figures 3 and 4 provide a checklist for some of the ART readiness assessment and activities.

Area	Question
Planning scope and context	Is the scope (product, system, technology domains) of the planning process understood? Have we identified our value stream(s) and ARTs?
Release Train Engineer (RTE)	Have we identified the RTE? Does the RTE understand the scope of the role in preparing the organization and prepping for the PI planning meeting?
Planning time frame, iteration and PI cadence	Have we identified the PI planning dates, the iteration cadence, and the PI cadence?
Agile Teams	Does each feature/component team have an identified Scrum Master and Product Owner?
Team makeup / commitment	Does every team have dedicated team members?
Agile Team attendance	Are all team members present in person, or are arrangements made to involve them remotely?
Executive, Business Owner participation	Do we know who will set the business context (Business Owners) and who will present the product/solution vision (typically Product Management)?
Business alignment	Is there reasonable agreement on priorities among the Business Owner and Product Management?
Vision and program backlog	Is there a clear vision of what we are building, at least over the next few PIs? Have we identified the top 10 or so features that are the subject of the first PI?

Figure 3. ART readiness checklist: needed items

Area	Question
System Team	Has the System Team been identified and formed?
Shared Services	Have the Shared Services (User Experience, Architecture, etc.) been identified?
Other attendees	Do we know what other key stakeholders (IT, infrastructure, etc.) should attend?
Agile project management tooling	Do we know how and where iterations, PIs, features, stories, status, etc., will be maintained?
Development infrastructure	Do we understand the impact on and/or plans for environments (for example, continuous integration and build environments)?
Quality practices	Is there a strategy for unit testing and test automation?

Figure 4. ART readiness checklist: helpful items

Most would agree that the majority of the items in Figure 3 are required for a successful launch. The items in Figure 4 are certainly desirable, but depending on your circumstances, they can be addressed easily over the first few PIs.

Prepare the Program Backlog

As previously mentioned, using the launch date as a forcing function increases the urgency of determining the scope and Vision for the PI. After all, no one wants to show up at the PI planning meeting without a solid sense of the mission. While it's tempting to assume that kind of understanding will be shared prior to the event, experience often shows otherwise. It's more likely that team members will have multiple opinions about what the new system is supposed to do, and it might take some time to converge those points of view prior to the launch date.

The scope of the PI, or 'what gets built,' is largely defined by the Program Backlog, which contains the set of upcoming features, NFRs, and architectural work that define the future behavior of the system. To that end, SPCs and Lean-Agile Center of Excellence (LACE) stakeholders often facilitate bringing the ART stakeholders together to prepare a common backlog. This is typically done in a series of backlog workshops and other activities, as illustrated in Figure 5.

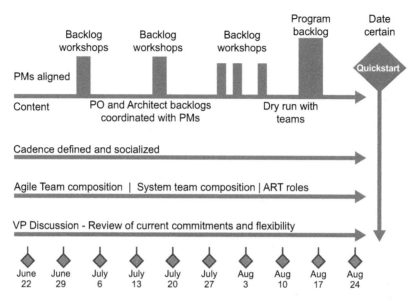

Figure 5. Preparing the program backlog and related activities

It's easy to over-invest in backlog readiness, so don't let that preparation bog you down: The act of planning with the teams will undoubtedly sort out many of these issues. Anyway, the teams typically know what's best. Our experience shows that a list of well-written features with initial acceptance criteria is sufficient. Many leaders tend to over-plan and create the stories ahead of time, but that tends to create waste and disappointment when the vision changes. It's also a sure way to demotivate the teams, as creating stories is a significant aspect of their contribution to PI planning.

Moving Forward

So far, it's been quite a journey. Here's what we've accomplished so far:

- Reached the tipping point
- Trained Lean-Agile change agents
- Trained executives, managers, and leaders
- Identified value streams and ARTs
- Created the implementation plan
- Prepared for the first ART launch

It's finally time to leave the station and launch this train. Are you ready? Good! Now you'll want to read the next chapter, Train Teams and Launch the ART.

LEARN MORE

[1] Thanks to SPCT Mark Richards for the ART Canvas inspiration.

[2] https://en.wikipedia.org/wiki/T-shaped_skill

[3] http://www.prettyagile.com/2017/01/facilitating-team-self-selection-safe-art.html

Train Teams and Launch the ART

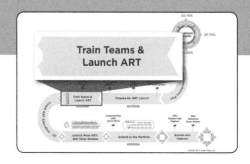

We often don't think through carefully enough what new behavior, skills, and attitudes will be needed when major changes are initiated. As a result, we don't recognize the kind and amount of training that will be required to help people learn those new behaviors, skills, and attitudes.

—*Kotter*

Train teams and launch trains.

—*The SAFe approach*

By now, key Agile Release Train (ART) stakeholders are trained and on board, and launch plans are in place. The Lean-Agile Center of Excellence (LACE) and various SAFe Program Consultants (SPCs) are ready and prepared to help. In this chapter, we'll discuss how to train the teams and launch the ART, so that the real business benefits of the change can start to occur.

Details

Kotter's quote reminds us that changing people's behaviors, attitudes, and skills—and in the end, the culture of an enterprise—is no small feat. Simply put, if we want people to do things differently, leaders must "shape the path" [1]. That requires training to show people the way and follow-up coaching to help them master these new skills, techniques, and attitudes.

Train the Agile Teams

We are now ready to turn our attention to the new and tentatively identified Agile Teams who will account for most of the train members. These are the people who actually build the systems needed by the business, so it's important that they fully grasp what's about to take place. They must have an understanding of their role in the ART and gain the Lean and Agile skills needed to be effective in their changing role. It's likely that some or all will have never participated in an Agile or SAFe environment, so the next significant task is to train all the teams in the SAFe way of working.

Scaled Agile, Inc.'s two-day SAFe for Teams (S4T) course is designed for this purpose. This team-building and training course features an introduction to Agile development, including an overview of the Agile Manifesto and its values and principles. It also includes:

- Core Scrum elements and an exploration of the roles of Scrum Master and Product Owner

- The purpose and mechanics of the basic events, including Iteration Planning (IP), Iteration Execution, Daily Stand-up (DSU), Iteration Review, and Iteration Retrospective

- Preparation for Program Increment (PI) Planning

- Building a Kanban board for tracking Stories

In addition, teams prepare their Team Backlog, which identifies the work needed for the upcoming PI planning event.

When approaching this training, keep in mind that many of the team members will likely have some degree of experience with Agile development and might feel that they are already equipped to work in SAFe. There could potentially be some resistance to what they might consider more basic Agile training. In reality, this team training is critically important for SAFe success, as it provides coaching that goes far beyond core Scrum practices. In particular, a number of elements of Agile at scale are unique to SAFe:

- The role of the team in PI planning, Inspect and Adapt (I&A), and the IP iteration

- Focus on and participation in the System Demo

- Applying Features, user stories, and acceptance criteria to define and validate system behavior

- Using story points as the measure of velocity and for estimating purposes

- Understanding the flow of work through the Kanban systems, including the team's local Kanban

- Collaboration with other teams and other roles, including Product Management and System Architecture

- Introduction/application of Built-In Quality practices, including Continuous Integration, Test-First with test automation, and pair work

- Building the larger team-of-teams that constitutes the ART

The Benefits of Big Room Training

In some rollouts, training is performed team by team over time. That strategy can sometimes be effective. Nevertheless, we strongly recommend a more accelerated approach, which includes training all the team members at the same time. This practice has raised some eyebrows in the industry. Many picture 100-plus people in a room being trained simultaneously, compare it to the more intimate setting of a small team with a single instructor, and can't imagine that it delivers equivalent benefits. In reality, it delivers far more:

- **Accelerated learning** – This training happens in two days, rather than over a period of months. That speeds up the timing and assimilation by all the members of the train, which accelerates the launch.

- **A common scaled Agile paradigm** – All team members receive the same training, at the same time, from the same instructor. This eliminates the variability of different training sessions over time, by different instructors, using different courseware.

- **Cost-efficiency** – One challenge with Agile implementation at scale has been the availability and expense of training. Talented, proven instructors are hard to find and not consistently available, and their value and cost are commensurately high. The Big Room approach is typically three to five times more cost-effective than individual team training.

- **Collective learning** – There is no substitute for the learning experience of big room training. Face-to-face interaction is one of the critical ingredients of Agile at scale. Training everyone together starts building the social network that the ART relies upon and creates a far better experience than what can be accomplished when participants work separately from each other. Such training can take on a transformative aspect, something you have to experience to believe.

To give you a feel for what's possible, following are some observations from Mark Richards, SAFe Program Consultant Trainer (SPCT) and a SAFe pioneer in Australia.

How on earth do you get a high-impact training experience with 100 people in the room? I was initially unconvinced, so I worked with my clients to schedule four or five SAFe team-level courses over the period leading up to the first PI planning. I'd request that they send entire teams to the same course so they could sit and learn together, and they would promise to do their best. Then the pain would start. Firstly, the teams would often be in flux up until the last moment. Then they would be too busy on current commitments to all come together, so they would dribble through two or three at a time. And distributed team members would go to different courses.

But I eventually got convinced enough to try it. After the first big room training, I was blown away and spent some time sorting through how on earth it could be so powerful.

Here are some of Mark's insights:

- **The teams will be fully formed.** The whole team can sit at the same table. Not only do they get to learn together and share insights, it's actually a very powerful team formation event. Teams choose their names on day one, and we watch team identity grow before our eyes.

- **Teams engage in collective learning.** The teams have a chance to resolve their different interpretations in discussions and exercises. They're not reliant on one mind—the Scrum Master—to ensure they get value from the Agile approach. Instead, teams have many minds, and each has different nuances.

- **The features for the PI will be ready.** The team training exercises involving the identification, splitting, and estimating of stories are done on the real features the teams will be dealing with in PI planning.

- **Teams form their own identities.** Teams sit together, choose a name for their team, and begin to form the shared identity of the ART. As team discussions and debriefs of exercises unfold, they start to learn about each other's worlds.

As different as it is, the all-in, big-room training approach remains one of our strongest recommendations and is one of SAFe's most cost-effective and valuable implementation strategies.

Launch the ART

There are many ways to successfully start an ART, and there's no specific timeline for the readiness activities we described in the previous chapter. However, experience has shown that the easiest and fastest way to launch an ART is through the ART Quickstart approach, as illustrated in Figure 1.

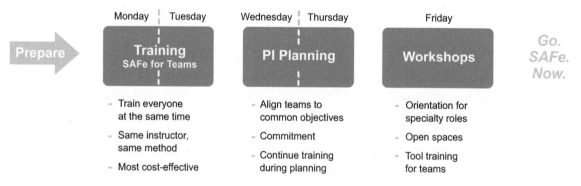

Figure 1. The one-week, all-in ART Quickstart approach

In this approach, the Agile teams are trained, and the first PI planning session is scheduled in a single week. While this may seem daunting, experience has shown that it is the easiest and most pragmatic way to help 100-plus people transition to the new way of working. There are three elements to this approach:

- **Days 1–2** – The Agile team big room training takes place, as described previously.

- **Days 3–4** – Team training is followed immediately by PI planning. This way, the teams are still present and in context, and their first PI planning experience builds on the prior day's training.

- **Day 5** – This day is reserved for mentoring people in their new roles, tool training, discussion of needed Agile technical practices, open space, and any other activities that the teams need to get ready for the first iteration.

The First PI Planning Session

During the Quickstart, PI planning serves to help build the teams' backlogs based on current priorities. It also reinforces the training they've just received. The very next week, the teams will plan their iteration in the normal fashion and start executing the PI.

Obviously, getting off to a good start with PI planning is essential to the success of the first PI. It demonstrates a commitment to the new way of working for all the teams and stakeholders. An effective session will have the following outcomes:

- Build confidence and enthusiasm in the new way of working

- Start to build the ART as a team-of-Agile-teams and the social network that it relies on

- Teach the teams how they can assume responsibility for planning and delivery

- Create full visibility into the mission and current context of the program

- Demonstrate the commitment of Lean-Agile Leaders to the SAFe transformation

This first planning session is, therefore, a critical event for SPCs, other leaders, and change agents. To ensure a good outcome, an experienced SPC will typically co-facilitate the session.

Moving Forward

With the teams and stakeholders trained and the new way of working now in effect, there's no going back. As you prepare to evolve and improve your practice of SAFe, keep this point in mind: Just because people have been initially trained in Agile, that doesn't actually make them *Agile*. Just as Agile value delivery is incremental in nature, so is becoming Agile. A mindset of continuous learning and adoption of 'inspect and adapt' practices is now essential to the health and well-being of the ART and the business goals of the enterprise.

It's important to actively support the individuals who make up the ART and provide them with an environment in which learning and growing are encouraged. To leave them to their own devices would be against our responsibility as Lean-Agile leaders and change agents.

We need to coach people on this new path, so they will be empowered to excel in this new working environment. That is the subject of the next chapter, Coaching ART Execution.

LEARN MORE

[1] Heath, Chip, and Dan Heath. *Switch: How to Change Things When Change Is Hard*. Crown Publishing Group, Kindle Edition.

Coach ART Execution

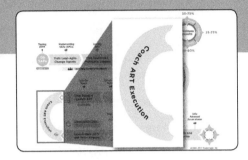

Whenever you let up before the job is done, critical momentum can be lost and regression may follow.

—John Kotter

At this stage of the implementation, the first big events are now in your rearview mirror. You've trained teams, launched the first Agile Release Train (ART), and held a Program Increment (PI) Planning session. The result of all this effort is an empowered, engaged, and aligned team-of-Agile-teams that is ready to begin building solutions that deliver value.

Before you move on to that critical work, it's important to understand that training and planning alone do not make the newly formed teams and ARTs *Agile*. They simply provide the opportunity to begin the journey of becoming Agile. To support this journey, leadership—and SAFe Program Consultants (SPCs), in particular—must be mindful that knowledge does not equal understanding. It takes time to achieve effective team-level Agile practices and behaviors, which is why significant effort must be made to coach ART execution.

Details

To reach this point, the enterprise has made a significant investment in developing SPC change agents and training stakeholders in the new way of working. Now is the time for that investment to pay off, as SPCs and Lean-Agile Leaders focus on what really matters: helping to assure the delivery of value in the shortest sustainable time, while producing the highest quality. That will start to happen when you begin team-level and ART-level coaching.

ART Coaching

Coaching the ART fosters progress in the following areas:

- Helping to build and maintain the Vision and Roadmap
- Defining and managing the Program Kanban and Program Backlog

- Coaching Product Managers, System Architects, and Release Train Engineers in their roles

- Supporting frequent system-level integration, including the System Demo

- Participating in the Scrum of Scrums, Product Owner (PO), and ART Sync meetings

- Helping to facilitate Inspect and Adapt (I&A) and to follow up on improvement items

- Fostering the System Team, Agile teams, and others in building a DevOps culture and implementing a Continuous Delivery Pipeline with the appropriate level of automation

- Maintaining a focus on the Architectural Runway

- Supporting Release Management in the new way of working

- Supporting or delivering additional training

Team Coaching

The teams, especially those new to Agile, will need significant help as well. Team coaching opportunities include the following activities:

- Helping teams plan, execute, review, and retrospect the first iterations

- Coaching new Scrum Masters and Product Owners in their roles

- Initiating and supporting Agile technical and Built-In Quality practices

- Helping teams establish the infrastructure, DevOps practices, and culture needed for the continuous delivery pipeline

- Encouraging and supporting Communities of Practice to help acquire new knowledge and skills

Clearly, there's no shortage of opportunities for SPCs and Lean-Agile Leaders to practice and demonstrate their new skills and mindset.

An important note: For first-line development and engineering managers, the move to SAFe and Lean-Agile adoption can be scary. Traditional daily and task-oriented supervision is no longer required. Instead, these new 'Lean-thinking manager-teachers' adopt a servant-leader approach and take on a different set and style of activities, as described in the Lean-Agile Leaders chapter. The short list of coaching opportunities also serves notice that the knowledge and skills of the organization's managers and leaders are incredibly valuable, as there is much work to be done. It just needs to be done differently.

Inspect and Adapt

There is no coaching opportunity more critical than the first Inspect and Adapt (I&A) workshop. That's where everyone will learn how the PI went, how the teams performed against their PI objectives, how well the organization is adopting SAFe, and how the solution they developed *really* worked at that point in time. In addition, SPCs and coaches can lead the first real corrective action and problem-solving workshop.

The I&A workshop gives teams the tools they need to improve their performance independently. It also allows them to work together—along with their management stakeholders—to collaboratively address the larger impediments that they face.

Moving Forward

For the first ART, then, it's on to the next PI. But for the reader, it's on to the next chapter: Launching More ARTs in the Value Stream.

Launch More ARTs and Value Streams

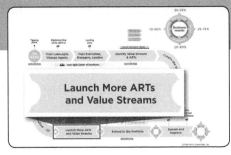

Consolidate gains and produce more change.

  —John Kotter

You can think of the next stage of the Implementation Roadmap as analogous to a train picking up steam and heading down the tracks at an accelerated pace. The larger business opportunity has arrived, enabling the enterprise to 'consolidate gains and produce more change' by launching more Agile Release Trains (ARTs) and Value Streams [1]. This allows the business to start realizing the fuller benefits of SAFe, effectively shifting to the next higher gear of the transformation.

Details

The first Program Increment (PI) Planning event, ART launch, and PI deliverables provide initial, measurable, and substantial business benefits. Business and development are now aligned to a common vision and mission; everyone has agreed to a new way of working and has adopted a common method, language, and cadence, as well as synchronized events; new roles and responsibilities are established; and a new level of employee engagement has emerged as teams take responsibility for planning their own future. Most importantly, the first PI deliverables have illustrated the effectiveness of adopting SAFe.

In addition, the first ART creates an effective pattern and the initial institutional 'muscle memory' needed to implement additional ARTs in the Value Stream. In this next critical move—launch more ARTs and value streams—the enterprise can start to realize an even greater return on its investment: faster time-to-market, higher quality, higher productivity, and increased employee engagement. These are the rewards that only a full and effective implementation of scaled Lean-Agile practices can deliver.

Launch More ARTs

By now, SAFe Program Consultants (SPC)s, the Lean-Agile Center of Excellence (LACE), and other stakeholders have the experience needed to launch more ARTs in the next selected value stream. After all, the more ARTs, the greater the return. The pattern is the same. Simply repeat the critical moves that worked the first time:

- Prepare for ART launch
- Train teams and launch the ART
- Coach ART execution

However, a cautionary note is warranted. The same attention and effort must be devoted to the next few ARTs as was paid to the first. Otherwise, there may be a tendency to assume that 'everyone knows how to do this now.' That kind of comfort level is unlikely to be in place so early in the transformation, and the stakeholders in the lead will need to give as much love and care to each subsequent ART as they did to their first.

Implement Large Solution Roles, Artifacts, and Events

As we described in the chapter Identifying Value Streams and ARTs, some value streams can be realized by a single ART. They already have the people, resources, and cross-functional skills needed to Release on Demand without additional coordination, integration with other ARTs, or added governance. In contrast, for larger value streams, some or all of the additional roles, events, and artifacts of the SAFe Large Solution Level will be required (Figure 1).

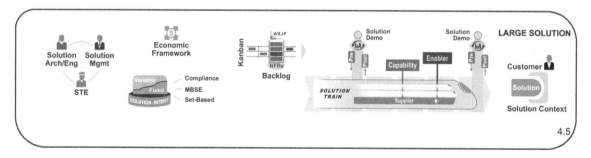

Figure 1. Large Solution Level

This is also true for high-assurance systems, where more rigor in system definition (Solution Intent) and other activities is likely to be required. In this case, the next stage of the rollout for these value streams will need to establish these additional practices.

Because these responsibilities, artifacts, and activities are new to the enterprise, the leaders, the SPCs, and the LACE will again play an active role. Their tasks may include the following:

- **Establishing roles** – Fill the three value stream roles—Solution Train Engineer (STE), Solution Management, and Solution Architect/Engineering.

- **Establishing solution intent and Solution Context** – Determine the responsibilities, process, and tooling to define and document solution intent and solution context. For high-assurance systems, establish and/or evolve Lean-Agile Verification and Validation practices (see Compliance).

- **Establishing value stream, Vision, Roadmap, and Metrics** – Many elements of the spanning palette may be required for large value streams, including vision, roadmap, metrics, Shared Services, System Team and DevOps strategies, User Experience (UX), Milestones, and releases.

- **Introducing Capabilities and the Solution Backlog** – Larger value streams will benefit from the use of the capabilities backlog item, in which case the Solution Kanban must also be established.

- **Implementing Pre- and Post-PI Planning, Solution Demo, value stream, and Inspect and Adapt (I&A)** – These events are required to prepare for individual ART PI planning, to follow up and coordinate Value Stream Objectives after planning, and to demonstrate the full solution to value stream stakeholders.

- **Integrating Suppliers** – Large value streams typically have internal and/or external suppliers. Whether they are already embracing Lean-Agile and SAFe principles or not, they must be integrated into the new way of working. Lean enterprises often take an active role in helping their suppliers adopt SAFe, as it improves the economics of the larger value stream. Whatever the case, the suppliers must at least be integrated into SAFe events at the Large Solution Level.

Launch More Value Streams

Launching the first full value stream is a major milestone in the transformation. Outcomes are improving. People are happier. The new way of working is being ingrained into the habits of the organization. The culture is evolving as well.

However, the job is far from done in the large enterprise. The other value streams may be entirely different businesses, operating units, or subsidiaries. They may be located in different countries, offer markedly different solutions and services, and have different chains of command that may converge only at the highest corporate level.

As a result, even the spread of good news to other value streams may not evoke an automatic embrace of SAFe across the enterprise. Many may think, "What worked there may not work here." So, in a sense, each new value stream represents the same challenge and opportunity to incorporate all the change management steps described so far. Likewise, each new value stream will need to go through the same series of steps that got you to this point, as illustrated in Figure 2.

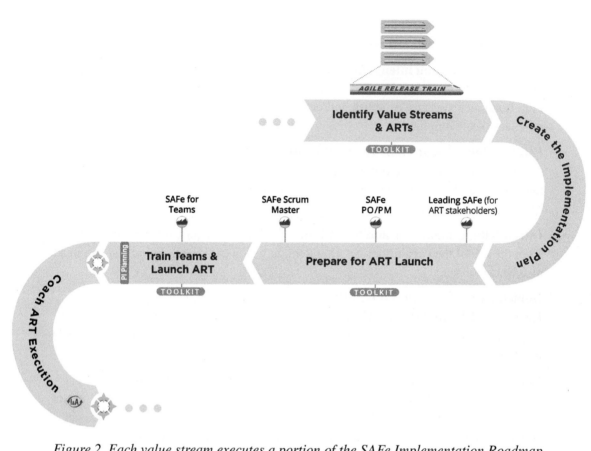

Figure 2. Each value stream executes a portion of the SAFe Implementation Roadmap

Accordingly, as the enterprise ponders the next big steps—where the change, impact, and business benefits will be the greatest—it's a good time to roll out the 'Invitation-Based Implementation Approach.' This approach is intended to generate the necessary buy-in and 'shape the path' that allows key stakeholders to assume the leadership roles they will need to succeed in the new way of working [2].

Also, given the scope of the effort ahead, now is a good time to reflect on earlier principles and apply Principle #6: Visualize and limit Work in Process (WIP), reduce batch sizes, and manage queue lengths. We'll see these principles at work in the SAFe Implementation Railway.

The SAFe Implementation Railway

A while ago, we had the opportunity to visit the folks at Northwestern Mutual. They were in the midst of one of the larger and most significant SAFe rollouts to date. We spent some time with the technical transformation team (similar to the LACE), sharing experiences and learning from each other. The Northwestern Mutual team showed us how they had managed their transformation rollout.

The highlight was a 10-foot-long Big Visible Information Radiator (BVIR). We mean *really big*, as illustrated in Figure 3.

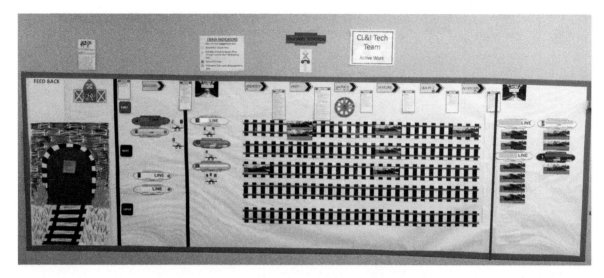

Figure 3. The SAFe Implementation Railway board ('cow board') at Northwestern Mutual (Reproduced with permission of Northwestern Mutual.)

We were greatly impressed by their Lean-Agile Mindset, the way they applied SAFe principles and practices, and the structured way they executed the implementation—so impressed that we asked if we could share their experience. They graciously agreed. One outcome was that Sarah Scott presented their work as a case study at the 2016 SAFe Summit. Further, we've taken those learnings and generalized their experience into guidance for what we call the SAFe Implementation Railway, depicted in Figure 4.

The Four States of the Railway

The railway operates as a Kanban board that contains a series of four major states, with one state—the tracks—having multiple steps for each ART. Each of the four major states is described next.

- **Input funnel** – Used for numerous purposes, this state's primary role is to act as an opportunity for stakeholders to volunteer their value streams for transformation. Other purposes include collecting feedback, offering suggestions for improvement or points of discussion, or identifying challenges—in short, whatever is needed. There are no WIP limits for the funnel. When it is ready, a value stream is pulled into the transformation backlog state.

(Note: At Northwestern Mutual, the funnel state also features the barn, a holding place for a small herd of what the team labels 'impediment cows,' which are explained later in this chapter.)

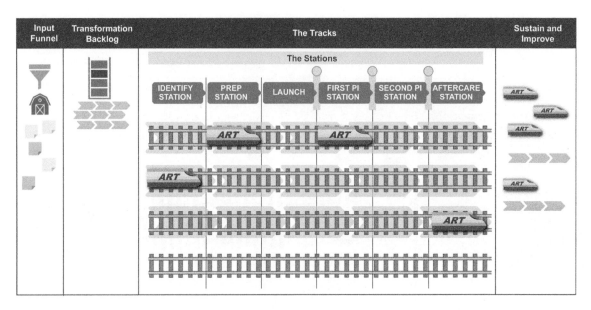

Figure 4. The SAFe Implementation Railway

- **Transformation backlog** – The transformation backlog is the to-do state—that is, where value streams are prioritized for transformation based on opportunity and support from relevant stakeholders. Value streams stay here until they meet the following exit criteria:

  - **Leadership prepared** – Value stream stakeholders have been trained in the new way of working, established and communicated a sense of urgency, built the guiding coalition, and developed and communicated the change vision.

  - **ARTs identified** – The operational and development value streams have been analyzed, and prospective ARTs have been identified (see Identifying Value Streams and ARTs).

  - **Value Stream Canvas defined** – The value stream itself is further defined and the value stream canvas is created (see Creating the Implementation Plan).

  - **SPCs trained** – To provide the knowledge and coaching expertise, additional SPCs in the value stream are trained (see Training Lean-Agile Change Agents). A coaching plan is created.

This state is WIP limited, ensuring adequate LACE and SPC support.

- **The tracks** – The tracks represent the doing state, where the ARTs are structured, launched, and operated to achieve the aim of the value stream. There are five intermediate stations on this track, described in the next section. The tracks are WIP limited in two ways: There are only a small number of tracks (value streams) available, and there can be no more than the specified number of trains on each track.

- **Sustain and improve** – Once an ART can run independently, without the constant attention of coaches, the train is moved to the sustain and improve state on the BVIR. This section displays all the SAFe value streams and ARTs in the organization that have been launched to date. This state is not WIP limited: The more, the merrier!

As the name indicates, the arrival of each train at its sustain and improve state is not the end of its journey. Such an event is only a milepost. Once it arrives, each train's relentless improvement journey begins.

The Tracks

The tracks are where most of the transformational work takes place. Each station on the track represents a state of maturity for an ART. While the number and definition of the stations can be adapted to each enterprise's context, we offer an example in Figure 5.

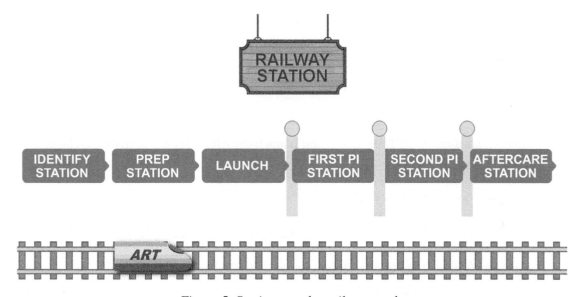

Figure 5. Stations on the railway tracks

The stations are as follows:

- **Identify station** – (See Create the Implementation Plan.) This station includes the following types of work:
    - Communication of the change vision
    - Identifying trains using the ART canvas
    - Preparing for the first ART launch, including setting the date for PI planning

- Confirming that the scope and structure of the ART are determined and the needed practitioners are identified

- Establishing a training plan

Data captured: The number of practitioners in each ART, including the PI cadence (start and end date) for each ART.

- **Preparation station** – (See Prepare for ART Launch.) Typical activities include:

    - Defining the ARTs

    - Organizing teams into feature and component teams

    - Performing Leading SAFe training

    - Training Product Owners, Product Managers, and Scrum Masters

    - Assessing and evolving launch readiness

    - Preparing the program backlog

Data captured: The PI cadence (start and end date) for each ART and the number of people trained for each role.

- **Launch station** – (See Train Teams and Launch the ART.) Typical activities include:

    - Conducting SAFe for Teams training

    - Conducting the first PI planning event

Data captured: The date of first PI planning and the total time (cycle time) for a train in this state.

- **First PI station** – (See Coach ART Execution.) Typical activities include:

    - Coaching the ART

    - Finalizing establishment of roles, including any specialty training required

    - Executing the first PI

    - Conducting the first system demo

    - Holding the first I&A workshop

    - Reinforcing the Lean-Agile mindset and SAFe principles

    - Successful ceremonies

Data captured: The start and end dates for each ART, the estimated date of second PI planning event, the estimated coaching end date, and the first PI predictability measure.

- **Second PI station** – (See Coach ART Execution.) Typical activities include:

  - Observing improvement items from the first I&A workshop

  - Completing the second I&A workshop

  - Assessing PI predictability and other relevant objective measures

  - Observing and coaching self-managing and self-improving behaviors

  - Assessing progress toward a relentless-improvement mindset

  - Observing significant events, including system demo, and ensuring that events are occurring on a regular cadence

  - Observing next PI planning event

Data captured: The PI predictability measure, the PI performance metrics, and the date of the second PI planning event.

- **Aftercare station** – (See Coach ART Execution.) The aftercare station timing is a little more subjective but usually occurs after two to four PIs. Typical activities and measures include:

  - PI predictability in achieving the target zone (80–100 percent)

  - Planning future coaching needs

  - Exhibiting self-reflection and relentless improvement

Data captured: The start and end dates for each ART in this state and the PI predictability measures.

Managing Impediments

This plan seems straightforward, assuming the training, change management, and cultural underpinnings are all there. Unfortunately, many impediments will naturally occur during the rollout. In their own words, here's how Northwestern Mutual had some fun with their series of challenges:

- **The impediment cow** – "It's important to include your organization's culture into the transformation. One key aspect of our culture was an impediment, which we call a 'cow on the tracks' [see Figure 6]."

- **The backstory of the cow** – "In 1859, two Northwestern Mutual policy owners were killed when a train hit a cow and derailed. A tragedy for sure. First death claims totaled $3,500. But the company had only $2,000 on hand. President Samuel Daggett personally borrowed the funds needed to cover the remaining balance, which was the inception of our focus on doing what's right for policy owners. Now whenever there is a significant challenge or impediment, people might say, 'Look out, there is a cow on the track!'

"In the context of both Northwestern Mutual and SAFe, whenever a train was facing a major problem, we took a cow out of the barn and placed it on the track. It was obvious, fun, and reinforced our culture. Most importantly, it immediately drew attention to the problem."

Figure 6. An impediment cow on the tracks
(Image courtesy of Northwestern Mutual. Source of cow: http://www.vectorportal.com/)

Moving Forward

Clearly, this portion of the roadmap represents the largest amount of work in a successful SAFe implementation. It requires leadership, urgency, persistence, and actively removing impediments. As the culture starts to shift to the new values and norms, patience is also essential.

With value streams and trains now running on a consistent basis, it's time to move on to the next critical move in the SAFe Implementation Roadmap: Extend to the Portfolio.

LEARN MORE

[1] Kotter, John P. *Leading Change*. Harvard Business Review Press, 1996.

[2] Heath, Chip, and Heath, Dan. *Switch: How to Change Things When Change Is Hard*. Crown Publishing Group, Kindle Edition.

Extend to the Portfolio

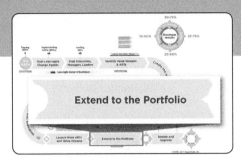

Anchor new approaches in the culture.

—*John Kotter*

It's quite an accomplishment for an organization to have implemented SAFe across a set of Value Streams. At this point, the new way of working is well on its way to becoming second nature to everyone who has a role in the implementation. Most importantly, the measurable benefits of time-to-market, quality, productivity, and employee engagement are now tangible and demonstrating real progress. As a result, the effectiveness of the entire enterprise starts to improve, and the larger goal is coming into sharper focus: a truly Lean-Agile enterprise with a fully implemented set of SAFe value streams. This is a telling phase in the rollout, as it tests the authenticity of the organization's commitment to transforming the business at all levels. Now is the time to expand the implementation across the entire Portfolio and anchor the new approach in the culture.

Details

In the last chapter, Launching More ARTs and Value Streams, we described how enterprise leaders drive and facilitate a wider implementation of SAFe. The success of these Agile Release Trains (ARTs) and value streams creates a buzz in the organization about the new and better way of working. This tends to stimulate greater scrutiny of some of the higher-level practices in the business, which often reveals legacy, phase-gated processes and procedures that impede performance. Inevitably, such discoveries put pressure on the portfolio and trigger the need for the additional changes that will be necessary to further improve the strategic flow across the portfolio. These issues typically include:

- Perpetual overload of demand versus capacity, which jeopardizes throughput and undermines strategy

- Project-based funding (bringing the people to the work), cost accounting friction, and overhead

- No understanding of how to apply capitalization in Agile

- Overly detailed business cases based on speculative, lagging return on investment (ROI) projections

- Strangulation by the iron triangle (fixed scope, cost, and date projects)

- Traditional Supplier management and coordination—focus on lowest cost, rather than on highest life-cycle value

- Phase-gate approval processes that don't mitigate risk and actually discourage incremental delivery

Nowhere is Lean-Agile Leadership more important than when addressing some of these remaining legacy challenges. If these approaches are not modernized, the enterprise will be unable to escape the inertia of traditional, legacy approaches, causing the organization to revert back to the old way of doing things. This inevitably leads to attempting Agile development with a non-Agile mindset, what is often referred to as "Agile in name only." The results can be seriously compromised.

But help is at hand! Figure 1 illustrates how these mindsets evolve with training and engagement in the process of implementing SAFe.

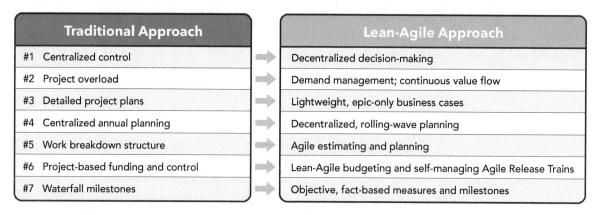

Traditional Approach	Lean-Agile Approach
#1 Centralized control	Decentralized decision-making
#2 Project overload	Demand management; continuous value flow
#3 Detailed project plans	Lightweight, epic-only business cases
#4 Centralized annual planning	Decentralized, rolling-wave planning
#5 Work breakdown structure	Agile estimating and planning
#6 Project-based funding and control	Lean-Agile budgeting and self-managing Agile Release Trains
#7 Waterfall milestones	Objective, fact-based measures and milestones

Figure 1. Evolving traditional mindsets to Lean-Agile thinking

Leading the Transformation

Many of these traditional mindsets exist throughout the organization and, if allowed to persist, can sabotage a fully realized implementation. To help the SAFe workforce embrace the new way of working, we've described how SAFe Program Consultants (SPCs) and Lean-Agile Leaders lead the transformation by providing the new knowledge needed to inspire an attitude that will embrace the new mindset. Since it is better to lead than follow, increasingly we have observed an emerging Lean-Agile Program

Management Office (PMO) taking an active, leadership role in the transformation. In so doing, these personnel establish exemplary Lean-Agile principles, behaviors, and practices:

- Lead the change and foster relentless improvement
- Align value streams with enterprise strategy
- Establish enterprise value flow
- Implement Lean financial management and budgeting
- Align portfolio demand with implementation capacity and Agile forecasting
- Evolve leaner and more objective governance practices
- Foster a leaner approach to contracts and supplier relationships

Each of these roles is described in the following sections.

Lead the Change and Foster Relentless Improvement

For many enterprises, the need for change and the knowledge of the new way of working is led by Lean portfolio and Agile PMO personnel. These team members sponsor and participate in the Lean-Agile Center of Excellence (LACE), become SPCs, and support or encourage the development of specialty Communities of Practice (CoPs) that focus on and advance the new roles, responsibilities, and behaviors.

Align Value Streams with Enterprise Strategy

Value streams exist for one reason: to meet the strategic goals of the portfolio. This can be ensured by implementing a process of establishing and communicating the Strategic Themes. Such an effort helps organize the portfolio into an integrated and unified solution offering. Strategic themes also inform value stream budgeting decisions, as described later.

Establish Enterprise Value Flow

Managing the flow of work from portfolio-level initiatives is an important step in the maturity cycle. It requires implementing the Portfolio Backlog and Kanban system, including filling the role of Epic Owners by adopting the Epics construct and Lean business case. In addition, Enterprise Architects establish enabler epics that provide common technological underpinnings, which support the broader use cases across the full portfolio.

Implement Lean Financial Management

Historically, enterprises were built by carefully controlling the definition and cost of development via the 'project' construct. In a sense, the project model provided 'temporary work for temporary people,' and the inevitable cost and schedule overruns caused personnel upheaval and financial churning.

As we improve our methods, and discover the long-lived nature of most of what we do, it becomes clear that we must move to a more persistent flow-based model. The new approach must minimize overhead, give people a stronger sense of purpose, and support the growth of institutional knowledge. This is the larger purpose of the portfolio's value streams, which are funded in accordance with SAFe Lean-Budget practices. In addition, to ensure that development costs are appropriately recorded without excessive overhead, a leaner approach to managing capital and expense costs is described in the CapEx and OpEx guidance chapter.

Align Portfolio Demand with Implementation Capacity and Agile Forecasting

Lean thinking teaches us that any system operating in a constant state of overload will deliver far less than its actual capacity. This is certainly true for any development process in which excess Work in Process (WIP) drives multiplexing (lowering productivity), unpredictability (lowering trust and engagement), and burnout (lowering everything).

By consistently applying the concept of velocity at the team, ART, and Solution Train levels, the emerging SAFe enterprise uses this invaluable knowledge to limit portfolio WIP until demand matches capacity. This increases the throughput and value delivered to the customer. Instead of attempting to establish detailed long-range commitments, the SAFe enterprise applies Agile forecasting to create a portfolio roadmap, a baseline of expectations that is communicated to internal and external stakeholders.

Evolve Leaner and More Objective Governance Practices

As shown in Figure 1, traditional governance practices were often implemented based on traditional, waterfall life-cycle development. This typically included passing various phase-gate milestones, along with proxy, paper-based measures of completion. The Lean-Agile model works differently. As explained in SAFe Lean-Agile Principle #5: Base milestones on objective evidence of working systems, the focus of governance moves to establishing and measuring the appropriate objective measures at each Program Increment (PI) boundary.

Foster a Leaner Approach to Contracts and Supplier Relationships

The Lean-Agile Mindset informs another group of business practices: how the enterprise treats its suppliers and customers.

The Lean enterprise takes the long view and enters into long-term partnerships with suppliers, which produces the lowest overall cost of ownership, instead of a series of near-term maneuvers that lower only the cost of a current deliverable. Indeed, the enterprise engages directly in helping its suppliers adopt Lean-Agile thinking, and may even participate in developing a supplier's capabilities in that area.

The SAFe enterprise also recognizes the critical importance of customers to the value stream. That realization means customers are included in such key events as PI Planning, System and Solution Demos, and Inspect and Adapt (I&A) workshops. Customers, in turn, take on the responsibilities expected of them in a Lean-Agile ecosystem. These relationships are fostered by adopting a leaner approach to Agile Contracts.

Moving Forward

By now, substantial business benefits are growing daily. Improvements in quality, productivity, time-to-market, and employee engagement are meeting or exceeding expectations. So how do you sustain this pattern over the long term? This is the subject of the next critical move: Sustain and Improve.

Sustain and Improve

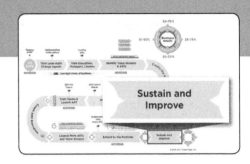

Excellent firms don't believe in excellence—only in constant improvement and constant change.

—Tom Peters

If you've followed the previous 11 steps in the SAFe Implementation Roadmap, congratulations! You have made substantial progress on this portion of your Lean-Agile transformation journey. Your accomplishments are many. A sufficiently powerful coalition of change agents is in place. The majority of stakeholders are trained. Agile Release Trains (ARTs) and Value Streams are transformed and delivering value. The new way of working is becoming a part of the culture all the way from the team to the portfolio level.

By now, substantial business benefits are accumulating every day. Improvements in quality, productivity, time-to-market, and employee engagement are meeting or exceeding expectations. So how do you sustain this trend over the long term? It's important to recognize that culture change can lose momentum as the 'new car smell' of a new initiative begins to fade.

To continue the practice of SAFe effectively, and ensure the ongoing engagement of the workforce, leaders must now expand their view of the implementation. They will need to maintain the energy and enthusiasm they are devoting to the short cycles of Iterations and Program Increments (PIs), while setting their sights on the distant horizon of long-term sustainability. The mindset and process of relentless improvement must now take root. This, of course, is synonymous with continuous change—a quest that can prove challenging for an enterprise.

In this chapter, we'll suggest some key activities the enterprise can use to continuously *sustain and improve* its business performance.

Details

Getting to this last step of the Implementation Roadmap is the beginning of another journey, one of relentless improvement. By now, the emerging Lean-Agile enterprise will have started to build a new operating model and culture, one in which relentless improvement is beginning to be the norm—but that state can't be taken for granted.

Sustaining and improving upon the benefits gained require dedication to basic and advanced practices, self-reflection, and retrospection. Here are a number of activities the enterprise can use to ensure relentless improvement:

- Foster relentless improvement and the Lean-Agile Mindset

- Implement Agile Human Resources (HR) practices

- Advance program execution and servant leadership skills

- Measure and take action

- Improve Agile technical practices

- Focus on Agile Architecture practices

- Improve DevOps and continuous delivery capability

- Reduce time-to-market with value stream mapping

Each of these activities is described in the following sections.

Relentless Improvement and the Lean-Agile Mindset

The effort continues right where it began with relentless improvement, Lean-Agile leadership, and the Lean-Agile mindset. Figure 1 illustrates the direct connection between leadership and relentless improvement.

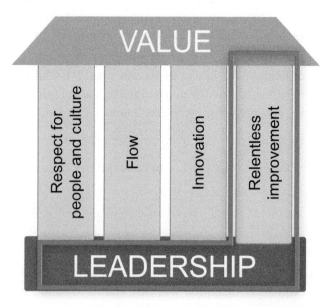

Leadership and relentless improvement are inseparable

"There is a constant sense of danger."

—Toyota

Figure 1. Lean leadership is the foundation for relentless improvement; you can't have one without the other

Extending the benefits requires that leaders set an example by providing a continuous sense of urgency for change.

Ongoing Leadership Training

No matter how extensive the rollout training was, it likely did not reach all of the stakeholders who need to understand and embrace the new way of working—in operations, HR, legal, finance and accounting, sales, marketing, and more.

If these key stakeholders don't understand or agree with the new culture, the transformation may continue, but you'll be driving with the brakes on. In other words, you'll have a traditional, non-Agile governance model working next to, but not integrated with, a Lean-Agile development workforce. Now is the time to extend the knowledge and culture by teaching Leading SAFe to all relevant stakeholders.

Continuing Role of the Lean-Agile Center of Excellence

Earlier in Part 2, we described the Lean-Agile Center of Excellence (LACE) as the engine of the "sufficiently powerful coalition for change." When the LACE is first established, its primary role is to implement the new way of working within the organization. Once that goal has been accomplished, the LACE becomes a long-lived center, a persistent energy source for continuous improvement.

Communities of Practice

As influential as it might be, the LACE is only one element of the coalition. If the enterprise is to effectively sustain and improve its operations, additional help is needed. As described in previous chapters, SAFe organizes people with different skills around a value stream. Organizing this way can have an unintended consequence: It can limit the opportunities to share knowledge and learn new skills with other people in the same role. Communities of Practice (CoPs) help overcome this limitation by bringing people together around a subject domain, work roles, or other areas of common interest.

Implement Agile HR Practices

Respect for people is a pillar of the House of Lean. It is people, after all, who build these critical systems we all depend on. They go to work intrinsically motivated to build high-quality, innovative systems. Given the importance of their contributions, management's challenge is to cultivate an environment in which they can prosper and do their best.

While SAFe provides many of the values and practices of that environment, it also puts extreme pressure on traditional human resources practices. It compels enterprises to embrace a new, Lean-Agile HR perspective to accommodate the modern knowledge worker. This new dynamic features six major themes:

1. Embrace a new talent contract, which explicitly acknowledges the need for value, autonomy, and empowerment.

2. Foster continuous engagement to both the business and technical mission.

3. Hire people for Agile attitude, team orientation, and cultural fit.

4. Eliminate annual performance reviews, replacing them with continuous, iterative performance feedback and evaluation.

5. Eliminate destructive individual financial incentives. Take the issue of money off the table by paying employees enough to focus on the work, not the money.

6. Support meaningful, impactful, and continuous learning and growth.

For more on this topic, read the SAFe guidance white paper, "Agile HR with SAFe: Bringing People Operations into the 21st Century with Lean-Agile Values and Principles"[2].

Advance Program Execution Leadership Skills

An effective SAFe implementation that leads to substantive results is built on effective Agile teams and ARTs. No roles are more important than Scrum Master and Release Train Engineer (RTE) when it comes to facilitation and servant leadership. Once these individuals become adept in handling their basic responsibilities, they will be ready to take the next step to advance and cultivate new skills.

Advanced Scrum Master Training

Scaled Agile, Inc.'s two-day SAFe Advanced Scrum Master course with SASM certification prepares current Scrum Masters for their leadership role in facilitating Agile team, program, and enterprise success. The course covers facilitation of cross-team interactions in support of program execution and relentless improvement. It enhances the Scrum paradigm with scalable engineering and DevOps practices, as well as the application of Kanban to facilitate the flow and support of interactions with architects, product management, and other critical stakeholders. The course offers actionable tools for building high-performing teams and explores practical ways of addressing Agile and Scrum anti-patterns in the enterprise.

Release Train Engineer Training

In a similar fashion, RTEs can improve their skills as Agile program managers, team coaches, and program-level facilitators. The SAFe Release Train Engineer course with RTE certification is designed just for this purpose.

In this three-day interactive course, attendees gain an in-depth understanding of the role and responsibilities of an RTE. They learn how to facilitate and enable end-to-end value delivery through ARTs and value streams. Attendees also learn how to build a high-performing ART by becoming a servant-leader and coach, and how to plan and execute a PI planning event (the primary enabler of alignment throughout all levels of a SAFe organization).

Measure and Take Action

Peter Drucker is credited with saying, "What's measured improves." We haven't focused much on measures as yet, but you can't knowingly improve what you can't measure. In this section we'll take a quick look at a few of the many opportunities to measure and take action on the results.

Inspect and Adapt

Inspect and Adapt (I&A) is the cornerstone event of program improvement. Unlike simpler forms of retrospectives, these events bring the key stakeholders—the people who can change the systems in which everyone works—into a corrective action workshop. They offer an objective demonstration, measurement, and structured root cause analysis. Leaders must actively encourage and participate in I&A problem-solving. This closes the loop on the PI learning cycles and is the basis for continuously improving enterprise performance.

Lean Metrics

Lean-Agile development is inherently more measurable than other methods used in the past. The Metrics chapter highlights many of the measures that enterprises can apply to objectively evaluate their progress toward better outcomes.

Enhance Performance with SAFe Self-Assessments

People don't generally like to be measured. After all, a person can be evaluated only by being compared to another person—and only the one at the top can feel good about that outcome.

What's more, many measures traditionally applied to the development process and its workers are now obsolete. Being measured by others goes against empowered, self-managing Agile thinking.

Instead, we suggest that teams self-assess their progress against agreed-to Agile values. SAFe provides a set of self-assessment worksheets for the Team, Program, and Portfolio levels.

See the Metrics chapter in Part 6 (Spanning Palette) for sample radar charts, which are used to show the results of an assessment. (Note: The self-assessment worksheets can be downloaded at scaledagileframework.com/metrics/.)

Improve Agile Technical Practices

We've often observed that within the first year or so of adoption of the SAFe Implementation Roadmap, teams can quickly reach an apparent velocity limit by implementing only the basic role and team project management practices. After that, further improvements in velocity and quality can occur through effective implementation of Agile technical practices.

Built-In Quality software practices include Continuous Integration, Test-First, and test automation. Mastering these practices takes an additional investment of time and focus, typically with the help of outside experts who have applied these practices in other contexts. Time must be allocated for this new learning to take place, and the Innovation and Planning (IP) iteration can often provide the dedicated time needed.

In addition, companies building really large and/or high-assurance systems need to focus on evolving fixed and variable Solution Intent and maintenance of architectural and other models that show how the system works. Implementing and advancing Model-Based Systems Engineering and Set-Based Design can help the enterprise develop and maintain these important artifacts.

For teams building high-assurance systems—where the cost of error is simply unacceptable—these practices should go all the way into, and through, verification, validation, and compliance. Guidance for these practices is described in the Compliance chapter.

Focus on Agile Architecture

Agile or not, it's impossible to build significant world-class systems without some degree of intentional architecture. Today, however, the Big Design Up-front (BDUF) practices of waterfall development are no longer relevant.

In today's enterprises, solution architecture must be evolved while building the solution. This includes creating the architectural underpinnings (Architectural Runway) and practices for incrementally evolving legacy systems into the new platforms of choice. In other words, we have to change the engine while driving to the destination.

Creating an Agile Architecture CoP can help the enterprise meet these challenges. This approach allows System and Enterprise Architects to come together to define and learn the leaner and more incremental approaches to establishing and evolving solution architecture, and to advancing their Agile architectural skills and craft. Along the way, the following topics are likely to be addressed:

- Review and adopt the SAFe Seven Principles of Agile Architecture

- Identify enabler Epics and Capabilities necessary to evolve the solution architecture

- Identify methods of splitting architectural epics into enabler capabilities and Features for incremental implementation

- Establish the decision-making framework and policies for architectural governance and capacity allocation

- Identify relevant Nonfunctional Requirements (NFRs)

In many enterprises, such workshops are run on the PI cadence, often aligned with the innovation and planning iteration. This timing conveniently makes development teams available for fast feedback spikes to help establish the technical feasibility of design alternatives. It also supports the pressing need to prepare architectural concepts and models for review in the upcoming PI planning session.

Improve DevOps and Continuous Delivery

Once ARTs are launched and value streams begin to operate better, the enterprise has greater visibility into the next set of bottlenecks and impediments. Often, 'leaning out' the development cycle just moves the bottleneck farther down the value stream toward release and deployment. Since DevOps is integral to the value stream, SAFe ARTs include operations and maintenance personnel and can release value independently. Together, they focus on improving delivery speed via a Continuous Delivery Pipeline. A number of recommended practices are described in the DevOps chapter, which involve shifting the company mindset and enabling a collaborative environment. This requires strong leadership from managers and subject-matter experts with the authority to create a culture for continuous value delivery. CoPs can also play a leading role in this effort.

Reduce Time-to-Market with Value Stream Mapping

Identifying the value streams and organizing release trains around them delivers another significant benefit: Each value stream provides an identifiable and measurable flow of value to a Customer. As such, it can be systematically improved to increase delivery velocity and quality.

The value stream is the most important organizational construct in SAFe. 'Taking a systems view of value delivery' means understanding all the steps from ideation and feature approval to development through deployment, all the way to release. The total average time for all these steps, including the delay times, is the average time-to-market for any new feature. This gives us one more important tool in our toolbox: the process of value stream mapping, an analytical process that teams can use to first understand, and then improve, time-to-market.

An important process, as the SAFe enterprise matures its thinking, is to map the value stream and make continuous improvements. The steps are as follows:

1. From the receipt of the customer request to the solution's release, map the current state by identifying all the steps, value-added times, handoffs, and delays.

2. Identify the largest sources of delays and handoffs as the feature moves through the system.

3. Pick the biggest delay. Perform root cause analysis. Create improvement backlog items to reduce the delay. Reduce batch sizes wherever possible.

4. Implement the new improvement backlog items.

5. Measure again, and repeat the process.

Using this process, the maturing Lean enterprise can systematically improve time-to-market aggressively and continuously for its own benefit. For example, what if the ride management system value stream/ART of Figure 2 was always the critical path, and even when the vehicle was ready for shipment the ride management software was not? That would be a high cost of delay!

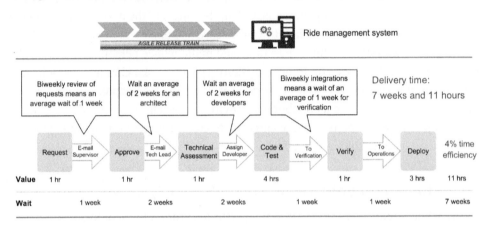

Figure 2. Ride management system value stream mapping example

In this case, the ride management ART would apply value stream mapping to identify the steps and flow through the system, and they might describe a flow such as that illustrated in Figure 2. The teams would quickly see that the amount of value-added touch time is only a small portion of the overall time it takes to deliver the end result. After all, it took them only 11 hours of work to create the new feature, yet it took *seven weeks* to deliver it! As the value stream mapping shows, the majority of the time is spent in handoffs and delays. The team members have been working hard, and apparently efficiently from the touch time, yet the overall flow through the system could not meet the demand. Coding and testing faster won't help. Rather, the teams must take the systems view and focus on the delays.

Reducing delays in the value stream is always the fastest way to reduce time-to-market.

ADDITIONAL RESOURCES

[1] Martin, Karen, and Mike Osterling. *Value Stream Mapping*. McGraw-Hill, 2014.

[2] www.http://www.scaledagileframework.com/agile-hr/

Part 3
The SAFe Principles

#1 – Take an economic view

#2 – Apply systems thinking

#3 – Assume variability; preserve options

#4 – Build incrementally with fast, integrated learning cycles

#5 – Base milestones on objective evaluation of working systems

#6 – Visualize and limit WIP, reduce batch sizes, and manage queue lengths

#7 – Apply cadence, synchronize with cross-domain planning

#8 – Unlock the intrinsic motivation of knowledge workers

#9 – Decentralize decision-making

scaledagileframework.com/**safe-lean-agile-principles**

Principle #1: Take an economic view

While you may ignore economics, it won't ignore you.

—Don Reinertsen, *Principles of Product Development Flow*

Achieving the goal of Lean—that is, the shortest sustainable lead time with the best quality and value to people and society—requires understanding the economics of the mission. Without that, even a technically competent system may cost too much to develop, take too long to deliver, or incur manufacturing or operating costs that cannot economically support efficient value.

To this end, the entire chain of leadership, management, and knowledge workers must understand the economic impact of the choices they're making. Traditionally, the economic constraints on their activities are known only to the decision-makers and authorities who understand the business, marketplace, and customer finances.

However, centralizing such knowledge means that a worker's everyday decisions are either made without this information or escalated to those who have it. The first choice directly undermines economic outcomes. The second increases delays in value delivery, which ultimately has the same effect.

Details

SAFe highlights the important role of economics in successful Solution development. Therefore, SAFe's first Lean-Agile principle is to take an economic view. It's Principle #1 for a reason: If the solution doesn't meet the Customer's or solution provider's economic goals, then its sustainability is suspect. Solutions fail for many reasons, and economics is a big one. This chapter describes the two essential aspects needed to achieve optimal economic outcomes via Lean-Agile methods:

- Deliver early and deliver often
- Understand the economic trade-off parameters for each program and Value Stream

Each of these steps is outlined in the following sections. In addition, SAFe represents many of these principles directly in its various practices, such as the 'Economic Framework' in part 7.

Deliver Early and Often

Enterprises decide to embrace Lean-Agile development either because their existing processes aren't producing the results they need, or because they anticipate that they won't do so in the future. By choosing a Lean-Agile path, they are embracing a model based on incremental development and early and continuous value delivery, as Figure 1 illustrates.

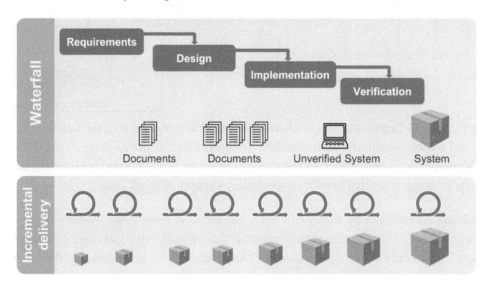

Figure 1. Moving to early and continuous delivery

That decision alone contributes perhaps the primary economic benefit, as illustrated in Figure 2.

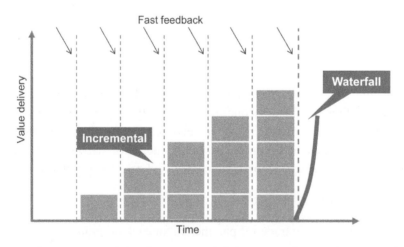

Figure 2. Incremental development and delivery produce value far earlier

Figure 2 shows how Lean-Agile methods deliver value to the customer much earlier in the process. Moreover, this value accumulates over time: The longer the customer has it, the more value the customer receives. Conversely, with the waterfall model, value can't even begin until the end of the planned development cycle.

This difference is a material economic benefit of SAFe. What is more, this picture does not take into account the advantages of receiving far faster feedback related to the solution and of eliminating the probability that the waterfall delivery would not occur on time or may not demonstrate fitness for use. Moreover, there is a third and final factor, as shown in Figure 3.

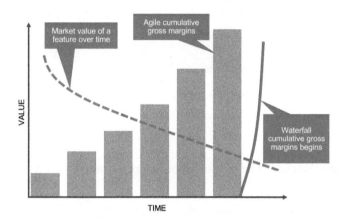

Figure 3. Value is higher early on, producing higher margins over a longer period of time

Figure 3 illustrates a key differentiator, as long as the quality is high enough: Products and services delivered to market early are typically more valuable. After all, if they arrive ahead of the competition, they aren't available from anyone else and the buyer perceives them as worth paying a premium. Over time, features become commoditized. Cost, not value differentiation, then rules the day. For this reason, even a Minimum Viable Product (MVP) can be worth more to an early buyer than a more fully featured product delivered later.

The net effect is that cumulative gross margins are higher. This is the premise of Lean-Agile development—one that is firmly entrenched in the Lean-Agile Mindset and that drives the development of the solution in the shortest sustainable lead time.

Understand Economic Trade-Off Parameters

The rationale discussed previously serves as motivation for adopting a more effective economic model of faster delivery. However, there is far more work to be done when executing a program. After all, economic decisions made throughout the life of the solution will ultimately determine the outcome. Therefore, it's necessary to take a more in-depth look at additional economic trade-offs. Reinertsen describes five factors that can be used when assessing the economic perspective of a particular investment, as shown in Figure 4 [1].

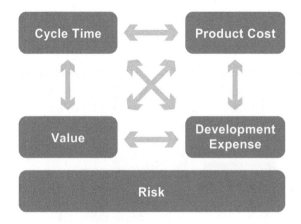

Figure 4. Five primary trade-off parameters for product development economics

In this illustration:

- **Development expense** – The cost of labor and materials required to implement a Capability
- **Cycle time** – The time to implement the capability (lead time)
- **Product cost** – The manufacturing cost (of goods sold) and/or deployment and operational costs
- **Value** – The economic worth of the capability to the business and the customer
- **Risk** – The uncertainty of the solution's technical or business success

Understanding these trade-offs helps optimize life-cycle profits, which is the key to unlocking optimal development economic value. At the same time, however, it requires a deeper project understanding. Here are two examples:

- A team building a home automation system estimates that moving more functionality to software can reduce the cost of electronic parts by $100. Doing so would delay the release lead time by three months. Should the team take this step? Clearly, the answer is 'it depends.' It depends on the anticipated volume of the product to be sold compared to the Cost of Delay (CoD) of not having the new release to market for three extra months. Some further analysis is required before that decision can be made.

- A large software system with substantial technical debt has become extremely difficult to maintain. The development expense is largely fixed. Focusing on the technical debt now will reduce the near-term value delivery. But it will also reduce lead time for future features. Should the team take this step? Again, the answer is 'it depends.' More quantitative thinking will need to be applied.

In addition to the trade-off parameters, Reinertsen describes a number of key principles that help teams make informed decisions based on economics:

- **The Principle of Quantified CoD** – If you quantify only one thing, quantify the CoD

- **The Principle of Continuous Economic Trade-Offs** – Economic choices must be made throughout the process

- **The Principle of Optimal Decision Timing** – Each decision has its ideal economic timing

- **The Sunk Cost Principle** – Do not consider money already spent

- **The First Decision Rule Principle** – Use decision rules to decentralize economic control

This last principle is particularly relevant to SAFe, and to the corollary Principle #9 – Decentralize decision-making, and is described further in the 'Economic Framework' chapter in part 7.

LEARN MORE

[1] Reinertsen, Donald. *The Principles of Product Development Flow: Second Generation Lean Product Development.* Celeritas Publishing, 2009.

Principle #2: Apply systems thinking

A system must be managed. It will not manage itself. Left to themselves, components become selfish, competitive, independent profit centers, and thus destroy the system. The secret is cooperation between components toward the aim of the organization.

—W. Edwards Deming

The three foundational bodies of knowledge that inform SAFe are systems thinking, Agile development, and Lean product development. Systems thinking takes a holistic approach to solution development, incorporating all aspects of a system and its environment into the design, development, deployment, and maintenance of the system itself.

Figure 1 illustrates the three primary aspects of systems thinking.

1. The solution itself is a system.	2. The enterprise building the system is a system, too.	3. Optimize the full Value Stream.

Figure 1. Three aspects of systems thinking

Understanding these concepts helps leaders and teams navigate the complexity of solution development, the organization, and the larger picture of total time-to-market. Each is described in the following sections.

The Solution Is a System

SAFe guides the development and deployment of complex software and cyber-physical systems. They are represented by the SAFe Solution object, the tangible object that delivers the end user's value and is the subject of each Value Stream—the application, satellite, medical device, or website. When it comes to such tangible systems, Deming's comment that "a system must be managed" leads to some critical insights:

- Team members must understand clearly where the boundaries of the system are, what the system is, and how it interacts with the environment and systems around it.

- Optimizing a component does not optimize the system. Components can become selfish and hog the resources—computing power, memory, electrical power, whatever—that other elements need.

- For the system to behave well as a system, intended behavior and some higher-level understanding of its architecture (how the components work together to accomplish the aim of the system) must be understood. Intentional design is fundamental to systems thinking.

- The value of a system passes through its interconnections. Those interfaces—and the dependencies they create—are critical to providing ultimate value. Continuous attention to those interfaces and interactions is vital.

- A system can evolve no faster than its slowest integration point. The faster the full system can be integrated and evaluated, the faster the system knowledge grows.

The Enterprise Building the System Is a System, Too

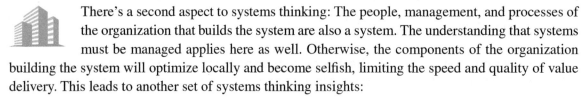 There's a second aspect to systems thinking: The people, management, and processes of the organization that builds the system are also a system. The understanding that systems must be managed applies here as well. Otherwise, the components of the organization building the system will optimize locally and become selfish, limiting the speed and quality of value delivery. This leads to another set of systems thinking insights:

- Building complex systems is a social endeavor. Therefore, leaders must cultivate an environment where people can collaborate on the best way to build better systems.

- Suppliers and customers are integral to the value stream. They must be treated as partners, based on a long-term foundation of trust.

- Optimizing a component does not optimize the system in this case, either. Likewise, optimizing local teams or functional departments does not necessarily enhance the flow of value through the enterprise.

- Value crosses organizational boundaries. Accelerating its delivery requires eliminating silos or creating cross-functional organizations, such as Agile Release Trains (ARTs).

Understand and Optimize the Full Value Stream

Value streams are fundamental to SAFe. A SAFe portfolio is essentially a collection of value streams, each of which delivers one or more solutions to the market. As illustrated in Figure 2, each value stream consists of the steps necessary to integrate and deploy a new concept through a new or existing system.

Principle #4: Build incrementally with fast, integrated learning cycles

The epiphany of integration points is that they control product development and are the leverage points to improve the system. When timing of integration points slips, the project is in trouble.

—Dantar P. Oosterwal

In traditional, phase-gated development, investment costs begin immediately and accumulate until a Solution is delivered. Often, little to no actual value is provided before all of the committed Features are available or the program runs out of time or money. During development, it's difficult to get any meaningful feedback, because the process just isn't designed for it. What's more, the development process itself isn't set up or implemented to allow incremental Capabilities to be evaluated by the customer. As a result, the risk remains in the program until the deadline, and even into deployment and after initial use.

No wonder the typical procedure is error-prone and problematic, often resulting in loss of trust with the customer. Attempting to adjust for this possibility, both parties try even harder to define the requirements and select the best design up-front. They also typically implement even more rigorous phase gates. Each of these remedies, unfortunately, actually compounds the underlying problem. This is a systems-level problem in the development process: It must be addressed from a systemic perspective.

Integration Points Create Knowledge from Uncertainty

Lean principles and practices approach the problem differently. Rather than pick a single requirements-and-design choice early on—assuming that this choice is feasible and will provide fitness for purpose—a range of requirements and design options (Principle #3) are considered while building the solution incrementally in a series of short timeboxes. Each timeboxed activity results in an increment of a working system that can be evaluated. Subsequent timeboxes build on the previous increments, and the solution evolves until it is finally released. The knowledge gained from integration points is not solely to establish technical viability. That is, integration points can also serve as minimum viable solutions or prototypes for testing the market, validating usability, and gaining objective customer feedback. Where necessary, these fast feedback points allow teams to pivot to an alternative course of action, one that should better serve the needs of the intended customers.

Integration Points Occur by Intent

The development process and the solution architecture are designed, in part, to focus on cadence-based integration points. Each point creates a 'pull event' that pulls the various solution elements into an integrated whole, even though it addresses only a portion of the system intent. Integration points pull the stakeholders together as well, creating a routine synchronization that helps assure that the evolving solution addresses the real and current business needs, as opposed to the assumptions established at the beginning of the process. Each integration point delivers its value by converting uncertainty into knowledge:

- Knowledge of the technical feasibility of the current design choice

- Knowledge of the potential sustainability of the solution, based on objective measures (Principle #5)

Faster Learning through Faster Cycles

Integration points are an example of Shewhart's plan–do–check–adjust cycle (Figure 1) and are the mechanism for controlling the variability of solution development [3].

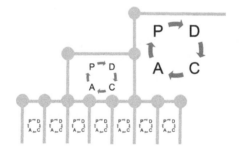

Figure 1. Plan–do–check–adjust cycle

The more frequent the points, the faster the learning. In complex systems development, local integration points are used to assure that each system element or capability is meeting its responsibilities to contribute to the overall Solution Intent. These local points must then be integrated at the next higher system level. The larger the system, the more such integration levels exist. Solution designers recognize that the top-level, least-frequent integration point provides the only true measure of system progress, and they work to create these points as frequently as possible. All stakeholders understand that when the timing of integration points slips, the project is in trouble. But even then, this knowledge helps spark the necessary adjustments to scope, technical approach, cost, or the delivery timing needed to redirect the project to meet revised expectations.

LEARN MORE

[1] Oosterwal, Dantar P. *The Lean Machine: How Harley-Davidson Drove Top-Line Growth and Profitability with Revolutionary Lean Product Development.* Amacom, 2010.

[2] Ward, Allan C., and Durward Sobek. *Lean Product and Process Development.* Lean Enterprise Institute, 2014.

[3] Deming, W. Edwards. *Out of the Crisis.* MIT Press, 2000.

Principle #5: Base milestones on objective evaluation of working systems

There was in fact no correlation between exiting phase gates on time and project success ... the data suggested the inverse might be true.

—Dantar P. Oosterwal, The Lean Machine

The Problem with Phase-Gate Milestones

Developing today's large systems requires substantial resources—investments that can total millions and even hundreds of millions of dollars. Developers and customers have a mutual fiduciary responsibility to ensure that investments in new Solutions will deliver the necessary economic benefits. Otherwise, why bother?

Clearly, stakeholders must collaborate in ways that help ensure the potential to realize the prospective economic benefit throughout the development process, versus engaging in wishful thinking until the end. The industry has generally applied a sequential phase-gated (waterfall) development process to address this challenge, measuring and controlling progress through a series of specific Milestones.

These phase-gate milestones are not arbitrary, but rather follow a seemingly logical and sequential process: discovery, requirements, design, development, test, and delivery. Of course, this approach doesn't always work out all that well, as Figure 1 shows.

Figure 1. The problem with phase-gate milestones

The cause of the problem is the failure to recognize the four critical errors about the assumption that phase gates reveal real progress and, therefore, to mitigate risk:

- Centralizing requirements and design decisions in siloed functions that may not be integral to the solution.

- Forcing too-early design decisions and false-positive feasibility [1]:

  - An early choice is made for the best-known option at that time.

  - Development proceeds under the assumption that everything is on track.

  - Later it's discovered that the chosen path is not feasible (see Principle #3).

- Assuming a point solution exists and can be built correctly the first time. This ignores the variability inherent in the process and provides no legitimate outlet for it. Variability will find a way to express itself.

- Making up-front decisions creates large batches of requirements, code, and tests, as well as long queues. This leads to large-batch handoffs and delayed feedback (Principle #6).

Base Milestones on Objective Evidence

Clearly, the phase-gate model does not mitigate risk as intended, so a different approach is needed. Principle #4, which calls for building incrementally with fast, integrated learning cycles, provides elements of the solution to this dilemma.

Throughout development, the system is built in increments, each of which is an integration point that demonstrates some evidence of the feasibility of the solution in process. Unlike phase-gated development, every milestone involves a portion of each step—requirements, design, development, testing; together, these steps produce an increment of value (Figure 2).

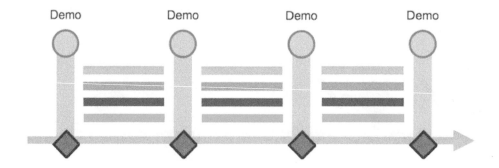

Figure 2. Milestones based on objective evaluation of working systems

Further, this is done routinely on a cadence (Principle #7), which provides the discipline needed to ensure periodic availability and evaluation, as well as predetermined time boundaries that can be used to collapse the field of less desirable options.

What is actually measured at these critical integration points is subject to the nature and the type of system being built. The key point is that the system can be measured, assessed, and evaluated by the relevant stakeholders frequently, and throughout the solution development life cycle. This provides the financial, technical, and fitness-for-purpose governance needed to ensure that the continuing investment will produce a commensurate return.

LEARN MORE

[1] Oosterwal, Dantar P. *The Lean Machine: How Harley-Davidson Drove Top-Line Growth and Profitability with Revolutionary Lean Product Development.* Amacom, 2010.

Principle #6: Visualize and limit WIP, reduce batch sizes, and manage queue lengths

Operating a product development process near full utilization is an economic disaster.

—Donald Reinertsen

To achieve the shortest sustainable lead time, Lean enterprises strive for a state of continuous flow, which allows them to move new system Capabilities quickly from concept to cash. Accomplishing this aim requires eliminating the traditional start–stop–start project initiation and development process, along with the incumbent phase gates that hinder flow (Principle #5).

There are three major keys to implementing flow:

- Visualize and limit work in process (WIP)
- Reduce the batch sizes of work items
- Manage queue lengths

Visualize and Limit WIP

Overloading teams and programs with more work than they can accomplish is a common and harmful practice. Having too much WIP confuses priorities, causes frequent context switching, and increases overhead. It overloads workers, scatters focus on immediate tasks, reduces productivity and throughput, and increases wait times for new functionality. Burnout is a painfully common result.

The first step to correct the problem is to make the current WIP visible to all stakeholders (see Figure 1). This Kanban board illustrates the total amount of work at each state and serves as an initial process diagnostic, showing the current bottlenecks. Often, simply visualizing the current volume is the wake-up call that causes practitioners to start addressing the systemic problems of too much work and too little flow.

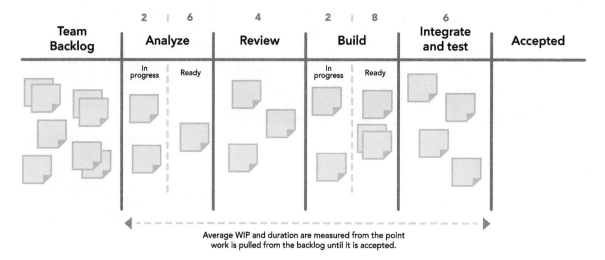

Figure 1. Visualizing work in progress

The next workflow state is to start balancing the amount of WIP against the available development capacity. When any step reaches its WIP limit, no new work is taken on.

Limiting WIP, however, requires knowledge, discipline, and commitment. It may even seem counter-intuitive to those who believe that the more work you put into the system, the more you get out. That relationship can hold true up to the point of nearly full capacity, but thereafter the system becomes turbulent and throughput decreases. There is no substitute for effectively managing WIP.

Reduce Batch Size

Another way to reduce WIP and improve flow is to decrease the batch sizes of the work—the requirements, designs, code, tests, and other work items that move through the system. Small batches go through the system more quickly and with less variability, which fosters faster learning. The reason for the faster speed is obvious. The reduced variability results from the smaller number of items in the batch. Since each item has some variability, the accumulation of a large number of items has more variability.

The economically optimal batch size depends on both the holding cost (the cost for delayed feedback, inventory decay, and delayed value delivery) and the transaction cost (the cost of preparing and implementing the batch). Figure 2 illustrates the U-curve optimization for batch size [1].

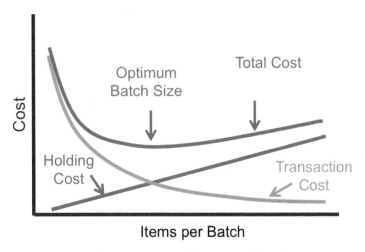

Figure 2. Determining the optimal batch size

To improve the economics of handling smaller batches—and thus increase throughput—teams must focus on reducing the transaction costs of any batch. This typically involves increasing the attention to and investment in infrastructure and automation, including considerations such as Continuous Integration and the build environment, DevOps automation, and system test setup times. Such a focus is integral to systems thinking (Principle #2) and a critical element in long-view optimization.

Manage Queue Lengths

The last method to achieve flow is to manage queue lengths and reduce them. Little's law—the seminal principle of queuing theory—tells us that the wait time for service from a system equals the ratio of queue length divided by the average processing rate. (While this might sound complicated, even the line at Starbucks proves the validity of Little's law.) Therefore, assuming any average processing rate, the longer the queue, the longer the wait.

For solution development, this means that the longer the queue of work awaiting implementation by the team, the longer the wait time, no matter how efficient the team. So, to achieve faster service, you must either reduce the length of the queue or increase the processing rate. While increasing the processing rate is a worthy goal, the easiest method to reduce wait time is to reduce the queue length. Keeping backlogs short and largely uncommitted allows new, higher-priority work to enter and leave the system with less wait time. Visualizing the work helps identify ways to streamline the process, while shortening the queue size decreases delays, reduces waste, and increases predictability of outcomes.

The three primary ways of implementing flow—visualizing and limiting WIP, reducing the batch sizes of work items, and managing queue lengths—provide powerful approaches to increase throughput. Implementing them can trigger fast and measurable improvements in customer satisfaction and employee engagement, benefiting Agile teams and their customers.

LEARN MORE

[1] Reinertsen, Donald G. *The Principles of Product Development Flow: Second Generation Lean Product Development.* Celeritas, 2009.

Principle #7: Apply cadence, synchronize with cross-domain planning

Cadence and synchronization limit the accumulation of variance.

—Don Reinertsen, *Principles of Product Development Flow*

Solution development is an inherently uncertain process. If it weren't, the solutions would already exist, and there would be no room for the next generation of innovations. This risk conflicts with the need for businesses to manage investments, track progress, and have enough confidence in future outcomes to plan and commit to a reasonable course of action.

Lean-Agile teams function in a 'safety zone,' where enough uncertainty actually provides the freedom to pursue innovation, while sufficient confidence allows the business to operate. The primary means to achieve this balance is through the knowledge of the current state gained in cadence, synchronization, and cross-domain planning.

Cadence

Cadence provides a rhythmic pattern, the steady heartbeat of the process. It makes routine everything that can be routine, so knowledge workers can just focus on managing the variable part of solution development. By transforming unpredictable events into expected events, cadence offers many additional benefits:

- Wait times become predictable. If the work you're waiting for isn't in this Program Increment (PI) timebox, it likely will be in the next one.

- By facilitating planning, cadence enables more efficient use of people and resources.

- It lowers the transaction costs of key events, including planning, integration, demos, feedback, and retrospectives.

Synchronization

Synchronization allows multiple perspectives to be understood, resolved, and integrated at the same time (Figure 1). As a result, it:

- Pulls the different assets of a system together to assess solution viability

- Aligns the development teams and business to a common mission

- Integrates the customers into the development process

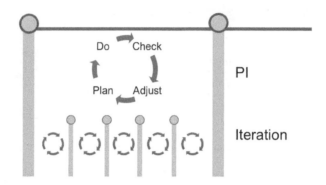

Figure 1. SAFe cadence and synchronization harmonics

Taken together, cadence and synchronization—and most importantly, the associated activities—help teams proceed confidently despite the risks described previously.

Synchronize with Cross-Domain Planning

Of all the events that occur, one is the most critical: Periodically, all stakeholders gather for cross-domain planning and synchronization. This event, known as PI Planning, is the fulcrum upon which all other events rest. It also gives the teams an opportunity to present and review their true knowledge of the current state.

The PI Planning event serves three primary purposes:

- **It assesses the current state of the solution.** An integrated, solution-level demonstration and assessment determines the objective knowledge of the current state. This typically occurs just before the planning event.

- **It realigns all stakeholders to a common technical and business vision.** Based on the current state, business and technology leaders reset the mission, with the minimum number of constraints (Principle #8 and Principle #9). This aligns all stakeholders to a common vision, in both the near term and the long term.

- **It facilitates planning and commits teams to the next program increment.** Based on the new knowledge, the teams plan what they can accomplish in the upcoming timebox. Sharing the planning and control empowers teams to create the best possible plans to achieve the best possible solution within the given constraints.

Developing large-scale systems is fundamentally a social activity, and this planning event provides a continuous opportunity to build and improve the social network.

There's no cure for the inherent uncertainty of solution development. If there were, it would surely be worse than the disease. However, applying cadence and synchronization, along with periodic cross-domain planning, provides the tools needed to operate in the safety zone.

LEARN MORE

[1] Reinertsen, Donald. *The Principles of Product Development Flow: Second Generation Lean Product Development.* Celeritas Publishing, 2009.

[2] Kennedy, Michael. *Product Development for the Lean Enterprise.* Oaklea Press, 2003.

Principle #8: Unlock the intrinsic motivation of knowledge workers

It appears that the performance of the task provides its own intrinsic reward … this drive … may be as basic as the others….

—Daniel Pink, Drive: The Surprising Truth About What Motivates Us

Lean-Agile Leaders must accept a relatively new, game-changing truth: The management of knowledge workers is an oxymoron. As Peter Drucker points out, "knowledge workers are individuals who know more about the work that they perform than their bosses" [2]. In that context, how can any manager seriously attempt to oversee or even coordinate the technical activities of people who are infinitely more capable than they are of defining the tasks necessary to accomplish their mission?

Indeed, they cannot. What managers *can* do is unlock the intrinsic motivation of knowledge workers. Some guidelines are provided in the following sections.

Leverage the Systems View

Before delving into additional motivational constructs, we must note a significant insight: The Lean-Agile principles of SAFe are themselves a system, too. Moreover, the elements of this system collaborate to create a new and empowering paradigm. With SAFe, knowledge workers are now able to:

- Communicate across functional boundaries
- Make decisions based on an understanding of the economics
- Receive fast feedback about the efficacy of their solution
- Participate in continuous, incremental learning and mastery
- Participate in a more productive and fulfilling solution development process—one of the most powerful motivations of all

Understand the Role of Compensation

Many organizations still operate from assumptions about human potential and individual performance that are outdated, rooted more in folklore than in science. They continue to pursue practices such as short-term incentive plans and pay-for-performance schemes in the face of mounting evidence that such measures usually don't work and often do harm.

   —Daniel Pink, *Drive: The Surprising Truth About What Motivates Us*

Pink, Drucker, and others have pointed out the fundamental paradox of compensation as a motivational factor for knowledge workers [1, 2]:

- If you don't pay enough, people won't be motivated.

- But after a point, money is no longer a motivator. That is the goal of intellectual freedom and self-actualization. When that state is achieved, the knowledge worker's mind is free to focus on the work, not the money.

After this point, adding incentive compensation elements can shift the focus to the money, rather than the work, resulting in poorer employee performance.

Lean-Agile Leaders understand that ideation, innovation, and deep workplace engagement aren't motivated by money, or even by the reverse—threats, intimidation, or fear. Such incentive-based compensation, often determined by individual management by objectives (MBO), causes internal competition and the potential destruction of the cooperation necessary to achieve the larger aim. In that competition, the enterprise is the loser.

Provide Autonomy with Purpose, Mission, and Minimum Possible Constraints

Pink asserts that knowledge workers have a need for autonomy—the ability to self-direct and to manage their own lives. Providing autonomy, while harnessing it to the larger aim of the enterprise, is an important leadership responsibility [1].

Managers and workers also know that the motivation of self-direction must occur within the context of the larger objective. To this end, leaders must provide some larger purpose—some connection between the aim of the enterprise and a knowledge worker's daily activities.

When building systems, knowledge workers collaborate as a team. Being part of a high-performing group is yet another critical motivation. Leaders can inspire teams to do their best by providing the following guidance [4]:

- The mission, a general goal and strategic direction, and a strong vision

- Little, minimal, or even no specific work or project plans

- Challenging requirements, along with the minimum possible constraints as to how teams meet these requirements

Create an Environment of Mutual Influence

"To effectively lead, the workers must be heard and respected" [2] in the context of an environment of mutual influence [4]. Leaders create this kind of environment by giving tough feedback supportively, by showing a willingness to become more vulnerable, and by encouraging others to engage in positive ways:

- Disagree where appropriate

- Advocate for the positions they believe in

- Make their needs clear and push to achieve them

- Enter into joint problem-solving with management and peers

- Negotiate, compromise, agree, and commit

We live in a new age, where the workers are smarter and have more local context than management can ever have. Unlocking this raw potential can significantly improve the lives of those doing the work, as well as provide better outcomes for customers and the enterprise.

LEARN MORE

[1] Pink, Daniel. *Drive: The Surprising Truth About What Motivates Us.* Riverhead Books, 2011.

[2] Drucker, Peter F. *The Essential Drucker.* Harper-Collins, 2001.

[3] Bradford, David L., and Allen Cohen. *Managing for Excellence: The Leadership Guide to Developing High Performance in Contemporary Organizations.* John Wiley and Sons, 1997.

[4] Takeuchi, Hirotaka, and Ikurijo Nonaka. "The New New Product Development Game." *Harvard Business Review,* January 1986.

Principle #9: Decentralize decision-making

Knowledge workers themselves are best placed to make decisions about how to perform their work.

—Peter F. Drucker

Delivering value in the shortest sustainable lead time requires decentralized decision-making. Any decision that must be escalated to higher levels of authority introduces a delay. Also, such decisions can decrease quality due to the lack of local context, plus changes to the facts on which they are based that occur during the waiting period.

Conversely, decentralizing decision-making reduces delays, improves product development flow and throughput, and facilitates faster feedback and more innovative solutions. Higher levels of empowerment are an additional, tangible benefit.

Centralize Strategic Decisions

Of course, not all decisions should be decentralized. Some decisions are strategic, have far-reaching impact, and are outside the scope, knowledge, or responsibilities of the teams. In addition, leaders are still accountable for outcomes. They also have the market knowledge, longer-range perspectives, and understanding of the business and financial landscape necessary to steer the enterprise.

Some decisions, then, should be centralized. Generally, they share the following characteristics:

- **Infrequent** – Made infrequently, these decisions typically are not urgent, and deeper consideration is appropriate (e.g., product strategy, international expansion).

- **Long-lasting** – Once made, these decisions are unlikely to change, at least in the short term (e.g., commitment to a standard technology platform, commitment to organizational realignment around Value Streams).

- **Provide significant economies of scale** – These choices deliver large and broad economic benefits (e.g., a common way of working, standard development languages, standard tooling, offshoring).

Leadership is charged with making these types of decisions, supported by the input of those stakeholders who are affected by the results.

Decentralize Everything Else

The vast majority of decisions do not reach the threshold of strategic importance. All other decisions should be decentralized. Characteristics of these types of decisions include:

- **Frequent** – The problems addressed by decentralized decisions are recurrent and common (e.g., Team and Program Backlog prioritization, real-time Agile Release Train scoping, response to defects and emerging issues).

- **Time-critical** – Delaying these types of decisions comes with a high cost of delay (e.g., point releases, customer emergencies, dependencies with other teams).

- **Require local information** – These decisions need specific local context, whether it be technology, organization, or specific customer or market impact (e.g., shipping a release to a specific customer, resolving a significant design problem, self-organization of individuals and teams to meet an emerging challenge).

Decentralized decisions should be made by the workers who have local context and detailed knowledge of the technical complexities of the current situation.

A Lightweight Thinking Tool for Decision-Making

Understanding how decisions are made helps enable knowledge workers to approach the decision-making process with a clearer point of view. Leadership's responsibility is to establish the rules for decision-making (including, for example, the Economic Framework) and then empower others to make them. A simple tool or exercise for thinking about whether decisions should be centralized or decentralized is shown in Figure 1.

① Consider three significant decisions you are currently facing.
② Rate each item using the table below.
③ Would you centralize or decentralize?

Decision	Frequent? Y=2 N=0	Time critical? Y=2 N=0	Economies of scale? Y=0 N=2	Total

▷ Scale: 0 to 2 (low to high)
▷ Then add the total: 0 to 3 = centralize | 4 to 6 = decentralize

Figure 1. A simple decision-making framework and exercise

Part 4
The Team Level

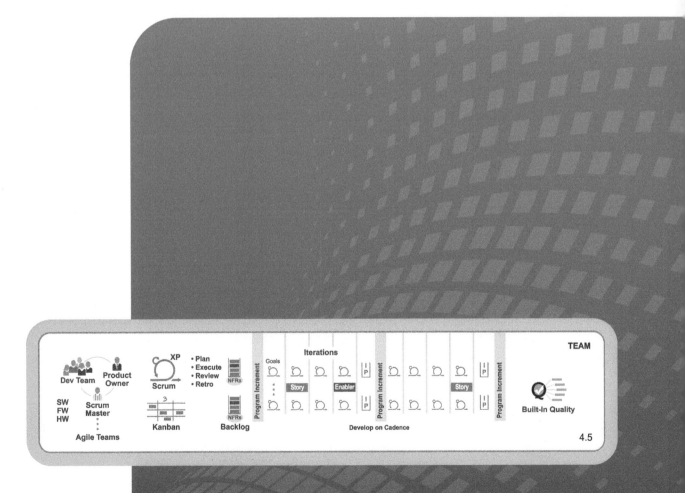

scaledagileframework.com/**team-level**

Team Level

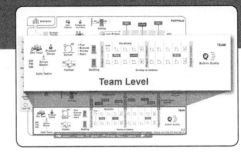

'Ba'—we, the work, and the knowledge are all one.

—*SAFe Authors*

The *Team Level* contains the roles, activities, events, and processes that Agile Teams build and deliver value in the context of the Agile Release Train (ART).

While depicted somewhat separately in the 'Big Picture,' the SAFe Team Level is a vital part of the Program Level. All SAFe teams are part of an ART—the primary construct of the program level.

Details

The team level describes how Agile teams power the train, as shown in Figure 1.

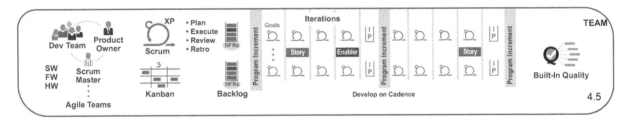

Figure 1. Team level

The ART roles and functions, including the Release Train Engineer (RTE), Product Management, System Architect/Engineering, System Team, and Shared Services support all the teams on the train. As a result, they are fully capable of defining, developing, testing, and delivering working and tested systems each Iteration.

Each Agile team is responsible for defining, building, and testing Stories from its Team Backlog. Using a shared iteration cadence and synchronization, the teams align to a series of fixed-length iterations to make sure the entire system is iterating. Teams use ScrumXP or Team Kanban, along with the Built-In Quality practices, to deliver high-quality systems, routinely producing a System Demo every two weeks. This ensures that all teams in the ART create an integrated and tested system that stakeholders can evaluate and respond to with fast feedback.

Each team has five to nine members and includes all the roles necessary to build a quality increment of value in each iteration. ScrumXP roles include the Scrum Master, Product Owner (PO), dedicated individual contributors, and any subject-matter experts the team needs to deliver value. Team Kanban roles are less strictly defined, though many SAFe Kanban teams implement the ScrumXP roles as well.

Highlights

Following are the highlights of the team level:

- **Iterations** – Fixed-length timeboxes that provide the development cadence for Agile teams building Features and components. Each iteration delivers a valuable increment of new functionality.

- **Program Increments (PIs)** – Establish common iterations for all teams on the ART to use the same duration, and start and end dates within the PI.

- **Develop on Cadence** – Uses the PI timebox to combine larger, system-wide functionality into valuable and measurable program increments. Programs should develop on cadence and Release on Demand.

- **ScrumXP** – A lightweight process for self-organizing and self-managing cross-functional teams of five to nine people. To continuously deliver value, ScrumXP uses the Scrum framework for project management and XP-derived software engineering practices.

- **Team Kanban** – A Lean method that helps teams facilitate the flow of value by visualizing workflow, establishing Work in Process (WIP) limits, measuring throughput, and continuously improving their processes. SAFe teams can choose to operate as ScrumXP or Kanban teams, or in a hybrid model.

- **Built-In Quality** – Practices largely inspired by Extreme Programming (XP), which ensures that software, firmware, and hardware solution increments are high in quality and can readily adapt to change.

Roles

The team-level roles help coordinate and synchronize team-level events, through which the Agile teams build and deliver value in the context of the Agile Release Train:

- **Agile Team** – A cross-functional ScrumXP or Kanban team that consists of the Dev Team as well as the Scrum Master and the Product Owner. This group of 5 to 11 people has the ability and authority to define, build, and test an element (story or Enabler) of solution value within an iteration.

- **Development Team (Dev Team)** – A small, cross-functional team of developers, testers, and other specialists who work collaboratively to deliver a vertical slice of functionality. The Dev Team is a subset of the Agile team.

- **Product Owner** – The role that has content authority for the team backlog. The Product Owner is responsible for defining stories and prioritizing the backlog and is the only team member empowered to accept stories as done.

- **Scrum Master** – A member of the Agile team who acts as both a servant leader and an Agile team coach. The Scrum Master helps the team remove impediments, facilitates team events, and fosters a supportive environment for high-performing teams.

Events

The team level uses several events to synchronize and coordinate activities among teams within the ART:

- **Iteration Planning** – An event in which an Agile team determines the Iteration Goals and decides how much of the team backlog they can commit to during an upcoming iteration. Team capacity determines the number of stories and enablers that are selected.

- **Iteration Review** – A cadence-based event in which the team inspects the increment at the end of the iteration and adjusts the team backlog based on feedback. All work done during the iteration is demoed during the iteration review.

- **Iteration Execution** – The means by which the Agile team develops an increment of an effective, high-quality, working, tested system within the timebox. Each day during execution, an Agile team holds a 15-minute timeboxed meeting called a Daily Stand-up (DSU). The goal of the DSU is to synchronize team members, review progress, and identify issues.

- **Iteration Retrospective** – An event held at the end of the iteration during which the Agile team reviews its practices and identifies ways to improve. The retrospective is based on the qualitative and quantitative information presented during the iteration review.

- **Backlog refinement** – An event held once or twice during the iteration to refine, review, and estimate stories and enablers in the team backlog.

- **Innovation and Planning (IP) Iteration** – An event that provides the teams with an opportunity for exploration and innovation, dedicated time for planning, and learning through informal and formal channels. In the case where a release is on the PI boundary, teams perform final system verification, validation, and documentation.

Artifacts

The following team-level artifacts help describe the business and technical value delivered by the teams during each iteration and PI:

- **Story** – The vehicle that carries Customer requirements through the Value Stream into implementation. The teams use stories to deliver value within an iteration, and the Product Owner has content authority over their creation and acceptance.

- **Enabler stories** – Support the activities needed to extend the Architectural Runway to provide future business functionality. Like any story, they must fit within an iteration and require acceptance criteria to clarify the requirements and support testing.

- **Iteration goals** – An output of the iteration planning event. These high-level summaries indicate the business and technical goals that the Agile team agrees to accomplish in an iteration. They help ensure alignment with the PI Objectives.

- **Team backlog** – User and enabler stories; most are identified during PI planning and backlog refinement meetings.

- **Team PI objectives** – Summary descriptions of the specific business and technical goals that an Agile team intends to achieve in the upcoming PI.

LEARN MORE

[1] Leffingwell, Dean. *Agile Software Requirements: Lean Requirements Practices for Teams, Programs, and the Enterprise*. Addison-Wesley, 2011.

Agile Teams

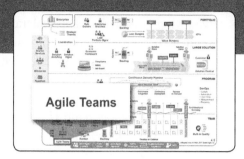

Nothing beats an Agile Team.
  —SAFe mantra

The SAFe *Agile Team* is a cross-functional group of 5 to 11 people who have the responsibility to define, build, test, and where applicable deploy some element of Solution value—all in a short Iteration timebox. Specifically, the SAFe Agile Team incorporates the Dev Team, Scrum Master, and Product Owner roles.

In SAFe, Agile Teams power the Agile Release Train (ART) and are responsible for delivering larger solution value. No train can exist without its teams. Likewise, all teams are on a train, contributing to its Vision and Roadmap, collaborating with other teams, and participating in ART events. In addition, they are largely responsible for building the Continuous Delivery Pipeline and ART DevOps capabilities.

The teams and the train are inseparable; the whole is greater than the sum of its parts.

Details

The Agile movement [1] represented a major turning point in the way software and systems were developed. SAFe builds on this change by empowering Agile Teams as the building blocks for creating and delivering value. Without effective Agile Teams, composed of empowered and motivated individuals, organizations cannot achieve the larger business benefits of Lean-Agile development.

Collectively, the members of an Agile Team have all the skills necessary to develop increments of value in a short timebox:

- **Define** – Elaborate and design features and components
- **Build** – Implement features and components
- **Test** – Run test cases to validate features or components
- **Deploy** – Moving features to 'staging' and 'production' environments

While operating within the context of the ART, teams are empowered, self-organizing, and self-managing. They are accountable to deliver results that meet the Customer's needs and expectations.

Teams develop software, hardware, firmware, or some combination of these outputs. Mostly, though, a team represents a collaboration of the cross-functional disciplines necessary to deliver Features or components.

By moving work to the teams and trains, instead of bringing people to the work, Enterprises can largely eliminate the 'project model' of working (see Lean Budgets) and instead create teams, and teams of teams, that are long-lived and dedicated to relentlessly improving their ability to deliver solutions. This is what makes SAFe different from the traditional approach, in which managers direct individuals to complete activities. SAFe teams—rather than their managers—determine which features and components they can build in an iteration and how to build them. Lean-Agile Leaders provide the vision, leadership, and autonomy necessary to foster and promote high-performing teams. Assigning work to individual team members is no longer required, because teams are largely self-organizing and self-managing. This enables decentralized decision-making all the way to the level of the individual contributor. The primary responsibility of Lean-Agile Leaders then becomes coaching and mentoring Agile Teams.

SAFe Teams Typically Blend Agile Methods

SAFe teams use Agile practices of choice, based primarily on Scrum, Kanban, and Extreme Programming (XP). Most SAFe teams apply Scrum with XP (see SAFe ScrumXP) as the basic framework. The Product Owner manages the Team Backlog. The Scrum Master facilitates the team in meeting its delivery objectives and helps build a high-performing and self-managing group.

Teams apply Lean UX feature development and Built-In Quality practices to drive disciplined development and quality. These practices—which include collective ownership, pair work, coding standards, test-first, and Continuous Integration—help to keep things Lean by embedding quality and operating efficiency directly into the process. Agile Architecture completes the picture for quality solution development.

SAFe is a flow-based system, so most teams also apply Kanban to visualize their work, establish Work in Process (WIP) limits, and use Cumulative Flow Diagrams (CFDs) to identify bottlenecks and key opportunities for improving throughput. Some teams—especially maintenance teams and System Teams—apply Kanban as their base practice. This approach is helpful because the planning and commitment elements of Scrum may not apply as efficiently for workloads that are activity and demand-based and in environments where priorities change more frequently.

Responsibilities

SAFe helps the organization move away from the traditional, phase-gated development model in which user value is delivered at the end of a long life cycle with input from separate functional silos (requirements, design, test, deploy). Instead, Agile Teams perform *all* of these functions while delivering value at every iteration. Agile Teams are responsible for managing their work and producing value across

Dev Team

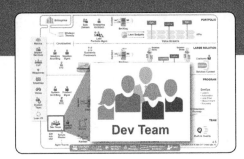

Everybody codes. Everybody tests.

The *Dev Team* is a subset of the Agile Team. It consists of the dedicated professionals who can develop and test a Story, Feature, or component. The Dev Team typically includes software developers and testers, engineers, and other dedicated specialists required to complete a vertical slice of functionality.

For consistency with the Scrum definition, the Dev Team does not include the Product Owner and the Scrum Master; these roles are part of the larger Agile Team.

Details

Developers and testers are the core of Agile development. They work in small, cross-functional teams and can quickly create working, tested code that delivers value. They build the systems we all depend on.

In traditional development, the developer and tester roles are typically differentiated, often with each reporting into a different management structure. In Agile development, the two roles are blended together. For example, Mike Cohn doesn't distinguish the roles and instead calls everyone 'developers' [1]. Engineers who develop hardware, firmware, and other components are also considered 'developers' in the context of SAFe. The line between development and test is purposely blurred; developers test and testers code.

Dev teams are empowered by the enterprise to manage and self-organize to accomplish their own work. Their members possess all the skills the team needs to create an increment of a working, tested solution.

Responsibilities

The Dev Team has the following responsibilities:

- Collaborate with the Product Owner to create and refine user stories and acceptance criteria

- Participate in PI Planning and create Iteration plans and Team PI Objectives

- Develop and commit to Team PI Objectives and Iteration plans

- Work with the Product Owner to confirm that the code and acceptance tests reflect the desired functionality; writing the code

- Conduct research, design, prototyping, and other exploration activities

- Create unit tests and automated acceptance tests

- Check new code into the shared source code repository

- Pair up to write code and automated acceptance test cases

- Execute acceptance tests and maintain the test cases in a shared repository

- Strive to continuously improve the team's process

Collocation, Collaboration, and Knowledge Sharing

The collocation of Agile team members and the blurring of the traditional roles optimizes velocity and quality. It also helps create empowered Agile teams. However, this means that developers no longer operate collectively from a shared resource pool, where theoretically it might be easier to learn, share, and advance collective competencies. To address this potential disadvantage, the Agile enterprise must consciously create a culture and environment in which best practices and knowledge are shared. This includes newfound Agile skills such as story writing, Continuous Exploration, Continuous Integration, Continuous Deployment, collective code ownership, and automated unit and acceptance testing, which are easily shared across teams. Such sharing is often facilitated by Communities of Practice.

Continuous Delivery

As implied earlier, the Dev Team is directly responsible for much of the culture and many of the practices necessary for building the Continuous Delivery Pipeline and implementing DevOps. To this end, the team's 'T-shaped' skill training includes developing and managing staging and deployment environments and mastering techniques for independently releasing elements of the larger Solution. The team members assume additional responsibilities for following the code downstream and into production. This approach further blends traditional siloed responsibilities such that Agile teams, and even individual developers, can master the ability to Release on Demand.

Design for Testability

Since all code is tested code, developers design and evolve the system to support testability and test automation. In practice, designing for testability and good design are synonymous and imply modularity, low coupling, and high cohesion of layers, components, and classes. This supports the testability of any separate fragment of logic, as well as the ability to create higher, system-level, integration tests. In a similar manner, the solution should be designed to make it easy to deploy and release.

LEARN MORE

[1] Cohn, Mike. *Succeeding with Agile: Software Development Using Scrum.* Addison-Wesley, 2009.

[2] Leffingwell, Dean. *Agile Software Requirements: Lean Requirements Practices for Teams, Programs, and the Enterprise.* Addison-Wesley, 2011.

Product Owner

Business people and developers must work together daily throughout the project.

—Agile Manifesto

The *Product Owner (PO)* is the member of the Agile Team who is responsible for defining Stories and prioritizing the Team Backlog to streamline the execution of program priorities, while simultaneously maintaining the conceptual and technical integrity of the Features or components for the team. The PO has a significant role in quality control and is the only team member empowered to accept stories as done. For most enterprises moving to Agile, this is a new and critical role, typically translating into a full-time job, requiring one PO to support each Agile team (or, at most, two teams).

The PO role has significant relationships and responsibilities outside the local team. For example, the PO works with Product Management, the role that is responsible for the Program Backlog, to prepare for the Program Increment (PI) Planning meeting.

Details

The PO is the member of the Agile team who serves as the Customer proxy. This person is responsible for working with Product Management and other stakeholders—including other POs—to define and prioritize stories in the team backlog. This activity ensures that the Solution effectively addresses program priorities (features and Enablers) while maintaining technical integrity. Ideally, the PO is collocated with the rest of the team members and typically shares the same management, incentives, and culture. In addition, the PO attends most relevant Product Management meetings about planning and Program Backlog/Vision refinement.

Responsibilities

The PO fulfills the following duties.

Preparation and Participation in PI Planning

- As a member of the extended Product Management team, the PO is heavily involved in program backlog refinement and preparations for PI planning, and also plays a significant role in the planning event itself. Before the planning event, the PO updates the team backlog and typically reviews and contributes to the program's Vision, Roadmap, and content presentations.

- During the event, the PO is involved with story definition, providing the clarifications necessary to assist the team members with their story estimates and sequencing. The PO also drafts the team's specific objectives for the upcoming PI.

Iteration Execution

- **Maintaining the team backlog** – With input from the System Architect/Engineering role and other stakeholders, the PO has the primary responsibility for building, editing, and maintaining the team backlog. Consisting mostly of user stories, it also includes defects and enablers. Backlog items are prioritized based on user value, time, and other team dependencies determined in the PI planning meeting and refined during the PI.

- **Iteration planning** – The PO reviews and reprioritizes the backlog as part of the prep work for Iteration Planning, including coordination of dependencies with other POs. During the iteration planning meeting, the PO is the primary source of story details and priorities and is responsible for accepting the final iteration plan.

- **Just-in-time story elaboration** – Most backlog items are elaborated into user stories for implementation. This may happen before the iteration, during iteration planning, or during the iteration. While any team member can write stories and acceptance criteria, the PO has the primary responsibility for maintaining the flow. It's usually a good idea to have approximately two iterations' worth of stories ready in the team backlog at all times. More would create a queue, while fewer might inhibit flow.

- **Supporting Acceptance Test–Driven Development (ATDD)** – POs participate in the development of story acceptance criteria, draft them when feasible, and provide examples in support of ATDD specification by example (see the Test-First chapter).

- **Accepting stories** – The PO is the only team member who can accept stories as done. This step requires validation that the story meets acceptance criteria, has the appropriate, persistent acceptance tests, and otherwise complies with its Definition of Done (DoD). In so doing, the PO also assures a level of quality, focusing primarily on fitness for use.

- **Understand enabler work** – Although POs are not expected to drive technological decisions, they are supposed to understand the scope of the upcoming enabler work and to collaborate with the System and Solution Architect/Engineering team to assist with decision-making and sequencing of the critical technological infrastructures that will host the new business functionality. This can often be best accomplished by establishing a capacity allocation, as described in the discussion of the team backlog.

- **Participate in team demos and retrospectives** – As the person responsible for requirements, the PO has an essential role in the team demos, reviewing and accepting stories. The PO also participates in the Iteration Retrospective, where the teams gather to improve their processes and are active in the Agile Release Train's (ART's) Inspect and Adapt (I&A) workshop.

Program Execution

- Iterations and Agile teams serve a larger purpose: They provide for the frequent, reliable, and continuous release of value-added solutions. During each PI, the PO coordinates dependencies with other POs. This often occurs in weekly PO sync meetings (see the PI chapter for more information).

- The PO also has an instrumental role in producing the System Demo for program and Value Stream stakeholders.

Inspect and Adapt

- Teams address their larger impediments in the I&A workshop. In that setting, the PO works across teams to define and implement improvement stories that will increase the velocity and quality of the program.

- The PI system demo is part of the I&A workshop. The PO has an instrumental role in producing the PI system demo for program stakeholders.

- To ensure that they will be able to show the most critical aspects of the solution to the stakeholders, POs also participate in the preparation of the PI system demo.

Content Authority

At scale, a single person cannot handle the entire product and market strategy while also being dedicated to an Agile team. Since Product Management and the PO share the content authority for the program, it's important to have a clear delineation of roles and responsibilities, as illustrated in Figure 1.

Product Manager	Product Owner	Team
▸ Market and customer facing. Identifies market needs. Collocated with marketing/ business. ▸ Owns vision and roadmaps, program backlog, pricing, licensing, ROI. ▸ Drives PI objectives and release content via prioritized features and enablers. ▸ Establishes feature acceptance criteria.	▸ Solution, technology, and team facing. Collocated with team(s). ▸ Contributes to vision and program backlog. Owns team backlog and implementation. ▸ Defines iterations and stories. Accepts iteration increments. ▸ Drives iteration goals and iteration content via prioritized stories. ▸ Establishes story acceptance criteria, accepts stories into the baseline.	▸ Customer/stakeholder facing. ▸ Owns story estimates and implementation of value. ▸ Contributes to intentional architecture. Owns emergent design. ▸ Contributes to backlog refinement and creation of stories. ▸ Integrates with other teams.

Figure 1. Release content governance

Fan-Out Model of Product Manager, Product Owner, and Agile Teams

Successful development is, in part, a game of numbers in the Enterprise. Without the right number of people in the right roles, bottlenecks will severely limit velocity. Therefore, the number of Product Managers, POs, and Agile teams must be roughly in balance to steer the ART. Otherwise, the whole system will spend much of its time waiting for definition, clarification, and acceptance. To maximize the chance of success, SAFe recommends a fan-out model, as illustrated in Figure 2.

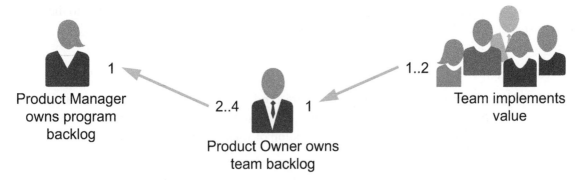

Product Manager owns program backlog — 1

2..4 — Product Owner owns team backlog — 1

1..2 — Team implements value

Figure 2. Fan-out model for Product Manager, PO, and Agile teams

Each Product Manager can usually support up to four POs, each of whom can be responsible for the backlog of one or two Agile teams.

LEARN MORE

[1] Leffingwell, Dean. *Agile Software Requirements: Lean Requirements Practices for Teams, Programs, and the Enterprise*. Addison-Wesley, 2011.

[2] Larman, Craig, and Bas Vodde. *Practices for Scaling Lean and Agile Development: Large, Multisite, and Offshore Product Development with Large-Scale Scrum*. Addison-Wesley, 2010.

Scrum Master

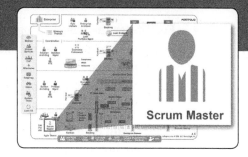

Good leaders must first become good servants.
  —*Robert K. Greenleaf*

Scrum Masters are servant leaders and coaches for an Agile Team. They help educate the team in Scrum, Extreme Programming (XP), Kanban, and SAFe, ensuring that the agreed Agile process is being followed. They also help remove impediments and foster an environment that supports high-performing team dynamics, continuous flow, and relentless improvement.

Although the Scrum Master role is mainly based on standard Scrum, Agile Teams—even those teams that are applying Kanban—establish this position to help the team meet its goals and coordinate activities with other teams. The primary responsibility of the team member who fills the Scrum Master role is assisting the self-organizing, self-managing team to achieve its goals. Scrum Masters do this by teaching and coaching team practices, implementing and supporting SAFe principles and practices, identifying and eliminating impediments, and facilitating flow.

Details

The Scrum Master role is a unique one, which is filled by an Agile team member who spends much of her time helping other team members communicate, coordinate, and cooperate. Stated generally, this person assists the team in meeting their delivery goals.

Responsibilities

An effective Scrum Master is a team-based servant leader who demonstrates the following characteristics:

- **Exhibits Lean-Agile leadership** – The Scrum Master demonstrates the behaviors of a Lean-Agile Leader with a Lean-Agile Mindset. This individual helps the team embrace SAFe Core Values, adopt and apply SAFe Principles, and implement SAFe practices.

- **Supports the team rules** – The rules of an Agile Team are lightweight, but they are rules nonetheless, and the Scrum Master is responsible for reinforcing them. These may include the rules of Scrum, Built-In Quality practices from Extreme Programming, Work in Process (WIP) limits from Kanban, and any other process rules the team has agreed.

- **Facilitates the team's progress toward team goals** – The Scrum Master is trained as a team facilitator and is continuously engaged in challenging the old norms of development to improve performance in the areas of quality, predictability, flow, and velocity. The person filling this role helps the team focus on daily and Iteration Goals in the context of current Program Increment (PI) Objectives.

- **Leads team efforts in relentless improvement** – The Scrum Master helps the team members improve and take responsibility for their actions and facilitates the team retrospective. This role also teaches problem-solving techniques and helps the team members become better problem-solvers both as a group and for themselves.

- **Facilitates meetings** – The Scrum Master facilitates all team meetings, including (where applicable) the Daily Stand-up, Iteration Planning, Iteration Review, and Iteration Retrospective.

- **Supports the Product Owner** – The Scrum Master helps the Product Owner manage the backlog and guide the team while facilitating a healthy team dynamic with respect to priorities and scope.

- **Eliminates impediments** – Many blocking issues will be beyond the team's authority or may require support from other teams. The Scrum Master actively addresses these issues so that the team can remain focused on achieving the objectives of the Iteration.

- **Promotes SAFe quality practices** – SAFe provides guidance to assist the teams in constantly improving the quality of their deliverables and meeting the Definition of Done (DoD). The Scrum Master helps foster the culture of technical discipline and craftsmanship that is the hallmark of effective Agile teams.

- **Builds a high-performing team** – The Scrum Master focuses on continually improving team dynamics and performance. This responsibility includes helping the team manage interpersonal conflicts, challenges, and opportunities for growth. The Scrum Master escalates 'people problems' to management where necessary, but only after internal team processes have failed to resolve the issue, and helps individuals and teams cope with personnel changes.

- **Protects and communicates** – The Scrum Master communicates with management and outside stakeholders, and helps protect the team from uncontrolled expansion of work.

- **Coordinates with other teams** – The Scrum Master is typically the representative in the Scrum of Scrums (SoS) meeting, passing information from that meeting back to the team (see the Program Increment chapter for more details). The person filling this role often coordinates with the System Team, User Experience, Architecture, and Shared Services roles. It is important to note, however, that the responsibility for inter-team coordination cannot be delegated entirely to the Scrum Master; every team member shares responsibility in that regard.

- **Facilitates preparation and readiness for ART events** – The Scrum Master assists the team in preparing for ART activities, including PI Planning, System Demos, and the Inspect and Adapt workshop.

- **Supports estimating** – The Scrum Master guides the team in establishing normalized estimates and helps the team understand how to estimate Features and Capabilities.

Sourcing the Role

The Scrum Master can be a part-time or full-time role, depending on the size of the team, the context, and other responsibilities. However, at Enterprise scale, it can be a challenge to sell the need for a full-time Scrum Master for each Agile team. After all, if the enterprise is organizing 100 new teams, it probably isn't economically or politically practical to take 100 full-time development team members and assign them to these new duties—duties that don't include development or testing. Nor is it economically viable to hire a full- or part-time consultant for each team to help its members learn and master the new methods. That could kill the transformation before it even gets started, and before the teams have had a chance to prove the value of the role.

SAFe takes a pragmatic approach and assumes, in general, that the Scrum Master is a part-time role. During initial SAFe adoption, the job may be more intensive. Thus, at this stage, the organization may find it beneficial to bring external consultants on board to coach the teams while they become experienced in Scrum and SAFe. These outside consultant Scrum Masters will often coach multiple teams in the organization.

LEARN MORE

[1] www.scrumalliance.org.

[2] Leffingwell, Dean. *Agile Software Requirements: Lean Requirements Practices for Teams, Programs, and the Enterprise*. Addison-Wesley, 2011.

Built-In Quality

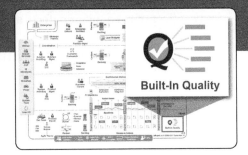

Built-In Quality

Inspection does not improve the quality, nor guarantee quality. Inspection is too late. The quality, good or bad, is already in the product. Quality cannot be inspected into a product or service; it must be built into it.

—W. Edwards Deming

Built-In Quality practices ensure that each Solution element, at every increment, meets appropriate quality standards throughout development.

The enterprise's ability to deliver new functionality with the shortest sustainable lead time and adapt to rapidly changing business environments depends on solution quality. It should come as no surprise, then, that built-in quality is one of the SAFe Core Values. Built-in quality is not actually unique to SAFe, but rather is a core principle of the Lean-Agile Mindset, where it helps avoid the cost of delays associated with the recall, rework, and defect fixing. The built-in quality philosophy applies systems thinking to optimize the system as a whole, ensuring a fast flow across the entire Value Stream, and makes quality everyone's job.

The Agile Manifesto emphasizes quality as well: "Continuous attention to technical excellence and good design enhances agility" [1]. Many of the practices mentioned in this chapter are inspired and described by Extreme Programming (XP). These practices help Agile teams ensure that the Solutions they build are high in quality, can readily adapt to change, and are designed for testing, deployment, and recovery. The collaborative nature of these practices, along with a focus on frequent validation, creates an emergent culture in which engineering and craftsmanship are key business enablers.

Software, hardware, and firmware all share the same goals and principles of built-in quality. However, the work physics and economics are somewhat different for hardware and firmware, requiring a different set of practices. They include a more intense focus on modeling and simulation, as well as more exploratory early iterations, more design verification, and frequent system-level integration.

Details

When Enterprises need to respond to change, software and systems built on good technical foundations are easier to change and adapt. For a large solution, this consideration is even more critical, as the cumulative effect of even minor defects and wrong assumptions can create unacceptable consequences.

Achieving high-quality systems is serious work that requires ongoing training and commitment. This investment is warranted because of its many business benefits:

- Higher customer satisfaction
- Improved velocity and delivery predictability
- Better system performance
- Improved ability to innovate, scale, and meet compliance requirements

The following sections summarize the recommended practices for achieving built-in quality for software, and hardware and firmware.

Software Practices

Software and systems built with high quality are easier to modify and adapt when an enterprise must rapidly respond to change. Many of the practices inspired by XP, along with a focus on frequent validation, create an emergent culture in which engineering and craftsmanship are key business enablers. These practices include:

- **Continuous Integration (CI)** – The practice of merging the code from each developer's workspace into a single main branch of code, multiple times per day. CI lessens the risk that integration issues will be deferred and, therefore, their potential impact on system quality and program predictability. Teams perform local integration at least daily. To confirm that the work is progressing as intended, full system-level integration should be achieved at least one or two times per iteration.

- **Test-First** – A set of practices that encourage teams to think deeply about intended system behavior, before implementing the code. Test-first methods can be further divided into two categories: (1) *Test-Driven Development (TDD)*, in which developers write an automated unit test first, run the test to observe the failure, and then write the minimum code necessary to pass the test, and (2) *Acceptance Test–Driven Development (ATDD)*, in which Story and Feature acceptance criteria are expressed as automated acceptance tests, which can be run continuously to ensure continued validation as the system evolves.

ScrumXP

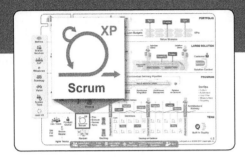

... a holistic or 'rugby' approach—where a team tries to go the distance as a unit, passing the ball back and forth—may better serve today's competitive requirements.

—*Nonaka and Takeuchi, "The New New Product Development Game"*

ScrumXP is a lightweight process to deliver value for cross-functional, self-organized teams within SAFe. It combines the power of Scrum project management practices with Extreme Programming (XP) practices.

Most Agile Teams use Scrum as their primary, team-based project management framework. A lightweight, yet disciplined and productive process, Scrum allows cross-functional, self-organized teams to operate within the SAFe construct. It prescribes three roles: Scrum Master, Product Owner (PO), and Development Team [2].

The Scrum Master is a servant leader who helps the team adhere to the rules of Scrum and works inside and outside of the team to remove impediments. The Product Owner is responsible for defining what gets built. When extended by Lean quality practices and XP engineering techniques, the ScrumXP team provides the basic Agile building blocks for SAFe.

Of course, ScrumXP teams do not work in isolation. Each such team is part of the larger Agile Release Train (ART) in which they cooperate in building the larger system.

Details

The ScrumXP Agile Team is a self-organizing, self-managing, cross-functional group of five to nine people, collocated when possible. The size and structure of the team are optimized for communication, interaction, and value delivery.

Self-organization implies that the team has no team leader or manager role that oversees the team members, estimates their work, commits them to specific objectives, or determines how exactly they will advance the Solution. Instead, the team is presented with the intent of the Iteration, then is solely responsible for determining how much of that scope the team can commit to and how the members will build that increment of value.

The cross-functional nature of the team means it possesses all the roles and skills needed to deliver a working solution. Together, the team's self-organization and cross-functional nature—when enhanced by constant communication, constructive conflict, and dynamic interaction—can create a productive and more enjoyable work environment for its members.

Scrum defines specific roles and unique sets of responsibilities for two members of the Agile Team: the Product Owner (PO) and the Scrum Master. Each of these roles is covered in its own chapter, with a brief summary of their responsibilities being provided here.

Product Owner

Each ScrumXP team has a Product Owner who is responsible for the Team Backlog. Focusing intensely on the team's efforts, the PO interacts with the team members every day. Therefore, the most effective model is to dedicate a PO to each team or to share one PO across no more than two teams. This allows the PO to support the team effectively during Iteration Execution by answering questions, providing more detail on the functionality under development, and reviewing and accepting the completed Stories into the baseline.

Scrum Master

The Scrum Master is the facilitator and Agile coach for the team. The primary responsibilities for this role are as follows:

- Ensuring that the ScrumXP process is followed

- Educating the team in Scrum, XP, and SAFe practices

- Providing the environment for continuous improvement

As a full- or part-time role for a team member, the Scrum Master is also typically charged with removing impediments. Alternatively, some dedicated Scrum Masters may support two to three Scrum teams.

The Scrum Process

The Scrum process is a lightweight project management framework that fosters quick, iterative advancement of the solution. To facilitate continuous improvement to support higher quality and productivity as well as better outcomes, it employs a series of iterations—that is, two-week timeboxes, during which the team defines, builds, tests, and reviews results. The Scrum process is further described in the following subsections. (Note: Scrum uses the term 'sprint,' while SAFe uses the more general term 'iteration.')

Planning the Iteration

The iteration starts with Iteration Planning, a timeboxed event of four hours or less in which the PO presents the stories for planning. The team then takes the following actions:

- Reviews the stories
- Defines the acceptance criteria
- Splits larger stories into smaller ones where necessary
- Estimates the stories in terms of story points
- Distills what they can build, based on their known velocity (story points per iteration), into Iteration Goals
- Commits to the iteration goals

Many teams further divide stories into tasks, estimating the tasks in terms of hours to better refine their understanding of the work ahead.

Even before the iteration starts, the ScrumXP team begins preparing content by refining the team backlog items. The objective of this preparation is to better understand the work to be delivered in the upcoming iteration.

Visualizing Work

During execution, the team builds and tests stories with the goal of delivering one or two every few days. This approach limits Work in Process (WIP) and helps avoid 'waterfalling' the iteration. Teams use Big Visual Information Radiators (BVIRs) to understand and track progress during iteration execution.

The team's storyboard visualizes the stories and the progress being made throughout the iteration. To do so, teams often use development steps as the columns, moving stories from left to right over time, as depicted in Figure 1.

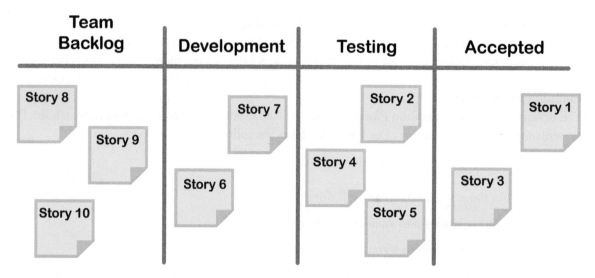

Figure 1. An example of a team's storyboard

Some teams also apply WIP limits to some steps to create a 'pull' process within the iteration and to continuously balance the work so as to increase throughput. Indeed, many teams integrate the best practices of Scrum and Kanban to facilitate the flow of work through the iterations. In such a case, the simple storyboard depicted in Figure 1 evolves into a more structured Kanban board. See the Team Kanban chapter for more on the use of Kanban by ScrumXP teams.

Coordinating with Daily Stand-up Meetings

Each day, the team has a formal ceremony—the Daily Stand-up (DSU) meeting—to understand where team members are, escalate problems, and get help from other team members. During this meeting, each team member describes what he or she did yesterday to advance iteration goals, what the member plans to work on today to achieve the iteration goals, and which, if any, blocks the member is encountering in meeting the iteration goals. As this is a daily coordination meeting, the Scrum Master has to keep it short and to the point. The DSU should take no more than 15 minutes and is done standing up in front of the storyboard.

Of course, team communication does not end there, as team members interact continuously throughout the iteration. Facilitating such communication is the main reason why ScrumXP prefers that the team be collocated whenever possible.

Demonstrating Value and Improving the Process

At the end of each iteration, the team conducts an Iteration Review and an Iteration Retrospective. During the iteration review, the team demonstrates each story accomplished, culminating with the team's increment of value for that iteration. This is not a formal status report, but rather a review of the tangible outcomes of the iteration. Thereafter, the team conducts a brief retrospective, which provides time to reflect on the iteration, the process, things that are working well, and current obstacles. Then the team comes up with improvement stories for the next iteration.

Building Quality In

A tenet of SAFe spells out the need for Built-In Quality (one of the Core Values of SAFe): "You can't scale crappy code." Quality begins at the code and component levels with the people creating the solution. Otherwise, it's difficult (or impossible) to ensure quality later, as the solution is integrated and scales from component to system and solution.

To make sure teams build quality into code and components, SAFe describes five engineering and quality practices that are inspired by the tenets of XP and that supplement the project management practices of Scrum: Continuous Integration, Test-First, Refactoring, pair work, and collective ownership. Some teams use other XP practices, such as pair programming and metaphors [3].

ScrumXP Teams Are on the Train

Although the teams are cross-functional, it isn't always realistic for a team of seven or eight people to deliver end-user value when a large system includes different technology platforms and a spectrum of disciplines. Achieving this goal may require development of hardware, software, and systems engineering components, and typically many more teams are required.

To address this need for collective efforts, SAFe Agile Teams operate within an ART, which provides mission alignment and a collaborative environment in which teams can cooperate with other teams to build the larger solution's capabilities. As part of the ART, all Agile Teams plan together, integrate and demo together, release and deploy together, and learn together, as illustrated in Figure 2.

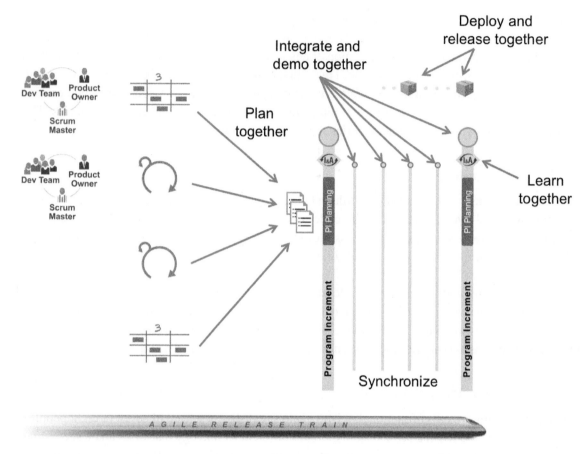

Figure 2. Together, Agile teams plan, integrate and demo, release and deploy, and learn

Each team's participation in this shared responsibility is further defined in the Agile Team chapter.

Leadership of ScrumXP Teams

Managers are typically not part of the cross-functional team. However, the initial organization of people around features, components, and subsystems—and the design and structure of the ART—is typically a management responsibility based on team input. Thereafter, team management undergoes a shift from 'manager as expert,' directing the team to specific technical achievements, to 'manager as a developer of people' and Lean-Agile Leader.

LEARN MORE

[1] Kniberg, Henrik. *Scrum and XP from the Trenches*. lulu.com, 2015.

[2] Sutherland, Jeff, and Ken Schwaber. Scrumguides.org.

[3] Beck, Kent, and Cynthia Andres. *Extreme Programming Explained: Embrace Change*, 2nd edition. Addison-Wesley, 2004.

Story

Stories act as a 'pidgin language,' where both sides (users and developers) can agree enough to work together effectively.

—Bill Wake, co-inventor of Extreme Programming

Stories are short descriptions of a small piece of desired functionality, written in the user's language. Agile Teams implement small, vertical slices of system functionality and are sized so they can be completed in a single Iteration.

Stories are the primary artifact used to define system behavior in Agile. They're not requirements, but rather short, simple descriptions of functionality usually told from the user's perspective and written in the user's language. Each story is intended to enable the implementation of a small, vertical slice of system behavior that supports incremental development.

Stories provide just enough information for the intent to be understood by both business and technical people. Details are deferred until the story is ready to be implemented. Through acceptance criteria, stories get more specific, helping to ensure system quality.

User stories deliver functionality directly to the end user. Enabler stories bring visibility to the work items needed to support exploration, architecture, infrastructure, and compliance.

Details

SAFe describes a four-tier hierarchy of artifacts that outline functional system behavior: Epic, Capability, Feature, and story. Along with Nonfunctional Requirements (NFRs), these Agile backlog items define the system and Solution Intent, model system behavior, and build up the Architectural Runway.

Epics, capabilities, features, and enablers are used to describe the larger intended behavior. In contrast, the detailed implementation work is described through stories, which make up the Team Backlog. Most stories emerge from business and enabler features in the Program Backlog, but others come from the team's local context.

Each story is a small, independent behavior that can be implemented incrementally and provides some value to the user or the Solution. It comprises a vertical (rather than horizontal) slice of functionality to ensure that every iteration delivers new value. Stories are split into smaller ones so they can be completed in a single iteration (see the Splitting Stories section).

Often, stories are first written on an index card or sticky note. The physical nature of the card creates a tangible relationship between the team, the story, and the user: It helps engage the entire team in story writing. Sticky notes offer other benefits as well: They help visualize work and can be readily placed on a wall or table, rearranged in sequence, and even passed off when necessary. Stories allow improved understanding of the scope and progress:

- "Wow, look at all these stories I'm about to sign up for." (scope)
- "Look at all the stories we accomplished in this iteration." (progress)

While anyone can write stories, approving them for entry into the team backlog and accepting them into the system baseline are the responsibility of the Product Owner. Of course, stickies don't scale well across the Enterprise, so stories often move quickly into Agile project management tooling.

There are two types of stories in SAFe: user stories and enabler stories.

Sources of Stories

Stories are typically driven by splitting business and enabler features, as Figure 1 illustrates.

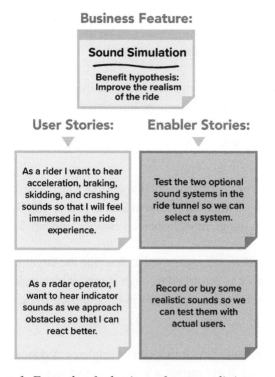

Figure 1. Example of a business feature split into stories

User Stories

User stories are the primary means of expressing needed functionality. They largely replace the traditional requirements specification. (In some cases, they serve to explain and develop system behavior that's later recorded to support compliance, traceability, or other needs.)

Because they focus on the user, rather than the system, as the subject of interest, user stories are value-centric. To support this perspective, the recommended form of expression is the user-voice form, as follows:

As a (user role), I want to (activity) so that (business value).

By using this format, teams are guided to understand who is using the system, what they are doing with it, and why they are doing it. Applying the 'user voice' format routinely tends to increase the team's domain competence; team members come to better understand the real business needs of the user. Figure 2 provides an example.

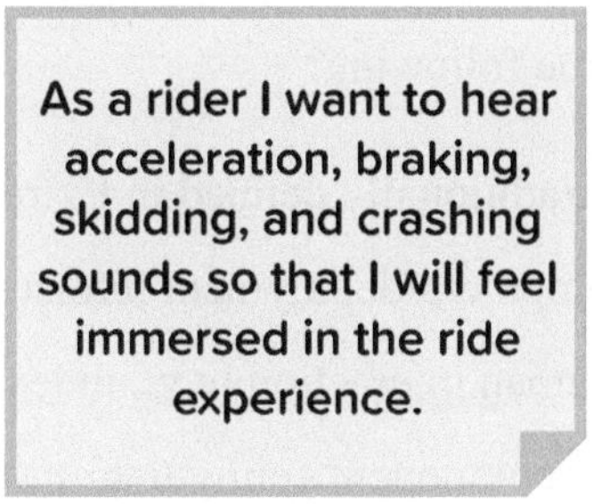

As a rider I want to hear acceleration, braking, skidding, and crashing sounds so that I will feel immersed in the ride experience.

Figure 2. Example user story in user voice form

While the user story voice is the common case, not every system interacts with an end user. Sometimes the 'user' is a device (e.g., printer) or a system (e.g., transaction server). In these cases, the story can take on the form shown in Figure 3.

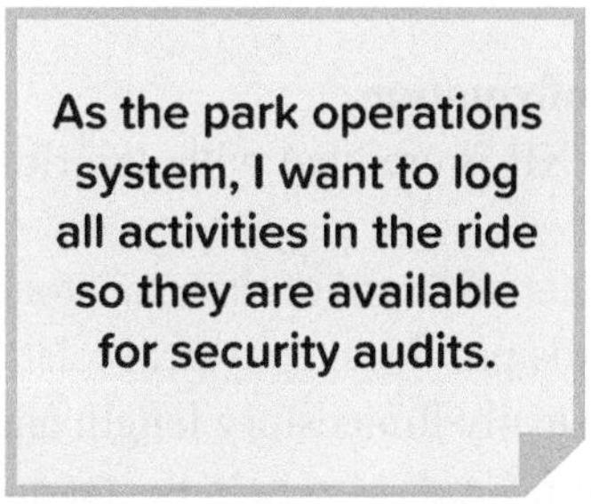

As the park operations system, I want to log all activities in the ride so they are available for security audits.

Figure 3. Example of a user story with a 'system' as a user

Enabler Stories

Teams may need to develop the architecture or infrastructure to implement some user stories or support components of the system. In this case, the story may not directly touch any end user. Such enabler stories can support exploration, architecture, or infrastructure, just like all other enablers. In these cases, the story can be expressed in technical rather than user-centric language, as shown in Figure 4.

Figure 4. Example enabler story

Enabler stories may include any of the following:

- Refactoring and Spikes (as traditionally defined in Extreme Programming [XP])

- Building or improving development/deployment infrastructure

- Running jobs that require human interaction (e.g., index one million web pages)

- Creating required product or component configurations for different purposes

- Verification of system qualities (e.g., performance and vulnerability testing)

Enabler stories are demonstrated just like user stories, typically by showing the artifacts produced or via the user interface, stub, or mock-up.

Writing Good Stories

The 3Cs: Card, Conversation, Confirmation
Ron Jeffries, one of the inventors of XP, is credited with describing the 3Cs of a story:

- **Card** – Captures the statement of intent of the user story on an index card, sticky note, or tool. The use of index cards provides a physical relationship between the team and the story. The card size physically limits story length and premature suggestions for the specificity of system behavior. Cards also help the team 'feel' upcoming scope, as there is something materially different about holding ten cards in one's hand versus looking at ten lines on a spreadsheet.

- **Conversation** – Represents a "promise for a conversation" about the story between the team, Customer/user, PO, and other stakeholders. Such discussion is necessary to determine more detailed behavior required to implement the intent. The conversation may spawn additional specificity in the form of attachments to the user story (e.g., mock-up, prototype, spreadsheet, algorithm, timing diagram). The conversation spans all steps in the story life cycle:

  - Backlog refinement

  - Planning

  - Implementation

  - Demo

  These discussions provide a shared understanding of scope that formal documentation does not provide. Specification by example replaces overly detailed documentation of functionality. Conversations also help uncover gaps in user scenarios and NFRs. Some teams use the confirmation section of the story card to write down what they will demo.

- **Confirmation** – Consists of acceptance criteria that provide the information needed to ensure that the story is implemented correctly and covers the relevant functional and NFRs. Figure 5 provides an example.

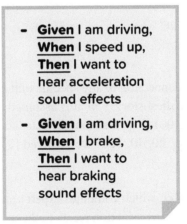

Figure 5. Story acceptance criteria

Agile teams automate acceptance tests wherever possible, often in business-readable, domain-specific language. Automation creates an executable specification to validate and verify the solution. Automation also provides the ability to quickly regression-test the system, thereby enhancing Continuous Integration, refactoring, and maintenance.

Invest in Good Stories

To remind themselves of the elements of a good story, teams often use the INVEST model, developed by Bill Wake [1, 2]:

- **I**ndependent (among other stories)

- **N**egotiable (a flexible statement of intent, not a contract)

- **V**aluable (providing a valuable vertical slice to the customer)

- **E**stimable (small and negotiable)

- **S**mall (fits within an iteration)

- **T**estable (understood enough to know how to test it)

Estimating Stories

Agile teams use story points and 'estimating poker' to value their work [2, 3]. A story point is a singular number that represents a combination of qualities:

- **Volume** – How much is there?

- **Complexity** – How hard is it?

- **Knowledge** – What's known?

- **Uncertainty** – What's unknown?

Story points are relative, without a connection to any specific unit of measure. The size (effort) of each story is estimated relative to the smallest story, which is assigned a size of '1.' A modified Fibonacci sequence (1, 2, 3, 5, 8, 13, 20, 40, 100) is applied that reflects the inherent uncertainty in estimating, especially when large numbers (e.g., 20, 40, 100) are involved [2].

Estimating Poker

Agile teams often use *estimating poker*, which combines expert opinion, analogy, and disaggregation to create quick but reliable estimates. Disaggregation refers to the process of splitting a story or features into smaller, easier-to-estimate pieces. A number of other methods are used as well.

The rules of estimating poker are as follows:

1. Participants include all team members.

2. Each estimator is given a deck of cards with 1, 2, 3, 5, 8, 13, 20, 40, 100, ∞, and ?.

3. The PO participates but does not estimate.

4. The Scrum Master participates but does not estimate, unless this person is doing actual development work.

5. For each backlog item to be estimated, the PO reads the description of the story.

6. Questions are asked and answered.

7. Each estimator privately selects an estimating card representing his or her estimate.

8. All cards are turned over at the same time to avoid bias and to make all estimates visible.

9. High and low estimators explain their estimates.

10. After a discussion, each estimator provides a new estimate by selecting either a different card or the same one as in the previous estimate.

11. The estimates will likely converge. If not, the process is repeated.

Although some amount of preliminary design discussion is appropriate, spending too much time on design discussions is often wasted effort. The real value of estimating poker is to come to an agreement on the scope of a story. It's also fun!

Velocity

The team's capacity for an iteration is equal to the sum of the points for all the completed stories that met their Definition of Done (DoD). Knowing the velocity assists with planning and helps limit Work in Process (WIP), as teams don't take on more stories than their prior velocity would allow. This measure is also used to estimate how long it will take to deliver epics, features, capabilities, and enablers, which are also forecasted using story points.

Starting Baseline for Estimation

In standard Scrum, each team's story point estimating—and the resulting velocity—is a local and independent concern. In contrast, in SAFe, story point velocity must share the same starting baseline, so that estimates for features or epics that require the support of many teams can be understood.

SAFe uses a starting baseline where one story point is defined roughly the same way across all teams. This means that work can be prioritized based on converting story points to costs. Of course, adjustments may be needed to account for the different average labor costs across geographies (e.g., United States, China, India, Europe). After all, there's no way to determine the potential return on investment (ROI) if there is no common 'currency.' *Normalized* story points provide a method for getting to an agreed starting baseline for stories and velocity as follows:

1. Give every developer-tester on the team '8' points (adjust for part-timers).

2. Subtract one point for every team member vacation day and holiday.

3. Find a small story that would take about a half-day to code and a half-day to test and validate. Call it a '1.'

4. Estimate every other story relative to that '1.'

As an example, assume there is a six-person team composed of three developers, two testers, and one PO, with no vacations or holidays on the team calendar. In this case, the estimated initial velocity = 5 × 8 points = 40 points/iteration. Note that it may be necessary to lower this estimate a bit if one of the developers and testers is also the Scrum Master.

In this way, story points are somewhat comparable to an ideal developer day, and all teams create estimates using the same method. Management can easily determine the cost for a story point for people in a specific geographic region, which in turn provides a meaningful way to figure out the cost estimate for an upcoming feature or epic.

Note: There is no need to recalibrate team estimation or velocity after that point. It is just a starting baseline.

While teams tend to increase their velocity over time—and that's a good thing—the number usually remains fairly stable. A team's velocity is far more affected by changing team size and technical context than by productivity variations. If necessary, financial planners can adjust the cost per story point a bit. Experience shows that this is a minor concern, versus the wildly differing velocities that teams of comparable size may demonstrate if they don't set a common starting baseline. That kind of variation simply doesn't work at enterprise scale, making it difficult to make economic decisions.

Splitting Stories

Smaller stories allow faster, more reliable implementation, since small things go through a system faster, reducing variability and managing risk. Splitting bigger stories into smaller ones is, therefore, a mandatory survival skill for every Agile team. It's both the art and the science of incremental development. Ten ways to split stories are described in Leffingwell's *Agile Software Requirements* [1]. A summary of these techniques follows:

- Workflow steps

- Business rule variations

- Major effort

- Simple/complex

- Variations in data

- Data entry methods

- Deferred system qualities

- Operations (ex., Create, Read, Update, Delete [CRUD])

- Use-case scenarios

- Break-out spike

Figure 6 illustrates an example of splitting by use-case scenarios.

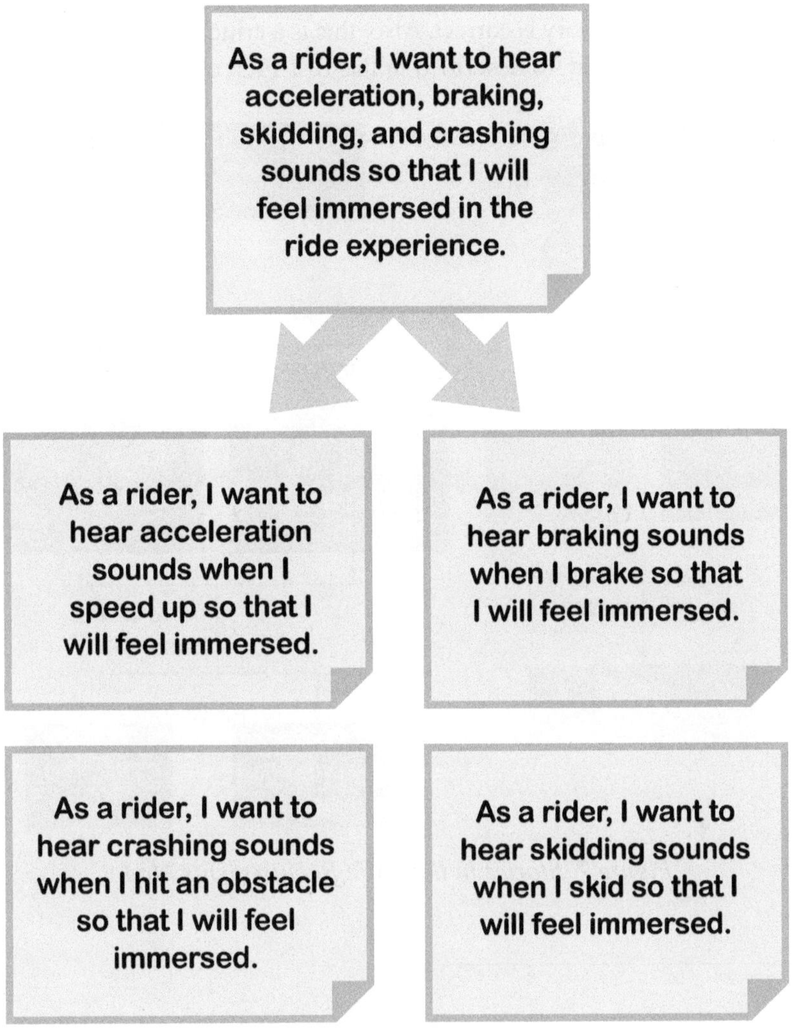

As a rider, I want to hear acceleration, braking, skidding, and crashing sounds so that I will feel immersed in the ride experience.

As a rider, I want to hear acceleration sounds when I speed up so that I will feel immersed.

As a rider, I want to hear braking sounds when I brake so that I will feel immersed.

As a rider, I want to hear crashing sounds when I hit an obstacle so that I will feel immersed.

As a rider, I want to hear skidding sounds when I skid so that I will feel immersed.

Figure 6. An example of splitting a big story into smaller stories

Stories in the SAFe Requirements Model

As described in the SAFe Requirements Model chapter in Part 9, the Framework applies an extensive set of artifacts and relationships to manage the definition and testing of complex systems in a Lean and Agile fashion. Figure 7 illustrates the role of stories in this larger picture.

Note that this figure uses Unified Modeling Language (UML) notation to represent the relationships between the objects: zero to many (0..*), one to many (1..*), one to one (1), and so on.

As shown in Figure 7, stories are often (but not always) created by new features and each has a story acceptance test. Further, each story should have a unit test. Unit tests primarily serve to ensure that the technical implementation of the story is correct. Also, this is a critical starting point for test automation, as unit tests are readily automated, as described in the Test-First chapter in Part 9.

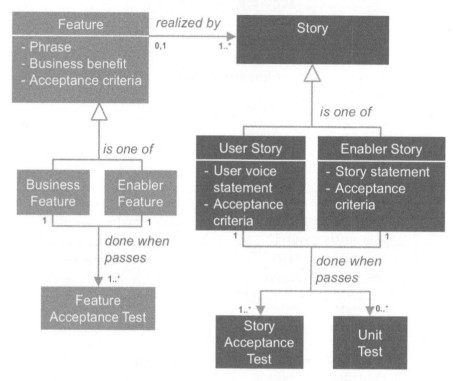

Figure 7. Stories in the SAFe Requirements Model

LEARN MORE

[1] Leffingwell, Dean. *Agile Software Requirements: Lean Requirements Practices for Teams, Programs, and the Enterprise.* Addison-Wesley, 2011.

[2] Cohn, Mike. *User Stories Applied: For Agile Software Development.* Addison-Wesley, 2004.

Iteration Planning

Stay committed to your decisions, but stay flexible in your approach.

—Tom Robbins

Iteration Planning is an event in which all team members determine how much of the Team Backlog they can commit to delivering during an upcoming Iteration. The team summarizes this work as a set of committed Iteration Goals.

Teams plan by selecting Stories from the team backlog and committing to execute a set of them in the upcoming iteration. The team's backlog will have been seeded and partially planned during the Program Increment (PI) Planning meeting. In addition, the teams have feedback available—not only from their prior iterations, but also from the System Demo and other teams. That information, and the natural course of changing fact patterns, provides the broader context for iteration planning. Iteration planning produces three outputs:

- The iteration backlog, consisting of the stories committed to the iteration, with acceptance criteria where appropriate
- A statement of iteration goals, typically a sentence or two stating the business objectives of the iteration
- A commitment by the team to the work needed to achieve the goals

Details

The purpose of iteration planning is to organize the work and define a realistic scope for the iteration. Each Agile Team agrees on a set of stories for the upcoming iteration (the iteration backlog) and summarizes those stories by creating a set of iteration goals. The iteration backlog and goals are based on the team's capacity and allow for consideration of each story's complexity, size, and dependencies on other stories and other teams. At the end of planning, the team commits to the goal of the iteration and adjusts stories as necessary to achieve the larger purpose. In return, management does not interfere or adjust the scope of the iteration, allowing the team to stay focused on its goals.

Inputs to Iteration Planning

In SAFe, iteration planning is a refinement of the level of detail and an adjustment of the initial iteration plans created during Agile Release Train (ART) PI planning. Teams approach iteration planning with a pre-elaborated team backlog. (They have usually held a backlog refinement meeting during the previous iteration.) The planning meeting has a number of inputs:

- The team and program PI Objectives, created at PI planning

- The team's PI plan backlog, which consists of stories that were identified during PI planning

- Additional stories that arise based on the local context, including items such as defects, refactors, and new stories that have emerged since the planning session

- Feedback from the prior iteration, including any stories that were not successfully completed (did not meet the Definition of Done; see "A Scaled Definition of Done" in the Release on Demand chapter) in that iteration

- Feedback from the system demo

Planning the Iteration

Prior to the meeting, the Product Owner (PO) will have prepared some preliminary iteration goals based on the team's progress in the program increment. Typically, the Product Owner starts the meeting by reviewing the proposed iteration goals and the higher-priority stories in the team backlog. During the meeting, the Agile team discusses implementation options, technical issues, Nonfunctional Requirements (NFRs), and dependencies and then plans the iteration. The Product Owner defines the *what*; the team members define *how* and *how much*.

Throughout the meeting, the team elaborates the acceptance criteria and estimates the effort needed to complete each story. Based on the estimated velocity, the team selects the candidate stories. Some teams choose to break each story down into tasks and estimate the effort needed to complete those tasks in hours to confirm that they have the capacity and skills to meet the iteration goal. The team then commits to the work and records the iteration backlog in a visible place, such as a storyboard, Kanban board, or tooling. Planning is timeboxed to a maximum of four hours for a two-week iteration.

Establishing Velocity

First, the team quantifies its capacity to perform work in the upcoming iteration. Each team member determines his or her availability, acknowledging time off and other potential duties. This activity also takes into account other standing commitments—such as maintenance—that are distinct from new story development (see the section about capacity allocation in the Team Backlog chapter).

Story Analysis and Estimating

Once team member capacity has been established, the team backlog is reviewed. Each story is discussed, including its relative difficulty, size, complexity, technical challenges, and acceptance criteria. Finally, the team agrees to a size estimate for the story. The team backlog typically includes other types of stories as well, such as Enablers that could constitute infrastructure work, refactoring, research Spikes, architectural improvements, and defects. These items are also prioritized and estimated.

Tasking Stories

Some teams break each story into tasks. As the tasks are identified, team members discuss the relevant details: who will be the best person(s) to accomplish the task, approximately how long it will take (typically in hours), and any dependencies it may have on other tasks or stories. Once all of these details are well understood, a team member takes responsibility for a specific task or tasks. As team members commit to tasks, they reduce their individual iteration capacity until it reaches zero. Often, toward the end of the session, some team members will find themselves overcommitted, while others will have some of their capacity still available. This situation leads to a further discussion among team members to evenly distribute the work.

While breaking stories into tasks is fairly common, it is optional and not mandated in SAFe. This approach is mostly used by beginner teams to learn their velocity and capabilities. With greater experience, it becomes unnecessary, such that team planning relies on only stories.

Developing Iteration Goals

Once the iteration backlog is understood, the team turns its attention to synthesizing one or more iteration goals that are based on the team and program PI objectives from the PI planning session and the iteration backlog. The closer this iteration is to the PI planning session, the more likely the program objectives are to remain unchanged.

Committing to Iteration Goals

When the team's collective capacity has been reached in terms of committed stories, no more stories are pulled from the team backlog. At this point, the Product Owner and team agree on the final list of stories that will be selected, and they revisit and restate the iteration goals. The entire team then commits to the iteration goals, and the scope of the work remains fixed for the duration of the iteration.

Attendees

The iteration planning meeting is attended by the following individuals:

- The Product Owner
- The Scrum Master, who acts as facilitator for this meeting

- The Development Team
- Any other stakeholders, including representatives from different Agile teams or the ART, and subject-matter experts

Agenda

An example agenda for iteration planning follows:

1. Calculate the available team capacity for the iteration
2. Discuss each story, elaborate acceptance criteria, and provide estimates using story points
3. Planning stops once the team runs out of capacity
4. Determine and agree on the iteration goals
5. Everyone commits to the goals

Acceptance criteria are developed through conversation and collaboration with the Product Owner and other stakeholders. Based on the story estimates, the Product Owner may change the ranking of the stories. Optionally, the team may break stories into tasks, estimated in hours, and take shared responsibility for those tasks' execution.

Guidelines

Tips for holding an iteration planning meeting follow:

- Timebox the meeting to four hours or less
- This planning session is organized by the team and is for the team
- A team should avoid committing to work that exceeds its historical velocity

Relative Estimating, Velocity, and Normalizing Story Point Estimating

Agile teams use story points to relatively estimate the scope of the various user stories [2, 3]. With relative estimating, the size (effort) for each backlog item is compared to other stories. For example, an 8-point story takes four times as much effort as a 2-point story. The team's velocity for an iteration is equal to the total points for all the stories completed in the prior iteration. Knowing a team's velocity assists with planning and helps limit Work in Process (WIP)—teams don't take on more stories than their prior velocity would allow. Velocity is likewise used to estimate how long it takes to deliver Features or Epics, which are also forecasted in story points.

Normalizing Story Point Estimating

In Scrum, each team's story point estimation (and the resultant velocity) is typically a local and independent matter. The fact that these estimates might vary significantly—a small team might estimate in such a way that its velocity is 50, while a larger team estimates that its velocity is 13—usually does not pose a concern.

In contrast, in SAFe, story point estimation must be normalized, so that estimates for features or epics that require the support of multiple teams are based on the same story point definition, allowing a shared basis for economic decision-making. One starting algorithm is as follows:

1. **Normalize story point estimation**

   - Find a small story that would take about a half-day to develop and a half-day to test and validate, and call it a '1'

   - Estimate every other story relative to that '1'

2. **Establish velocity before historical data exists**

   - For every full-time developer and tester on the team, give the team 8 points (adjust for part-timers)

   - Subtract '1' point for every team member vacation day and holiday in the iteration

Example: Assuming a six-person team composed of three developers, two testers, and one PO, with no vacations, the estimated initial velocity equals 5 × 8 points or 40 points per iteration. (Note: The team may need to lower this estimate a bit if one of the developers and testers is also the Scrum Master.)

Normalized estimation is particularly helpful in initial PI planning, as many teams will be new to Agile and will need a way to estimate the scope of work in their first PI. There is no need to recalibrate team estimating or velocities after that point; this baseline is just used as a common starting point. In this way, all teams estimate the size of work in a common fashion, so management can quickly estimate the cost for a story point for teams in a specific region. Managers then have a meaningful way to establish the aggregate cost estimate for an upcoming feature or epic.

Teams tend to increase their velocity over time—and that is a good thing. Nevertheless, this velocity usually remains fairly stable, and is far more affected by changing team size, makeup, and technical context than by productivity changes. If necessary, financial planners can adjust the cost per story point a bit to account for these changes. This is a minor concern compared to the wildly differing velocities that teams of comparable size may have in the non-normalized case.

LEARN MORE

[1] Leffingwell, Dean. *Agile Software Requirements: Lean Requirements Practices for Teams, Programs, and the Enterprise.* Addison-Wesley, 2011.

[2] Leffingwell, Dean. *Scaling Software Agility: Best Practices for Large Enterprises.* Addison-Wesley, 2007.

[3] Cohn, Mike. *Agile Estimating and Planning.* Robert C. Martin Series. Prentice Hall, 2005.

Iteration Goals

Clarity adorns profound thoughts.

   —Luc de Clapiers

Iteration Goals are a high-level summary of the business and technical goals that the Agile Team agrees to accomplish in an Iteration. They are vital to coordinating an Agile Release Train (ART) as a self-organizing, self-managing team of teams.

Iteration goals provide the following benefits:

- They align the team members and the Product Owner to the mission.
- They align the people to the Program Increment (PI) Objectives.
- They provide context for understanding and addressing cross-team dependencies.

Whether the teams apply Scrum or Kanban, iteration goals give program stakeholders, management, and Agile teams a shared language for maintaining alignment, managing dependencies, and making necessary adjustments during the execution of the program increment.

Details

As described in the Iteration Planning chapter, the planning process produces three outputs:

- The Iteration backlog, consisting of the Stories committed to the iteration
- A statement of iteration goals, as shown in Figure 1
- A commitment to the work needed to achieve the team's goals

Iteration goals often reflect the following factors:

- Features, feature slices, or feature aspects, such as research and necessary infrastructure
- Business or technical Milestones
- Architectural, infrastructure, exploration, and compliance activities
- Routine jobs and other things, such as maintenance and documentation

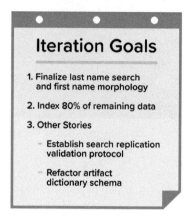

Figure 1. One team's iteration goals

Iteration goals are achieved by completing backlog items, even though it may not be necessary to finish every story to meet the goals. In other words, the goals for the iteration override the concerns related to any particular story. On occasion, it may even be necessary to add new user stories to achieve the iteration's goals.

Why Iteration Goals?

In the Agile Release Train (ART) context, iteration goals help in understanding and maintaining a larger view of what the team intends to accomplish in each iteration, and what to present in the upcoming System Demo.

Iteration goals support three of the four SAFe Core Values—namely, transparency, alignment, and program execution. Simply committing to complete a set of stories in an iteration is insufficient. Instead, the team must continually review the business value of each iteration, and then be able to communicate it in business terms to the Business Owners, management, and other stakeholders.

Although Kanban teams don't typically use iterations in the same way that ScrumXP teams do, iteration goals still provide transparency and alignment when they are part of an ART.

Align Team Members to a Common Purpose

The execution of an iteration goes by very quickly. It's a fast and furious process. Iteration goals help the team and Product Owner reach agreement on the initial business value they intend to deliver, align the team and program PI objectives, and ground everyone in the shared purpose, as summarized in Figure 2.

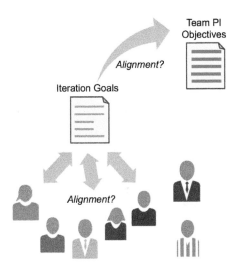

Figure 2. Iteration goals help align the team to the program PI objectives

Align Teams to Common PI Objectives and Manage Dependencies

Agile teams are not islands of agility, but rather integral parts of the broader Program Level context and purpose. As a result, the intent of upcoming iterations requires communication with other teams and the Release Train Engineer (RTE). Iteration goals facilitate alignment with the program PI objectives. In addition, they provide the necessary context for discovering dependencies and developing a resolution, as shown in Figure 3.

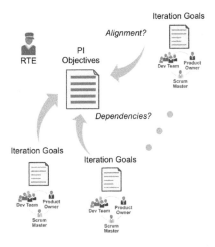

Figure 3. Iteration goals align teams and help identify dependencies

Provide Continuous Management Information

Scaling to the program level requires the creation of a leaner, more empowered organization in which management can handle more responsibility, using organization skills to eliminate impediments and drive improvements. However, management cannot and should not relinquish its responsibility to understand what the teams are doing and why they are doing it. Managers are still accountable for the effectiveness of the development organization and the value delivery outcomes. Moreover, aggregating iteration goals for a train provides a simple two-week summary of what's happening, as depicted in Figure 4.

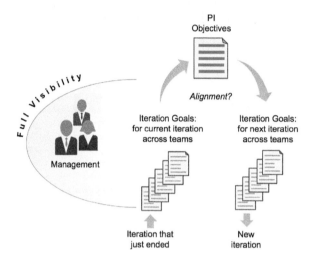

Figure 4. Iteration goals provide visibility and communication with management

---

LEARN MORE

[1] Leffingwell, Dean. *Agile Software Requirements: Lean Requirements Practices for Teams, Programs, and the Enterprise.* Addison-Wesley, 2011.

Iteration Execution

Vision without execution is hallucination.

—*Thomas Edison*

Iteration Execution is how Agile Teams manage their work throughout the Iteration timebox, resulting in a high-quality, working, tested system increment.

Developing high-quality systems is a challenge for every Agile team, Agile Release Train (ART), and Solution Train. No matter the preparation and no matter the planning, without effective iteration execution, scaling is nearly impossible and solution quality is compromised.

During the iteration, each team collaborates to define, build, and test the Stories developed in the course of Iteration Planning. The team members track the iteration's progress and improve the flow of value by using story and Kanban boards and Daily Stand-up (DSU) meetings. They deliver stories throughout the iteration and avoid 'waterfalling' the timebox. They apply Built-In Quality practices to build the system right.

These completed stories are demoed throughout the iteration and at the Iteration Review. During the Iteration Retrospective, the Agile Team reflects on its practices and challenges and makes small improvements at every increment. The team also works effectively with other teams on the train and participates in the System Demo.

Details

Empowering Agile Teams to focus on rapid value delivery fuels them with energy, motivation, and purpose. It instills a better sense of mission than traditional management and development models. The centerpiece of this approach is the development of high-quality system increments during the iteration. Teams employ a variety of practices to achieve that result, but the focus is always the same: to deliver the stories they committed to during iteration planning to meet the Iteration Goals.

But even with good, local execution, teams are always part of a larger purpose—namely, optimizing *program execution*, one of the four Core Values of SAFe. Agile Teams operate in the context of the ART, which guides teams toward the agreed-to team and Program PI Objectives. All teams use the same iteration *cadence* and duration to *synchronize* their work for integration, evaluation, and demonstration during the iteration review and system demo.

Successful iteration execution relies on the following activities:

- **Tracking iteration progress** – The team uses either a storyboard or a Kanban board to follow the progress of the iteration.

- **Building stories serially and incrementally** – This practice avoids mini-waterfalls within the iteration.

- **Constant communication** – Continuous communication and synchronization via DSU meetings are key elements.

- **Improving flow** – The team optimizes flow by managing Work in Process (WIP), building quality in, and continuously accepting stories throughout the iteration.

- **Program execution** – Teams work together as an ART to achieve program PI objectives.

Tracking Iteration Progress

Tracking iteration progress requires visibility into the status of user stories, defects, and other team activities. For this purpose, most teams use a *Big Visible Information Radiator (BVIR)* on a wall in the team room. Kanban teams use their Kanban board, while ScrumXP teams would use a storyboard, perhaps one similar to Figure 1.

With this simple storyboard, the team just moves the red ribbon to the current day, providing an easy-to-understand visual assessment of iteration progress. In Figure 1, it's clear that the iteration is at risk; the team can use the storyboard to figure out the best way of completing the iteration. The storyboard can be shared with remote participants or stakeholders using a webcam, email, wiki, or Agile project management tooling, although this means of communication usually complements the BVIR, rather than replacing it.

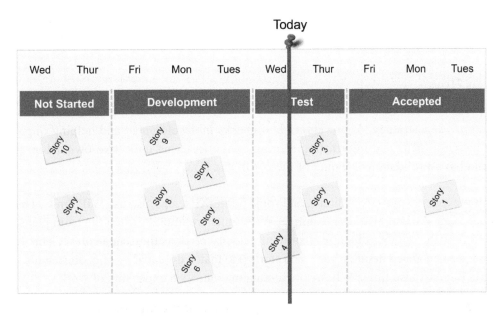

Figure 1. Tracking progress with a team storyboard

Constant Communication

An open work environment and collocation of team members are essential to collaboration. Otherwise, delays in value delivery will rule the day. If a team is geographically distributed, they can improve communication by leaving webcams, instant messaging, and other collaboration tools in an always-on state.

The Daily Stand-up

Each day, the team members meet at the same time and place to coordinate their work by having each member answer the following questions:

- What did I do yesterday to advance the iteration goals?

- What will I be able to complete today to advance the iteration goals?

- What's preventing us from completing the iteration goals?

The DSU is key to team synchronization and self-organization. It's most useful when held in front of a BVIR that highlights the stories that are part of the team's PI objectives. The DSU is strictly timeboxed to 15 minutes and is not a problem-solving or status meeting for management. Instead, its purpose is to coordinate the team's activities and raise blocking issues and dependencies, many of which need to be resolved afterward. The Scrum Master writes down topics that need further discussion on the 'meet after' board. During the 'meet after,' only the involved parties stay to talk. Ineffective DSUs are symptoms of deeper problems that require a systematic approach for resolution, which often becomes the responsibility of the Scrum Master.

Note: Although the DSU is a Scrum construct, many Kanban Teams also hold a DSU in front of their Kanban board to coordinate and inspect it for bottlenecks or WIP problems.

Improving Flow

Managing WIP

WIP limits provide a strategy for preventing bottlenecks in development and helping improve flow. They also increase focus and information sharing, while fostering collective ownership. All SAFe teams should have a solid understanding of their WIP and flow.

Kanban teams explicitly apply WIP limits, and some ScrumXP teams also use WIP limits. These limits can be either explicit or implicit. For example, WIP limits are implicit when the team plans its work and takes on only the number of stories that their velocity predicts they can achieve. This forces the demand (i.e., the negotiated iteration goals and stories) to match the capacity (e.g., the team's velocity). The iteration timebox also limits WIP by preventing uncontrolled expansion of work.

In an alternative approach, some ScrumXP teams may use explicit WIP limits on their storyboard. For example, in the situation depicted in Figure 1, what would a developer do if there were no WIP limits and he or she finished story 5? The developer would probably start another story. But if a WIP limit of 3 was imposed on the in-process and test stages, the developer would need to help test stories instead, and throughput would increase. To understand more about WIP limits, refer to SAFe Principle #6.

Building Quality In

ARTs execute and deliver new functionality with the shortest sustainable lead time. To do so, they must create high-quality systems that promote a predictable development velocity. SAFe prescribes a set of five quality and engineering practices that contribute to the built-in quality of even the most significant Solutions:

- Test-First
- Continuous Integration
- Refactoring
- Pair work
- Collective ownership

Ensuring that quality is built in from the beginning makes the delivery of value quicker, easier, and less costly.

Continuously Accepting Stories

Accepting stories on a continuous basis improves flow. With this approach, problems can be addressed quickly and efficiently and the team avoids building new functionality on top of work that is not fit for purpose. Further, the team avoids the context switching that might otherwise occur when rework is required. When it continuously accepts stories, the team reworks stories that are not accepted. Figure 1 illustrates an example of an iteration with too much WIP and insufficient flow: After six days, this team has moved only one story to the 'done' state.

Test Automation

Where possible, the criteria for acceptable system behavior, as specified by the Product Owner and the Agile Team members, should be converted to automated story-acceptance tests. As the system evolves, continuously running these tests helps assure that the solution previously developed and tested still performs the same way after it has been changed or interfaced with other components. Automation also provides the ability to quickly regression-test the system, which in turn enhances continuous integration, refactoring, and maintenance. Documenting acceptance criteria as human-readable, executable specifications encourages closer collaboration, helping teams keep the business goals in mind at all times.

Continuous Integration and Deployment

Continuous integration at the team, system, and solution levels, as well as migrating work to a staging environment and even deploying to production, allow for a faster flow of value and validation of the expected benefits. The Continuous Integration and Continuous Deployment chapters describe these practices in more detail.

Building Stories Serially and Incrementally

Avoiding the Iteration Waterfall

Teams should avoid the temptation to waterfall the iteration. Instead, they should ensure that they are completing multiple define–build–test cycles in the course of the iteration, as shown in Figure 2.

This is an inter-iteration waterfall:

Iteration 1	Iteration 2	Iteration 3	Iteration 4	Iteration 5
Define	Build	Test		
	Define	Build	Test	
		Define	Build	Test

X

This is an intra-iteration waterfall:

Iteration 1	Iteration 2	Iteration 3	Iteration 4	Iteration 5
Define Build Test	Define Build Test	Define Build Test		

X

These are cross-functional iterations:

Iteration 1	Iteration 2	Iteration 3	Iteration 4	Iteration 5
D B T	D B T	D B T		
D B T	D B T	D B T		
D B T	D B T	D B T		

✓

Figure 2. Avoid the inter- and intra-waterfall by implementing cross-functional iterations

Building Stories Incrementally

Figure 3 illustrates how implementing stories in thin, vertical slices is the foundation for incremental development, integration, and testing.

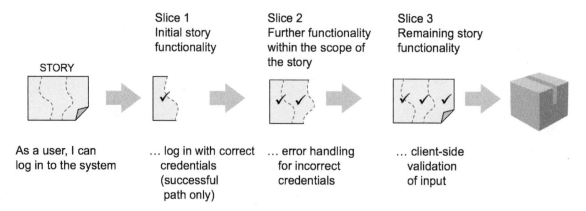

Figure 3. Implementing stories in vertical slices is the key to incremental development

Building stories this way enables a short feedback cycle and allows the Dev Teams to work with a smaller increment of the working system, which in turn facilitates continuous integration and testing. This approach helps Dev Team members refine their understanding of the functionality, and it supports pairing and more frequent integration of working systems. The dependencies within and across teams and even trains can be managed more effectively, as the dependent teams can consume the new functionality sooner. Incrementally implementing stories helps reduce uncertainty, validates architectural and design decisions, and promotes early learning and knowledge sharing.

Focusing on Program Execution

The ultimate goal of all Agile Teams is the successful execution of the ART's PI objectives. Figure 4 shows that teams plan, integrate, and demo together; deploy and release together; and learn together. Collectively, these actions help teams avoid focusing solely on their own local concerns.

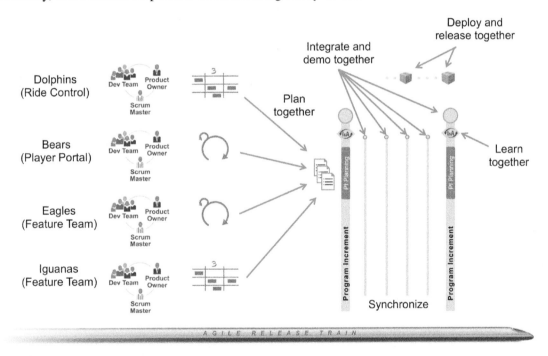

Figure 4. Agile Teams collaborate to achieve the program PI objectives

The Agile Teams and Dev Team chapters further describe these teams' role in program execution.

LEARN MORE

[1] Leffingwell, Dean. *Agile Software Requirements: Lean Requirements Practices for Teams, Programs, and the Enterprise.* Addison-Wesley, 2011.

Iteration Review

Seeing is believing.

—*Anonymous*

The *Iteration Review* is a cadence-based event, in which each team inspects the increment at the end of every Iteration to assess progress and then adjusts its backlog for the next iteration.

During the iteration review, each Agile Team measures and then demonstrates its progress by showing working stories to the Product Owner (PO) and other stakeholders to get their feedback. Teams demo every new Story, Spike, Refactor, and Nonfunctional Requirement (NFR). The preparation for the iteration review begins during Iteration Planning, when teams start thinking about how they will demo the stories to which they have committed. 'Beginning with the end in mind' facilitates iteration planning and alignment, fostering a more thorough understanding of the functionality needed before iteration execution.

Details

The iteration review provides a way to gather immediate, contextual feedback from the team's stakeholders on a regular cadence. The iteration review serves three important purposes:

- It brings closure to the iteration timebox, to which many individuals have contributed to provide new value to the business

- It gives teams an opportunity to show the contributions they have made to the business and to take some satisfaction and pride in their work and progress

- It allows stakeholders to see working stories and provide feedback to improve the product

Process

To begin the iteration review, the team goes over the Iteration Goals and discusses their status. A walk-through of all the committed stories then follows. Each completed story is demoed in a working, tested system—preferably in a staging environment that closely resembles the production environment.

Spikes are demonstrated via a presentation of findings. Stakeholders provide feedback on the stories that are demoed, which is the primary goal of the review process.

After the demo, the team reflects on which stories were *not* completed, if any, and why the team was unable to finish them. This discussion usually results in the discovery of impediments or risks, false assumptions, changing priorities, estimating inaccuracies, or over-commitment. In turn, these findings may lead to further study in the Iteration Retrospective about how the next iterations can be better planned and executed. Figure 1 illustrates an iteration review in action.

Figure 1. Showing a working, tested team increment at the Iteration Review

In addition to reflecting on how well it did within this latest iteration, the team determines how it is progressing toward its Program Increment (PI) Objectives. It finishes the event by refining the Team Backlog before the next iteration planning.

Attendees

Attendees at the iteration review include the following parties:

- The Agile Team, which includes the Product Owner and the Scrum Master
- Stakeholders who want to see the team's progress, which may also include other teams

Although Agile Release Train (ART) stakeholders may attend, their interests and level of detail are usually better aligned with the System Demo.

Guidelines

Following are some tips for the iteration review:

- Limit demo preparation by team members to about one to two hours.

- Timebox the meeting to about one to two hours.

- Minimize the use of slides. The purpose of the iteration review is to get feedback on working software functionality, hardware components, and other outputs.

- Verify completed stories meet the Definition of Done (DoD).

- Demo incomplete stories, if enough functionality is available to get feedback.

- If a significant stakeholder cannot attend, the Product Owner should follow up to report progress and get feedback.

- Encourage constructive feedback and celebration of the accomplishments.

Teams that are practicing Continuous Delivery or Continuous Deployment should also do more frequent story or Feature review. Once functionality has reached the ready-for-deployment state, key stakeholders should review it.

LEARN MORE

[1] Leffingwell, Dean. *Agile Software Requirements: Lean Requirements Practices for Teams, Programs, and the Enterprise.* Addison-Wesley, 2011.

[2] Leffingwell, Dean. *Scaling Software Agility: Best Practices for Large Enterprises.* Addison-Wesley, 2007.

Iteration Retrospective

At regular intervals, the team reflects on how to become more effective, then tunes and adjusts its behavior accordingly.

—Agile Manifesto

The *Iteration Retrospective* is a regular meeting in which Agile Team members discuss the results of the Iteration, review their practices, and identify ways to improve.

At the end of each iteration, Agile teams that apply ScrumXP (and many teams that use Kanban) gather for an iteration retrospective, during which the team members discuss their practices and identify ways to improve. Timeboxed to an hour or less, each retrospective seeks to uncover what's working well, what isn't, and what the team can do better next time.

Each retrospective yields both quantitative and qualitative insights. The quantitative review gathers and evaluates any metrics the team is using to measure its performance. The qualitative part discusses the team practices and the specific challenges that occurred during the last iteration or two. When issues have been identified, root cause analysis is performed, potential corrective actions are discussed, and improvement Stories are entered into the Team Backlog.

Details

Agile teams use the iteration retrospective to reflect on the iteration just completed and to develop new ideas to improve the process. This helps instill the concept of relentless improvement—one of the pillars of the SAFe Lean-Agile Mindset—in the individuals and the team. In addition, it helps ensure that every iteration yields some small improvements in the team's process.

The whole team participates in the retrospective, with the Scrum Master facilitating and applying the tools and processes for data collection and problem-solving. The team conducts the retrospective in two parts:

- **Quantitative review** – The team assesses whether they met the Iteration Goals. This is a binary measure: yes or no. Team members also collect any other metrics they agreed to analyze. This information should include velocity—both the portion that is available for new development and the part devoted to maintenance. Agile teams collect and apply other Iteration Metrics for visibility and to help with process improvement. These data also serve as the context for the qualitative review that follows.

- **Qualitative review** – First the team reviews the improvement stories they had identified in the prior retrospective. Next it analyzes the current process, with a focus on finding one or two things it can do better in the next iteration. Since many improvement items have a significant scope, the team should divide them into smaller improvement stories, so that they can focus on what they can improve during an iteration.

As organizations move closer to implementing DevOps and a Continuous Delivery Pipeline, Agile teams will have a robust list of improvement opportunities, including but not limited to the following:

- Test automation and Continuous Integration
- Architectural approaches for decoupling development from deployment
- Automating the deployment process
- Building telemetry and recovery techniques into systems

Lean-Agile Leaders are responsible for preserving and protecting the time that teams need during each Program Increment (PI) to focus on cultivating these skills, in addition to delivering new features. The Innovation and Planning (IP) Iteration is a great time to create opportunities for teams to advance their skill levels in these new domains.

Retrospective Formats

Several techniques have been introduced for eliciting subjective feedback on the success of the iteration (also see [1], [3], [4,], [5]):

- **Individual** – Individually write feedback on Post-it notes and then find patterns as a group.

- **Appreciation** – Note whether someone has helped you or helped the team.

- **Conceptual** – Choose one word to describe the iteration.

- **Rating** – Rate the iteration on a scale of 1 to 5, and then brainstorm how to make the next iteration become a 5.

- **Simple** – Open a discussion and record the results under three headings.

The last is the familiar method in which the Scrum Master simply puts up three sheets of paper labeled 'What Went Well,' 'What Didn't,' and 'Do Better Next Time,' and then facilitates an open brainstorming session. Such a discussion can be conducted fairly easily, making all accomplishments and challenges visible, as illustrated in Figure 1.

Figure 1. One team's retrospective results (Image courtesy of Scaled Agile, Inc.)

Teams may choose to rotate the responsibility for facilitating retrospectives. If this is done, a fun practice is to allow each person to choose his or her own retrospective format when it's that individual's turn to lead. This not only creates shared ownership of the process but also keeps the retrospective fresh. Team members are more likely to remain engaged when formats are new and different.

Guidelines

Following are some tips for holding a successful iteration retrospective:

- Keep the meeting timeboxed to an hour or less. Remember, it will come up every two weeks. The goal is to make small, continuous improvement steps.

- Pick only one or two things that can be done better next time and add them as improvement stories to the team backlog, targeted for the next iteration. The other targets for improvement can always be addressed in future iterations if they resurface in retrospectives.

- Make sure everyone speaks.

- The Scrum Master should spend time preparing the retrospective, as it's a primary vehicle for improvement.

- Focus on items that the team can address, not on how others can improve.

- To show progress, make sure improvement stories from the previous iteration are discussed either at the Iteration Review or at the beginning of the quantitative review.

- The retrospective is a private meeting for the team and should be limited to Agile team members only (Development Team, Scrum Master, and Product Owner).

LEARN MORE

[1] Derby, Esther, and Diana Larson. *Agile Retrospectives: Making Good Teams Great*. Pragmatic Bookshelf, 2006.

[2] Leffingwell, Dean. *Scaling Software Agility: Best Practices for Large Enterprises*. Addison-Wesley, 2007.

[3] Fun Retrospectives. www.funretrospectives.com.

[4] TastyCupcakes.org. http://tastycupcakes.org/tag/retrospective/.

[5] Agile Retrospective Resource Wiki. www.retrospectivewiki.org.

Team Backlog

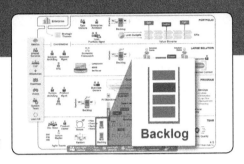

The *Team Backlog* contains user and Enabler Stories that originate from the Program Backlog, as well as stories that arise locally from the team's local context. It may include other work items as well, representing all the things a team needs to do to advance its portion of the system.

The Product Owner (PO) is responsible for the team backlog. Since it includes both user stories and enablers, it's essential to allocate capacity in a way that balances investments across conflicting needs. The allocation takes into account the needs of both the Agile Release Train (ART) and the specific team.

Details

While 'backlog' seems to be a simple notion, it includes some critical concepts:

- It contains all things undone. If an item is in there, it might get done. If it isn't, there is no chance that it will get done.

- It's a list of 'want to do' items, not a commitment. Items can be estimated (preferable) or not, but neither case implies a specific time commitment for completion.

- It has a single owner—the Product Owner—who protects the team from the problem of multiple stakeholders, each with potentially divergent views of what's important.

- All team members can enter stories into the backlog.

- The backlog contains user, enabler, and improvement stories; the last are those stories that capture the results of the team's Iteration Retrospective.

The team backlog conveniently hides some of the complexity of Agile at scale. Figure 1 depicts the team backlog and its three primary input sources.

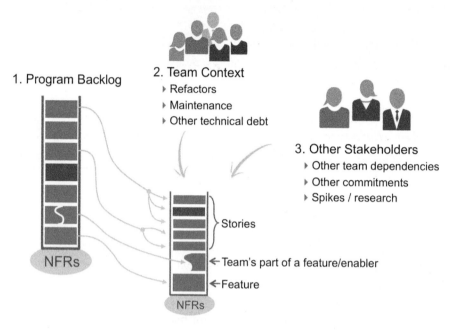

Figure 1. Input sources for a team backlog

The program backlog consists of upcoming Features that are planned to be delivered by an ART. During Program Increment (PI) Planning, the candidate features for the PI are split into stories by the teams and tentatively scheduled into upcoming Iterations in the team backlog.

Teams in the ART are not islands, and their backlogs will contain some stories that support other teams' work and the ART's PI Objectives. These can include spikes for research and estimation of features, Capabilities, and even Epics.

In addition to the stories needed to fulfill features, the team typically has a backlog of local stories representing new functionality, refactors, defects, research, and other technical debt. These are written as enabler stories, which are estimated and prioritized like user stories.

Optimizing Value Delivery with Capacity Allocation

Just like the ART itself, every team faces the problem of how to balance the backlog of internally facing work—maintenance, refactors, and technical debt—with the new user stories that deliver more immediate business value.

Focusing solely on business functionality may work for a bit and even provide immediate gratification to the market, but this will be short-lived, as delivery velocity eventually will be slowed by a crushing load of technical debt. Teams then must continuously invest in both evolving the architecture of the solution and keeping existing customers happy with bug fixes and enhancements, so as to avoid the need for wholesale replacement of the system due to technological obsolescence.

Balancing the different types of work complicates the challenge of prioritization, as the PO is trying to compare the value of unlike things: defects, refactors, redesigns, technology upgrades, and new user stories. And there is no upper limit to the demand for any of these things!

Similar to the program backlog, teams use 'capacity allocation' to determine how much of their total effort can be applied to each type of activity for a given time period, as Figure 2 illustrates. The PO, in collaboration with the team, selects the highest-priority backlog items for each 'slice' of the capacity allocation to implement in an iteration.

For stories that are committed to the program, sequencing is probably already predetermined by PI planning commitments. In contrast, for a specific team's local stories, the PO can sequence those using 'value/size' or even apply full Weighted Shortest Job First (WSJF) where beneficial. Also, to balance long-term product health and value delivery, the percentage allocation to each 'slice' can be changed over time. Such changes typically occur at PI boundaries.

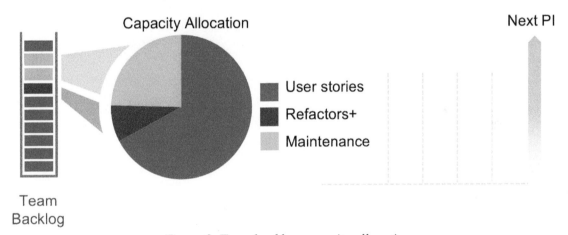

Figure 2. Team backlog capacity allocation

Backlog Refinement

Since the team backlog must always contain some stories that are essentially ready for implementation, without significant risk or surprise, backlog refinement should be a continuous process. Agile teams take a flow-based approach to maintaining this level of backlog readiness, typically by having at least one team backlog refinement workshop per week; avoid limiting backlog refinement to just a single meeting. The sole focus of this workshop is to look at upcoming stories (and features, as appropriate), discuss and estimate their scope, and establish an initial understanding of acceptance criteria.

Teams applying Acceptance Test–Driven Development (ATDD) will typically invest even more time up-front in developing specific acceptance tests, sometimes in sessions often called 'specification workshops.' Also, given that multiple teams will be doing backlog refinement, new issues, dependencies, and stories are likely to emerge. In this way, backlog refinement helps surface problems with the current plan, which can then be discussed in ART sync meetings.

LEARN MORE

[1] https://www.merriam-webster.com/dictionary/backlog.

[2] Leffingwell, Dean. *Agile Software Requirements: Lean Requirements Practices for Teams, Programs, and the Enterprise.* Addison-Wesley, 2011.

Team Kanban

The only way you can create excess inventory is by having excess manpower.

—Eli Goldratt

Or perhaps overspecialization?

—SAFe Authors

Team Kanban is a method that helps teams facilitate the flow of value by visualizing workflow, establishing Work In Process (WIP) limits, measuring throughput, and continuously improving their process.

SAFe teams have a choice of Agile methods. Most use Scrum, a lightweight and popular method for managing work. Teams that develop new code also apply Extreme Programming (XP) practices to bring focus to software engineering and code quality. Other teams—particularly System Teams, operations, and maintenance teams—choose to apply Kanban as their primary method. In these contexts, the rapid-fire nature of the work, the fast-changing priorities, and the lower value of planning activities for the next Iteration all lead them to this choice.

Kanban systems are applied to the Portfolio, Large Solution, Program, and Team levels of SAFe, even though it's for different reasons. This chapter describes a Kanban system well suited to Agile Teams. However, these teams are on the train, and some additional rules must apply.

Details

Kanban is a 'pull system,' meaning that teams pull work when they know they have the capacity for it, rather than having scope pushed on them. A Kanban system is made up of workflow steps. Most steps have WIP limits, such that a work item can be pulled into a step only when the number of items at that step is lower than the WIP limit. A few steps (typically beginning and end steps) may not be limited. WIP limits are defined and adjusted by the team, allowing it to adapt quickly to the variations in the flow of complex system development.

In SAFe, team Kanban is applied together with the cadence and synchronization requirements of the Agile Release Train (ART). This facilitates alignment, dependency management, and fast, integration-based learning cycles. These efforts provide the objective evidence needed to advance the broader Solution.

Kanban Description

Kanban, which means 'visual signal,' is a method for visualizing and managing work. While there are many interpretations of how to apply Kanban in development, most would agree that the primary aspects include the following:

- The system contains a series of states that define the workflow.

- The progress of items is tracked by visualizing all work.

- Teams agree on specific WIP limits for each state and change them when necessary to improve flow.

- Policies are adopted to specify the management of work.

- Flow is measured. Work items are tracked from the time they enter the system to the time they leave, providing continuous indicators of the amount of WIP and the current lead time—in other words, how long, on average, it takes an item to get through the system.

- Classes of service are used to prioritize work based on the Cost of Delay (CoD).

Visualizing Flow and Limiting WIP

To get started, teams typically build an approximation of their current process flow and define some initial WIP limits. Figure 1 shows an example of one team's initial Kanban board, which captures the current workflow steps: analyze, review, build, and integrate and test.

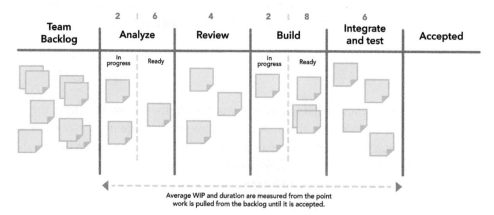

Figure 1. One team's initial Kanban board

In Figure 1, the team has also decided to create two buffers (the 'Ready' columns) to better manage flow variability. One precedes the 'Review' step, which might require external subject-matter experts (Product Management or others), whose availability may be limited and uneven. The other buffer precedes the 'Integrate & test' state, which, in this case, requires the use of shared test fixtures and resources. Since integration and testing are performed by the same people on the same infrastructure, the two steps are treated as a single step. Also, to justify the transaction cost, the team allows reasonably higher WIP limits for the review and integrate and test steps.

A team's Kanban board evolves iteratively. After defining the initial process and WIP limits and executing for a while, the team's bottlenecks should surface. If not, the team refines the process or further reduces some WIP limits until it becomes evident that a workflow state either is 'starving' or is too full. This helps the team continually adjust the process to optimize the flow—for example, by changing WIP limits and merging, splitting, or redefining workflow states.

Measuring Flow

Kanban teams use objective measures, including average lead time, WIP, and throughput, to understand and improve their flow and process. The Cumulative Flow Diagram (CFD), illustrated in Figure 2, is an area graph that depicts the quantity of work in a given state, showing arrivals, time in a state, quantity in a state, and departure.

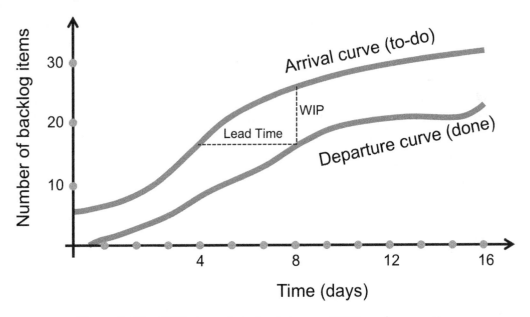

Figure 2. The CFD shows how lead time and WIP evolve over time

Each work item is date stamped, both when it enters the Kanban (pulled from the team backlog to begin implementation) and when it is completed. The arrival curve shows the rate at which backlog items are pulled into work. The departure curve shows when these items have been accepted. The *x*-axis shows the average lead time—how long it takes, on average, for an item to get through the system. The *y*-axis shows the WIP—the average number of items in the system at any point in time.

Throughput—the number of Stories completed per specified period of time—represents another critical metric. Since Kanban teams in SAFe operate on an Iteration cadence, they measure throughput in terms of the number of stories per iteration.

The CFD provides the data that the team uses to calculate its current iteration throughput. To arrive at the average number of stories processed per day, the team divides the average WIP by the average lead time. Next they multiply this value by 14, which is the number of days in a two-week iteration. This provides the average throughput of stories per iteration, which helps with planning. (This metric is also important in calculating derived velocity, as described later in this chapter.)

The CFD also provides an important visualization of significant flow variations. Such variations may be the result of systemic internal impediments of which the team is unaware or external forces that impede the flow. The CFD is an excellent example of an objective measure that facilitates relentless improvement for Kanban teams.

Improving Flow with Classes of Service

Teams also need to be able to manage dependencies and ensure alignment with Milestones. Kanban uses the concept of classes of service to help teams optimize the execution of their backlog items. Classes of service help differentiate backlog items based on their CoD. Each class of service has a specific execution policy that the team agrees to follow. For example:

- **Standard** – Represents the baseline *class of service*, applicable to work items that are neither *expedited* nor *fixed date*. Most backlog items should fall into this category. The CoD is linear for standard items, meaning that value cannot be achieved until delivery occurs, but there's no fixed-date requirement.

- **Fixed date** – Describes work item*s* that must be delivered on or before a specific date. Typically, the COD of these items is nonlinear and highly sensitive to small changes in the delivery date; these items must be actively managed to mitigate the schedule risk. As a consequence, they are pulled into development when necessary to be finished on time. Some items may require additional analysis to refine the expected lead time. Some need to be reclassified into the expedite class if the team falls behind.

- **Expedite** – Includes items with an unacceptable CoD that require immediate attention. Such an item can be pulled into development, even in violation of current WIP limits. Typically, there can be only one expedite item in the system at a time, and teams may set a policy to swarm on that item to make sure it moves through the system rapidly.

If teams find that many items require expediting, then the system may be overloaded. In this situation, either demand exceeds capacity, or the input process may need more discipline. Whatever the case, the process needs to be adjusted.

As illustrated in Figure 3, classes of service are typically visualized as 'swim lanes.'

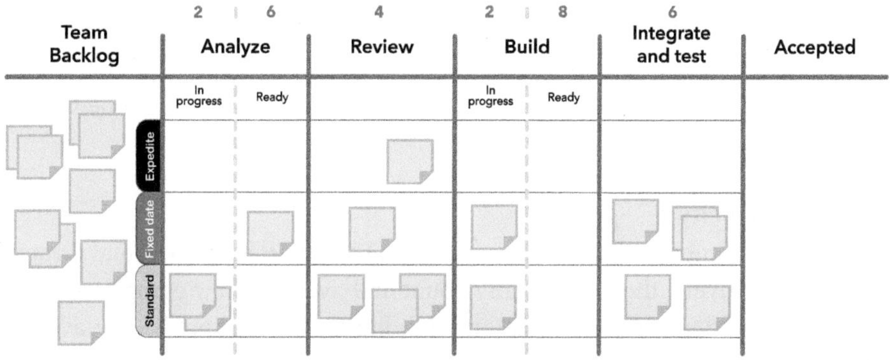

Figure 3. Classes of service on the Kanban board

Also, teams may use specific colors for different types of backlog items, such as new functionality, research spikes, and modeling. This adds clarity to the work being performed, as described in the Program Increment (PI) Planning chapter.

Close attention to the process of flow enables Kanban teams to recognize and capitalize on improvement opportunities that might otherwise pass unnoticed. For example, changes in the CFD may suggest increasing average WIP (which will cause an increase in lead time). While this may just be a symptom of a deeper problem, the team now has a way of spotting it. Regular reflection on and adaptation of the process are necessary to realize the benefit of high visibility of flow.

The SAFe Kanban Team Is on the Train

Kanban teams operate in a broader context, building a solution that requires multiple Agile teams and/or the collaboration within a Solution Train. To accomplish this, the team needs to adhere to specific SAFe rules in addition to the regular Kanban guidelines. The rules are that the teams plan together, integrate and demo together, and learn together, as is described in the Agile Teams chapter. Planning together is one element that warrants further discussion, as described in the next section.

Estimating Work

Kanban teams don't invest as much time in estimating or tasking as Scrum teams do. Instead, they take a look at the work needed, split the bigger items where necessary, and push the resulting stories to completion, mostly without much concern for their size. However, SAFe teams must be able to estimate the demand against their capacity for PI planning and also help estimate larger backlog items.

Moreover, forecasting requires estimating the team's velocity in a manner that's consistent with the methods used by other teams on the train and the total ART velocity.

Establish a Common Starting Point for Estimation

Initially, a new Kanban team does not know its throughput, as that is a trailing measure based on history. To get started, team members need a way to estimate work, often beginning in the first PI planning session. In a manner consistent with Scrum teams, estimation of initial capacity begins with normalized estimating (as described in Iteration Planning). Kanban teams then add their estimated stories into iterations, just as the Scrum teams do. Their starting capacity is their assumed velocity, at least for the first PI.

Calculating Derived Velocity

After this starting point, Kanban teams can use their CFD to calculate their actual throughput in stories per iteration. Alternatively, they can simply count and average their completed stories. Kanban teams then calculate their derived velocity by multiplying the throughput by the average story size (typically 3 to 5 points). In this way, both SAFe ScrumXP and Kanban teams can participate in the larger Economic Framework, which in turn provides the primary economic context for the portfolio.

Estimating Larger Work Items

At the portfolio and large solution levels, it is often necessary to estimate larger work items to determine their potential economic viability (Epics and Capabilities). Also, developing a program Roadmap requires two inputs:

- A knowledge of estimating (How big is the item?)
- ART velocity (How much capacity does the ART have to do it?)

Larger items tend to be harder to estimate, which increases risk. When faced with such items, the team splits them into user stories, just as ScrumXP teams do, to improve understanding, increase the accuracy of estimation, and make it easier for the PO to prioritize the work. Stories are then estimated in normalized story points. This provides the ability for the Enterprise to combine estimates from various types of teams, without excessive debate about their merits.

LEARN MORE

[1] Anderson, David. *Kanban: Successful Evolutionary Change for Your Technology Business.* Blue Hole Press, 2010.

[2] Kniberg, Henrik. *Lean from the Trenches: Managing Large-Scale Projects with Kanban.* Pragmatic Programmers, 2012.

Part 5
The Program Level

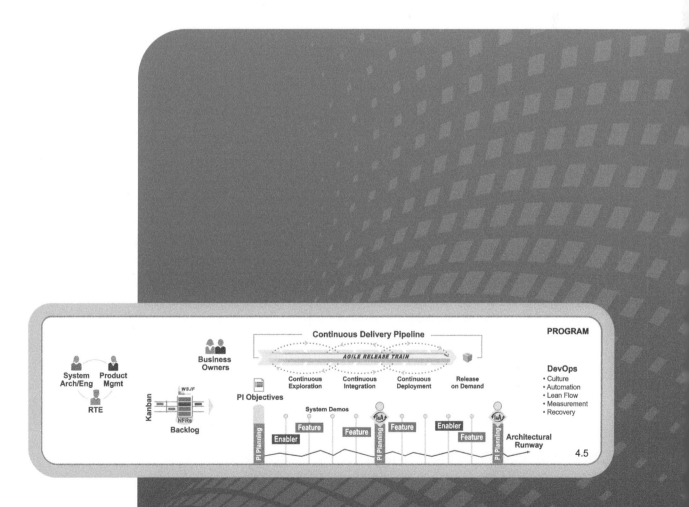

scaledagileframework.com/**program-level**

Introduction to the Program Level

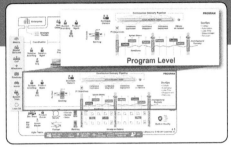

A system must be managed. It will not manage itself. Left to themselves, components become selfish, competitive, independent profit centers, and thus destroy the system. ... The secret is cooperation between components toward the aim of the organization.

—W. Edwards Deming

The *Program Level* contains the roles and activities needed to continuously deliver solutions via an Agile Release Train (ART).

The program level is where development teams, stakeholders, and other resources are devoted to some important, ongoing solution development mission. The ART metaphor describes the program-level teams, roles, and activities that incrementally deliver a continuous flow of value. ARTs are virtual organizations formed to span functional boundaries, eliminate unnecessary handoffs and steps, and accelerate value delivery by implementing SAFe Lean-Agile principles and practices.

Although they operate at the program level, ARTs are long-lived and, therefore, have a more persistent self-organization, structure, and mission than a traditional program. Usually, a program has a definitive start and end date, as well as temporarily assigned resources.

Details

The program level (Figure 1) is where ARTs deliver a portion of a Solution or in some cases, the entire solution. The long-lived, flow-based, self-organizing nature of the ART is what powers SAFe.

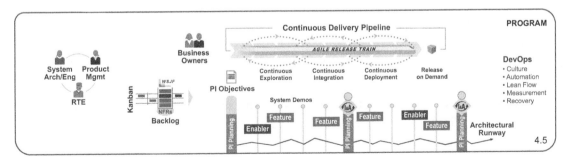

Figure 1. Program level

Many trains are virtual in nature, spanning organizational and geographic boundaries. Others follow a line of business or product line management reporting structure.

Highlights

The highlights of the program level include the following components:

- **Agile Release Train** – Is the key organizational element of the program level and aligns the people and the work around a common program vision, mission, and backlog.

- **Agile Teams** – Each ART is composed of 5–12 Agile teams (50–125 people, and sometimes more or less) and includes the roles and infrastructure necessary to deliver fully working and tested software and systems.

- **Program Increment (PI)** – A timebox in which an ART delivers incremental value. PIs are typically 8–12 weeks long. The most common pattern for a PI is four development Iterations, followed by one Innovation and Planning (IP) iteration.

- **Continuous Delivery Pipeline** – The workflows, activities, and automation needed to provide a constant release of value to the end user.

- **DevOps** – A mindset, culture, and set of technical practices. It provides communication, integration, automation, and close cooperation among all the people needed to plan, develop, test, deploy, release, and maintain a solution.

Roles

ARTs are self-managing and self-organizing teams of Agile teams that plan, commit, and execute together. Nevertheless, a train needs guidance and direction. The program-level roles help align people to a shared mission, coordinate the ARTs, and provide the necessary Lean governance:

- **System Architect/Engineer** – An individual or small cross-disciplinary team that truly applies Principle #2, Apply systems thinking. This role defines the overall architecture for the system, helps define Nonfunctional Requirements (NFRs), determines the major elements and subsystems, and helps design the interfaces and collaborations among them.

- **Product Management** – The internal voice of the Customer. This role works with customers and Product Owners to understand and communicate their needs, define system features, and participate in validation. Product Management is also responsible for the Program Backlog.

- **Release Train Engineer (RTE)** – A servant leader and the chief Scrum Master for the train. The RTE helps optimize the flow of value through the program by using various mechanisms, such as PI Planning, the Program Kanban, and the Inspect and Adapt (I&A) workshop.

- **Business Owners** – A small group of stakeholders who assume the business and technical responsibility for fitness for use, governance, and return on investment (ROI) for a Solution developed by an ART. They are primary stakeholders in the ART and actively participate in ART events.

Events

The program level uses three main activities to help coordinate the ART:

- **PI Planning** – A cadence-based, face-to-face planning event that serves as the heartbeat of the ART, aligning all the teams on the ART to the mission.

- **System Demo** – An activity that provides an integrated view of new features for the most recent iteration delivered by all the teams in the ART. Each demo provides ART stakeholders with an objective measure of progress during a PI.

- **Inspect and Adapt** – A significant event during which the current state of the solution is demoed and evaluated. Teams then reflect and identify improvement backlog items via a structured problem-solving workshop.

Artifacts

The following program-level items help coordinate the ART:

- **Features** – A series of systems or services that fulfill stakeholder needs. Each includes a name, benefits hypothesis, and acceptance criteria. Features are sized to fit within a PI.

- **Program Epics** – The epics for a single ART.

- **Program Backlog** – The holding area for upcoming features, which are intended to address user needs and deliver business benefits for a single ART. It also contains the enabler features necessary to build the Architectural Runway.

- **Program Kanban** – The method that visualizes and manages the flow of features and enablers through the Continuous Delivery Pipeline.

- **PI Objectives** – Summary descriptions of the specific business and technical goals that an ART intends to achieve in the next PI.

- **Architectural Runway** – The existing code, components, and technical infrastructure necessary to support the implementation of prioritized, near-term features, without excessive redesign and delay.

Managing the Flow of Value through the ART

The program Kanban system is a method to visualize and facilitate the flow of features from ideation to analysis, implementation, and release through the continuous delivery pipeline. Once approved, features are maintained and prioritized in the program backlog. Upon implementation, they are sized to fit in a PI such that each delivers new functionality with conceptual integrity. Features are realized by Stories, which are handled by a single team within an iteration.

Connection to the Portfolio and Value Stream

The program vision and roadmap provide a view of the features to be developed, reflecting customer and stakeholder needs and the approaches that are proposed to address those needs. However, for Solutions Trains, the program vision and roadmap are not created in isolation, but rather are developed with the help of Product and Solution Management and must be synchronized with all ARTs that form the Solution Train. Lean Portfolio Management (LPM) and Product and Solution Management also collaborate on the development of the respective roadmaps and visions.

LEARN MORE

[1] Leffingwell, Dean. *Agile Software Requirements: Lean Requirements Practices for Teams, Programs, and the Enterprise.* Addison-Wesley, 2011.

Agile Release Train

The more alignment you have, the more autonomy you can grant. The one enables the other.

—Stephen Bungay, author and strategy consultant

The *Agile Release Train (ART)* is a long-lived team of Agile teams, which, along with other stakeholders, develops and delivers solutions incrementally, using a series of fixed-length Iterations within a Program Increment (PI) timebox. The ART aligns teams to a common business and technology mission.

Each ART is a virtual organization (50–125 people, sometimes more or less) whose members plan, commit, and execute together. ARTs are organized around the enterprise's significant Value Streams and exist solely to realize the promise of that value by building Solutions that deliver benefit to the end user.

Details

ARTs are cross-functional and have all the capabilities—software, hardware, firmware, and other—needed to define, implement, test, and deploy new system functionality. An ART operates with a goal of achieving a *continuous flow of value*, as shown in Figure 1.

Figure 1. The long-lived Agile Release Train

The ART aligns teams to a common mission and helps manage the inherent risk and variability of solution development. ARTs operate on a set of common principles:

- **A fixed schedule** – The train departs the station on a known, reliable schedule, as determined by the chosen PI cadence. If a Feature misses a train, it can catch the next one.

- **A new system increment every two weeks** – Each train delivers a new system increment every two weeks. The System Demo provides a mechanism for evaluating the working system, which is an integrated increment from all the teams.

- **A fixed PI timebox** – All teams on the train are synchronized to the same PI length (typically 8–12 weeks) and have common iteration start/end dates and duration.

- **A known velocity** – Each train can reliably estimate how much cargo (new features) can be delivered in a PI.

- **Agile Teams** – Agile Teams embrace the Agile Manifesto and the SAFe values and principles. They apply Scrum, Extreme Programming (XP), Kanban, and other Built-In Quality practices.

- **Dedicated people** – Most people needed by the ART are dedicated full time to the train, regardless of their functional reporting structure.

- **Face-to-face PI Planning** – The ART plans its own work during periodic, largely face-to-face PI Planning events.

- **Innovation and Planning (IP)** – IP iterations provide a guard band (buffer) for estimating and a dedicated time for PI planning, innovation, continuing education, and infrastructure work.

- **Inspect and Adapt (I&A)** – An I&A event is held at the end of every PI. The current state of the solution is demonstrated and evaluated. Teams and management then identify improvement backlog items via a structured, problem-solving workshop.

- **Develop on Cadence; Release on Demand** – ARTs apply cadence and synchronization to help manage the inherent variability of research and development. However, releases are typically decoupled from the development cadence. ARTs can release a solution, or elements of a solution, at any time, subject to governance and release criteria.

Additionally, in larger value streams, multiple ARTs collaborate to build larger solution capabilities via a Solution Train. Some ART stakeholders participate in Solution Train events, including the Solution Demo and Pre- and Post-PI Planning.

Organization

ARTs are typically virtual organizations that have all the people needed to define and deliver value. This arrangement breaks down any traditional functional silos (Figure 2) that may exist.

In the traditional functional organization, developers work with developers, testers work with other testers, and architects and systems engineers work with each other. While there are reasons why organizations have evolved in this way, value doesn't flow easily within this type of structure, as it must cross all the silos. The daily involvement of managers and project managers is necessary to move the work across. As a result, progress is slow, and handoffs and delays rule.

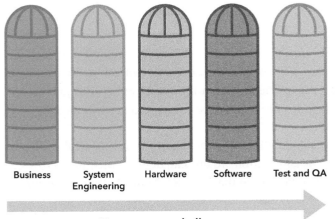

- Value delivery is inhibited by hand-offs and delays

- Political boundaries can prevent cooperation

- Silos encourage geographic distribution of functions

- Communication across silos is difficult

Figure 2. Traditional functional organization

In contrast, the ART applies systems thinking and builds a cross-functional organization that is optimized to facilitate the flow of value from ideation to deployment, as shown in Figure 3. Collectively, this fully cross-functional organization—whether physical (direct organizational reporting) or virtual (line of reporting is unchanged)—has everyone and everything it needs to define and deliver value. It is self-organizing and self-managing. This approach creates a far leaner organization, one where traditional daily task and project management is no longer required. Value flows more quickly, with a minimum of overhead.

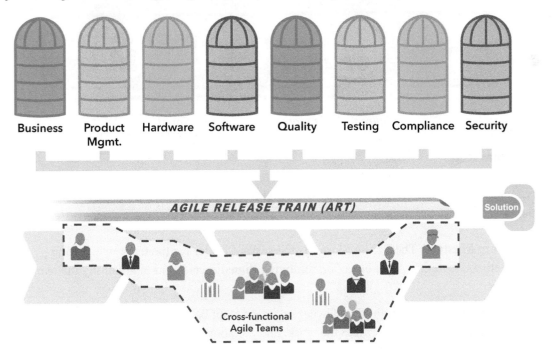

Figure 3. Agile Release Trains are fully cross-functional

Agile Teams Power the Train

ARTs include the teams that define, build, and test features and components. SAFe teams have a choice of Agile practices, based primarily on Scrum, XP, and Kanban. Software quality practices include continuous integration, test-first, refactoring, pair work, and collective ownership. Hardware quality is supported by exploratory early iterations, frequent system-level integration, design verification, modeling, and Set-Based Design. Agile architecture supports software and hardware quality.

Each Agile team includes five to nine dedicated individual contributors, covering all the roles necessary to build a quality increment of value for an iteration. Teams can deliver software, hardware, and any combination thereof. Of course, Agile teams within the ART are themselves cross-functional, as shown in Figure 4.

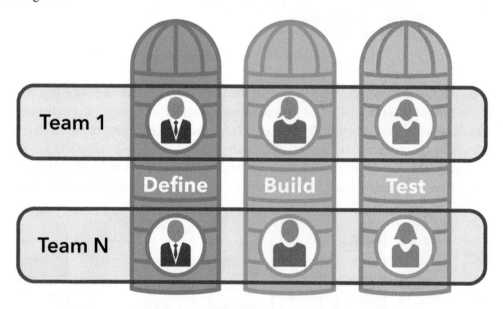

Figure 4. Agile teams are cross-functional

Critical Team Roles

Each Agile team has dedicated individual contributors, covering all the roles necessary to build a quality increment of value for an iteration. Most SAFe teams apply a ScrumXP and Kanban hybrid, with the three primary Scrum roles:

- **Scrum Master** – The Scrum Master is the servant leader for the team, facilitating meetings, fostering Agile behavior, removing impediments, and maintaining the team's focus.

- **Product Owner** – The Product Owner owns the team backlog, acts as the Customer for developer questions, prioritizes the work, and collaborates with Product Management to plan and deliver solutions.

- **Development Team** – The Development Team consists of three to nine dedicated individual contributors, covering all the roles necessary to build a quality increment of value for an iteration.

Critical Program Roles

The following program-level roles, in addition to the Agile teams, help ensure successful execution of the ART:

- **Release Train Engineer (RTE)** – The servant leader who facilitates program-level execution, impediment removal, risk and dependency management, and continuous improvement.

- **Product Management** – Responsible for 'what gets built,' as defined by the Vision, Roadmap, and new features in the Program Backlog. Product Management works with customers and Product Owners to understand and communicate their needs and also participates in solution validation.

- **System Architect/Engineer** – An individual or team that defines the overall architecture of the system. This role works at a level of abstraction above the teams and components and defines Nonfunctional Requirements (NFRs), major system elements, subsystems, and interfaces.

- **Business Owners** – Key stakeholders of the ART who have the ultimate responsibility for the business outcomes of the train.

- **Customers** – The ultimate buyers of the solution.

In addition to these critical program roles, the following functions play an important part in ART success:

- **The System Team** – Typically provides assistance in building and maintaining the development, continuous integration, and test environments.

- **Shared Services** – Are specialists—for example, data security experts, information architects, and database administrators (DBAs)—who are necessary for the success of an ART but cannot be dedicated to a specific train.

- **Release Management** – Has the authority, knowledge, and capacity to foster and approve releases. In many cases, Release Management includes Solution Train and ART representatives, as well as representatives from marketing, quality, Lean Portfolio Management, IT Service Management, operations, deployment, and distribution. This team typically meets regularly to evaluate content, progress, and quality. Its members are also actively involved in scope management.

Develop on Cadence

ARTs also address one of the most common problems with traditional Agile development: Teams working on the same solution operate independently and asynchronously. That kind of operation makes it extremely difficult to routinely integrate the full system. In other words, "The teams are sprinting, but the system isn't." This increases the risk of late discovery of issues and problems, as shown in Figure 5.

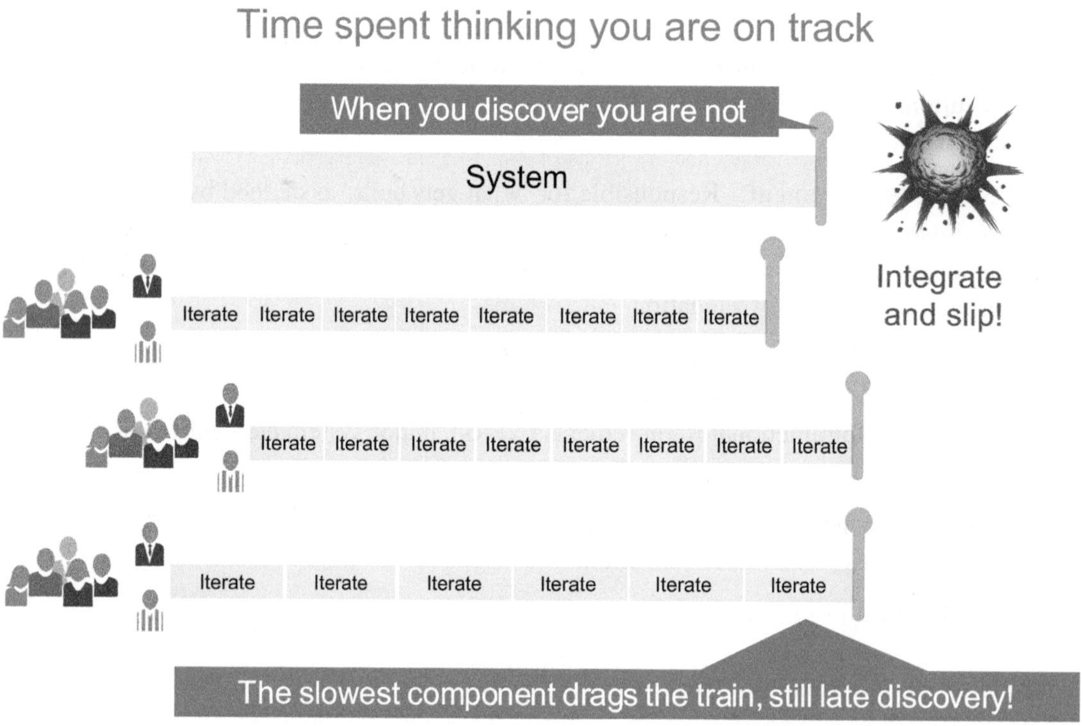

Figure 5. Asynchronous Agile development

Instead, the ART applies cadence and synchronization to assure that the system is sprinting as a whole, as shown in Figure 6.

Cadence and synchronization assure that the focus is constantly on the evolution and objective assessment of the full system, rather than its individual elements. The system demo, which occurs at the end of the iteration, provides the objective evidence that the system is moving forward.

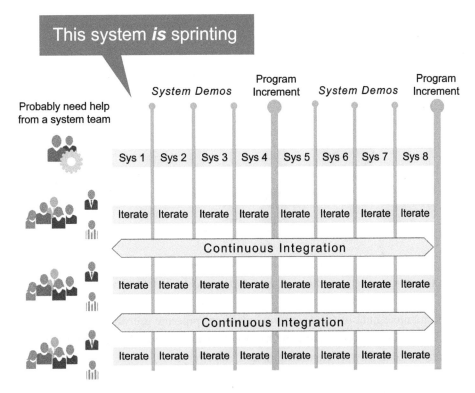

Figure 6. Aligned development: this system is sprinting

ART Execution, DevOps, and Continuous Delivery

Every two weeks (and in aggregate, with every PI), the ART delivers a new system increment of value. This delivery cycle is supported by a Continuous Delivery Pipeline, which contains the workflows, activities, and automation needed to provide the availability of new features release. Figure 7 illustrates how these processes run concurrently and continuously, supported by the ART's DevOps capabilities.

Each ART builds and maintains (or shares) a pipeline with the assets and technologies needed to deliver solution value as independently as possible. The first three elements of the pipeline work together to support delivery of small batches of new functionality, which are then released to meet market demand.

- **Continuous Exploration** – The process of constantly exploring market and user needs and defining a vision, roadmap, and set of features that address those needs.

- **Continuous Integration** – The process of taking features from the program backlog and developing, testing, integrating, and validating them in a staging environment so that they are ready for deployment and release.

- **Continuous Deployment** – The process that takes validated features from continuous integration and deploys them into the production environment, where they are tested and readied for release.

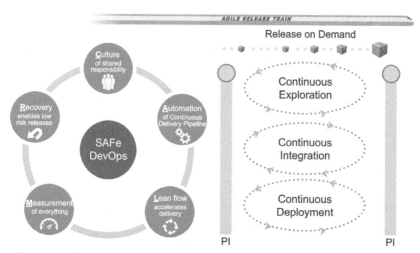

Figure 7. Continuous exploration, continuous integration, and continuous deployment are continuous, concurrent, and supported by DevOps capabilities

Development and management of the continuous delivery pipeline are supported by DevOps, a capability of every ART. SAFe's approach to DevOps uses the acronym 'CALMR' to reflect the aspects of Culture, Automation, Lean flow, Measurement, and Recovery.

Flow through the system is visualized, managed, and measured by the Program Kanban.

Release on Demand

Releasing is a separate concern from the development cadence. While many ARTs choose to release on the PI boundary, more typically, releases occur independently of this cadence. Moreover, for larger systems, a release is not an all-or-nothing event; that is, different parts of the solution (e.g., subsystems, services) can be released at different times, as described in Release on Demand.

ARTs Deliver All or Part of a Value Stream

The organization of an ART determines who will plan and work together, as well as which products, services, features, or components the train will deliver. Organizing ARTs is part of the 'art' of SAFe. This topic is covered extensively in the Implementation Roadmap chapters, particularly in Identifying Value Streams and ARTs and Creating the Implementation Plan.

A primary consideration with ART organization is size. Effective ARTs typically consist of 50–125 people. The upper limit is based on Dunbar's number, which suggests a limit on the number of people with whom one can form effective, stable social relationships. The lower limit is based mostly on empirical observation. However, trains with fewer than 50 people can still be very effective and provide many advantages over legacy Agile practices for coordinating Agile teams.

Given the size constraints, two primary patterns tend to occur (Figure 8):

- Smaller value streams can be implemented by a single ART.

- A larger value stream must be supported by multiple ARTs.

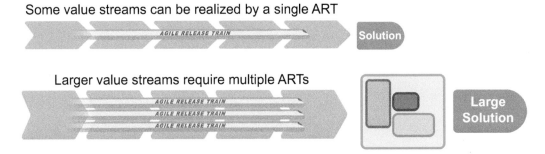

Figure 8. ARTs realize all or part of a value stream

In the latter case, enterprises apply the elements and practices of the Large Solution Level and create a Solution Train to help coordinate the contributions of ARTs and Suppliers to deliver some of the world's largest systems.

LEARN MORE

[1] Knaster, Richard, and Dean Leffingwell. *SAFe Distilled: Applying the Scaled Agile Framework for Lean Software and Systems Engineering.* Addison-Wesley, 2017.

[2] Leffingwell, Dean. *Agile Software Requirements: Lean Requirements Practices for Teams, Programs, and the Enterprise.* Addison-Wesley, 2011.

[3] Leffingwell, Dean. *Scaling Software Agility: Best Practices for Large Enterprises.* Addison-Wesley, 2007.

Business Owners

Business Owners are a small group of stakeholders who have the primary business and technical responsibility for governance, compliance, and return on investment (ROI) for a Solution developed by an Agile Release Train (ART). They are key stakeholders on the ART who must evaluate fitness for use and actively participate in certain ART events.

Business Owners can be identified by asking the following questions:

- Who is ultimately responsible for business outcomes?

- Who can steer this ART to develop the right solution?

- Who can speak to the technical competence of the solution now and into the near future?

- Who should participate in planning, help eliminate impediments, and speak on behalf of development, the business, and the customer?

- Who can approve and defend a set of Program Increment (PI) plans, knowing full well that they will never satisfy everyone?

- Who can help coordinate the efforts with other departments and organizations within the enterprise?

The answers to these questions will identify the Business Owners, who will play a key role in helping the ART deliver value. Among other duties, they have specific responsibilities during PI Planning, where they participate in mission setting, planning, drafting plan reviews, conducting management reviews, and problem-solving. They assign business value to Program PI Objectives and approve the PI plan. But they don't simply disappear after planning: Active and continuous involvement by Business Owners is a determining factor in the success of each train.

Details

Self-managing, self-organizing Agile Teams and ARTs are essential to the success of SAFe. Their presence leads to a significant change in the management mindset. Managers no longer need to directly supervise development by assigning tasks and activities. Instead, they lead by establishing mission and Vision. They help the teams with coaching and skill development but largely decentralize execution authority to the members of the ART. However, transformation to a Lean-Agile way of working does not relieve managers of their ultimate responsibilities. They remain accountable for the growth of the organization and its people, operational excellence, and business outcomes.

To facilitate this goal, SAFe defines the responsibilities of Business Owners, the key managers who guide the ART to the appropriate outcomes. The recommended activities for Business Owners in SAFe enable them to fulfill their obligations to the enterprise while empowering the teams to do their best work. Business Owners are Lean-Agile Leaders who share accountability for the value delivered by a specific ART. They are responsible for understanding the Strategic Themes that influence the train. They have knowledge of the current Enterprise and Value Stream context, and they are involved in driving or reviewing the program vision and Roadmap.

Responsibilities

An effective Business Owner is an active and involved Business Owner, fulfilling SAFe responsibilities on a daily basis. The following sections describe their tasks from the perspective of incremental development and execution through Program Increments (PIs).

Prior to PI Planning

The time prior to PI planning is a busy period for Business Owners. During this time, they will engage in the following activities:

- Participate in Pre-PI Planning as needed

- Understand and help ensure that business objectives are comprehended and agreed to by key stakeholders of the train, including the Release Train Engineer (RTE), Product Management, and System Architects

- Prepare to communicate the business context, including Milestones and significant external dependencies, such as those of Suppliers

During PI Planning

The importance of the Business Owner's role during PI planning cannot be overstated. Business Owners have the following responsibilities in this setting:

- Provide relevant elements of the business context in the defined PI planning agenda timebox

- Participate in key activities, including presenting the vision, reviewing the draft plan, assigning final business value to program PI objectives, and approving final plans

- Play a primary role in the draft plan review, understanding the bigger picture and recognizing how these plans, when taken together, do or do not fulfill the current business objectives

- Watch for significant external commitments and dependencies

- Actively circulate during planning, communicating business priorities to the teams, and maintaining agreement and alignment among the stakeholders regarding key objectives of the train

- Participate in the management review and problem-solving meeting to review and adjust scope, and compromise as necessary

Assigning Business Value

Assigning business value during planning requires an essential face-to-face dialogue between the team and its most important stakeholders, the Business Owners. This is an opportunity to develop personal relationships between Agile teams and Business Owners, identify common concerns around which to gain mutual commitment, and better understand business objectives and their value. An example is provided in Figure 1.

When assigning business value, Business Owners typically rank the user-facing Features highest. Nevertheless, they also should include technical experts who know that architectural and other concerns will increase the team's velocity in producing future business value. Assigning business value to Enablers helps drive velocity and shows support for the team's legitimate technical challenges.

Because the road after PI planning inevitably takes twists and turns, ranking objectives by business value guides the teams in making trade-offs and minor scope adjustments. It allows them to deliver the maximum possible business benefit. These numbers also later inform the PI Predictability Measure, a key indicator of program performance and reliability.

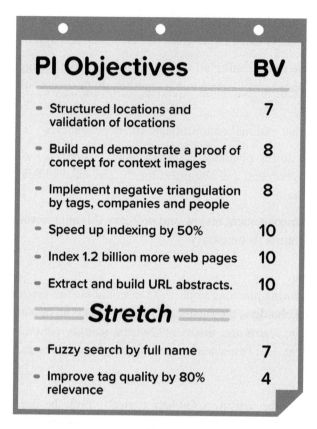

PI Objectives	BV
• Structured locations and validation of locations	7
• Build and demonstrate a proof of concept for context images	8
• Implement negative triangulation by tags, companies and people	8
• Speed up indexing by 50%	10
• Index 1.2 billion more web pages	10
• Extract and build URL abstracts.	10
Stretch	
• Fuzzy search by full name	7
• Improve tag quality by 80% relevance	4

Figure 1. An example of a team's PI objectives ranked by business value

At the Inspect and Adapt Event

The Inspect and Adapt (I&A) workshop is the larger, cadence-based opportunity for the members of the ART to come together to address the systemic impediments they face—many of which cannot be addressed without the involvement of Business Owners. During this event, Business Owners help assess actual value achieved versus plan, and they participate in the problem-solving workshop that follows.

During PI Execution

The Business Owners' job is not complete when PI planning is done; they have an ongoing role to help assure the success of the PI. Business Owners' responsibilities in this phase include the following activities:

- Actively participate in ongoing agreements to maintain business and development alignment as priorities and scope inevitably change

- Help validate the definition of Minimum Viable Products (MVPs) for Program Epics and guide the pivot-or-persevere decision based on delivery of the MVP

- Attend the System Demo to view progress and provide feedback

- Attend Agile Team Iteration Planning and Iteration Retrospective meetings, as appropriate

- Participate in Release Management, focusing on scope, quality, deployment options, release, and market considerations

Other Responsibilities

Business Owners may have additional duties beyond those described previously, including the following:

- Participate and provide feedback from the Solution Demo regarding the capabilities and subsystems being built by the ART

- Actively address impediments—especially those that escalate beyond the authority of the key stakeholders on the train

- Participate in Pre- and Post-PI Planning for the Solution Train and assist in adjusting the ART's PI plans as needed

- Participate, in some cases, in Lean Portfolio Management (LPM), Product Management, and System Architecture, and serve as an Epic Owner, where appropriate

- Help drive investment in the Continuous Delivery Pipeline to improve the responsiveness and quality of the ART

- Help break silos to align development and operations to create a DevOps culture of shared responsibilities

It cannot be emphasized enough: Active participation of Business Owners is critical to the success of the train.

Product and Solution Management

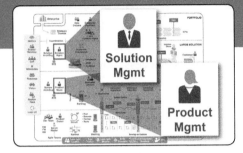

Decentralize decision-making.

  —SAFe Lean-Agile Principle #9

Product Management has content authority for the Program Backlog. These managers are responsible for identifying Customer needs, prioritizing Features, guiding the work through the Program Kanban, and developing the program Vision and Roadmap.

Solution Management has content authority for the Solution Backlog. These managers work with customers to understand their needs, prioritize Capabilities, create the Solution vision and roadmap, define requirements, and guide work through the Solution Kanban.

This chapter describes the roles that Product Managers and Solution Managers play in SAFe. While the roles are similar in most respects, they manage different levels of concern.

Details

Lean enterprises focus on delivering the right solutions to customers with the highest quality in the shortest sustainable lead time. This requires people with explicit content authority to take responsibility for continuously defining, prioritizing, and validating requirements. Working closely with development professionals in short, integrated learning cycles, Product and Solution Management bring the voice of the customer to the developers and the voice of the developers to the customer.

Following Principle #9, Decentralize decision-making, SAFe offers a chain of content authority that spans three levels:

1. **Team** – Product Owners make fast, local content decisions on behalf of the Agile Team.

2. **Program** – Product Management is accountable for content decisions for the Agile Release Trains (ARTs).

3. **Large Solution** – Solution Management has content authority for Solution Trains.

Product Management and Solution Management prioritize work using the Weighted Shortest Job First (WSJF) formula, schedule Features and Capabilities for Release using the Roadmap, validate customer response, and provide fast feedback.

A Lean-Agile Approach to Content Management

What SAFe describes as content has traditionally been represented by a Marketing Requirements Document (MRD), Product Requirements Document (PRD), and System Requirements Specifications (SRS).

In traditional development, these artifacts were typically created up-front, with an expectation that all the requirements could be established before the start of Solution development. This method had limited success, however, and its shortcomings were a significant driver of Lean and Agile practices.

We now understand that assumptions about requirements, design, and architecture all need to be validated through actual solution development, testing, and experimentation. Further, Agile teams must be open to emerging knowledge that can be quickly fed back into the solution [1]. In SAFe, Continuous Exploration is the process used to explore the market and user needs on an ongoing basis and to define a vision, roadmap, and set of features and capabilities that address those needs.

Responsibility	Traditional	Agile
Understand customer need	Up-front and discontinuous	Constant interaction with the customer, who is part of the Value Stream. Other techniques include customer visits, Gemba walks, elicitation (ex. interviews and surveys, brainstorming, trade studies, and market research)
Document requirements	Fully elaborated in documents, handed off	High-level Vision, constant Product and Solution Backlog refinement and informal face-to-face communication with Agile teams
Schedule	Created in hard-committed Roadmaps and Milestones at the beginning	Continuous near-term 'Roadmapping'
Prioritize requirements	Not at all or perhaps one-time only. Requirements often found in document form	Reprioritized at every Program Increment (PI) boundary via WSJF, constant scope triage
Validate requirements	Not applicable, quality assurance (QA) responsibility	Primary role, involved with Iteration and PI System Demos, acceptance criteria included, fitness for purpose understood
Manage delivery schedule	Typically one time, fixed well in advance	Released frequently, whenever there is enough value
Manage change	Change avoided – weekly change control meetings	Change embraced, adjusted at PI and iteration boundaries

Table 1. Changes in Product and Solution Management behavior in a Lean-Agile enterprise

As described in the Solution Intent chapter, some of the requirements of the solution are likely to be well understood and fixed from the beginning, while others are variable and can be recognized only during the product development process. Managing this new approach is the primary responsibility of Product and Solution Management. In the Lean Enterprise, these duties must be fulfilled in a far more Agile manner, as outlined in Table 1.

Responsibilities of Product Management

This section describes the primary responsibilities of the Product Manager in the context of a single Agile Release Train (ART). The responsibilities of Solution Management are described later.

- **Understand customer needs and validate solutions** – Product Management is the internal voice of the customer for the ART and works with customers (as well as Product Owners) to constantly understand and communicate their needs and participate in the validation of the proposed solutions.

- **Understand and support portfolio work** – Every ART lives in the context of a portfolio, so Product Management has a responsibility to understand the budget for the upcoming fiscal period, understand how Strategic Themes influence the strategic direction, and work with Epic Owners to develop the Lean business case for Epics that affect their ART.

- **Develop and communicate the program vision and roadmap** – Product Management continuously develops and communicates the vision to the development teams and defines the features of the system. In collaboration with System and Solution Architect/ Engineering, these managers also define and maintain the Nonfunctional Requirements (NFRs) to help ensure that the solution meets relevant standards and other system quality requirements. They are responsible for the roadmap, which illustrates, at a high level, how features will be implemented over time.

- **Manage and prioritize the flow of work** – Product Management manages the flow of work through the program Kanban and into the program backlog. These managers are responsible for making sure that there are enough features ready in the backlog at all times. For example, they specify feature acceptance criteria that can be used to establish that a feature meets its Definition of Done (DoD). Since judicious selection and sequencing of features is the key economic driver for each ART, the backlog is reprioritized with WSJF before each Program Increment (PI) Planning session.

- **Participate in PI planning** – During each PI planning session, Product Management presents the vision, which highlights the proposed features of the solution, along with any relevant upcoming Milestones. These managers also typically participate as Business Owners for the train, with the responsibility of approving PI Objectives and establishing business value.

- **Define releases and program increments** – Owning the 'what' means that Product Management is largely responsible for release definition as well, including new features, architecture, and allocations for technical debt. This is accomplished through a series of Program Increments and releases, whose definition and business objectives are also determined by Product Management. Product Management works with Release Management, where applicable, to decide when enough value has been accrued to warrant a release to the customer.

- **Work with System Architect/Engineering to understand Enabler work** – While Product Management is not expected to drive technological decisions, these managers are expected to understand the scope of the upcoming enabler work and to work with System and Solution Architect/Engineering to assist with decision-making and sequencing of the technological infrastructures that will host the new business functionality. This is typically done by establishing a capacity allocation, as described in the Program and Solution Backlogs chapter.

- **Participate in demos and Inspect and Adapt (I&A) events** – The Product Management role is an active participant in biweekly System Demos, including the final system demo at the end of the PI. These managers are also involved in the assessment of Metrics, including evaluation of business value achieved versus plan, and are active participants in the Inspect and Adapt workshop.

- **Build an effective Product Manager/Product Owner team** – Although the Product Owner and Product Management roles may report to different organizations, forming an effective extended Product Management/Product Owner team is the key to efficient and effective development. Such a team also contributes materially to the job satisfaction that comes with being part of a high-performing team, one that routinely delivers on its quality and vision commitments.

Product Management's Participation in Large Value Streams

The preceding section highlighted the role of Product Management in the context of the ART. For teams building large solutions that require multiple ARTs, Product Management has additional responsibilities:

- **Collaborate with Solution Management** – At the Large Solution Level, Solution Management plays a similar role, but with a focus on the capabilities of the larger solution. Ultimately, the ability to build an effective solution depends on the quality of the collaboration between the two roles. This collaboration involves participating in solution backlog refinement and prioritization, as well as splitting capabilities into features and NFRs, as the case may be.

- **Participate in Pre- and Post-PI Planning** – Product Management participates in the Pre-PI planning meeting, working with the Solution Train stakeholders to define the inputs, milestones, and high-level objectives for the upcoming PI planning session. In the Post-PI planning session, Product Management helps summarize findings into an agreed-to set of solution PI objectives.

- **Participate in the Solution Demo** – Product Management participates in the solution demo, often demonstrating the capabilities that the managers' own ART has contributed and reviewing the contributions of the other ARTs, always with a systems view and always with an eye toward fitness of purpose.

- **Collaborate with Release Management** – In larger-scale systems, Release Management also plays a significant role. Product Management works with the key stakeholders on progress, budget, release strategy, and release readiness of their elements of the solution.

Responsibilities of Solution Management

Solution Management plays a similar role to Product Management, but works at the large solution level and has content authority over capabilities instead of features. Responsibilities include working with portfolio stakeholders, customers, ARTs and Solution Trains to understand needs and build and prioritize the solution backlog. These managers have a similar vision, roadmap, solution Kanban, and solution demo activities as well.

The Solution Management, Solution Train Engineer, and Solution Architect/Engineering roles form a trio that shares much of the responsibility for the success of a Solution Train. Solution Management is responsible for the solution intent, which captures and documents fixed and variable solution-level behaviors. These managers also work with Release Management where applicable.

Solution Management has a crucial role in pre- and post-PI planning, as well as large solution-level I&A workshops. These managers also work with Suppliers, making sure the requirements for supplier-delivered capabilities are understood and assisting with the conceptual integration of these concerns.

LEARN MORE

[1] Ries, Eric. *The Lean Startup: How Today's Entrepreneurs Use Continuous Innovation to Create Radically Successful Businesses.* Crown Business, 2011.

[2] Leffingwell, Dean. *Agile Software Requirements: Lean Requirements Practices for Teams, Programs, and the Enterprise.* Addison-Wesley, 2011.

Release Train Engineer and Solution Train Engineer

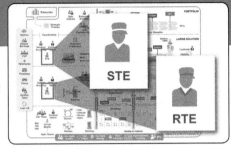

It is a misuse of our power to take responsibility for solving problems that belong to others.

—Peter Block

The *Release Train Engineer (RTE)* is a servant leader and coach for the Agile Release Train (ART). The RTE's major responsibilities are to facilitate the ART events and processes and to assist the teams in delivering value. RTEs communicate with stakeholders, escalate impediments, help manage risk, and drive relentless improvement.

The *Solution Train Engineer (STE)* plays an equivalent role in a Solution Train, facilitating and guiding the work of all ARTs and Suppliers in the Value Stream.

Although ARTs and Solution Trains are composed of self-organizing and self-managing teams, trains don't drive or steer themselves on autopilot. That responsibility falls to the RTE or the STE. Both of these roles operate most effectively as servant leaders. They have a solid grasp of how to scale Lean and Agile practices and understand the unique opportunities and challenges associated with facilitating and continuously aligning a large development program.

Details

The RTE and the STE facilitate ART and Solution Train processes and execution, respectively. They escalate impediments, manage risk, help ensure value delivery, and help drive relentless improvement. Many also participate in the Lean-Agile transformation, coaching leaders, teams, and Scrum Masters in the new processes and mindsets. They help configure SAFe to the organization's needs, standardizing and documenting practices.

Responsibilities

RTEs and STEs typically fulfill the following responsibilities:

- Manage and optimize the flow of value through the ART and Solution Train using various tools, such as the Program and Solution Kanbans and other information radiators

- Establish and communicate the annual calendars for Iterations and Program Increments (PIs)

- Facilitate PI Planning readiness by fostering the preparation of Vision and Backlogs, and through Pre- and Post-PI Planning meetings

- Facilitate the PI planning event

- Summarize the Team PI Objectives into Program PI Objectives (the RTE) and publish them for visibility and transparency

- Summarize the program PI objectives into Solution PI Objectives (the STE) and publish them for visibility and transparency

- Assist in tracking the execution of features and capabilities (see Metrics)

- Facilitate periodic synchronization meetings, including the ART sync at the Program Level and the value stream sync for Solution Trains

- Assist with economic decision-making by facilitating feature and capability estimation by teams and the roll-up to Epics, where necessary

- Coach leaders, teams, and Scrum Masters in Lean-Agile practices and mindsets

- Help manage risks and dependencies

- Escalate and track impediments

- Provide input on resourcing to address critical bottlenecks

- Encourage collaboration between teams and System and Solution Architects/Engineering

- Work with Product and Solution Management, Product Owners, and other stakeholders to help ensure strategy and execution alignment

- Improve the flow of value through value streams using the Continuous Delivery Pipeline and DevOps

- Help drive the Lean User Experience (UX) innovation cycle

- Report status to Lean Portfolio Management(LPM) and support related activities

- Understand and operate within Lean Budgets

- Facilitate System Demos and Solution Demos

- Drive relentless improvement via Inspect and Adapt workshops; assess the agility level of the ART and Solution Train and help these trains improve their agility

- Foster Communities of Practice and the use of engineering and Built-In Quality practices

Reporting Structure

SAFe doesn't prescribe a reporting structure, but the RTE and STE typically report to the development organization or an Agile Program Management Office (APMO). In SAFe, the APMO is considered a part of LPM. In contrast, enterprises with a traditional PMO organization, a program manager often plays this role.

RTEs and STEs Are Servant Leaders

While new RTEs and STEs typically have the organizational skills necessary to perform their roles, they may need to learn and adopt Lean-Agile Mindsets. In addition, they may need to transition from directing and managing activities to acting as a servant leader. Servant leadership is a philosophy that implies having a comprehensive view of the quality of people, work, and community spirit [1]. The focus is on providing the support needed by the teams, ARTs, and Solution Trains to be self-organizing and self-managing. Servant leaders typically demonstrate the following characteristics:

- Listen and support teams in problem identification and decision-making
- Create an environment of mutual influence
- Understand and empathize with others
- Encourage and support the personal development of each individual and the development of teams
- Coach people with powerful questions rather than use authority
- Think beyond day-to-day activities; apply systems thinking
- Support the teams' commitments
- Be open and appreciate openness in others

As Robert Greenleaf, the father of servant leadership, said, "Good leaders must first become good servants." Just as there are Lean-Agile transformational patterns for the LPM function, so there are also transformational patterns for a traditional manager moving to a servant leader. This transition involves the following 'from' and 'to' states:

- From *coordinating* team activities and contributions to *coaching* the teams to collaborate
- From *deadlines* to *objectives*
- From *driving* toward specific outcomes to *being invested* in the program's overall performance
- From *knowing* the answer to *asking* the teams for the answer
- From *directing* to *letting* the teams self-organize and hit their stride
- From *fixing* problems to *helping* others fix them

LEARN MORE

[1] See the article on Servant Leadership at http://en.wikipedia.org/wiki/Servant_leadership.

[2] Leffingwell, Dean. *Agile Software Requirements: Lean Requirements Practices for Teams, Programs, and the Enterprise.* Addison-Wesley, 2011.

[3] Trompenaars, Fons, and Ed Voerman. *Servant-Leadership across Cultures: Harnessing the Strengths of the World's Most Powerful Management Philosophy.* McGraw-Hill, 2009.

System and Solution Architect/Engineering

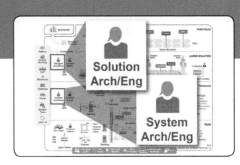

Engineering is a great profession. There is the satisfaction of watching a figment of the imagination emerge through the aid of science to a plan on paper. Then it moves to realization in stone or metal or energy. Then it brings homes to men or women. Then it elevates the standard of living and adds to the comforts of life. This is the engineer's high privilege.

—Herbert Hoover

The *System and Solution Architect/Engineering* role is filled by an individual or small team that defines a shared technical and architectural vision for the Solution under development. These people participate in determining the system, subsystems, and interfaces; validate technology assumptions; and evaluate alternatives; all while working closely with the Agile Release Train (ARTs) and Solution Train.

These individuals, or cross-disciplinary teams, take a 'systems view' of solution development (SAFe Lean-Agile Principle #2). They participate in defining the higher-level functional and Nonfunctional Requirements (NFRs) by analyzing technical trade-offs, determining the primary components and subsystems, and identifying the interfaces and collaborations between them. They understand the Solution Context and work with the teams, Customers, and Suppliers to help ensure fitness for purpose.

Collaborating with Solution and Product Management, Architect/Engineers play a critical role in aligning teams in a shared technical direction geared toward the accomplishment of the Vision and Roadmap. And, of course, Architect/Engineers are Lean-Agile Leaders who understand the complexities of large-scale solution development and apply SAFe Lean-Agile principles and practices to address them.

Details

Architect/Engineering personnel support solution development by providing, communicating, and evolving the broader technology and architectural view of the solution.

Architect/Engineering teams are found at both the Program and Large Solution Levels. System Architect/Engineering operates mainly in the context of the ART, where these personnel work with Agile Teams and provide technical enablement concerning subsystems and capability areas for an ART. Solution Architect/Engineering teams provide technical leadership for evolving architectural capabilities of the entire solution.

Both roles engage in close collaboration with business stakeholders, teams, customers, suppliers, and third-party stakeholders to define the technology infrastructure, decompose it into components and subsystems, and define interfaces between subsystems and between the solution and solution context.

While providing a general view of solution architecture, Architect/Engineering enables those who implement value by empowering them to make local decisions, thereby allowing a faster flow of work and better economics.

Responsibilities

Architect/Engineering teams are Lean-Agile Leaders who typically have the following responsibilities:

- Participate in planning, definition, and high-level design of the solution and explore solution alternatives

- Actively participate in the Continuous Exploration process as part of the Continuous Delivery Pipeline, especially with enabler Epics

- Define subsystems and their interfaces, allocate responsibilities to subsystems, understand solution deployment, and communicate requirements for interactions with solution context

- Work with customers, stakeholders, and suppliers to establish high-level Solution Intent, along with the solution intent information models and documentation requirements

- Establish critical NFRs at the solution level, and participate in the definition of other NFRs

- Operate within the Economic Framework to validate the economic impact of design decisions

- Work with portfolio stakeholders—most notably the Enterprise Architect—to develop, analyze, split, and realize the implementation of enabler epics

- Participate in Program Increment (PI) Planning and Pre- and Post-PI Planning, System and Solution Demos, and Inspect and Adapt (I&A) events

- Define, explore, and support the implementation of ART and Solution Train Enablers to evolve solution intent, working directly with Agile teams to implement them

- Plan and develop the Architectural Runway in support of new business Features and Capabilities

- Work with Product and Solution Management to determine capacity allocation for enablement work

- Support technology/engineering aspects of Program and Solution Kanbans

- Provide oversight and foster Built-In Quality

The Origin of the Roles in SAFe

Role of the System Architect

Architects routinely participate in software development efforts, and this function is part of SAFe. Architects work at the program and large solution levels, with their role often extending beyond the software domain to include responsibilities that enable value delivery in a technically diverse and heterogeneous multi-domain solution environment.

Role of Systems Engineering

Enterprises building cyber-physical systems (e.g., embedded systems) also rely on systems engineering—which typically encompasses multiple disciplines, including hardware, electrical and electronic, mechanical, hydraulic, and optical, as well as the software elements. The International Council on Systems Engineering defines systems engineering as follows [1]:

> ... an interdisciplinary approach and means to enable the realization of successful systems. It focuses on defining customer needs and required functionality early in the development cycle, documenting requirements, then proceeding with design synthesis and system validation while considering the complete problem, including operations, performance, test, manufacturing, cost and schedule, training and support, and disposal. Systems engineering integrates all the disciplines and specialty groups into a team effort, forming a structured development process that proceeds from concept to production to operation. Systems engineering considers both the business and the technical needs of all customers with the goal of providing a quality product that meets the user needs.

A Leaner Approach

It is impossible to reason about how to build complex solutions without including the roles of software architecture and systems engineering. However, a significant note of caution is warranted. The dominant, traditional methods for both strongly favor phase-gated, point-solution Big Design Upfront (BDUF) approaches. This preference is understandable because these solutions are big systems and someone has to know how to go about building them—and the BDUF model has the best available one in the past.

As noted in the SAFe Lean-Agile Principles, the BDUF approach is not supportive of product development flow, and it doesn't produce the optimal economic outcomes. SAFe, by comparison, views software architecture and systems engineering as enabling functions for continuous product development flow. In the Lean-Agile Mindset, these roles focus on cross-disciplinary collaboration, building systems incrementally through fast, feedback-driven learning cycles, understanding and leveraging the inherent variability of the product development process, and decentralizing control.

The Compliance chapter in Part 7 elaborates on the shift from traditional phase-gated governance models to a Lean-Agile process that enables flow while still meeting regulatory and compliance concerns.

Decentralized Decision-Making

Design decisions vary significantly regarding their impact, urgency, and frequency of occurrence. This diversity suggests a need to balance centralized and decentralized decision-making (see Principle #9, Decentralize decision-making). In terms of system design, this has two implications:

- Certain larger-scale architectural decisions should be centralized. These decisions include the definition of primary system intent, subsystems, and interfaces; allocation of functions to subsystems; selection of platforms; elaboration of solution-level NFRs; and elimination of redundancy.

- Most design decisions are the responsibility of Agile teams, who must balance applying emergent design in conjunction with intentional architecture (see Agile Architecture).

Frequent collaboration supports system design, whether in the form of informal and continuous face-to-face discussions or, more regularly, in PI planning, system, and solution demos, I&A workshops, and specification workshops.

In any case, Architect/Engineers exhibit the traits of Lean-Agile Leaders:

- Collaborate with, enable, and empower engineers and subject-matter experts with decision-making

- Educate team members in design-related disciplines and lead technical Communities of Practice that foster open exchange of ideas with practitioners across ARTs

- Demonstrate Lean and Agile principles, as applied to system design—for example, Set-Based Design (SBD)

An Empirical Approach

The success of any solution development program also depends on the organization's ability to embrace the learnings from empirical evidence. This paradigm can challenge the traditional mindsets that support detailed, committed, early design based on reasoned but unverified hypotheses and implementation strategies. In the case where contrary evidence exists, those responsible for the initial design tend to defend the solution and ignore the evidence.

The Lean-Agile Architect/Engineering mindset relies on the firm belief that if a problem arises with the design, the problem does not lie with the people who created it. No one could have anticipated the new learnings—it's research and development, after all. Everyone learns together. This belief is further fostered by:

- Fact-based governance, based on frequent integration and objective evidence

- Continuous exploration to identify alternatives for enablers necessary to support the Minimal Marketable Features (MMFs) included in the Minimum Viable Product (MVP) of an epic

- SBD, where a spectrum of possible solutions to a problem is considered, instead of a single idea picked too early

- Learning Milestones that are planned and executed with the specific purpose of validating the technical and business hypotheses

- A bias toward economic decision-making, where trade-offs between architectural capabilities of the system and business outcomes are made continuously and in collaboration with stakeholders

LEARN MORE

[1] International Council on Systems Engineering. "What Is Systems Engineering?" http://www.incose.org/AboutSE/WhatIsSE.

[2] Leffingwell, Dean. *Agile Software Requirements: Lean Requirements Practices for Teams, Programs, and the Enterprise.* Addison-Wesley, 2011.

Program and Solution Backlogs

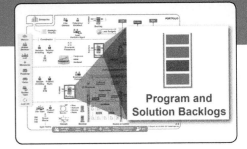

The emphasis should be on why we do a job.
   —W. Edwards Deming

The *Program Backlog* is the holding area for upcoming Features, which are intended to address user needs and deliver business benefits for a single Agile Release Train (ART). It also contains the Enabler features necessary to build the Architectural Runway.

The *Solution Backlog* is the holding area for upcoming Capabilities and enablers, each of which can span multiple ARTs and is intended to advance the Solution and build its architectural runway.

Product Management has responsibility for the Program Backlog, while Solution Management is responsible for the Solution Backlog. The items in these backlogs result from research activities and active collaboration involving various stakeholders—Customers, Business Owners, Product Management, Product Owners, System and Solution Architects/Engineering, and more.

The backlog items are managed through their respective Program and Solution Kanban systems. The work travels through the states of 'funnel' and 'analyzing,' with the highest-priority features and capabilities, after being sufficiently elaborated and approved, then moving to the 'backlog' state. There, these items are prioritized relative to the rest of the backlog and await implementation.

Effectively identifying, refining, prioritizing, and sequencing backlog items using Weighted Shortest Job First (WSJF) is the key to the economic success of the solution. Since the backlog contains both new business functionality and the enablement work necessary to extend the architectural runway, a 'capacity allocation' is used to help ensure immediate and long-term value delivery, combined with adequate velocity and quality.

Details

The program and solution backlogs are the repositories for all the upcoming work that affects the behavior of the Solution. Product and Solution Management develop, maintain, and prioritize the program and solution backlogs, respectively. The backlogs are essentially short-term holding areas for features and capabilities that have gone through their respective Kanban systems and been approved for implementation. Backlog items are estimated in story points, as Figure 1 illustrates.

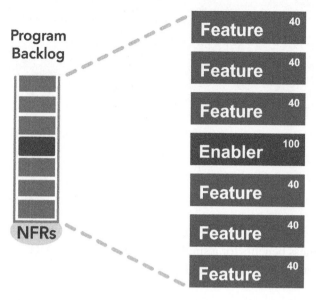

Figure 1. Exploded view of Program Backlog, with story point size estimates

Refining the Backlog

ARTs and Solution Trains maintain a steady 8- to 12-week Program Increment (PI) cadence of planning, execution, demo, and Inspect and Adapt (I&A) events. This regular rhythm is the heartbeat that drives backlog readiness as well. Appearing at a Pre-PI Planning or a PI Planning without a well-elaborated backlog adds unacceptable risk to the upcoming PI.

The time between PI planning events is a busy time for Product and Solution Management, as these managers are always in the process of refining their backlogs in preparation for the next PI planning. Making this process visible and achieving backlog readiness for the upcoming PI are the primary purposes of the program and solution Kanbans.

Backlog refinement typically includes the following activities:

- Reviewing and updating backlog item definitions and developing acceptance criteria and benefit hypotheses

- Working with the teams to establish technical feasibility and scope estimates

- Analyzing ways to split backlog items into smaller chunks of incremental value

- Identifying the enablers required to support new features and capabilities and establishing their capacity allocation

Prioritizing the Backlogs

Prioritizing the program and solution backlogs is a critical economic driver for the solution. To this end, Product and Solution Management use the WSJF prioritization method for job sequencing. To recap, WSJF ultimately translates to a simple formula, shown in Figure 2.

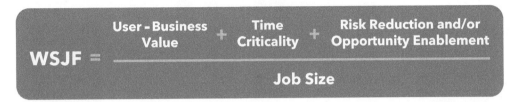

$$WSJF = \frac{\text{User - Business Value} + \text{Time Criticality} + \text{Risk Reduction and/or Opportunity Enablement}}{\text{Job Size}}$$

Figure 2. A formula for calculating WSJF

Preparing for PI Planning

The week or two before PI planning is a hectic time. Product and Solution Management personnel do the final backlog preparation, update the vision briefings, and work with Product Owners to further discuss the backlog before the event. System and Solution Architect/Engineering personnel update enabler definitions and models and often develop use cases that illustrate how the features and capabilities work together to deliver the end-user value.

Optimizing Value and Solution Integrity with Capacity Allocation

One challenge that every ART and Solution Train faces is how to balance the backlog of business features and capabilities with the need to continuously invest in the architectural runway, provide time for exploration of requirements and design for future PIs, and create prototypes and models to enhance visibility into any problem areas. To avoid velocity reduction and to defer the need for wholesale replacement of components due to technological obsolescence, ARTs must invest continuously in implementing the enablers of the solution. This complicates the prioritization of work, as different people may pull the teams in different directions (see Figure 3).

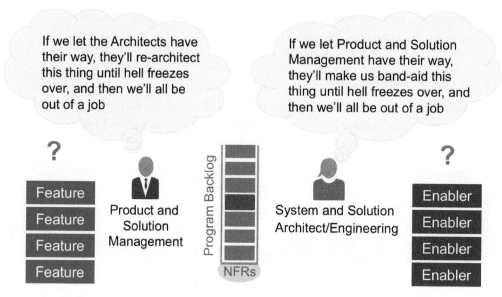

Figure 3. Business versus enabler backlog items dilemma

To address this problem, teams apply capacity allocation—a process by which they decide how much of the total effort can be used for each type of activity for an upcoming PI. Further, they agree to determine how the work is performed for each activity type. Examples of the results are given in Figure 4 and Table 1.

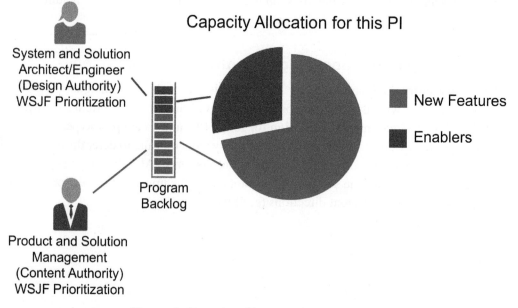

Figure 4. Capacity allocation for a single PI

- At each PI boundary, we agree on the percentage of resources to be devoted to new features or capabilities versus enablers.

- We agree that System and Solution Architects/Engineering have authority to prioritize enabler work.

- We agree that Product and Solution Management have authority to prioritize business backlog items.

- We agree to jointly prioritize our work based on economics. We agree to collaborate on sequencing work in a way that maximizes customer value.

Table 1. Sample policies for managing enabler and feature capacity allocation

While the agreed-to policies can persist for some time, the amount of capacity allocated should change periodically based on the context. In the context of an ART, this decision can be revisited as part of backlog refinement in preparation for each PI planning session, while Solution Management and Solution Architect/Engineering make similar choices for the solution as a whole before pre-PI planning.

On Backlogs, Queues, Little's Law, and Wait Times

At this point, we'll take a brief detour to discuss the relationships among a backlog, wait times, and flow. Principle #6, Visualize and limit WIP, reduce batch sizes, and manage queue lengths, explains these relationships in detail. We'll summarize that discussion here, because the program and solution backlogs can have the most significant impact on delivery time and throughput:

- *Little's law* illustrates that the average wait time for an item in a queue is equal to the average length of the queue divided by the average processing rate for an item in a queue (see Figure 5). Thus, the longer the queue, the longer the wait time, and the higher the variability.

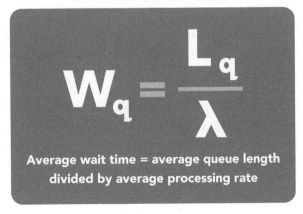

$$W_q = \frac{L_q}{\lambda}$$

Average wait time = average queue length divided by average processing rate

Figure 5. Little's law

- *Think of the line at Starbucks*: If each of the 10 people ahead of you orders a tall coffee, you are going to be out of there in minutes. If each buys an extra-hot vanilla latte and a toasted bagel, you might be late for your meeting. Ultimately, the outcome is not under your control.

- *Long queues are all bad*, causing decreased motivation, poor quality, longer cycle times, higher variability (think Starbucks), and increased risk [2] (Figure 6).

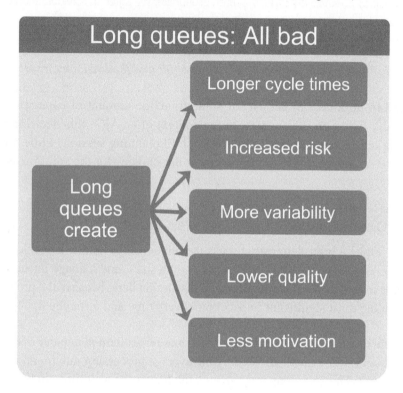

Figure 6. Long queues are bad

Your program and solution backlogs are *not* queues, as some items can leapfrog others for faster delivery, and you can always choose not to service everything in the backlog. (Note that neither of these tactics works at Starbucks.)

However, if all the items in your backlog are committed to stakeholders, then your backlog behaves like a queue—and the longer it is, the longer your stakeholders will have to wait for service. Of course, if they have to wait too long, they are likely to seek out another coffee shop, as your shop just can't meet their rapidly changing market needs.

For this reason, teams must actively manage their backlogs and keep them short so that the development program is both fast and responsive. Teams also must limit their commitment to longer-term work, because some other item may come along that's more important than a prior commitment. If a team has too many fixed and committed requirements in the backlog, it cannot respond quickly, no matter how efficient the team members are.

Teams can be both reliable and fast only if they actively manage the backlog and keep it short.

LEARN MORE

[1] Leffingwell, Dean. *Agile Software Requirements: Lean Requirements Practices for Teams, Programs, and the Enterprise.* Addison-Wesley, 2011.

[2] Reinertsen, Don. *Principles of Product Development Flow: Second Generation Lean Product Development.* Celeritas Publishing, 2009.

Features and Capabilities

There's innovation in Linux. There are some really good technical features that I'm proud of. There are capabilities in Linux that aren't in other operating systems.

—Linus Torvalds, creator of Linux

A *Feature* is a service that fulfills a stakeholder need. Each feature includes a benefit hypothesis and acceptance criteria and is sized or split as necessary so that it can be delivered by a single Agile Release Train (ART) in a Program Increment (PI).

A *Capability* is a higher-level solution behavior that typically spans multiple ARTs. Capabilities are sized and split into multiple features to facilitate their implementation in a single PI.

Features also lend themselves to the Lean UX process model, which includes a definition of the Minimum Marketable Feature (MMF), a benefit hypothesis, and acceptance criteria. The MMF helps limit the scope and investment, enhances agility, and provides fast feedback. Capabilities behave the same way as features. However, they are at a higher level of abstraction and support the definition and development of large Solutions.

Details

Features and capabilities are central to the SAFe Requirements Model. They are critical to defining, planning, and implementing Solution value. Figure 1 provides the broader context for these work items.

As shown in Figure 1, solutions are developed using features. Each reflects a service provided by the system that fulfills some important stakeholder need. The features are maintained in the Program Backlog and are sized to fit in a PI so that each delivers new value. Features can originate either from the local context of the ART or from splitting Epics or capabilities.

The Program and Solution Kanban systems support the flow of features and capabilities, where they progress through the funnel, analyzing, backlog, implementing, validating, deployment, and release states. This process provides reasoned economic analysis, technical impact, and strategy for incremental implementation.

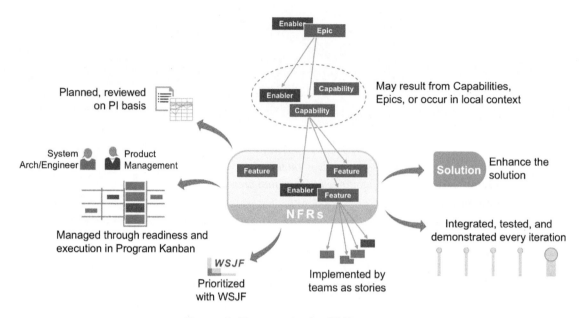

Figure 1. Features in the SAFe context

Product Management and System Architect/Engineering own the features and enablers, respectively. Nonfunctional Requirements (NFRs) define system attributes such as security, reliability, performance, maintainability, scalability, and usability. NFRs serve as constraints or restrictions on the design of the system across the different backlogs. Features are prioritized using the Weighted Shortest Job First (WSJF) method and are planned and reviewed at PI boundaries. They are split into Stories, and are implemented, integrated, tested, and demoed as the functionality becomes available.

Describing Features

Features are defined using a Features and Benefits (FAB) Matrix:

- **Feature** – A short phrase giving a name and context

- **Benefit hypothesis** – The proposed measurable benefit to the end user or business

It's best to avoid defining features with the 'user story voice' format that is designed to support one user role, because features typically provide functionality for multiple user roles. Furthermore, using the same method to describe user stories and features may confuse the Business Owners, since they are not usually familiar with stories.

Figure 2 illustrates an example FAB matrix with four different features.

Feature	Benefit Hypothesis
In-service software update	Significantly reduced planned downtime
Hardware VPN acceleration	High-performance encryption for secure WAN
Traffic congestion management	Improve overall quality of service across different protocols
Route optimization	Improve quality of service due to faster and more reliable connectivity

Figure 2. Features and benefits matrix

Creating and Managing Features

Product Managers, in collaboration with Product Owners and other key stakeholders, define features in the local context of an ART. Some of these features may arise as a result of splitting epics.

System Architects typically create enabler features, which are then maintained in the program backlog alongside the business features. Enablers may pave the Architectural Runway and support exploration, or they may provide the infrastructure needed to develop, test, and integrate the initiative.

Just like business features, enabler features may originate from epics or emerge locally at the ART level. Enablers that make it through the Kanban system will be subject to capacity allocation in the program backlog to ensure that enough emphasis is placed on both delivering the solution and extending the architectural runway. At each PI boundary, the percentage of resources to be allocated to new features (or capabilities) versus enablers is estimated to guide the train.

Prioritizing Features

The WSJF prioritization model is used to sequence jobs (e.g., features, capabilities) based on the economics of product development flow. Since implementing the *right jobs* in the *right sequence* produces the maximum economic benefit, it is hard to overestimate the importance of this critical process.

Product and Solution Management have authority to prioritize features, while System and Solution Architects and Engineering have authority to prioritize enabler features.

Estimating Features

Feature estimation supports forecasting value delivery, applying WSJF prioritization, and sizing epics by splitting them into features and summing their individual estimates. This process usually occurs within the analysis state of the Program Kanban and relies on normalized estimation techniques, similar to the methods used by Agile teams (see the Iteration Planning chapter for more detail). During analysis, subject-matter experts from the ART engage in exploration activities and preliminary sizing. While in this state, sizing of features does not require splitting them into stories or including all the teams that might develop them.

Accepting Features

Acceptance criteria are used to determine whether the implementation is correct and delivers the business benefits. Figure 3 provides an example.

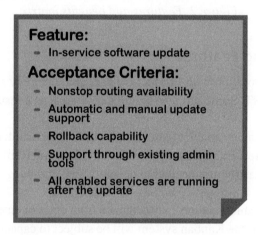

Figure 3. Feature with acceptance criteria

Acceptance criteria are intended to mitigate implementation risks and enable early validation of the benefit hypothesis. Moreover, acceptance criteria are typically the source of various stories as well as functional tests, which are developed and automated to support refactoring and regression testing.

Product Management is responsible for accepting the features. These managers use acceptance criteria to determine whether the functionality is properly implemented and the nonfunctional requirements are met.

Capabilities

Most of this chapter is devoted to describing the definition and implementation of features, as they are the most commonly encountered descriptions of system behavior. Capabilities exhibit the same characteristics and practices as features:

- Capabilities are described using a phrase and benefit hypothesis.

- They are sized to fit within a PI, although they often take multiple ARTs to implement.

- They are reasoned about and approved using the Solution Kanban. The Solution Backlog holds approved capabilities.

- Capabilities have associated enablers to describe and bring visibility to all the technical work necessary to support efficient development and delivery of business capabilities.

- They are accepted by Solution Managers, who use the acceptance criteria to determine whether the functionality is fit for purpose.

Capabilities may originate in the local context of the solution or arise from splitting of portfolio epics that may cut across more than one Value Stream. Another potential source of capabilities is the Solution Context, where some aspect of the environment may require new solution functionality.

Splitting Features and Capabilities

Capabilities must be decomposed into features to be implemented. These features, in turn, are split into stories that can be handled by teams within an iteration. SAFe provides 10 patterns for splitting work, as described in Leffingwell [1], Chapter 6.

1. Workflow steps
2. Business rule variations
3. Major effort
4. Simple/complex
5. Variations in data
6. Data methods
7. Deferring system qualities
8. Operations
9. Use-case scenarios
10. Breaking out a spike

Figure 4 illustrates splitting a capability into features.

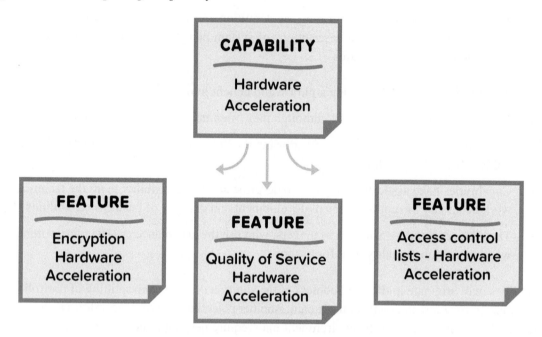

Figure 4. A capability split into features

LEARN MORE

[1] Leffingwell, Dean. *Agile Software Requirements: Lean Requirements Practices for Teams, Programs, and the Enterprise.* Addison-Wesley, 2011.

Enablers

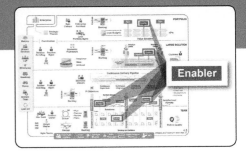

Luck is what happens when preparation meets opportunity.

   —Seneca

Enablers support the activities needed to extend the Architectural Runway so as to provide future business functionality. These activities include exploration, infrastructure, compliance, and architecture development. The enablers are captured in the various backlogs and occur at all levels of the Framework.

Details

Enablers bring visibility to all the work necessary to support efficient development and delivery of future business requirements. Primarily, enablers are used for exploration, evolving the architecture, ensuring Compliance, and improving the infrastructure. Since they reflect the real work (and sometimes plenty of it), they cannot remain invisible. Rather, enablers are treated like all other value-added development activities—and are subject to estimating, visibility and tracking, Work in Process (WIP) limits, feedback, and presentation of results.

Type of Enablers

Enablers can be used for any activities that support upcoming business requirements, but generally fall into one of four categories:

- **Exploration enablers** – Support research, prototyping, and other activities needed to develop an understanding of Customer needs, to explore prospective Solutions, and to evaluate alternatives.

- **Architectural enablers** – Created to build the architectural runway, which allows smoother and faster development.

- **Infrastructure enablers** – Created to build, enhance, and automate the development, testing, and deployment environments. They facilitate faster development, higher-quality testing, and a faster Continuous Delivery Pipeline.

- **Compliance enablers** – Facilitate managing specific compliance activities, including Verification and Validation (V&V), documentation and sign-offs, and regulatory submissions and approvals.

Creating and Managing Enablers

Enablers exist at all levels of the Framework and are written and prioritized to follow the same rules as their respective epics, capabilities, features, and stories.

- **Enabler Epics** – Are written using the Epic Hypothesis Statement format, in the same way as business epics. Enabler epics typically cut across Value Streams and Program Increments (PIs). To support their implementation, they must include a Lean Business Case and are identified and tracked through the Portfolio Kanban system. Enabler epics may also occur at the Large Solution and Program levels.

- **Enabler Capabilities and Features** – Occur at the Large Solution and Program levels and are intended to capture work of that type. Since these enablers are a type of Feature or Capability, they share the same attributes, including a phrase, benefit hypothesis, and acceptance criteria. They also must be structured to fit within a single PI.

- **Enabler Stories** – Must fit in Iterations like any Story. Although they may not require the user voice format, their acceptance criteria clarify the requirements and support testing.

Enablers are often created by architects or by systems engineering at the various levels—for example, by Enterprise Architects at the portfolio level, or by Solution and System Architects/Engineering at the large solution and program levels. These architects steer their enablers through the Kanban systems, providing the guidance necessary to analyze them and the information needed to estimate and implement them.

To improve the existing solution, some enablers may emerge locally from the needs of the Agile Teams, Agile Release Trains (ARTs), or Solution Trains to ensure that enough emphasis is placed on developing the solution and extending the architectural runway. Those enablers that make it through the Kanban systems will be subject to capacity allocation in the Program and Solution Backlogs. This prioritization can be applied to enabler work as a whole, or it can distinguish between different types of enablers.

Using Enablers

Exploration

Applying enablers for exploration provides a way for development teams to flesh out the details of requirements and design. The nature of the Solution Intent is that many requirements begin as variables. After all, at the beginning of development, little is known about what the customer needs or how to implement it. Customers themselves often don't understand exactly what they want. Only through iterative product development and demos do they begin to figure out what they actually need.

On the solution side, many technical possibilities are available for implementing a business need. Those alternatives must be analyzed and are often evaluated through modeling, prototyping, or even concurrent development of multiple solution options (also known as Set-Based Design).

Architecture

The architectural runway is one of the constructs that SAFe uses to implement the concepts behind Agile Architecture. It is the basis for developing business initiatives more quickly, on appropriate technical foundations. Because this technical foundation is constantly being updated as a result of implementing new functionality, the architectural runway must be maintained. Enablers are the backlog items used to maintain and extend the runway.

Some architectural enablers fix existing problems with the solution—for example, the need to enhance performance. These enablers start out in the backlog but may become Nonfunctional Requirements (NFRs) after their implementation. In fact, many NFRs come into existence as a result of architectural enablers and tend to evolve over time, as shown in Figure 1.

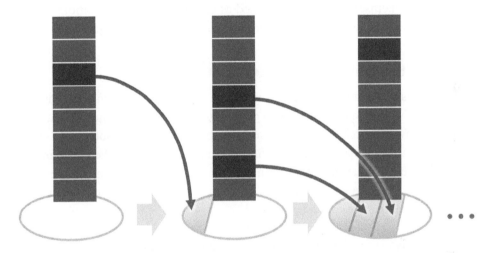

Figure 1. Many NFRs appear over time as a result of enablers

Infrastructure

Agile development relies on frequent integration: Agile teams integrate their work with other teams on the ART at the System Demos in every iteration; the trains integrate every PI for the Solution Demo. Many Enterprises implement Continuous Integration and Continuous Deployment to ensure that the solution is always running. This reduces the risk at the integration points and permits rapid deployment and early release value.

To support such frequent or continuous integration and testing, a supportive infrastructure is needed at the team, program, and large solution levels. Agile teams, working with the System Team, are responsible for building and maintenance of this infrastructure. Infrastructure enablers are used as backlog items to advance this work and continuously enhance it, both to support new scenarios and to enhance the agility of the enterprise.

Compliance

By incrementally building the necessary artifacts in the solution content over a series of PIs, SAFe supports continuous Verification and Validation. Verification activities are implemented as part of the flow (e.g., backlog items or Definition of Done [DoD]). While the artifacts will satisfy the objective evidence needed at the end of development, they are created iteratively throughout the life cycle. Validation occurs when Product Owners, customers, and end users participate in ART planning and system demos, validating the solution's fitness for purpose.

For example, suppose that regulations require design reviews and that all actions need to be recorded and resolved. The design review enabler backlog item offers evidence of the required review, and its DoD ensures that actions are recorded and resolved according to the Lean Quality Management System. If needed, the actions themselves could be tracked as enabler stories. Regulations may also require that all changes be reviewed, which is addressed by a compulsory peer review DoD for all stories.

Implement Architectural Enablers Incrementally

The size and demands of architectural enabler work can make these challenges seem overwhelming. For this reason, such work needs to be broken down into smaller stories that fit in an iteration. This can be difficult, however, as architectural and infrastructure changes can potentially stop the existing system from working until the new architecture/infrastructure is in place. When planning enabler work, make sure to organize it so that the system can operate for most of the time on the old architecture or infrastructure. That way, teams can continue to work, integrate, demo, and even release while the enabler work is happening.

As described in the System and Solution Architect/Engineering chapter and in [1], there are three options for tackling architectural enabler work:

- **Case A** – The enabler is big, but there is an incremental approach to implementation. The system always runs (operates).

- **Case B** – The enabler is big but can't be implemented entirely incrementally. The system will need to take an occasional break.

- **Case C** – The enabler is *really* big and can't be implemented incrementally. The system runs when needed. In other words, do no harm.

Examples of incremental patterns are also described in [2], where the legacy subsystems are gradually 'strangled' over time, using proven patterns such as asset capture or event interception.

By creating the technology platforms that deliver business functionality, enablers drive better economics. Of course, innovative product development cannot occur without risk-taking. In turn, initial technology-related decisions cannot always be correct, which is why the Agile enterprise must be prepared to change course on occasion. In these cases, the principle of sunk costs [3] provides essential guidance: Do not consider money already spent. Incremental implementation helps, as the corrective action can be taken before the investment grows too large.

Implement Enablers Epics across ARTs and Value Streams

Enabler epics and enabler capabilities can cut across multiple value streams or ARTs. During the analysis phase of the Kanban system, one of the most important decisions is whether to implement the enabler in all ARTs and Solution Trains at the same time or to do so incrementally. This decision involves a trade-off between the risk reduction of implementing one solution or system at a time and the Cost of Delay (CoD) caused by not having the full enabler (as shown in Figure 2).

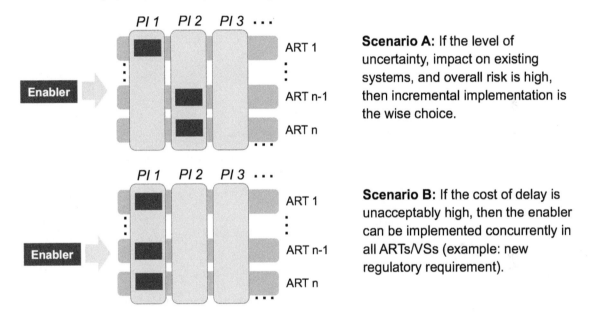

Scenario A: If the level of uncertainty, impact on existing systems, and overall risk is high, then incremental implementation is the wise choice.

Scenario B: If the cost of delay is unacceptably high, then the enabler can be implemented concurrently in all ARTs/VSs (example: new regulatory requirement).

Figure 2. Two scenarios for implementing large enablers

LEARN MORE

[1] Leffingwell, Dean. *Agile Software Requirements: Lean Requirements Practices for Teams, Programs, and the Enterprise.* Addison-Wesley, 2011.

[2] Fowler, Martin. Strangler Application. http://martinfowler.com/bliki/StranglerApplication.html.

[3] Reinertsen, Donald. *The Principles of Product Development Flow: Second Generation Lean Product Development.* Celeritas Publishing, 2009.

Nonfunctional Requirements

The devil is in the details.

—*Common proverb*

Nonfunctional Requirements (NFRs) define system qualities such as security, reliability, performance, maintainability, scalability, and usability. They serve as constraints or restrictions on the design of the system across the different backlogs.

In contrast, *functional requirements* are largely expressed in user stories, features, and capabilities. This is where most of the work occurs. Teams build systems that deliver value to the user, and most of the time and effort in solution development are devoted to that goal.

NFRs, however, ensure the usability and effectiveness of the entire system. Failing to meet any one of them can result in systems that fail to satisfy internal business, user, or market needs, or that do not fulfill mandatory requirements imposed by regulatory or standards agencies.

Details

One way to think about all the types of requirements that affect a solution's overall fitness is the 'FURPS' categorization described in Managing Software Requirements [5]: Functionality, Usability, Reliability, Performance, and Supportability.

NFRs are persistent qualities and constraints that, unlike functional requirements, are typically revisited as part of the Definition of Done (DoD) for each Iteration, Program Increment (PI), or release. NFRs exist in all backlogs: Team, Program, Solution, and Portfolio.

Proper definition and implementation of NFRs is critical. Over-specify them, and the solution may be too costly to be viable; under-specify or underachieve them, and the system will be inadequate for its intended use. Applying an adaptive and incremental approach to exploring, defining, and implementing NFRs is a vital skill for Agile teams.

NFRs are just as important as functional requirements to system success. NFRs can be considered constraints on new development, in that each eliminates some degree of design freedom for the people who are building the system. For example, SAML-based Single Sign-on (SSO) may be a requirement for all products in a particular suite. In this case, SSO is a functional requirement, while SAML is a constraint.

NFRs can cover a wide range of business-critical issues that are often poorly addressed by functional requirements. As a reminder to system designers, a comprehensive list of such potential NFRs is provided in [1].

NFRs Occur at All Levels

NFRs are associated with backlogs at all levels of SAFe, as Figure 1 illustrates.

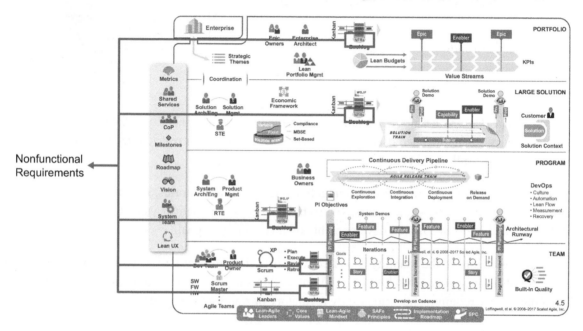

Figure 1. NFRs occur at all levels

Because NFRs are significant attributes of the solution that the Agile Release Train (ART) and Value Streams create, their most obvious representation is at the program and large solution levels. System and Solution Architect and Engineering specialists are often responsible for defining and refining these NFRs.

All teams must be aware of the special attributes they're creating for the system. Accelerating NFR testing, rather than postponing it, helps foster Built-In Quality practices. Teams include the relevant NFRs into their DoD, use them as constraints on local design and implementation decisions, and take responsibility for some level of NFR testing on their own. Otherwise, the solution may not satisfy key NFRs, and the costs of corrections that occur late in the process can be very high.

Team backlog NFRs can also be important, as they create constraints and performance requirements on the features and the subsystems that emerge. The portfolio backlog may require NFRs as well. This is often the case for cross-system qualities, as in the single sign-on case. Other examples include restrictions on open source usage, security requirements, and regulatory standards. If a specific portfolio-level NFR hasn't been achieved, it may require Enablers to implement it. NFRs are defined in the 'epic hypothesis statement' that is used to describe business and enabler Epics.

NFRs as Backlog Constraints

NFRs are modeled as backlog constraints in the framework, as illustrated in Figure 2.

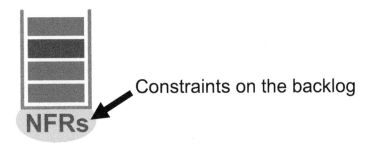

Figure 2. Backlogs are constrained by NFRs

Moreover, the SAFe Requirements Model specifies that NFRs may constrain zero, some, or many backlog items. Further, to verify that the system is compliant with the constraint, most NFRs require one or more system qualities tests, as shown in Figure 3.

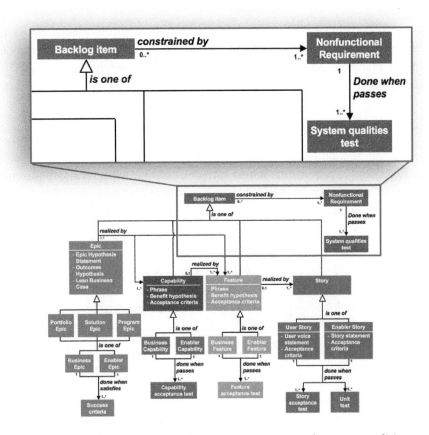

Figure 3. Relationships among backlog items, NFRs, and system qualities tests

Many NFRs begin as enablers that need to be addressed. After that, they constrain the system and all new backlog items going forward.

The Impact of NFRs on Solution Development

Nonfunctional requirements can have a substantial impact on solution development and testing. NFRs are tricky to specify; it's easy to go overboard. For example, a statement such as '99.999 percent availability' may increase development effort exponentially more than a statement such as '99.98 percent availability.' Sometimes that exacting level of detail is necessary, but at other times it's not. Nevertheless, the impact of the NFR must be well understood by those persons who are defining the solution requirements. Similarly, if not given enough thought, physical constraints such as weight, volume, or voltage may cause the solution to be overly complicated and costly.

The Economic Framework of the solution should contain criteria to evaluate NFRs. NFRs should be viewed in the context of trade-offs with costs and other considerations. NFRs also affect Suppliers, as declaring them incorrectly, or without the full trade-off ramifications of the economic framework, could lead to unnecessarily complex and costly systems and components.

It's also important to reevaluate NFRs regularly. Unlike other requirements, NFRs are persistent constraints on the backlog, rather than backlog items themselves. As a result, they may not always be addressed during PI Planning. NFRs do change during development, however, and it's important to ensure they are addressed.

NFRs and Solution Intent

Solution Intent is the single source of truth about the solution, as shown in Figure 4. As such, it includes NFRs as well as functional requirements. It also includes links between NFRs, requirements that they impact, and tests used to verify them. NFRs play a key role in understanding the economics of fixed versus variable solution intent.

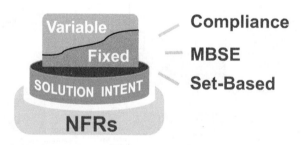

Figure 4. Solution intent

Early on, some of the functionality is likely to be unclear and will need to be tested and negotiated with Customers during development. The same goes for NFRs. Some are fixed and well known in advance; others will evolve with the solution.

By imposing constraints, NFRs may affect a wide range of system functionality. Therefore, they're an important factor to consider in the following circumstances:

- Analyzing business epics, capabilities, and features

- Planning and building the Architectural Runway

- Refactoring to better reflect increasing solution domain knowledge

- Imposing DevOps constraints on manufacturing, deployment, support, installation, maintainability, and so on

The tools used to help develop the solution intent provide some mechanisms to establish an economic approach to define and implement NFRs:

- **Compliance** – This is the proof that the system or solution meets regulatory, industry, and other relevant standards and guidelines.

- **Model-Based Systems Engineering (MBSE)** – MBSE can be used to simulate the effect of NFRs and can link to the tests that validate them.

- **Set-based Design (SBD)** – SBD provides different options for achieving NFRs and can guide a range of edge-case testing to support design decisions.

Specifying NFRs

Considering the following criteria helps define NFRs:

- **Bounded** – When they lack bounded context, some NFRs are irrelevant (or even harmful). For example, performance considerations can be critical for the main application but may be unnecessary or too expensive for administration and support applications.

- **Independent** – NFRs should be independent of each other so that they can be evaluated and tested without consideration of or impact from other system qualities.

- **Negotiable** – Understanding NFR business drivers and bounded context requires that NFRs have some degree of negotiability.

- **Testable** – NFRs must be stated with objective, measurable, and testable criteria because if you can't test it, you can't ship it.

Implementation Approaches

Many NFRs mandate that some additional work be done—either now or in the future—to satisfy them. Sometimes the NFR must be implemented all at once; at other times the teams can take a more incremental approach. The trade-offs described in the economic framework should influence the implementation approach. Implementation should occur in a way that will allow several learning cycles to ascertain the right level of NFR.

- **All at once** – Some NFRs appear as new concerns and will require immediate implementation. For example, a new regulatory rule for derivative trading, if not immediately incorporated into the solution, could take the company completely out of the market or cause a regulatory violation.

- **Incremental story-by-story path** – Teams sometimes have options for addressing NFRs. For example, the need for substantially improved performance can be dealt with over time, one story at a time (as shown in Figure 5).

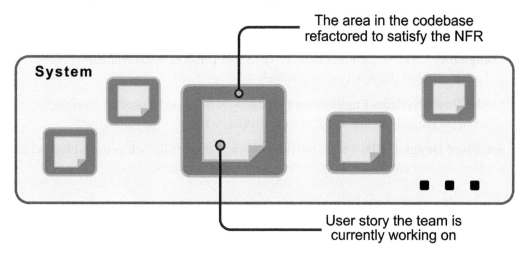

Figure 5. Incremental implementation of an NFR

NFR implementation is also impacted by the way ARTs have been organized. ARTs built around architectural layers will find it challenging to implement and test an NFR in its entirety. By comparison, trains organized around capabilities will find it easier to implement, test, and maintain systemic NFRs.

Using Agile Architecture supports the development of NFRs and helps maintain flexibility as the requirements evolve.

Testing Nonfunctional Requirements

Of course, to verify that a system complies with NFRs, it must be tested. Testing NFRs is most easily viewed from the perspective of the four Agile testing quadrants, as shown in Figure 6 [2, 3].

Quadrant 4, 'system qualities tests,' is the home of most NFR tests. Due to their scope and importance, NFR tests often require collaboration between the System Team and the Agile Teams. To prevent technical debt, teams should automate testing wherever possible so that these tests can be run continuously, or at least on demand.

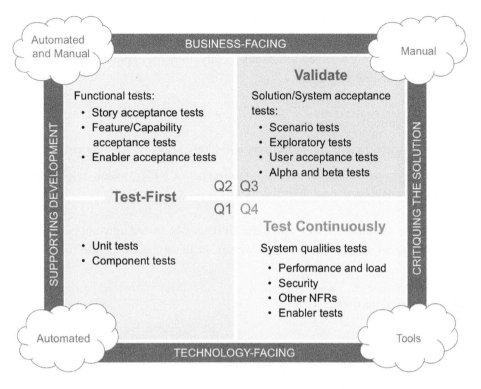

Figure 6. Agile testing quadrants (adapted from [2] and [3])

Over time, however, the increasing number of regression tests, even when automated, may consume too much processing time and too many resources. Even worse, it can mean that NFR testing may be practical only on occasion or only with the use of specialty resources or personnel. To ensure practicality and continuous use, teams often need to create reduced test suites and test data, as illustrated in Figure 7.

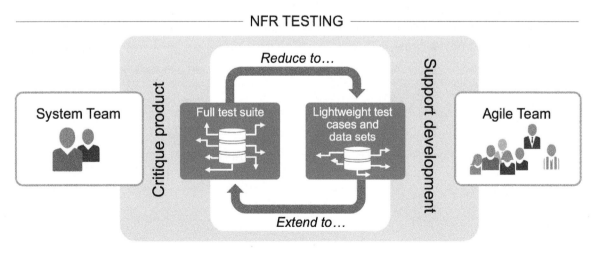

Figure 7. Collaboration with the system team and Agile teams to create a more practical NFR testing strategy

Although partial testing sounds less than ideal, it can be beneficial in increasing system quality:

- When teams can apply reduced test suites locally, they may spot inconsistencies in the test data or the testing approach.

- Teams may create new and unique tests, some of which may be adopted by the System Team to help build the larger set.

- Testing infrastructure and configurations will likely improve continuously.

- Teams gain a practical understanding of the impact of NFRs, which helps improve estimating of business and enabler features.

Even so, in some cases, the environment where the NFRs can be tested may not be available on a daily basis (e.g., field testing of vehicle guidance software). In these instances, the following approaches can be used [4]:

- Using virtualized hardware

- Creating simulators

- Creating similar environments

In all cases, efficiently testing NFRs requires some thought and creativity. A lack of NFR testing, in contrast, may increase the risk of substantial technical debt or, worse, system failure.

LEARN MORE

[1] https://en.wikipedia.org/wiki/Non-functional_requirement.

[2] Leffingwell, Dean. *Agile Software Requirements: Lean Requirements Practices for Teams, Programs, and the Enterprise*. Addison-Wesley, 2011.

[3] Crispin, Lisa, and Janet Gregory. *Agile Testing: A Practical Guide for Testers and Agile Teams*. Addison-Wesley, 2009.

[4] Larman, Craig, and Bas Vodde. *Practices for Scaling Lean and Agile Development: Large, Multisite, and Offshore Product Development with Large-Scale Scrum*. Addison-Wesley, 2010.

[5] Leffingwell, Dean, and Don Widrig. *Managing Software Requirements: A Use Case Approach* (2nd ed.). Addison-Wesley, 2003.

Weighted Shortest Job First

If you only quantify one thing, quantify the Cost of Delay.

—Don Reinertsen

Weighted Shortest Job First (WSJF) is a prioritization model used to sequence jobs (e.g., Features, Capabilities, and Epics) so as to produce maximum economic benefit. In SAFe, WSJF is estimated as the Cost of Delay (CoD) divided by job size.

Agile Release Trains (ARTs) provide an ongoing, continuous flow of work that makes up the Enterprise's incremental development effort. This approach avoids the overhead and delays caused by the start–stop–start nature of traditional projects, where authorizations and phase gates control the program and its economics.

While this continuous flow model speeds the delivery of value and keeps the system Lean, priorities must be updated continuously to provide the best economic outcomes. In a flow-based system, job sequencing—rather than theoretical, individual job return on investment—produces the best result. To that end, WSJF is used to prioritize backlogs by calculating the relative CoD and job size (a proxy for the job's duration). Using WSJF at Program Increment (PI) boundaries continuously updates backlog priorities based on user and business value, time factors, risk, opportunity enablement, and effort. WSJF also conveniently and automatically ignores sunk costs, a fundamental principle of Lean economics.

Details

Reinertsen describes a comprehensive model, called weighted shortest job first, for prioritizing jobs based on the economics of product development flow [2]. WSJF is calculated by dividing the CoD by the job's duration. Jobs that can deliver the most value (or CoD) and are of the shortest length are selected first for implementation. When applied in SAFe, the WSJF model supports some additional principles of product development flow:

- Taking an economic view
- Ignoring sunk costs
- Making financial choices continuously

- Using decision rules to decentralize decision-making and control

- If quantifying only one thing, quantify the Cost of Delay

Figure 1 shows the impact of correctly applying WSJF (see [2] for a full discussion). The areas shaded in blue illustrate the total CoD in each case. As can be seen in the figure, applying the WSJF algorithm delivers the best overall economics.

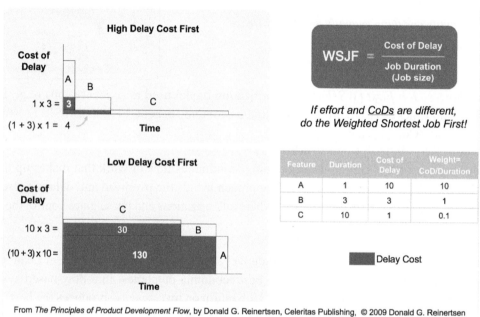

From *The Principles of Product Development Flow*, by Donald G. Reinertsen, Celeritas Publishing, © 2009 Donald G. Reinertsen

Figure 1. Applying the WSJF algorithm delivers the best overall economics

Calculating the Cost of Delay

In SAFe, our jobs are the epics, features, and capabilities we develop, so we need to establish both the Cost of Delay and the duration. Three primary elements contribute to the Cost of Delay:

- **User-business value** – Do our users prefer this over that? What is the revenue impact on our business? Is there a potential penalty or other adverse consequences if we delay this job?

- **Time criticality** – How does the user/business value decay over time? Is there a fixed deadline? Will the Customer wait for us, or will the customer move to another solution? Are there Milestones on the critical path impacted by this job?

- **Risk reduction-opportunity enablement value** – What else does this job do for our business? Does it reduce the risk of this or a future delivery? Is there value in the information we will receive? Will this feature open up new business opportunities?

Moreover, since we are in a continuous flow and should have a large enough backlog to choose from, we needn't worry about the absolute numbers. We can just compare backlog items relative to each other using the modified Fibonacci numbers we use in 'estimating poker.' Then the relative CoD is calculated as shown in Figure 2.

$$\text{Cost of Delay} = \text{User-Business Value} + \text{Time Criticality} + \text{Risk Reduction and/or Opportunity Enablement}$$

Figure 2. A formula for the relative CoD

Duration

Next, we need to understand job duration. That amount of time can be relatively difficult to determine, especially early on when we might not know who is going to do the work or how capacity is allocated among the teams. Fortunately, we have a ready proxy for job duration in systems with fixed resources—namely, job size. (If I'm the only person mowing my lawn, and the front yard is three times bigger than the backyard, it's going to take three times longer.) We already know how to estimate item size in story points (see the Features and Capabilities chapter). Using job size, we can perform a reasonably straightforward calculation to compare jobs via WSJF, as shown in Figure 3.

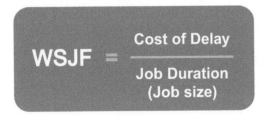

$$\text{WSJF} = \frac{\text{Cost of Delay}}{\text{Job Duration (Job size)}}$$

Figure 3. A formula for WSJF

Then, for example, we can create a simple table to compare jobs (three jobs, in this case), as shown in Figure 4.

To use the table in Figure 4, the team rates each feature relative to the others for each of the three parameters. (Note: With relative estimating, you look at one column at a time, set the smallest item to '1,' and then set the others' values relative to that item.) It then divides the CoD by job size. The job with the highest WSJF is the next most important item to do.

This model encourages splitting large items into multiple smaller ones that can compete against other smaller, low-risk items. But that's just Agile at work. Since the implementation is incremental, whenever a continuing job doesn't rank higher than its peers, then you have likely satisfied that particular requirement sufficiently that you can move on to the next one.

Feature	User- business value	Time criticality	RR | OE value	CoD	Job size	WSJF
	+	+	=	÷	=	
	+	+	=	÷	=	
	+	+	=	÷	=	

- Scale for each parameter: 1, 2, 3, 5, 8, 13, 20
- Note: Do one column at a time, start by picking the smallest item and giving it a "1."
- There must be at least one "1" in each column!
- The highest priority is the highest WSJF.

Figure 4. A sample spreadsheet for calculating WSJF

Another advantage of the WSJF model is that it is not necessary to determine the absolute value of any of these numbers. Instead, you simply need to rate the parameters of each item against the other items from the same backlog. Finally, as the backlog estimates should include only the remaining job size, the frequent reprioritization means that the system will automatically ignore sunk costs.

A Note on Job Size as a Proxy for Duration

Job size does not always make a good proxy for the *duration* of the *WSJF model*. For example:

- If availability of resources means that a more significant job may be delivered more quickly than some other item with roughly equal value, then we probably know enough about the work to use estimated duration and obtain a more accurate result. (If three people are available to mow my front lawn, while I do the backyard, then these items may have about the same duration, but not the same cost.)

- A small job may have multiple dependencies with other things and may take longer to complete than a bigger item.

We rarely need to worry about these edge cases, however: If we make some small error in selection, that next important job will make its way up the priorities list soon enough.

LEARN MORE

[1] Leffingwell, Dean. *Agile Software Requirements: Lean Requirements Practices for Teams, Programs, and the Enterprise*. Addison-Wesley, 2011.

[2] Reinertsen, Don. *Principles of Product Development Flow: Second Generation Lean Product Development*. Celeritas Publishing, 2009.

Program Increment

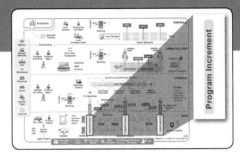

Doing is a quantum leap from imagining.

—Barbara Sher

A *Program Increment (PI)* is a timebox during which an Agile Release Train (ART) delivers incremental value in the form of working, tested software and systems. PIs are typically 8–12 weeks long. The most common pattern for a PI is four development Iterations, followed by one Innovation and Planning (IP) Iteration.

A *Program Increment is to an ART (or Solution Train)* as an Iteration *is to the* Agile Team. In other words, the PI is a fixed timebox for building and validating a full system increment, demonstrating value, and getting fast feedback. Each PI uses cadence and synchronization to accomplish the following goals:

- Facilitate planning
- Limit Work in Process (WIP)
- Summarize newsworthy value for feedback
- Assure consistent, Program Level retrospectives

Due to its scope, the PI provides several observations appropriate for Portfolio Level consideration and 'roadmapping.'

Details

SAFe divides the development timeline into a set of Iterations within a PI. The Big Picture illustrates how a PI is initiated by a PI Planning session, which is then followed by four execution iterations, concluding with one Innovation and Planning iteration. This pattern is suggestive but arbitrary, and there is no fixed rule for how many iterations are included in a PI. Experience has shown, however, that a PI duration between 8 and 12 weeks works best, with a bias toward the shortest duration.

A Solution Train and its associated Agile Release Trains use the same PI cadence, as shown in Figure 1.

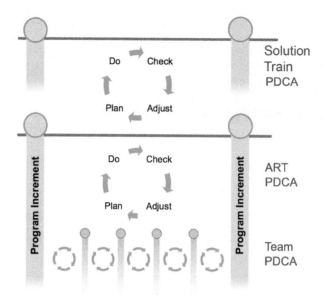

Figure 1. The Solution Train and Agile Release Trains follow the same PI cadence

The PI represents the outer loop of Shewhart's PDCA cycle, as shown at the top of Figure 1. It combines the value developed by each Agile Team into a meaningful Milestone to objectively measure the Solution under development.

The PDCA learning cycle (shown in Figure 1) is represented by the following events in SAFe for the PI (outer loop):

- **Plan** – The PI Planning event is the *plan* step of the cycle.
- **Do** – PI execution is the *do* step.
- **Check** – The System Demo is the *check* step.
- **Adjust** – The Inspect and Adapt (I&A) event is the *adjust* step.

Develop on Cadence; Release on Demand

Continuous execution of PIs provides the rhythm for trains, and the assets they create grow iteratively and incrementally. Releasing solutions, however, is a separate concern, which is covered in the Release on Demand chapter. While trains determine the best product development rhythm, the business is enabled to deploy releases whenever it, or the market, requires.

The cadence for the PI can be different from the release cadence. However, in some situations, the PI and release cadences are the same, which can be a major convenience. Other ARTs may need to release less or more frequently than the PI cadence. Still others will have multiple, independent release cycles for the solution's various components.

Executing the Program Increment

When it comes to PI execution for a single ART, a sequence of program events creates a closed-loop system to keep the train on the tracks, as illustrated in Figure 2. Each program event is described in the following sections.

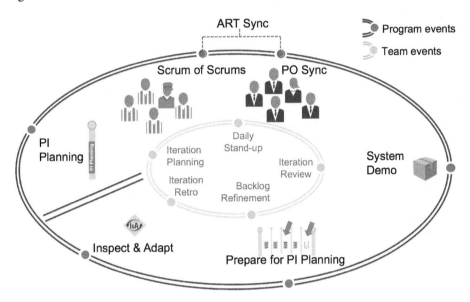

Figure 2. Program execution events

PI Planning

Each PI begins with a PI planning event. Since PI planning occurs on a fixed cadence, the entire calendar year of events can be scheduled well in advance. By scheduling PI planning events in advance, the enterprise can lower the cost of travel and logistics. In addition, this advance scheduling helps people on the train, especially Business Owners, to manage their personal calendars to assure they can be present for these critical events.

During PI planning, the teams estimate what will be delivered and highlight their dependencies with other Agile teams and trains. PI planning also creates a rhythm for integration of work and system demos. One outcome of the PI planning is a set of program PI Objectives, detailing what the ART should have ready for integration and demo at the end of the PI. Of course, Agile teams continuously integrate their work and demo it during the Iteration Review and System Demo (or Solution Demo for Solution Trains).

Scrum of Scrums

The Release Train Engineer (RTE) typically facilitates a weekly (or more frequent, as needed) Scrum of Scrums (SoS) meeting. The SoS helps coordinate the dependencies of the ARTs and provides visibility into progress and impediments. The RTE, Scrum Masters, and others (where appropriate) meet to review their progress toward milestones, program PI objectives, and internal dependencies among the teams. The meeting is timeboxed for less than 30 minutes and is followed by a 'meet after' to solve any problems that emerge during the SoS. A suggested agenda for the SoS meeting is described in Figure 3.

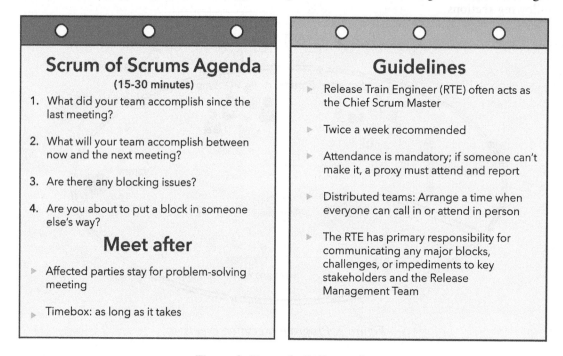

Figure 3. Example SoS agenda

Product Owner Sync

Similar to the SoS, a *PO sync* meeting is often held for POs and Product Managers. This meeting typically occurs weekly, or more frequently, as needed. The PO sync is also timeboxed (30–60 minutes) and is followed by a 'meet after' to solve any problems.

The PO sync may be facilitated by the RTE or Product Manager. The purpose is to get visibility into how well the ART is progressing toward meeting the program PI objectives, to discuss problems or opportunities with Feature development, and to assess any scope adjustments. The meeting may also be used to prepare for the next PI (discussed later in this chapter) and may include Program Backlog refinement and Weighted Shortest Job First (WSJF) prioritization before the next PI planning meeting.

Note: As shown in Figure 2, sometimes the SoS and the PO sync are combined into one meeting, often referred to as an ART sync.

Release Management Meetings

Release management meetings provide governance for any upcoming releases, as well as communication to management. To learn more, read the Release on Demand chapter.

System Demo

A system demo is a biweekly event that provides feedback from the stakeholders about the effectiveness and usability of the system under development. This demo also helps ensure that integration between teams on the same ART occurs on a regular basis, no less frequently than every iteration. Given that "integration points control product development [1]," the PI is the routine point at which the meaningful, emergent behavior of the full system or solution can be evaluated.

Prepare for the Next PI Planning Event

While we note this function as an event in Figure 3, preparing for the upcoming PI is actually a continuous process, with three primary focus areas:

- Management alignment and organizational readiness for planning

- Backlog readiness

- The actual logistics for the event—for example, facility readiness

Since any one of these factors can interfere with the desired outcome—that is, a specific and committed PI plan—careful consideration of all three factors is necessary.

Inspect and Adapt

The PI is done when its timebox expires. Each PI is followed by a *final system demo*, a newsworthy event that illustrates all the Features that have been accomplished during the PI. This demo is usually done as part of the I&A workshop, which offers a regularly scheduled time to reflect, problem-solve, and take on improvement actions needed to increase the velocity, quality, and reliability of the next PI. The result of the workshop is a set of improvement backlog features or Stories that can be added to the backlog for the upcoming PI planning. In this way, every ART improves every PI.

Solution Train PI Execution

The Large Solution Level has additional important events and activities, which bring a similar focus to the progress of the solution. These events and activities are described next.

Pre- and Post-PI Planning

Pre- and Post-PI Planning events are used for preparation and coordination of PI planning across multiple ARTs and Suppliers in a Solution Train. The purpose of these events is to create a common Vision and mission as well as a set of features that will advance the solution in alignment.

The *pre-PI planning* event is used to coordinate input (e.g., objectives, key milestones, business context, and Solution Context) for the ART planning sessions. The *post-PI planning* event is used to integrate the results from individual ART planning sessions into the vision and Roadmap for the Solution Train. At the end of the post-PI planning meeting, there should be an agreed set of solution PI objectives that are expected to be implemented by the end of the PI and demoed at the next solution demo.

Solution Increment and Solution Demo

During the PI timebox, the ARTs build multiple increments of value, which grow into solution Capabilities. The new capabilities must be designed, developed, tested, and validated holistically, along with the existing capabilities of the system. The solution demo is a critical aspect of the PI learning cycle. This high-profile event allows large solution stakeholders, Customers (or their internal proxies), and senior management to view the progress that the solution has made during the past PI.

At this event, the Solution Train demos its accomplishments for the entire PI. Senior managers and stakeholders review the progress in the broader solution context. It may also inform decisions about whether to pivot or persevere with capabilities, as well as whether to change the Lean Budgets for the various Value Streams.

Inspect and Adapt for the Solution Train

At the end of the PI, an additional I&A workshop may be required for the Solution Train. It follows the same format as the ART I&A. Due to the number of people involved, the Solution I&A workshop cannot include all stakeholders from the ARTs, so the most appropriate representatives are selected to address that context. This group includes the primary stakeholders of the Solution Train, as well as representatives from the various ARTs and suppliers.

LEARN MORE

[1] Oosterwal, Dantar P. *The Lean Machine: How Harley-Davidson Drove Top-Line Growth and Profitability with Revolutionary Lean Product Development.* Amacom, 2010.

Innovation and Planning Iteration

Inertia is the residue of past innovation efforts. Left unmanaged, it consumes the resources required to fund next-generation innovation.

  —Geoffrey Moore

100% utilization drives unpredictability.

  —Don Reinertsen

The *Innovation and Planning (IP) Iteration* occurs every Program Increment (PI) and serves multiple purposes. Specifically, it acts as an estimating buffer for meeting PI Objectives and provides dedicated time for innovation, continuing education, PI Planning, and Inspect and Adapt (I&A) events.

SAFe has an intense focus on continuous customer value delivery, and people within the organization will be busy working on the Features they committed to during PI planning. Every Iteration counts and the teams are mostly heads down, delivering near-term value. One iteration after another, the Solution marches closer to market. The attention on solution delivery is intense and unrelenting.

Of course, a focus on one thing—delivery—can lead to a lack of focus on another—innovation. Given the constant urgency for delivery, there's a risk that the 'tyranny of the urgent iteration' will override any opportunity to innovate. To address this possibility, SAFe provides dedicated IP iterations.

Details

Understand the IP Iteration Activities

IP iterations provide a regular, cadence-based opportunity, with every PI, for teams to work on activities that are difficult to fit into a continuous, incremental value delivery pattern. These activities may include the following considerations:

- Time for innovation and exploration, beyond the iterations dedicated to delivery
- Work on technical infrastructure, tooling, and other impediments to delivery
- Education to support continuous learning and improvement

- A dedicated time for the PI System Demo, I&A workshop, PI planning events, and backlog refinement, including final prioritization of Features using the Weighted Shortest Job First (WSJF) model

- Final integration of the solution, including verification and validation, if releasing it on the PI boundary

- Final user acceptance testing and documentation, and any other readiness activities that are neither feasible nor economical to perform at every iteration

IP iterations fulfill another critical demand by providing an estimating buffer for meeting PI objectives and enhancing the predictability of PI performance.

Members of Agile Release Trains (ARTs) typically report that their overall efficiency, velocity, and job satisfaction are enhanced by regular opportunities to 'recharge their batteries and sharpen their tools.'

Allow Time for Innovation

One of the pillars of the SAFe Lean-Agile Mindset is innovation, but finding time for ideation and change in the midst of delivery deadlines can be difficult. To this end, many enterprises use IP iterations for research and design activities and hackathons. There are two simple rules for hackathons:

- People can work on whatever they want, with whomever they want, so long as the work reflects the mission of the company.

- The teams demo their work to others at the end of the hackathon.

The learnings from hackathons routinely make their way into Program Backlogs and often help drive innovation. They're fun, too!

Dedicate Time to PI Events

Performing the I&A and PI planning during the IP iteration avoids a reduction in velocity of the regular iterations. More importantly, these events can follow a specific cadence so that their occurrence is better guaranteed. Also, it's likely that some just-in-time, last-responsible-moment Program and Solution Backlog refinement and Feature and Capability elaboration during this period can significantly increase the productivity of the upcoming planning session.

Integrate the Complete Solution

When a solution includes hardware (and other components), it becomes more difficult to integrate the solution in an end-to-end manner continuously. Full integration at the Program Level, as well as the Large Solution Level, may be feasible only during the IP iteration. In these cases, it's just common sense to plan for that prospect.

Nevertheless, the IP iteration should not be the only attempt to integrate the assets into the system. Full or partial integration happens over the course of the PI, with a total solution integration occurring at least once per PI. This approach validates the assumptions early enough that the teams can respond to significant problems and risks within the PI.

The final PI system demo occurs at the end of each PI. This integrated presentation of the work of all teams on the train is done in a staging environment and emulates the envisioned production as much as possible. In large Solution Trains, the system demo feeds into the aggregate Solution Demo.

The IP iteration is also a placeholder for the final integration and Solution Demo. It's a more structured and formal affair, as it demonstrates the accumulation of all the features developed over the course of the entire PI for a Solution Train.

Typically, the solution demo, which is part of the Solution Train's I&A event, feeds into the retrospective and the collection of various PI progress Metrics.

Advance the Development Infrastructure

Lean delivery puts increased pressure on the development infrastructure: New continuous integration environments require provisioning; new test automation frameworks must be implemented and maintained; Agile project management tooling must be adopted; cross-team and train communications systems must be upgraded or enhanced; and the list goes on.

It's often more efficient to improve the infrastructure or perform a migration at a time when there isn't a critical iteration demo just a few days away. (Many times, the improvement stories come from the team's Iteration Retrospective or Enablers.)

We all understand that we have to sharpen our tools from time to time; Agile teams are no different. Indeed, they have an even higher dependency on their working environments, so time must be spent continuously improving them.

Enable Continuous Learning

Lean engineers and leaders are lifelong learners. Changes in technology, as well as changes in methods and practices, are routine; opportunities for continuing education, however, arise far less frequently. Also, the initial move to a Lean-Agile framework typically requires many new techniques and skills:

- Feature and Story writing
- Building in quality
- Automated testing

- Collective ownership
- Agile Architecture
- Continuous Integration
- Pair work
- Mastering the Product Owner and Scrum Master roles
- Team building

Making time for continuing education gives teams and leaders a welcome opportunity to learn and master these new techniques. These sessions can also be used to launch and support Communities of Practice devoted to these and other topics. The net results benefit both the individual and the Enterprise: Employee mastery and job satisfaction increase, velocity increases, and time-to-market decreases.

Leverage the Built-In Estimation Buffer

Lean flow teaches us that operating at "100 percent utilization drives unpredictable results" [1]. Simply put, planning for everyone to work at full capacity does not allow people to flex when problems occur, as they inevitably do. The result is unpredictability and delays in value delivery. As a countermeasure, the IP iteration offers a 'guard band' (or small buffer) to prevent unfinished work from the current PI from carrying over to the next PI.

During PI planning, the ART does not plan features or stories for the IP iteration, providing a buffer (extra time) to the teams for responding to unforeseen events, delays resulting from dependencies, and other issues, and thereby increasing their ability to meet Team and Program PI Objectives. This buffer substantially increases the predictability of the program's outcomes, which is extremely important to the business. However, routinely using that time for completing the work is a *failure pattern*. Doing so defeats the primary purpose of the IP iteration, and innovation will likely suffer. Teams must take care that the estimating guard does not simply become a crutch to meeting the PI goals.

A Sample IP Iteration Calendar

IP iterations take on a somewhat standard schedule and format. Figure 1 provides an example IP iteration calendar. The items in orange represent Solution Train events, while the blue and green ones are for a single ART.

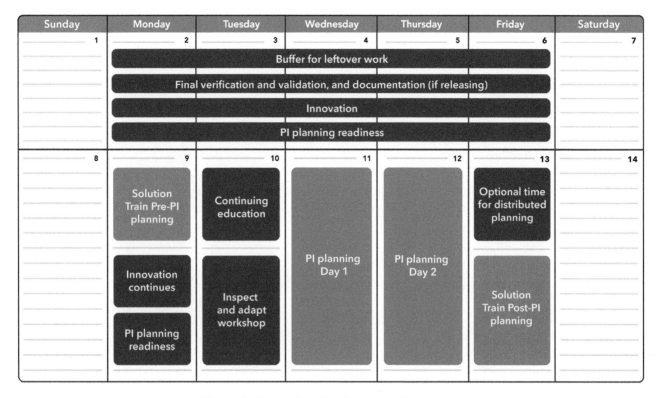

Figure 1. Example calendar for an IP iteration

LEARN MORE

[1] Reinertsen, Donald G. *The Principles of Product Development Flow: Second Generation Lean Product Development.* Celeritas Publishing, 2009.

[2] Leffingwell, Dean. *Agile Software Requirements: Lean Requirements Practices for Teams, Programs, and the Enterprise.* Addison-Wesley, 2011.

Develop on Cadence

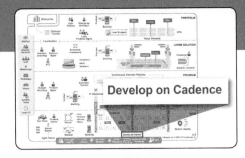

Control flow under uncertainty.

—Don Reinertsen

Develop on Cadence is an essential method for managing the inherent variability of systems development in a flow-based system by making sure important events and activities occur on a regular, predictable schedule.

The effects of cadence can be seen directly in the Big Picture—with fast synchronized short Iterations being completed and then integrated into larger Program Increments (PIs). Cadence assures that important events such as PI Planning, System and Solution Demos, and Inspect & Adapt (I&A) workshops happen on a regular, predictable schedule. It also lowers the cost of these standard events by enabling them to be planned well in advance.

Details

Cadence, along with synchronization, is a key construct used to build system and Solution assets in SAFe. Cadence is the use of a regular, predictive development rhythm, while synchronization causes multiple, potentially dependent events to happen at the same time.

Thanks to Don Reinertsen's *principles of product development flow* [1], we can explain why cadence and synchronization are critical to effective solution development. Some of these principles are summarized in Tables 1 and 2, along with the relevant SAFe practices that implement them.

Principles of Flow: Cadence	SAFe Practices
F5: Use a regular cadence to limit the accumulation of variance	Planning at regular PI intervals limits variances to a single PI timebox, increasing Agile Release Train (ART) and Solution Train predictability.
F6: Provide sufficient capacity margin to enable cadence	In order to reliably meet PI objectives, the Innovation and Planning (IP) iteration has no planned scope and provides a schedule margin (buffer). In addition, uncommitted but planned-for stretch goals also provide capacity margin (scope buffer). Together, they offer a way to reliably meet PI goals.
F7: Use cadence to make waiting times predictable	If a Feature doesn't make it into a PI, but remains a high priority, its delivery can be scheduled for the next PI (or another scheduled, frequent release). This avoids the temptation to load excess Work in Process (WIP) into the current increment.
F8: Use a regular cadence to enable small batch sizes	Short iterations help control the number of Stories in the iteration batch. Feature batch sizes are controlled by short PIs and frequent releases, providing high system predictability and throughput.
F9: Schedule frequent meetings using a predictable cadence	PI planning, System Demos, Inspect and Adapt (I&A), ART Sync, Iteration Planning, backlog refinement, and architecture discussions are examples of things that benefit from frequent meetings. Each meeting needs to process only a small batch of new information. Cadence helps lower the transaction costs of these meetings.

Table 1. Cadence principles applied in SAFe

Principles of Flow: Synchronization	SAFe Practices
F10: Exploit economies of scale by synchronizing work from multiple projects	Individual Agile Teams are aligned to common iteration lengths. Work is synchronized by system and solution demos. Portfolio business and Enabler Epics drive common infrastructure and Customer utility.
F11: Capacity margin enables synchronization of deliverables	The Innovation and Planning (IP) iteration enables the final PI system demo, and solution demo to occur without taking velocity away from ARTs or Solution Trains.
F12: Use synchronized events to facilitate cross-functional trade-offs	ART and Solution Train events synchronize customer feedback and enable resource and budget adjustments, mission alignment, continuous improvement, and program oversight and governance. They also drive collaboration and team building.
F13: To reduce queues, synchronize the batch size and timing of adjacent processes	Teams are aligned to common timeboxes and similar batch sizes. The ART and solution system teams support integration on a regular cadence. To facilitate rapid delivery of new ideas, backlogs are kept short and uncommitted.
F14: Apply nested cadence harmonic multiples to synchronize work	Teams integrate and evaluate on iteration boundaries (at least). ARTs and Solution Trains evaluate on PI boundaries.

Table 2. Synchronization principles applied in SAFe

Taken together, cadence and synchronization are critical concepts that help us manage the inherent variability of our work. They create a more reliable, dependable solution development and delivery process, one that our key business stakeholders can come to rely on.

But Release on Demand

As we have seen, developing on cadence delivers many benefits. But when it comes to actually releasing value, a different set of rules may apply. Given a reliable cadence of PIs, the next and even larger consideration is to understand when and how to actually release all that accumulating value to the end user. As described in the Continuous Delivery Pipeline and Release on Demand chapters, every ART and Solution train needs a strategy for releasing solutions that suits its development and business context.

Toward Continuous Delivery

For many organizations, the prospect of continuous delivery is highly desirable. After all, none of us panics when an automatic update becomes available for our mobile phone. Rather, we assume it will deliver value, and we press that update button without much thought or concern. Surely there is as much or more software in that phone as in some of our enterprise systems.

Nevertheless, the enterprise world often marches to a different drummer. Perhaps, for reasons related to security and availability, or for financial or safety-critical systems, the customer's operational environment is ill suited to continuous updates of significant new value. Perhaps our enterprise's development and release capabilities have not advanced to a point where such updates are a largely a risk-free proposition for our customers. Perhaps, for whatever reason, continuous updating just doesn't make economic sense.

In addition, systems that support continuous delivery must be designed for that outcome. Even then, releasing is not an all-or-nothing event. For example, even the simple SAFe website has multiple release cadences. If, however, we updated the Big Picture every week, the people supporting SAFe with tooling and courseware would think that was a bad approach. However, without the ability to roll out new content (through the blog, supplemental guidance articles, and updates to existing articles), we'd undermine our goal of continuous value delivery. We couldn't be as Agile. In short, you have to design for these things.

In all cases, enterprises that apply SAFe can rest easy knowing that development and releasing are separate concerns. They can release any quality asset, as needed, to meet business conditions.

LEARN MORE

[1] Reinertsen, Don. *Principles of Product Development Flow: Second Generation Lean Product Development.* Celeritas Publishing, 2009.

[2] Leffingwell, Dean. *Scaling Software Agility: Best Practices for Large Enterprises.* Addison-Wesley, 2007, chapter 16.

[3] Leffingwell, Dean. *Agile Software Requirements: Lean Requirements Practices for Teams, Programs, and the Enterprise.* Addison-Wesley, 2011.

Release on Demand

Develop on Cadence. Release on Demand.

   —A SAFe mantra

Release on Demand is the process by which Features deployed into production are released incrementally or immediately to Customers based on market demand. It is the fourth and last element in the four-part Continuous Delivery Pipeline, shown in Figure 1.

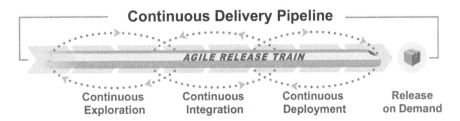

Figure 1. The final element of the continuous delivery pipeline: release on demand

The three processes that precede release on demand in Figure 1 help ensure that the value is ready to be deployed in the production environment. But since tangible development value occurs only when end users are operating the Solution in their environment, delivery value at the right time is critical for the enterprise to gain the real benefits of agility. The decision to release is a key economic driver that requires careful consideration. While deployed features may be immediately available to all end users in some situations, more often the release is a decoupled on-demand activity, occurring for specific users, timed for when they need it.

Details

The ability to release on demand is a critical aspect of the continuous delivery pipeline, which raises three questions that allow Agile Release Trains (ARTs) to embrace Principle #3, Assume variability and preserve options:

1. When should we release?
2. Which elements of the system should be released?
3. Which end-users should receive the release?

Having all three options accelerates the delivery process and provides flexibility in delivering value. Further, release on demand 'closes the loop' by evaluating the benefit hypothesis proposed during the Continuous Exploration stage of the pipeline. Releasing provides the data needed to decide whether further exploration of an idea is warranted, or if new functionality should be added, or if perhaps a different approach is warranted.

Practicing release on demand requires the organization to develop the following capabilities:

- Decoupling the release from the development cadence
- Decoupling the release elements from the solution
- Designing the solution to support incremental releases

The following sections describe each of these capabilities.

Decouple the Release from the Development Cadence

Develop on cadence is the other half of a strategy that allows ARTs and the Solution Trains to operate in a predictable pattern and synchronize the efforts of multiple development teams. When it comes to releasing value, though, a different set of rules may apply.

Once we have a reliable stream of value through the Continuous Deployment process, the next consideration is when and how to release. The release strategy is decoupled from the development cadence, as shown in Figure 2.

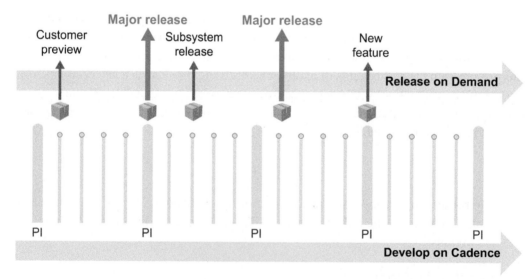

Figure 2. Decoupling development concerns from release concerns

Several release strategies may apply depending on the context and situation:

- **Releasing on the Program Increment (PI) cadence** – In the simplest case, the enterprise releases on the PI boundaries. With this strategy, PI planning, releasing, and Inspect and Adapt will have predictable calendar dates. Also, the Innovation and Planning Iterations can be timed, designed, and organized to support the more extensive release activities. The IP iterations may include final, Verification and Validation (V&V), User Accepted Testing (UAT), and training and release documentation.

- **Releasing less frequently** – In many cases, releasing on a fast PI cadence may not be possible or even desirable. For example, in some enterprise settings, deployed systems constitute critical infrastructure for an operating environment. Even if the customer would like to have the new software, the service level and license agreements may rule out this kind of release. Moreover, the organization must take into account the overhead and disruption associated with deployment. In other cases, the timeline for building complex systems that include both software and hardware (e.g., mobile phones or geophysical mapping satellites) is driven by those systems' hardware components (displays, chipsets, and the like), which typically have longer lead times. The new hardware must be available first, which means releasing early and incrementally may not be an option. In these cases, releasing on a PI cadence may not be practical, and the planning and releasing activities are entirely decoupled.

- **Releasing more frequently** – For many organizations, the goal is to release as often as possible—hourly, daily, weekly, and so on. Achieving frequent releases requires DevOps capabilities, an efficient continuous delivery pipeline, and architecture that supports incremental delivery. Even then, the periodic planning function still provides the cadence, synchronization, and alignment the enterprise needs to manage variability and limit deviations from expectations.

- **Release on demand** – For organizations building complex solutions (e.g., systems of systems), the preceding cases are probably overly simplistic. Big systems often contain different types of components and subsystems, each of which may leverage its own release model. In that case, the most general model is this: Release whatever you want and whenever it makes sense, within an appropriate governance and business model.

Decouple Release Elements from the Solution

Applying different release frequencies raises another question: Is a release a monolithic, all-or-nothing process? If so, the release strategy would be limited. Fortunately, that's not the case. In fact, even simple solutions will have multiple release elements, each operating with different release strategies, as Figure 3 illustrates.

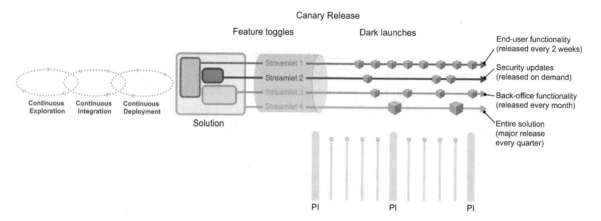

Figure 3. Decoupling release elements from the solution

For example, the SAFe website has multiple release cycles:

- Its authors can make a fix to a deployed version or address security at any time (ad hoc, but expedited).

- Its authors can update any article at any time and simply notify readers via blog post (high frequency).

- Its authors can add new articles to the Advanced Topics section whenever significant new content is available (medium frequency).

- Significant revisions to the framework are made only periodically, based on new content, new ways to render the Big Picture, and most importantly, when the market is ready for a new release (low frequency).

We call these separate flows value *streamlets*, as they represent a full, end-to-end flow of value within a Value Stream. Each streamlet (or value stream segment) can and should be managed to deliver value according to its own needs and pace. Identifying streamlets is critical to enable release on demand, as they allow the different elements of the solution to be released independently in a separate cadence.

Architect the Solution for Incremental Release

Achieving the different release strategies requires solutions to be designed for component (or service-based) deployability, releasability, and fast recovery. Intentional design of these attributes requires the collaboration of System Architects, Agile Teams, and deployment operations. The goal is a quick and flawless delivery process, ideally requiring little manual effort.

The following capabilities allow for a more flexible release process:

- **Feature toggles** – Feature 'toggles or switches' enable deployment of features into production without making them visible to the end user. They help avoid the need for multiple code branches, allowing developers to deploy new features to production but activate them only when the enterprise is ready to consume them. After the feature has been released and deemed stable, the toggles are removed to avoid technical debt.

- **Canary releases** – This technique reduces the risk associated with introducing a release in production, by slowly rolling out the change first to a small subset of users, and only then rolling it out to the entire user base. Canary releases allow selective production testing and feature validation without impacting everyone.

- **Dark launches** – In some situations, it's important to test new functionality in a production setting before making it available to customers, especially when there is high uncertainty on how well the system will meet its Nonfunctional Requirements (NFRs) under a production load.

Implementing these capabilities may require the organization to upgrade its infrastructure and architecture, including moving to standard technology stacks, decoupling monolithic applications with micro-services, ensuring data preparation and normalization, engaging with third-party APIs and data exchange, and implementing logging and reporting tools.

Close the Loop on the Feature Hypothesis

Finally, after the feature is released, it's time to evaluate the benefit hypothesis. Were the intended outcomes achieved? For example, should a canary release be extended to more customers? Should the organization turn off the feature toggles? The feature is considered done once we have an understanding of the production results. However, it may be necessary to add new backlog items to extend the functionality (persevere), or pivot (remove the feature) to find a different solution.

Building the Release

Building large-scale systems that are ready for release and fit for use requires an incremental development approach, as Figure 4 illustrates. The four types of increments are described next.

Team Increment

The first step in this process is that each Agile team ensures that it produces a working increment for the stories, features, and components the team is responsible for by doing the following:

- Completing user stories from the Team Backlog, while assuring that each meets its local (story) Definition of Done (DoD)

- Applying Continuous Integration practices with test automation to monitor and confirm progress

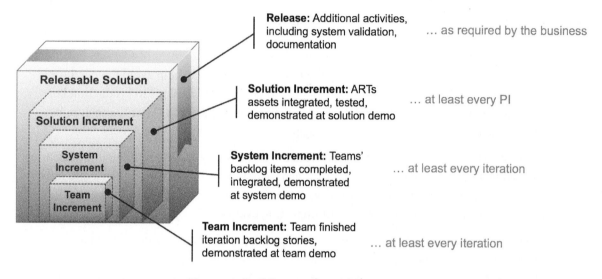

Figure 4. Building a releasable solution

System Increment

Every two weeks, teams build a system increment—that is, an integrated stack of new functionality, representing all the backlog items completed by the ART during the current and all previous iterations. During the System Demo, stakeholders review the system increment and provide feedback. In this way, new features are added incrementally to the system, usually a few per iteration.

Solution Increment

When developing large solutions, ARTs typically contribute to only a part of the solution, whether it's a set of subsystems, some solution capabilities, or a mix of the two. When integrated, verified, and validated, the solution increment must satisfy both the functional and Nonfunctional Requirements. Such a solution increment is the subject of the all-important Solution Demo, which brings all the system increments together into a working system.

Release Increment

Building solutions incrementally affects the release increment as a whole. As discussed earlier, decoupling solution elements allows for smaller, independent releases of the solution. These items might be at the team, system, or solution levels, so the same logic should be applied across the entire integration stack.

Some additional activities might be required when releasing increments—namely, final, V&V, release notes, UAT, documentation, and training materials, as well as marketing activities. As much as possible, these activities are part of the DoD of previous increments. Some, however, will remain as release activities.

A Scaled Definition of Done

The continuous development of incremental system functionality requires a scaled DoD. An example is shown in Table 1.

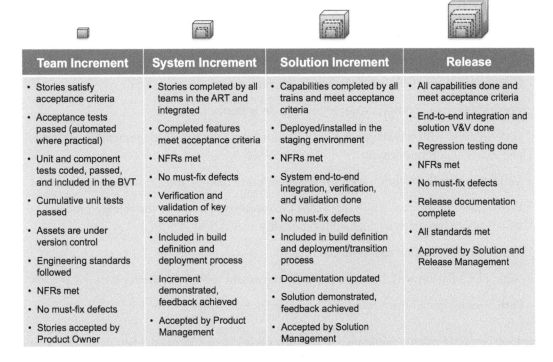

Team Increment	System Increment	Solution Increment	Release
• Stories satisfy acceptance criteria	• Stories completed by all teams in the ART and integrated	• Capabilities completed by all trains and meet acceptance criteria	• All capabilities done and meet acceptance criteria
• Acceptance tests passed (automated where practical)	• Completed features meet acceptance criteria	• Deployed/installed in the staging environment	• End-to-end integration and solution V&V done
• Unit and component tests coded, passed, and included in the BVT	• NFRs met	• NFRs met	• Regression testing done
• Cumulative unit tests passed	• No must-fix defects	• System end-to-end integration, verification, and validation done	• NFRs met
• Assets are under version control	• Verification and validation of key scenarios	• No must-fix defects	• No must-fix defects
• Engineering standards followed	• Included in build definition and deployment process	• Included in build definition and deployment/transition process	• Release documentation complete
• NFRs met	• Increment demonstrated, feedback achieved	• Documentation updated	• All standards met
• No must-fix defects	• Accepted by Product Management	• Solution demonstrated, feedback achieved	• Approved by Solution and Release Management
• Stories accepted by Product Owner		• Accepted by Solution Management	

Table 1. Example of a scalable DoD

Release Management

Release management is the process of planning, managing, and governing solution releases, which helps guide the value stream toward the business goals. In some enterprises, especially those that must meet significant regulatory and compliance criteria, a centralized, portfolio-level team or function is present that assures releases meet all the relevant business criteria. In other circumstances, ART and Solution Train leadership and stakeholders from development operations, quality, sales, and other stakeholders should own some of the release management and governance responsibilities.

In either case, the release management function facilitates the activities needed to help internal and external stakeholders receive and deploy the new solution. It also ensures that the most critical governance quality elements are appropriately addressed before deployment—particularly internal and external security, regulatory, and other compliance guidelines.

Release planning is part of the PI planning process. But that's the easy part; the hard part is coordinating the implementation of all the capabilities and features over multiple iterations within a release. This is especially true when new issues, roadblocks, dependencies, and gaps in Vision and backlogs are uncovered. Due to these challenges, the scope of each release must be continually managed, revalidated, and communicated. Primary considerations include the following:

- Ensuring that the organization's release governance is understood and adhered to
- Communicating release status to external stakeholders
- Ensuring that an appropriate deployment plan is in place
- Coordinating with marketing and with Product and Solution Management on internal and external communications
- Validating that the solution meets relevant solution quality and Compliance criteria
- Participating in Inspect and Adapt (I&A) workshops to improve the release process, value stream productivity, and solution quality
- Providing final authorization for the release
- Acting as a liaison with Lean Portfolio Management (LPM), as appropriate
- Participating in and overseeing the final release activities

Many enterprises hold *release management* meetings weekly to address the following questions:

- Is the vision still understood, and are the trains and teams aligned for that purpose?
- Does everyone understand what they are building, and is their understanding aligned with the purpose of the Value Stream and current Strategic Themes?
- Are the trains tracking to the scheduled release dates?
- Is the appropriate quality built into the solution?
- Which impediments must be addressed to facilitate progress?

This weekly meeting provides senior management with regular visibility into the release progress. It's also the place to approve any scope, timing, people, or resource adjustments necessary to assure the release. In a more continuous delivery environment, the participants closely monitor the release section of the Program Kanban, making sure items are released when needed, to the right audiences; managing dark and canary releases; verifying that hypotheses are evaluated; and ensuring that feature toggles are removed after production verification.

LEARN MORE

[1] Kim, Gene, Jez Humble, Patrick Debois, and John Willis. *The DevOps Handbook: How to Create World-Class Agility, Reliability, and Security in Technology Organizations.* IT Revolution Press, 2016.

Architectural Runway

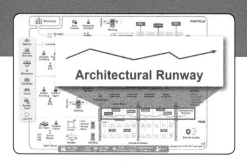

While we must acknowledge emergence in design and system development, a little planning can avoid much waste.

—James Coplien and Gertrud Bjørnvig, Lean Architecture for Agile Software Development

The *Architectural Runway* consists of the existing code, components, and technical infrastructure needed to implement near-term features without excessive redesign and delay. It provides the necessary technical foundation for developing business initiatives and implementing new Features and Capabilities. The architectural runway is one of the primary tools used to implement the Framework's Agile Architecture strategy.

Since the development of new features and capabilities consumes the architectural runway, continual investment must be made to extend it by implementing Enablers. Some enablers fix existing problems with the Solution, such as improving the performance or User Experience. Others might provide foundational capabilities that will be used to support future functionality.

Details

Agile development avoids Big Design Up-front (BDUF) and replaces it with a simple belief that "the best architectures, requirements, and designs emerge from self-organizing teams" [3]. This perspective fosters the practice of emergent design—the process of discovering and extending the architecture only as necessary to implement and validate the next increment of functionality.

However, organizations must respond simultaneously to new business challenges with larger-scale architectural initiatives that require some intentionality and planning. As a result, emergent design alone may not be able to handle the complexity of large-scale system development, such that the following problems start to occur:

- Excessive redesign and delays reduce velocity.

- Systems become difficult to integrate, validate, and maintain.

- System qualities, known as Nonfunctional Requirements (NFRs), begin to decline.

- Reduced collaboration and synchronization among teams becomes apparent.

- There are low reuse rates for common components and redundancy of solution elements.

All of these problems can result in poor solution performance, unfavorable economics, and slower time-to-market.

Intentional Architecture Supports the Bigger Picture

It just isn't possible for teams to anticipate all the changes that may occur well outside their environment. Nor can individual teams fully understand the entire system and avoid producing redundant and conflicting designs and implementations. Simply put, no one team in a larger Enterprise can see the whole picture or reasonably anticipate all the changes headed their way—many of which arise outside their local control. For this reason, teams need some intentional architecture—a set of purposeful, planned architectural guidelines that enhance solution design, performance, and usability—and direction for cross-team design while syncing implementation.

Applied together, intentional architecture and emergent design allow Agile Release Trains (ARTs) to create and maintain large-scale solutions. Emergent design enables fast, local control so that teams can react appropriately to changing requirements without excessive attempts to future-proof the system. Intentional architecture provides the guidance needed to ensure that the whole system has conceptual integrity and is fit for its purpose. Achieving the right balance of emergent design and intentional architecture is the key to developing large-scale systems effectively.

Enable Flow and Agility with Architecture

Enterprise Architects define enablers at the Portfolio Level, while System and Solution Architects/Engineering typically define them at the Program and Large Solution Levels.

The architects who define the enablers help steer them through the Kanban systems, providing the guidance needed to analyze, estimate, and implement them. This support ensures that the affected elements—subsystems, components, functions, protocols, and internal system functions—have the architecture necessary to support the near-term features and capabilities identified on the Roadmap.

To avoid the BDUF approach, the enterprise commits to implementing architecture incrementally. Thus, enabler epics are split into enabler features or capabilities, which are ultimately implemented by ARTs. Each enabler feature must be completed within a Program Increment (PI), ensuring that the system always runs—meaning it's potentially deployable, even during its development.

In some cases, new architectural initiatives are implemented incrementally. (They may not even be made visible to the users in the PI in which they are implemented.) In this way, the architectural runway can be implemented and tested behind the scenes, while still allowing shipment throughout. The new architecture can be exposed to users when it's ready to support new business epics and features.

PI cadence and synchronization help manage the inherent variability of research and development. This way, ARTs have new products constantly available for potential release. The enterprise is then free to decide whether to ship those assets based on mostly external factors. Having high-quality, deployable, system-level solutions at PI boundaries, at the very least, is critical.

In turn, some amount of architectural runway *must exist* prior to the PI Planning session. Otherwise, there's a danger that architectural rework—followed by the build-out of new features reliant on that rework—may add unacceptable risk and delay to the program.

To mitigate that threat, programs must ensure that the underlying architecture for the most innovative new features is already in the system when planning for the PI. As we'll see in the following sections, that's achieved in three ways:

- Building some amount of runway

- Using the runway

- Extending the runway

Building the Architectural Runway

When developing new platforms, especially ones that are particularly innovative, as well as in the case of entirely new development, it's common for the System or Solution Architect/Engineer to play a role in defining and building out the runway. Usually, the new infrastructure is initially put in place with just a few Agile Teams—sometimes with the Architect/Engineer serving as Product Owner during a few Iterations, as illustrated in Figure 1.

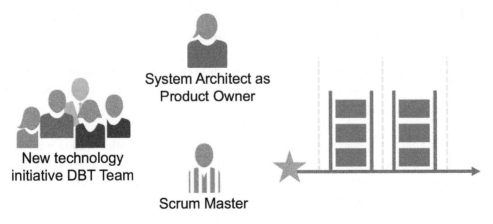

Figure 1. Initiating the architectural runway

The rules for building the runway are both simple and Agile:

- The teams that build the runway complete iterations just like every other Agile team in the program.

- Credit goes to working solutions, not models and designs.

- Time is of the essence. It should take no more than a few iterations to implement and prove the new architecture.

- After that point, the program is rapidly expanded to include some feature teams who test the new architecture with the initial, consumable features, as illustrated in Figure 2.

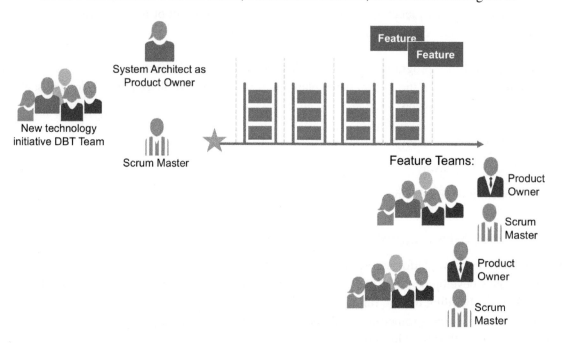

Figure 2. Implementing some new features on the new runway

In the meantime, the teams build the additional architectural runway needed, as illustrated in Figure 3.

To support a stable velocity, the architectural runway needs to be continuously maintained and extended. Capacity allocations are used to ensure continuous investments in enablers—that is, the activities required to extend the runway.

Although Product/Solution Management and Architects/Engineers, in collaboration with the affected teams, define many of these enablers, implementation of the enablers is the responsibility of the ARTs. While supporting successful near-term delivery, the architectural runway should not overly constrain development with long-range technical commitments. Just the right amount of architectural runway is required:

- Too much, and the architecture limits the teams and is too disconnected from the current context

- Too little, and the teams will have trouble making and meeting their near-term commitments

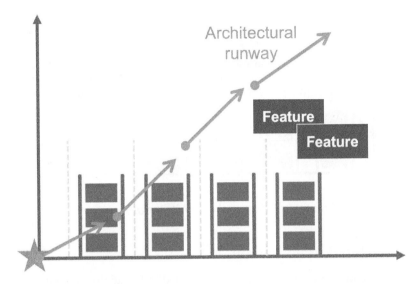

Figure 3. Progress in building the architectural runway

Consuming the Architectural Runway

With a new architecture in place and valuable features already deployed, the teams can take pride in their accomplishments. This initial success can be temporary, however, as a number of natural forces will tend to consume the architecture over time:

- **Agile teams are fast.** They have an unparalleled focus and ability to deliver new features, thus consuming the existing runway.

- **Product Owners and Product/Solution Management are impatient.** They've invested some time in internal system capabilities, and they will quickly move backlog priorities to the features that users are willing to pay for.

- **Architecture itself is fragile and needs to be continuously evolved.** Technologies change rapidly and may become outdated.

- **Customer needs change quickly.** In today's fast-paced digital economy, opportunities and threats emerge quickly, and customer requirements are constantly evolving.

Unless the Agile teams are really on their game, the result will be the pattern shown in Figure 4.

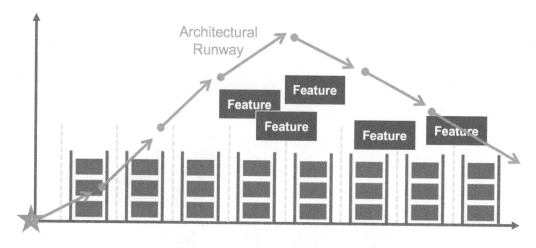

Figure 4. Using up the architectural runway

Extending the Architectural Runway

How can teams avoid ending up right back where they started? By realizing that investing in architecture cannot be a one-time or infrequent event. After all, ARTs operate in a continuous flow process using various Kanban systems. Therefore, teams must commit to continuous elaboration, analysis, and implementation of enablers. In addition, Architects/Engineers and Agile teams must acquire the skills needed to split enablers into small slices that can be implemented during the course of each iteration and PI, so that they continuously deliver value to the customer (see the System and Solution Architect/ Engineering chapter in Part 5 and *Agile Software Requirements*, chapters 20 and 21 [2], for incremental implementation strategies).

Backstory of the Architectural Runway

The term 'architectural runway' started as an analogy while observing PI-level burn-down charts. Often, when a sufficient architectural runway is lacking when teams start a PI, any features dependent on the new architecture pose a high risk.

ARTs can't always 'land those PIs' (i.e., bring the burn-down to zero at the end of the PI). In such a case, they won't meet the PI objectives. A PI, like an airplane, needs enough runway to safely land.

In the SAFe Big Picture, the architectural runway is depicted as a line going up and down over time, because the team builds up some runway, then uses some, builds some more, and then uses that, too. In short, there has to be just about the right amount of runway at any point in time.

To extend the runway metaphor, the bigger the aircraft (system) and the faster the flying speed (velocity), the more runway is needed to land the PI safely. The architectural runway is explored further in the Agile Architecture chapter in Part 9.

LEARN MORE

[1] Leffingwell, Dean. *Scaling Software Agility: Best Practices for Large Enterprises.* Addison-Wesley, 2007.

[2] Leffingwell, Dean. *Agile Software Requirements: Lean Requirements Practices for Teams, Programs, and the Enterprise.* Addison-Wesley, 2011.

[3] Manifesto for Agile Software Development. http://www.agilemanifesto.org.

PI Planning

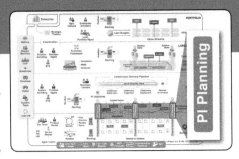

Future product development tasks can't be predetermined. Distribute planning and control to those who can understand and react to the end results.

—Michael Kennedy, *Product Development for the Lean Enterprise*

There is no magic in SAFe . . . except maybe for PI Planning.

—Authors

Program Increment (PI) Planning is a cadence-based, face-to-face event that serves as the heartbeat of the Agile Release Train (ART), aligning all the teams on the ART to a shared mission and Vision. For geographically distributed ARTs, this planning event may occur at multiple locations simultaneously by maintaining constant audio and video communication between the sites.

Details

The Agile Manifesto states, "The most efficient and effective method of conveying information to and within a development team is a face-to-face conversation." SAFe takes this to the next level with PI planning—a routine, face-to-face event, with a standard agenda that includes a presentation of business context and vision, followed by team planning breakouts where the teams create their Iteration plans and objectives for the upcoming PI.

Facilitated by the Release Train Engineer (RTE), this event includes all members of the ART, whenever possible. It takes place over two days and occurs within the Innovation and Planning (IP) Iteration. Holding the event during the IP iteration avoids affecting the scheduling or capacity of other iterations in the PI.

PI planning is essential to SAFe: If you are not doing it, you are not doing SAFe. This is quite a significant occasion, as Figure 1 implies.

Figure 1. Face-to-face PI planning. Remote teams are planning at the same time using video conferencing (Image courtesy of Scaled Agile, Inc.)

Business Benefits of PI Planning

PI planning delivers many business benefits:

- Establishes face-to-face communication across all team members and stakeholders
- Builds the social network on which the ART depends
- Aligns development to business goals with the business context, Vision, and Team and Program PI objectives
- Identifies dependencies and fosters cross-team and cross-ART collaboration
- Provides the opportunity for 'just the right amount' of architecture and Lean User Experience (UX) guidance
- Matches demand to capacity, eliminating excess Work in Process (WIP)
- Facilitates fast decision-making

Following are highlights of the ART Readiness Checklist [1].

Inputs and Outputs of PI Planning

Inputs to PI planning include the following items:

- Business context (see the 'Content Readiness' section)
- Roadmap and vision
- Top 10 Features of the Program Backlog

A successful PI planning event delivers two primary outputs:

- **Committed PI objectives** – This set of SMART objectives is created by each team, with the business value being assigned by the Business Owners.

- **Program board** – This board highlights the new feature delivery dates, feature dependencies among teams and with other ARTs, and relevant Milestones.

Preparation

PI planning is a significant event that requires preparation, coordination, and communication. Event attendees include Business Owners, Product Management, Agile Teams, System and Solution Architect/Engineering, the System Team, and other stakeholders who must be notified in advance so that they can be well prepared.

For the event to be successful, preparation is required in three major areas:

- **Organizational readiness** – Strategic alignment and setup of teams and trains
- **Content readiness** – Management and development preparedness
- **Facility readiness** – The actual space and logistics for the event

Organizational Readiness

Before planning, Programs must have strategy alignment among participants, stakeholders, and Business Owners. Critical roles should also be assigned. To address these issues in advance, event organizers must answer the following questions:

- **Planning scope and context** – Is the scope (product, system, technology domain) of the planning process understood? Do we know which teams need to plan together?
- **Business alignment** – Is there reasonable agreement on priorities among the Business Owners?
- **Agile teams** – Do we have Agile teams? Are there dedicated developer and test resources and an identified Scrum Master and Product Owner for the team?

Content Readiness

It's equally important to ensure that there are a clear vision and context and that the right stakeholders can participate. Therefore, the PI planning must include these elements:

- **Executive briefing** – A briefing that defines the current business context
- **Product vision briefing(s)** – Briefings prepared by Product Management, including the top 10 features in the Program Backlog
- **Architecture vision briefing** – A presentation made by the CTO, Enterprise Architect, or System Architect to communicate new Enablers, features, and Nonfunctional Requirements (NFRs)

Facility Readiness

Securing the physical space and technical infrastructure necessary to support a large number of attendees isn't a trivial matter—especially if there are remote participants. Considerations include the following elements:

- **Facility** – The facility must be roomy enough to accommodate all attendees, with breakout rooms if necessary.

- **Facilities/tech support** – These people need to be identified in advance and reachable during setup and testing, as well as during the event itself.

- **Communication channels** – For distributed planning meetings, primary and secondary audio, video, and presentation channels must be available.

Standard Agenda

The meeting follows an agenda similar to that shown in Figure 2. Descriptions of each item follow.

Figure 2. Standard two-day PI planning agenda

Day 1 Agenda
- **Business context** – A senior executive/line-of-business owner describes the current state of the business and presents a perspective on how well existing solutions are addressing current Customer needs.

- **Product/solution vision** – Product Management presents the current program vision (typically represented by the top 10 upcoming features) and highlights any changes from the previous PI planning meeting, as well as any forthcoming Milestones.

- **Architecture vision and development practices** – System Architect/Engineering presents the architecture vision. Also, a senior development manager may introduce Agile-supportive changes to development practices, such as test automation, DevOps, Continuous Integration, and Continuous Deployment, which are being advanced in the upcoming PI.

- **Planning context and lunch** – The Release Train Engineer presents the planning process and expected outcomes of the meeting.

- **Team breakouts #1** – In the breakout, teams estimate their capacity (velocity) for each Iteration and identify the backlog items they will likely need to realize the features. Each team creates its draft plans, which are made visible to all, iteration by iteration.

During this process, teams identify risks and dependencies and draft their initial team PI objectives. The PI objectives typically include 'stretch objectives,' which are goals built into the plan (e.g., stories that have been defined and included for these objectives) but not committed to by the team because of too many unknowns or risks.

Stretch objectives are *not* extra things to do in case the team has extra time. Instead, they increase the reliability of the plan and give management an early warning of goals that the ART may not be able to deliver. The team also adds the features to the program board, as shown in Figure 3.

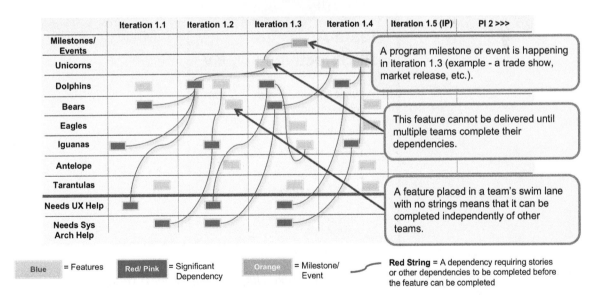

Figure 3. Program board

- **Draft plan review** – During the tightly timeboxed draft plan review, teams present key planning outputs, including draft objectives, potential risks, and dependencies. Business Owners, Product Management, and other teams and stakeholders review and provide input.

- **Management review and problem-solving** – It's likely that the draft plans present challenges such as scope, people and resource constraints, and dependencies. During the problem-solving meeting, management may negotiate scope changes and resolve other problems by agreeing to various planning adjustments. The RTE facilitates and keeps the primary stakeholders together for as long as necessary to make the decisions needed to reach achievable objectives.

In multi-ART Solution Trains, a similar meeting may be held after the first day of planning to solve cross-ART issues that have come up. Alternatively, the RTEs of the involved trains may talk with each other to raise issues that are then resolved in the ART's management problem-solving meetings. The Solution Train Engineer (STE) helps facilitate and resolve issues across the ARTs.

Day 2 Agenda

- **Planning adjustments** – The next day, the meeting begins with managers describing any changes to planning scope and resources.

- **Team breakouts #2** – Teams continue planning based on their agenda from the previous day, making the appropriate adjustments. They finalize their objectives for the PI, to which the Business Owners assign business value, as shown in Figure 4.

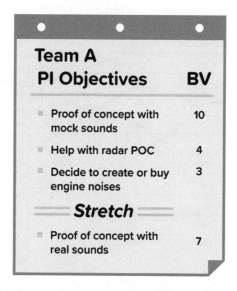

Figure 4. A team's PI objectives sheet with assigned business values

- **Final plan review and lunch** – During this session, all teams present their plans to the group. At the end of each team's time slot, the team states its risks and impediments, but there is no attempt to resolve them in this short timebox. If the plan is acceptable to the customers, the team brings its program PI objectives sheet and program risks sheet to the front of the room so that all can see the aggregate objectives unfold in real time.

- **Program risks** – During planning, teams will have identified program-level risks and impediments that could impact their ability to meet their objectives. These potential problems are resolved in a broader management context in front of the whole train. One by one, the risks are addressed with honesty and transparency, and then categorized into one of the following categories:

    - **Resolved** – The teams agree that the issue is no longer a concern.

    - **Owned** – Someone on the train takes ownership of the item since it cannot be resolved at the meeting.

    - **Accepted** – Some risks are just facts or potential problems that must be understood and accepted.

    - **Mitigated** – Teams identify a plan to reduce the impact of an item.

- **Confidence vote** – Once program risks have been addressed, teams vote on their level of confidence in their ability to meet their program PI objectives (Figure 5).

Figure 5. Confidence vote for an ART (Image courtesy of Scaled Agile, Inc.)

Each team conducts a 'fist of five' vote. If the average is three fingers or more, then management accepts the commitment. If this average is less than three, the team reworks the plan. Any person voting two fingers or fewer should be given an opportunity to voice his or her concerns. This might add to the list of risks, require some additional planning, or simply be informative.

- **Plan rework** – If necessary, teams rework their plans until they reach a high confidence level regarding their ability to meet the objectives. This is one occasion where alignment and commitment are valued more highly than adhering to a timebox.

- **Planning retrospective and moving forward** – Finally, the RTE leads a brief retrospective for the PI planning event to capture what went well, what didn't, and what can be done better next time (Figure 6).

Figure 6. Planning retrospective (Image courtesy of Scaled Agile, Inc.)

- Typically, a discussion about the next steps, along with final instructions to the teams, follows. This might include the following actions:

  - Cleaning up the rooms used for planning

  - Capturing the team PI objectives and user stories in the Agile project management tool

  - Reviewing team and program calendars

  - Determining Daily stand-up (DSU) meeting times and locations

  - Reviewing the locations for the Iteration Planning meetings

After the planning event is complete, the RTE and other ART stakeholders summarize the individual team PI objectives into a set of program PI objectives (Figure 7) and use this summary to communicate externally about the teams' plans and to track progress toward the goals.

Product Management uses the program PI objectives to update the roadmap and to improve the forecast for the next two PIs based on what was just learned.

The program board is often used during the Scrum of Scrums meetings to track dependencies. In other cases, it may not be maintained (manually) after the PI planning event. This depends upon the Agile project management tooling in place and the needs of the ART.

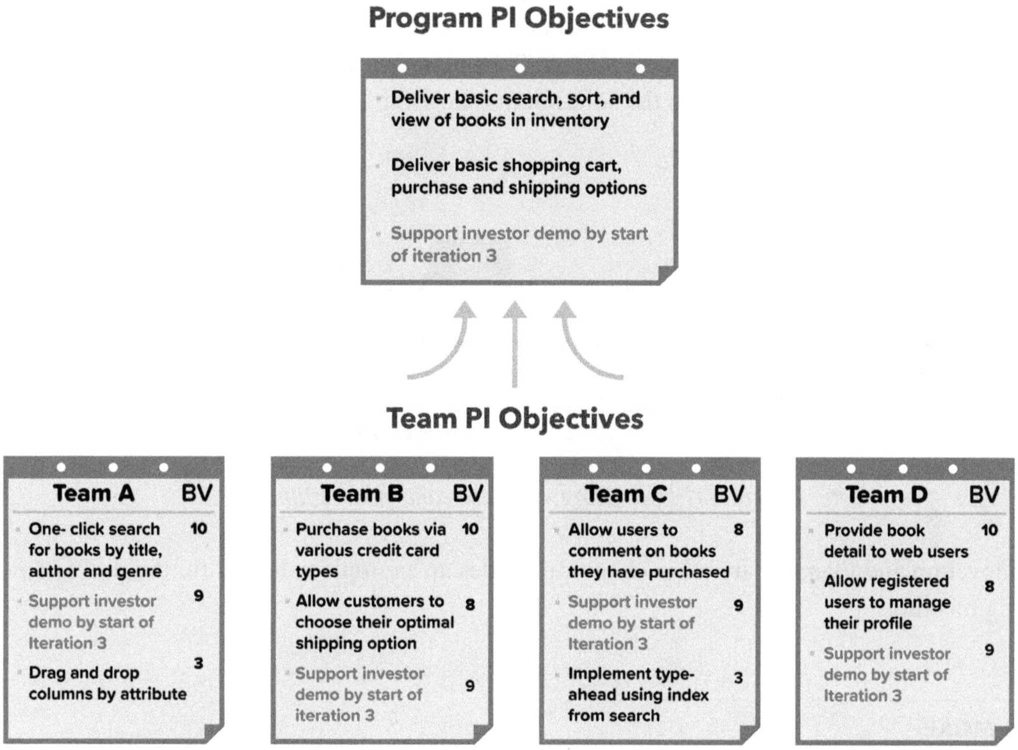

Figure 7. Summarizing team PI objectives into a set of program PI objectives

Teams leave the PI planning event with a prepopulated iteration backlog for the upcoming PI. They take their team's PI objectives, iteration plans, and risks back to their regular work area. Program risks remain with the RTE, who ensures that the people responsible for owning or mitigating a risk have captured the information and are actively managing that risk.

Most important, the program proceeds to execute the PI, tracking progress and adjusting as necessary to the changes that occur as new knowledge emerges. Execution of the PI begins with all the teams conducting planning for the first iteration using their PI plans as a starting point. These plans serve as fresh input for the Iteration Planning processes that follow. Since the iteration plans did not take into account the story acceptance criteria, it's likely that adjustments will be needed to the first and subsequent iteration plans.

Solution Train PI Planning

This chapter focuses on the planning activities of a single ART. However, large Value Streams may include multiple ARTs and suppliers. In this case, the Solution Train provides coordination via a Pre-PI Planning meeting, which sets the context and input objectives for the individual ART PI planning sessions. A Post-PI Planning session follows the ART PI planning and is used to integrate the planning results of the ARTs that contribute to the solution (as shown in Figure 8).

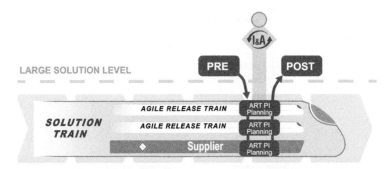

Figure 8. PI planning with pre- and post- planning

The Innovation and Planning Iteration chapter provides an example calendar for the pre- and post-PI planning meetings.

LEARN MORE

[1] Leffingwell, Dean. *Agile Software Requirements: Lean Requirements Practices for Teams, Programs, and the Enterprise.* Addison-Wesley, 2011.

[2] Kennedy, Michael. *Product Development for the Lean Enterprise.* Oaklea Press, 2003.

PI Objectives

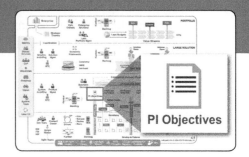

Making and meeting small commitments builds trust. Ba must be energized with its own intentions.

—Nonaka and Takeuchi, The Knowledge-Creating Company

Program Increment (PI) Objectives are a summary of the business and technical goals that an Agile Team or train intends to achieve in the upcoming Program Increment (PI).

During PI planning, teams create PI objectives, which provide several benefits:

- Provide a common language for communicating with business and technology stakeholders

- Align the train with a shared mission

- Create the near-term vision, which teams can rally around and develop during the PI

- Enable the ART to assess its performance and the business value achieved via the Program Predictability Measure

- Communicate and highlight each team's contributions to business value

- Expose dependencies that require coordination

Note: The Role of PI Objectives chapter in Part 9 explains the differences between Team PI Objectives and Features and provides additional insights on their usage and value.

Details

SAFe relies on a rolling wave of *short-term* commitments from Agile teams and trains to assist with business planning and outcomes, resulting in improved alignment and trust between development and business stakeholders. However, PI objectives should not be confused with a set of fixed, inflexible, long-term deliverables.

For the business to do any meaningful planning, teams must do some amount of reliable, predictable forecasting. Too little, and critics will complain, "Those ARTs can't commit to anything useful." Too much, and critics will proclaim, "Those ARTs never do what they say they will." Neither of these shortcomings is good, as both increase the distrust between business and development. That significantly hinders business success, not to mention the joy of work.

We need something in between—and that is a primary purpose of PI objectives. In addition to helping with alignment, the process of setting realistic objectives helps the organization avoid having too much Work in Process (WIP) in the system.

PI objectives and Iteration plans are built from the bottom up by Agile teams who estimate and identify their part of the solution during the PI Planning. They are summarized at the Program Level and then rolled up again at the Large Solution Level, if the ART is part of a Solution Train (Figure 1).

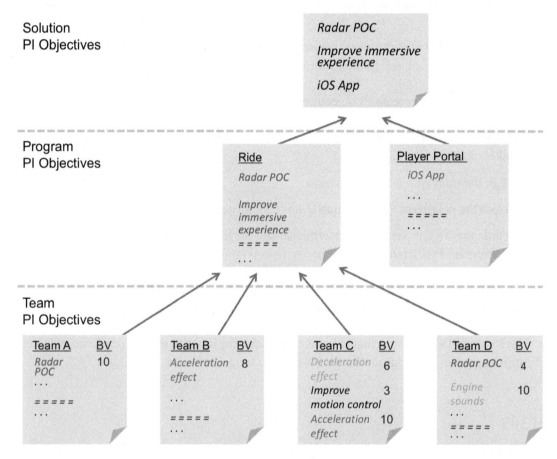

Figure 1. Roll-up of team and program PI objectives

Building the Team PI Objectives

During PI planning, the teams review the Program Vision and new features and plan the stories they need to deliver. In so doing, they also identify their specific team PI objectives.

Creating team PI objectives is not a trivial effort. It requires reasonable estimating and planning, a well-understood velocity, analysis of upcoming Features, definition of Stories for the Team Backlog, and, finally, summarizing of the information into simple business terms that can be understood by everyone.

Figure 2 illustrates an example of one team's PI objectives.

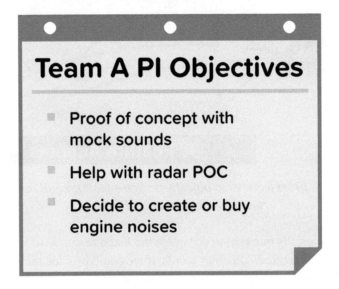

Figure 2. A team's PI objectives

Differentiate between Features and PI Objectives

The team's PI objectives often relate directly to the system's intended features; indeed, many objectives and features are the same. However, the mapping is not always straightforward, since some features require the collaboration of multiple teams (as shown in Figure 3).

Note that some features (such as Feature A in Figure 3) can be delivered by individual teams; others (Feature B) require collaboration. In addition to features and inputs to features, other team objectives will appear in the mapping. These can include technical objectives (for example, the proof of concept in Figure 2) that enable future features, enhancements to development infrastructure, and Milestones. All the results of this process are captured in the affected team's objectives.

Features and acceptance criteria are excellent tools to help teams understand, capture, and collaborate around the work that needs to be done, but it's all too easy to get caught up in 'finishing the features' and missing the overall goals hidden inside them. PI objectives help shift the focus away from developing features and toward achieving the desired business outcomes.

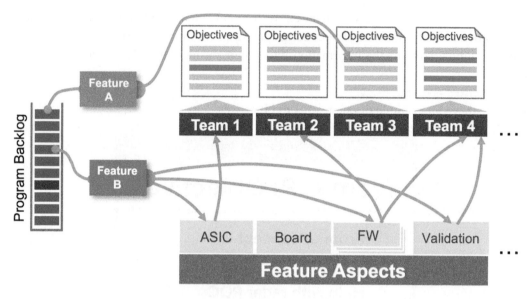

*Figure 3. From features to objectives: Some features will appear on
more than one team's objectives*

The core question becomes, "Is our goal to complete the listed features, or is our goal to provide the outcomes desired by those features?" In other words, if we could provide the same value with half the amount of work, and without building all of the features, would this outcome be acceptable?

A better understanding of the intent can be obtained by engaging in direct conversations with the Business Owners. This often results in the teams providing new perspectives to System Architects/ Engineering and Product Management and quickly finding ways to apply their expertise to create better solutions.

Use Stretch Objectives

Stretch objectives help improve the predictability of delivering business value since they are *not* included in the team's commitment or counted against teams in the program's predictable measures.

- Stretch objectives are used to identify work that can *vary* within the scope of a PI. Stretch objectives are *not* a way for stakeholders to load the teams with more work than they can do. They are not extra stuff to do, just in case time permits.

- If a team has low confidence in its ability to meet a PI objective, it should consider categorizing it as a stretch objective.

- If an item has many unknowns, consider moving it to the set of stretch objectives, and plan spikes early in the PI to reduce uncertainty about the team's ability to meet the PI objective for that item.

Ultimately, teams agree to do their best to deliver the stretch objectives, and they are included in the capacity for the PI. Since these objectives might not be finished in the PI, however, stakeholders must plan accordingly.

Stretch objectives provide several benefits:

- **Improved economics** – Without stretch objectives, a team must commit to a 100 percent scope in a fixed timebox. This forces teams to trade off quality or build other buffers into the system. The other buffers can accumulate, and convert uncertain early completion of the work to certain late delivery, resulting in less overall throughput.

- **Increased reliability** – Stretch objectives have variable scope, allowing confidence in the delivery of the main priorities. In turn, delivering commitments is the most important factor in building trust between the teams and the stakeholders (stretch objectives are not committed objectives).

- **Adaptability to change** – To enable the team to reliably deliver on a cadence, stretch objectives provide the capacity margin needed to meet commitments, yet alter priorities if necessary, when fact patterns change.

Typically, the total allowance for stretch objectives is 10–15 percent of the total capacity. The team must also constantly keep in mind that stretch objectives are used to identify what can vary within the scope of a plan.

Write SMART PI Objectives

Team PI objectives are a summary of a team's plan for the PI. Sometimes this causes their description to consist of fuzzy and non-verifiable 'chunks of intent.' As a countermeasure, teams make their objectives SMART:

- **Specific** – State the intended outcome concisely and explicitly as possible. (Hint: Try starting with an action verb.)

- **Measurable** – It should be clear what a team needs to do to achieve the objective. The measures may be descriptive, yes/no, quantitative, or provide a range.

- **Achievable** – Achieving the objective should be within the team's control and influence.

- **Realistic** – Recognize factors that cannot be controlled. (Hint: Avoid making 'happy path' assumptions.)

- **Time-bound** – The time period for achievement must be within the PI, so all objectives must be scoped appropriately.

Communicate Business Value with PI Objectives

As objectives are finalized during PI planning, Business Owners collaboratively assign business value to each of the team's individual objectives in a face-to-face conversation.

The value of this particular conversation with the team cannot be overstated, as it communicates the strategy and context behind these weighting decisions. Business Owners use a scale from 1 (lowest) to 10 (highest) when assigning business value. Business value should not be confused with any other measures, such as the associated effort or total story points associated with an objective.

Thus, business value is assigned, not calculated, and serves as an input to execution considerations. Many of the team's objectives provide direct and immediate value to the solution. Others, such as Enablers (e.g., advances in infrastructure, development environments, and quality initiatives) allow for the faster creation of future business value. All of these factors must be weighed in the final balance.

Finalize the Team PI Objectives

When objectives have been made 'smarter,' stretch objectives have been identified, and business value has been established, then the objectives in Figure 2 might evolve to look like those in Figure 4.

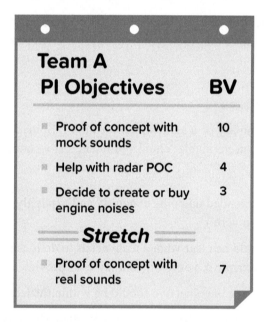

Figure 4. Objective sheet with business value and stretch objectives

Commit to PI Objectives

A vote of confidence is held near the end of PI planning, when the teams commit to the PI objectives. The commitment sought must be a reasonable thing to ask of the people who do the work. Therefore, the SAFe commitment has the following parts:

- Teams agree to do everything in their power to meet the committed objectives.

- The teams agree to escalate issues immediately that might prevent objectives from being met.

- During the course of the PI, if it's discovered that some objectives are not achievable, the teams agree to escalate the issue immediately so that corrective action can be taken.

In this way, all stakeholders know that either the program results will be achieved as planned, or they will be provided with sufficient notice so as to be able to mitigate and take corrective action, thereby minimizing business disruption. That's about as good as it gets, because this is, after all, research and development.

Creating Program and Solution PI Objectives

The result of the PI planning process will be some number of approved objectives, with one set of objectives for each team. Teams vote on the confidence level for the objectives as a set, and if confidence is high enough, the aggregate set of objectives becomes the committed ART plan. The Release Train Engineer summarizes the team objectives into the program PI objectives in a format suitable for communicating them to management.

The summarized objectives should be SMART, much like the team PI objectives, and have stretch objectives. Also, like the team PI objectives, these might be business Capabilities the ART is working on, enablers, or other business or technical goals.

During the Post-PI Planning meeting, after all the ARTs have planned, objectives are further rolled up to the large solution level by the Solution Train Engineer, and the solution PI objectives are synthesized and summarized. This is the top level of PI objectives in SAFe; such summaries communicate to stakeholders what the value stream as a whole will deliver in the upcoming PI. Figure 1 illustrates this summary from team to program and from program to solution PI objectives.

It's important that business value is assigned only to team PI objectives. The predictability metric itself is rolled up to determine predictability at a higher level.

Reduce WIP with Realistic PI Objectives

During the review of the team PI objectives, not everything that was envisioned by the various business stakeholders will likely be achieved within the PI timebox. Therefore, some of the current in-flight development work (WIP) will need to be reevaluated in conjunction with Business Owners to gain agreement to the PI objectives.

Those lower-priority work items are moved back into the Program Backlog. Decreasing excess WIP reduces overhead and thrashing and increases productivity and velocity. The net result is a feasible set of PI objectives that are agreed to by all business stakeholders and team members, as well as increased efficiency and a higher probability of delivery success. That's something that most everyone should be able to commit to.

Planning at the large solution level can work similarly. The planning of the various ARTs will likely create some conflicts, with some work being pushed back into the Solution Backlog for reevaluation in a later PI.

LEARN MORE

[1] Leffingwell, Dean. *Agile Software Requirements: Lean Requirements Practices for Teams, Programs, and the Enterprise.* Addison-Wesley, 2011.

[2] Reinertsen, Donald. *The Principles of Product Development Flow: Second Generation Lean Product Development.* Celeritas Publishing, 2009.

System Demo

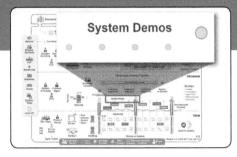

Base milestones on objective evaluation of working systems.

   —*Lean-Agile Principle #5*

The *System Demo* is a significant event that provides an integrated view of new Features for the most recent Iteration delivered by all the teams in the Agile Release Train (ART). Each demo gives ART stakeholders an objective measure of progress during a Program Increment (PI).

A system demo is a critical event. It provides a way to gather immediate, ART-level feedback from the people doing the work—as well as from sponsors, stakeholders, and Customers. The one real measure of value, velocity, and progress is the demo of the fully integrated work from all the teams during the prior iteration.

Planning for and presenting a useful system demo requires some work and preparation by the teams. Despite the effort required, the outcome is worth it: The system demo is the only way to get the fast feedback needed to build the right Solution.

Details

The purpose of the system demo is to test and evaluate the full system in the staging environment in which the ART is working and getting feedback from the primary stakeholders. These stakeholders include Business Owners, executive sponsors, other Agile Teams, development management, and customers (and their proxies) who provide input on the fitness for purpose of the solution under development. Their feedback is critical, as only they can give the guidance the train needs to stay on course or take corrective action, as shown in Figure 1.

The system demo occurs at the end of every iteration. It provides an integrated, comprehensive view of the new features that have been delivered by all the teams on the train in the most recent iteration. It offers the ART a fact-based measure of current, system-level progress within the PI. It's the only real measure of ART velocity. Achieving this intended purpose requires implementing the scalable engineering practices necessary to support integration and synchronization across the ART.

Figure 1. The system demo

At the end of each PI, the ART holds a final PI system demo. This event is a somewhat structured and formal affair, as it demos an increment that includes all the features developed over the course of the PI. This demo is usually part of the Inspect and Adapt (I&A) event, which feeds into the retrospective and various PI progress Metrics, including the 'program predictability measure' and 'program performance metrics.'

The staging environment is best suited to be the venue for the system demo, as this environment usually mirrors production as much as possible. In large value streams, the system demo feeds into the Solution Demo performed by the Solution Train.

Timing of the System Demo

The system demo occurs as close to the end of the iteration as possible—ideally, the next day. In some cases, however, certain complications can make that timing impractical:

- Typically, the results of the full integration effort are available only at the end of the iteration. (Of course, the goal is to strive for Continuous Integration across the entire stack, but that isn't always feasible.)

- Each new increment may require extensions to the demo environment, new interfaces, third-party components, simulation tools, and so forth. Of course, the System Team and the Agile teams can plan for that possibility, but some late-breaking items that may thwart the system demo are inevitable.

Ultimately, though, the system demo must occur within the time bounds of the following iteration. Otherwise, feedback to the teams will be delayed, potentially putting the PI at risk. The ART must make all the necessary investments to allow the system demo to happen in a timely cadence.

Balancing Integration Effort and Feedback

The goal of the system demo is to learn from the most recent development experience and adjust the course of action. However, when the concerns for an ART span software, hardware, mechanical systems, and supplier-provided components, integrating all assets every two weeks may consume too much capacity and create an unacceptable transaction cost. Simply put, continuous integration may not be economical or practical in such environments.

Nevertheless, deferred integration, or no integration at all, is far worse. It significantly inhibits learning and creates a false sense of security and velocity. Thus, if a system demo is not practical, it's critical to find the right balance and to continuously improve integration and testing automation to lower the cost of future integrations. Figure 2 shows a 'U-curve' cost optimization for integration efforts.

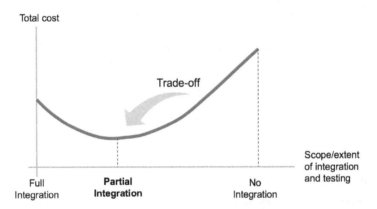

Figure 2. Integration U-curve cost optimization

When full integration at every iteration is too costly, the teams should consider the following options:

- Integrating a subset of Capabilities, components, or subsystems
- Integrating to illustrate a particular feature, capability, or Nonfunctional Requirement (NFR)
- Partial integration with the support of prototypes and mock-ups
- Less frequent integration (e.g., every other iteration) until it's feasible to do it more often

It's also important to remember that continuous integration represents a natural challenge for groups still transitioning to Lean and Agile methods. That's normal and should not be an excuse to reduce the scope or extent of integration. Most of the challenges should disappear as the train matures—but only if the teams start embracing continuous integration as a goal immediately.

Process and Agenda

Having a set agenda and fixed timebox helps lower the transaction costs of the system demo. A sample agenda follows:

- Briefly, review the business context and the PI Objectives (approximately 5–10 minutes)
- Briefly, describe each new feature before demoing it (approximately 5 minutes)
- Demo each new feature in an end-to-end use case (approximately 20–30 minutes total)
- Identify current risks and impediments
- Discuss questions and feedback
- Wrap up by summarizing progress, feedback, and action items

Attendees

Attendees at the system demo typically include the following personnel:

- Product Managers and Product Owners, who are usually responsible for running the demo
- One or more members of the System Team, who are often responsible for setting up the demo in the staging environment
- Business Owners, executive sponsors, customers, and customer proxies
- System Architect/Engineering, IT operations, and other development participants

Following are some tips for a successful system demo:

- Timebox the demo to one hour. A short timebox is critical to maintain the continuous, biweekly involvement of key stakeholders. It also illustrates team professionalism and system readiness.
- Share demo responsibilities among the team leads and Product Owners who have new features to demo.
- Demo features using the staging environment.
- Minimize the use of slides; instead, demonstrate only working, tested solutions.
- Discuss the impact of the current solution on NFRs.

LEARN MORE

[1] Leffingwell, Dean. *Agile Software Requirements: Lean Requirements Practices for Teams, Programs, and the Enterprise.* Addison-Wesley, 2011.

[2] Leffingwell, Dean. *Scaling Software Agility: Best Practices for Large Enterprises.* Addison-Wesley, 2007.

Inspect and Adapt

Kaizen is about changing the way things are. If you assume that things are all right the way they are, you can't do kaizen. So change something!

—Taiichi Ohno

The *Inspect and Adapt (I&A)* workshop is a significant event, held at the end of each Program Increment (PI), in which the current state of the Solution is demonstrated and evaluated by the train. Teams then reflect and identify improvement backlog items via a structured, problem-solving workshop.

One statement from the Agile Manifesto summarizes how important the philosophy of continuous improvement is to the SAFe Lean-Agile approach: "At regular intervals, the team reflects on how to become more effective, then tunes and adjusts its behavior accordingly."

SAFe emphasizes the importance of this philosophy by taking it a step further—that is, by including relentless improvement as one of the four pillars of the SAFe House of Lean. While opportunities to improve can and should occur continuously (e.g., Iteration Retrospectives), applying some structure, cadence, and synchronization helps ensure that time is set aside to consider what can be done better during the Agile Release Train (ART) I&A event.

Details

All program stakeholders participate with the Agile Teams in the ART I&A workshop. The result is a set of improvement backlog items that the teams add to the backlog for the next PI Planning event. In this way, every ART improves every PI. For large solutions, a similar I&A workshop also occurs for the Solution Train.

The I&A workshop consists of three parts:

1. PI System Demo
2. Quantitative measurement
3. Retrospective and problem-solving workshop

Participants in the ART I&A workshop should include, wherever possible, *all* the people involved in building the system:

- The Agile Teams
- Release Train Engineer (RTE)
- System and Solution Architect/Engineering
- Product Management, Business Owners, and others on the train

Additionally, Value Stream stakeholders may attend this workshop.

PI System Demo

The PI System Demo is the first part of the ART I&A workshop. This demo is a little different from the biweekly ones that precede it, in that it is intended to show all the Features that the ART has developed over the course of the PI. Typically, the audience is broader; for example, additional Customer representatives may choose to attend this demo. Therefore, the PI system demo tends to be a little more formal, and some extra preparation and staging are usually required. Like any other system demo, though, it should be timeboxed to an hour or less, with the level of abstraction remaining high enough to keep stakeholders actively engaged and providing feedback.

During the PI system demo, Business Owners, customers, and other vital stakeholders collaborate with each Agile team to rate their actual business value achieved as shown in Figure 1.

Objectives for PI 3	Business Value	
	Plan	Actual
• Structured locations and validation of locations	7	7
• Build and demonstrate a proof of concept for context images	8	8
• Implement negative triangulation by: tags, companies and people	8	6
• Speed up indexing by 50%	10	5
• Index 1.2 billion more web pages	10	8
• Extract and build URL abstracts	7	7
=== *Stretch Objectives* ===		
• Fuzzy search by full name	7	0
• Improve tag quality to 80% relevance	4	4
Totals:	50	45
% Achievement: 90%		

*Figure 1. Business Owners collaborate with each team to rate their
PI objectives during the PI system demo*

Quantitative Measurement

In the second part of the workshop, teams review any quantitative Metrics they have agreed to collect and then discuss these data and any trends. In preparation for this part of the workshop, the RTE and the Solution Train Engineer are often responsible for gathering the necessary information, analyzing it to identify potential issues, and facilitating the presentation of the findings to the ART.

One primary measurement is the program predictability measure. Each team's planned versus actual business value is rolled up to the program level in the program predictability measure, as shown in Figure 2.

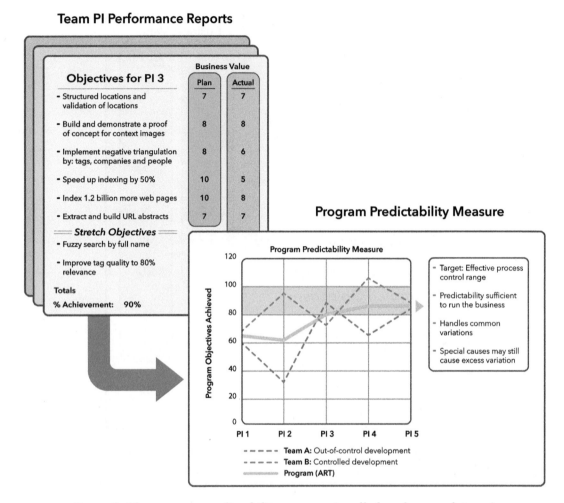

Figure 2. The program predictability measure is rolled up from each team's planned versus actual business value

Reliable trains should operate in the 80–100 percent range; this allows the business and its outside stakeholders to plan effectively. Note that stretch objectives don't count toward the commitment but do count toward the actual score, as can also be seen in Figure 1.

Retrospective

The teams then run a brief (30 minutes or less) retrospective, whose goal is to identify whatever issues they would like to address. There is no one way to do this; several different Agile retrospective formats can be used [3]. The objective of the retrospective is to identify a few significant problems that the teams can potentially address.

Based on the attendees present at the retrospective and the nature of the problems identified, the facilitator helps the group decide which issues they want to tackle. Each team then has a choice of resolving Team Level problems or, more typically, selecting a program-level problem and joining others who wish to work on the same issue. This self-selection helps provide cross-functional and differing views of the problem, and it seeds the problem-solving workshop with those who are most likely to be impacted and those who are best motivated to address the issue.

Key ART stakeholders—including Business Owners, customers, and management—join the teams in the retrospective and problem-solving workshop that follow. Often the Business Owners, acting alone, can unblock the impediments that exist outside the team's control.

Problem-Solving Workshop

To address program-level problems, the ART holds a structured, root cause problem-solving workshop. Root cause analysis provides a set of problem-solving tools that can be used to identify the actual causes of a problem, rather than just addressing the symptoms. This session is typically facilitated by the RTE, or another facilitator, in a timebox of two hours or less. Figure 3 illustrates the steps in the problem-solving workshop and the following sections describe each step in more detail.

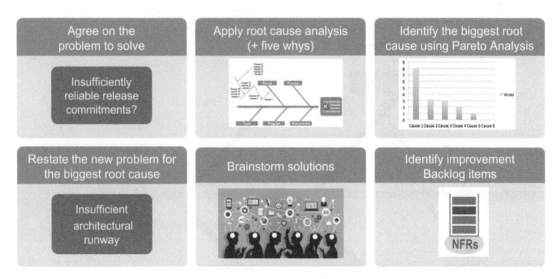

Figure 3. Problem-solving workshop format

Agree on the Problem(s) to Solve

American inventor Charles Kettering is credited with the statement that "a problem well stated is a problem half solved." At this point, the teams have self-selected the problem they want to address. But do they agree on what the problem is, or (more likely) do they have differing perspectives? To clarify their understanding, the teams should spend a few minutes stating the problem, thinking about the what, where, when, and impact as succinctly as they can. Figure 4 illustrates a Baja Ride systems engineering example.

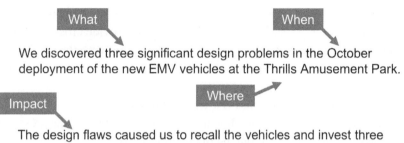

What

When

We discovered three significant design problems in the October deployment of the new EMV vehicles at the Thrills Amusement Park.

Where

Impact

The design flaws caused us to recall the vehicles and invest three months in materials, redesign, and testing. We delivered late, paid substantial penalties, and lost credibility with the customer.

Concept contributed by Beth Miller

Figure 4. Example problem statement

Perform Root Cause Analysis

Effective problem-solving tools include the fishbone diagram and the 'Five Whys.' Also known as an Ishikawa Diagram, a fishbone diagram is a visual tool that is used to explore the causes of specific events or sources of variation in a process. Figure 5 illustrates the fishbone diagram, in which the problem statement is written at the head of the 'fish.'

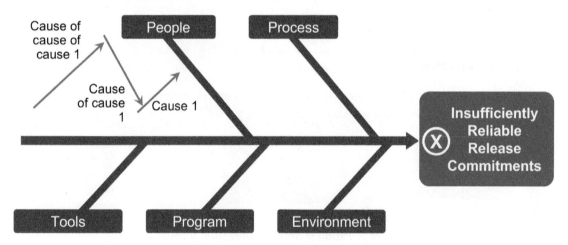

Figure 5. Fishbone diagram with major sources identified

In the problem-solving workshop, this diagram is preloaded with the main bones—that is, the categories of people, process, tools, program, and environment. Causes are identified and then grouped into categories as bones off the main bone. However, these may be adapted as appropriate.

Team members then brainstorm factors that they think contribute to the problem to be solved. Once a root cause is identified, its cause is identified with the 'Five Whys' technique. By simply asking why as many as five times, each cause-of-a-cause becomes easier to discover and can be added to the diagram.

Identify the Biggest Root Cause
Pareto Analysis, also known as the 80/20 rule, is a technique used to narrow down the number of actions that produce the most significant overall effect. It uses the principle that 20 percent of the causes are responsible for 80 percent of the problem. Pareto analysis is especially useful when many possible courses of action are competing for attention, which is almost always the case with complex, systemic issues.

Once all the possible causes-of-causes have been identified, team members cumulatively vote on the item they think is the most significant factor causing the end problem. They can do this by placing stars (five stars are allocated to each group member, which can be spread among one or more items as they see fit) on the causes they think are most problematic. The team then summarizes the votes in a Pareto chart (as shown in Figure 6), which illustrates their collective consensus on the most significant root cause.

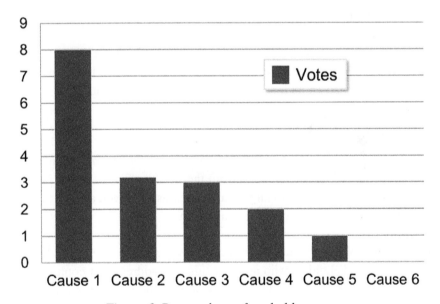

Figure 6. Pareto chart of probable causes

Restate the New Problem
The next step is to pick the largest cause from the list and restate it clearly as a problem. This should take only a few minutes or so, as the teams are very close the root cause now.

Brainstorm Solutions

At this point, the root cause will start to imply some potential solutions. The working group brainstorms as many possible corrective actions as they can think of within a fixed timebox (about 15–30 minutes). The rules of brainstorming apply here:

- Generate as many ideas as possible.

- Do not allow criticism or debate.

- Let the imagination soar.

- Explore and combine ideas.

Create Improvement Backlog Items

The team then cumulatively votes on up to three most likely solutions. These solutions will serve as improvement stories and features to be fed directly into the PI planning session that follows. During that session, the RTE helps ensure that the relevant improvement stories are loaded onto the iteration plans, thereby ensuring that action will be taken and resources allocated to them, as with any other backlog item. This closes the loop on the retrospective and ensures that people and resources are dedicated as necessary to improve the current state.

In this way, problem-solving becomes routine and systematic at both the program and large solution levels. Team members, program stakeholders, and large solution stakeholders can be assured that the value stream is solidly launched on its journey of relentless improvement.

Inspect and Adapt for the Solution Train

The preceding sections described a rigorous approach to problem-solving in the context of a single ART. The ART I&A often includes key stakeholders from the Solution Train, which is the recommended path to facilitate solution development. In larger value streams, however, an additional Solution Train I&A workshop may be required, following the same format.

Due to the number of people in a Solution Train, not everyone can attend the Solution Train I&A workshop. Instead, those stakeholders who are best suited to address that context are invited to participate. This group includes the primary stakeholders of the Solution Train, as well as representatives from the ARTs and Suppliers.

LEARN MORE

[1] Leffingwell, Dean. *Agile Software Requirements: Lean Requirements Practices for Teams, Programs, and the Enterprise.* Addison-Wesley, 2011.

[2] Leffingwell, Dean. *Scaling Software Agility: Best Practices for Large Enterprises.* Addison-Wesley, 2007.

[3] Derby, Esther, and Diana Larsen. *Agile Retrospectives: Making Good Teams Great.* Pragmatic Bookshelf, 2006.

Program and Solution Kanban

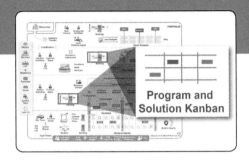

It is said that improvement is eternal and infinite. It should be the duty of those working with Kanban to keep improving it with creativity and resourcefulness without allowing it to become fixed at any stage.

—Taiichi Ohno

The *Program and Solution Kanban* systems are a method to visualize and manage the flow of Features and Capabilities from ideation to analysis, implementation, and release through the Continuous Delivery Pipeline. The Kanban systems help Agile Release Trains (ARTs) and Solution Trains match demand to capacity based on Work in Process (WIP) limits, and visualizing bottlenecks in each process state helps identify opportunities for *relentless improvement* described in the SAFe House of Lean (see the Lean-Agile Mindset chapter). The Kanban system also includes policies governing the entry and exit of work items in each state.

Details

Implementation and management of the program and solution Kanban systems occur with the support of Product and Solution Management. Implementing the Kanban systems requires an understanding of Lean and Agile development and how capacity is available for new development, business-as-usual maintenance, and support activities. When these issues are well understood, the Enterprise can then evaluate Program and Large Solution level initiatives logically and pragmatically, supporting their analysis and forecasted timing for implementation based on Metrics.

Kanban systems are the primary mechanism to achieve SAFe Principle #6, Visualize and limit WIP, reduce batch sizes, and manage queue length, as well as the Lean concept of flow. These systems provide many benefits:

- Increase visibility into existing and upcoming work, and help teams better understand the flow of work

- Ensure continuous refinement of new value definition and acceptance criteria

- Foster collaboration across disciplines, functions, and levels

- Support economic decision-making by setting the policies for the pull-based mechanism

- Establish connections between the ARTs, Solution Train, and Portfolio

The Program Kanban

The program Kanban facilitates the flow of *features* through the continuous delivery pipeline. Figure 1 illustrates a typical program Kanban, as well as example policies and WIP limits governing each state.

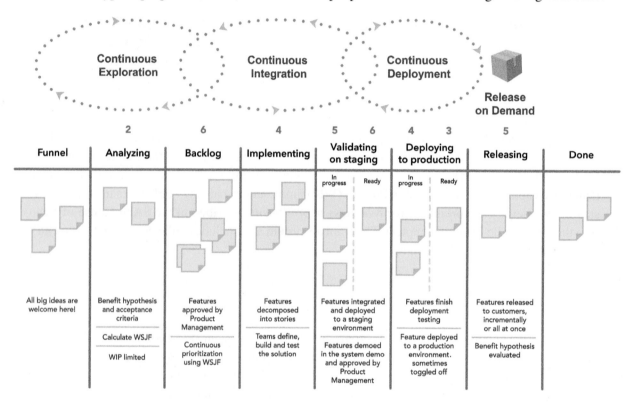

Figure 1. A typical program Kanban

Features begin with Continuous Exploration and may originate locally from the ART or come from an upstream Kanban (e.g., solution or Portfolio Kanban). The local content authority, Product Management, and System Architects collectively manage this Kanban. The following process states describe its flow:

- **Funnel** – All new features are welcome here. They may include new functionality, enhancement of the existing system functions, or Enabler features.

- **Analyzing** – New features that align with the Vision and support the Strategic Themes are further explored by Agile Teams when they have available capacity. Refinement includes collaboration to define a feature's description, business benefit hypothesis, acceptance criteria, and size in normalized story points. The feature may require prototyping or other forms of exploration by Agile Teams. The WIP limit for this state must account for the availability of Product Management, the capacity of teams and other subject-matter experts.

- **Program Backlog** – The highest-priority features that were analyzed and approved by Product Management advance to this state, where they are prioritized, using the Weighted Shortest Job First (WSJF) model, relative to the rest of the backlog, and await implementation.

- **Implementing** – At every Program Increment (PI) boundary, the ART pulls the top features from the program backlog and moves them into the implementing state. Through the PI Planning process, these features are split into stories, planned into iterations, and subsequently implemented by teams during the PI.

- **Validating on staging** – At the end of every iteration, while the ART prepares for the System Demo, features that are ready for feedback get pulled into this state. The teams integrate and test them with the rest of the system in a staging environment (or its closest proxy), and the features are presented to Product Management and other stakeholders for approval at the system demo. Approved features move to the 'ready' part of this state, where they are prioritized again using WSJF to await deployment.

- **Deploying to production** – When capacity becomes available for deployment activities (or immediately in a fully automated continuous delivery environment), the feature gets moved to production. If it's deployed but turned off (see the Release on Demand chapter for more details), then it moves to the 'ready' part of this state to await release. This state is WIP limited to avoid the buildup of features that are deployed but not yet released.

- **Releasing** – When there's sufficient value, market need, and opportunity, features are released to some or all of the customers. At that point, evaluation of the benefit hypothesis happens. While the feature moves to the 'done' state, new work items may be created to support the Minimum Viable Products (MVPs) and Minimal Marketable Features (MMFs).

The Kanban system described here provides a good starting point for most ARTs. However, it should be customized to fit the ART's process, including the definition of WIP limits and the specific policies for each process state.

Program Epic Kanban

Some ART initiatives are simply too big to be completed in a single PI. These initiatives, known as Program Epics, are instead identified and managed in a separate Kanban system, as shown in Figure 2. Also, some portfolio epics may need to be split into solution and program epics to facilitate their incremental implementation. While mainly a local concern, program or solution epics may have impacts on financial, human, and other resources that are large enough to warrant a Lean business case, discussion, and financial approval from Lean Portfolio Management (LPM). That's what makes an epic 'an epic.'

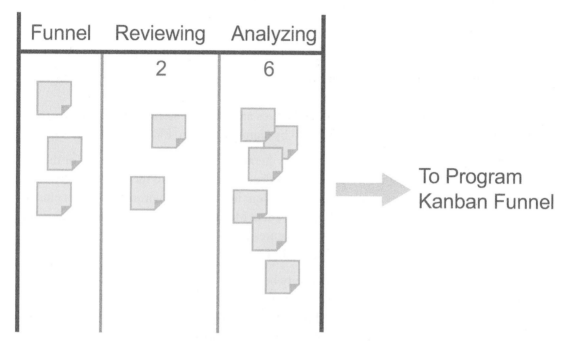

Figure 2. A typical program epic Kanban

The primary purpose of this Kanban system is to analyze and approve program epics, splitting them into features that will be further explored and implemented using the program Kanban. Depending on how frequently program epics occur in the local context of the ART, this Kanban system may not be required.

A program Kanban typically requires the engagement of large solution or portfolio stakeholders to explore and approve the program epics. The process states in this Kanban usually follow those in the Portfolio Kanban:

- **Funnel** – All big program initiatives are welcome in the 'funnel' state. There is no WIP limit.

- **Reviewing** – Subject-matter experts and stakeholders perform the review of the epics and prioritize them using WSJF to determine which ones should move on for more in-depth exploration. Again, WIP limits apply.

- **Analyzing** – During this diagnostic and exploration state, subject-matter experts and stakeholders are encouraged to:

  - Refine size estimates and WSJF relative to other epics

  - Consider solution alternatives

  - Identify possible MVPs and MMFs

  - Determine the costs, technology and architectural enablement, and infrastructure involved, using a Lean business case

Guided by analysis and insights, Business Owners (and typically Lean Portfolio Management personnel) approve or reject the epics. Approved epics then get split into features and transitioned to the funnel of the program Kanban, where they are prioritized based on WSJF. WIP limits also apply to the analyzing state.

As in the portfolio level, program epics may require Epic Owners to help with their definition, exploration, and implementation.

Managing the Program Kanban with the ART Sync

One significant program event is the ART sync meeting, in which Scrum Masters and Product Owners review the program Kanban system and pull in more work based on the available capacity at each state. Participants discuss new work, prioritize work, and make deployment and release decisions as needed.

In addition, the Program Board (see the PI Planning chapter) facilitates reviewing items in the 'implementing' state, including discussion of dependencies and execution.

The Solution Kanban Systems

This chapter has described the program Kanban systems in depth. For organizations using the Large Solution level or configuration, the *solution Kanban* follows the same structure and process used for the program level. However, Solution Management and Solution Architects manage this Kanban, which operates with Capabilities instead of features. Also, where useful, Solution Trains employ a *Solution Epic Kanban* for solution epics that mirror the program epic Kanban.

DevOps

Imagine a world where product owners, Development, QA, IT Operations, and Infosec work together, not only to help each other, but also to ensure that the overall organization succeeds. By working toward a common goal, they enable the fast flow of planned work into production, while achieving world-class stability, reliability, availability, and security.

—The DevOps Handbook

DevOps is a mindset, a culture, and a set of technical practices. It provides communication, integration, automation, and close cooperation among all the people needed to plan, develop, test, deploy, release, and maintain a Solution.

SAFe enterprises implement DevOps to break down silos and empower each Agile Release Train (ART) and Solution Train to continuously deliver new Features to their end users. Over time, the separation between development and operations is significantly reduced, and trains operate with an automated Continuous Delivery Pipeline. This mechanism seamlessly defines, implements, and delivers solution elements to the end user, without handoffs or excessive external production or operations support.

The goal is simple: Deliver value more frequently. This is indeed achievable, as "high-performing IT organizations deploy 30 × more frequently with 200 × shorter lead times. … [and] 60 × fewer failures and recover 168 × faster" [1].

Details

DevOps is a combination of two words, *development* and *operations*. Without a DevOps approach, there's often significant tension between those who create new features and those who maintain the stability of the production environment. The development team is measured on the business value delivered to end users, while IT service management is measured on the health and stability of the production environment. When each group has seemingly opposing business objectives, delivery inefficiency and organizational friction may rule the day.

DevOps ends this silo approach, thereby providing an enterprise with the ability to develop and release small batches of functionality to the business or customer in a flow process called the continuous delivery pipeline. DevOps is integral to every Value Stream and, by definition, is integral to SAFe.

Many SAFe concepts and principles—systems thinking, small batch sizes, short iterations, fast feedback, and more—directly support DevOps principles. In addition, the SAFe practices of Continuous Exploration, Continuous Integration (CI), Continuous Deployment, and Release on Demand directly support this business need.

The Goal of DevOps

From planning through delivery, the goal of DevOps is to improve collaboration between Development and IT Operations by developing and automating a continuous delivery pipeline. In doing so, DevOps:

- Increases the frequency and quality of deployments

- Improves innovation and risk-taking by making it safer to experiment

- Achieves faster time to market

- Improves solution quality and shortens the lead time for fixes

- Reduces the severity and frequency of release failures

- Improves the Mean Time to Recovery (MTTR)

SAFe's CALMR approach to DevOps covers the five main aspects of the DevOps environment (Figure 1). Each aspect is described in the following sections.

Figure 1. SAFe's CALMR approach to DevOps

Culture of Shared Responsibility

In SAFe, DevOps leverages the culture created by adopting the Lean-Agile values, principles, and practices of the entire framework. Just about every principle of SAFe—from Principle #1, Take an economic view, to Principle #9, Decentralize decision-making—applies to DevOps. Adoption of this perspective allows some operating responsibilities to be shifted upstream, while following development work downstream into deployment, and operating and monitoring the solution in production. Such a culture includes the following characteristics:

- **Collaboration and organization** – DevOps relies on the ability of Agile teams and IT Operations teams to collaborate effectively in an ongoing manner, ensuring that solutions are developed and delivered more rapidly and more reliably. This cohesiveness is achieved, in part, by including operations personnel and capabilities on every ART.

- **Risk tolerance** – DevOps requires a tolerance for failure and rapid recovery and rewards risk-taking.

- **Self-service infrastructures** – Infrastructure empowers development and operations to act independently without blocking each other.

- **Knowledge sharing** – Sharing discoveries, practices, tools, and learning across silos is encouraged.

- **Automate everything mindset** – DevOps relies heavily on automation to provide speed, consistency, and repeatable processes and environment creation, as described in the next section.

Automate Everything

DevOps simply recognizes that manual processes are the enemy of fast value delivery, high productivity, and safety. But automation is not just about saving time: It also enables the creation of repeatable environments and processes that are self-documenting and, therefore, easier to understand, improve, secure, and audit. The entire continuous delivery pipeline is automated to achieve a fast, Lean flow.

Automation facilitates faster learning and responses to market demand and customer feedback. Builds, testing, deployments, and packaging that are automated improve the reliability of processes that can be made routine.

This goal is accomplished, in part, by building and applying an integrated and automated 'tool chain' shown in Figure 2. This chain typically contains the following categories of tools:

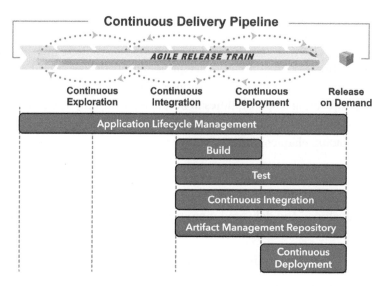

Figure 2. DevOps tool chain within the CD Pipeline

- **Application Life Cycle Management (ALM)** – Application and Agile life-cycle management tools create a standardized environment for communication and collaboration between development teams and related groups. Model-Based Systems Engineering provides similar information in many contexts.

- **Artifact Management Repository** – These tools provide a software repository for storing and versioning binary files and their associated metadata.

- **Build** – Build automation is used to script or automate the process of compiling computer source code into binary code.

- **Testing** – Automated testing tools include unit and acceptance testing, performance testing, and load testing.

- **Continuous integration** – CI tools automate the process of compiling code into a build after developers have checked their code into a central repository. After the CI server builds the system, it runs unit and integration tests, reports results, and typically releases a labeled version of deployable artifacts.

- **Continuous deployment** – Deployment tools automate application deployments to the various environments. They facilitate rapid feedback and continuous delivery while providing the required audit trails, versioning, and approval tracking.

- **Additional tools** –Numerous other important DevOps support tools are available: configuration, logging, management and monitoring, provisioning, source code control, security, code review, and collaboration.

Lean Flow

SAFe teams strive to achieve a state of continuous flow, enabling new features to move quickly from concept to cash. The three primary keys to implementing flow are summarized in Principle #6: Visualize and limit WIP, reduce batch sizes, and manage queue lengths. All three are integral to systems thinking (Principle #2) and long-term optimization. Each is described next in the DevOps context.

- **Visualize and limit Work in Process (WIP)** – Figure 3 illustrates an example Program Kanban board, which makes WIP visible to all stakeholders. This board helps teams identify bottlenecks and balance the amount of WIP against the available development and operations capacity, as work is completed when the new feature or functionality is running successfully in production.

- **Reduce the batch sizes of work items** – Another way to improve flow is to decrease the batch sizes of the work. Small batches go through the system faster and with less variability, which fosters faster learning and deployment. This strategy typically involves focusing more attention on and increasing investment in infrastructure and automation. It also reduces the transaction cost of each batch.

- **Manage queue lengths** – Faster flow may also be achieved by managing, and generally reducing, queue lengths. For solution development, this means that the longer the queue of work awaiting implementation or deployment, the longer the wait time, no matter how efficiently the team is processing the work. Conversely, the shorter the queue, the faster the deployment.

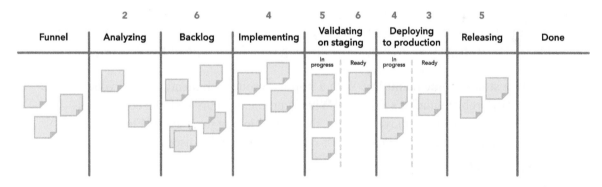

Figure 3. The program Kanban helps visualize and limit WIP

Measure the Flow of Value

In a DevOps environment, problem resolution is less complex, because changes are made more frequently and in smaller batches. Telemetry—that is, automated collection of real-time data related to the performance of solutions—helps the teams quickly assess the impact of frequent application changes. Resolution happens faster because teams don't need to wait for a different group to troubleshoot and fix the problem.

It's important to implement application telemetry to automatically collect data on the business and technical performance of the solution. Indeed, basing decisions on data, where 'the facts are always friendly,' rather than on intuition, leads to an objective, blameless path toward improvement. Data should be transparent, accessible to everyone, meaningful, and easily visualized so as to spot problems and trends.

The goal is to build applications that perform the following functions:

- Collect data on business, application, infrastructure, and client layers
- Store logs in ways that enable analysis
- Use different telemetry for different stakeholders
- Broadcast measurements and are hyper-transparent
- Overlay measurements with events (deploys, releases)
- Continuously improve telemetry during and after problem-solving

It's also important to measure the flow of value through the continuous delivery pipeline. See the Metrics chapter for specific recommendations on DevOps measures.

Recover: Enable Low-Risk Releases

To support the continuous delivery pipeline and the concept of Release on Demand, the system must be designed for low-risk component or service-based deployability, releasability, and fast recovery from operational failure. Techniques to achieve a more flexible release process are described in the Release on Demand chapter. In addition, the following techniques support fast recovery:

- **Have a stop-the-line mentality.** With a stop-the-production mentality, everyone swarms to fix any problem until it's resolved. When a problem occurs with the continuous delivery pipeline or a deployed system, the same thinking must apply. Findings are integrated immediately into the process or product as they're discovered.

- **Plan for and rehearse failures.** When it comes to large-scale IT applications, failure is not just an option, but it is actually guaranteed at some point. A proactive approach to experiencing failures will increase the team's response practices and foster built-in resilience into the systems. (See the 'Chaos Monkey' discussion in [2]).

- **Build the environment and capability to fix forward or roll back.** Since mistakes will be made and servers will fail, teams need to develop the capability to quickly 'fix forward' and, where necessary, roll back to a prior known good state. In the latter case, planning and investment must be made to revert any data changes back to the prior state, without losing any user transactions that occurred during the process.

To achieve these recovery capabilities, the organization will typically need to undertake certain enterprise-level initiatives to enhance architecture, infrastructure, and other nonfunctional considerations to support deployment readiness, release, and production.

LEARN MORE

[1] Kim, Gene, Jez Humble, Patrick Debois, and John Willis. *The DevOps Handbook: How to Create World-Class Agility, Reliability, and Security in Technology Organizations*. IT Revolution Press, 2016.

[2] 2015 State of DevOps Report. https://puppet.com/resources/whitepaper/2015-state-devops-report?link=blog.

Continuous Delivery Pipeline

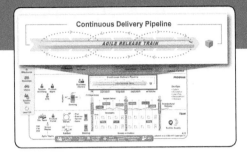

Our highest priority is to satisfy the customer through early and continuous delivery of valuable software.

—Agile Manifesto

The Continuous Delivery Pipeline (also referred to as 'the pipeline') represents the workflows, activities, and automation needed to provide a continuous release of value to the end user. The pipeline consists of four elements: Continuous Exploration (CE), Continuous Integration (CI), Continuous Deployment (CD), and Release on Demand, as shown in Figure 1.

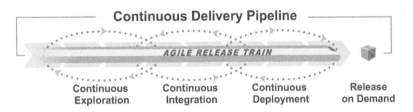

Figure 1. The SAFe continuous delivery pipeline

Each Agile Release Train (ART) builds and maintains (or shares) a pipeline with the assets and technologies needed to deliver solution value as independently as possible. The first three elements of the pipeline work together to support delivery of small batches of new functionality, which are then released in accordance with market demand.

Details

The Continuous Delivery Pipeline represents the ability to deliver new functionality to users far more frequently than is possible with the currently used processes. For some software systems, 'continuous' means daily releases or even releasing multiple times per day. For others, 'continuous' may mean weekly or monthly releases.

For large and complex systems, releasing the solution incrementally avoids taking an 'all-or-nothing' approach. Consider a satellite system consisting of the satellite, the ground station, and a web farm to feed the acquired satellite data to end users. Some elements may be released continuously—perhaps the web farm functionality. Other elements, such as the hardware components of the satellite itself, may be released only once per launch cycle.

In a sense, then, continuous delivery means what you need it to mean—*as long as the goal is to deliver far more frequently than is happening now*. In our satellite example, the more capability that gets moved to software, the more continuous the delivery can become, as those elements can then be decoupled from physical launch constraints. In all cases, the goal should be clear: more frequent delivery of value to the end user.

Fostering Innovation with the Lean Startup Cycle

The Lean Startup [1] movement has captured the imagination of business and technical leaders around the world. Inspired in part by the emergence of Agile methods, Lean Startup advocates recognized that Big Design Up-Front (BDUF), in tandem with big financial commitment up-front, is a poor way to foster innovation. Such an approach assumes and commits too much time, people, and resources before having any validated learning.

Instead, the Lean Startup movement embraces the highly iterative 'hypothesize–build–measure–learn' cycle, which fits quite naturally into SAFe. Specifically, we can apply this model to any Epic, whether it arises at the Portfolio, Large Solution, or Program Level. No matter the source, the scope of an epic calls for a sensible and iterative approach to investment and implementation, as reflected in Figure 2.

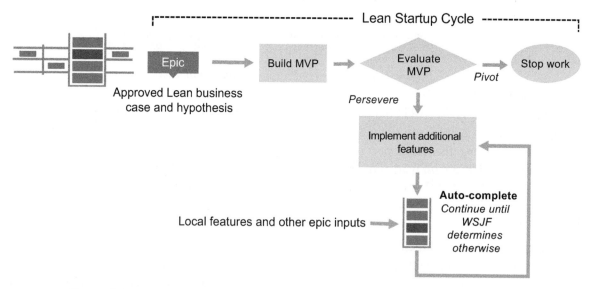

Figure 2. Iterative and incremental approach for epics in the Lean Startup cycle

As Figure 2 implies, approved epics deserve additional investment—but not a fully committed investment up-front. After all, the work up to that point has been analytical and exploratory. The proof is in validated learning, and for that, we need to apply the steps in the hypothesize–build–measure–learn cycle:

- **Hypothesize** – Each epic has a Lean business case, which includes the hypothesis that describes the assumptions and potential measures that can be used to assess whether an epic will deliver business value commensurate with the investment needed to complete that epic.

- **Build an MVP** – Based on the hypothesis of the epic, the next step is to implement a Minimum Viable Product (MVP)—that is, the minimum effort necessary to sufficiently validate or invalidate the hypothesis. In SAFe, this translates to the minimum Feature set required to deliver some holistic, but minimal, solution.

- **Evaluate the MVP** – Once the feature set is implemented, teams evaluate the MVP against the hypothesis. However, this evaluation is not based on Return on Investment (ROI), as that is a trailing economic indicator. Instead, teams apply 'innovation accounting' [1] and design the systems to provide fast feedback on the leading indicators of future success. These indicators might include usage statistics, system performance, or anything else that would be a useful metric.

- **Pivot or persevere** – With the objective evidence in hand, teams and stakeholders can decide what to do next. Specifically, should they *pivot*—stop doing that work and start doing something else—or should they *persevere*—define features to further develop and refine the innovation?

- **Implement additional features** – Choosing to persevere means work continues until new epic-inspired features that hit the backlog can't compete with other features. This will occur naturally when the Weighted Shortest Job First (WSJF) model is used. WSJF also has the unique advantage of ignoring sunk costs on the epic to date, as the job size includes only the work remaining.

The Continuous Delivery Pipeline Learning Cycle

In short, the pipeline doesn't operate in a strict linear sequence. Rather, it's a learning cycle that allows teams to establish a number of hypotheses, build a solution to test each hypothesis, and learn from that work, as depicted in Figure 3.

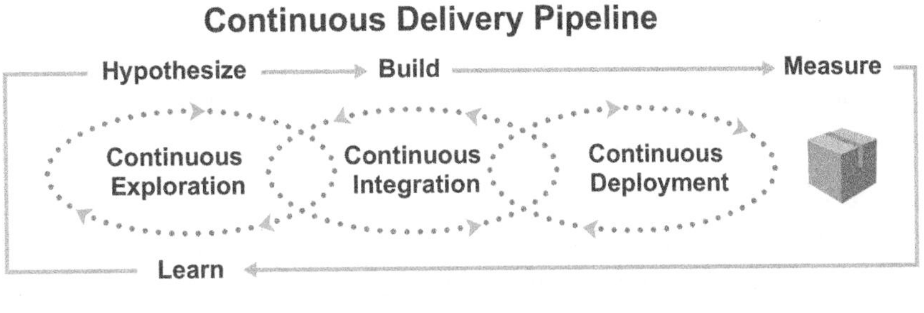

Continuous Delivery Pipeline

Hypothesize ⟶ Build ⟶ Measure

Continuous Exploration · Continuous Integration · Continuous Deployment

Learn ⟵

Figure 3. The continuous delivery pipeline is a mechanism for continuous learning and value delivery

Now, let's move on to summarizing the activities of continuous exploration, continuous integration, continuous deployment, and release on demand.

Continuous Exploration

Continuous exploration is the process of constantly exploring the market and user needs and defining a Vision and a set of features that address them. This process is summarized in Figure 4.

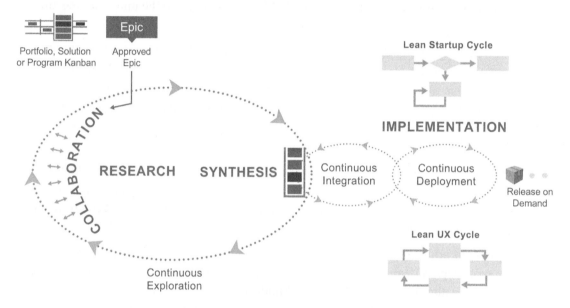

Figure 4. Summary of the continuous exploration cycle

This cycle includes four major elements:

- **Collaboration** – Product Management enables and facilitates a continuous and collaborative process that solicits input from a diverse group of stakeholders. These stakeholders include Customers, Agile Teams, Product Owners, Business Owners, portfolio epics, and System and Solution Architects/Engineering.

- **Research** – In addition to the direct input, Product Management uses a variety of research activities and techniques to help establish the vision. These include customer visits, Gemba walks, active requirements, elicitation techniques, trade studies, and original and applied market research.

- **Synthesize** – Product Management synthesizes their findings into the key SAFe artifacts—namely, the vision, Roadmap, and Program Backlog. The net result is a set of features in the backlog that are ready for implementation.

- **Implementation** – Now the work of implementation begins. At the strategic level, work follows the Lean Startup cycle, which consists of an initial MVP feature set, followed by additional features until the higher priorities of other work take over.

Continuous Integration

The next cycle in the pipeline is continuous integration—the process of taking features from the program backlog and developing, testing, integrating, and finally validating them in a staging environment. Each feature implementation follows the Lean UX cycle [3], producing an initial Minimum Marketable Feature (MMF), followed by whatever extensions deliver appropriate and additional economic value.

Continuous integration often requires a three-tier approach: story integration, system integration, and solution integration, as shown in Figure 5.

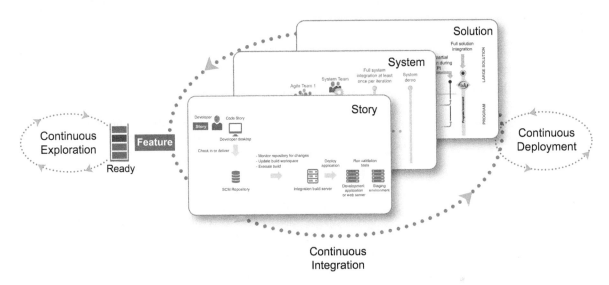

Figure 5. Three-tier continuous integration

Story Integration

Since features are too abstract to be coded directly, they must be converted into Stories during PI Planning. Each story is defined, coded, tested, and integrated into the baseline. Team members integrate their individual work frequently and apply automated continuous integration environments. To ensure that the new stories are compatible with the existing functionality, the overall system must be continually tested as well. Thus, teams apply automated testing and Test-First Development.

System Integration

Agile teams implement the features and components for which they are responsible. Of course, that isn't enough to ensure compatibility and overall progress. With the support of the System Team, the work of all teams on the ART must be integrated frequently to assure that the *system* is evolving as anticipated. At the all-important System Demo, this small batch of work is evaluated objectively.

Solution Integration

Finally, the largest solutions require an additional level of integration, as the work from all ARTs and Suppliers must be integrated together. In the Solution Demo event, the results are made visible to the customer and other stakeholders. To be able to routinely perform solution demos, ARTs and Solution Trains invest in solution-level integration, testing, and supporting infrastructure. Even then, the extent of integration and testing may be less than 100 percent and may need to vary across multiple early integration points.

Continuous Deployment

Continuous deployment is the process that takes features that have passed through continuous exploration and continuous integration and deploys them into the staging and production environments, where those features are readied for release.

Figure 6 identifies six general practices that can help an organization implement a continuous deployment environment and process. The labels for each of these practices are somewhat self-explanatory. Each is described in further detail in the Continuous Deployment chapter.

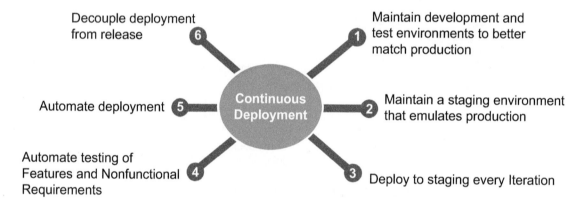

Figure 6. Six recommended practices for continuous deployment

Release on Demand

Release on Demand is the process that releases deployed features gradually or immediately to customers and evaluates the hypothesis from the continuous exploration stage. But, as we describe in the Release on Demand chapter, continuously releasing is not always automatic. Nor is it an 'all-or-nothing' proposition, as Figure 7 illustrates.

Instead, elements of the system are released as they become available and as the market demands. This approach is further facilitated by contemporary release strategies, including techniques such as feature toggles, dark releases, and canary releases [4], all of which are described in the Release on Demand chapter.

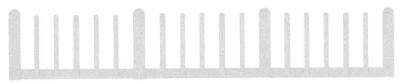

Develop on cadence

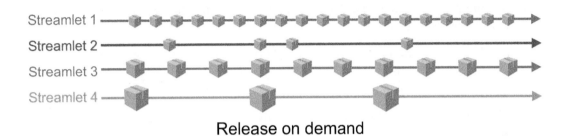

Release on demand

Figure 7. Develop on cadence, but release on demand

Tracking Continuous Delivery

When viewed as a whole, continuous delivery is an extensive process. Indeed, it may be the most important capability of every ART and Solution Train. And while it's automated to the extent possible, it's important that stakeholders can visualize and track the ongoing work. They need the ability to establish Work in Process (WIP) limits to improve throughput and identify and address bottlenecks. That's the role of the Program Kanban, as shown in Figure 8.

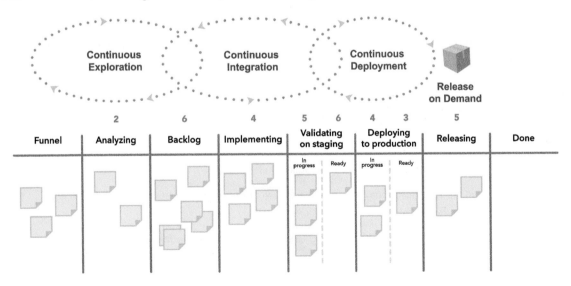

Figure 8. An example program Kanban

The Kanban systems consist of the following series of states:

- **Funnel** – This is the capture state for all new features or enhancement of existing system features.

- **Analyzing** – Features that best align with the vision are pulled into the analyzing step for further exploration. Here they're refined with key attributes, including the business benefit hypothesis and acceptance criteria.

- **Program backlog** – After analysis, higher-priority features move to the backlog, where they're prioritized.

- **Implementing** – At every Program Increment (PI) boundary, top features from the program backlog are pulled into the implementing stage, where they're developed and integrated into the system baseline.

- **Validating on staging** – Features that are ready for feedback get pulled into the validating on staging step to be integrated with the rest of the system in a staging environment and are then tested and validated.

- **Deploying to production** – When capacity is available, features are deployed into the production environment, where they await release.

- **Releasing** – When sufficient value meets market opportunity, features are released and the benefit hypothesis is evaluated.

- **Done** – When the hypothesis has been satisfied, no further work on the feature is necessary, so it moves to the done column.

Summary

Together, continuous exploration, continuous integration, continuous deployment, and release on demand provide an integrated Lean and Agile strategy for rapidly accelerating the releases of value to the customer.

LEARN MORE

[1] Manifesto for Agile Software Development. http://agilemanifesto.org/.

[2] Ries, Eric. *The Lean Startup: How Today's Entrepreneurs Use Continuous Innovation to Create Radically Successful Businesses*. Random House. Kindle Edition.

[3] Gothelf, Jeff, and Josh Seiden. *Lean UX: Designing Great Products with Agile Teams*. O'Reilly Media. Kindle Edition.

[4] Kim, Gene, Jez Humble, Patrick Debois, and John Willis. *The DevOps Handbook: How to Create World-Class Agility, Reliability, and Security in Technology Organizations*. IT Revolution Press, 2016.

Continuous Exploration

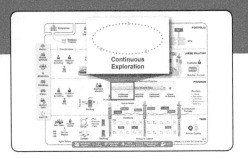

Specifically, you can take the time to develop and bring to the table an outside-in, market-centric perspective that is so compelling and so well informed that it can counterbalance the inside-out company-centric orientation of last year's operating plan.

—Geoffrey Moore, Escape Velocity

Continuous Exploration (CE) is the process of continually exploring the various market and user needs, and defining a Vision, Roadmap, and set of Features that address those needs. It's the first element in the four-part Continuous Delivery Pipeline, as shown in Figure 1.

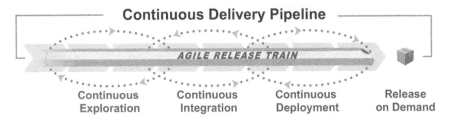

Figure 1. Continuous exploration is the first element of the continuous delivery pipeline

New features are initially captured and defined during the continuous exploration process. When each feature is ready, it is entered into the Program Backlog, and the continuous integration process pulls the highest-priority features into implementation. Thereafter, the continuous deployment cycle pulls the features into the staging or deployment environment, where they are validated and made ready for release.

Inputs to continuous exploration come from Customers, Agile Teams, Product Owners, Business Owners, stakeholders, and portfolio concerns. Under the direction of Product Management, various research and analysis activities are used to further define and evaluate each feature. The result of this process is a set of outputs, including the vision, a set of features in the backlog sufficiently defined for implementation, and a preliminary roadmap forecast of how those features might be delivered over time.

Details

SAFe avoids the traditional 'waterfall' approach to development, thereby eliminating the extensive up-front definition of the work to be done. Instead, it applies a continuous exploration process, providing a consistent flow of new work that is sufficiently ready for the teams to implement. This way, new functionality is available in small batches that can travel easily through continuous integration, continuous deployment, and on to release.

Continuous Exploration Process

The continuous exploration process may be considered to consist of three separate activities—collaborate, research, and synthesize, as shown in Figure 2.

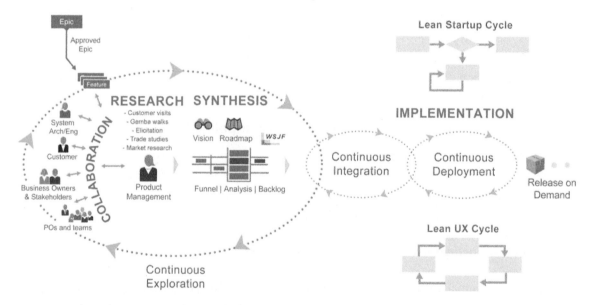

Figure 2. Continuous exploration process

Collaborate

To create a compelling and differentiated vision, Product Management enables and facilitates a continuous and collaborative process that solicits input from a diverse group of stakeholders. Primary sources of input include the following collaborators:

- **System Architects/Engineers** – System Architects/Engineers have in-depth technical knowledge of the solution and are responsible for understanding it at the system level, as well as its 'use cases' and Nonfunctional Requirements (NFRs). Although it's natural to view these roles as technically and internally inclined, the most capable—in our experience—also involve significant and ongoing customer engagement.

- **Customers** – By voting with their wallets or their feet, customers are the ultimate judge of value. They're the most obvious and primary source of input. But a note of caution is warranted: Customers are heavily bound to their current solution context, so they are often motivated to improve things incrementally. In other words, the sum total of customer input does not a strategy make. At the same time, failing to meet real and evolving customer needs sets an organization on the path to extinction. A sense of balance is required. As the SAFe Lean-Agile mindset says, "Producers innovate. Customers validate."

- **Business Owners and stakeholders** – Business Owners have the business and market knowledge needed to set the mission and vision. They also have specific responsibilities throughout the development process. A solution that doesn't meet their expectations is probably no solution at all.

- **POs and teams** – Product Owners and teams include some of the foremost experts in the domain. In most cases, they developed the existing solution and are closest to both technical and user concerns. Their input is integral and invaluable.

Agile Release Trains (ARTs) operate in a larger portfolio context. Strategic Themes drive new Epics to improve portfolio differentiation.

Research

In addition to this direct input, Product Management uses a variety of research activities and techniques to help establish the vision:

- **Customer visits** – There's no substitute for first-person observation of the daily activities of the people doing the work. Whether their investigations are structured or informal, Product Managers and Product Owners are responsible for understanding how people actually use systems in their actual work environments. They can't do that at their own desks—there is no substitute for observing users in their specific Solution Context.

- **Gemba walks** – Many times, customers are the internal people who implement the operational values streams that the organization's development systems support. In this case, developers can use the Gemba walk ('Gemba' is the place where the work is performed [4]) to observe how these stakeholders execute the steps and specific activities in their operational value streams.

- **Elicitation** – Product Management and Product Owner professionals use a variety of structured elicitation techniques to generate input and prioritize user needs. These include research methods such as interviews and surveys, brainstorming and idea reduction, questionnaires, and competitive analysis. Other techniques include requirements workshops, user experience mock-ups, user personas, review of customer requests, and use-case modeling [2, 3].

- **Trade studies** – Teams engage in trade studies to determine the most practical characteristics of a solution. They review numerous solutions to a technical problem, as well as vendor-provided products and services that address the subject area or an adjacent need. Alternative solutions are then evaluated against the benefit hypothesis to determine which ones are the most effective for a particular context.

- **Market research** – To broaden their thinking, teams conduct original market research, analyze secondary research and market/industry trends, identify emerging customer segments, interview industry analysts, and review competitive solutions.

Synthesize

Based on this collaboration and research, Product Management synthesizes their findings into the vision, roadmap, and program backlog. The Program Kanban helps manage this work. The default Kanban states of funnel, analysis, and backlog are good starting points to establish the workflow. Features that make it to the program backlog are ready for Weighted Shortest Job First (WSJF) prioritization to determine which ones should be pulled into Program Increment (PI) planning.

Implementation

The Lean UX chapter describes a simple, four-step process for implementing features:

1. Define a benefit hypothesis
2. Design collaboratively
3. Implement a Minimum Marketable Feature (MMF)
4. Evaluate the MMF against the hypothesis

While this model was developed and described in the context of user-facing functionality, it isn't reserved exclusively for that environment; all features can benefit from this approach. For example, an Enabler feature such as "In-service software update" might not be user-facing at all, as shown in Figure 3.

With a solid feature definition in hand, the next process, continuous integration, pulls features from the program backlog and implements them. In accordance with the Lean UX process [5], each MMF is collaboratively designed, developed, and delivered incrementally. Incremental delivery leads to the fast feedback that teams need to refactor, adjust, and redesign—or even pivot to abandon a feature, based solely on real objective data and user feedback. This creates a closed-loop Lean UX process that iterates toward a successful outcome, driven by objective evidence of whether a feature fulfills the hypothesis.

Feature: In- service software update

Benefit Hypothesis:
- Downtime decreased by 80%

Acceptance Criteria:
- Nonstop routing availability
- Automatic and manual update support
- Rollback capability
- Support through existing admin tools
- All enabled services are running after the update

Figure 3. Enabler feature definition

LEARN MORE

[1] Ries, Eric. *The Lean Startup: How Today's Entrepreneurs Use Continuous Innovation to Create Radically Successful Businesses.* Random House, Inc.

[2] Leffingwell, Dean. *Agile Software Requirements: Lean Requirements Practices for Teams, Programs, and the Enterprise (Agile Software Development Series).* Pearson Education.

[3] http://www.innovationgames.com.

[4] Womack, Jim. *Gemba Walks: Expanded 2nd Edition.* Lean Enterprise Institute.

[5] Gothelf, Jeff, and Josh Seiden. *Lean UX: Designing Great Products with Agile Teams.* O'Reilly Media, 2016.

Continuous Integration

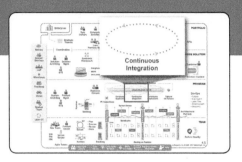

The epiphany of integration points is that they control product development. They are the leverage points to improve the system. When timing of integration points slips, the project is in trouble.

—Dantar Oosterwal, The Lean Machine

Continuous Integration (CI) is the process of taking features from the Program Backlog and developing, testing, integrating, and validating them in a staging environment where they are ready for deployment and release. CI is the second element in the four-part Continuous Delivery Pipeline (see Figure 1).

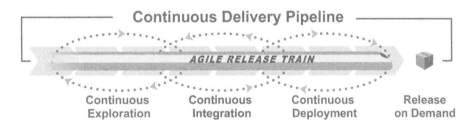

Figure 1. Continuous integration in the context of the continuous delivery pipeline

CI is a critical technical practice for each Agile Release Train (ART). It reduces risk and establishes a fast, reliable, and sustainable development pace.

Details

With continuous integration, the "system always runs"—meaning it's potentially deployable, even during development of the Solution. CI is most readily applied to software solutions where small, tested vertical threads can deliver value independently. In larger, multiplatform software systems, the challenge of CI becomes much greater. Each platform has its own technical constructs, and the platforms themselves must be continuously integrated to prove new functionality.

In complex systems—those with mechanical subsystems, software, electrical/electronic subsystems, Suppliers, subassemblies, and the like—CI is harder still. However, integrating and testing collaborating components together *frequently* is the only practical way to fully validate a solution. As Dantar Oosterwal points out in *The Lean Machine*, "integration points control product development" [1].

Thus, teams need a balanced approach—one that allows them to build quality in, yet receive fast feedback from the integrated increments. For the software elements, truly continuous integration can be more easily applied. For larger and complex systems, in particular, CI requires economic trade-offs between frequency of integration, scope of integration, and testing.

A Three-Tiered Solution Integration Strategy

The level of effort and strategy for CI depends on the size and complexity of the solution. When building at the Large Solution Level, CI becomes a three-tiered approach (Figure 2).

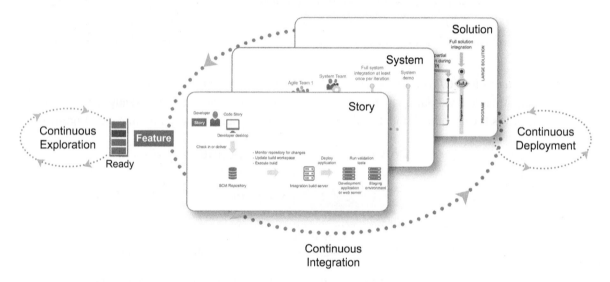

Figure 2. Three-tiered continuous integration

Integrate and Test Stories

The role of the CI process is to pull features from the program backlog so that the team can design, implement, integrate, test, and validate them in a staging environment. But as we know, features are often too big and abstract to be coded directly. Instead, features are converted into Stories during Program Increment (PI) Planning, as shown in Figure 3.

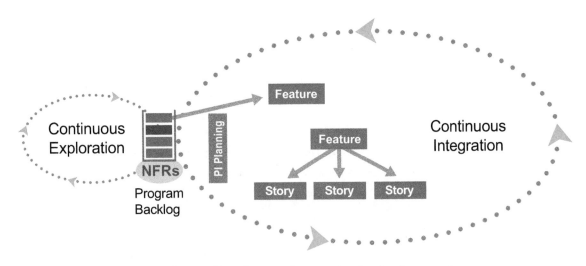

Figure 3. Breaking features into stories for implementation

Thereafter, each story is defined, coded, tested, and integrated into the baseline. To support this effort, team members integrate their individual work frequently, applying automated continuous integration environments like that illustrated in Figure 4 [1].

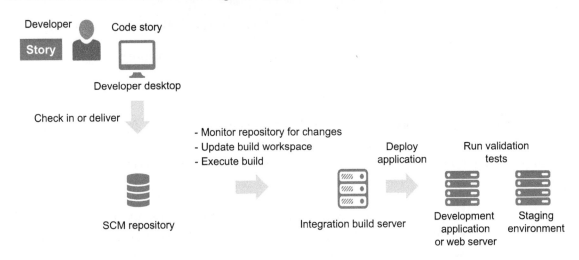

Figure 4. An automated continuous integration environment

Automate Story Tests

Developing incrementally means that the system must be continually tested as well; otherwise, there is no way to assure that the new stories will work (and be compatible) with all the existing functionality. To this end, teams apply Test-First development, which includes creating unit and acceptance tests for each story that gets implemented. To avoid building 'technical debt,' Agile teams develop and apply these tests in the same Iteration in which they implement the story (see Figure 5). Passing versus not-yet-passing and broken automated tests are the real indicators of progress.

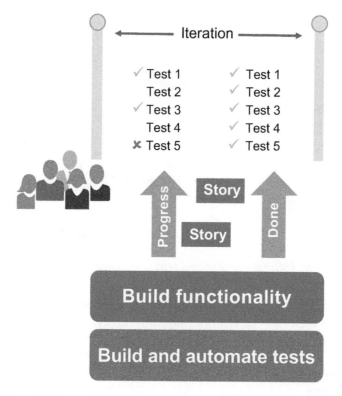

Figure 5. Teams build and automate tests for each new story

Integrate and Test the System

While critical, such local story integration and testing aren't enough. To fully test the features, system-level integration and testing are required. With the support of the System Team, the work of all teams on the ART must be frequently integrated to assure that the system is evolving as anticipated (Figure 6).

System-level testing happens as frequently as possible during the iteration, ideally daily. Even if it occurs less often, such full-system integration must be accomplished at least once per iteration. Otherwise, the late discovery of defects and issues will have ripple effects that reach all the way back to earlier iterations, causing substantial rework and delays. All this work comes together in the System Demo, which demonstrates the accumulated features and is the true indicator of ART progress.

Automate Feature Tests

As with user stories, features must be continuously tested against their acceptance criteria, to assure that new functionality is developed. Again, the test-first philosophy is applied, in this case by automating as many of the feature tests as possible.

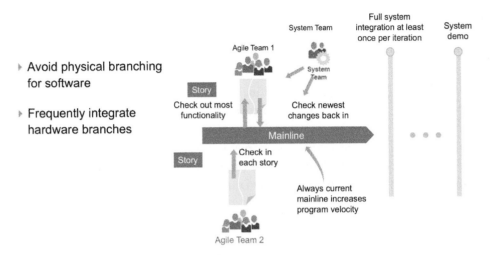

- Avoid physical branching for software

- Frequently integrate hardware branches

Figure 6. Integrating the work of all teams on the ART

Integrate and Test the Solution

Finally, building large solutions—those that require multiple ARTs and Suppliers to develop them—requires an additional level of integration to pull all the work together. Full or partial integration happens over the course of the PI, with a full solution integration occurring at least once per PI (see Figure 7).

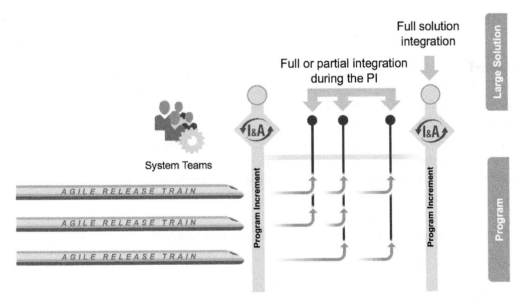

Figure 7. Full solution-level integration at least once per PI

The solution integration and demo are the joint responsibility of the ART and solution system teams. During the Solution Demo event, the aggregated results are made visible to the Customer and other stakeholders.

To be able to demonstrate the full solution routinely, ARTs typically make additional investments in integration, testing, and supporting infrastructure. In many cases, the extent of integration and testing may be less than 100 percent and may need to vary across multiple early integration points. To assist in this effort, teams can leverage virtualization, environment emulation, mocks, stubs, reduced test suites, and other testing-related techniques. The time and effort for such extensive integration and demonstration may need to be explicitly allocated during PI Planning.

Synchronize with Suppliers

Suppliers make unique contributions to the development effort that can have a large impact on lead time and value delivery. Their work must be continuously integrated as well. Tips for accomplishing this integration include the following:

- ARTs and suppliers should jointly plan integration points.

- Adopt a common integration cadence; establish objective evaluation milestones.

- Foster collaboration between the system teams of ARTs and suppliers.

- Foster collaboration and synchronization between System and Solution Architects/ Engineers of ARTs and suppliers.

- Participate in Pre- and Post-PI Planning and solution demos.

Optimizing Integration Trade-Offs

Each ART's goal is to fully integrate features across all teams in each iteration. As described earlier, however, achieving that goal can be difficult due to the solution's complexity and heterogeneity; issues with the availability of specialty testers, laboratories, equipment, and third-party components; and so on. Given these challenges, teams may perceive that the goal of integrated iteration is not realistic—at least initially. But that can't be an excuse for accepting late-in-the cycle integration and testing. Following are some suggestions for how to achieve most of the benefits, even when full, fast CI isn't immediately practical.

- Integrate different aspects of the solution at different intervals

- Integrate all assets, but run only a subset of tests

- Use virtual or emulated environments, stubs, and mocks, until the actual functionality is available

Enabling Continuous Integration

Continuously integrating large and complex systems is a journey that takes time. The following suggestions will help build a successful CI culture and practice.

- **Integrate often** – The more frequently teams integrate, the more quickly they find problems. The harder it is to do, the more often they need to do it—eliminating impediments and adding automation along the way. This results in faster learning cycles and less rework.

- **Make integration results visible** – When the integration process breaks, everyone should know how and why it broke. And when it's fixed, new tests should be added to detect the problem earlier and prevent it from happening again.

- **Fixing failed integrations is a top priority** – If teams just keep working during an integration failure, that continuation of their normal routine doesn't create the right sense of urgency and importance to fix the problem. To highlight the problem, teams often use flashing lights to draw attention to a broken build, and visible indicators displaying the percentage of the time the system remains broken.

- **Establish a common cadence** – Integration points are easier when all the teams are moving at the same consistent rhythm. That's why all PIs use the same iteration cadence within an ART and a Solution Train. If full CI can't be accomplished during the course of an iteration, teams can make near-term trade-offs on what can be integrated, while continuously improving their techniques and infrastructure to move them further toward this goal.

- **Develop and maintain the proper infrastructure** – Effective continuous integration depends on the availability of test and staging environments (see Continuous Deployment). Infrastructure is, of course, an investment. Lean-Agile Leaders take the long view and make the investments necessary today to increase velocity for the marathon ahead.

- **Apply supportive engineering practices** – Continuous integration is easier when the system is designed with those concerns in mind. Test-first development and designing for testability call for better solution modularity and separation of concerns, as well as the use of primary interfaces and physical test points.

Start Now!

It's also important to note that continuous system integration and frequent solution integration represent a special challenge for groups early in their transition to SAFe. They just haven't done it previously, nor have they built the necessary infrastructure. Even so, the current state cannot be an excuse to simply reduce the scope of integration. Most of these challenges will disappear in a better, future state, but *only if the teams start now*.

LEARN MORE

[1] Oosterwal, Dantar P. *The Lean Machine: How Harley-Davidson Drove Top-Line Growth and Profitability with Revolutionary Lean Product Development*. Kindle Edition.

[2] Leffingwell, Dean. *Scaling Software Agility: Best Practices for Large Enterprises (Agile Software Development Series)*. Pearson Education. Kindle Edition.

[3] Kim, Gene, Jez Humble, Patrick Debois, and John Willis. *The DevOps Handbook: How to Create World-Class Agility, Reliability, and Security in Technology Organizations*. IT Revolution Press. Kindle Edition.

Continuous Deployment

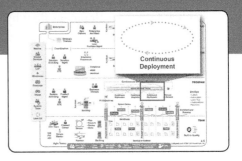

In order for you to keep up with customer demand, you need to create a deployment pipeline. You need to get everything in version control. You need to automate the entire environment creation process. You need a deployment pipeline where you can create test and production environments, and then deploy code into them, entirely on demand.

—Erik to Grasshopper, The Phoenix Project [1]

Continuous Deployment (CD) is the process that takes validated Features from Continuous Integration and deploys them into the production environment, where they are tested further and readied for release. It is the third element in the four-part Continuous Delivery Pipeline (see Figure 1).

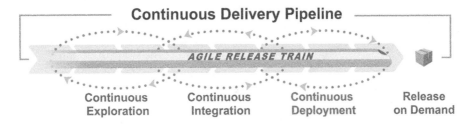

Figure 1. Continuous deployment in the context of the Continuous Delivery Pipeline

Since tangible value occurs only when end users are successfully operating the Solution in their environment, CD is a critical capability for each Agile Release Train (ART) and Solution Train. It demands that the complex routine of deploying to production receive early and meaningful attention during development.

By calling out specific mechanisms for continuously maintaining deployment readiness throughout the feature development timeline, the chapters describing continuous exploration and continuous integration led us directly to this point. The result is smaller batches of features, some of which are always ready for deployment and release. Now we just need to continuously deploy these valuable assets so that they can be available immediately in production. This gives the business the ability to release more frequently, with the best possible quality in the shortest sustainable lead time.

Details

The goal is always the same: to deliver increasingly valuable solutions to the end users as frequently as possible. A leaner and more Agile approach to the development process, as SAFe describes, helps establish faster development flow by systematically reducing time in the development cycle and by introducing Built-In Quality approaches.

In many cases, however, development teams still deliver solutions to deployment or production in large batches. There, the actual deployment and release of the new solution is likely to be manual, error prone, and unpredictable, adversely affecting release-date commitments and delivered quality.

To address these shortcomings, the development and operations teams must collectively focus their attention on the downstream deployment process. By reducing the transaction cost and risk at that point, the business can move toward a more continuous deployment process, tuned to deliver smaller batch sizes more economically. That is the final key to unlocking a more continuous delivery process.

Six Recommended Practices for Continuous Deployment

SAFe recommends six specific practices to help establish a more efficient and continuous deployment process, as highlighted in Figure 2. Each is described in the following sections.

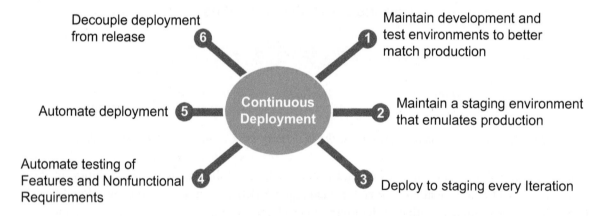

Figure 2. Six recommended practices for continuous deployment

Maintain Development and Test Environments That Better Match Production

Often teams discover that what seemed to work well in development does *not* work in production. This results in much time spent frantically fixing new defects directly in the production environment, typically in emergency mode.

One root cause of this dilemma: Development environments often don't match production environments. For example, as Em Campbell-Pretty notes from her experience in adopting SAFe at Telstra [2], "The team quickly made a surprising discovery: Only 50 percent of the source code in their development and test environments matched what was running in production."

Part of the reason for the differing environments is practicality and cost. For example, it may not be feasible to have a separate load balancer or production-equivalent data set for every development team. However, most software configurations can be affordably replicated across all environments. Therefore, all changes in the production environment (such as component or supporting application upgrades, new development-initiated configuration/environment changes, and changes in system metadata) must be replicated back to all development environments. This can be accomplished with the same workflow and pipeline that are used for continuous delivery of the production solution.

To support this, all configuration changes need to be captured in version control. Likewise, all new actions required to enable the deployment process should be documented in scripts and automated wherever possible.

Maintain a Staging Environment That Emulates Production

This leads to a second issue. For many reasons, development environments will never be identical to production environments. In production, for example, the application server is behind a firewall, which is preceded by a load balancer. The much larger-scale production database is clustered, and media content lives on separate servers. The list of differences goes on and on. Once again, Murphy's law will prevail: Deployment will fail, and debugging and resolution will demand an unpredictable amount of time.

This typically creates the need for a staging environment that bridges the gap. Even though pursuing production equivalency may never be financially prudent—for example, replicating the hundreds or thousands of servers required—there are numerous ways to achieve the functional equivalent without such an investment.

For example, it may be sufficient to have only two instances of the application server, instead of 20, and a cheaper load balancer from the same vendor. In a cyber-physical system—that of a crop harvesting combine, for instance—all the electronics subsystems, drive motors, and hardware actuators that operate the machine can be practically provisioned as a staging environment, without the 15 tons of iron.

Deploy to Staging Every Iteration

It's impossible to understand the true state of any system increment unless it can be operated and tested in a production-like environment. So, one suggestion seems obvious: Do all System Demos within the staging environment. That way, deployability becomes part of the Definition of Done (DoD).

While continuous deployment readiness is critical to establishing a reliable delivery process, the real benefits of shortening the lead time come from actually deploying to production more frequently. This also helps eliminate long-lived production support branches and the resulting extra effort needed to merge and synchronize all instances where changes are needed.

Automate Testing of Features and Nonfunctional Requirements

Of course, when you deploy more frequently, you have to test more frequently. That calls for testing automation, including the ability to run automated regression tests on all the unit tests associated with the stories that implement the feature. Running automated acceptance tests at the feature level is also required.

Deploying incrementally also means that teams will be deploying partial functionality—individual stories, parts of features, features that depend on other yet-to-be-developed features, and features that depend on external applications and the like. Therefore, some of what teams need to test against will not be present in the system at the time they need to test it. Fortunately, there are many evolving techniques for addressing this issue, including applying mocks, stubs, and service virtualization.

Finally, while automating 100 percent of nonfunctional tests may not be practical, what can be automated should be automated—especially in those areas where new functionality might affect system performance. Otherwise, some change could have an unanticipated and detrimental effect on performance, reliability, compliance, or any other system quality.

Note: For more on test-driven development (TDD), acceptance test-driven development (ATDD), deployment testing, test automation, and testing Nonfunctional Requirements (NFRs), see the Test-First chapter in Part 9 and references [3] and [4].

Automate Deployment

By now, it should be clear that the actual deployment process itself also requires automation. This includes all the steps in the flow—building the system, creating the test environments, executing the automated tests, and deploying and validating the verified code and associated systems and utilities in the target environment. This final, critical automation step is achievable only via an incremental process, one that requires the organization's full commitment and support, as well as creativity and pragmatism, as the teams prioritize target areas for automation. The end result is an automated deployment process, as Figure 3 illustrates.

As shown in Figure 3, three main processes must be automated:

1. **Automatically fetch version-controlled development artifacts** – The first step is to automatically fetch all necessary artifacts from the CI process, including code, scripts, tests, supporting configuration items, and metadata—all of which must be maintained under version control. This includes the new code, all required data (e.g., dictionaries, scripts, look-ups, mappings), all libraries and external assemblies, configuration files, and databases. Test data must also be version controlled and manageable enough for the teams to update every time they introduce, create, or test a new scenario.

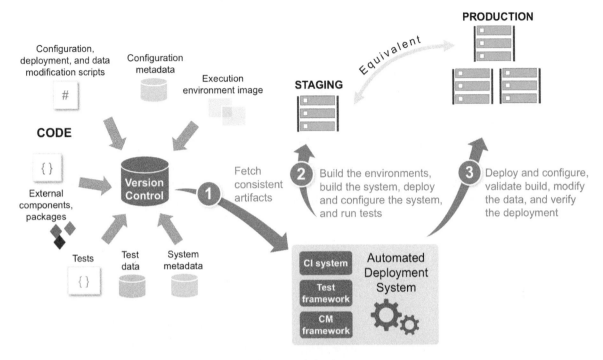

Figure 3. Automated deployment process

2. **Automatically build the system and its environments** – Many deployment problems arise from the error-prone, manually intensive routines needed to build the actual runtime system and its environments. They include preparing the operating environment, applications, and data; configuring the artifacts; and initiating the required jobs in the system and its supporting systems. To establish a reliable deployment process, the environment setup process itself needs to be fully automated. This can be facilitated largely by virtualization, using Infrastructure as a Service (IaaS) and applying special frameworks for automating configuration management jobs.

3. **Automatically deploy to production** – The process of deploying and validating all the assets moved to the production environment must also be automated, without disrupting service to the end users. Deployment techniques are further discussed in the Release on Demand chapter in Part 5.

Decouple Deployment from Release

One myth about continuous delivery is exactly that: the myth that you must deliver continuously to the end users, whether or not you—or they—like it. But that exaggerates the case and ignores the basic economic and market factors, which mandate that the act of releasing a solution is dependent on more than just the state of the system. Many factors affect the timing of releases, including customer readiness, channel and supplier support, trade shows and market events, and compliance demands. These issues are further explored in the Release on Demand chapter.

LEARN MORE

[1] Kim, Gene, et al. *The Phoenix Project: A Novel about IT, DevOps, and Helping Your Business Win*. IT Revolution Press, 2013.

[2] Kim, Gene, Jez Humble, Patrick Debois, and John Willis. *The DevOps Handbook: How to Create World-Class Agility, Reliability, and Security in Technology Organizations*. IT Revolution Press, 2016.

[3] Humble, Jez, and David Farley. *Continuous Delivery: Reliable Software Releases through Build, Test, and Deployment Automation*. Addison-Wesley, 2010.

[4] Gregory, Janet, and Lisa Crispin. *More Agile Testing: Learning Journeys for the Whole Team.* Addison-Wesley Signature Series (Cohn). Pearson Education. Kindle Edition.

Part 6
The Spanning Palette

scaledagileframework.com

Metrics

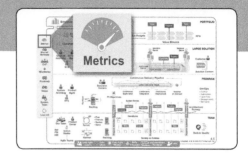

The most important things cannot be measured. The issues that are most important, long term, cannot be measured in advance.

—W. Edwards Deming

Working software is the primary measure of progress.

—Agile Manifesto

Metrics are agreed-upon measures used to evaluate how well the organization is progressing toward the Portfolio, Large Solution, Program, and team's business and technical objectives.

Thanks to its work physics, timeboxes, and fast feedback, Agile is inherently more measurable than its proxy-based predecessor, the waterfall process. Moreover, with Agile, 'the system always runs.' So, the best measure comes directly from the objective evaluation of the working system. Continuous delivery and DevOps practices provide even more things to measure. All other measures—even the extensive set of Lean-Agile metrics outlined in this chapter—are secondary to the overriding goal of focusing on *rapid delivery of high-quality solutions*.

Nevertheless, metrics are important in the enterprise context. SAFe provides metrics for each level of the Framework.

Portfolio Metrics

Lean Portfolio Metrics

The set of Lean portfolio metrics provided here is an example of a comprehensive but Lean group of measures that can be used to assess internal and external progress for an entire portfolio. In the spirit of 'the simplest set of measures that can work,' Table 1 provides the metrics that a few Lean-Agile portfolios are using effectively to evaluate the overall performance of their transformations.

Benefit	Expected Result	Metric Used
Employee engagement	Improved employee satisfaction; lower turnover	Employee survey; HR statistics
Customer satisfaction	Improved Net Promoter Score	Net promoter score survey
Productivity	Reduced average feature cycle time	Feature cycle time
Agility	Continuous improvement in team and program measures	Team, program, large solution and portfolio self-assessments; Release predictability measure
Time-to-market	More frequent releases	Number or releases per year
Quality	Reduced defect counts and support call volume	Defect data and support call volume
Partner health	Improved ecosystem relationships	Partner and vendor surveys

Table 1. Lean Portfolio Metrics

Portfolio Kanban Board

The primary purpose of the Portfolio Kanban board is to ensure that Epics are weighed and analyzed before reaching a Program Increment (PI) boundary. This way, they can be prioritized appropriately and have established acceptance criteria to guide a high-fidelity implementation. Further, the business and enabler epics can then be tracked to understand their progress.

Epic Burn-up Chart

The epic burn-up chart tracks progress toward an epic's completion. There are three measures:

- **Initial estimate line (blue)** – Estimated Story points from the lean business case
- **Work completed line (red)** – Actual story points rolled up from the epic's child Features and stories
- **Cumulative work completed line (green)** – Cumulative story points completed and rolled up from the epic's child features and stories

Figure 1 illustrates these measures.

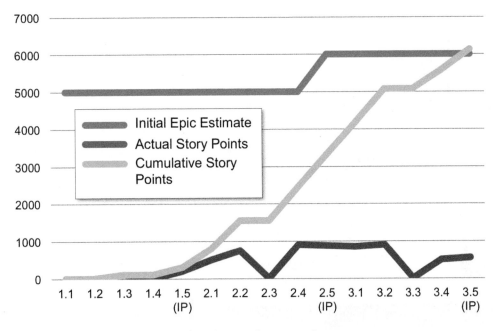

Figure 1. Epic burn-up chart

Epic Progress Measure

This report provides an at-a-glance view of the status of all epics in a portfolio.

- **Epic X** – Represents the name of the epic. Business epics are blue, and enabler epics are red.

- **Bar length** – Represents the total current estimated story points for an epic's child features/stories. The dark green shaded area represents the actual story points completed; the light shaded area depicts the total story points that are in progress.

- **Vertical red line** – Represents the initial epic estimate, in story points, from the Lean business case.

- **0000/0000** – The first number represents the current story point estimate (summarized from its child features/stories); the second number represents the initial story point estimate (also represented by the vertical red line).

Figure 2 illustrates these measures.

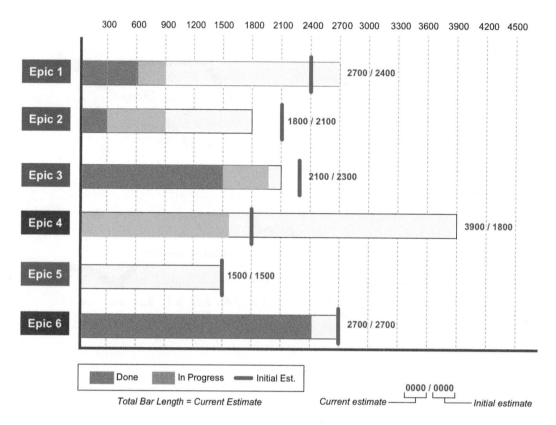

Figure 2. Epic progress measure

Enterprise Balanced Scorecard

The enterprise balanced scorecard provides four perspectives to measure performance for each portfolio—although the popularity of this approach has been declining over time in favor of Lean Portfolio Management (LPM), as discussed in the next subsection. These measures are:

- Efficiency
- Value delivery
- Quality
- Agility

These results are then mapped into an executive dashboard, as illustrated in Figures 3 and 4.

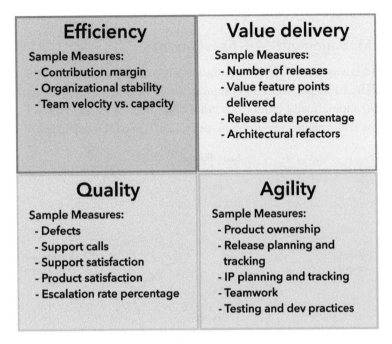

Figure 3. A balanced scorecard approach, dividing measures into four areas of interest

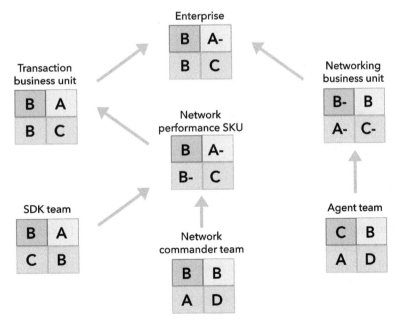

Figure 4. Converting the metrics in Figure 3 to an alphabetical rating and summarizing the data to the enterprise provides a broader picture of performance

For more on this approach, see chapter 22 of *Scaling Software Agility: Best Practices for Large Enterprises* [2].

Lean Portfolio Management Self-Assessment

The Lean Portfolio Management (LPM) continuously assesses and improves the methods being used by the Enterprise. The LPM periodically conducts a self-assessment questionnaire to measure their performance, which automatically produces a radar chart like the one shown in Figure 5. It highlights the relative strengths and weaknesses of the organization's portfolio practices.

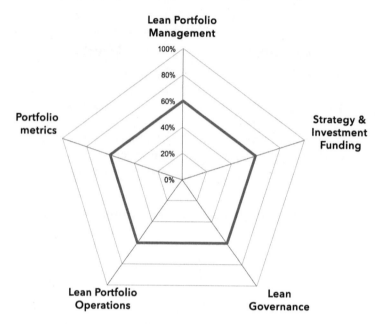

Figure 5. Portfolio self-assessment radar chart

Large Solution Metrics

Solution Kanban Board

For organizations using the Large Solution level or configuration, the Solution Kanban follows the same structure and process used for the program level (see Figure 9). However, Solution Management and Solution Architects manage this Kanban, which operates with Capabilities instead of features. Also, where useful, Solution Trains employ a Solution Epic Kanban for solution epics. It essentially works the same as the Program Epic Kanban.

Solution Train Predictability Measure

The Agile Release Trains (ARTs) predictability measures are summarized to calculate the Solution Train's predictability measure, as illustrated in Figure 6.

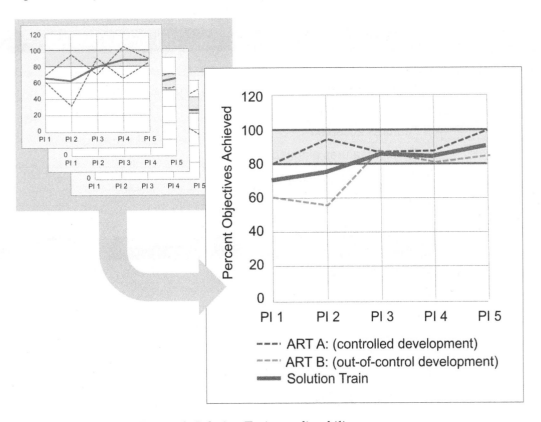

Figure 6. Solution Train predictability measure

Solution Train Performance Metrics

The ARTs performance metrics are summarized to calculate the Solution Train's performance metrics, as shown in Figure 7.

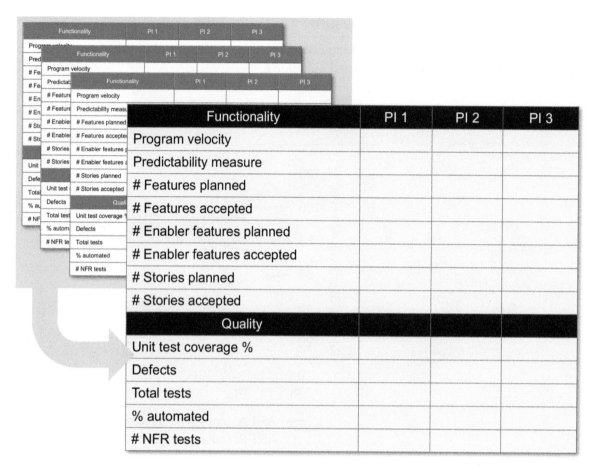

Functionality	PI 1	PI 2	PI 3
Program velocity			
Predictability measure			
# Features planned			
# Features accepted			
# Enabler features planned			
# Enabler features accepted			
# Stories planned			
# Stories accepted			
Quality			
Unit test coverage %			
Defects			
Total tests			
% automated			
# NFR tests			

Figure 7. Solution Train performance metrics

Program Metrics

Feature Progress Report

The feature progress report tracks the status of features and enablers during PI execution. It indicates which features are on track or behind at any point in time. The chart has two bars:

- **Plan** – Represents the total number of stories planned.
- **Actual** – Represents the number of stories completed. The bar is shaded red or green, depending on whether the item is on track.

Figure 8 gives an example of a feature progress report.

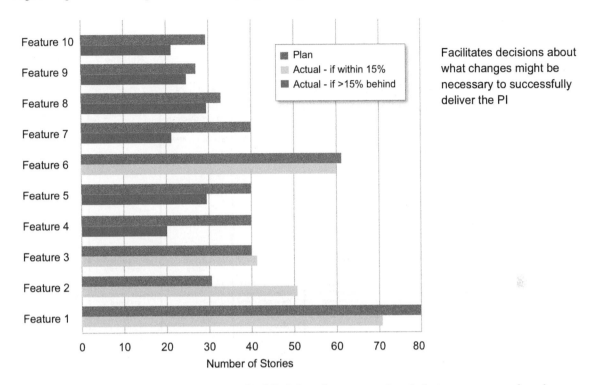

Facilitates decisions about what changes might be necessary to successfully deliver the PI

Figure 8. Feature progress report, highlighting the status of each feature compared to the program increment plan

Program Kanban Board

The Program Kanban facilitates the flow of features through the continuous delivery pipeline. Figure 9 illustrates a typical program Kanban, as well as example policies and WIP limits governing each state. However, the Kanban process states and WIP limits will need to evolve iteratively as the ART learns how to improve its process and resolve bottlenecks. Also, where useful, ARTs employ a Program Epic Kanban for initiatives that are too large to fit in a PI.

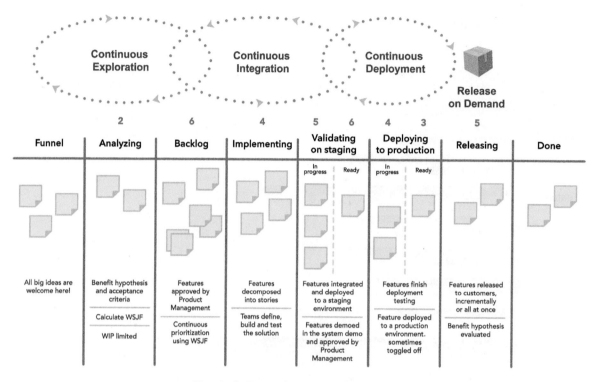

Figure 9. Typical Kanban for an ART

Program Predictability Measure

The team PI performance reports are summarized to determine the program predictability measure, as illustrated in Figure 10.

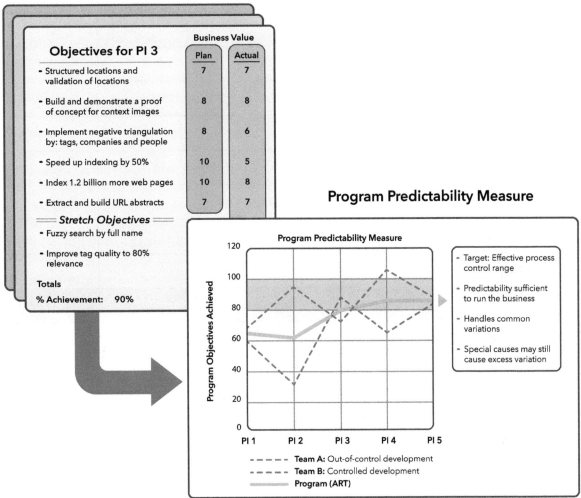

Team PI Performance Reports

Objectives for PI 3

	Business Value	
	Plan	Actual
• Structured locations and validation of locations	7	7
• Build and demonstrate a proof of concept for context images	8	8
• Implement negative triangulation by: tags, companies and people	8	6
• Speed up indexing by 50%	10	5
• Index 1.2 billion more web pages	10	8
• Extract and build URL abstracts	7	7

Stretch Objectives
- Fuzzy search by full name
- Improve tag quality to 80% relevance

Totals
% Achievement: 90%

Program Predictability Measure

- Target: Effective process control range
- Predictability sufficient to run the business
- Handles common variations
- Special causes may still cause excess variation

Team A: Out-of-control development
Team B: Controlled development
Program (ART)

Figure 10. Program predictability measure, showing two of the teams on the train and program (cumulative)

The report compares actual business value achieved to planned business value (see Figure 23 later in this chapter).

For more on this approach, see chapter 15 of *Agile Software Requirements: Lean Requirements Practices for Teams, Programs, and the Enterprise* [1].

Program Performance Metrics

The end of each PI is a natural and significant measuring point for an ART. Figure 11 shows a set of program performance metrics for a PI.

Functionality	PI 1	PI 2	PI 3
Program velocity			
Predictability measure			
# Features planned			
# Features accepted			
# Enabler features planned			
# Enabler features accepted			
# Stories planned			
# Stories accepted			
Quality			
Unit test coverage %			
Defects			
Total tests			
% automated			
# NFR tests			

Figure 11. One ART's chart of performance metrics

PI Burn-Down Chart

The PI burn-down chart shows the progress toward the PI timebox. It's used to track the work planned for a PI against the work accepted.

- The horizontal axis of the PI burn-down chart shows the iterations within the PI.
- The vertical axis shows the amount of work, in story points, remaining at the start of each iteration.

Figure 12 depicts a train's burn-down measure.

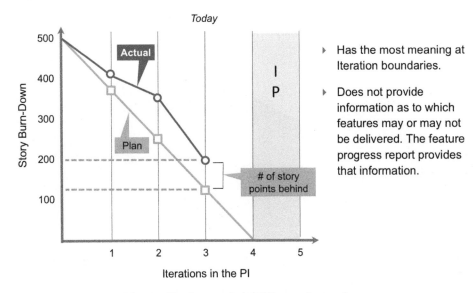

Figure 12. One train's PI burn-down chart

Although the PI burn-down chart shows the progress toward the PI timebox, it does not reveal which features are lagging behind. The feature progress report provides that information (refer to Figure 8).

Cumulative Flow Diagram

The Cumulative Flow Diagram (CFD) is made up of a series of lines or areas that show the amount of work in different Kanban states. For example, the typical states included in the program Kanban are as follows:

- Funnel
- Analyzing
- Backlog
- Implementing
- Validating on staging
- Deploying to production
- Releasing
- Done

Figure 13 shows the number of features in each Kanban state by day. The thicker areas in the CFD represent potential bottlenecks.

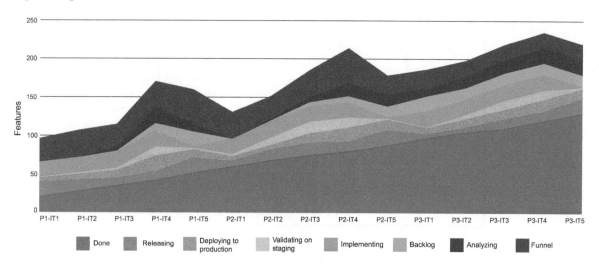

Figure 13. Example program Kanban CFD

Agile Release Train Self-Assessment

As program execution is a core value of SAFe, the ART continuously strives to improve its performance. The Release Train Engineer (RTE) fills out the self-assessment questionnaire at PI boundaries or anytime the train wants to pause and reflect on the teams' progress. Trending these data over time provides a key performance indicator. Figure 14 gives an example of the results in a radar chart.

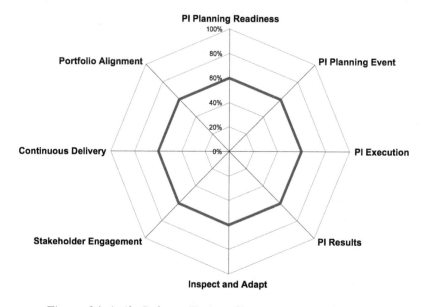

Figure 14. Agile Release Train self-assessment radar chart

Continuous Delivery Pipeline Efficiency

The pipeline efficiency compares the amount of touch time versus wait time. The *touch time* represents when the team is adding value. Typically, touch time is only a small proportion of the total production time; most of the time is spent waiting, such as when moving work, waiting in queues, and so on.

Some of this information can be sourced automatically from tools, especially Continuous Integration and Continuous Deployment tools, while other data require manually recording in a spreadsheet. The value stream mapping technique is often applied to analyze problems identified in this report. Figure 15 depicts the efficiency of the continuous delivery pipeline for one organization.

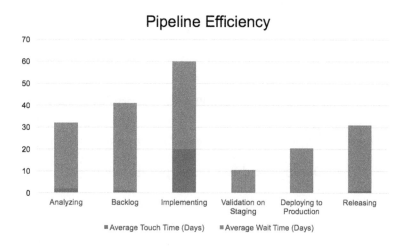

Figure 15. Continuous delivery pipeline efficiency

Deployments and Releases per Timebox

The deployments and releases per timebox metric is meant to demonstrate whether the program is making progress toward deploying and releasing more frequently. It can be viewed on a PI basis, as shown in Figure 16. Alternatively, we can zoom in to see how releases are handled in mid-PI, as shown in Figure 17.

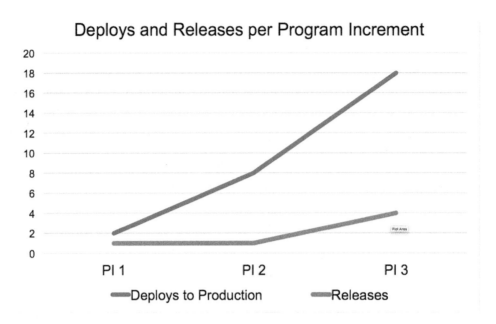

Figure 16. Deployments and releases per program increment

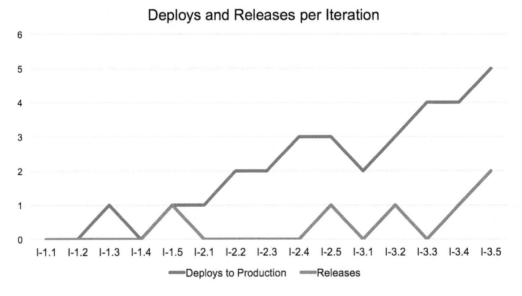

Figure 17. Deployments and releases per iteration

Recovery over Time

The report of recovery over time measures the number of rollbacks that occurred either physically or by turning off feature toggles. The date when a solution was deployed or released to production is also plotted to determine whether there is a relationship between the two. Figure 18 provides an example.

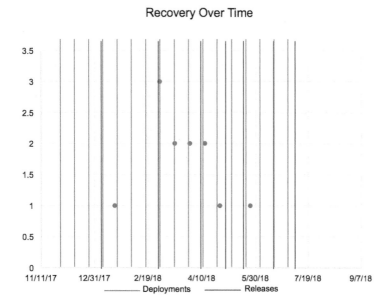

Recovery Over Time

Figure 18. Recovery over time

Innovation Accounting and Leading Indicators

One of the goals of the continuous delivery pipeline is to enable the organization to run experiments quickly, thereby allowing Customers to validate the hypotheses. Both Minimal Marketable Features (MMFs) and Minimal Viable Products (MVPs) must define the leading indicators so that progress toward the benefit hypothesis can be measured. Avoid relying on vanity metrics that do not measure real progress.

Figure 19 shows some metrics that were gathered from the SAFe website to demonstrate leading indicators for our development efforts.

	6/21/17	6/26/17	7/1/17	7/6/17	7/11/17	7/16/17	7/21/17	7/26/17	7/31/17	8/5/17
Visits to the site	4000	5500	6500	6000	4500	4600	4000	4200	4200	5500
New visits	42%	10%	12%	12%	30%	40%	42%	42%	40%	60%
Bounce rate	50%	15%	17%	15%	25%	45%	51%	50%	51%	50%
Time on site	7:01	12:01	14:47	12:23	8:47	6:34	6:59	6:58	6:32	7:02
Number of articles visited	3.24	7.5	8.7	7.7	6.5	4.5	3.7	3.86	3.6	3.7

SAFe 4.5
release

Guidance
articles
on front
page

Figure 19. Leading indicators for SAFe website innovation accounting

Hypotheses Tested over Time

The primary goal of hypothesis-driven development is to create small experiments that are validated as soon as possible by customers or their proxies. Figure 20 shows the number of verified hypotheses versus failures in a PI. In an environment of quick testing (see [3] for more information), a high failure rate may indicate that the team is rapidly learning to progress toward a good outcome.

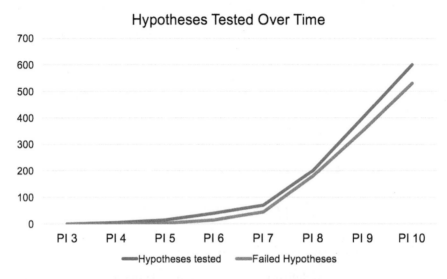

Figure 20. Hypotheses tested over time

Team Metrics

Iteration Metrics

Each Agile Team gathers the iteration metrics that team has agreed to collect. This occurs in the quantitative part of the team retrospective. Figure 21 illustrates the measures for one team.

Functionality	Iteration 1	Iteration 2	Iteration 3
Velocity planned			
Velocity actual			
# Stories planned			
# Stories accepted			
% Stories accepted			
Quality			
Unit test coverage %			
# Defects			
# New test cases			
# New test cases automated			
Total tests			
Total % tests automated			
# Refactors			

Figure 21. One team's chart of iteration metrics

Team Kanban Board

After a team determines its initial Kanban process (e.g., define, analyze, review, build, integrate, test) and Work in Process (WIP) limits, the process states will need to evolve iteratively as the team learns how to improve its process and resolve bottlenecks. Figure 22 illustrates a Kanban board for one team.

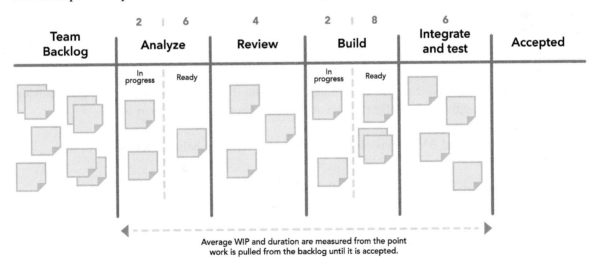

Figure 22. One team's initial Kanban board

Team PI Performance Report

During the final PI System Demo, the Business Owners, customers, Agile Teams, and other key stakeholders rate the actual business value (BV) achieved for each team's PI Objectives, as shown in Figure 23.

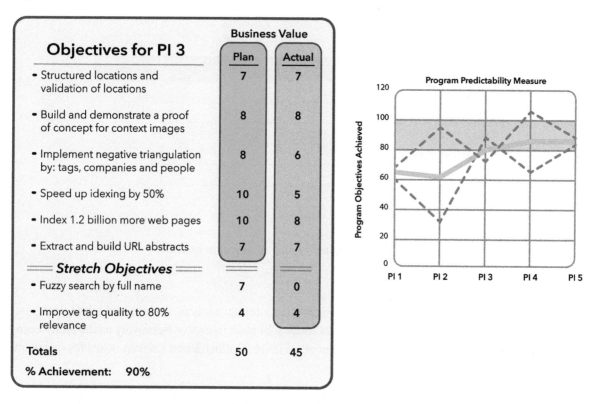

Figure 23. Team PI performance report

Reliable trains should operate in the 80–100 percent range; this allows the business and its outside stakeholders to plan effectively. Following are some notes about how the report works:

- The planned total BV does not include stretch objectives to help the reliability of the train

- The actual total BV does include stretch objectives

- The achievement percentage is the actual BV divided by the planned BV

- A team can achieve greater than 100 percent (as a result of stretch objectives achieved)

Individual team totals are rolled up into the program predictability measure (see Figure 9).

SAFe Team Self-Assessment

Agile teams continuously assess and improve their process. One tool they use for this purpose is a simple SAFe team practices assessment. When the team completes the spreadsheet, it will automatically produce a radar chart like the one shown in Figure 24, which highlights the team's relative strengths and weaknesses.

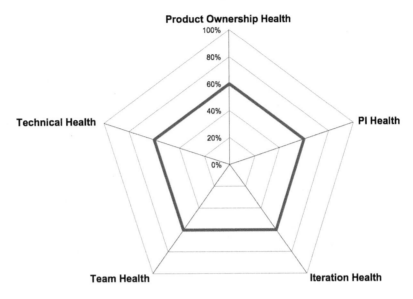

Figure 24. SAFe Team self-assessment radar chart

LEARN MORE

[1] Leffingwell, Dean. *Agile Software Requirements: Lean Requirements Practices for Teams, Programs, and the Enterprise.* Addison-Wesley, 2011.

[2] Leffingwell, Dean. *Scaling Software Agility: Best Practices for Large Enterprises.* Addison-Wesley, 2007.

[3] https://www.youtube.com/watch?v=VOjPpeBh40s.

Shared Services

A specialist is a man who knows more and more about less and less.

—William J. Mayo

Shared Services represents the specialty roles, people, and services that are necessary for the success of an Agile Release Train (ART) or Solution Train but that cannot be dedicated such a train on a full-time basis. Because these resources are specialized—often single-sourced and typically quite busy—each ART and Solution Train must plan to engage the shared services personnel it needs, when it needs them.

Details

The focus that comes from assembling all the necessary skills and abilities needed to deliver value is what characterizes ARTs and, by extension, Solution Trains. However, in many cases, it's just impractical to devote some specialty functions to a single ART. There may be a shortage of a particular skill, or the needs of the ART may fluctuate, making full-time availability impractical. To address these issues, Shared Services supports development by quickly focusing specialty expertise on the areas of the system or Solution that require unique knowledge and skills.

In some cases, the effort must occur ahead of the Agile Teams (e.g., security, information architecture) so that it may contribute directly to the Architectural Runway that supports new Capability or Feature development. In other cases, the resources can trail core development a bit (e.g., customer training, localizations). In some cases, merely being supportive and reacting quickly is sufficient.

In either case, without timely support and synchronization, the programs will struggle to meet their objectives. While not dedicated to the train, Shared Services must travel with it, as the train has to carry some of their cargo, too.

Summary Role Description

Potential members of Shared Services typically include people with the following types of specialized skills:

- Agile and software/systems engineering coaches
- Application/web portal management

- Configuration management

- Data modeling, data engineering, and database support

- Desktop support

- End-user training

- Enterprise architecture

- Information architecture

- Infrastructure and tools management

- Internationalization and localization support

- IT service management and deployment operations

- Security specialist (Infosec)

- System quality assurance and exploratory testing

- Technical writers

Responsibilities

Shared Services personnel engage in the following type of activities:

- Participating in Program Increment (PI) Planning as well as Pre- and Post-PI Planning

- Driving requirements where necessary, adding to solution intent and taking ownership of their portion of dependent backlog items

- Collaborating with Agile Teams to fulfill the dependencies that occur during PI execution

- Participating in System Demos, Solution Demos, and Inspect and Adapt (I&A) workshops, when appropriate, as many improvement backlog items may reflect challenges with the availability of specialized skills and dependencies

Occasionally, members of Shared Services may choose to operate as a single team. In that case, they would iterate on the same cadence as the ARTs and work like any other Agile team.

Maintain Specialized Training

Because shared technical resources are highly specialized (as opposed to the 'generalized specialists' found in an Agile team), their skills must be continuously refined to keep up with advancements in their respective fields. Shared Services should receive training with the Agile Teams during the ART launch.

Periodically Embed in Agile Teams

Supporting Agile Teams requires either sustained or transitional specialty expertise. Shared Services personnel may temporarily become part of an Agile team for short periods of time. In this case, they have the benefit of experiencing the Agile dynamic, as well as an understanding of the speed of development and the quality of the product produced. Their membership on the team, while temporary, also accelerates the broader teams-of-Agile-teams dynamic that—only by acting together—can deliver Enterprise value. Also, having Shared Services personnel embedded in the team for short periods of time enables knowledge transfer, which reduces the ART's dependence on specialized skills.

LEARN MORE

[1] Leffingwell, Dean. *Agile Software Requirements: Lean Requirements Practices for Teams, Programs, and the Enterprise.* Addison-Wesley, 2011.

Communities of Practice

It's said that a wise person learns from his mistakes. A wiser one learns from others' mistakes. But the wisest person of all learns from others' successes.

—Zen proverb, adapted by John C. Maxwell

Communities of Practice (CoPs) are organized groups of people who have a common interest in a specific technical or business domain. They collaborate regularly to share information, improve their skills, and actively work on advancing the general knowledge of the domain.

Healthy CoPs have a culture built on professional networking, personal relationships, shared knowledge, and common skills. Combined with voluntary participation, CoPs provide knowledge workers with opportunities to experience autonomy, mastery, and purpose beyond their daily tasks on an Agile Release Train (ART) [2].

CoPs enable practitioners to exchange knowledge and skills with people across the entire organization. This open membership offers access to a wide range of expertise to help resolve technical challenges, fuel continuous improvement, and provide for more meaningful contributions to the larger goals of the Enterprise. The result is that the organization benefits from rapid problem-solving, improved quality, cooperation across multiple domains, and increased retention of top talent.

Details

According to Wenger [1], CoPs must have three distinct traits to be considered a community of practice (see Figure 1):

- **Domain** – An area of shared interest
- **Practice** – A shared body of knowledge, experiences, and techniques
- **Community** – A self-selected group of individuals who care enough about the topic to participate in regular interactions

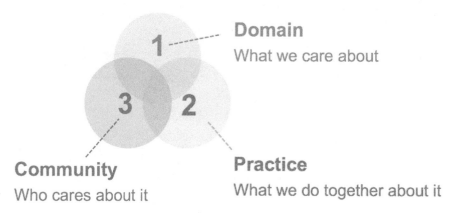

Figure 1. Three distinct traits of communities of practice

Lean-Agile principles and practices promote cross-functional teams and programs that facilitate value delivery in the enterprise. Similarly, Lean thinking emphasizes organizing people with different skills around a Value Stream. However, developers need to talk with other developers, testers need to talk with other testers, Product Owners need to communicate with their peers from other Agile Teams, and so on. This is critical for leveraging the multiple experiences and different types of practical knowledge available from a variety of people. That is what drives craftsmanship and continuous learning, facilitating the adoption of new methods and techniques.

Such domain-focused interactions are often supported by CoPs—informal networks designed specifically for efficient knowledge-sharing and exploration across teams, trains, and the entire organization. Figure 2 provides an example of role-based CoPs, one of the most common types of communities.

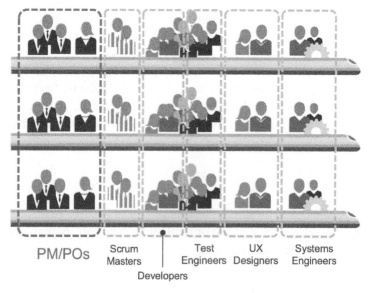

Figure 2. Role-based communities of practice

For example, Scrum Masters from different Agile teams may form a CoP to exchange practices and experiences in building highly productive Agile teams. As CoPs start to gain acceptance and participation, topic-based communities like those shown in Figure 3 often begin to emerge.

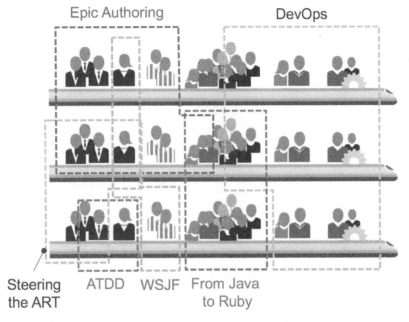

Figure 3. Topic-based communities of practice

The membership of these CoPs can be far more diverse. A CoP on the topic of DevOps, for example, could attract participants from almost any role in an organization.

An automated testing CoP could consist of test engineers and developers interested in advancing these skills. An Agile architecture and design CoP could foster the adoption of practices such as emergent design, intentional system architecture, Continuous Integration, and refactoring. It could also support the effort put into building and maintaining the Architectural Runway, foster design thinking, and support designing for testability and deployment, application security, and more. Still other CoPs may form around Agile coaching, DevOps and the Continuous Delivery Pipeline, Compliance, Built-In Quality practices, and other new processes.

Organizing a Community of Practice

CoPs are highly organic. Like most living organisms, they have a natural life cycle, beginning with an idea for a new community and ending when the community members feel the group has achieved its objectives or is no longer providing value. Figure 4 shows the typical life cycle of a CoP.

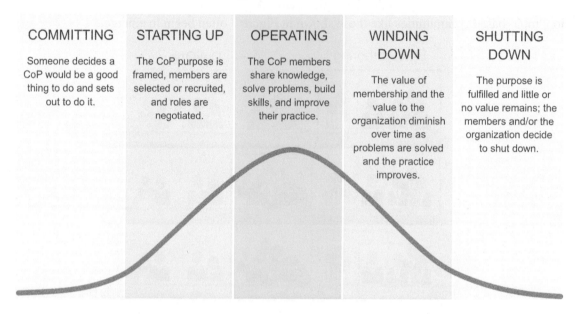

CoP stages of development

COMMITTING

Someone decides a CoP would be a good thing to do and sets out to do it.

STARTING UP

The CoP purpose is framed, members are selected or recruited, and roles are negotiated.

OPERATING

The CoP members share knowledge, solve problems, build skills, and improve their practice.

WINDING DOWN

The value of membership and the value to the organization diminish over time as problems are solved and the practice improves.

SHUTTING DOWN

The purpose is fulfilled and little or no value remains; the members and/or the organization decide to shut down.

Figure 4. CoPs typically follow a five-stage life cycle, from conceptualization to closure [3]

CoPs are formed in the committing stage by a small, core group of practitioners who share a common passion and need for a particular domain. As shown in Figure 5, CoP members exhibit multiple levels of participation. Each level is described next:

- **Core team** – The core team forms the heart of the community that will organize, charter, market, nurture, and operate the community.

- **Active** – These members work closely with the core team to help shape the definition and direction of the CoP. This includes defining the community's shared vision, purpose, roles, strategies for interaction, marketing, and communications.

- **Occasional** – These members participate when specific topics of interest are addressed or when they have something to contribute to the group. They are often the largest group within the community.

- **Peripheral** – These members feel a connection to the community but engage on a limited basis. They could be newcomers or individuals who have a more casual interest in community activities.

- **Transactional** – These members are the least connected to the community and may connect only to access CoP resources or to provide a specific service to the CoP (for example, website support).

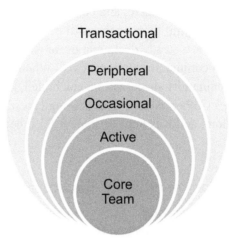

Figure 5. CoP members exhibit multiple levels of participation and can move freely across the levels as needs and interests evolve

It's common for people to move between different levels of participation and commitment over time. CoPs are self-organizing, and their members have the freedom to determine their own level of engagement—an aspect of these groups' organization that is different from other work groups, such as tiger teams, task forces, and committees. Natural movement of people among communities and levels is healthy. It allows new knowledge and fresh ideas to flow across the organization in ways that are different, but complementary, to formal information-sharing.

Operating a Community of Practice

Since CoPs are informal and self-managing by nature, community members are empowered to design the types of interactions and determine the frequency of interaction that best meets their needs. For developers, this could involve hackathons, coding dojos, and tech talks. Other formats might include meetups, brown bags, webinars, and independent communications through social business platforms such as Slack, Confluence, and Jive.

In the operating stage of a CoP, community members continuously evolve by engaging in periodic retrospectives similar to those used by Agile teams. Core team members focus on maintaining the health of the community in the following ways:

- Keeping things simple and informal

- Fostering trust

- Ensuring the rapid flow of communication and shared awareness

- Increasing the shared body of knowledge developed in the CoP

Eventually, individual CoPs will run their course, and community members should consider retiring the CoP, allowing practitioners to commit their energies to other communities. Signals that a community has reached this stage include a steady decline in event participation and reduced activity on collaboration sites and input from community retrospectives. When a CoP is retired, leaders should make it a positive event where community successes are celebrated, key contributors are recognized, and ongoing participation in other CoPs is encouraged. Through these celebrations, CoP experiences often become part of company lore, and it is not uncommon for a healthy CoP retirement to spawn three to five new communities.

Fostering Engagement in Communities of Practice

The Innovation and Planning (IP) Iteration offers great opportunities for CoPs to hold learning sessions, formal or informal, as well as to engage in other activities such as 'coding dojos,' coaching clinics, and the like.

The role of Lean-Agile Leaders is to encourage and support people's desire to improve. This helps the enterprise as a whole improve and unlocks the intrinsic motivation of knowledge workers, as discussed in SAFe Principle #8. CoPs embrace the ideals of respect for people, innovation, flow, and relentless improvement described in the House of Lean.

By fostering CoP formation, Lean-Agile Leaders can show support by continuously communicating the value of CoPs, highlighting success stories, and recognizing the efforts of community volunteers. Leaders can also support CoPs by providing meeting spaces, logistical support, and funding for meetups, tooling, and communications infrastructure.

LEARN MORE

[1] Wenger, Etienne. *Communities of Practice: Learning, Meaning, and Identity*. Cambridge University Press, 1999.

[2] Pink, Daniel H. *Drive: The Surprising Truth About What Motivates Us*. Riverhead Books, 2011.

[3] The Distance Consulting Company. *Community of Practice Start-Up Kit*. 2000.

Milestones

Base milestones on objective evaluation of working systems.

—SAFe Lean-Agile Principle #5

Milestones are used to track progress toward a specific goal or event. They mark specific progress points on the development timeline, and they can be invaluable in measuring and monitoring the evolution and risk of a program. In the past, many progress milestones were based on phase-gate activities. In SAFe, however, progress milestones are better indicated by the fixed cadence of Iterations and Program Increments (PIs).

Planning in SAFe often takes three types of milestones into account:

- **PI milestones** – These support the ability to objectively evaluate progress toward the technical or business hypothesis. They occur on the PI cadence.

- **Fixed-date milestones** – Not everything, however, occurs on cadence. Software and systems engineering involves many factors that rely on external events, third-party deliverables, and external constraints. These often call for fixed-date milestones that are distinct from the development cadence.

- **Learning milestones** –These milestones help validate business opportunities and hypotheses.

When applied properly, each type of milestone can bring focus to the work, help provide effective governance, and enable better business outcomes.

Details

The development of today's large systems requires substantial investment—an investment that can reach millions, tens of millions, and even hundreds of millions of dollars. Together, Customers, development teams, and other stakeholders have a fiduciary responsibility to ensure that the investment in new Solutions will deliver the necessary economic benefit. Otherwise, there is no reason to make the investment. Clearly, active engagement of stakeholders is needed *throughout* the development process to help ensure the realization of the proposed economic benefit, rather than just relying on wishful thinking that all will be well at the end.

The Problem with Phase-Gate Milestones

To address this challenge, industry has historically employed phase-gated (waterfall) development processes, whereby progress is measured—and control is exercised—via a series of specific progress *milestones*. These milestones are not arbitrary, but are generally document based; they follow the apparently logical and sequential process of discovery, requirements, design, implementation, test, and delivery.

But as Oosterwal notes in *The Lean Machine* [1], such milestones don't really work. The cause of this problem is the failure to recognize some *critical errors* with the basic assumption that phase gates reveal real progress and thereby mitigate risk. For example:

- Using documents as a proxy for solution progress. Not only do these documents create a false sense of security for solution progress, but they also drive various measures and Metrics, such as work breakdown structures, earned value measures, and others, that may actually impede flow and real value delivery.

- Centralizing requirements and design decisions in siloed functions that may not be integrally involved in building the solution.

- Forcing too-early design decisions and "false-positive feasibility" [1].

- Assuming that a 'point' solution exists, early in 'cone of uncertainty,' and that it can be built right the first time.

These examples highlight the flaws with phase-gate milestones, which typically do not reduce risk. Instead, they encourage picking a 'point' solution far too early in the development process, resulting in the late discovery of problems (see Figure 1).

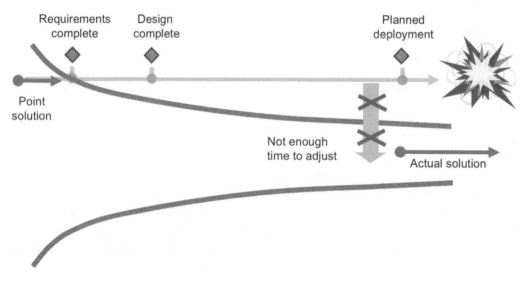

Figure 1. The problem of phase-gate milestones

Against this backdrop, it becomes clear that a different approach to milestones is needed, as is described in the rest of this chapter.

PI Milestones: Objective Evidence of Working Systems

SAFe provides a number of means to address the problems associated with the traditionally used milestones. In particular, Principle #4: Build incrementally with fast, integrated learning cycles, especially when used in conjunction with set-based design, provides elements of the solution.

With this approach, the system is built in increments, each of which is an integration and knowledge point that demonstrates evidence of the viability of the current in-process solution. Further, this is done routinely, on the PI *cadence*, which provides the discipline needed to ensure periodic availability and evaluation, as well as predetermined time boundaries that can be used to collapse the field of less desirable options. Each PI creates an objective measure of progress, as illustrated in Figure 2.

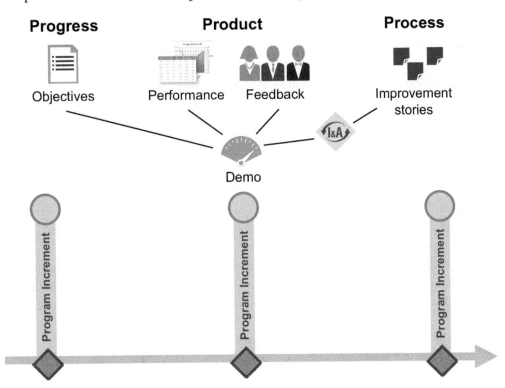

Figure 2. PI milestones provide objective evidence

This is true for both the Program and Large Solution levels, where solution/system integration and validation happen. Of course, what is actually measured at these critical integration points depends on the nature and type of the system being built. Nevertheless, the system can be measured, assessed, and evaluated frequently by the relevant stakeholders throughout development. Most importantly, changes can be made while there is still time to make them, as shown in Figure 3.

This provides the financial, technical, and fitness-for-purpose governance needed to ensure that the continuing investment will produce a commensurate return.

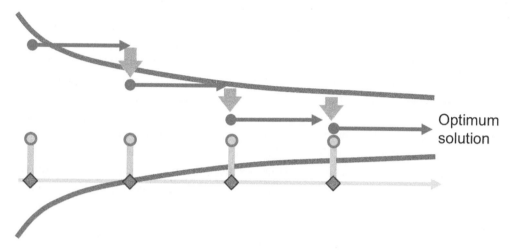

Figure 3. PI milestones guide system developers to the optimal solution

In SAFe, the PI milestones are the most critical learning milestones that control solution development—so critical that they are simply assumed as credible and objective milestones. In other words, every PI is a learning milestone of a sort. But there are other milestones as well, as described in the following sections.

Other Learning Milestones

In addition to the PI milestones, other learning milestones can be used to support the central goal of building a solution that satisfies customer needs and generates value for the business. It is critical that the value proposition behind a new solution, or a large initiative, is treated as a *hypothesis* that requires conceptualization and validation against actual market conditions. Translating a hypothesis into business demand is the science and art of Lean-Agile product management. It involves a great deal of intermediate organizational learning. Learning milestones can help. For example:

- Do the new product Capabilities have a market that is ready to pay for them?

- Do they solve the user problem for the users being targeted?

- Are the necessary nonfinancial accounting measures available to demonstrate real progress [2]?

- How much revenue can the organization expect?

- Is there a viable business model to support the new product or capability?

These and many other business concerns formulate the basic hypothesis for any large initiative. Learning milestones provide the necessary means to understand the feasibility of the solution and frame the right set of capabilities. Testing a concept of a new capability with a focus group, building and releasing a Minimum Viable Product (MVP), and validating Lean UX assumptions for a Minimum Marketable Feature (MMF) are examples of learning milestones. Such milestones do not necessarily occur on PI boundaries and may require significant effort to achieve, not only from the product development organization but also from other business functions in the enterprise, such as sales, marketing, operations, and finance.

Every learning milestone assumes that there is a certain degree of uncertainty that needs to be translated into knowledge and, ultimately, into business benefits for the organization. This requires set-based design thinking and the ability to pivot, if necessary, to a different concept of the solution.

Since the outcome of any learning milestone impacts the understanding of intent, milestones are planned incrementally, as Figure 4 suggests. Other elements, including the solution Vision, Solution Intent, and the Economic Framework, also evolve with the learning.

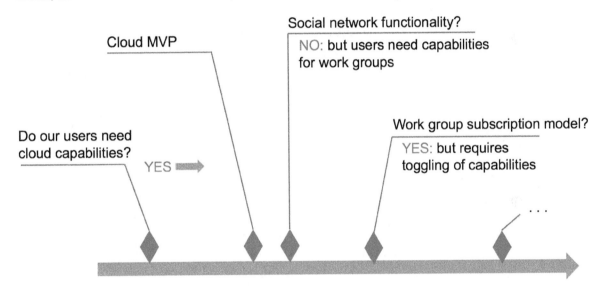

Figure 4. Learning milestones help evaluate progress toward the goal

But learning doesn't stop even when new product capabilities hit the market and start to generate business benefits. Every new capability and every significant nonfunctional aspect of the system needs facts to replace assumptions about anticipated value. In a Lean Enterprise environment, learning is an integral part of development, even for mature products. Meaningful learning milestones can help.

Fixed-Date Milestones

Every Lean-Agile enterprise wants to operate with minimal constraints. In part, that's the driving force for pursuing agility. The real world, however, has different concerns, and fixed-date milestones are common in both traditional and Lean-Agile development. For example, fixed dates may arise from the following sources:

- Events such as trade shows, customer demos, user group meetings, and preplanned product announcements

- Release dates that are controlled by other internal or external business concerns

- Contractually binding dates for delivery of value, intermediate milestones, payment, and demonstrations

- Scheduling of larger-scale integration issues, including hardware, software, supplier integration, and anything else where a fixed date provides an appropriate forcing function to bring together assets and validate their interoperability

Many more examples could be cited, of course. In Lean terms, fixed dates have a nonlinear cost of delay. That is, required system Features become a much higher priority as the date comes closer, as failure to meet the milestones has negative economic consequences. This is directly incorporated into Program and Solution Backlog prioritization via the Weighted Shortest Job First (WSJF) model; the 'time criticality' parameter gets higher as the fixed date gets closer, thereby increasing WSJF priorities for elements dependent on that date. In any case, any fixed-date milestones should be reflected on the relevant program or value stream Roadmap so all stakeholders can plan and act accordingly.

Other Milestones

In addition to the milestones discussed previously, other concerns must often be addressed to ensure the economic success of product development, such as filing patents, certifying the system, auditing certain regulatory requirements, and so on. In many instances these milestones influence content or priorities of work; they may even alter the development *process* itself. For example, the need to perform solution certification may increase the transaction cost of accepting a new Release into production and may drive teams to seek alternative ways of acquiring feedback before release. Again, any such milestones should appear on the relevant roadmap.

Planning and Executing Against Milestones

An understanding of which types of milestones are required to support value creation may originate from different sources. It may be communicated to portfolios from the enterprise, or identified during the analysis state in the Portfolio or Solution and Program Kanban systems, or even specified during the planning and roadmapping process for value streams and Agile Release Trains. Eventually, teams will have to create a specific plan of action during the PI planning process, build specific Stories in support of a milestone, reflect the milestone in their roadmaps and PI Objectives, understand and address dependencies with other teams and trains, and negotiate scope and time trade-offs with program stakeholders. Thereafter, execution of milestones happens incrementally. Progress is demoed every PI.

Measuring Success

Successful execution of milestones requires having criteria for what 'success' means, so there can be value in associating specific measures and metrics with milestones. For example, a milestone of 'capturing 25 percent market share' may require an understanding of revenue or usage indicators. A learning milestone of 'a search engine being able to reliably identify persons' names on a web page' could be supported by a limited percentage of false positives across the pages in the 'gold collection' of web data. In any case, thoughtful measures make for more meaningful milestones.

LEARN MORE

[1] Oosterwal, Dantar P. *The Lean Machine: How Harley-Davidson Drove Top-Line Growth and Profitability with Revolutionary Lean Product Development*. Amacom, 2010.

[2] Ries, Eric. *The Lean Startup: How Today's Entrepreneurs Use Continuous Innovation to Create Radically Successful Businesses*. Crown Business, 2011.

Roadmap

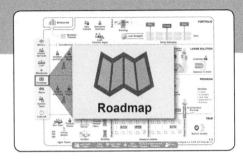

Prediction is very difficult, especially if it is about the future.

—Niels Bohr, Danish physicist

The *Roadmap* is a schedule of events and Milestones that communicate planned Solution deliverables over a timeline. It includes commitments for the planned, upcoming Program Increment (PI) and offers visibility into the deliverables forecasted for the next few PIs.

Of course, predicting the future is a hazardous business, and a Lean-Agile Enterprise must be able to respond to changing facts, learning, and business conditions. The real world, however, occasionally demands some certainty. As a consequence, it may be necessary for enterprises to predict on a longer-term basis. Some initiatives take years to develop, and some degree of commitment must be made to Customers, Suppliers, and partners. Moreover, SAFe provides some guidance for forecasting over the longer term, based on the estimated scope of new work, the velocity of the Agile Release Trains (ARTs) and Solution Trains, and the current predictability of program execution. (See the discussion of the program predictability measure in the Metrics chapter.)

The desired forecasting horizon must be balanced carefully. Too short, and the enterprise may jeopardize alignment and the ability to communicate important new future Features and Capabilities. Too long, and the enterprise is basing assumptions and commitments on an uncertain future.

Details

"Responding to change over following a plan" is one of the four values of the Agile Manifesto [1]. To live up to that value, it is quite important to have a plan—otherwise, everything is a change, and the backlog is the tail of the dog that is constantly wagged by changes that could have been readily anticipated. In turn, this causes thrashing, excess rework, and too much Work in Process (WIP). Such a situation is demotivating to all. Planning helps eliminate unnecessary thrashing—and that's a good thing!

The roadmap provides a plan that helps the teams understand their current commitments and the plan of intent in a broader context. The ability to routinely execute those plans provides a sense of personal satisfaction and increases morale. It also offers the extra mental and physical capacity necessary to respond to the *real changes*, those that could not have been anticipated.

The SAFe roadmap consists of a series of planned PIs with various milestones called out, as shown in Figure 1. Each element on the roadmap is a milestone—either a learning milestone that has been defined by the teams or a fixed-date milestone that may be driven by external events.

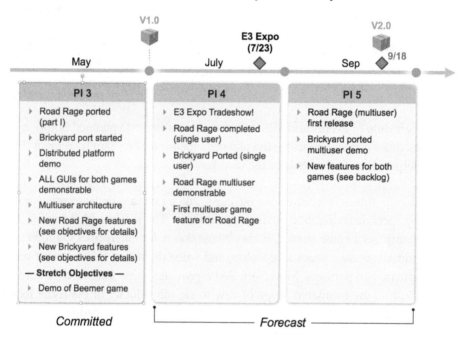

Figure 1. An example PI roadmap for a game company

Building the PI Roadmap

Figure 1 shows a roadmap that covers three PIs or approximately 30 weeks. In many enterprises, this is about the sweet spot—there's enough detail to be able to run the business, yet a short enough time frame to keep long-term commitments from interfering with the ability to flex to changing business priorities. This roadmap consists of a committed PI and two forecasted PIs, as described in the following sections. It's important to note that a forecast does not represent a commitment.

The Committed PI

During PI Planning, teams commit to meeting the program PI Objectives for the next PI. Therefore, the current PI plan is a high-confidence plan; the enterprise should be able to confidently plan for the impact of the upcoming new functionality. For ARTs that are new to SAFe and have yet to reach high confidence levels with their PI plans, the System Demo and Inspect and Adapt (I&A) workshop will help increase confidence in each PI. In any case, achieving predictable delivery of the upcoming PI is a key capability for every ART.

Forecast PIs

Forecasting the next two PIs is a little more interesting. ARTs and Solution Trains typically plan only one PI at a time. For most, it's simply unwise to plan in detail much further out (except perhaps for some Architectural Runway), since the business and technical context changes so quickly.

However, the Program and Solution Backlogs contain Features and Capabilities (which are future milestones) that have been working their way through the Kanban systems. They have been reasoned, have been socialized with the teams, have acceptance criteria and a benefit hypothesis, and have preliminary estimates for size in Story points. Given knowledge of the ART velocities, the PI predictability measure, relative priorities, and the history of how much work is devoted to maintenance and other business-as-usual activities, ARTs can generally lay the future features into the roadmap without too much difficulty. As a result, most trains have roadmaps with a reasonable degree of confidence over about a three-PI period.

Long-Term Forecasting

The previous discussion highlighted how enterprises can have a reasonable, near-term plan of intent for all the ARTs in the portfolio. However, for many enterprises, especially those building large, complex systems, complete with suppliers, long hardware lead times, major subsystems, critical delivery dates, external customer commitments, and so on, that amount of roadmap will be inadequate. Simply put, building a satellite, an intelligent combine harvester, or a new car takes a lot longer than the time span covered by the PI roadmap, and the enterprise must plan realistically for the longer-term future.

Also, even when external events do not necessarily drive the requirement for long-term forecasting, enterprises need to be able to plan their investments in future periods. They need to understand the potential resource and development bottlenecks in support of the longer-term business demands and the waxing and waning of investments in particular Value Streams.

The conclusion, then, is inevitable: It is most likely necessary to extend the forecast well beyond the PI planning horizon, even though the future work is largely unplanned.

Estimating Longer-Term Initiatives

Fortunately, Agile work physics gives us a means to forecast longer-term work. Of course, to forecast the work, estimation is required. Agile teams can use story points, based on normalized estimating to forecast larger initiatives at the Epic level.

Epics are split into potential features during the Portfolio Kanban 'analysis' state. Typically, Product Management and System Architect/Engineering estimates the features based on history and relative size. Individual Agile teams are engaged in this estimation as needed.

Figure 2 depicts how Epics are split into Features, which are then estimated in story points. The features estimates are rolled up into the epic story point estimate as part of the Lean business case.

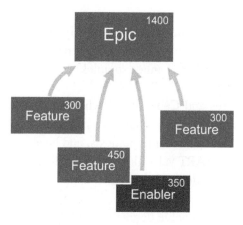

1. Epics are broken down into potential features during the Portfolio Kanban analysis stage

2. Potential features are estimated in story points
   – Typically performed by PM and System Architects, based on history and relative size
   – Individual teams are engaged as necessary

3. Feature estimates are aggregated back into the epic estimate as part of the lightweight business case

Figure 2. Epics are estimated in story points rolled up from feature estimates

Given the story points, a knowledge of ART velocities, and some sense of the capacity allocation that can be provided to new initiatives, the business can then play out a what-if analysis, as Figure 3 illustrates.

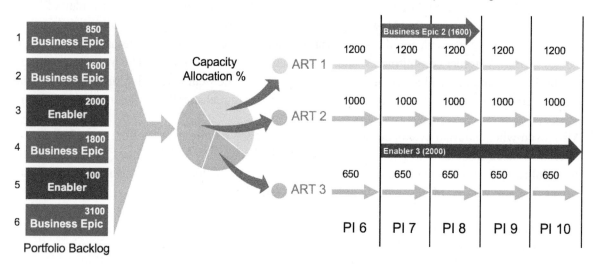

Figure 3. Epic estimates, capacity allocations, and Agile Release Train velocities are used for longer-term forecasting

Using this forecasting approach, the enterprise can build a roadmap that goes as far into the future as it needs. However, every enterprise must be very careful about such forecasts. While many see long-term predictability as the goal, Lean-Agile Leaders know that every long-term commitment decreases the enterprise's agility.

Even in a case in which requirements can be fairly well established in advance, the unpredictability and variability of innovation, the tendency to estimate only the known activities, and the difficulty of predicting future capacity, unforeseen events, and other factors all conspire to create a bias for under-estimating reality. The net effect is that while fixed, long-term plans and commitments may feel good, and may even be required in some circumstances, they absolutely limit the ability of the enterprise to pivot to a new, and potentially more economically beneficial, outcome. You can't have it both ways.

Ultimately, the Lean-Agile enterprise strives to establish the right amount of visibility, alignment, and commitment, while enabling the right amount of flexibility. The correct balance can be obtained via a willingness to convert long-term commitments into forecasts and to continually reevaluate priorities and business value, as needs dictate, at each PI boundary.

Avoid Turning the Roadmap into a Queue

Lean-Agile Leaders must understand the queuing theory discussed in SAFe Principle #6: Visualize and limit WIP, reduce batch sizes, and manage queue lengths, and be aware of the impact that long queues have on delivery time. Simply put, the longer the committed queue, the longer the wait for any new initiative.

For example, in Figure 1, the second PI on the roadmap does not appear to be fully loaded. The math tells us that the wait time for a new, unplanned feature is 10–20 weeks; it can't be in the current PI, but it can be scheduled for the next PI.

The roadmap in Figure 4 tells a different story. For example, if all the items on this roadmap are fully committed and the teams are running at nearly full capacity, then the wait time for a new capability is in excess of 50 weeks! (This assumes a 10-week PI duration.) The enterprise, while thinking it's Agile, is really stuck in a traditional mindset, if its leaders do not understand Little's law of queueing theory.

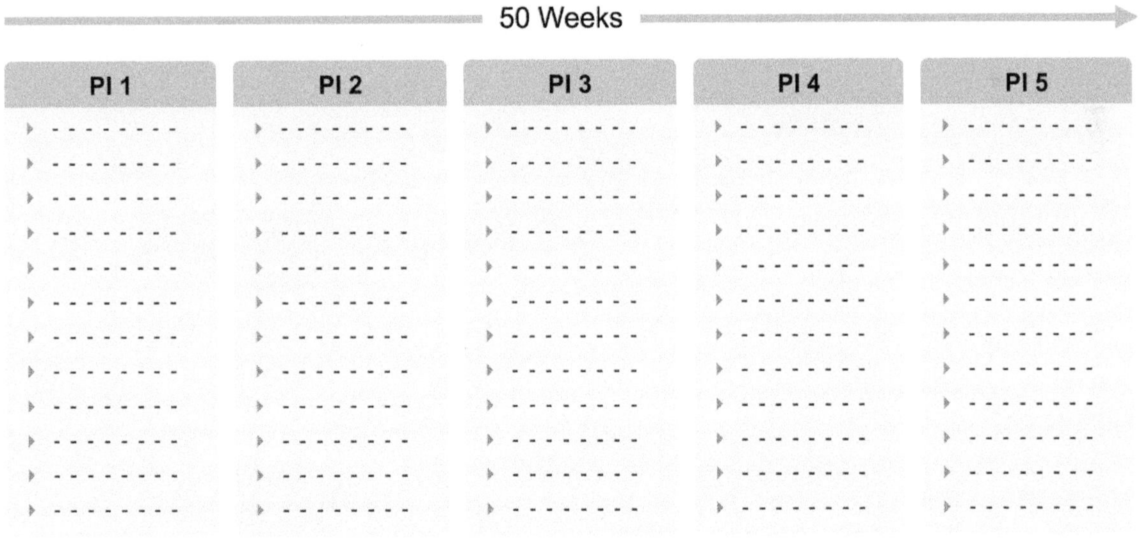

Figure 4. A fully committed roadmap becomes a queue

LEARN MORE

[1] The Agile Manifesto. http://agilemanifesto.org.

Vision

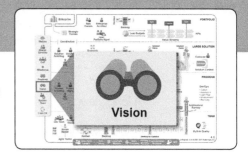

People at work are thirsting for context, yearning to know that what they do contributes to a larger whole.

—Daniel Pink

The *Vision* is a description of the future state of the Solution under development. It reflects Customer and stakeholder needs, as well as the Feature and Capabilities proposed to meet those needs.

The vision is both aspirational and achievable, providing the broader context—an overview and purpose—of the solution under development. It describes the markets, customer segments, and user needs. It sets the boundaries and context for new features, Nonfunctional Requirements (NFRs), and other work.

The vision applies to any level of SAFe, which explains why it's on the spanning palette. While its focus is typically on the solution, a portfolio vision is also clearly relevant, reflecting how the Value Streams will cooperate to achieve the Enterprise objectives. Agile Release Trains (ARTs) and Agile Teams may also have their own visions to communicate their part in developing the solution.

Details

Few question the benefit of Lean-Agile's focus on near-term deliverables and fast value delivery, which favors deferring decisions until the last responsible moment and limiting Work in Process (WIP). This approach also avoids Big Design Up-Front (BDUF), future-proofing architectures, and overly detailed plans. There is no substitute for a bias for action: 'Let's build it, and then we'll know.'

However, in the context of large solutions, every individual contributor makes many decisions. Therefore, continuously developing, maintaining, and communicating the vision is critical to creating a shared understanding of the program's goals and objectives, especially as those ideas evolve due to ever-shifting market needs and business drivers.

Portfolio Vision

The portfolio vision sets a longer-term context for near-term decisions in a way that is both practical and inspirational: 'This is something worth doing.' Understanding the longer-term view helps the

Agile teams make more informed choices about the development of functionality in both the short term and the long run.

Lean-Agile Leaders have the most responsibility for setting the strategic direction of the company and establishing the mission for the teams that will implement that strategy. The authors of *Switch* call this view a 'Destination Postcard' (Figure 1) [1].

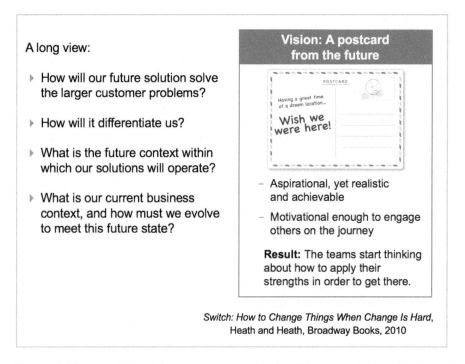

A long view:

▸ How will our future solution solve the larger customer problems?

▸ How will it differentiate us?

▸ What is the future context within which our solutions will operate?

▸ What is our current business context, and how must we evolve to meet this future state?

Vision: A postcard from the future

POSTCARD

Having a great time at a dream location...

Wish we were here!

– Aspirational, yet realistic and achievable

– Motivational enough to engage others on the journey

Result: The teams start thinking about how to apply their strengths in order to get there.

Switch: How to Change Things When Change Is Hard, Heath and Heath, Broadway Books, 2010

Figure 1. The portfolio vision is an enterprise-level 'postcard from the future.'

A portfolio vision exhibits the following characteristics:

- **Aspirational, yet realistic and achievable** – It must be compelling and somewhat futuristic, yet practical enough to be feasible over some meaningful time frame.

- **Motivational to engage others on the journey** – The vision must align with the Strategic Themes, as well as with the individual team's purpose.

Business Owners (or C-level executives) typically present this longer-term view and business context during the Program Increment (PI) Planning event. These leaders can inspire and align the teams, increasing their engagement and fostering their creativity to achieve the best results.

Solution Vision

Product and Solution Management have the responsibility for translating the portfolio vision into a solution vision, indicating the reason and direction behind the chosen solution. Doing so requires specific questions to be asked and answered:

- What will this new solution do?

- Which problems will it solve?

- Which features and benefits will it provide?

- For whom will it provide them?

- Which Nonfunctional Requirements will it satisfy?

Inputs to the Solution Vision

Product and Solution Management work directly with Business Owners and other stakeholders to synthesize all the inputs and integrate them into a holistic and cohesive vision, as illustrated in Figure 2. These inputs include the following resources:

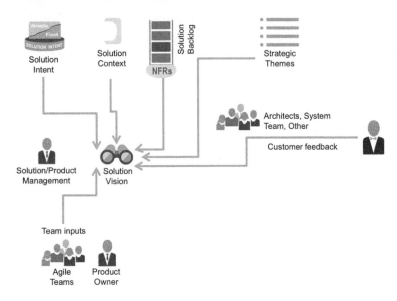

Figure 2. Solution vision input sources

- **Customers** – End users and Customers provide fast feedback and have intimate knowledge of what is needed.

- **Strategic themes** – The strategic themes provide direction and serve as decision-making filters.

- **Solution Context** – The solution context indicates how the solution interacts with the customer's context.

- **Solution Backlog** – The solution backlog contributes direction and guidance to the vision.

- **Solution Intent** – The solution intent contains some of the vision and is the destination for new elements.

- **Architect/Engineers** – The system and solution architects/engineers support the continuous evolution of the Architectural Runway, which in turn supports current and near-term features.

- **Agile Teams** – The foremost experts in the domain are typically the Agile teams themselves.

- **Product Owners** – The Product Owners continuously communicate and integrate emerging requirements and opportunities back into the program vision.

Capturing Vision in Solution Intent

Given the SAFe practice of cadence-based, face-to-face PI planning, vision documentation (various forms of which can be found in [2], [3], and [4]) is augmented—and sometimes replaced—by rolling-wave vision briefings. These briefings provide routine, periodic presentations of the short- and longer-term vision to the teams. During PI planning, Large Solution level stakeholders, such as Solution Management, describe the current overall solution vision, while Product Management provides the specific ART context and vision.

The relevant elements of the vision, along with details of the current and specific behaviors of the system, are captured in solution intent.

Program Vision

When using Full SAFe or Large Solution SAFe, each ART will likely have its own vision, detailing the direction of the specific capabilities or subsystems that it produces. This vision should be tightly coupled to the solution vision it supports.

Roadmap View

Having a sense of direction is critical to planning and engagement. Of course, unless there is some realistic plan for how teams will fulfill the vision, people won't actually know what they must do. That purpose is filled by the Roadmap. Figure 3 provides an example.

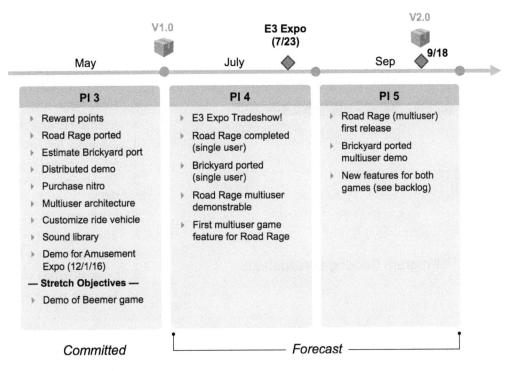

Figure 3. The roadmap is part of the vision

PI Planning Vision: The Top 10 Features

The roadmap is indeed helpful—but for action and execution, the immediate steps must be clear. Product and Solution Management have the responsibility to provide the direction for these next steps. In the SAFe context, this translates into a series of incremental steps forward, one PI at a time and one feature at a time, as illustrated in Figure 4.

To achieve this, Product Management constantly updates feature priorities using the Weighted Shortest Job First (WSJF) model. Then, during PI planning, they present the top 10 features to the team. The team won't be surprised by the new list, as they will have seen the vision evolve over time and will be aware of the new features that are headed their way. Further, the Program Kanban is used to explore the scope of features, their benefit hypotheses, and their acceptance criteria; thus, when features reach this boundary, they are fairly well formed and vetted. Architect/Engineering has already reviewed them, and various Enablers have already been implemented.

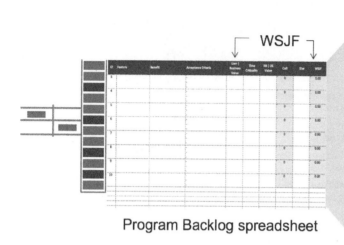

WSJF

Program Backlog spreadsheet

Top 10 Features
for PI 3+

1. Reward points
2. Road Rage ported
3. Estimate Brickyard port
4. Demo for Amusement Expo 12/1/2016
5. Distributed platform demo
6. Purchase nitro
7. Spike new GUI
8. Multiuser architecture
9. Customize ride vehicle
10. Enhance sound library

Figure 4. Vision is achieved one PI at a time, via the 'Top 10 Features for the next PI.'

However, everyone understands that the top 10 list is an input to the planning process, rather than an output of, and recognizes that what can be achieved in the next PI is subject to capacity limitations, dependencies, knowledge that emerges during planning, and more. Only the teams can plan and commit to a course of action, one that is summarized in the PI Objectives.

But these features are ready for implementation. And feature by feature, the program marches forward toward the accomplishment of the vision.

Likewise, Solution Management presents a similar top 10 capabilities list during Pre-PI Planning to align the ARTs within a Solution Train.

LEARN MORE

[1] Heath, Chip, and Dan Heath. *Switch: How to Change Things When Change Is Hard.* Broadway Books, 2010.

[2] Leffingwell, Dean. *Agile Software Requirements: Lean Requirements Practices for Teams, Programs, and the Enterprise.* Addison-Wesley, 2011.

[3] Leffingwell, Dean. *Scaling Software Agility: Best Practices for Large Enterprises.* Addison-Wesley, 2007.

[4] Leffingwell, Dean, and Don Widrig. *Managing Software Requirements.* Addison-Wesley, 2001.

System Team

The whole is greater than the sum of its parts.

—Aristotle

The *System Team* is a specialized Agile Team that assists in building and using the Agile development environment, including Continuous Integration, test automation, and Continuous Deployment. The System Team supports the integration of assets from Agile teams, performs end-to-end Solution testing where necessary, and assists with deployment and release.

In SAFe, Agile teams are not stand-alone units. Instead, they are part of the Agile Release Train (ART), responsible collectively for delivering larger system and solution value. During the transition to Agile, additional infrastructure work is typically required to integrate solution assets more frequently. To accomplish this, one or more specialized System Teams are often formed. They help build the environments and assist with system and solution integration. They also help demo the solution as it evolves.

Once the infrastructure matures, System Teams are sometimes eliminated from an ART, and the development teams take on the responsibilities for maintenance and use. In larger solutions, it's more likely that specialty expertise remains with one or more System Teams, where the combination of people, skills, and technical assets delivers the best economic value.

Details

The System Team assists in building and using the Agile development environment infrastructure—including continuous integration—as well as integrating assets from Agile teams and performing end-to-end solution testing. The members of this team often participate in the System Demo at the end of each Iteration and in the Solution Demo at the end of each Program Increment (PI), or more frequently if necessary. The demos support the teams and other stakeholders by providing quick feedback concerning the fitness for use and integrity of the evolving end-to-end solution. System Teams may also assist with releasing and the coordination of Solution Trains.

However, the System Team and Agile teams share this responsibility. Otherwise, the System Team will become a bottleneck, and the Agile teams will not be fully capable of or accountable for real value delivery.

The System Team in Solution Trains

For large, multi-ART value streams that need the constructs of the Solution Train, System Teams are particularly useful. Depending on the scope and complexity of the value stream there are three main patterns for structuring the System Team:

- There is one System Team per ART, which coordinates the solution integration and validation without additional help.

- There is a System Team only for the Solution Train, which can fulfill these responsibilities for each of its ARTs.

- There are System Teams for both the ARTs and the Solution Train.

The decision regarding which pattern to use depends on the specific context of the value stream. Factors include the ART structure within the value stream (built around features or components), solution architecture, branching and integration policies across the ARTs, system testability, and development infrastructure.

Responsibilities

The System Team's primary responsibilities are described next.

Building Development Infrastructure

Good infrastructure supports high ART velocity, so the System Team may do the following:

- Create and maintain infrastructure, including continuous integration, automated builds, and automated build verification testing

- Create platforms and environments for solution demos, development, quality assurance, user acceptance testing, and staging

- Create products, utilities, and scripts to automate deployment

- Facilitate the technical aspects of collaboration with third parties, such as data or service providers and hosting facilities

System Integration

Complex solutions also require that the System Team do the following:

- Participate in PI Planning and the Pre- and Post-PI Planning meetings at the Large Solution Level, and in backlog refinement to define integration and test backlog items

- Determine and help maintain decisions and policies for appropriate branching models

- Run solution-level integration scripts or manually integrate areas where automation is not yet possible

- Assist component teams in defining intercomponent interfaces

- Attend other teams' stand-ups to support daily activities

End-to-End and Solution Performance Testing

The System Team may also perform some automated testing duties:

- Create newly automated test scenarios

- Extend test scenarios to data sets that more closely match production

- Organize test cases designed by individual teams into ordered suites

- Perform manual testing and run automated tests for new features and Stories

- Prioritize time-consuming tests, refactor, and run reduced test suites where applicable

- Help teams create reduced test suites that they can run independently

- Test solution performance against Nonfunctional Requirements (NFRs) and assist System and Solution Engineering in identifying system shortfalls and bottlenecks

System and Solution Demos

At the appropriate time during every iteration, the ART demonstrates the current, whole system to stakeholders in the system demos. Likewise, the Solution Train must integrate the work completed to date and show progress at the solution demo. The System Team typically helps prepare the technical environments, so that team members can adequately and reliably demo the new solution functionality.

Release

The System Team members often have unique skills and experience related to the evolving solution. They may include senior quality assurance personnel; perhaps the System Architect/Engineer serves as a member of this team. These team members have seen the solution progress across multiple iterations, which means they understand what it is, what it does, and how well it meets the intended requirements. With this perspective, the System Team is likely to be directly involved in supporting the PI. As part of DevOps and the Continuous Delivery Pipeline activities, they will be doing whatever is necessary to help the ART or Solution Train prepare, package, and deploy a solution into the target environment.

Balancing Solution Integration and Testing Effort

The System Team, however, can never be the entire solution to the integration challenge. Agile teams must also envision the bigger picture of what they are creating. Otherwise, not even the local excellence of Agile teams will result in good economic outcomes. Efficient solution development requires sharing best practices. For example, if just the System Team is testing NFRs, and individual teams don't perform even lightweight performance testing, then the entire ART velocity will be slowed by the rework necessary to pass these critical quality tests. Similarly, if Agile teams are not continuously integrating, at a minimum, the immediate components they interface with, the System Team effort will be a long and painful process. Maximizing ART velocity requires maintaining an effective balance between Agile Teams and System Teams (see Figure 1). With maturity and automation, the optimal point for integration responsibility moves to the left.

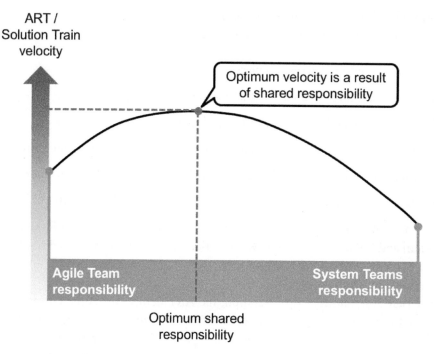

Figure 1. The optimal balance of integration effort between Agile teams and System Teams

---

LEARN MORE

[1] Leffingwell, Dean. *Agile Software Requirements: Lean Requirements Practices for Teams, Programs, and the Enterprise*. Addison-Wesley, 2011.

Lean UX

*What if we found ourselves building something that nobody wanted?
In that case, what did it matter if we did it on time and on budget?*

—Eric Ries

Lean User Experience (Lean UX) design is a mindset, a culture, and a process that embraces Lean-Agile methods. It implements functionality in minimum viable increments and determines success by measuring results against a benefit hypothesis.

Lean UX design extends the traditional UX role beyond merely executing design elements and anticipating how users might interact with a system. Instead, it encourages a far more comprehensive view of why a Feature exists, which functionality is required to implement it, and which benefits it delivers. By getting immediate feedback to understand whether the system will meet the real business objectives, Lean UX provides a closed-loop system for defining and measuring value.

Details

Generally, UX represents a user's perceptions of a system—ease of use, utility, and the effectiveness of the user interface (UI). UX design focuses on building systems that demonstrate a deep understanding of end users. It takes into account what users need and want, while making allowances for those users' context and limitations.

A common problem, when using Agile methods, is how best to incorporate UX design into a rapid Iteration cycle that results in a full-stack implementation of the new functionality. When teams attempt to resolve complex and seemingly subjective user interactions, while simultaneously trying to develop incremental deliverables, they can often churn through many designs, which can become a source of frustration with Agile development.

Fortunately, the Lean UX movement addresses these issues by combining Agile development with Lean Startup implementation approaches. The mindset, principles, and practices of SAFe reflects this new thinking. This process often begins with the Lean Startup Cycle described in the Epic chapter in Part 8 and continues with the development of features and Capabilities using the Lean UX process described here.

As a result, Agile teams and Agile Release Trains (ARTs) can leverage a common strategy to generate rapid development, fast feedback, and a holistic user experience that delights users.

The Lean UX Process

In *Lean UX*, Gothelf and Seiden [2] describe a model that we have adapted to our context. This model is illustrated in Figure 1.

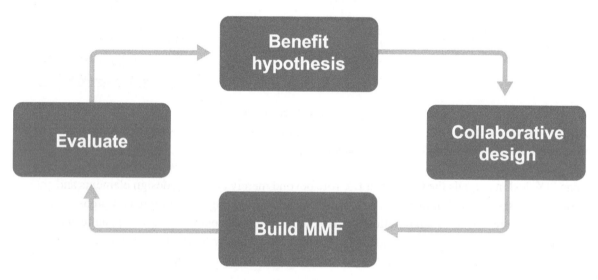

Figure 1. The Lean UX process (adapted from [2])

Benefit Hypothesis

The Lean UX approach starts with a benefit hypothesis: Agile teams and UX designers accept the reality that the 'right answer' is unknowable up-front. Instead, teams apply Agile methods to avoid Big Design Up-Front (BDUF), focusing on creating a hypothesis about the feature's expected business result, and then they implement and test that hypothesis incrementally.

The SAFe Feature and Benefit matrix (FAB) can be used to capture this hypothesis as it moves through the Continuous Exploration cycle of the Program Kanban:

- **Feature** – A short phrase giving a name and context
- **Benefit hypothesis** – The proposed measurable benefit to the end user or business

Measuring the outcome is best done using leading indicators (see the 'Innovation Accounting' discussion in [1]) to evaluate how well the new feature is progressing toward its benefits hypothesis. For example, the indicator might state, 'We believe the administrator can add a new user in half the time it took before.'

Collaborative Design

Traditionally, UX design has been an area of specialization. People who had an eye for design, a feel for user interaction, and specialty training were often placed in charge of the entire design process. The goal was 'pixel-perfect' early designs, done in advance of the implementation. Usually, this work was done in silos, apart from the very people who knew the most about the system and its context. Success was measured by how well the implemented user interface complied with the initial UX design. In Lean UX, that situation changes dramatically:

> "Lean UX literally has no time for heroes. The entire concept of design as hypothesis immediately dethrones notions of heroism; as a designer, you must expect that many of your ideas will fail in testing. Heroes don't admit failure. But Lean UX designers embrace it as part of the process." [2]

Agile teams apply Principle #2: Apply systems thinking to their Lean UX design activities, moving from a siloed specialist approach to a collaborative, cross-functional design model. Agile Teams and ARTs are ideally suited for this model, which should include all the design–build–test cross-functional skills. The design perspectives of Product Management, System Architecture, Business Owners, information security, operations, and Shared Services should also be included, thereby ensuring a solution that is fit for use both for the end-user and supports deployment operations and for customer support.

Principle #9: Decentralize decision-making provides additional guidance for the Lean UX process: Agile teams are empowered to do collaborative UX design and implementation, and that significantly improves business outcomes and time-to-market. Moreover, another important goal is to deliver a consistent user experience across various system elements or channels (e.g., mobile, web, kiosk) or even across different products from the same company. Making this consistency a reality requires some centralized control (following Principle #9) over certain reusable design assets. A design system [2] is a set of standards that contains whatever UI elements the teams find useful, including the following:

- Editorial rules, style guides, voice and tone guidelines, naming conventions, standard terms, and abbreviations

- Branding and corporate identity kits, color palettes, usage guidelines for copyrights, logos, trademarks, and other attributions

- UI asset libraries, which include icons and other images, standard layouts, and grids

- UI widgets, which include the design of buttons and other similar elements

Making these assets more accessible allows the team to 'do the right thing,' as part of their natural workflow without friction. Moreover, this approach supports decentralized control, while realizing that some elements of the design system need to be centralized. After all, these decisions are infrequent, have long-lasting effects, and provide significant economies of scale, as described in Principle #9.

Build MMF

With a hypothesis and design in place, teams can proceed to implement the functionality in a Minimum Marketable Feature (MMF). The MMF should be the minimum functionality that the teams can build to learn whether the benefit hypothesis is valid or not. By doing this, ARTs apply Principle #4: Build incrementally with fast, integrated learning cycles to implement and evaluate the feature.

In some cases, the MMF could initially be extremely lightweight and not even functional (e.g., paper prototypes, low-fidelity mockups, simulations, API stubs). In other cases, a vertical thread (full stack) of just a portion of an MMF may be necessary to test the architecture and get fast feedback at a System Demo. However, in some instances, functionality may need to proceed all the way through to deployment and Release, where application instrumentation and telemetry provide feedback data from production users.

(Note: Telemetry is an automated process by which measurements and other data are collected at remote or inaccessible points and transmitted for monitoring and analysis. Telemetry could apply to both technical and business aspects of the functionality. For example: performance monitoring of solution components and automated A/B testing.)

User Stories

SAFe teams implement features via user Stories. Conveniently, user stories are written using a format that supports the outcome–hypothesis approach of Lean UX:

> *As a <user role> I can <activity> so that <business value>.*

Incremental implementation of features using stories enables continuous testing of the results against the benefit hypothesis.

Personas

To better understand their users, Agile teams apply user personas, which are representations of the characteristics, goals, and behaviors of different types of end users. Developing and maintaining a deep understanding of primary and secondary user personas is a common practice of successful Agile teams. (For more on personas, see [3].)

Evaluate

When implementing an MMF, there are a variety of ways to determine whether the feature delivers the right outcomes:

- **Observation** – Wherever possible, directly observe the actual usage of the system; it's an opportunity to understand the user's context and behaviors.

- **User surveys** – When direct observation isn't possible, a simple end-user questionnaire can obtain fast feedback.

- **Usage analytics** – Lean-Agile teams may build analytics directly into their applications, which helps validate initial use and provides the application telemetry needed to support a Continuous Delivery model. Telemetry offers constant operational and user feedback from the deployed system.

- **A/B testing** – This form of statistical hypothesis compares two samples, while acknowledging that user preferences are unknowable in advance. Recognizing this fact is truly liberating, eliminating endless arguments between designers and developers— who likely won't use the system. Teams follow Principle #3: Assume variability; preserve options to keep their design options open as long as possible. Wherever it's practical and economically feasible, they should implement multiple alternatives for critical user activities. Then they can test those other options with mockups, prototypes, or even full-stack implementations. In the last case, differing versions may be deployed to multiple subsets of users, perhaps sequenced over time and measured via analytics.

In short, measurable results deliver the knowledge that teams need to refactor, adjust, redesign, or even pivot to abandon a feature, based solely on objective data and user feedback. Measurement creates a closed-loop Lean UX process that iterates toward a successful outcome, driven by actual evidence of whether a feature fulfills the hypothesis.

LEARN MORE

[1] Ries, Eric. *The Lean Startup: How Today's Entrepreneurs Use Continuous Innovation to Create Radically Successful Businesses*. Random House. Kindle Edition.

[2] Gothelf, Jeff, and Josh Seiden. *Lean UX: Designing Great Products with Agile Teams*. O'Reilly Media, 2016.

[3] Leffingwell, Dean. *Agile Software Requirements: Lean Requirements Practices for Teams, Programs, and the Enterprise*. Addison-Wesley, 2011.

Part 7

The Large Solution Level

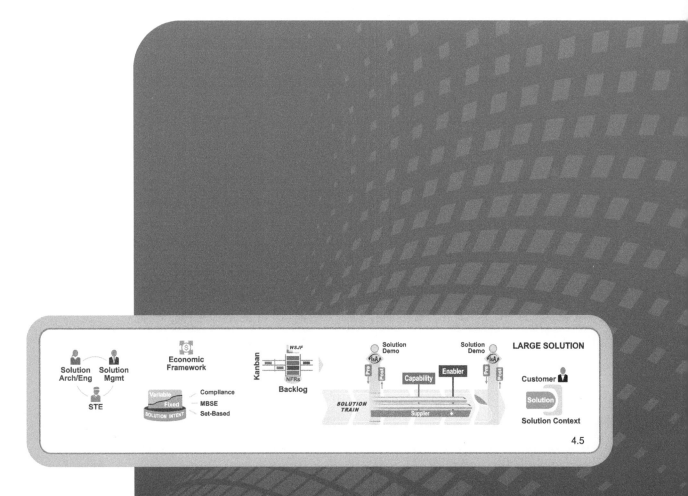

Introduction to the Large Solution Level

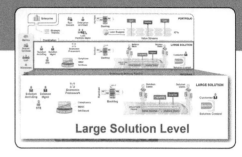

Large Solution Level

Everything must be made as simple as possible. But not simpler.

— Albert Einstein

The *Large Solution Level* contains the roles, artifacts, and processes needed to build large and complex solutions. This includes a stronger focus on capturing requirements in Solution Intent, the coordination of multiple Agile Release Trains (ARTs) and Suppliers, and the need to ensure compliance with regulations and standards.

Einstein's quote reminds us that we should strive to make things as simple as possible, but not simpler than what is needed. Similarly, when building large and complex systems, theoretically the simplest thing that could *possibly* work would be a single team. Of course, we know that even teams with more than 10 people are problematic. And a single 'team' of hundreds, or even thousands, of people just isn't feasible. Instead, we scale by organizing people into ARTs (a team-of-Agile-teams) and Solution Trains (a team of multiple ARTs). Coordinating the work of a Solution Train to build large and complex solutions requires additional roles, events, and artifacts, which is the purpose of the large solution level.

Details

The large solution level (see Figure 1) is meant for enterprises that face the biggest challenges—building large-scale solutions that are beyond the scope of a single ART to develop. Building these solutions requires additional roles, artifacts, events, and coordination.

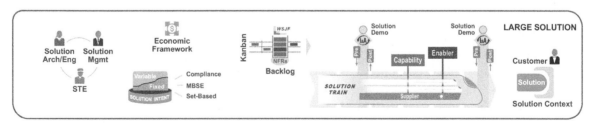

Figure 1. Large solution level

Highlights

Following are the highlights of the large solution level:

- **Solution** – Each Value Stream produces one or more solutions, which are products, services, or systems delivered to the Customer, whether internal or external to the enterprise.

- **Solution Train** – The key organizational element of the large solution level, it aligns the people and the work around a common solution vision, mission, and backlog.

- **Economic Framework** – The economic framework is a set of decision rules that aligns everyone to the financial objectives of the Solution and guides the economic decision-making process.

- **Solution Intent** – This repository for current and future solution behaviors can be used to support verification, validation, and Compliance. Solution intent is also used to extend Built-In Quality practices with systems engineering disciplines, including Set-Based Design, Model-Based Systems Engineering (MBSE), Compliance, and Agile Architecture.

- **Solution Context** – This context describes how the system will interface and be packaged and deployed in its operating environment.

- **Solution Kanban and Backlog** – The Solution Kanban and Solution Backlog are used to manage the flow of solution Epics and Capabilities.

Roles

The large solution level roles provide governance and help coordinate multiple ARTs and suppliers:

- **Customer** – The ultimate buyer of every solution. An integral part of the Lean-Agile development process and value stream, customers have specific responsibilities in SAFe.

- **Solution Architect/Engineering** – An individual or small team that defines a shared technical and architectural vision for the solution under development.

- **Solution Management** – The representative of the customer's overall needs across ARTs, as well as the communicator of the portfolio's Strategic Themes. This individual collaborates with Product Management to define capabilities and split them into features. Solution Management, as the primary content authority for the solution backlog, also contributes to the economic framework that governs ARTs and Agile teams.

- **Solution Train Engineer (STE)** – A servant leader and coach who facilitates and guides the work of all ARTs and suppliers.

- **Supplier** – An internal or external organization that develops and delivers components, subsystems, or services, which in turn help Solution Trains deliver solutions to customers.

Events

The large solution level uses three major activities to help coordinate multiple ARTs and suppliers:

- **Pre- and Post-PI Planning** – An event used to prepare for, and follow up after, Program Increment (PI) Planning for ARTs and suppliers in a Solution Train.

- **Solution Demo** – An event in which the results of all the development efforts from multiple ARTs—along with the contributions from suppliers—are integrated, evaluated, and made visible to customers and other stakeholders.

- **Inspect & Adapt (I&A)** – A significant event where the current state of the solution is demonstrated and evaluated. Teams then reflect and identify improvement backlog items via a structured problem-solving workshop.

Artifacts

The following large-solution-level artifacts help coordinate multiple ARTs and suppliers:

- **Capabilities** – Higher-level solution behaviors that typically span multiple ARTs. They are sized and split into multiple features so that they can be implemented in a single PI.

- **Solution Epics** – Epics that apply specifically to one Solution Train.

- **Nonfunctional Requirements (NFRs)** – System qualities such as security, reliability, performance, maintainability, scalability, and usability; they are incorporated in the solution intent.

- **Solution Backlog** – The holding area for upcoming capabilities and enablers, each of which can span multiple ARTs and is intended to advance the solution and build its architectural runway.

- **Solution Kanban** – A method used to visualize and manage the flow of business and enabler capabilities from ideation to analysis, implementation, and release.

Solution Trains Deliver Value

The Solution Train is the organizational vehicle that is used to coordinate the efforts of multiple ARTs and suppliers to deliver the world's largest and most complex systems. These trains align and coordinate ARTs and suppliers so that they can collaborate like a single team but have all the advantages inherent in organizing using small teams and ARTs to scale the development and release effort.

Apply Large Solution Elements to Other SAFe Configurations

A number of unique elements are present at the large solution level, yet any individual element of this level may also be applied to the Essential SAFe or Portfolio SAFe configurations. For example, solution intent and compliance might be used by a single ART that is building a medical device of modest scale. As illustrated in Figure 2, this is part of SAFe's scalability and configurability.

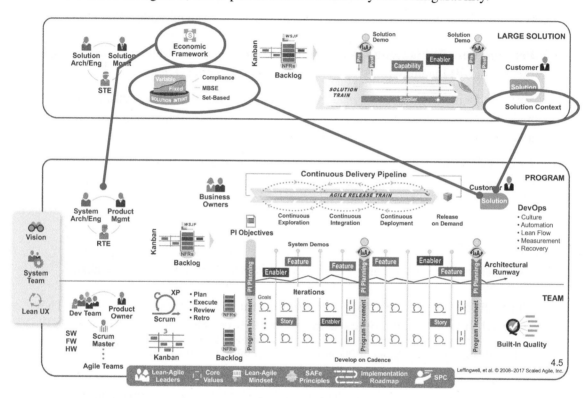

Figure 2. Applying large solution level elements to other SAFe configurations

Solution Train

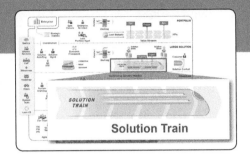

Principle of Alignment: There is more value created with overall alignment than with local excellence.

—Don Reinertsen

The *Solution Train* is the organizational construct used to build large and complex Solutions that require the coordination of multiple Agile Release Trains (ARTs), as well as the contributions of Suppliers. It aligns ARTs with a shared business and technology mission using the solution Vision, Backlog, and Roadmap, and an aligned Program Increment (PI).

The Solution Train builds large and complex solutions (often described as a 'system of systems'), which may require the efforts of hundreds or even thousands of people to develop. Examples include medical devices, automobiles, commercial aircraft, banking systems, and aerospace and defense systems. The Solution Train provides the additional roles, events, and artifacts necessary to coordinate the building of some of the world's largest and most important systems. Failure of such a system often has unacceptable social or economic consequences, so an additional degree of development rigor is required. Many of these systems are subject to industry and regulatory standards, and they must provide objective evidence of their Compliance.

Details

Solution Trains allow businesses to build large and complex solutions, including cyber-physical systems (e.g., embedded systems) in a Lean-Agile manner. By aligning ARTs to a shared mission and coordinating the efforts of ARTs and suppliers, the Solution Train helps manage the inherent risk and variability of large-scale solution development and requires the support of additional SAFe roles, artifacts, and events, as illustrated in Figure 1.

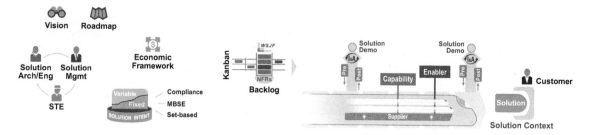

Figure 1. The Solution Train

Solution Trains, like ARTs, operate on the following set of principles:

- **Fixed cadence** – All ARTs on the Solution Train depart the station together, on a known, reliable schedule, as determined by the chosen PI cadence. If a Capability misses a train, it can catch the next one.

- **A new solution increment every PI** – During the PI, the Solution Train integrates as much of the solution as is economically feasible, and within the constraints of the Iteration timeboxes. At the end of the PI, the Solution Train delivers a fully integrated solution increment. The Solution Demo provides a mechanism for evaluating the working solution, which is an integrated solution increment from all the ARTs.

- **Solution** - Each Value Stream produces one or more solutions, which are products, services, or systems delivered to the Customer, whether internal or external to the Enterprise.

- **Solution Intent** – The Solution Intent is the repository for storing, managing, and communicating the knowledge of the current and intended Solution behavior. The Solution Context identifies the environment in which the solution operates.

- **Compliance** – Compliance describes how to use solution intent to achieve high quality while meeting regulatory and industry requirements using a Lean-Agile approach.

- **Suppliers** – Often playing a pivotal role in solution development, a supplier's agility influences the Solution Train's agility.

- **PI timebox** – All ARTs on the Solution Train use the same PI duration and iteration start/end dates.

- **Use of an Economic Framework** – The economic framework is a set of decision rules that aligns everyone to the financial objectives of the Solution and guides the economic decision-making process.

- **ARTs power the Solution Train** – ARTs build the components of the solution using Lean-Agile principles and practices.

- **Inspect and Adapt** – The current state of the solution is demoed and evaluated at the Inspect and Adapt (I&A) event, which is held at the end of every PI for individual ARTs and the Solution Train. Solution Management then identifies improvement backlog items via a structured, problem-solving workshop.

- **Develop on cadence; release on demand** – Solution trains use cadence and synchronization (Develop on Cadence) to help manage the inherent variability of research and development. However, releasing is typically decoupled from the development cadence. Solution trains can Release on Demand a solution, or elements of a solution, at any time—subject to requisite governance and release criteria.

- **Solution Kanban and Backlog** – The Solution Kanban and Solution Backlog are used to manage the flow of solution Epics and Capabilities.

Agile Release Trains Power the Solution Train

Each ART within a Solution Train contributes to the development of the solution, as shown in Figure 2. All development activities typically occur within each ART and are coordinated by the Solution Train, as described next.

Figure 2. ARTs power the Solution Train

Solution Train Roles

Three primary Solution Train roles help facilitate successful execution:

- **Solution Train Engineer (STE)** – The servant leader of the Solution Train. The STE's oversight allows the train to run smoothly by identifying and resolving bottlenecks across the entire solution. The STE facilitates the large-solution-level events and monitors the solution Kanban and solution health via its Metrics. This role also works with Release Train Engineers (RTEs) to coordinate delivery.

- **Solution Management** – The representative of the customer's overall needs across ARTs, as well as the communicator of the portfolio's Strategic Themes. This individual collaborates with Product Management to define capabilities and split them into features. Solution Management, as the primary content authority for the solution backlog, also contributes to the economic framework that governs ARTs and Agile teams.

- **Solution Architect/Engineering** – An individual or small team that defines a shared technical and architectural vision for the solution under development across ARTs.

Also, the following roles play an essential part in the Solution Train's success:

- **Customers** – The ultimate buyers of the solution, who are involved at every level of SAFe. Customers are part of the value stream and are inseparable from the development process. They work closely with Solution and Product Management and other key stakeholders to shape the solution intent, the vision, and the economic framework in which development occurs.

- **System Team** – This team is often formed to help the Solution Train address the integration issues across ARTs.

- **Shared Services** – Specialists—data security, information architects, and database administrators (DBAs), for example—who are necessary for the success of a solution but cannot be dedicated to a specific train.

Defining the Solution

Solution behavior and decisions are managed in the solution intent, which serves as the single source of truth and the container for requirements as they move from variable to fixed. In addition to the vision and roadmap, the development of the solution intent in an adaptive manner is supported by three additional practices, as shown in Figure 3 and described below.

Figure 3. Solution intent

- **Compliance** – Describes how SAFe uses the solution intent to achieve high quality and meet regulatory and industry standard requirements using Lean-Agile development.

- **Model-Based Systems Engineering (MBSE)** – Describes how emergent requirements and design can be developed, documented, and maintained in more flexible and accessible models.

- **Set-Based Design (SBD)** – Describes practices that support preservation of options and the move from variable to fixed requirements over time, while deferring decisions to the last responsible moment.

Building Solution Capabilities

Building large and complex solutions is not a trivial matter. Such systems often require additional constructs beyond those provided by a single ART:

- Solution intent, as the repository for intended and actual solution behavior

- Solution context, which describes the way a solution fits in the deployment environment

- Capabilities and enablers, which are needed to realize the vision and roadmap for the value stream, and more importantly, to satisfy the needs of customers

The solution is described as having a set of capabilities. Similar to features, capabilities represent a higher level of solution behaviors that typically require the efforts of multiple ARTs to implement, as shown in Figure 4. Like features, they are sized to fit within a PI.

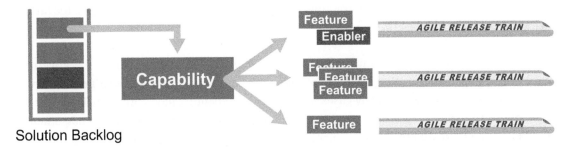

Solution Backlog

Figure 4. Capabilities are split into features that are implemented by multiple ARTs

The solution Kanban is used to manage the flow of work to assure the evaluation and analysis of capabilities before they reach the solution backlog, where they await implementation. This Kanban system also helps limit Work in Process (WIP), thereby ensuring that all the ARTs are synchronized and have the capacity to deliver value together. Larger initiatives defined as solution epics are broken down into capabilities during the analysis state in the Kanban.

Coordinating ARTs and Suppliers

Solution trains coordinate the development of solutions within a PI, and they provide for cadence and synchronization of ARTs and suppliers, including PI Planning meetings and the solution demo. In many cases, large solutions require suppliers who develop components, subsystems, or capabilities for the value stream; these suppliers participate in the Solution Train events.

At the start of each PI, planning takes place for all ARTs at the same time, with each ART conducting its own individual PI planning meeting. To gain alignment and create a single plan across all trains, as well as to manage dependencies between the trains, Pre- and Post-PI Planning meetings also take place. These events result in summarized solution PI Objectives that can subsequently be communicated to the various stakeholders.

The Solution Train holds a solution demo at the end of each PI (sometimes at the start of the next PI). During this event, it presents an integrated solution across all ARTs and suppliers to customers and stakeholders from the portfolio and other value streams. After this demo, an I&A workshop is held to improve the process of the entire value stream.

Lean-Agile suppliers can be treated as another ART, participating in all Solution Train events. In contrast, suppliers that rely on traditional methodologies work against Milestones but are still expected to attend pre- and post-PI planning, solution demos, and Solution Train I&A. SAFe enterprises help suppliers improve their processes and become more Lean and Agile, to the economic benefit of both organizations.

Releasing and Release Governance

As noted earlier, Solution Trains apply cadence and synchronization to manage development. Ultimately, these trains can deploy an entire solution, or the elements of a solution, at any time the business and market dictate.

In support of this practice, each Solution Train must establish—or operate within the governance of—a release management function. Release management has the authority, knowledge, and capacity to foster and approve releases. In many cases, release management includes Solution Train and ART representatives, as well as representatives from marketing, quality, Lean Portfolio Management, IT Service Management, operations, deployment, and distribution. This team typically meets regularly to evaluate content, progress, and quality. Its members are also actively involved in scope management. In addition, release management may be concerned with other elements of the whole solution, including internationalization, packaging and deployment, training requirements, internal and external communications, and ensuring compliance conformance to regulatory and standards requirements.

LEARN MORE

[1] Knaster, Richard, and Dean Leffingwell. *SAFe 4.0 Distilled: Applying the Scaled Agile Framework for Lean Software and Systems Engineering.* Addison-Wesley, 2017.

Customer

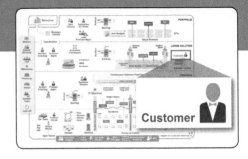

Even when they don't yet know it, customers want something better, and your desire to delight customers will drive you to invent on their behalf. No customer ever asked Amazon to create the Prime membership program, but it sure turns out they wanted it, and I could give you many such examples.

—*Jeff Bezos*

Customers are the ultimate buyer of every Solution. They are an integral part of the Lean-Agile development process and Value Stream and have specific responsibilities in SAFe.

Whether internal or external, customers are increasingly demanding. They have choices. They expect solutions to work well and to solve their current needs. They also expect their solution providers to continuously improve the quality of their products and services.

Details

Customers provide support for SAFe principles, and their active engagement and continuous participation in solution development is essential for a successful business outcome.

Customer Responsibilities

Either in person or by proxy, customers fulfill the following responsibilities:

- Participate as a Business Owner in PI Planning

- Attend the Solution Demo and possibly System Demos; help evaluate the solution increment

- Participate in Inspect and Adapt (I&A) workshops; assist in removing some systemic impediments

- Interact with analysts and subject-matter experts during specification workshops

- Collaboratively manage scope, time, and other constraints with Product and Solution Management

- Help define the Roadmap, Milestones, and Releases

- Communicate the economic logic behind the solution and help validate assumptions in the Economic Framework

- Review the technical and financial status of the solution

- Participate in beta testing, User Acceptance Testing (UAT), and other forms of solution validation

The Customer Is Part of the Value Stream

The Lean-Agile Mindset extends beyond the development organization to encompass the entire value stream, which includes the customer. Engaging customers in the development process depends on the type of solution and the customer's impact. Consider these examples:

- An *internal customer* might request that the IT department build an application for the customer's use

- An *external customer* might be the buyer of a custom-built offering (e.g., a government purchasing a defense system) or part of a larger class of buyers (e.g., an independent software vendor that sells a suite of products)

Internal Customer

For those teams that build solutions for an internal end user (e.g., internal IT department), the *customer* is part of the *operational value stream*, as illustrated in Figure 1. An example would be a marketing director who is responsible for the partner enrollment value stream. The partner is the ultimate end user of the workflow and is the customer. However, to the development team, the marketing director and those who operate the value stream are the customers.

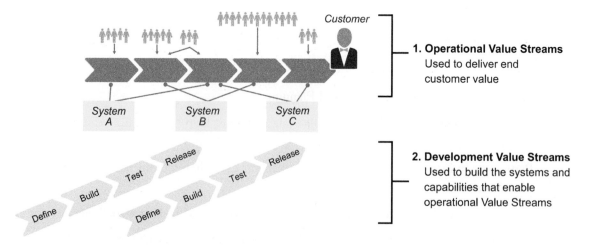

Figure 1. The internal customer is part of the operational value stream

External Customer

For those teams that build solutions for an external end user, the customer is the direct buyer of the solution, as illustrated in Figure 2. In this case, the development value stream and the operational value stream are one and the same. The solution can be a final product that's sold or deployed directly. In other cases, the solution may need to be embedded into a broader Solution Context, such as a system of systems.

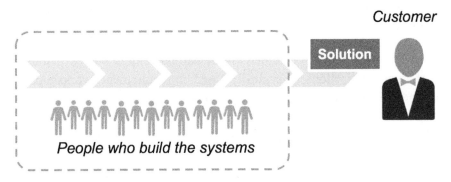

Figure 2. External customers are direct buyers

Customer Engagement Drives Agile Success

Lean-Agile development depends on a high degree of customer engagement—much higher than the degree assumed in traditional development models. However, the methods of engagement are different. Notably, they are determined by the nature of the solution:

- **General solution** – A solution designed to be used by a *significant number* of customers

- **Custom-built solution** – A solution built and designed for an *individual* customer

Figure 3 illustrates the relative level of indirect or direct customer engagement in each case.

Figure 3. Customer engagement models in general and custom-built solutions

General Solutions

Because general solutions must address the needs of a larger audience, no single customer is an adequate proxy for the whole market. In this case, Product and Solution Management become the indirect customer proxy; they have the authority over solution content. It's their responsibility to facilitate external interactions and make sure that the voice of the customer will be heard and that the organization continuously validates new ideas. Scope, schedule, and budget for development are generally at the discretion of the internal Business Owners.

Since it's unlikely that any particular customer will be participating in regular planning and system demo sessions, customer interactions are typically based on requirements workshops, focus groups, usability testing, and limited beta releases. The solution evolves through feedback from user behavior analysis, metrics, and business intelligence to validate the various hypotheses. During PI planning, a group of internal and external stakeholders acts as the Business Owners—the ultimate internal customer proxy within a specific value stream.

Custom-Built Solutions

For custom-built solutions, the external customer typically defines the solution with the support of Product and Solution Management. However, even though the customer is leading the effort, it is critical to establish a collaborative approach when determining the scope and prioritization. This fosters incremental learning and exhibits a willingness to adjust the course of action as needed.

Active participation of the external customer in PI planning, the solution demo, and selected specification workshops is required. This will often reveal inconsistencies in requirements and design assumptions, with potential contractual problems. This process should drive the customer and Agile Release Trains (ARTs) toward a more collaborative and incremental approach.

Demonstrating results of the program increment to the customer, in the form of a fully integrated solution increment, establishes a high degree of trust (e.g., 'These teams can really deliver'). It also provides the opportunity to empirically validate the current course of action. Based on the measured predictability and velocity of trains, forecasting is significantly improved.

Transitioning toward an Agile contract model will also help increase trust and reduce the win–lose focus of traditional contracts. One such model is the 'SAFe managed investment model,' in which the customer commits the funding for a PI or two, then adjusts that funding based on objective evidence and incremental deliveries. This requires a fair bit of trust going in, but then trust is built incrementally, based on a continuous flow of value received.

LEARN MORE

[1] Ward, Allen, and Durward Sobek. *Lean Product and Process Development.* Lean Enterprise Institute, 2014.

Supplier

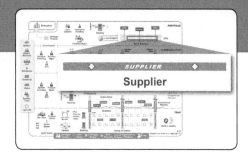

A long-term relationship between purchaser and supplier is necessary for best economy.

—W. Edwards Deming

A *Supplier* is an internal or external organization that develops and delivers components, subsystems, or services that help Solution Trains provide Solutions to their Customers.

Lean-Agile teams deliver value to their customers in the shortest possible lead time, with the highest possible quality. Wherever applicable, they engage suppliers to develop and deliver components and subsystems that help them achieve their mission. Suppliers possess competencies and distinctive skills and solutions. They are experts in their technology and can provide a high leverage point for fast and economical delivery. For all these reasons, suppliers participate in most Solution Trains, and value delivery depends heavily on their performance.

This chapter discusses how suppliers are integrated into the solution. The means by which this is accomplished depends somewhat on the supplier's development and delivery methods. Nonetheless, the SAFe Enterprise treats suppliers as long-term business partners, involving them deeply in the solution. Further, these enterprises actively work with suppliers to help them adopt Lean-Agile Mindsets and practices, which in turn increases the economic benefit to both parties.

Details

Suppliers play a critical role in SAFe. Due to their unique Capabilities and solutions, they are the source of significant economic value opportunities. When their efforts are directed toward achieving the overarching goal of delivering value to customers in the shortest sustainable lead time, suppliers can have a considerable impact on the enterprise's Value Streams.

Suppliers can be external to the enterprise, or they can be other value streams within the organization. Enterprises, however, are well aware that suppliers have their own mission and their own solutions to deliver to other clients, not to mention their own Economic Framework. For both organizations to achieve optimal results, close collaboration and trust are required.

Historically, industries have suffered from the many problems associated with delegating supplier selection and contracting to purchase. With this approach, there may be more focus on pricing than on whether the supplier's solutions and services are an optimal fit for the buyer's purpose and culture, both now and in the future. Moreover, it can even be customary to routinely switch suppliers in search of the *lowest price* and to seek out suppliers across the globe in the most economical *cost venue*. Then, after a business secures a supplier, that supplier is often held at arm's length and notified of information only on a need-to-know basis. With little discussion of the organization's aims or rationale, suppliers are regularly assigned specifications, timelines, and even pricing.

The Lean-Agile enterprise takes a different view—one that maintains a longer-term economic perspective via a collaborative, ongoing, and trusted relationship with suppliers. In such a relationship, suppliers become an extension of the culture and ethos of the enterprise; they are treated as true partners. Their capabilities, policies, and economics are surfaced and understood.

Reaching this state can pose a challenge if the supplier's basic mindset, philosophy, and development approach are materially different from that of the buyer. There are two cases to be considered: one in which the supplier has embraced and adopted Lean-Agile development, and the other in which the supplier has not. Most typically, the larger enterprise must address both prospects, but the goal is the same—a more cooperative, long-term, adaptive, and transparent partnership.

Working with Lean-Agile Suppliers

Involving Lean-Agile suppliers as contributors to a portfolio value stream is the easier case. The working models and expectations are largely the same, and many current Lean-Agile practices can be simply assumed and extended:

- The supplier is treated like an Agile Release Train (ART) and works in the same cadence as the other ARTs.

- The supplier participates in the Program Increment (PI) Planning and Pre- and Post-PI Planning meetings, where it presents what it plans to deliver in the next Program Increment, along with an indication of what will be delivered in each Iteration.

- The supplier demos its subsystem or components in the System Demo, participates in the Solution Demo, and continually integrates its work with the rest of the value stream, providing feedback to other trains.

- The supplier participates in Inspect and Adapt (I&A) events, both to improve the value stream as a whole and to help improve its own Lean-Agile practices.

In addition to their usual responsibilities and their contributions to the solution, suppliers treat the entire enterprise as their customer. As a consequence, they will and should expect routine involvement from the customer (the enterprise/buyer) in the supplier's own development value stream.

Working with Suppliers Using Traditional Methodologies

It's a little trickier to work with suppliers that employ traditional, phase-gated methods for development. It simply isn't reasonable or practical for a Lean-Agile enterprise to assume a supplier will instantly transition to a Lean-Agile paradigm. After all, some suppliers are much larger than their customers, and change is not always easy in the larger enterprise. (However, such an expectation may exist for the longer term.)

Due to differences in working models (e.g., larger batch size, non-incremental development), the enterprise may need to adjust its expectations:

- Some initial up-front design time will be needed in the early PIs to allow suppliers to build their plans and to establish Milestones that they can demo or deliver. The suppliers may expect more formal requirements and specifications.

- The suppliers will likely not deliver incrementally.

- Changes to requirements and design need to be understood earlier, and the response time can be expected to be longer.

However, some expectations and behaviors can and should be imposed on these suppliers:

- In the pre-PI planning meeting, they should indicate the upcoming milestones and their progress toward them.

- In the solution demos, suppliers should present their accomplishments during the PI timebox, even if these are documents and not working systems. They should also provide feedback on the demos of the other trains.

- Involvement in the I&A workshop is crucial, as many of these suppliers will have longer learning cycles. They should use this opportunity to raise problems encountered in their working process.

In addition, suppliers may have limited flexibility in adjusting their plans. As a result, other trains will have to be flexible to accommodate their needs.

Note: For more information on working with suppliers using traditional methods, see the guidance articles on the SAFe website: "Mixing Agile and Waterfall Development" and "Technical Strategies for Agile and Waterfall Interoperability at Scale."

Applying Systems Thinking and Decentralizing Decision-Making

Since the goal is to improve the Solution Train and the flow of value as a whole, it's important to apply systems thinking at all levels of decision-making about how and how much to involve suppliers. The cadence of integration with the supplier, for example, is impacted by the supplier's method of work as well as by the transaction cost of the integration. Likewise, how far decisions can be decentralized to suppliers depends on the Solution Context. For example, if the supplier is creating a subsystem that interfaces with the solution through well-established standards, it's easier to let the supplier take more control. In contrast, if it's a proprietary interface that impacts several other suppliers, and thus has economies of scale, more negotiation is required. Also, in a highly dynamic environment, constant collaboration and integration are more important than in more static environments.

In addition, setting very specific design requirements might be important in certain contexts but might lead to poor outcomes in situations in which capabilities and Nonfunctional Requirements (NFRs) cross several trains. There, over-specification could cause the supplier to over-invest in an NFR.

It is important for each Solution Train to incorporate such thinking into its economic framework and manage its relationships with suppliers accordingly.

Collaborating with Suppliers

Collaboration with suppliers occurs at all levels of SAFe. It starts by sharing Strategic Themes. As Liker and Choi state, "Honda tells the suppliers what kinds of products it intends to introduce and what types of markets it plans to cultivate in the coming years" [4]. If suppliers are to become aligned with the enterprise, it is important that solution developers share what they're going to build.

It's also important to make sure that suppliers understand the economic framework that the Solution Train is working under. It is equally vital for the purchaser to understand the economic framework of each supplier so that win–win relationships can be built. Liker and Choi state, "Toyota uses the term *genchi genbutsu* or *gemba* (actual location and actual parts or materials) to describe the practice of sending executives to see and understand for themselves how suppliers work" [4].

Collaboration continues by building the requirements together with the suppliers. Solution Management works with suppliers continuously and collaboratively to write capabilities and then decompose them into Features. Solution Architect/Engineering works with their supplier counterparts to design the solution. Again quoting Liker and Choi, "At the Toyota Technical Center, the 'design-in' room houses suppliers who work in the same room on the same project" [4].

The same collaboration should cascade down. Agile Teams develop the actual solution, so it is important to have open communication channels with the supplier's engineers to collaborate on the best design, given the constraints of the architecture and the economic framework. As Toyota's supplier guidelines state, "Automobile manufacturing at Toyota is a joint endeavor with suppliers and Toyota. To succeed in that endeavor, we and our suppliers need to work together as a single company. We must maintain close communication, exchanging ideas frankly and coming to terms with each other on all matters of importance" [2].

To enable early integration and improve quality, suppliers and ARTs need to share interfaces, tests, and simulators. All such interfaces should be documented in the Solution Intent so that the information is available to everyone.

Suppliers should, to the greatest degree possible, participate in Continuous Exploration and in relentless improvement by delivering smaller batches into the Continuous Delivery Pipeline.

Selecting Suppliers

As solutions have become ever more complex, there has been a general market shift away from suppliers that create parts and components and toward suppliers that create higher-value, integrated systems. Even in industries where suppliers provide work for hire, there has been a shift from hiring individuals to sourcing whole Agile teams, and even to sourcing entire ARTs.

This trend makes selecting the right suppliers even more critical. It's a long-term, high-value proposition. To make the right choice, multiple participants from engineering and purchasing will need to be involved in supplier selection. Since the Lean-Agile enterprise will generally seek fewer suppliers, but ones with which it has enduring relationships, these perspectives can better consider the long-term culture and process fit of the two organizations.

Helping Suppliers Improve

It's easier and more productive to work with Lean-Agile suppliers; they can better fit their own cadence within the cadence of the enterprise and adapt their plans as needed. In addition, trying to improve the value stream without improving supply chains is not optimal. To solve these problems, Lean-Agile enterprises work with their suppliers to improve their processes and results, to the benefit of both companies. Liker and Choi observe, "While other automakers devote one day to a week to developing suppliers, Honda commits 13 weeks to its development program.... Honda's best practices program has increased suppliers' productivity by about 50 percent, improved quality by 30 percent, and reduced costs by 7 percent. That isn't entirely altruistic; suppliers have to share 50 percent of the cost savings with Honda" [4].

Inviting suppliers to join I&A workshops and other relentless improvement activities, as well as sending engineers who are proficient in Lean and Agile approaches to help suppliers improve their processes, can have a major impact on lead times and costs.

Agile Contracts

To forge effective working relationships with suppliers, it's important to build an environment of trust between the parties. Unfortunately, that's hard to do when the contracts governing the relationship assume something entirely different.

Traditional contracts often lead to undesirable results. Deming notes, "There is a bear trap in the purchase of goods and services based on a price tag that people don't talk about. To run the game of cost-plus in industry, a supplier offers a bid so low that he is almost sure to get the business. He gets it. The customer discovers that an engineering change is vital. The supplier is very obliging, but 'regrets,' he discovers, that this change will double the cost of the items" [1].

While this practice is still somewhat common in today's market, it does not optimize the economic benefit for either party. Instead of adopting this win–lose philosophy, Lean-Agile buyers and suppliers collaborate and embrace change, to the benefit of both parties. These relationships are built on trust. Increasingly, these relationships can be built via Agile Contracts, which provide a better way of working. This isn't new; as Toyota notes, "Contracts governing the relationships are ambiguous, consisting of general statements and nonbinding targets" [3].

LEARN MORE

[1] Deming, W. Edwards. *Out of the Crisis*. MIT Center for Advanced Educational Services. 1982.

[2] "Toyota Supplier CSR Guidelines." 2012. http://www.toyota-global.com/sustainability/society/partners/supplier_csr_en.pdf.

[3] Aoki, Katsuki, and Thomas Taro Lennerfors. "New, Improved Keiretsu." *Harvard Business Review*. September 2013.

[4] Liker, Jeffrey, and Thomas Y. Choi. "Building Deep Supplier Relationships." *Harvard Business Review*. December 2004.

Economic Framework

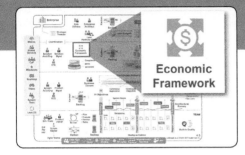

Take an economic view.

—SAFe Lean-Agile Principle #1

The *Economic Framework* is a set of decision rules that align everyone to the financial objectives of the Solution and guide the economic decision-making process. It contains four primary constructs: Lean Budgets, Epic funding and governance, decentralized decision-making, and job sequencing based on the Cost of Delay (CoD).

SAFe Lean-Agile Principle #1: Take an economic view highlights the key role of economics in successful solution development. This chapter describes the primary aspects of taking an economic view, delivering early and often, and understanding other economic trade-off restrictions. In addition, Principle #9: Decentralize decision-making is another cornerstone of SAFe.

These principles come together in this chapter, which describes the economic framework, a set of decision rules aligning everyone to the mission and its financial constraints. That includes budget considerations driven by the program portfolio, as well as trade-offs that affect a particular solution. In this context, portfolio fiduciaries can delegate decision-making authority to others, knowing that the resulting decisions will align with the agreed-to economic guidelines.

Details

The primary purpose of the economic framework is to support effective, fast decision-making within the bounds of the larger economic picture. In turn, that requires three things:

- An understanding of the rules for decision-making
- The current local context
- Relevant decision-making authority

To this end, many of the needed economic decision rules are embedded in various SAFe practices. Figure 1 summarizes where these rules and authorities occur. Each of these areas is described in the sections that follow.

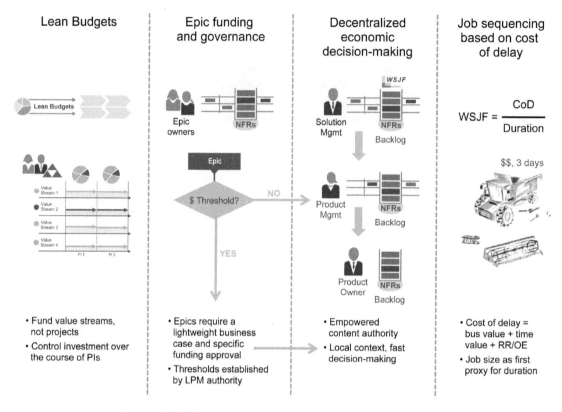

Figure 1. SAFe constructs for economic decision-making

Lean Budgets

The first decision is a big one, as the Lean-Agile enterprise moves from project-based, cost-center accounting to a more streamlined, leaner budget process, where the funding is allocated to long-lived Value Streams. Thereafter, the cost for each Program Increment (PI) is largely fixed, and the scope is varied as necessary. Each value stream budget can then be adjusted over time at PI boundaries, based on the relative value that each value stream provides to the portfolio. This process is described further in the Lean Budgets chapter.

Epic Funding and Governance

Allocating funds to the value streams (and thereby to the Agile Release Trains [ARTs]) is all well and good. But what happens when there are substantial, crosscutting concerns, such as portfolio epics? Or significant local investment concerns, as represented by solution or program epics? Empowered funding requires the parallel responsibility to communicate the need for any unexpected investments—the primary purpose of the Portfolio Kanban System. Each epic requires a Lean business case and an explicit approval process (see the Epic chapter and the discussion of Lean portfolio governance in the Lean Portfolio Management chapter).

Decentralized Economic Decision-Making

With these budget elements in place, the Enterprise then empowers people—particularly Product and Solution Management—with the relevant context, knowledge, and authority necessary to make content decisions at each level of the Framework. Of course, they don't act alone, but rather collaborate with the larger stakeholder community to determine the best path. But in the end, the decision is theirs. That is their primary responsibility and authority.

Job Sequencing Based on Cost of Delay

Every significant program has a host of new backlog Features and Capabilities, just waiting to be implemented to increase the effectiveness of the solution. But SAFe is a flow-based system, whose economics are optimized by job-sequencing rather than theoretical job return on investment, or worse, first-come, first-served job selection. Picking the right next job is where the greatest economic benefit lies. This ability is enabled by the Program and Solution Kanban systems and the Program and Solution Backlog holding areas. Jobs are pulled into implementation based on the Weighted Shortest Job First (WSJF) model, using job size as the proxy for the job duration.

Practices Provide the Form; People Make the Decisions

This chapter has described the constructs that provide a comprehensive foundation for effective decision-making based on the economics of the portfolio and value stream. SAFe also defines the roles and responsibilities of those who live in the decision-making chain. Of course, these decisions don't make themselves. Lean-Agile Leaders continually apply these constructs and educate others in their use. This way, responsible decision-making happens throughout the development organization, bringing the full economic benefits of Lean-Agile development to the enterprise.

LEARN MORE

[1] Reinertsen, Donald G. *The Principles of Product Development Flow: Second Generation Lean Product Development.* Celeritas Publishing, 2009.

Pre- and Post-PI Planning

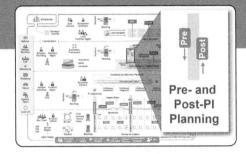

Apply cadence, synchronize with cross-domain planning.
  —SAFe Lean-Agile Principle #7

Pre- and Post-Program Increment (PI) Planning events are used to prepare for, and follow up after, PI Planning for Agile Release Trains (ARTs) and Suppliers in a Solution Train.

Program Increment (PI) planning is a critical, cadence-based synchronization point for every ART. For Solution Trains, however, there are two additional activities: pre- and post-PI planning. These activities support and coordinate the various ARTs involved in the Solution Train. Planning at this higher level helps align Solution development as a whole and provides direction and visibility into where the trains are going in the next PI.

Details

Pre- and post-PI planning events allow ARTs and Suppliers in large Value Streams to build a unified plan for the next PI. The pre- and post-PI planning events serve as a wrapper for the PI planning at the Program Level, where the actual detailed planning takes place and is incorporated into the Innovation and Planning (IP) Iteration calendar.

The *pre-PI planning* event is used to coordinate input objectives, Milestones, and business and solution context for the ART PI planning sessions.

The *post-PI planning* event is used to integrate the results of ART planning into the Vision and Roadmap for the value stream. At the end of the post-PI planning event, all parties should agree on a set of solution PI Objectives that will be implemented by the end of the PI and demoed at the next Solution Demo. Like PI planning, the pre- and post-PI planning events deliver several business benefits:

- Provide open and productive communication through face-to-face alignment
- Synchronize ARTs with Solution Train vision via the ART and solution PI objectives
- Identify dependencies and foster cross-ART coordination

- Provide the opportunity for just the right amount of solution-level architecture and user experience guidance (see the Lean UX chapter)

- Match solution demand to ART capacities

Another benefit is team building across the Solution Train, which helps create the social fabric necessary to achieve high performance. Also, as planning is based on known velocities, the post-PI planning event is a critical step in continuously assessing and removing Work in Process (WIP).

Inputs and Outputs

Inputs to pre- and post-PI planning include the solution roadmap, vision, Solution Intent, and the top Capabilities from the Solution Backlog. Attendees include the following individuals:

- Solution stakeholders, including the Solution Train Engineer (STE), Solution Management, Solution Architect/Engineering, solution System Team, and Release Management

- Representatives from all the ARTs and suppliers, usually Release Train Engineers (RTEs), Product Management, System Architect/Engineering, Customers, and other primary stakeholders

Outputs include three primary artifacts:

1. A set of aggregated specific, measurable, achievable, realistic, time-bound (SMART) PI objectives for the solution

2. A solution planning board, which highlights the capabilities, anticipated delivery dates, and any other relevant milestones for the solution

3. A confidence vote (commitment) to the solution PI objectives

This cadence-based planning process guides delivery through the inevitable technical obstacles and the many twists and turns found in the business and technology environment.

Gain Context in the Solution Demo

The solution demo is to the Solution Train what the System Demo is to the ART. In particular, it offers a regular opportunity to evaluate the fully integrated solution. This event is usually hosted by Solution Management, and solution stakeholders typically attend (including Solution Management, the Solution Train Engineer, and the customer). The insights from the demo will enable these stakeholders to understand the current, objective assessment of solution progress, performance, and potential fitness for use. While the timing of the solution demo will vary based on the solution context, it provides critical objective inputs for the pre- and post-PI planning events.

Prepare for Pre- and Post-PI Planning

The pre- and post-PI planning events bring together stakeholders from all parts of the Solution Train. They require advance content preparation, coordination, and communication. The actual agendas and timelines listed in this section are a suggested way to run these events, but various value streams may adapt these recommendations to their specific capabilities and locations.

Regardless of how the timing and physical logistics are arranged, all elements of these events must happen to achieve the right alignment across the trains and suppliers. It's critical that there are a clear vision and a context in which the right stakeholders participate and in which the primary activities take place. These activities include the following:

- **Executive briefing** – Defines the current business, solution, and customer context
- **Solution vision briefing(s)** – Prepared by Solution Management, including the top capabilities in the solution backlog
- **Milestones definitions** – Clearly explain upcoming events and Metrics

Set Planning Context in Pre-PI Planning

The pre-PI planning event is used to develop the context that the ARTs and suppliers can use to create their individual plans. A suggested agenda is shown in Figure 1, and each item is described next.

Figure 1. Example pre-PI planning agenda

- **PI summary reports** – Each ART and supplier presents a brief report of the accomplishments of the previous PI. This review doesn't replace the solution demo, but it does provide the context of what has been achieved for the planning process.

- **Business context and solution vision** – A senior executive presents a briefing about the current state of the solution and portfolio. Solution Management presents the current solution vision and highlights changes from the previous PI. They may also present the roadmap for the next three PIs, as well as milestones that occur during that period, to ensure that they are known and addressed.

- **Solution backlog** – Solution Management reviews the top capabilities for the upcoming PI. Solution Architect/Engineering discusses upcoming Enabler capabilities and Epics.

- **Next PI features** – Each ART's Product Management presents the Program Backlog that they prepared for the next PI and discusses potential dependencies with other trains.

Solution Stakeholders Participate in ART PI Planning

The practical logistics of large solution planning may rule out the participation of all solution stakeholders in all aspects of these events. However, it's critical that key stakeholders—particularly Solution Management, the Solution Train Engineer, and Solution Architect/Engineering—participate in as many of the ART PI planning sessions as possible. In many cases, ART planning sessions are concurrent, and these solution stakeholders may attend by circulating among the ART PI planning sessions. Suppliers and customers play a critical role as well, and they should be represented in ART PI planning.

Summarize Results in Post-PI Planning

The post-PI planning event occurs after the ARTs have run their respective planning sessions. It is intended to synchronize the ARTs' efforts and create the overall solution plan and roadmap. Participants include solution and key ART stakeholders. A sample agenda is shown in Figure 2.

9:00 ▷ 12:00	PI planning report
12:00 ▷ 1:00	Lunch
1:00 ▷ 2:00	Plan review, risk analysis, and confidence vote
2:00 ▷ ???	Plan rework if necessary
▷ ▷ ▷	Planning retrospective and moving forward

Figure 2. Example post-PI planning agenda

- **PI planning report** – Product Management from each ART presents that train's PI planning plans, explaining the PI objectives and when each is anticipated to be available. RTEs place their information on their ART's row of the solution planning board and discuss dependencies with other ARTs or suppliers.

- **Plan review, risk analysis, and confidence vote** – All participants review the complete plan. During PI planning, ARTs will have identified critical risks and impediments that might affect their ability to meet their objectives. Relevant risks are addressed in a broader solution context in front of the full group. One by one, risks are categorized and addressed in a clear, honest, and visible manner:

  - **Resolved** – The issue is no longer a concern

  - **Owned** – Someone takes ownership since the problem cannot be immediately resolved

  - **Accepted** – Some risks are facts or issues that must be understood and accepted

  - **Mitigated** – The impact of the risk can be reduced by implementing a contingency plan

Once all risks have been addressed, the Solution Train rates its confidence in meeting the solution's PI objectives. A fist-of-five vote is held to assess confidence. If the average is three or more fingers, then management should accept the commitment. If the average is fewer than three fingers, then adjustments should be made, and plans reworked. Any individuals voting with two fingers or fewer should be given time to voice their concerns, which might add to the list of risks.

- **Plan rework as necessary** – If necessary, the group revises its plans for as long as it takes to achieve a commitment from each ART. This could cascade into follow-up meetings with the ARTs, as teams will need to be involved in any change to the plans.

- **Planning retrospective and moving forward** – Finally, the STE leads a brief retrospective of the pre- and post-PI planning sessions to capture *what went well*, *what didn't*, and *what could be done better next time*. Then, subsequent steps are discussed, including capturing objectives, use of Agile project management tooling, and finalizing the schedule of upcoming Solution Train activities and events.

Create the Right Outcomes

A successful event delivers three primary artifacts:

- A set of *'SMART' solution PI objectives* for the Solution Train, with the business value set by Solution Management, Solution Architect/Engineering, and customers. This may include stretch objectives, which are goals built into the plan but not committed to by the solution. Stretch objectives provide the flexible capacity and scope management options needed to increase the reliability and quality of PI execution.

- A *solution planning board*, which highlights the anticipated delivery dates for capabilities, capability dependencies among ARTs and any other relevant milestones, including those aggregated from the program boards. Figure 3 provides an example.
- A *commitment* based on the confidence vote for meeting the solution PI objectives.

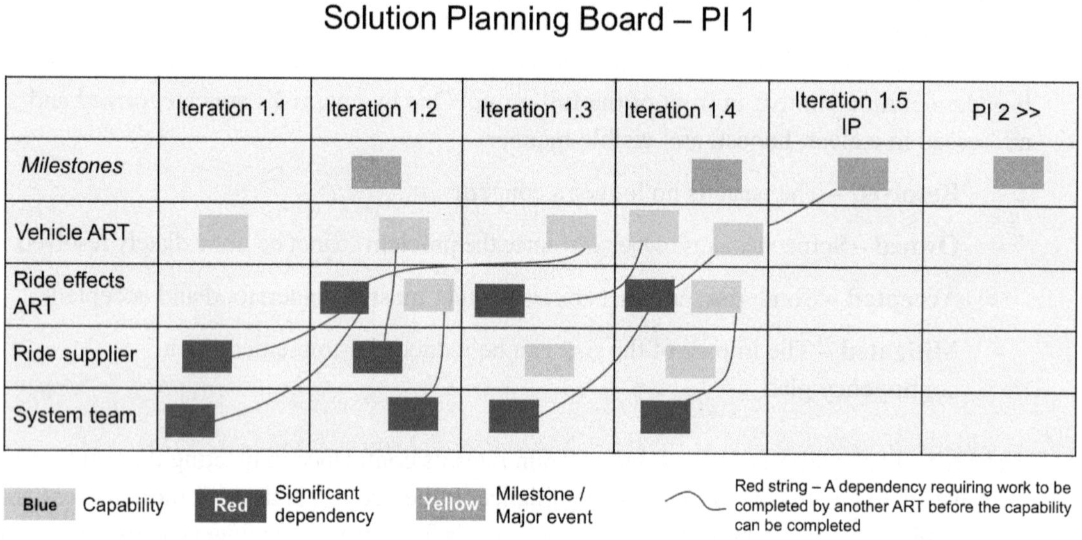

Solution Planning Board – PI 1

	Iteration 1.1	Iteration 1.2	Iteration 1.3	Iteration 1.4	Iteration 1.5 IP	PI 2 >>
Milestones		▇		▇	▇	▇
Vehicle ART	▇	▇	▇	▇		
Ride effects ART		▇ ▇	▇	▇ ▇		
Ride supplier	▇	▇	▇			
System team	▇	▇	▇	▇		

Blue Capability   **Red** Significant dependency   **Yellow** Milestone / Major event   Red string – A dependency requiring work to be completed by another ART before the capability can be completed

Figure 3. Example solution planning board

Next, the solution roadmap is updated based on the objectives for the planned PI. This is usually done by the STE and Solution Management after the post-PI planning session.

Coordinating Solution Train and ART Planning Events in the IP Iteration

Completing all the necessary refinement, pre- and post-PI planning, PI planning, and Inspect and Adapt (I&A) workshops for a Solution Train and its ARTs can present a logistical challenge. Sequencing the events in the optimal order requires precise planning by the STE and all RTEs to ensure the correct stakeholders are present during planning. Figure 4 shows a sample schedule of a two-week IP iteration with all the solution and ART events sequenced to ensure the ideal flow of inputs and outputs for each. Depending on the scope and complexity of the solution, some organizations will find this pattern to be too simplistic and may require multiple pre-PI planning sessions to be held 4–6 weeks in advance. Remember, SAFe is a framework, and you should use its principles as a guide to adapt your own planning as needed.

For geographically distributed trains, scheduling the I&A event for the day before PI planning is a common pattern, as many people might need to travel to a central location to participate. For cost-effective travel and venue scheduling, this usually requires an adjacent time block to conduct I&A and PI planning.

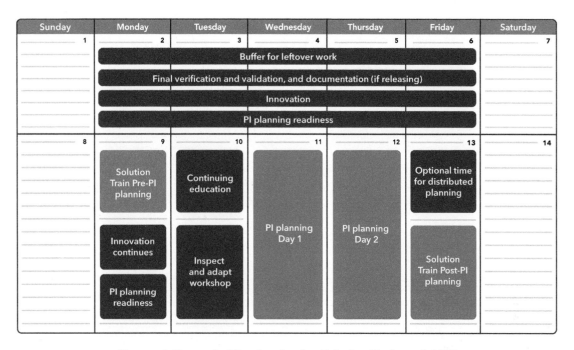

Figure 4. Example IP calendar for Solution Train and ARTs

When logistics are not the overriding consideration, an alternative is to hold ART-level I&A workshops before the Solution Train I&A. This allows the outputs of the ART I&As—including demos, metrics, and problem-solving workshops—to flow into the Solution Train's I&A process as inputs. The benefit is that solution stakeholders will have the most current picture of the state of the solution going into their planning events. Consider the design of the logistics to be a hypothesis—and evaluate it, inspect it, and adapt it as needed.

Solution Demo

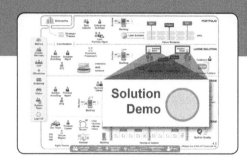

The objective of the pull event was simple. It was designed to focus the development organization on a tangible event to force completion of a learning cycle with the objective to physically demonstrate it.

—Dantar P. Oosterwal

The *Solution Demo* is where the results of development efforts from the Solution Train are integrated, evaluated, and made visible to Customers and other stakeholders. It is where the results of the combined development efforts of multiple Agile Release Trains (ARTs)—along with the contributions from Suppliers and other solution participants—are shown to customers and other stakeholders. This demo is a critical event for the Solution Train, as it offers an opportunity for objective evaluation and feedback. It's also a moment to celebrate the accomplishments of the last PI.

Each solution demo represents a significant learning point in the history of the solution, converting some product development uncertainty to knowledge. Results of this demo determine the future course of action for the investment in the portfolio.

Details

During the solution demo, development teams demonstrate the solution's new Capabilities, its compliance with Nonfunctional Requirements (NFRs), and its overall fitness for purpose. The solution demo provides essential input to near-term Value Stream and Portfolio Level investment decisions. The only real measure of progress, it mitigates investment risk.

Solution Demo as a 'Pull' Event

As the quote that opens this chapter suggests, the solution demo is a deliberate, mandatory, and high-profile 'pull event.' In other words, it pulls together various aspects of the solution and helps ensure that the ARTs and suppliers are creating an integrated and tested solution, fit for its intended purpose. In this way, it accelerates the integration, testing, and evaluation of the solution under development—something that's all too easy to defer until too late in the development life cycle.

Within a portfolio, Enterprises sometimes create even larger pull events, during which several Solution Trains come together for a 'roadshow' of their accomplishments (see [1] for an example). There, the senior managers, stakeholders, and other portfolio fiduciaries review the progress in the broader portfolio context and make decisions about the continuation (or cancellation) of initiatives. Alternatively, they might decide to make changes in the investments made in the various value streams.

Overview

Preparation

Such a critical event requires a good amount of preparation, which often begins at Pre- and Post-PI Planning, where the results of the most recent solution demos are available. Those results inform the people staging the demo about which specific capabilities and other aspects of the solution can and should be demonstrated. Also, even though the solution demo may not have a large group of attendees (scope considerations usually prevent most development team members from attending), logistics do matter. Those who do attend are important to the value stream supported by the solution, and attention to logistics, timing, presentation format, and professionalism will enhance their experience. It may even influence the outcome of the demo.

Attendees

Attendees at the solution demo typically include the following people:

- Solution Management

- Solution Train Engineer (STE)

- Solution Architects/Engineering

- Customers

- ART stakeholders, Product Management, the System Team, Product Owners, and key representatives of the Development teams themselves (to experience the customer feedback firsthand)

- Lean Portfolio Management (LPM) representatives

- Large Solution Level stakeholders, executive sponsors, and senior management

- Deployment Operations representatives

Event Agenda

A typical event agenda includes the following activities:

- Briefly, review the Solution Train PI Objectives for the PI (10 minutes)

- Demo each PI objective and capability in an end-to-end use case (30–60 minutes total)

- Identify the business value completed for each PI objective

- Initiate an open forum for questions and comments

- Wrap up by summarizing progress, feedback, and action items

In the case where multiple solutions are demoed together, the day can be even more interesting. A popular format is the 'science fair,' in which an area is provided to demo the progress of each solution and allow stakeholders to ask questions and provide feedback. Each solution has a one-hour timebox to demo its accomplishments to a set of specific stakeholders following the agenda described previously, but all solutions are constantly available for demo. Members of other solution teams and other stakeholders can attend one another's demos to get a less formal demo and provide informal feedback.

Guidelines

Here are a few tips to keep in mind for a successful demo:

- Timebox the demo to one to two hours. Any longer, and the attention of the stakeholders is likely to dwindle. Sticking to the allotted timebox demonstrates professionalism, respect for people's time, and solution readiness.

- Share demo responsibilities among different lead engineers and team members who have new capabilities to demo.

- Minimize the use of PowerPoint slides; demonstrate only working, tested capabilities.

- Discuss the impact of the current PI on the solution NFRs and Solution Intent.

- Demonstrate in the Solution Context (discussed in the next subsection).

Demonstrate the Solution in Its Solution Context

The last bullet point is particularly critical, as different solutions may have varying degrees of coupling with their solution context. In some cases, a solution is mainly independent of its environment, and an isolated solution demo may be adequate. However, when the system is highly dependent on the solution context (a system of systems, for example), then the isolated approach is inadequate and may even be misleading. In such a case, the solution should be demoed in an environment that is fully representative of the solution context. When that's not practical, development should plan for some cadence of integration with the broader solution context.

Strategy, Investment, and Timing of Solution Demos

Big systems can be challenging to integrate. Routinely demonstrating a solution increment requires teams to invest in integration, testing, and supporting infrastructure. Even then, the extent of integration and testing may be less than 100 percent and may need to vary across multiple integration points. Often critical components of the solution are not ready, requiring teams to leverage virtualization, environment emulation, mockups, stubs, and reduced test suites to demo the completed parts. Also, some effort required for integration and demo, along with time to invest in the supporting environment, may need capacity allocation during PI Planning.

As for timing, the solution demo may lag slightly behind the last system demos in the PI. This creates a delayed feedback loop that increases risk and decreases Solution Train velocity. Here are some tips for minimizing this kind of lag:

- Plan to demonstrate just a subset of the PI scope, which may require some staging and configuration management to support the partial demonstration.

- Set aside time during the Innovation and Planning (IP) Iteration for this high-level integration.

- ARTs that broaden their areas of responsibility for integration and testing can create more overlap with the subsystems and capability areas of other trains. As a result, even the individual system demos are likely to offer a better approximation of the fully integrated solution demo.

Finally, the solution itself may be designed to better support integration and testing, which significantly lowers the demo cost. Elements such as standard interfaces, strictly defined APIs, and containers can help teams spot problems and inconsistencies early on, making end-to-end integration and testing of subsystems easier.

LEARN MORE

[1] Oosterwal, Dantar P. *The Lean Machine: How Harley-Davidson Drove Top-Line Growth and Profitability with Revolutionary Lean Product Development.* Amacom, 2010.

Solution

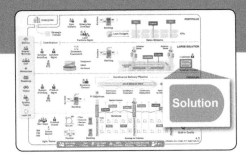

Click. Boom. Amazing!
  —*Steve Jobs*

Each Value Stream produces one or more *Solutions*, which are products, services, or systems delivered to the Customer, whether internal or external to the Enterprise.

All the words, pages, roles, activities, and artifacts in SAFe exist for only one purpose: to help development teams continuously deliver solutions that provide value to their customer. That, in turn, enables customers to achieve their goals, which is the ultimate purpose of every solution development enterprise.

However, even when teams and trains apply SAFe guidance and operate effectively within their disciplines, the value of the solution isn't guaranteed. After all, customers do not buy Capabilities or Features, but rather whole product solutions that deliver their desired business outcomes. For that reason, a solution is one of the central concepts in SAFe and requires taking a systems view regarding value delivery.

Details

Developing an effective solution—one that is fit for its intended purpose—is the larger aim of SAFe. As described in the Value Streams chapter, a solution is either a final product or a set of systems that enable the realization of an operational value stream within the organization. In either case, the work is largely the same: to determine the end user's needs and to reliably, efficiently, and continuously produce a flow of value that meets those needs.

Overview of Solution Development in SAFe

Solution development is the subject of each Agile Release Train (ART) and value stream. In the Essential SAFe and Portfolio SAFe configurations, each ART has the ability to deliver a largely independent solution to the customer.

The Large Solution Level supports solutions that require multiple ARTs, and typically Suppliers, to build them. At this level, solution development involves several core practices and elements of SAFe (see Figure 1).

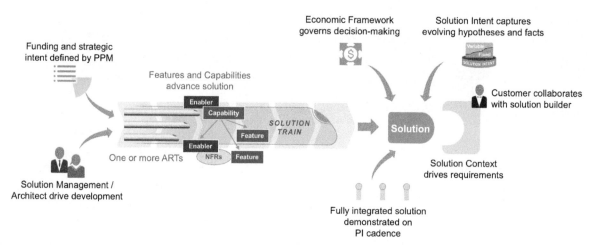

Figure 1. Overview of solution development

Large solutions are delivered by multiple ARTs operating together as a Solution Train. ARTs function simultaneously to build the solution in fully integrated increments, with their progress being measured via a Solution Demo that occurs at least during every Program Increment (PI). Solution Intent captures evolving hypotheses on what to build and how to build it. In addition, it facilitates exploring and defining fixed and variable requirements and designs that are derived, in part, from the Solution Context.

The customer interacts with the development teams to clarify intent, validate assumptions, and review progress. Solution Management and Architects help drive development, make scope and priority decisions, and manage the flow of features and capabilities and Nonfunctional Requirements (NFRs).

Governance is provided, in part, by the Economic Framework, which establishes the decision rules that govern the financial objectives of the solution and guide the economic decision-making process. Lean Budgets and Strategic Themes provide additional boundaries and input. In other words, developing an economically viable solution requires a systems approach to defining, planning, implementing, and reviewing the solution, as described next.

Effective Solution Development Requires Systems Thinking

Principle #2: Apply systems thinking guides the organization to institute scalable and forward-looking practices around value definition, architecture, development practices, and process improvement. Many elements of the Framework facilitate this approach, as described in the following subsections.

Solution Capabilities, Features, Enablers, and NFRs

Capabilities and features are the end-to-end solution services that help achieve user goals. Implemented via vertical, end-to-end slices of value, they support incremental solution development. The distinction between capabilities and features is simply that features can be realized by a single ART, whereas capabilities are realized by multiple ARTs within a Solution Train. Both capabilities and features must be completed within a single PI. Enablers allow exploration of new capabilities, contribute to solution infrastructure and architecture, and enhance NFRs. Their implementation triggers early value delivery and helps build robust architecture.

Solution Intent

The solution intent initiates and captures a full view of the solution. It also incorporates different aspects that govern value definition, including structural, behavioral, functional, and other views. Model-Based Systems Engineering (MBSE) provides an effective way of reasoning about the solution and is an efficient tool through which to share knowledge. Both fixed and variable solution intent enable ARTs and Solution Trains to enhance the overall solution intent based on the objective knowledge that emerges over the course of many learning cycles.

Customer and Solution Context

Taking a systems view requires understanding the solution context—that is, the broader ecosystem in which the solution operates. It provides the additional pieces that determine operational requirements and constraints.

Of course, customers are part of the value stream. They participate in defining the solution intent and solution context, and they help validate assumptions and fitness for use.

Building an Economically Viable Solution

Building a complex solution requires informed and effective decision-making. The trade-offs within the economic framework help guide solution development. In addition, a continuous exploration process that includes learning Milestones, customer feedback loops, and Set-Based Design informs and streamlines the learning process by validating good options and eliminating less practical ones.

Integrating, Testing, Demonstrating, and Releasing

Solution development is effective only when stakeholders and teams frequently evaluate integrated increments of the entire solution. While the Solution Demo occurs on a fixed PI cadence, all of the activities in the Continuous Delivery Pipeline work to support the continuous creation of value and Release on Demand. To accomplish this objective, development teams continuously enhance their DevOps capabilities as well as integration and testing practices, configuration management, automation, and virtualization.

Managing Multiple Solutions in the Portfolio

Each SAFe Portfolio contains multiple value streams. Many are largely independent, while others may have many cross-cutting concerns and dependencies (see Figure 2).

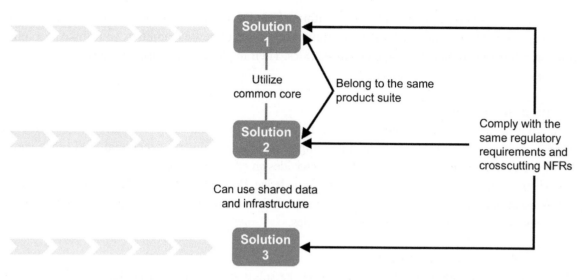

Figure 2. An example of crosscutting solution concerns in a portfolio

Sometimes these crosscutting concerns provide enhanced capabilities that allow strategy differentiation. At other times, they are just dependencies that must be addressed as part of the solution offering. When this is the case, coordination across value streams is required, as described in the Value Stream Coordination chapter.

Solution Context

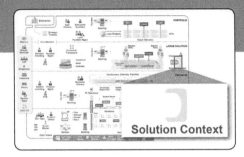

Context is the key—from that comes the understanding of everything.

—Kenneth Noland

Solution Context identifies critical aspects of the operational environment for a Solution. It provides an essential understanding of requirements, usage, installation, operation, and support of the solution itself. The solution context heavily influences opportunities and constraints for releasing on demand.

Understanding the solution context is crucial to value delivery. It impacts development priorities, Solution Intent, Capabilities, Features, and Nonfunctional Requirements (NFRs). It provides opportunities, limits, and constraints for the Continuous Delivery Pipeline and other solution-level Release on Demand activities.

The solution context is often driven by factors outside the control of the organization that develops the solution. The level of coupling between the solution and its context generally represents an architectural and business challenge, that of finding the right balance between flexibility and tightly coupled interaction with the environment—interactions that often cross internal, Supplier, and Customer organizational boundaries.

Details

Rarely are systems built for one's own use; instead, they are built for others, whether those others be internal operational Value Streams or external customers. This means that no single person typically controls, or fully understands, the complete context for the system's deployment and use. Rather, a system is shipped, deployed, installed, and maintained in an environment unlike that in which it was developed. Even in the case of internal IT systems, newly developed systems are typically hosted by the IT maintenance and operations teams. In this case, for many reasons, the production environment may not be the same as the development environment (see the DevOps chapter). Therefore, understanding the solution context is critical to reducing risk and achieving fitness for purpose.

Understanding and aligning the solution and solution intent with the solution context requires frequent interaction with the customer. The customer understands the Vision and has the decision-making authority with respect to solution context. As Figure 1 illustrates, collaboration is required, and the level of this collaboration depends heavily on the level of coupling between the solution and its environment.

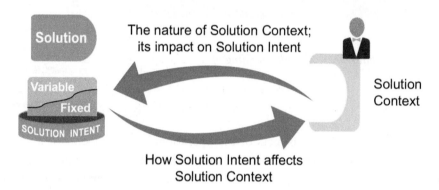

Figure 1. Solution intent and context inform each other

To ensure this alignment, the customer should participate in Program Increment (PI) Planning (and Pre- and Post-PI Planning where applicable) and Solution Demos as frequently as possible. In addition, the customer should regularly integrate the solution in the customer's own context. This regular cadence of interaction and integration allows for building solution increments based on correct assumptions and provides validation of the result within the customer's environment. Both sides play a role in adapting the context to achieve the best economic result (see the Economic Framework chapter).

Solution Context Drives the Solution Intent

The customer's context drives requirements and puts constraints on design and implementation decisions. Many of these contextual requirements are non-negotiable (often driven by Compliance concerns) and may render the solution unusable if not included. These requirements fall under the fixed category of the solution intent. Many aspects of the solution context surface as NFRs and need to be included as part of the Definition of Done for a solution increment.

The solution context may also stipulate specific content that the solution intent must address. In a hierarchical system of systems, the system intents may be hierarchically dependent (see the 'System of Systems Intent' section in the Solution Intent chapter). The system context defines how the solution intent must be organized, packaged, and integrated for use by the customer to meet any compliance, certification, and other objectives.

Fixed versus Evolving Solution Context

Some solution contexts are established customer environments that the solution must simply fit into (e.g., 'This is the way our system works; you have to fit in right here'). In that case, all solution context requirements are imposed on the solution via the solution intent.

In many other cases, new solutions may require the evolution of the customer's deployment environment, requiring those changes to be tracked. In such a case, it's important to actively track those changes, as both the system and the deployment environment must evolve to a common state. Fixed versus variable thinking and the preservation of options via multiple potentially viable solution contexts (see the 'Moving from Variable to Fixed Solution Intent' section in the Solution Intent chapter) are tools to manage risk in these circumstances. Simply put, a more variable and evolving solution context requires more continuous collaboration.

Types of Solution Contexts

Understanding the customer's solution context helps determine how the customer's system will be packaged and deployed in its ultimate operating environments. Examples of solution contexts might include environments such as the following:

- System of systems (e.g., avionics system as part of the aircraft), product suite (e.g., word processor as part of an office suite)

- IT deployment environments (e.g., cloud environment where the solution is deployed)

- Single solution used in different usage models (e.g., a single airliner that can fly both domestic and international routes economically)

Solution Context for a System of Systems

The solution supplier-to-customer relationship in large system-of-systems contexts is a unique and cascading thing, as Figure 2 shows.

Each organization in the supply chain delivers its solution to the customer's context, which specifies how the solution is packaged, deployed, and integrated. That customer, in turn, provides a solution in context to its own customer, and so on. In Figure 2, for example, a vehicle navigation system supplier operates first in the infotainment supplier's contexts, then in the vehicle manufacturer's context, and finally in the consumer's context. All these contexts can impact the viability of the solution, so one must be aware of the full end-to-end value chain.

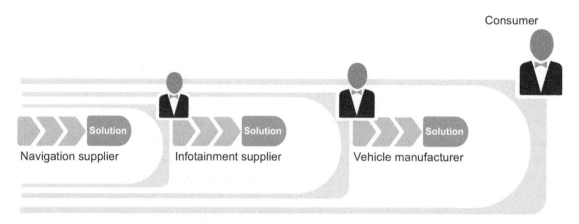

Figure 2. Solution contexts wrap in a system of systems

Solution Context for IT Deployment Environments

When developing software solutions for internal use, the customer may be internal, but delivering solutions into the production environment still requires context. The deployment must consider specific interfaces, deployed operating systems, firewalls, APIs to other applications, hosted or cloud infrastructure, and other factors, as Figure 3 shows.

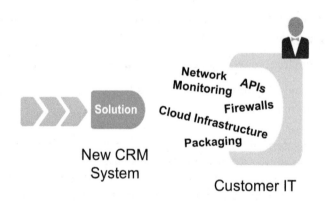

Figure 3. Solution context for internal IT deployment

Making deployment as routine as possible is the primary purpose of DevOps and the Continuous Delivery Pipeline.

In the example shown in Figure 3, the new customer relationship management (CRM) system should reflect the required interfaces, as well as how the application is packaged, released, hosted, and managed in the end environment.

Solution Context Includes Portfolio-Level Concerns

There is one final consideration. Generally, the products and services of an Enterprise must work together to accomplish the larger objectives of the solution. Therefore, most solutions do not stand alone; they are also a Portfolio Level concern. Thus, emerging initiatives, typically in the form of portfolio Epics, drive solution intent and impact the solution's development and deployment.

For internally hosted systems, interoperability with other solutions is often required, further extending the solution context. For example, larger operational value streams (see the Value Streams chapter) often use solutions from multiple development value streams, as illustrated in Figure 4. Each of those subject solutions must collaborate and integrate with the others to provide the operational value stream with a seamless, end-to-end solution.

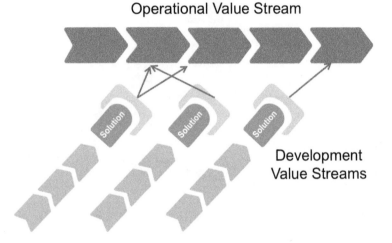

Figure 4. Solutions work together to support the full operational value stream

Continuous Collaboration Ensures Deployability

Ensuring that a solution will operate correctly in its context and deployed environment requires continuous feedback (see the Continuous Delivery Pipeline chapter). Cadence-based development frequently integrates the entire system-of-systems solution to demonstrate progress toward the top-level context's Milestone and release commitments. Continuous collaboration helps ensure that the solution can be deployed in the ultimate customer's context:

- The customer raises and discusses context issues during PI planning and solution demos.

- Solution Management and the customer continually ensure that the vision, solution intent, Roadmap, and Solution Backlog align with the solution context.

- Issues discovered in the customer's context are run through the Solution Kanban system to determine their impact and resolution.

- The partners understand and share relevant solution context knowledge, environment, and infrastructure, such as interface mockups, test and integration environments, and test and deployment scripts.

- Solution Architect/Engineering ensures technical alignment with the solution context—interfaces, constraints, and other aspects of the system.

Consequently, there are many collaboration points between the development teams and the various roles within the customer organization. Several SAFe roles carry that responsibility along with their customer counterparts, as shown in Figure 5.

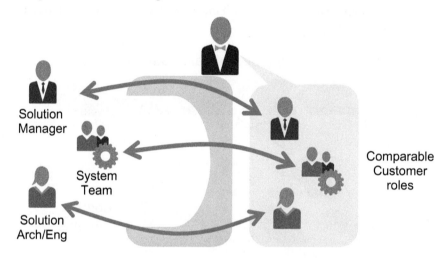

Figure 5. Collaboration between SAFe and customer roles

In summary, effective collaboration between customer and SAFe roles helps ensure that the system meets the customer's needs in the customer's context.

Solution Intent

Quality begins with the intent.

—W. Edwards Deming

Solution Intent is the repository for storing, managing, and communicating the knowledge of current and intended Solution behavior. Where required, this includes both fixed and variable specifications and designs; references to applicable standards, system models, and functional and nonfunctional tests; and traceability.

Building large-scale software and cyber-physical systems is one of the most complex and challenging endeavors in the industry today. It requires alignment on two central questions:

- What exactly is this thing we are building?
- How are we going to build it?

What's more, these two questions are interrelated and have an impact on each other. If you don't know 'how' to build something in an economically or technically feasible way, then 'what' is being built must be reconsidered in the context of the 'how.' SAFe labels this critical knowledge pool the *solution intent*; it is the basic understanding of the current and evolving requirements, design, and intent—that is, the larger purpose of the solution.

Some solution intent is fixed, with non-negotiable requirements for what it must do or already does. Other solution intent is variable, subject to further discussion and exploration as facts surface. Understanding and navigating these differences, and allowing variability to proceed (even late into the timeline), are key to unlocking agility in large-scale solution development.

Details

When building systems that have an unacceptably high cost of failure, the need for a more rigorous definition and validation of system behavior is a significant barrier to Agile adoption. Although many practitioners find that their own views resonate with the Agile Manifesto [1] value statement of "working software over comprehensive documentation," that concept can generate conflicting priorities for enterprises that need both.

Engineering complex and highly reliable solutions requires and creates large amounts of technical information. Much of this information reflects the intended behavior of the solution—Features and Capabilities, Stories, Nonfunctional Requirements (NFRs), system architecture, domain-level models and designs (e.g., electrical and mechanical), system interfaces, customer specifications, tests and test results, and traceability. Other relevant information records some of the key decisions and findings of the system. This may include information from trade studies, results of experiments, the reasoning for design choices, and other items. In many cases, this information must become part of the official record, whether by necessity or by regulation.

Capture Knowledge in Solution Intent

The solution intent is a critical knowledge repository in which to store, manage, and communicate 'what is being built' and 'how it will be built.' It serves many purposes:

- Provides a single source of truth regarding the intended and actual behavior of the solution

- Records and communicates requirements, design, and system architecture decisions

- Facilitates further exploration and analysis activities

- Aligns the Customer, Dev Team, and Suppliers to a common mission and purpose

- Supports Compliance and contractual obligations

Future and Current Solution Intent

Figure 1 illustrates the complex nature of the solution intent, including the following elements:

- **Current and future states** – Developers of complex systems must constantly know two things: what exactly the current system does now, and which changes are intended for a future state.

- **Specifications, designs, and tests** – Knowledge of both the current and future states can be captured in any form suitable—as long as it includes the three primary elements of specifications (documented definition of system behavior), design, and tests.

When building systems that must behave exactly as intended—including life-critical, mission-critical, and other systems governed by regulatory standards—traceability helps confirm that the system will behave as intended. It connects the elements of solution intent to each other and to the components of the systems realizing its full behavior. The solution intent itself is created collaboratively and evolves based on learning, as illustrated in Figure 1.

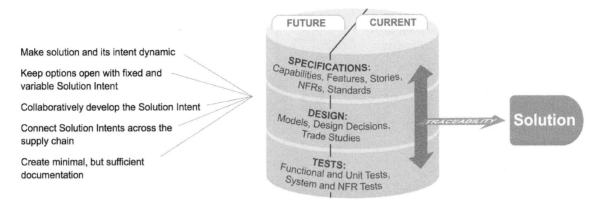

Figure 1. Anatomy of the solution intent

The specific elements of the solution intent can be realized in many forms, ranging from documents, spreadsheets, and whiteboard sessions to formal requirements and modeling tools, as described in the Model-Based Systems Engineering (MBSE) chapter. At the same time, the solution intent is a means to the end of building the solution, so methods for capturing it should not create unnecessary overhead and waste (see the 'Create Minimal But Sufficient Documentation' section later in this chapter).

Make the Solution Intent Dynamic

Traditionally, a set of detailed, up-front, fixed requirements has served as the proxy for the solution intent. SAFe Principle #3: Assume variability; preserve options, however, tells us that defining requirements and designs too tightly up-front leads to less successful outcomes. A different approach is needed—one that supports understanding what's known, yet allows what's unknown to emerge over the course of development.

The solution intent is not a static, one-time statement, but rather must support the entire development process and continue to evolve. Figure 2 contrasts the traditional early, fixed requirements decomposition with a Lean-Agile approach, in which decomposition is done at the appropriate time by the people doing the work.

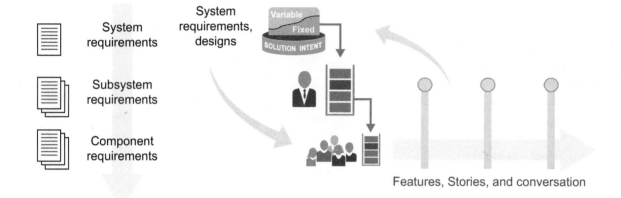

Figure 2. Solution intent evolves with and supports all the steps in solution development

The solution intent serves as a vision of the future system that aligns these teams and their backlogs. It provides the detail needed to establish the current vision but allows teams the flexibility to explore unknowns in building the solution. The resulting knowledge (Can we build the future system? What did we learn from exploration?) provides feedback on the to-be system and offers an opportunity to adapt based on the learnings.

Keep Options Open with Fixed and Variable Solution Intent

The solution intent serves a variety of purposes, but none of them mandates creating fully defined 'point-solution' specifications up-front. Such early decisions restrict the exploration of better economic alternatives and often lead to waste and rework [2]. To prevent this problem of settling too early, SAFe describes two elements of solution intent, fixed and variable, that support the general adaptive requirements and design philosophy needed to create the best economic outcome.

Fixed intent represents the 'knowns.' They may be non-negotiable, or they may have emerged during the course of development. Examples include:

- Certain performance specifications ('the pacemaker waveform must be as follows')

- Compliance standards ('comply with all PCI compliance credit card requirements')

- Core capabilities defining the solution ('the Baja Adventure Ride holds four adult riders')

Variable intent represents the elements that allow the exploration of the economic trade-offs of requirements and design alternatives that could meet the need. Once established, these new insights will eventually become fixed requirements.

Moving from variable to fixed solution intent requires gaining the knowledge needed to make decisions. Enablers are SAFe's vehicle to explore unknowns and record knowledge and decisions in the solution intent. Following Set-Based Design practices, teams explore alternatives to arrive at an optimal economic decision. These decisions enable development of downstream features in the Roadmap (Figure 3).

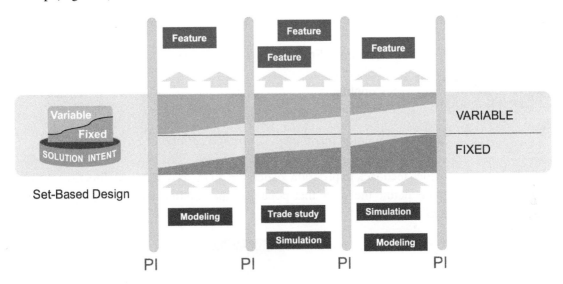

Figure 3. Moving from variable to fixed solution intent

At each Program Increment (PI) in this roadmap, teams are simultaneously building what we know, while exploring what we don't yet know. Fixed knowledge doesn't start off at zero because even at the left side of Figure 3, a lot is known. For example, it may be possible to reuse elements from previously developed systems. Then, through the course of development, more becomes known as fast as Iterations, PIs, and Solution Demos show what the system is capable of. In this way, variable intent becomes fixed over time and a solid understanding of what the system does and needs to do emerges.

Collaboratively Develop the Solution Intent

Developing solution intent requires a collaborative effort between teams and program leadership. Product and Solution Management, along with a Solution Architect and Systems Engineering, are responsible for the highest-level, system-wide decisions (system decomposition, interfaces, and allocations of requirements to various subsystems and capabilities). They also establish the solution intent's organizational structure to support future analysis and compliance needs. In turn, the solution intent helps drive localized decisions in the teams' backlogs, as shown in Figure 4.

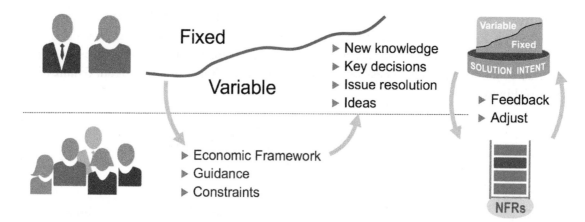

Figure 4. Solution intent evolves through collaboration

The resulting work provides feedback to program leadership on the progress and direction. As shown in Figure 5, backlog items define the work that populates the solution intent, moving the variable assumptions toward fixed decisions.

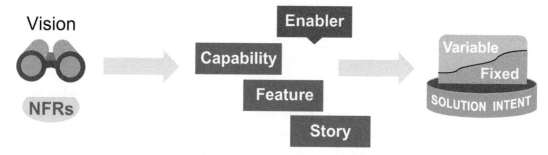

Figure 5. Developing solution intent

The solution intent begins with a Vision that describes the solution's purpose and key capabilities, along with the system's nonfunctional requirements. This knowledge and the emerging roadmap and critical Milestones guide teams in creating backlogs and planning their work. But the roadmap and solution intent are filled with assumptions. SAFe's guidance for continuous delivery validates assumptions through Minimum Viable Products (MVPs) that provide validated learning through frequent, quantifiable experiments. (Note: Although the validated learning in the solution intent is mostly technical, the Lean Startup principle of 'Leap–Test–Measure–Pivot' still applies.)

Connect Solution Intents across the Supply Chain

A system's solution intent does not necessarily stand alone. Many solutions are systems that participate in a higher-level system of systems. In that case, other systems, as well as suppliers, provide unique knowledge and solution elements that accelerate development. Suppliers, for example, will often have separate and independent requirements, designs, and other specifications for their own subsystems or capabilities. From their perspective, that is their solution intent. As a result, the ultimate (top-level) solution intent must include the relevant supplier knowledge and information necessary to communicate decisions, facilitate exploration, align teams, and support compliance. This 'daisy chain' of requirements moves design decisions up and down the system hierarchy, as illustrated in Figure 6.

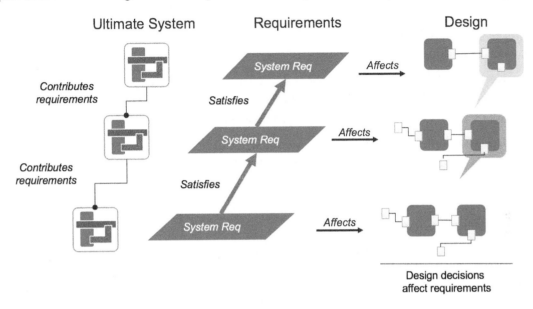

Figure 6. Solution intent hierarchy

Create Minimal But Sufficient Documentation

Solution intent is a means to an end—it's a tool to guide, facilitate, and communicate decisions, and to demonstrate compliance. Planning of the solution intent's content, organization, and documentation strategies should begin with those ends in mind. Nevertheless, more is not necessarily better. When documenting requirements, design, and architecture, the Lean-Agile community recommends keeping it light [5]. Best practices include the following:

- **Favor models over documents** – An environment of continuous change challenges a document-centric approach to organizing and managing solution intent. When applied properly, models (including those produced by modern practices such as design thinking and user-centered design) can provide more easily maintained ways to manage, as discussed in detail in the MBSE chapter.

- **Keep the solution intent collaborative** – There's no monopoly on innovation, and the solution intent is not the exclusive domain of the Product and Solution Managers, Architects, and Engineers. Many team members participate in the creation, feedback, and refinement of solution intent information.

- **Keep options open** – Defer decisions to local concerns, and make them as late as possible. An adaptive approach to requirements and design keeps promising options open as long as is economically feasible. Set-based design practices help avoid committing to design and requirements too early.

- **Document items in only one place** – Record any requirements and design decisions in one place, a single source of truth that serves as the repository of record for everyone and everything.

- **Keep it high level** – Communicate at as high a level of abstraction as possible, and don't over-specify. Provide a range of acceptable behaviors. Describe solution behavior with intent, not specificity. Decentralize requirements and design decision-making authority.

- **Keep it simple** – Record only what's needed. Solution intent is a method for building a product while meeting compliance and contractual obligations. Less is more.

LEARN MORE

[1] Manifesto for Agile Software Development. http://agilemanifesto.org/.

[2] Ward, Allen, and Durward Sobek. *Lean Product and Process Development*. Lean Enterprise Institute, 2014.

[3] Reinertsen, Don. *Principles of Product Development Flow: Second Generation Lean Product Development.* Celeritas Publishing, 2009.

[4] Leffingwell, Dean, and Don Widrig. *Managing Software Requirements: A Use Case Approach.* Addison-Wesley, 2003.

[5] Ambler, Scott. "Agile Architecture: Strategies for Scaling Agile Development." Agile Modeling, 2012. http://agilemodeling.com/essays/agileArchitecture.htm.

Compliance

Trust, but verify.

—*Ronald Reagan, citing a Russian proverb*

Compliance refers to a strategy and a set of activities and artifacts that allow teams to apply Lean-Agile development methods to build systems that have the highest possible quality, while simultaneously assuring they meet any regulatory, industry, or other relevant standards.

Enterprises use SAFe to build some of the world's largest and most important systems, many of which have unacceptable social or economic costs of failure. Examples of these high-assurance systems include medical devices, automobiles, avionics, banking and financial services, and aerospace and defense. To protect the public safety, these systems are often subject to extensive regulatory or customer oversight and rigorous compliance requirements. In addition, many enterprises are subject to other government regulations (e.g., Sarbanes-Oxley Act, Health Insurance Portability and Accountability Act [HIPAA], Affordable Care Act [ACA], state insurance regulations) that require similar attention and audits to ensure compliance.

Historically, organizations operating under such regulations have relied on comprehensive quality management systems (QMS). Based on phase-gated development models, they're intended to reduce risk and ensure compliance. Unfortunately, these traditional approaches don't scale, even when some teams follow Agile practices. Nor do they keep pace with accelerating time-to-market demands. Of greater concern is that even when the higher Cost of Delay (CoD) is accepted, these traditional approaches often do not increase quality or eliminate risk. As Deming notes, "Inspection is too late. The quality good, or bad, is already in the product."

This chapter offers guidance on how to apply Lean-Agile methods to build these systems faster and better, while also addressing critical compliance requirements.

Details

Traditional waterfall practices often mandate that full system specifications are defined and committed to in detail, up-front, long before all the real system behaviors can be known. Even worse, the sequential nature of phase-gated development produces large batches of work, long cycles between system integration points, and late feedback. In addition, compliance activities are typically deferred until the end of the project, providing little insight into compliance progress.

Collectively, these practices often result in missed deadlines, disappointing business or mission outcomes, lower quality, and substantial (and late) compliance challenges. In contrast, high-assurance Lean-Agile development builds in quality incrementally—early and throughout the development lifecycle. Moreover, it does so while including the very elements and activities necessary to ensure compliance.

The Role of the Quality Management System

To satisfy compliance requirements, organizations must demonstrate that their system meets its intended purpose and has no unintended consequences that might cause harm. They must also develop the objective evidence required to prove that the system conforms to those standards. To that end, organizations that build high-assurance systems define their approved practices, policies, and procedures in a QMS. These systems are intended to ensure that development activities and outcomes comply with all relevant regulations and provide the required documentation to prove it.

Unfortunately, the QMSs of many organizations are still heavily influenced by traditional phase-gated waterfall methods. This seriously inhibits, and can even prevent, the adoption of newer methods, as the older methods are hard-coded into the *only* approved way of working. As Figure 1 illustrates, SAFe describes an incremental approach to both development and compliance. It means those who want the benefits of Lean-Agile development (faster time-to-market and higher quality, to name two of these benefits) will typically have to evolve a Lean QMS.

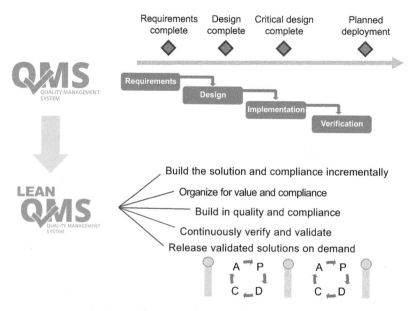

Figure 1. A Lean-Agile quality management system improves quality and makes compliance more predictable

The remainder of this chapter provides guidance on Lean-Agile strategies and patterns that develop these high-assurance systems.

Build the Solution and Compliance Incrementally

Even with a set of robust specifications, engineering teams never have all the answers when development begins. Instead, they have a set of hypotheses that must be tested through a series of short, iterative experiments, which provide validated learning to ideally advance toward the ultimate solution. Figure 2 highlights SAFe's incremental development approach, comparing Shewhart/Deming's plan–do–check–adjust (PDCA) learning cycles with a traditional waterfall model.

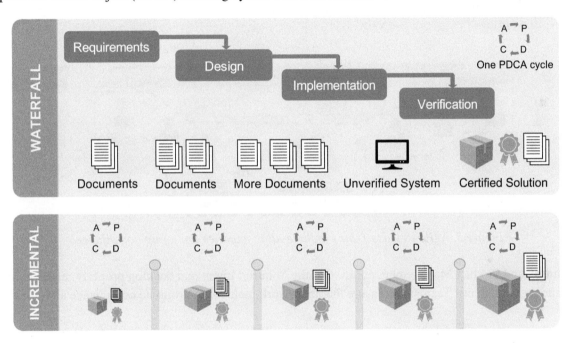

Figure 2. Rapid plan–do–check–adjust learning cycles increase quality and reduce risk

Figure 2 highlights two important implications for compliance. First, building smaller, working parts of the solution early allows compliance activities to also begin early, removing the large bow wave of performing such actions at the end. Each increment assesses the viability of the current solution, as well as progress toward compliance, providing early feedback on the system's ultimate fitness for use. Second, specifications are created and evolved over time in small batches, with faster feedback on decisions and the opportunity for continuous review and assessment.

Organize for Value and Compliance

Agile Release Trains (ARTs) are the primary value-delivery organizations in SAFe. Each train requires all the skills necessary to build and release the Solution, including those responsible for quality assurance (QA), security, testing, and Verification and Validation (V&V). (While some regulations require independent, objective assurance, compliance representatives can still participate continuously as members of the ART.) The result is an ART designed in the manner illustrated in Figure 3.

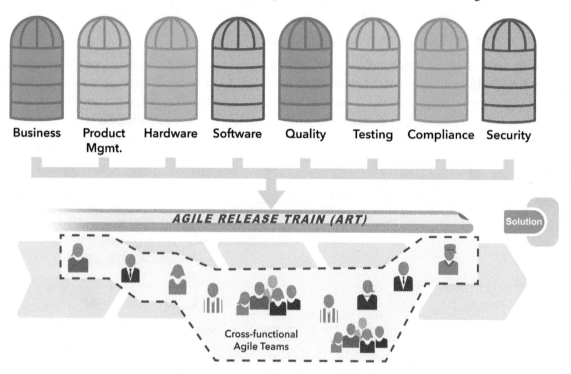

Figure 3. Agile Release Trains include all disciplines including compliance

Solution and Product Management ensure that the Solution Intent and backlog properly reflect compliance requirements. Teams also ensure that their work includes appropriate compliance activities.

Build in Quality and Compliance

Built-In Quality is one of SAFe's four Core Values and a core tenet of the Lean-Agile Mindset. SAFe describes the use of built-in quality practices, including automation to detect compliance and quality problems and, when detected, stopping the entire system to focus everyone on resolving the problem. This philosophy applies systems thinking by 'optimizing the whole,' ensuring fast flow across the entire value stream and making quality everyone's job. From this perspective, quality is a culture, not a job title.

To that end, compliance concerns are also built directly into the development process, and automated wherever possible, as illustrated in Figure 4.

Not all compliance activities can be automated, however, as some regulatory requirements mandate manual reviews, including activities like Failure Mode and Effects Analysis (FMEA) and audits. These activities are simply planned as part of the team backlog. The goal is to conduct these reviews as the solution is being built, reducing the last sign-off activity from a large, extended event to a quick and boring 'non-event.'

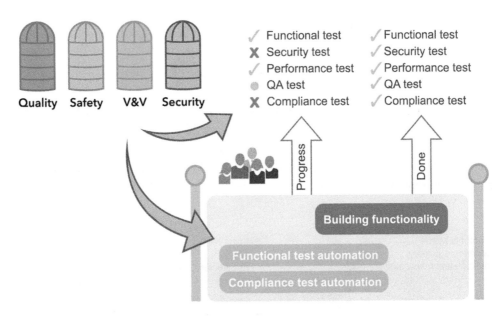

Figure 4. Building compliance into design–build–test automation

With this approach, the program receives fast feedback on the degree to which the team's compliance activities are being met and, conversely, how those activities may be impacting team performance. Figure 5 shows the feedback cycle between team activities and the practices defined by the Lean QMS.

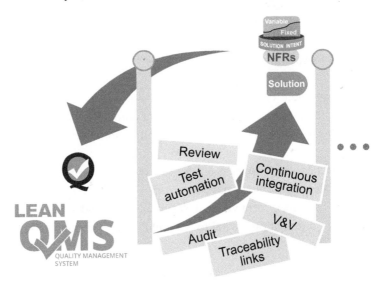

Figure 5. Program increments provide a feedback loop for compliance activities and practices

Continuously Verify and Validate

Most high-assurance systems require V&V to ensure that two criteria are met:

- The system works as designed (verification).

- The system meets the needs of the user (validation).

V&V must always occur against a known set of requirements. Otherwise, there is nothing to verify and validate against. As Figure 6 illustrates, SAFe uses solution intent as the repository for existing and emerging requirements and designs.

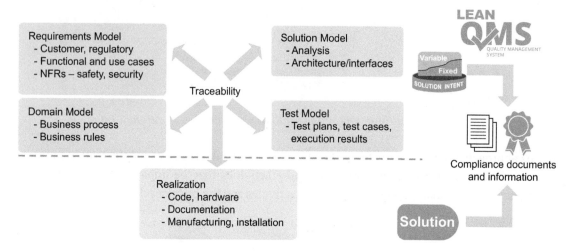

Figure 6. SAFe's solution intent provides support for verification and validation

Traceability from solution intent ensures that the artifacts produced during each Program Increment (PI)—the actual software, hardware components, and other outputs—address regulatory and compliance specifications, providing end-to-end evidence that V&V requirements have been met.

The SAFe Requirements Model Supports V&V

In SAFe, all elements of the requirements have test cases (see Figure 7), which are created at the same time as the functionality. Each increment yields new functionality and, consequently, adds new tests. As the number of tests grows, automation is vital to prevent testing activities from becoming bottlenecks.

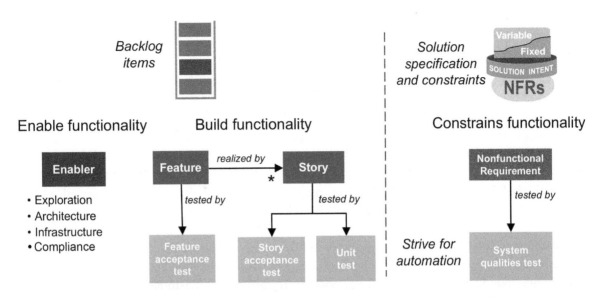

Figure 7. SAFe's requirements meta-model supports verification and validation

Make V&V and Compliance Activities Part of Regular Flow

By incrementally building the necessary artifacts in the solution content over a series of PIs, SAFe supports continuous verification. Figure 8 illustrates how this process works.

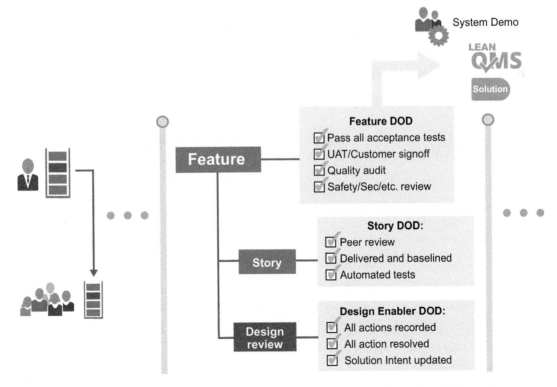

Figure 8. Verification and validation activities are part of the value delivery flow

Verification activities are implemented as part of the flow of value delivery (e.g., backlog items or Definition of Done [DoD] as described earlier). While the artifacts will satisfy the objective evidence needed at the end of development, they are created iteratively throughout the life cycle. Validation occurs when Product Owners, Customers, and end users participate in ART planning, demos, and validation of fitness for purpose.

In the example in Figure 8, regulations require design reviews and specify that all actions be recorded and resolved. The 'design review' Enabler backlog item offers evidence of the review, and its DoD ensures that actions are recorded and resolved per the Lean QMS. If needed, the actions themselves could be tracked as enabler stories. Regulations may also require that all changes be reviewed, which is addressed by a compulsory peer review DoD for all stories.

SAFe recommends building the integrated solution frequently (or elements of the system for cyber-physical solutions), at least at every iteration for the System Demo. Building and integrating frequently allows continuous validation from User Acceptance Testing (UAT), customers, and end users. For each iteration, the system demo provides objective evidence that the integrations perform as intended and that the entire system has advanced forward while maintaining quality and compliance standards.

Release Validated Solutions on Demand

SAFe recognizes that although the product development process happens in a predictable cadence (Develop on Cadence), the release process (Release on Demand) may require additional activities:

- Validation testing of the final release candidate (e.g., medical trial, flight test)
- Review of the objective evidence required before production approval and release
- Customer, regulatory, UAT, sign-offs, or other document submissions

Even then, Lean-thinking organizations always strive to fully automate delivery and, where possible, build in automated final release checks as part of a SAFe Continuous Delivery Pipeline and release on demand.

LEARN MORE

[1] Leffingwell, Dean. *Agile Software Requirements*. Pearson Education, 2011.

[2] "Achieving Regulatory and Industry Standards Compliance with SAFe" [White paper]. http://scaledagileframework.com/achieving-regulatory-and-industry-standards-compliance-with-safe/.

[3] "Achieving Regulatory and Industry Standards Compliance with SAFe" [Webinar]. https://www.youtube.com/watch?v=-7rVOWTHZEw&feature=youtu.be.

Model-Based Systems Engineering

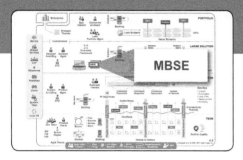

All models are wrong, but some are useful.

—George E. P. Box

Model-Based Systems Engineering (MBSE) is the practice of developing a set of related system models that help define, design, and document a system under development. These models provide an efficient way to explore, update, and communicate system aspects to stakeholders, while significantly reducing or eliminating dependence on traditional documents.

MBSE is the application of modeling requirements, design, analysis, and verification activities as a cost-effective way to explore and document system characteristics. By testing and validating system characteristics early, models facilitate timely learning about properties and behaviors, enabling fast feedback on requirements and design decisions.

Although models are never a perfect representation of a system, they provide knowledge and feedback sooner and more cost-effectively than implementation alone. In practice, engineers use models to gain knowledge (e.g., performance) and to serve as a guide for system implementation (e.g., SysML, UML). In some cases, they use them to directly build the actual implementation (e.g., electrical CAD, mechanical CAD).

Details

Lean practices support fast learning through a continuous flow of small pieces of development work to gain fast feedback on decisions. MBSE is a discipline and a Lean tool that allows engineers to quickly and incrementally learn about the system under development before the cost of change gets too high.

Models are used to explore the structure and behavior of system elements, evaluate design alternatives, and validate assumptions faster and as early as possible in the system life cycle. They are particularly useful for large and complex systems—satellites, aircraft, medical systems, and the like—where the solution must be proven practical beyond all possible doubt before, for example, launching into space or connecting to the first patient. Models also record and communicate decisions that will be useful to others. This information serves as documentation for Compliance, impact analysis, and other needs. In SAFe, model information is recorded as part of the Solution Intent, most often created by the work of Enablers.

The following sections provide guidance on adopting MBSE.

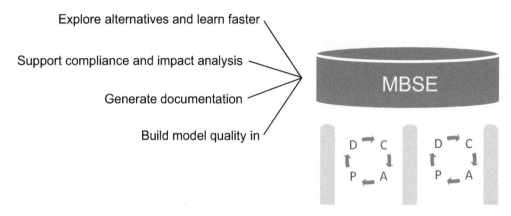

Figure 1. MBSE accelerates learning

Explore Alternatives and Learn Faster

MBSE supports fast learning cycles (see SAFe Principle #4: Build incrementally with fast, integrated learning cycles) and helps mitigate risks early in the product life cycle. Models facilitate early learning by testing and validating specific system characteristics, properties, or behaviors, thereby enabling the organization to obtain fast feedback on design decisions.

Dynamic, solid, graphs, equations, simulation, and prototypes—models come in many forms. As Figure 2 illustrates, each provides a different perspective into one or more system characteristics that enable the creation of future Capabilities and Features.

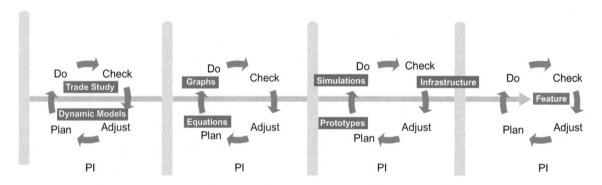

Figure 2. Models and learning cycles

Models may predict performance (response time, reliability) or physical properties (heat, radiation, strength). Some may explore design alternatives for user experience or response to an external stimulus. But models don't address just technical design alternatives: The practices of design thinking and user-centered design are synergistic with MBSE and help validate assumptions sooner.

Support Compliance and Impact Analysis

Historically, decisions on requirements, designs, tests, interfaces, allocations, and other factors have been maintained in a variety of sources, including documents, spreadsheets, and domain-specific tools, and sometimes even on paper. MBSE takes a holistic, system approach to managing system information and data relationships, treating all information as a model. Figure 3 shows a generic structure linking information from multiple types of models.

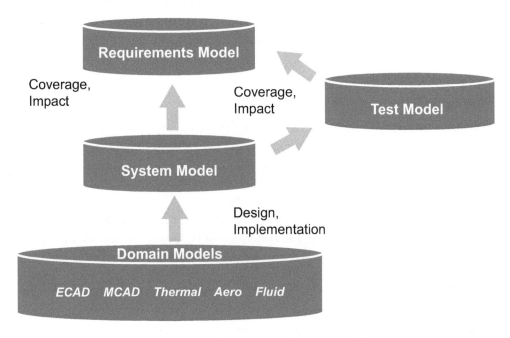

Figure 3. Linking cross-domain models

The practice of traceability is used to quickly and reliably understand the impact of changes to the system, or the impact of a change at the domain level on other parts of the system and requirements. For example, teams and System Architect/Engineers use model information to support the Epic review process. Traceability also provides the objective evidence needed to address many regulatory and contractual compliance concerns.

A Lean, continuous-change environment amplifies the need for related models. While manual solutions to manage related information for coverage and compliance may suffice in a phase-gate process, they will be quickly overwhelmed in an Agile environment that encourages frequent and constant change.

Generate Documentation

Although SAFe prefers that models are used to validate assumptions early and to record system decisions, many product domains require documents for regulatory compliance (e.g., Federal Aviation Administration, Food and Drug Administration) or contractual obligations (e.g., contract data requirements lists [CDRLs] in government contracting). Therefore, SAFe recommends generating documents from the information in system models. These models act as a single source of truth for system decisions and ensure consistency among many documents. Also, such models can create documents targeting different stakeholders, who may have individual system perspectives, or who have access to view only selected portions of the system information (e.g., Suppliers).

While all products and programs will likely require formal documents, System Engineers are encouraged to work with Customers and/or regulatory agencies on the minimum set sufficient to meet their obligations. The source of most, if not all, of the information resides in engineering models that can and should be used, where possible, for inspections and formal reviews.

Build Model Quality In

Due to the diversity and number of people contributing information, models can suffer a notable challenge: Continuous changes made by many people can cause a drop in quality if proper oversight is lacking. The System Architect/Engineer works with teams to define quality practices—model standards and model testing—and to ensure that they are followed.

The quality practices discussed here facilitate early learning cycles. As SAFe notes, "You can't scale crappy code," and the same is true for system models. Quality practices and strong version management allow engineers to confidently and frequently make model changes and contribute to the system intent.

Model Standards

Model standards help control quality and guide teams on how best to model. They may specify the following criteria:

- Which information should be captured

- Modeling notations (e.g., SysML) and parts of those notations (e.g., use case) to use or exclude

- Where modeling information should be placed for solution and subsystem elements

- Meta-information that should be stored with different types of model elements

- Links within the model or with other cross-disciplinary models

- Common types and dimensions used across the system

- Modeling tool properties and configuration

- Collaboration practices with any underlying version control system(s) (if relevant)

If documents are being generated from the models, the document templates should be defined early, as they will influence many of these decisions. System designers need to know where to store the model elements and which metadata or links may be used for queries, document generation, or compliance.

As a best practice, the organization should create an example high-level, full-system model early on. Ideally, this example will be a skeleton model across the solution (one that defines all subsystems). Here, one element can illustrate how to model the structure and behavior of a single subsystem. Run any document generation tests against this configuration early to ensure it envisions the whole system, thereby helping the organization avoid wasteful rework due to missed information.

Create Testable and Executable Models

SAFe Test-First practices help teams build quality into their products early, facilitating the continuous small changes we find in Agile software development. A test-first approach creates a rich suite of cases that allow developers to more reliably make changes without causing errors elsewhere in the system. Rich, automated tests are critical to the movement toward a Continuous Delivery Pipeline.

Lean practices encourage testable, executable models (when feasible) to reduce the waste associated with downstream errors. Models should be testable against whatever assessment criteria exist for the domain or discipline:

- Mechanical models test for physical and environmental issues.

- Electrical models test for logic.

- Software models test for anomalies.

- Executable system models test for system behavior.

Most tools provide the ability to check models or to create scripts that can iterate across the models and look for anomalies.

Testing Requirements Models

Textual requirements are used in almost every system and, under the current practice, are typically reviewed manually. The community has long sought executable specifications, in which requirements are itemized in a test-ready format. Success, however, has been limited to specific domains where the problem is well defined. Agile practices advocate for an option called Acceptance Test–Driven Development (ATDD). Some exploratory work has emerged to support ATDD for systems development. While promising for testing requirements, ATDD's use has been limited at a large scale. Automate where possible, and make requirements and tests one and the same.

Testing Analysis and Design Models

Designs represented in models can be tested using tools that have static analyzers or 'checkers' that identify something that deviates from what is standard, normal, or expected. Teams may add their own rules—model organization, modeling conventions and standards, required meta-information (e.g., SysML tags, stereotypes), and so on. If analyzers don't exist, scripts can iterate over the models to look for problems in the static model.

Models can also be tested dynamically. The models from engineering disciplines have their own solutions for assessing the quality and should be leveraged as part of testing practice.

Testing Traceability

To ensure proper queries, document generation, and compliance, models must comply with the linking structure.

Document Generation

While possibly redundant with the traceability scripts mentioned previously, document generation functions may have scripts to ensure that the model is structured properly and that all data exist to support all document templates. With large models, it's often easier to debug a script than a document template.

Set-Based Design

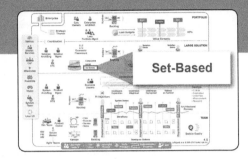

Assume variability; preserve options.

  —SAFe Lean-Agile Principle #3

Set-Based Design (SBD) is a practice that keeps requirements and design options flexible for as long as possible during the development process. Instead of choosing a single point solution up-front, SBD identifies and simultaneously explores multiple options, eliminating poorer choices over time. It enhances flexibility in the design process by committing to technical solutions only after validating assumptions, which produces better economic results.

System development can be described as a process of continuously converting uncertainty to knowledge. No matter how well a system is initially defined and designed, real customer needs and technological choices are both uncertain and evolving. Therefore, understanding of how a system needs to be implemented must adapt over time.

Details

SBD maintains multiple requirements and design options for a longer period in the development cycle. As the timeline advances, SBD uses empirical data to narrow the focus to the final design option. Through this approach, one can embrace Principle #3: Assume variability; preserve options for as long as possible, providing maximum flexibility.

Conversely, point-based design commits to a set of requirements and a single design strategy too early in the process. This practice often leads to late discoveries that require substantial rework as the deadline approaches. It may require shortcuts, quality compromises, and—worse—missed program commitments and deadlines. Using the Continuous Delivery Pipeline to provide feedback and learning along with SBD is often the optimal approach.

SBD is an important practice for economic efficiency in Lean product development, as described further in [1] and [2]. Figure 1 shows the conceptual difference between the set-based and point-based design approaches.

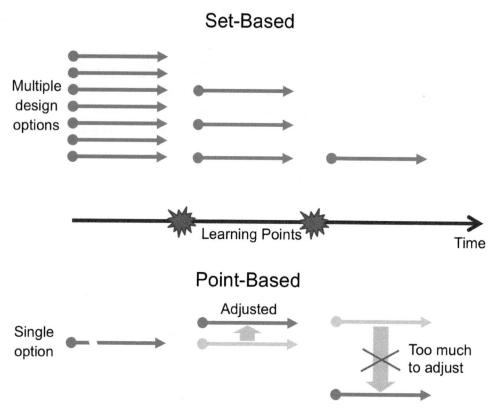

Figure 1. Comparing set-based and point-based design approaches

Increase Economic Efficiency with Set-Based Design

Employing SBD along with the teams, the System Architect/Engineering defines the subsystems and components for the solution and identifies architecture options for each. The teams then explore multiple alternative concepts for each subsystem, filtering out options that provide less economic value, are flawed in some way that cannot meet the targets, violate laws of physics, or fall short in some other way [1].

In SAFe, teams explore set-based design alternatives, applying a hypothesis-driven Minimum Viable Product (MVP) approach with a Lean Startup mindset (see the Continuous Delivery Pipeline chapter). Design alternatives include hypotheses and assumptions. MVPs may also define experiments intended to yield the knowledge that allows teams to validate or invalidate those hypotheses, filter alternatives, and arrive at the optimal economic decision.

Figure 2 provides an example of a significant learning Milestone (a deadline for the decision) in which designers of a future autonomous vehicle have to select the technology to support a new initiative that prevents forward collisions. In this example, the teams are exploring alternatives for a new 'Obstacle Detection System' (ODS) vehicle subsystem using lidar, radar, and camera technologies. With their corresponding hypothesis statement, they create Enablers that explore cost trade-offs, support for environmental and weather conditions, impact on vehicle design and manufacturing, quality of detection, and other issues. The teams record the results in the Solution Intent and filter the design alternatives based on validated learning.

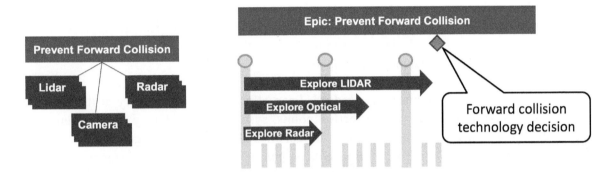

Figure 2. Example where a future autonomous vehicle has a significant learning milestone

Of course, exploring multiple design options comes at a cost—namely, the cost to develop and maintain those options, even if they are mostly model or paper-based. Reinertsen points out that maintaining multiple design options is one form of U-curve optimization, and sometimes the optimal number on the curve is 1 [3].

However, if there's a high degree of innovation, significant variability, or immovable deadlines (e.g., the crop combine must ship in January), a set-based design may be the best choice. In this case, design efficiency depends on several factors:

- **Flexibility** – Preserving a broad set of design options for as long as possible

- **Cost** – Minimizing the cost of multiple options through modeling, simulation, and prototyping

- **Speed** – Facilitating learning through early and frequent validation of design alternatives

Recommended practices to achieve design efficiency are described next.

Increase Flexibility in Interfaces and Design

Complex systems are built out of subsystems and component elements that collaborate to produce system behavior. Traditionally, specifications have been defined early when there are minimal understanding of what is possible and less concern for design trade-offs. A set-based approach, in contrast, makes trade-off decisions based on validated learning. Final designs and specifications emerge from teams' efforts toward exploring alternatives and understanding the trade-offs.

The System Architect/Engineering function typically defines the connections between subsystems and provides the context for teams to negotiate their own interfaces. In Figure 2, the system has a new ODS component responsible for preventing forward collisions. But teams must determine their own interfaces between the ODS and other subsystems—such as the chassis (sensor mounting), powertrain (deceleration), braking, and lighting (brake lights).

Interfaces are not rigid specifications. Indeed, Lean allows interfaces to vary at the points of subsystem intersection. At these intersection points, system engineers may specify ranges for negotiation (e.g., what's possible with an additional allocation of space, weight, or power?). This approach allows system engineers to manage the system-level allocations while teams make their own detailed decisions, creating a collaborative environment for system-level learning, negotiation, and economic decisions.

Modeling, Simulation, and Prototyping

The process of modeling, simulating, and prototyping allows for early empirical system validation, and it provides the initial learning points that will help eliminate some design alternatives and confirm others. Model-Based Systems Engineering (MBSE) supports set-based design through a disciplined, comprehensive, and rigorous approach. It incorporates a broad spectrum of modeling techniques specific to the industry and product type, including design thinking and user-centered design. These techniques should be applied to the parts of the system where the risk is highest, as they can significantly reduce the cost of maintaining design alternatives for a longer period of time.

Frequent Integration Points

During development periods when new designs are being explored, uncertainty abounds and actual knowledge is scarce. The only way to resolve the uncertainty is to test the design through the early and frequent integration of the system components. Integration points are driven in part by System Demos, which occur on a fixed two-week cadence, and by Solution Demos, which typically occur on the longer Program Increment (PI) cadence.

In fact, without this frequent integration, SBD practices may create a false sense of security. They may even increase risk, as it's possible that none of the design alternatives will really meet the identified targets. Frequent integration supports empirical learning, with the new insights being used to reduce options as the system evolves (Figure 3).

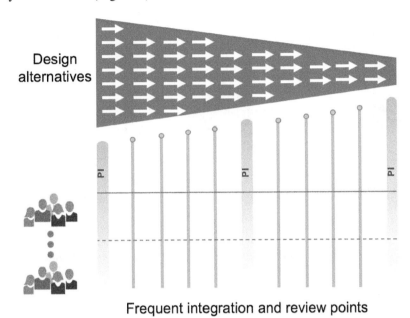

Figure 3. Frequent integration provides critical learning points that narrow design alternatives

Take a Systems View

On large systems, decisions may span many initiatives. For example, the ODS technology decision for the autonomous vehicle should consider more than the current initiative to avoid front collisions. System Architect/Engineering owns the technical vision and helps ensure that the system meets future goals. As Figure 4 illustrates, these personnel must guide the teams' understanding of the larger solution when making significant technology decisions.

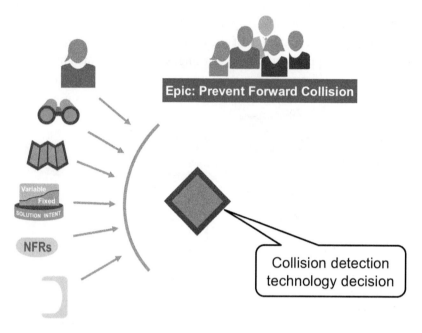

Figure 4. Technology decisions must look beyond the current initiative

As mentioned earlier, a set-based design has a cost. Exploring options can even increase the overall Cost of Delay (CoD). System Architect/Engineering must balance the possibility of over-engineering the solution (e.g., wasteful future-proofing) with the risk of being unprepared for near-term capabilities that may incur larger costs and rework ahead. Like every decision in SAFe, how much exploration is undertaken should be an economic decision.

Use Set-Based Design in Fixed-Schedule Programs

SBD is particularly effective for programs that require a high degree of fixed schedule commitments. Even if some of the more reliable design options don't provide the degree of innovation or enhanced performance that the system developers would prefer, it makes sense to keep multiple design options present, since the schedule is unmovable. When the deadline is unyielding, teams must do what they can within the schedule.

Adapting Planning

Explicit and regular planning provides the opportunity for evaluating different design alternatives and directly supports set-based thinking. PI Planning defines the overall intent for the PI, fostering alignment on the constraints and requirements that will govern the design alternatives under consideration. Iteration Planning plays a more tactical role. It allows teams to adjust during PI execution as they learn more from frequently integrating and reviewing increments of value.

Economic Trade-Offs in Set-Based Design

Different design options have different economic implications, so understanding SBD requires knowledge of the macroeconomic goals and benefits of the system. One way to look at these trade-offs is to place the alternatives on a spectrum, where a certain weight can be associated with each option.

Some of the significant economic indicators may include the following:

- Cost of development
- Cost of manufacturing
- Performance and reliability
- Cost of support
- Development time
- Technical risks

These indicators help team members identify which design options provide the greatest benefits. For instance, in the earlier collision prevention example, the trade-off between the accuracy of various detection technologies and the cost of manufacture can make a big difference, as shown in Figure 5.

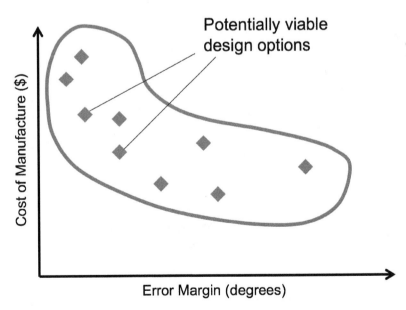

Figure 5. A trade-off curve between cost and a performance requirement (error margin) provides guidance for choosing among set-based designs

In summary, up-front commitment to a specific, detailed design can rarely survive contact with empirical evidence. A proper understanding of the economic trade-offs and SBD provides an adaptive approach that yields a wider systems perspective, better economic choices, and more adaptability to existing constraints.

LEARN MORE

[1] Ward, Allen, and Durward Sobek. *Lean Process and Product Development.* 2nd ed. Lean Enterprise Institute, 2014.

[2] Oosterwal, Dantar P. *The Lean Machine: How Harley-Davidson Drove Top-Line Growth and Profitability with Revolutionary Lean Product Development.* Amacom, 2010.

[3] Reinertsen, Don. *Principles of Product Development Flow: Second Generation Lean Product Development.* Celeritas Publishing, 2009.

Part 8
The Portfolio Level

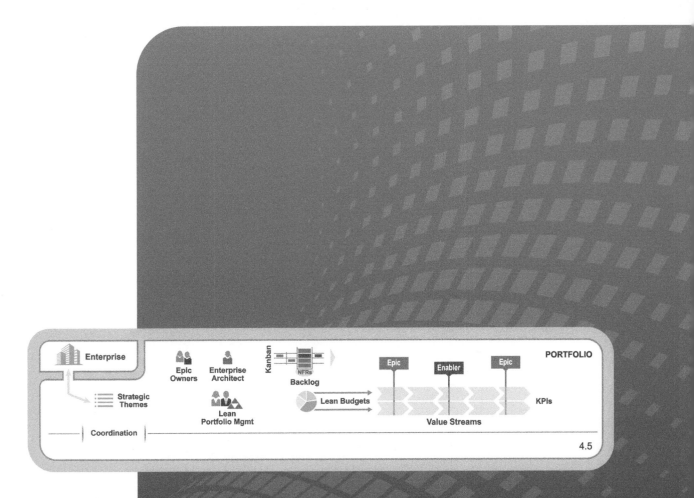

scaledagileframework.com/**portfolio-level**

Introduction to the Portfolio Level

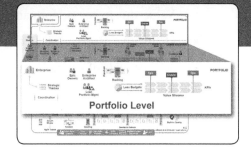

To succeed in the long term, focus on the middle term.

　—Geoffrey Moore

The *Portfolio Level* contains the principles, practices, and roles needed to initiate and govern a set of development Value Streams. This is where *strategy and investment funding* are defined for value streams and their Solutions. This level also provides *Agile portfolio operations* and *Lean governance* for the people and resources needed to deliver solutions.

The portfolio level aligns enterprise strategy to portfolio execution by organizing the Lean-Agile Enterprise around the flow of value through one or more value streams. Delivering the basic budgeting and necessary governance mechanisms, it assures that investment in solutions will provide the return on investment (ROI) the enterprise needs to meet its strategic objectives. In the large enterprise, there may be multiple SAFe portfolios.

Details

The SAFe portfolio level (Figure 1) contains the people and processes necessary to build the systems and solutions that the Enterprise needs to meet its strategic objectives.

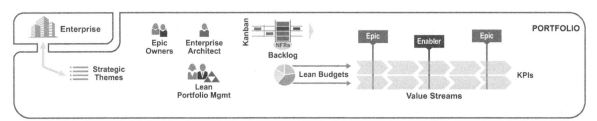

Figure 1. SAFe portfolio level

Each SAFe portfolio has a two-way connection to the enterprise. The first way establishes the Strategic Themes for the portfolio that guide it through ever-changing business objectives. The second way provides a constant flow of feedback from the portfolio back to the enterprise stakeholders. This feedback includes:

- The current state of the portfolio's solutions

- Value stream key performance indicators (KPIs)

- Qualitative assessments of the current solution's fitness for purpose

- Assessments of strengths, weaknesses, opportunities, and threats present across the portfolio

Highlights

Highlights of the portfolio level include:

- **Lean Budgets** – Lean budgeting allows fast and empowered decision-making, with appropriate financial control and accountability.

- **Value Streams** – Every value stream has to fund the people and resources necessary to build Solutions that deliver the value to the business or customer. Each is a long-lived series of steps (system definition, development, and deployment) that build and deploy systems that provide a continuous flow of value.

- **Portfolio Kanban** – The portfolio Kanban system makes the work visible and creates Work-in-Process (WIP) limits to help assure that demand is matched to the actual value stream and Agile Release Train (ART) capacities.

Roles

The portfolio-level roles provide the highest level of accountability and governance, including the coordination of multiple value streams.

- **Lean Portfolio Management (LPM)** – This function represents the individuals with the highest level of decision-making and financial accountability for a SAFe portfolio. This group is responsible for three primary areas: strategy and investment funding, Agile portfolio operations, and Lean governance.

- **Epic Owners** – These individuals take responsibility for coordinating portfolio Epics through the portfolio Kanban system.

- **Enterprise Architect** – This person works across value streams and programs to help provide the strategic technical direction that can optimize portfolio outcomes. The Enterprise Architect often may act as an Epic Owner for enabler epics.

Artifacts

The following portfolio-level artifacts help describe the strategic intent of the portfolio solution set:

- **Business epics** – Capture and reflect the new business capabilities that can be provided only through cooperation among value streams.

- **Enabler epics** – Reflect the architectural and other technology initiatives that are necessary to enable new Features and Capabilities.

- **Strategic themes** – Provide specific, itemized business objectives that connect the portfolio to the evolving enterprise business strategy.

- **Portfolio Backlog** – Is the highest-level backlog in SAFe. It holds approved business and enabler epics that are required to create a portfolio solution set. This provides the competitive differentiation and/or operational efficiencies necessary to address the strategic themes and facilitate business success.

LEARN MORE

[1] Leffingwell, Dean. *Agile Software Requirements: Lean Requirements Practices for Teams, Programs, and the Portfolio.* Addison-Wesley, 2011.

Enterprise

A strategic inflection point is that moment when some combination of technological innovation, market evolution, and customer perception requires the company to make a radical shift or die.

—Andy Grove, *Only the Paranoid Survive*

The *Enterprise* represents the business entity to which each SAFe portfolio belongs. In the small-to-midsize enterprise, one SAFe portfolio can typically govern the entire technical solution set. In larger enterprises, typically those with more than 500 to 1,000 technical practitioners, there can be multiple SAFe portfolios, typically one for each line of business. In either case, the portfolio is not the entire business, and it's important for the enterprise to ensure that each portfolio solution set evolves to meet its needs.

Details

Each portfolio within an enterprise exists for just one reason: to fulfill its contribution toward realizing the overall enterprise strategy. SAFe offers three primary constructs for connecting the enterprise strategy to a portfolio:

- The budget is the total funding provided to a portfolio for operating and capital expenditures. The portfolio budget is then allocated to individual value streams by Lean Portfolio Management authorities.

- Strategic Themes are specific, differentiated business goals that communicate aspects of the strategic intent from the enterprise to the portfolio.

- The portfolio context (described later in this chapter) provides constant feedback to support governance and inform the ongoing strategy development.

Enterprise Strategy Drives Portfolio Strategy

Developing the business strategy, and investing in the solutions that enable it, is a mostly centralized concern—the primary responsibility of the executives accountable for business performance. After all, portfolios don't form themselves or fund themselves; they exist solely to fulfill the larger enterprise purposes.

Small Enterprises May Have a Single SAFe Portfolio

In small enterprises, a single portfolio (a single instance of SAFe) may be enough to deliver a set of solutions for the entire organization. This portfolio is connected to the business strategy by strategic themes and the budget, and it provides feedback to the enterprise via portfolio context (Figure 1).

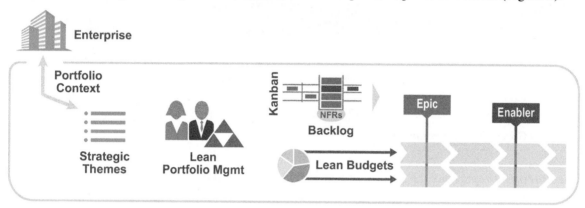

Figure 1. Enterprise view of a single SAFe portfolio

Large Enterprises Will Have Multiple Portfolios

SAFe is successfully applied by many of the world's largest enterprises. Many of these enterprises have thousands, and even tens of thousands, of IT, system, application, and solution development practitioners. Of course, these practitioners are not all working on the same solutions or within the same value streams. More likely, IT and development are organized to support various lines of business, internal departments, customer segments, or other business goals. To achieve the larger purpose, the enterprise will have multiple SAFe portfolios, each with its own budget and strategic themes reflecting that unit's portion of the business strategy (see Figure 2).

In this case, each SAFe portfolio exists in this broader enterprise context, which is the source of the business strategy it must address. The enterprise also provides the more general funding and governance model for all the portfolios. The strategy, however, is a two-way street.

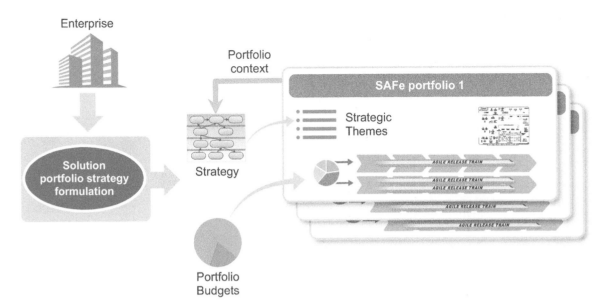

Figure 2. Enterprise view of multiple SAFe portfolios

Strategy Formulation

Defining the portfolio budget is a strategy development exercise (see the Strategic Themes chapter) that requires extensive collaboration. Many philosophies, trends, and influences are apparent in the tech sector, including those described by Geoffrey Moore's series of books [1] and *The Lean Startup* [2]. A variety of more specific strategy approaches are in vogue as well, including the Business Model Canvas and the Lean Canvas [3].

One example is described in *Beyond Entrepreneurship,* by Jim Collins [4]. The output of this process is a set of strategic themes that provides an ongoing strategy snapshot, which communicates evolving intent and a budget for the portfolio. Figure 3 highlights the main aspects of that approach when adapted to the SAFe context.

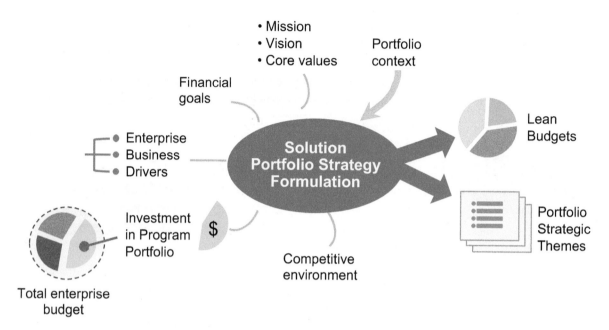

Figure 3. Solution portfolio strategy formulation

Each aspect of the solution portfolio strategy formulation is discussed briefly here:

- **Total enterprise budget** – As part of the organization's total operating budget, people and other resources are allocated to technical solutions across all SAFe portfolios. This budgeting process may include guidelines for capital and operating expenses (see the CapEx and OpEx guidance chapter).

- **Enterprise business drivers** – Enterprise business drivers reflect the evolving enterprise strategy. Since the current business and solution portfolio context is largely understood, there's no need to repeat the obvious. Instead, these drivers should express the additions to the current strategy. Business drivers such as 'integrate the capabilities of the new acquisition into the suite' (for a security company) and 'move applications to the cloud' are typical examples.

- **Financial goals** – Whether measured in revenue, profitability, market share, or other Metrics, financial performance goals should be clear. These goals must be communicated to the portfolio stakeholders.

- **Mission, vision, and core values** – A clear, unifying mission and set of core values provide the purpose and objectives that act as boundaries for creating the strategy.

- **Portfolio context** – The most effective strategies are developed while working in the complete portfolio context. Key performance indicators (KPIs), SWOT (strengths, weaknesses, opportunities, threats) analysis, and more provide the background. But strategic differentiation is what provides the enterprise's competitive advantage—it's the cultural and technical DNA that delivered the business's current success.

- **Lean Budgets** – A budget is allocated to each value stream to increase empowerment and decrease overhead by moving the day-to-day spending decisions (and associated resource decisions) to the people closest to solution development.

- **Competitive environment** – Competitive analysis will help identify the largest threats and areas of opportunity.

- **Strategic Themes** – Strategic themes are differentiating, specific business objectives that connect a portfolio to the strategy of the enterprise. They provide the business context for decision-making and serve as inputs to the vision, budget, and backlogs. The primary purpose of strategic themes is to drive portfolio innovation and differentiation.

As shown in Figure 3, portfolio budgets and strategic themes are an output of a process—a process in which the business executives and other stakeholders systematically analyze a set of inputs *before* arriving at conclusions.

Portfolio Context Informs Enterprise Strategy

The strategy also has some emergent properties—some elements that simply can't be known just centrally or up-front and that depend on the challenges and opportunities embedded in the current solution set and in the local market conditions they address. To respond to this kind of dynamic environment, strategy development requires continuous collaboration, communication, and alignment with downstream portfolios. In other words, it demands full and complete awareness of the *portfolio context*. This may include the following elements:

- **Key performance indicators** – The portfolio is responsible for providing feedback on the allocated investment. These KPIs can include quantitative and financial measures, such as return on investment (ROI), market share, customer net promoter score, and innovation accounting [2].

- **Qualitative data** – These data often include the outputs of SWOT analysis and, most important, the accumulated solution, market, and business knowledge of the portfolio stakeholders.

Strategy Formulation Is Largely Centralized; Portfolio Execution Is Decentralized

In keeping with SAFe Principle #9: Decentralize decision-making, forming a business strategy is largely centralized but also collaborative. Business executives and key portfolio stakeholders play a vital role. Executing solution strategy, however, is decentralized to the portfolio. Supported by transparency, constant feedback, KPIs, and appropriate portfolio metrics, only these people have the local knowledge necessary to define, evolve, and budget for value streams. They're in the best position to apply the Economic Framework and to manage the development of the solutions necessary to address changing Customer needs and new market opportunities.

LEARN MORE

[1] Moore, Geoffrey. *Crossing the Chasm* (1991, 2014), *Inside the Tornado* (1995, 2004), and *Escape Velocity* (2011). Harper Business Essentials.

[2] Ries, Eric. *The Lean Startup: How Today's Entrepreneurs Use Continuous Innovation to Create Radically Successful Businesses*. Random House, 2011.

[3] Maurya, Ash. *Running Lean: Iterate from Plan A to a Plan That Works.* O'Reilly Media, 2012.

[4] Collins, Jim, and William Lazier. *Beyond Entrepreneurship: Turning Your Business into a Great and Enduring Company.* Prentice Hall, 1992.

Value Streams

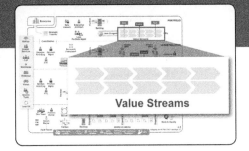

Shortest sustainable lead time with the best possible quality and value to people and society.

  —*House of Lean*

Value Streams represent the series of steps that an organization uses to build Solutions that provide a continuous flow of value to a Customer. SAFe value streams are used to define and realize Portfolio-Level business objectives and organize Agile Release Trains (ARTs) to deliver value more rapidly.

The primary role of a SAFe portfolio is to fund and nurture a set of development value streams. These value streams either deliver end-user value directly or support internal business processes.

Organizing around value offers substantial benefits to the organization, including faster learning, shorter time-to-market, higher quality, higher productivity, and leaner budgeting mechanisms. It results in value streams that are a better fit for the intended purpose. In SAFe, organizing around value is accomplished by first understanding value streams and then launching ARTs to fulfill them. Realizing value streams via ARTs is the 'art' and science of SAFe.

Value stream mapping can also be used to identify and address delays and non-value-added activities in a value stream to accomplish the Lean-Agile goal: shortest sustainable lead time.

Details

Lean-Agile methods focus intensely on continuous value delivery, where the value is achieved only when the end user, customer, or internal business process receives the business benefit of some new solution or Capability. In Lean, identifying and understanding the various flows of value is the most critical step—indeed, the starting point—for improving overall Enterprise performance. After all, if the enterprise doesn't have a clear picture of what it delivers and how, is it possible to improve the organization's performance? This brief background gives SAFe its primary incentive to organize development portfolios around flows of value called value streams.

A value stream is a long-lived series of steps used to deliver value, from concept or customer order to delivery of a tangible result for the customer. Figure 1 illustrates the anatomy of a value stream.

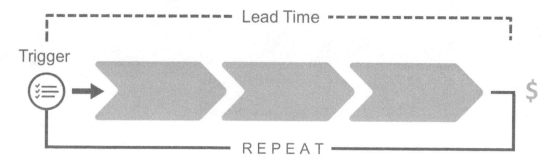

Figure 1. Anatomy of a value stream

As shown in Figure 1, a value stream begins when a significant event triggers the flow of value—perhaps a customer purchase order or new Feature request. It ends when some value has been delivered—a shipment, customer purchase, or solution deployment. The steps in the middle are the activities that the enterprise uses to accomplish this feat. A value stream contains the people who do the work, the systems they develop or operate, and the flow of information and materials. The time from the trigger to the value delivery is the lead time. Shortening the lead time reduces the time-to-market. That is the focus.

Types of Value Streams

In the context of SAFe, there are often two types of value streams present in the enterprise (Figure 2):

- **Operational value streams** – The steps used to provide goods or services to customers, be they internal or external [2]. This is how the company makes its money.

- **Development value streams** – The steps used to develop new products, systems, or services capabilities.

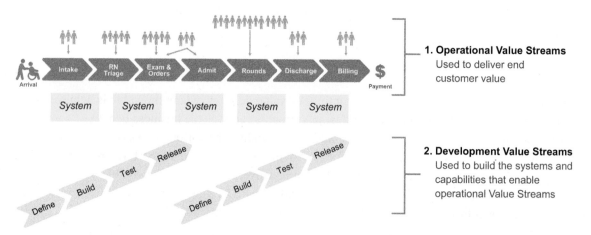

Figure 2. Development value streams build the systems that operational value streams use to deliver value

Sometimes the operational and development streams are the same, as when a solution provider develops a product for sale and feeds distribution directly (e.g., a small software as a service [SaaS] company). In that case, there is only one value stream: The development and operational value streams are the same stream.

However, understanding both types of value streams is critical, as the development value stream feeds the operational value stream, as illustrated in Figure 2. This is particularly true in the context of a big IT shop.

While the primary purpose of SAFe is guiding the people who build the systems, it's essential first to understand the overall flow of value, so that teams can develop and optimize solutions to accelerate the business result. Further, many of the critical requirements for the development value streams are not just functionality, but also solution and enterprise architecture, which are driven directly by the operational value streams.

To this end, identifying value streams and ARTs is one of the first steps in implementing SAFe. This process is described in the Identifying Value Streams and ARTs chapter.

Lean Budgeting for Development Value Streams

Identifying the value streams and understanding the flow through the organization is an essential step in improving value delivery. It also unlocks the opportunity to implement Lean Budgets, which can substantially reduce overhead and friction and further accelerate flow.

In support of this aim, each portfolio in SAFe contains a set of development value streams, each of which has a budget. Lean Portfolio Management (LPM) helps manage the budget for each value stream following Lean-Agile budgeting principles. Over time, LPM adjusts budgets for each value stream, based on changing business conditions. The Lean Budgets chapter describes dynamic budgets. Figure 3 shows the independent budgets for different development value streams.

Figure 3. Lean Portfolio Management allocates a budget to each development value stream

Value Stream KPIs

A Lean budgeting process can substantially simplify financial governance, empower decentralized decision-making, and increase the flow of value through the enterprise. It's a bold move to go from funding projects to allocating budgets to value streams. Naturally, this new approach raises a question: How does the enterprise know it's achieving an appropriate return on that substantial investment?

To help answer this question, each value stream defines a set of criteria, or key performance indicators (KPIs), which can be used to evaluate the ongoing investment. The type of value stream drives under consideration drives the KPIs that the business will need:

- Some value streams produce revenue, or end-user value directly, in which case revenue may be an appropriate measure. Other metrics, such as market share or solution usage, may provide additional insight.

- Other value streams, or elements of a value stream, create new offerings. In this case, potential return on investment (ROI) is a lagging economic measure. With these value streams leading to emergent offerings, using nonfinancial, innovation accounting KPIs to get fast feedback may be a better choice.

- Some development value streams are merely cost centers, which serve internal operational value streams and are not independently monetized. In this case, measures such as customer satisfaction, net promoter score, team/ART self-assessment, and feature cycle time may be more relevant.

- At the most significant scale, a value stream may establish an even broader set of measures, such as those represented by the sample Lean-Agile portfolio Metrics.

Value Stream Coordination

Two types of coordination activities are typically required with value streams:

- **Coordinating multiple value streams with a portfolio** – Value streams, by design, should be as independent as possible. However, there is likely to be some coordination required to ensure that the enterprise moves forward with each value stream in lockstep with the enterprise objectives. Value stream coordination is the topic of the Coordination chapter.

- **Coordinating multiple ARTs within a value stream** – Typically, in most large value streams there are some dependencies among the ARTs. How does the enterprise coordinate these activities to create a single, holistic solution set? Doing so can require an extensive degree of cooperation. For example:

  - Implementation of new, crosscutting capabilities, using a common Solution Backlog, managed by Solution Management

  - Collaboratively defining the technology and architecture that connect the solution across ARTs with the help of System and Solution Architects/Engineers

- Additional solution integration with full and partial Solution Demos

- Special considerations for Pre- and Post-PI Planning activities facilitated by the Solution Train Engineer

- Different degrees and types of DevOps and Continuous Delivery Pipeline support and collaboration

Coordinating multiple ARTs within a value stream is one of the primary challenges of the more significant Lean-Agile enterprise and is the subject of the Solution Train chapter, which is part of the Large Solution Level.

Reducing Time-to-Market with Value Stream Mapping

Identifying the value streams and organizing ARTs around them has another significant benefit: Each value stream provides an identifiable and measurable flow of value to a customer. As such, it can be systematically improved using value stream mapping [2] to increase delivery velocity and quality. Value stream mapping is further described in the Sustain and Improve chapter.

LEARN MORE

[1] Ward, Allen, and Durward Sobeck. *Lean Product and Process Development.* Lean Enterprise Institute, 2014.

[2] Martin, Karen, and Mike Osterling. *Value Stream Mapping.* McGraw-Hill, 2014.

[3] Poppendieck, Mary, and Tom Poppendieck. *Implementing Lean Software Development: From Concept to Cash.* Addison-Wesley, 2007.

Strategic Themes

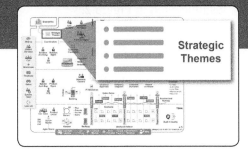

Innovation distinguishes between a leader and a follower.
—Steve Jobs

Strategic Themes are differentiating business objectives that connect a portfolio to the strategy of the Enterprise. They provide business context for decision-making and serve as inputs to the Vision, budget, and backlogs for the Portfolio, Large Solution, and Program Levels. The primary purpose of strategic themes is to drive portfolio innovation and differentiation.

Details

Strategic themes don't need to restate the obvious, as most elements of a portfolio vision are understood. That is, Portfolio stakeholders know quite well what the portfolio is for, and they establish and manage their mission and vision. Instead, strategic themes provide the enterprise with the differentiators needed to move from the current state to a more desirable, future state. They help drive innovation and competitive differentiation achievable only through effective portfolio Solutions.

Can you list ten things to get done in your portfolio that are important? When push comes to shove, what are the three (or five) most important of these items? Strategic themes provide the business objectives that highlight changes to the enterprise strategy affecting a particular solution portfolio. They are a significant communication mechanism between the enterprise and its solution portfolios (Figure 1).

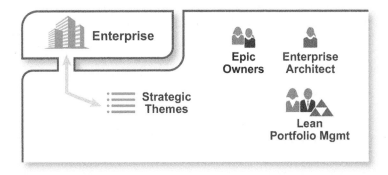

Figure 1. Strategic themes connect a portfolio to the broader enterprise context

Formulating Strategic Themes

Strategic themes are an output of a collaborative process in which the enterprise's executives and fiduciaries work with portfolio stakeholders to analyze a set of inputs before arriving at conclusions as illustrated in Figure 2.

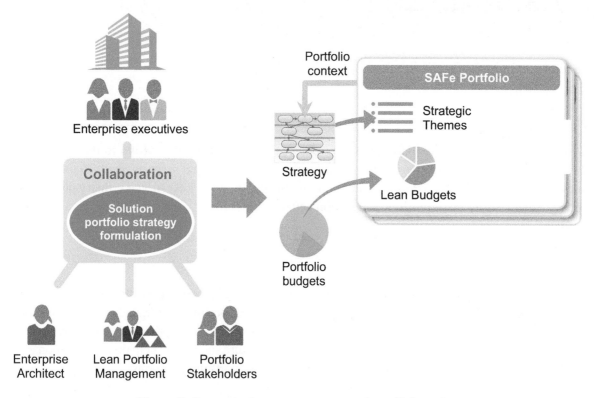

Figure 2. Strategic themes are outputs of a collaboration

Some examples of these themes follow:

- Appeal to a younger demographic (online retailer)

- Implement product and operational support for trading foreign exchange securities (securities company)

- Standardize on three software platforms (large IT shop)

- Lower warehouse costs (online retailer)

- Establish single sign-on from portfolio applications to internal enterprise apps (independent software vendor)

Strategic themes are a vital tool for communicating strategy to the entire portfolio, providing a simple, memorable message that influences everyone involved in solution delivery.

The Influence of Strategic Themes

Strategic themes are primary inputs to other portfolio elements (Figure 3). They affect the following aspects of the enterprise's operations:

- The value stream budgets
- The content in the Program and Solution Backlogs
- The ART and Solution Train vision and Roadmap
- The Economic Framework

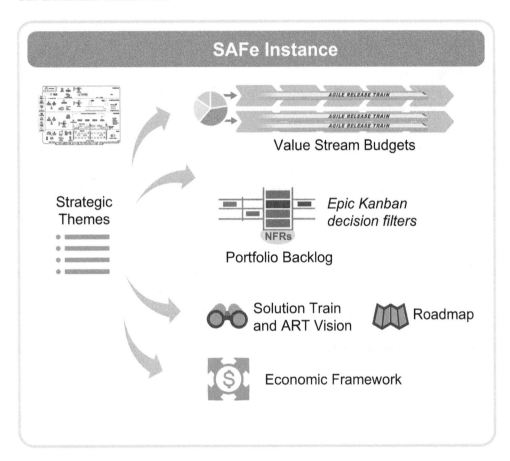

Figure 3. Influence of strategic themes

Value Streams Budgets

Strategic themes profoundly influence value stream budgets, which provide the investment and allocation of people needed to accomplish the strategic intent. Organizations should keep the following questions in mind when making those decisions:

- Do the current investments in value streams reflect the changes to the existing business context?

- Are we investing the appropriate amounts in new products and services? Are the capabilities of our current products and services sufficient or is more investment warranted? Are our maintenance and support activities sufficiently funded?

- Which other adjustments are required based on the new themes?

Portfolio Backlog

Strategic themes provide *decision-making* filters in the Portfolio Kanban system that influence the portfolio backlog. Within this system, they have the following implications:

- Impact the identification, success criteria, and prioritization of Epics in the funnel and backlog states

- Warrant consideration and discussion in the Lean business case (see the Epic chapter)

- May impact splitting and implementation of epics

Vision and Priorities

Strategic themes influence the ART and Solution Train vision and roadmap and help determine the attributes of Weighted Shortest Job First (WSJF) prioritization for items in the Program and Solution Backlogs. Solution and program epics that flow from the portfolio, or arise locally, are also influenced by the current themes. Moreover, strategic themes provide vital conceptual alignment between the trains. Due to their importance, they are often presented by the Business Owners during Program Increment (PI) Planning.

Economic Framework

Finally, because they can affect any major element of the pipeline—including development cycle time, product cost, product value, development expense, and risk—strategic themes may have a significant impact on the economic framework.

Measuring Progress against Strategic Themes

Identifying desired business outcomes for strategic themes can establish a context for assessing progress toward the strategic intent. However, many desirable measures of intent are trailing indicators. Measures of success, such as return on investment (ROI) and new markets penetrated, can take a long time to reach the desired levels.

Instead, the organization needs fast feedback from early indicators, many of which are not financial metrics. Lean organizations apply innovation accounting to address this challenge [1]. Innovation accounting is a thoughtful look at which early indicators are likely to produce the desired long-term results. It includes implementing the tooling, functionality, testing, or other mechanisms needed to collect those data.

In addition, certain criteria for success can be based on investment or activity. For example, an online retail store might want to reach a younger demographic. In this case, the success criteria could consist of a mix of investments, activities, and early indicators. A first learning Milestone might be to test the hypothesis of whether extending online capabilities to mobile platforms would appeal to the target audience. This could be measured easily with feedback from focus groups or analysis of mobile platform traffic data. From there, a second step might be to increase the budget for the mobile platform teams. To start trending the data, an epic Minimum Viable Product (MVP) could also be employed to capture the ages of users across all purchasing points.

Strategic theme outcome criteria provide indicators that allow the people managing the portfolio to understand the solutions involved, validate technical and business hypotheses, and, where necessary, pivot toward a better solution. The PI cadence offers an excellent timebox for experimenting with new approaches and gathering the feedback needed to show that investments in new strategic themes are likely to produce the desired long-term results.

LEARN MORE

[1] Ries, Eric. *The Lean Startup: How Today's Entrepreneurs Use Continuous Innovation to Create Radically Successful Businesses.* Crown Business, 2011.

Lean Budgets

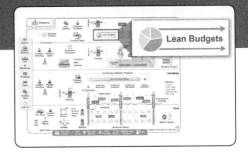

Agile software development and traditional cost accounting don't match.

—*Rami Sirkia and Maarit Laanti*

Lean Budgets is a set of practices that minimize overhead by funding and empowering Value Streams rather than projects while maintaining financial and fitness-for-use governance. This is achieved through objective evaluation of working systems, active management of Epic investments, and dynamic budget adjustments.

Each SAFe Portfolio exists for a purpose: to realize some set of Solutions that enable the business strategy. Each portfolio must work within an approved budget, as the operating costs for solution development are a primary factor in economic success.

Many traditional organizations quickly realize, however, that the drive for business agility through Lean-Agile development conflicts with current methods of budgeting and project cost management and accounting. The result may be that the move to Lean-Agile development—and realizing the potential business benefits—is compromised. Even worse, it may simply be unachievable.

SAFe provides strategies for Lean budgeting that eliminates the overhead of traditional project-based funding and cost accounting. In this model, Lean Portfolio Management (LPM) fiduciaries have control of spending, yet programs are empowered for rapid decision-making and flexible value delivery. This way, enterprises can have the best of both worlds: a development process that is far more responsive to market needs, along with professional and accountable management of technology spending.

Details

Every SAFe portfolio operates within an approved budget, which is a fundamental principle of financial governance for the development and deployment of products, services, and IT business solutions (software, hardware, firmware) within a SAFe portfolio. As described in the Enterprise chapter, the budget for each portfolio results from a strategic planning process (see Figure 1).

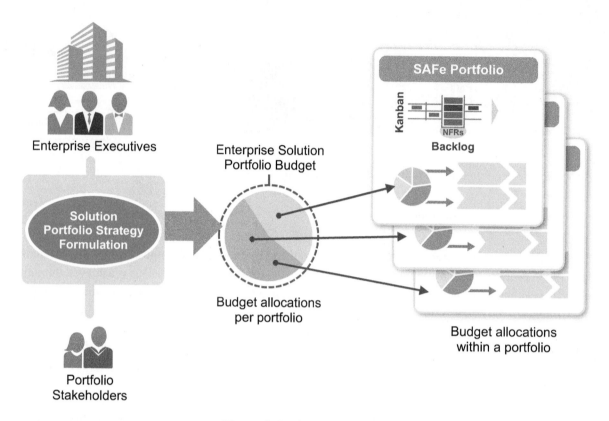

Figure 1. Budgeting overview

SAFe recommends a dramatically different approach to budgeting—one that reduces the overhead and costs associated with traditional cost accounting, while empowering Principle #9: Decentralize decision-making. With this new way of working, portfolio-level personnel no longer plan the work for others, nor do they track the cost of the work at the project level. Instead, the Lean enterprise moves to a new paradigm: *Lean budgeting, beyond project cost accounting*. This approach provides effective financial control over all investments with far less overhead and friction and supports a much higher throughput of development work (see Figure 2).

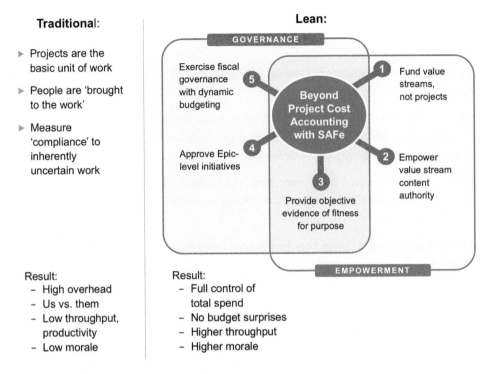

Traditional:

- Projects are the basic unit of work
- People are 'brought to the work'
- Measure 'compliance' to inherently uncertain work

Lean:

GOVERNANCE

Exercise fiscal governance with dynamic budgeting

5

Beyond Project Cost Accounting with SAFe

Approve Epic-level initiatives

4

3

Provide objective evidence of fitness for purpose

1 Fund value streams, not projects

2 Empower value stream content authority

EMPOWERMENT

Result:
- High overhead
- Us vs. them
- Low throughput, productivity
- Low morale

Result:
- Full control of total spend
- No budget surprises
- Higher throughput
- Higher morale

Figure 2. Empowerment and governance with Lean-Agile budgeting

Figure 2 illustrates the *five major steps* to this future state:

1. Fund value streams, not projects.

2. Empower value stream content authority (e.g., Solution Management).

3. Provide continuous objective evidence of fitness for purpose.

4. Approve epic-level initiatives.

5. Exercise fiscal governance with dynamic budgeting.

Each of these steps is discussed in the next sections.

The Problem of Traditional Project Cost Accounting

First, however, it's important to understand the problems caused by the traditional project approach to technology funding:

Cost-Center Budgeting Creates Multiple Challenges

Figure 3 represents the budgeting process of most enterprises before they move to Lean-Agile development. As shown in this figure, the enterprise is organized into cost centers. Each cost center must contribute to project spending or people (the primary cost element) to the new effort. This model creates some problems:

- The project budget process is slow and complicated. It requires many individual cost-center budgets to fund the project.

- It drives teams to make fine-grained decisions far too early in the 'cone of uncertainty.' If they can't identify all the tasks, how can they reasonably estimate how many people are needed, and for how long? Their hand is forced.

- People are assigned on a temporary basis. After the project is complete, people return to their organizational silo for future assignment within their cost center. And if they don't, other planned projects will suffer.

- The traditional model drives cost center managers to make sure everyone is fully allocated to one or more projects. However, running product development at 100 percent utilization creates an economic disaster [2], resulting in high variability between forecasted and actual time and costs.

- The model prevents individuals and teams from working together for longer than the duration of a single project. This hinders learning, team performance, and employee engagement. Moreover, collocation is out of the question. If the project takes longer than planned—which it often does—many people will have moved on to other projects, and further delays will occur.

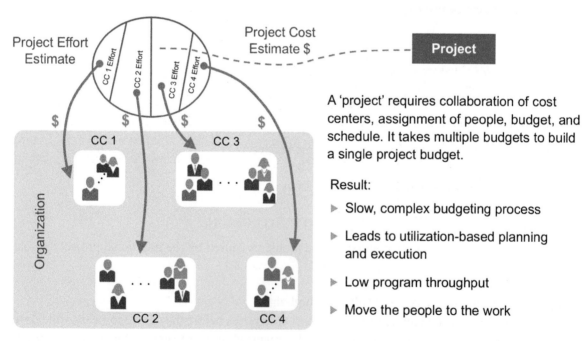

Figure 3. Traditional project-based cost budgeting and cost accounting model

Project-Based Constraints Impede Adaptability and Positive Economic Outcomes

Once the project is initiated, the challenges continue. The needs of the business and the project change quickly. However, because the budgets and personnel are fixed for the project term, the projects can't flex to the changing priorities (Figure 4).

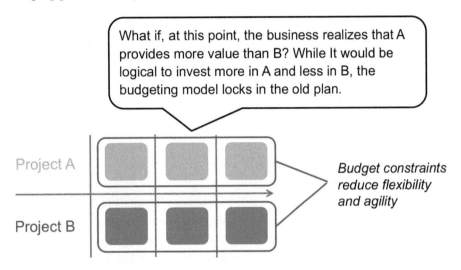

Figure 4. Project funding inhibits the ability to react to change

The result is an organization that is unable to adapt to changing business needs without incurring the overhead associated with re-budgeting and reallocating personnel. The Cost of Delay (CoD)—the cost of not doing the thing that you should be doing—increases.

Delays Happen—and Things Get Even Uglier

But we are not done. The product development personnel cannot innovate without taking risks [2]. Because this effort contains a high degree of technical uncertainty, it's challenging to estimate product development. And everyone knows that most things take longer than planned. Moreover, even when things go well, stakeholders may want more of a specific feature. That requires approval from a change control board, which adds further delay. Again, project-based funding hinders progress, culture change, and transparency (Figure 5).

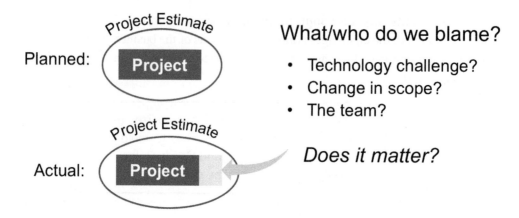

Figure 5. *When overruns happen, project accounting and re-budgeting increase CoD and negatively impact culture*

When schedule overruns occur for any reason, it's necessary to analyze the variances, re-plan the schedule, and adjust budgets. Resources are scrambled. Personnel are reassigned. As a result, other projects are negatively impacted. Now, the 'blame game' sets in, pitting project managers against each other and financial analysts against the teams. Any project overrun has a budget impact, but the real casualties are transparency, productivity, and morale.

Beyond Project Cost Accounting with SAFe

Traditional cost accounting undermines the goal of faster delivery and better economic outcomes. SAFe, however, provides five major steps to a better future state.

1. Fund Value Streams, Not Projects

The first step is to increase empowerment and decrease overhead by moving the day-to-day spending and resource decisions to the people closest to the solution domain. Each value stream is assigned a budget (Figure 6).

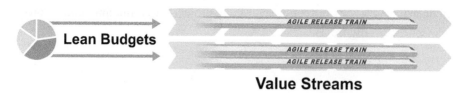

Figure 6. *Operating budgets (people and other resources) are defined for each value stream*

This is a significant step, and it delivers several benefits to the Lean enterprise:

- Value stream stakeholders, including the Solution Train Engineer (STE) and Lean Portfolio Management (LPM), are empowered to allocate the budget to the personnel and resources that make sense based on the current backlog and Roadmap.

- Since value streams and Agile Release Trains (ARTs) are long-lived, people work together for an extended time, increasing their engagement, knowledge, competency, and productivity.

- Self-organizing ARTs and value streams enable people to move from one ART and Agile Team to another, without requiring permission from management above the Program or Large Solution levels.

- The budget is still controlled. In most cases, the expenses across a Program Increment (PI) are fixed or easy to forecast. As a consequence, all stakeholders know the anticipated spending for the upcoming period, regardless of which features are implemented. If development of a feature takes longer than planned, there's no impact on the budget, and personnel decisions are a local concern (Figure 7).

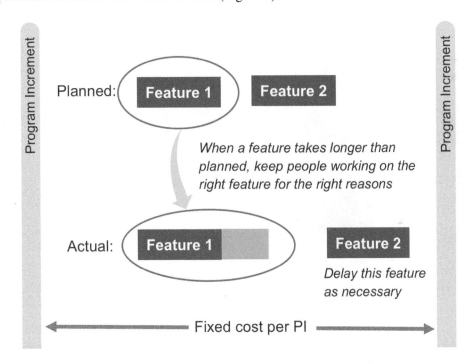

Figure 7. The budget for a program increment is fixed. If things take longer than anticipated, resources are not moved and the budget is not affected

2. Empower Value Stream Content Authority

Step 1 is a giant leap forward. Budgeting concerns aside, however, the enterprise still needs assurance that the value streams are building the right things. That's one of the reasons the project model was created. SAFe provides for this possibility not through increased overhead of projects, but rather through the empowerment and responsibilities of Product and Solution Management. To give visibility to everyone, all upcoming work is conducted, contained, and prioritized in the Program and Solution Backlogs (Figure 8).

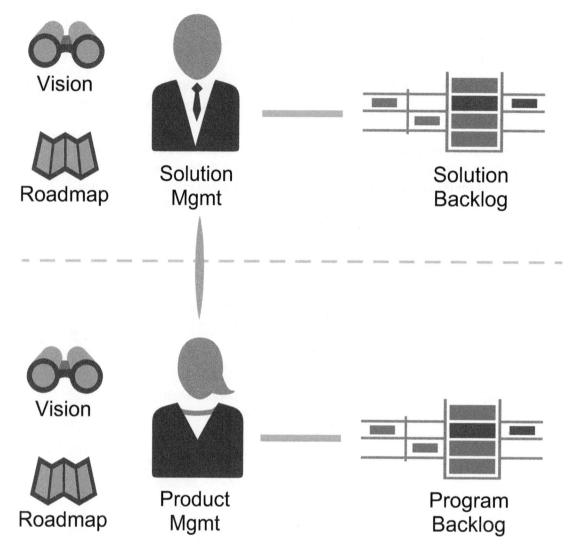

Figure 8. Transparent content decision-making authority by Product and Solution Management

Work is pulled from the backlogs based on Weighted Shortest Job First (WSJF) economic prioritization. This model assures that sound and logical economic reasoning support these critical decisions and that the right stakeholders are involved.

3. Provide Objective Evidence of Fitness for Purpose

Principle #5: Base milestones on objective evaluation of working systems provides the next piece of the puzzle. While the budget might be allocated in value stream–sized chunks, it's reasonable for all involved to want fast feedback on how the investment is tracking. Fortunately, SAFe provides regular, cadence-based opportunities to assess progress every PI via the Solution Demo and, if necessary, every two weeks via the System Demo. Participants include such key stakeholders as the Customer, Lean Portfolio Management, Business Owners, and the teams themselves. Any fiduciary party can participate and receive assurance that the right thing is being built in the right way and that it's meeting the customer's business needs, one PI at a time.

4. Approve Epic-Level Initiatives

While the rule is that each value stream is funded, there is an exception to that rule. By their very definition, epics are large enough and impactful enough to require additional approval. Often these initiatives affect multiple value streams and ARTs, and their costs may run into many millions of dollars. That is why all epics need review and LPM approval through the Kanban system and a Lean business case, whether they arise at the portfolio, Program, or Large Solution level (Figure 9).

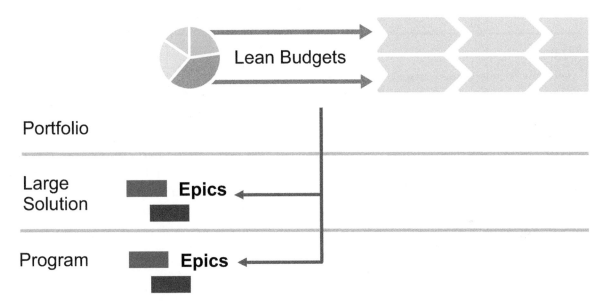

Figure 9. Epics require approval

Epics may be funded by tapping a portfolio budget reserve, by reallocating people or money from one value stream to another, or by simply accepting that an epic will consume a significant portion of an existing value stream budget. In any case, epics are large enough to require analysis, as well as strategic and financial review and decision-making. That scale, along with the Lean business case, is what makes an epic, an epic.

5. Exercise Fiscal Governance with Dynamic Budgeting

Although value streams are largely self-organizing and self-managing, they do not launch or fund themselves. As a result, LPM has the authority to set and adjust the value stream budgets within the portfolio. To respond to change, funding will vary based on business needs (Figure 10).

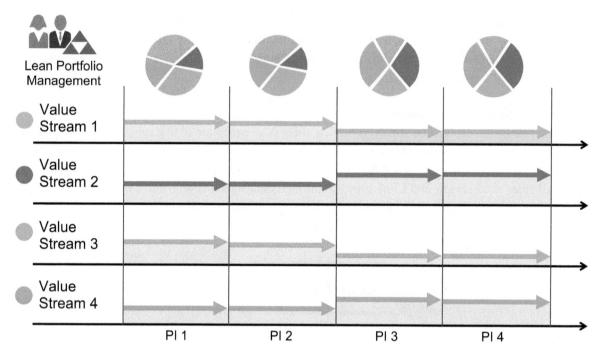

Figure 10. Value stream budgets are adjusted dynamically over time

Nominally, these budgets can be adjusted twice annually. Less frequently, and spending is fixed for too long, limiting agility. More frequently, and the enterprise may seem to be very Agile, but people are standing on shifting sand. That creates too much uncertainty and an inability to commit to any near-term course of action.

LEARN MORE

[1] Special thanks to Rami Sirkia and Maarit Laanti for an original white paper on this topic, which you can find at http://pearson.scaledagileframework.com/original-whitepaper-lean-agile-financial-planning-with-safe/.

[2] Reinertsen, Don. *Principles of Product Development Flow: Second Generation Lean Product Development.* Celeritas Publishing, 2009.

Epic

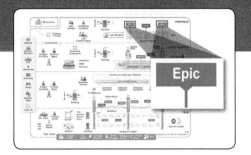

What if we found ourselves building something that nobody wanted? In that case, what did it matter if we did it on time and on budget?

  —Eric Ries

An *Epic* is a container for a Solution development initiative large enough to require analysis, the definition of a Minimum Viable Product (MVP), and financial approval prior to implementation. Implementation occurs over multiple Program Increments (PIs) and follows the Lean Startup 'build–measure–learn' cycle.

Epics are integral to Lean Portfolio Management (LPM) and Lean Budgeting models. They require an Epic Owner and Lean business case. Epics typically do not require a traditional scope completion end state. Instead, work continues until the optimal economic benefit is achieved.

SAFe defines two types of epics: business epics and enabler epics. Each type may occur at the Portfolio, Large Solution, and Program Levels. Although this chapter primarily describes the definition, approval, and implementation of portfolio epics, solution and program epics follow a similar pattern.

Details

Epics are the containers that capture and manage the largest initiatives that occur within a portfolio. Epics and the Value Streams they affect are the primary concern of the Portfolio level. Business epics directly deliver business value, while enabler epics are used to advance the Architectural Runway to support upcoming business epics.

Fostering Innovation with the Lean Startup Cycle and Lean Budgeting

Based in part on the emergence of Agile methods, the Lean Startup [1] strategy recommends a highly iterative 'build–measure–learn' cycle for product innovation and strategic investments. Applying this model to epics provides the economic and strategic advantages of a Lean Startup—managing investment and risk incrementally—while leveraging the flow and visibility constructs that SAFe provides (see Figure 1; for further discussion of this figure, see the Continuous Delivery Pipeline chapter).

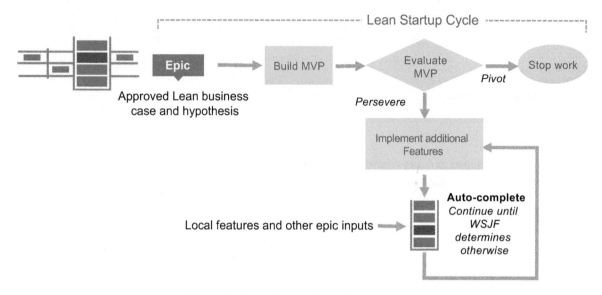

Figure 1. Epics in the Lean Startup cycle

In addition, the empowerment and decentralized decision-making associated with Lean Budgets depend on certain checks and balances. Even in the context of an approved value stream budget, epics still require visibility and approval of an MVP estimate prior to implementation. Thereafter, further investment in the epic is controlled locally via ongoing Feature prioritization of the Program Backlog.

Overview of the Portfolio Kanban

Portfolio epics are made visible, developed, and managed through the Portfolio Kanban, where they proceed through various states of maturity until they're approved or rejected. Understanding the Kanban system is fundamental to the understanding of portfolio epics. The states of the Portfolio Kanban are summarized here:

- **Funnel** – In this capture state, all big opportunities are welcome.

- **Review** – The review develops preliminary estimates of opportunity, effort, and cost of delay.

- **Analysis** – The analysis establishes viability, business outcome hypotheses, MVP, development and deployment impact, Lean business case, and 'go/no-go' decision approval.

- **Portfolio Backlog** – Approved epics move to the Portfolio Backlog until they are pulled by one or more Agile Release Trains (ARTs).

- **Implementing** – Implementation begins when capacity from one or more ARTs becomes available.

- **Done** – Once its business outcome hypotheses have been evaluated, the epic is considered done. If the hypothesis is proved true, more work will be done by implementing additional Features and Capabilities, or possibly new epics. If the hypothesis is proved false, however, the portfolio pivots to another approach or drops the initiative altogether.

Defining Epics

Reasoning about a potential epic must be based on a definition and intent that stakeholders can agree to. Figure 2 provides an epic hypothesis statement template that can be used to capture, organize, and communicate key information about an epic.

Epic Hypothesis Statement	
For	<customers>
who	<do something>
the	<solution>
is a	<something – the "how">
that	<provides this value>
Unlike	<competitor, current solution, or nonexistent solution>
our solution	<does something better – the "why">
Business outcome hypothesis:	• •
Leading indicators:	• (early innovation accounting measures) •
NFRs:	• •

Figure 2. Epic hypothesis statement

Analyzing and Approving Epics

Epics must be analyzed before being committed to implementation. Epic Owners take responsibility for this important task, while Enterprise Architects shepherd the enabler epics that support the technical considerations for business epics. The worthiest epics in the funnel pass to the analysis state when the queue has space.

The result of the analysis phase is a Lean business case. A Lean business case sample format is provided in Figure 3.

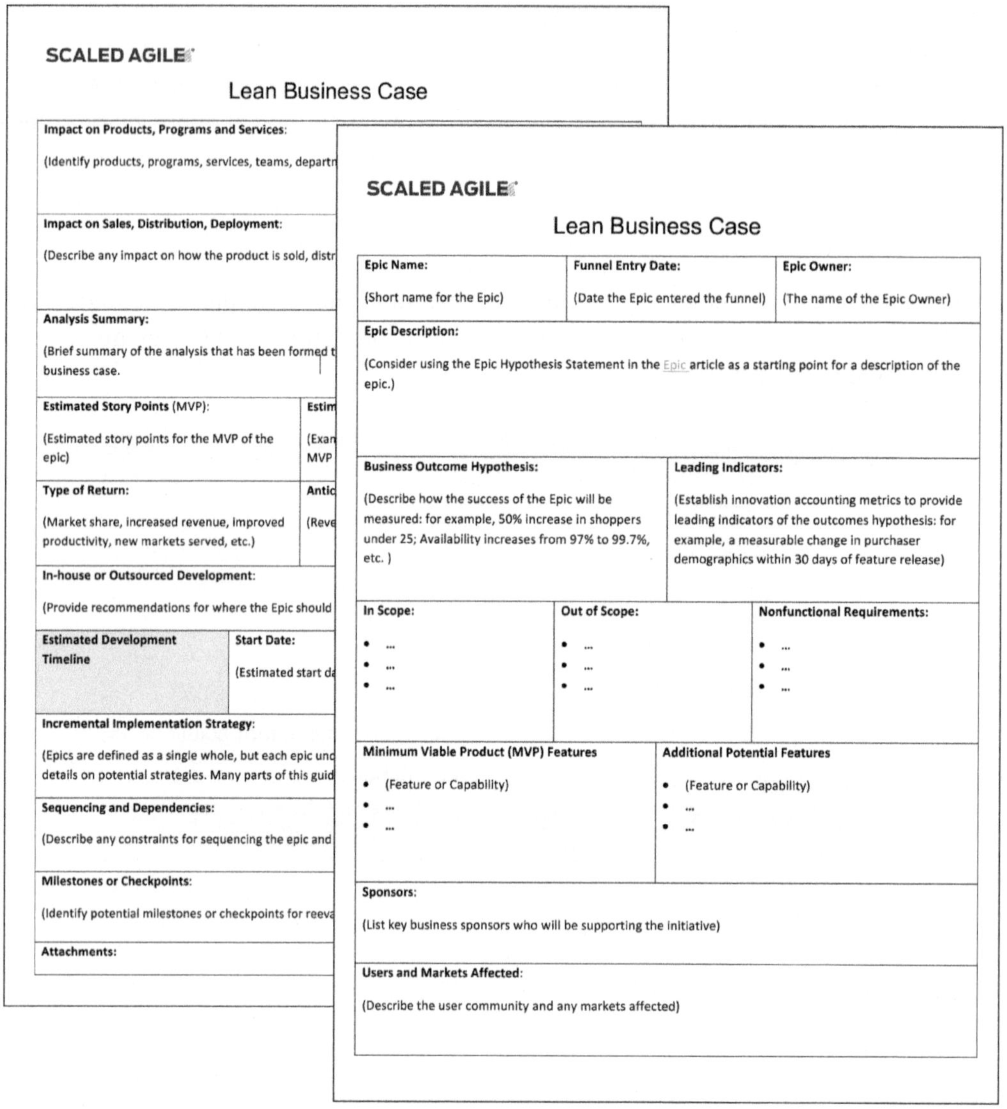

SCALED AGILE

Lean Business Case

Impact on Products, Programs and Services:

(Identify products, programs, services, teams, departm...

Impact on Sales, Distribution, Deployment:

(Describe any impact on how the product is sold, distr...

Analysis Summary:

(Brief summary of the analysis that has been formed t...
business case.

Estimated Story Points (MVP): | **Estim**

(Estimated story points for the MVP of the epic) | (Exan MVP

Type of Return: | **Antic**

(Market share, increased revenue, improved productivity, new markets served, etc.) | (Reve

In-house or Outsourced Development:

(Provide recommendations for where the Epic should

Estimated Development Timeline | **Start Date:**

| (Estimated start d

Incremental Implementation Strategy:

(Epics are defined as a single whole, but each epic und
details on potential strategies. Many parts of this guid

Sequencing and Dependencies:

(Describe any constraints for sequencing the epic and

Milestones or Checkpoints:

(Identify potential milestones or checkpoints for reeva

Attachments:

SCALED AGILE

Lean Business Case

Epic Name:	Funnel Entry Date:	Epic Owner:
(Short name for the Epic)	(Date the Epic entered the funnel)	(The name of the Epic Owner)

Epic Description:

(Consider using the Epic Hypothesis Statement in the Epic article as a starting point for a description of the epic.)

Business Outcome Hypothesis:	Leading Indicators:
(Describe how the success of the Epic will be measured: for example, 50% increase in shoppers under 25; Availability increases from 97% to 99.7%, etc.)	(Establish innovation accounting metrics to provide leading indicators of the outcomes hypothesis: for example, a measurable change in purchaser demographics within 30 days of feature release)

In Scope:	Out of Scope:	Nonfunctional Requirements:
• ... • ... • ...	• ... • ... • ...	• ... • ... • ...

Minimum Viable Product (MVP) Features	Additional Potential Features
• (Feature or Capability) • ... • ...	• (Feature or Capability) • ... • ...

Sponsors:

(List key business sponsors who will be supporting the initiative)

Users and Markets Affected:

(Describe the user community and any markets affected)

Figure 3. Lean business case for epics

The appropriate LPM authorities then review the Lean business case to make a go/no-go decision for the epic.

Implementing Epics

Once approved, portfolio epics stay in the portfolio backlog until implementation capacity becomes available from one or more ARTs. The Epic Owner or Enterprise Architect has the responsibility to work with the Product and Solution Management and System Architect/Engineering to define the MVP. Further, epics may be split into program or solution-level epics, or directly into feature or capability backlog items.

Splitting Epics

The incremental implementation of epics means that they must be split into smaller backlog items that represent the incremental value. Table 1 suggests nine methods for splitting epics, along with examples for each.

1. Solution / Subsystem / Component – Epics often affect multiple solutions, subsystems, or large components. In such cases, splitting by these aspects can be an effective implementation technique.	
Multiple user profiles	*... Multiple profiles in the opt-out website* *... Multiple profiles in the admin system*

2. Business Outcome Hypotheses – The epic business outcome hypotheses often provide hints as to how to incrementally achieve the anticipated business value.	
Implement new artifact in search results: Location hypotheses: a) Locations should provide additional filtering method when other disambiguation methods aren't useful b) Provide detailed location of a person	*... Provide state information in the search results (criteria [a] is partially satisfied, as states alone already provide some good filtering capability)* *... Implement compound location: State and city (entire success criteria is satisfied)*

3. Major Effort First – Sometimes an epic can be split into several parts, where most of the effort will go toward implementing the first one.	
Implement single sign-on across all products in the suite	*... Install PINGID protocol server and test with mock identity provider* *... Implement SSO management capability in our simplest product* *... Implement SSO in our most complex product* *... Proliferate as quickly as backlog capacity allows*

4. Simple/Complex – Capture that simplest version as its own epic, and then add additional program epics for all the variations and complexities.	

5. Variations in Data – Data variations and data sources are other aspects of scope, complexity, and implementation management.	
Internationalize all end-user facing screens	*... in Spanish* *... in Japanese* *... prioritize the rest by then-current market share*

6. Market Segment / Customer / Class of User – Segmenting the market or customer base is another way to split an epic. Do the one that has the higher business impact first.	
Implement opt-in functionality	*... For current partners* *... For all major marketers*

7. Defer Solution Qualities (NFRs) – Sometimes the initial implementation isn't all that hard, and the major part of the effort is in making it fast—or reliable or more precise or more scalable—so it may be feasible to achieve the solution qualities (NFRs) incrementally.	
8. Risk Reduction | Opportunity Enablement – Given their scope, epics can be inherently risky; use risk analysis and do the riskiest parts first.	
Implement filtering search results by complex user-defined expression	*... Implement negative filtering* *... Implement complex filtering expressions with all logical operations*
9. Use Case Scenarios – Use cases [1] can be used in Agile to capture complex user-to-solution or solution-to-solution interaction; split according to specific *scenarios* or *user goals* of the use case.	
Transitive people search functionality	*(Goal 1 ~) Find connection to a person* *(Goal 2 ~) Find connection to a company* *(Goal 3 ~) Distinguish strong and weak connections*

Table 1. Methods for splitting epics

Solution and Program Epics

The preceding discussion describes the largest kind of epics, portfolio epics. These epics are typically crosscutting efforts that affect multiple ARTs and value streams. Some portfolio epics may require splitting them into solution and program epics to facilitate incremental implementation.

In addition, epic-level initiatives may arise at the large solution or program levels. While mainly a local concern, these epics may have impacts on financial, human, and other resources that are large enough to warrant a Lean business case, discussion, and financial approval from LPM. That's what makes an epic an epic.

Methods for managing epics at these levels are discussed in the Program and Solution Kanban chapter.

LEARN MORE

[1] Ries, Eric. *The Lean Startup: How Today's Entrepreneurs Use Continuous Innovation to Create Radically Successful Businesses*. Random House, 2011.

[2] Leffingwell, Dean. *Agile Software Requirements: Lean Requirements Practices for Teams, Programs, and the Enterprise*. Addison-Wesley, 2011.

Epic Owners

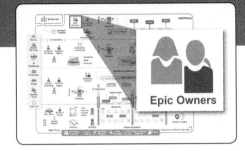

To be in hell is to drift; to be in heaven is to steer.
  —*George Bernard Shaw*

Epic Owners are responsible for coordinating portfolio Epics through the Portfolio Kanban system. They define the epic, its Minimum Viable Product (MVP), and Lean business case, and when approved, facilitate implementation of the epic.

If an epic is accepted, the Epic Owner works directly with the Agile Release Train (ART) and Solution Train stakeholders to define the Features and Capabilities that realize the value. This role may also have some responsibility for supporting the initiative as it moves downstream through the Continuous Delivery Pipeline to Release on Demand.

Details

In SAFe, epics drive a significant amount of the economic value for the enterprise. Epic Owners are responsible for formulating and elaborating the epic and analyzing its cost and impact. They define an MVP where applicable and secure approval (or rejection) of the epic.

Summary Role Description

The Epic Owner is responsible for driving individual epics from identification through the portfolio Kanban system and on to the go/no-go decisions of Lean Portfolio Management (LPM). After accepting the epic for implementation, the Epic Owner works with the Agile Teams to initiate the development activities necessary to realize the epic's business benefits. After the epic's initiation, the Epic Owner may have some ongoing responsibilities for stewardship and follow-up. As the features and capabilities that define the epics are incorporated into the Solution, the Epic Owner returns to other duties or takes responsibility for other emerging epics. After that point, the ARTs have the responsibility for implementing the new epic into the solution.

Typically, an Epic Owner works with the one or two epics at a time that fall within this role's area of expertise and current business mission.

Responsibilities

The Epic Owner role in SAFe is just that—a responsibility assumed by an individual, rather than a job title. The Epic Owner assumes the responsibilities outlined in this section.

Preparing the Epic

The Epic Owner's responsibilities begin early in the epic's life cycle. Responsibilities related to preparing the epic include the following:

- Working with stakeholders and subject-matter experts to define the epic value statement, the potential business benefits, a specific outcome hypothesis, the MVP, the Cost of Delay (CoD), and business sponsors

- Working with development teams to size the epic and provide input for economic prioritization based on the Weighted Shortest Job First (WSJF) model, the Lean business case, and the Economic Framework

- Shepherding epics through the portfolio Kanban system and creating the Lean business case [1]

- Preparing to present the business case to LPM for a go/no-go decision

Presenting the Epic

The Epic Owner has the primary responsibility for presenting the merits of the epic to LPM. Approval is not a rubber stamp process, however, as enterprises typically have ideas and opportunities that far exceed their capacity. That's one of the many arguments that favor Lean business cases; they should not create too high an emotional investment for the people analyzing them. Specific potential epics can and should be rejected in favor of more promising opportunities [1].

Implementation

If the epic is approved, then the following implementation activities begin:

- Work with Product and Solution Management to split the epic into ART and solution epics or features. Epic owners help prioritize these backlog items in their respective backlogs.

- Provide the context for the epic's target features.

- Participate in Program Increment (PI) Planning, System Demo, and Solution Demo whenever there is critical activity related to the epic.

- Work with Agile Teams that perform research Spikes, and create proofs of concept, mockups, and other artifacts.

- Coordinate and synchronize epic-related activities with sales, marketing, and other business units.

- Understand and report on the progress of the epic with key stakeholders.

Finally, to assess the outcomes against the hypothesis, the Epic Owner may follow the epic downstream through the Continuous Delivery Pipeline and during the release on demand process.

The Collaborative Nature of the Epic Owner Role

An Epic Owner can be effective only by collaborating closely with other groups in the enterprise. This role helps fill in the gaps that often occur when high-level initiatives descend from the top of the organization for implementation. Key collaborators are highlighted in Figure 1. By working closely with these key stakeholders, Epic Owners can create a realistic and compelling vision, appropriate economic priorities, and a consistent set of features and capabilities.

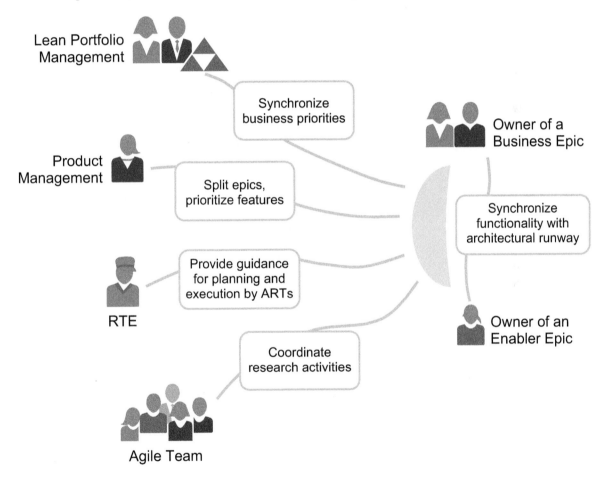

Figure 1. The collaborative nature of the Epic Owner role

LEARN MORE

[1] Leffingwell, Dean. *Agile Software Requirements: Lean Requirements Practices for Teams, Programs, and the Enterprise.* Addison-Wesley, 2011.

Enterprise Architect

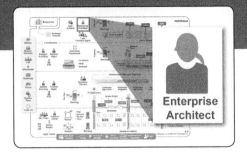

All men can see these tactics whereby I conquer, but what none can see is the strategy out of which victory is evolved.

 —Sun Tzu

The *Enterprise Architect* promotes adaptive design and engineering practices and drives architectural initiatives for the portfolio. Enterprise Architects also facilitate the reuse of ideas, components, services, and proven patterns across various solutions in a portfolio.

Poor strategic technical planning, communication, and visibility can result in suboptimal systems performance across the enterprise, prompting significant redesign. To prevent this undesirable outcome, and to support current and near-term business needs, these systems will benefit from having some Architectural Runway and architectural governance (e.g., to drive common usability and behavioral constructs across the Enterprise's solution). To address parts of this problem, SAFe highlights the roles of System and Solution Architects, who provide much of this guidance at the Program and Large Solution Levels.

At the Portfolio Level, the challenge is even larger. Mergers and acquisitions, changes in underlying technologies and competition, emerging standards, and other factors often push businesses in directions that go beyond the scope of Agile Teams. To help the organization cope with that stretching of its collective capabilities, Enterprise Architects have the authority and knowledge to work across Solution Trains and Agile Release Trains (ARTs). They can provide the strategic technical direction that can improve results. Aspects of this strategy may include recommendations for development and delivery of technology stacks, interoperability, APIs, and hosting strategies. These approaches produce results because Enterprise Architects foster incremental implementation while staying connected with the team's work.

Details

Enterprise Architects work with business stakeholders and Solution and System Architects to implement technology initiatives across Value Streams. They rely on continuous feedback, foster adaptive design and engineering practices, and rally programs and teams around a common technical vision.

Responsibilities

The Enterprise Architect focuses primarily on the following responsibilities:

- Collaborating with Lean Portfolio Management to provide a high-level, all-inclusive vision of enterprise solutions and development initiatives

- Defining key technical initiatives that support Lean Budgets via Enabler Epics

- Participating in the strategy for building and maintaining the Architectural Runway

- Understanding and communicating Strategic Themes, and other key business drivers for architecture, to System Architects and nontechnical stakeholders

- Driving architectural initiatives in the Portfolio Kanban system and participating in epic analysis where applicable

- Influencing common modeling, design, and coding practices

- Promoting Continuous Delivery Pipeline and DevOps capabilities

- Collecting, generating, and analyzing innovative ideas and technologies to use across the business

- Facilitating the reuse of code, components, and proven patterns

- Synchronizing the following disciplines across Solutions whenever applicable:
  - System and data security and quality
  - Production infrastructure
  - Solution user experience (Lean UX)
  - Scalability, performance, and other Nonfunctional Requirements (NFRs)

Enterprise Architecture Strategy

The enterprise's ability to embrace organizational change is a key competitive advantage, and the enterprise architectural strategy is a vital element of this ability. Figure 1 illustrates five key aspects of such a strategy; each element is briefly described in the following subsections.

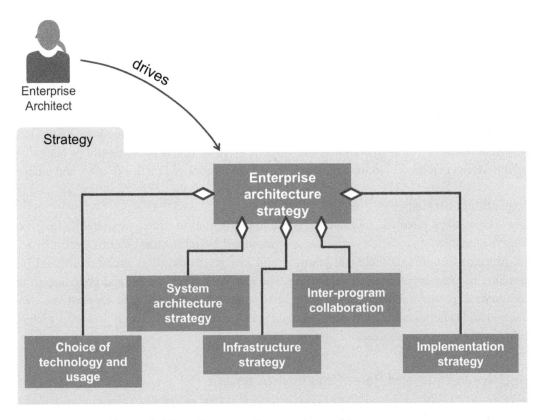

Figure 1. Five elements of enterprise architecture strategy

Choice of Technology and Usage

Choosing appropriate technologies is a key element of strategy formulation. Supporting activities include research and prototyping, understanding applicability and scope, and assessing the maturity of innovative new technologies.

Solution Architecture Strategy

The Enterprise Architect works closely with the Solution and System Architects to ensure that individual program and product strategies align with business and technical objectives. For example, emerging solutions to local problems should be consistent with the overall enterprise strategy. When that's not the case, decisions should be made explicit, as the inconsistent option may well influence future enterprise strategy.

Infrastructure Strategy

When it fulfills its function properly, development and deployment infrastructure goes unnoticed. However, the strategy for building and maintaining the infrastructure is a key challenge, overlapping with System Architect responsibilities. Some of these responsibilities include the reuse of configuration patterns, common physical infrastructure, knowledge sharing across ARTs and Solution Trains, and—especially—System Teams. In addition, some of the development and deployment infrastructure will likely intersect with internal IT systems. The Enterprise Architect can provide direction there as well.

Inter-program Collaboration

Various aspects of architecture work occur in different teams and programs, which is why it's helpful to ensure that common technology, design practices, and infrastructure are used when applicable. However, it's also important that value streams and ARTs have sufficient degrees of freedom; otherwise, innovation will decrease. Thus, both common and variable architectural aspects should be actively shared among the ARTs via joint design workshops, design Communities of Practice (CoPs), and other means.

Implementation Strategy

The importance of an effective, incremental Agile implementation strategy can hardly be overstated. Building the technical foundation for business epics into the Architectural Runway must be an incremental process. Continuous technical learning and fast feedback allow architecture and business functionality to grow synchronously over time. The ability of Agile Teams and programs to refactor as necessary and preserve multiple possible design options wherever practical supports this evolution. Abstraction and generalization help avoid binding specificity too early, which preserves architectural flexibility for future business needs.

Respect for People and Relentless Improvement

The Lean-Agile Mindset creates a healthy environment in which everyone operates on facts, not assumptions. This is particularly important for Enterprise Architects, who operate one (or two!) steps removed from day-to-day development activities. The Enterprise Architect is wise to maintain personal connections to each ART, Solution Train, and architect through the following activities:

- Receiving feedback on current enterprise-wide initiatives

- Participating in architecture and design CoPs

- Attending demos whenever critical redesign or foundation work is in progress

Developers and testers will be more likely to trust strategy driven by a person who knows their current challenges and context. Likewise, the Enterprise Architect will better trust teams that provide full visibility of their current context.

LEARN MORE

[1] Leffingwell, Dean. *Agile Software Requirements: Lean Requirements Practices for Teams, Programs, and the Enterprise.* Addison-Wesley, 2011.

[2] Bloomberg, Jason. *The Agile Architecture Revolution.* Wiley, 2013.

[3] Coplien, James, and Gertrud Bjørnvig. *Lean Architecture for Agile Software Development.* Wiley, 2010.

Lean Portfolio Management

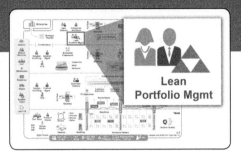

Most strategy dialogues end up with executives talking at cross-purposes because … nobody knows exactly what is meant by vision and strategy, and no two people ever quite agree on which topics belong where. That is why, when you ask members of an executive team to describe and explain the corporate strategy, you frequently get wildly different answers. We just don't have a good business discipline for converging on issues this abstract.

—Geoffrey Moore, Escape Velocity

The *Lean Portfolio Management (LPM)* function has the highest level of decision-making and financial accountability for the products and Solutions in a SAFe portfolio. An effective LPM function is necessary for SAFe success, but it is typically a function, not an organization. The people who fulfill these responsibilities may have various titles and roles. Usually, though, this function includes the business managers and executives who understand the Enterprise's financial position and are ultimately responsible for portfolio strategy, operations, and execution.

LPM is significantly different than traditional portfolio management. In many cases, an existing legacy mindset—with annual planning and budgeting cycles and traditional measures of progress—severely inhibits the enterprise's transition to agility. In response, SAFe recommends seven transformational patterns to move the organization to the leaner, more effective approach described in the Extending to the Portfolio chapter. With this context in mind, we can move on to describing LPM.

Details

As shown in Figure 1, every SAFe portfolio has an LPM function with three primary responsibilities: strategy and investment funding, Agile portfolio operations, and Lean governance.

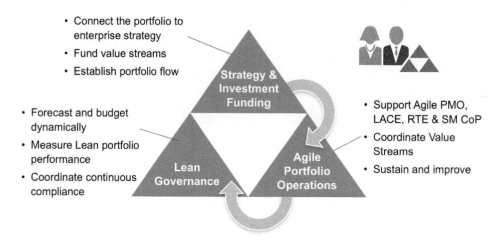

- Connect the portfolio to enterprise strategy
- Fund value streams
- Establish portfolio flow

- Forecast and budget dynamically
- Measure Lean portfolio performance
- Coordinate continuous compliance

Strategy & Investment Funding

Lean Governance

Agile Portfolio Operations

- Support Agile PMO, LACE, RTE & SM CoP
- Coordinate Value Streams
- Sustain and improve

Figure 1. Primary responsibilities of Lean Portfolio Management

Strategy and Investment Funding

Of these three primary responsibilities, strategy and investment funding is arguably the most important. Only by allocating the right investments to building the right things can an enterprise achieve its ultimate business objectives. Achieving this goal requires the focused and continued attention of LPM. As described in the Enterprise chapter, key stakeholders collaborate, create, and communicate the portfolio strategy. The Value Streams must then receive appropriate funding to develop and maintain portfolio products and services.

Effective strategy and investment funding requires extensive cooperation between enterprise executives, Business Owners, and Enterprise Architects. They can provide the longer-term view of the technology necessary to support the evolving business strategy, as described in Figure 2. Their responsibilities during this collaboration include connecting the portfolio strategy to the enterprise strategy, funding value streams, and establishing portfolio flow.

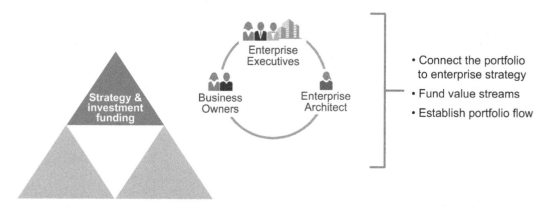

Strategy & investment funding

Enterprise Executives

Business Owners

Enterprise Architect

- Connect the portfolio to enterprise strategy
- Fund value streams
- Establish portfolio flow

*Figure 2. The Lean Portfolio Management collaboration and strategy and
investment funding responsibilities*

Connecting the Portfolio Strategy to the Enterprise Strategy

It's critical that the portfolio strategy both supports and informs the enterprise's broader business objectives. An effective strategy also relies on the existing assets and distinctive competencies of the portfolio's solutions. Thus, these strategies are interdependent. One key output of the collaboration between enterprise executives, Business Owners, and Enterprise Architects is the vital Strategic Themes that provide the differentiation needed to achieve the desired future state. To ensure that the entire portfolio is aligned to the overall business strategy, these themes must be developed and communicated broadly within the portfolio.

Funding Value Streams

The primary role of a SAFe portfolio is to identify, fund, and nurture a set of development value streams that deliver end-user value directly or that support internal business processes. This is one of the most critical activities in SAFe. Once established, Lean Budgets provide value stream funding aligned with the business strategy and current strategic themes. This eliminates the need for traditional project-based funding and cost accounting. Moving away from these legacy approaches reduces friction, delays, and overhead. Because this represents a significant change for many organization, it often requires some analysis and definition of the enterprise's value streams, as described in the Identifying Value Streams and Agile Release Trains (ARTs) chapter.

Establishing Portfolio Flow

To implement the business objectives, the flow of work originating from the portfolio must be balanced with the extensive work that arises as each ART and Solution Train responds to customer needs. Portfolio business and enabler Epics are used to capture, analyze, and approve new business and technology initiatives that require the collaboration of multiple value streams, or that cause the formation of entirely new ones. The Portfolio Kanban system is designed to visualize and limit Work in Process (WIP), reduce batch sizes of work, and control the length of longer-term development queues. Epic Owners, Enterprise Architects, and—where applicable—Solution Portfolio Management support this particular Kanban system. Successful implementation relies on knowing the total capacity for each ART in the portfolio, as well as understanding how much capacity is available for new development work versus ongoing maintenance and support activities. When this is understood, the enterprise can then evaluate and originate portfolio-level initiatives in a logical, objective, and practical sequence.

Agile Portfolio Operations

Managing investments and assuring alignment and consistency across the portfolio is a constant and urgent concern for managers and executives. Historically, much of this work was centralized, along with planning, program management, and solution definition. Such an approach ensured that solution development aligned with portfolio strategy to help foster consistent approaches to critical elements like information security, common platforms, and financial and progress reporting. Often, a centralized Program Management Office (PMO) took charge of these responsibilities.

In contrast, the SAFe Lean-Agile Mindset fosters the decentralization of strategy execution to empowered ARTs and Solution Trains. Even then, systems thinking must be applied to ensure that ARTs and Solution Trains operate within the larger enterprise context. As a consequence, some form of Agile portfolio operations is typically required in the larger enterprise. Figure 3 illustrates the collaboration and responsibilities of this function, which are discussed in the following subsections.

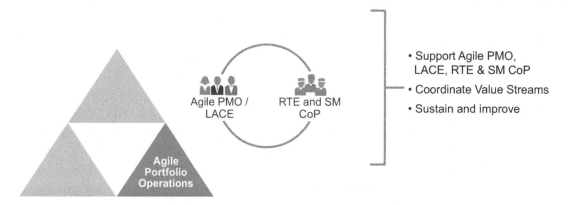

Figure 3. Agile portfolio operations collaboration

Support Agile PMO, LACE, RTEs, Scrum Masters, and Communities of Practice

As mentioned earlier in this chapter, the centralization and traditional mindsets potentially associated with the PMO function may undermine the move to SAFe. In response, some enterprises have abandoned the PMO approach, distributing all the responsibilities to ARTs and Solution Trains, often accompanied by a Release Train Engineer (RTE) and a Community of Practice (CoP). In some case, this ambitious reorganization effort can be 'a bridge too far,' particularly in the larger enterprise. Other organizations appear to be better served by redesigning the traditional PMO to become an Agile PMO (APMO), one that provides a consistent context for delivering in a more Lean and Agile manner.

In general, we recommend supporting an Agile PMO, a Lean-Agile Center of Excellence (LACE), RTEs, Scrum Masters, and CoPs. Moreover, we now see many enterprises in which the APMO drives the new way of working. In this case, the APMO often takes on additional responsibilities as part of the 'sufficiently powerful coalition for change':

- Sponsor and communicate the change vision

- Participate in the rollout (some members may even deliver training)

- Lead the move to objective milestones and Lean-Agile budgeting

- Foster more Agile Contracts and leaner Supplier and Customer partnerships

- Provide consistent support for effective program execution

The latter suggestions can be accomplished, in part, by sharing common and consistent enterprise patterns and practices for optimal value delivery. Standardizing such work is one of Lean's most effective tools. "By documenting the current best practice, standardized work forms the baseline for kaizen or continuous improvement. Improving standardized work is a never-ending process" [1]. Essential SAFe practices provide the guidance for program execution, often anchoring the Agile PMO in a consistent approach to value delivery.

The APMO may also sponsor or serve as a home for an ongoing CoP for RTEs, Solution Train Engineers, and Scrum Masters. Alternatively, these CoPs may form and operate independently. In either case, the CoPs provide a forum for sharing effective Agile program execution practices and other general institutional knowledge.

Also, the APMO can establish and maintain the systems and reporting capabilities that ensure the smooth deployment and operation of the value stream investment. In this role, it acts as a communication and advisory link regarding strategy, offers key performance indicators, and provides financial governance. It also supports management and people operations/human resources in hiring and staff development.

Coordinate Value Streams
In theory, value streams could be independent. Cooperation among a set of solutions, however, can provide some notable portfolio-level capabilities and benefits that competitors can't match. Indeed, in some cases, this is the ultimate goal: to offer a set of differentiated solutions where new cross-cutting patterns of use may emerge to respond to expanding end-user needs. In addition, some level of coordination may be necessary to assure that value streams don't build overlapping solutions that can confuse the market and dilute the return on investment. Similarly, coordinating component strategies may support efficient reuse, minimizing total investment. Value streams may also require coordination when they depend on scarce skill sets and Shared Services (such as security or compliance expertise).

Ultimately, this means that the value streams need some level of portfolio coordination, which may be another responsibility of an APMO. In larger portfolios, coordination of value streams may even require additional roles and responsibilities, such as a Solution Portfolio Manager, as well as the need to apply cadence and synchronization across value streams. This is further described in the Value Stream Coordination chapter.

Sustain and Improve
LPM—or, by proxy, the APMO—also has a leadership role in helping the organization relentlessly improve and achieve its business goals. This is often accomplished through a persistent Lean-Agile Center for Excellence. Whether it is a stand-alone group or part of the APMO, the LACE serves a continuous source of energy that can help power the enterprise through the necessary organizational changes. Additionally, since the evolution of a Lean-Agile enterprise is an ongoing journey, rather than

a fixed destination, the LACE often morphs into a longer-term center for continuous improvement. The Lean-Agile Center for Excellence chapter provides many suggestions on how to integrate SAFe practices with the LACE operation. More opportunities for improvement are also described in the Sustain and Improve chapter.

Lean Governance

As Figure 4 illustrates, another important SAFe collaboration influences spending, future expense forecasts and milestones, and other Lean governance. Its stakeholders include the relevant enterprise executives, the ART and Solution Train Business Owners and other stakeholders, and the APMO. Together they share the responsibilities described in the following subsections.

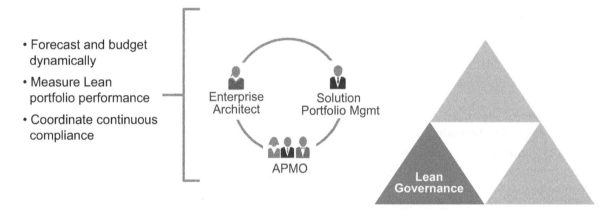

Figure 4. Lean governance collaboration and responsibilities

Forecast and Budget Dynamically
As described in the Lean Budgets chapter, in SAFe, a leaner, more Agile and fluid process replaces the fixed, long-range budget cycles, financial commitments, and fixed-scope expectations of the legacy mindset. Agile approaches to estimating, forecasting, and longer-term planning are described in the Roadmap chapter. Although traditional project cost accounting should not be required, any significant variation of spending versus planning for relatively long-lived value streams must be discussed and understood, as it may reflect a lack of alignment or a level inconsistent with the strategy.

Measure Lean Portfolio Performance
Each portfolio must establish the minimum Metrics needed to assure that the strategy is being implemented, spending is aligned with agreed boundaries, and results are constantly improving. The Metrics chapter describes a set of Lean portfolio metrics that are used to assess internal and external progress for an entire portfolio.

Coordinate Continuous Compliance
No portfolio is an island unto itself. Each operates in the context of its larger environment, typically containing auditing and Compliance requirements. These requirements may include internal or external

financial audits, industry, and legal and/or regulatory requirements. Such obligations impose significant constraints on solution development and operations. Traditional approaches to compliance tend to defer these activities to the end of development, subjecting the enterprise to the risk of late discovery, rework, and even compromising regulatory or legal exposure. A more continuous approach to assure compliance with relevant standards is required, as is described in the Compliance chapter.

Summary

In summary, the three aspects of Lean portfolio management—strategy and investment funding, Agile portfolio operations, and Lean governance—provide a leaner, more Agile, and yet fully comprehensive governance approach that can help assure each portfolio fulfills its role in helping the enterprise achieve its larger business objectives.

LEARN MORE

[1] Lean Enterprise Institute. https://www.lean.org/Workshops/WorkshopDescription.cfm?WorkshopId=20.

Portfolio Backlog

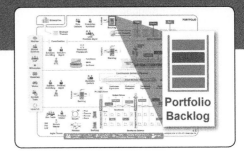

Innovation comes from the producer, not the customer.

—W. Edwards Deming

The *Portfolio Backlog* is the highest-level backlog in SAFe. It provides a holding area for upcoming business and enabler Epics intended to create a comprehensive set of Solutions, which provides the competitive differentiation and operational improvements needed to address the Strategic Themes and facilitate business success.

Portfolio epics are made visible, developed, and managed through the Portfolio Kanban, where they proceed through various process states until they are approved or rejected by Lean Portfolio Management (LPM). Approved epics move to the Portfolio Backlog, where they await implementation by one or more Agile Release Trains (ARTs).

Details

Due to their scope and typically crosscutting nature, epics usually require substantial investment and have a considerable impact on both the development programs and business outcomes. Given their broad implications for the business, epics are analyzed in the portfolio Kanban to establish feasibility, a Lean business case, and a Minimum Viable Product (MVP).

The portfolio backlog holds epics that have been approved and prioritized for implementation. These epics have made it through the portfolio Kanban system with 'go' approval (Figure 1).

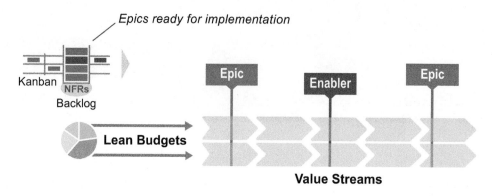

Figure 1. The Portfolio backlog holds epics that are ready for implementation

Operating under LPM leadership, the portfolio backlog brings visibility to upcoming business and enabler epics that have been approved but await implementation capacity. Epics in the portfolio backlog are reviewed periodically and scheduled for implementation based on the availability of capacity in the affected ARTs.

Managing the Portfolio Backlog

As Figure 2 illustrates, the portfolio backlog may contain several epics, so additional reasoning must be applied before any of them are scheduled for implementation. This reasoning includes considerations for sequencing work, sizing in Story points, and ranking the epics relative to each other, typically by one final, Weighted Shortest Job First (WSJF) prioritization. In this case, business and enabler epics are typically compared only against each other, inside the capacity allocation for each type. Those that rise to the top are then ready for implementation and are pulled from the portfolio backlog when trains have available capacity. In addition to job size, available program capacity must be taken into consideration when launching epics, because the job duration (the denominator in WSJF) is heavily dependent on the capacity available for implementation.

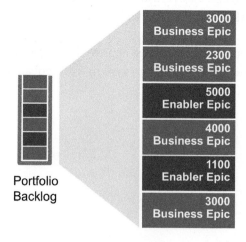

Figure 2. Estimates of business and enabler epics in the portfolio backlog

Forecasting

SAFe enhances the enterprise's adaptability, enabling it to respond more quickly to changing market opportunities. For its part, Agile delivery seems to work best when we fix the date and 'float' the scope. This supports frequent incremental delivery and avoids the inevitable quality trade-offs when all aspects—scope, time, and resources—are fixed. Yet, in the enterprise, Agile or not, some sense of the future is required:

- The enterprise, its partners, and customers need to plan for upcoming releases.

- Visions must define and track to the evolving enterprise strategy.

- Roadmaps capture strategic intent in forecasted deliverables.

Thus, the ability to do effective, Agile forecasting is a major economic driver and a key ability of the Lean-Agile enterprise.

Forecasting Requires Estimating

As described in other parts of SAFe, Agile Teams use story points and relative estimating to quickly arrive at estimates of the size and duration for user stories. At the program level, Product Managers and System Architects—working with Product Owners and teams wherever appropriate—can use historical data to quickly estimate the size of Features in story points as well. In addition, whenever the economics justify further investment in estimating, teams can break larger features into stories to get a more granular view.

Further, as illustrated in Figure 2, feature estimates, which are identified during the portfolio Kanban analysis state, can then be rolled up into epic estimates in the portfolio backlog. This approach ensures that the economics of a potential epic are understood before its implementation begins.

Finally and most importantly, given knowledge of program velocities, portfolio managers and other planners can use capacity allocation for ARTs to estimate how long a portfolio epic to implement might take under various scenarios. This provides a reasonable model for long-term planning and forecasting, as shown in Figure 3.

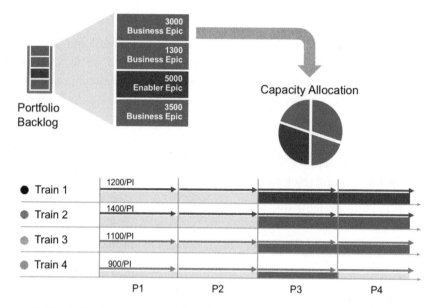

Figure 3. Portfolio forecasting with epic size estimates, ART capacity allocation, and program velocities

Whether an enterprise is Agile or not, no crystal ball is available for estimating epics—that is, there is no method that can guarantee high-fidelity estimation of large-scale software programs. While certainly not perfect, SAFe provides mechanisms for estimating and planning that have shown themselves to be more reliable than those historically applied with waterfall development methods.

Moving to Implementation

As resources become available within the affected programs, prioritized epics are moved from the 'portfolio backlog' state to the 'implementation' state of the portfolio Kanban. The Epic Owner shepherds this process forward and works with Product and Solution Management and System and Solution Arch/Engineering to split the epics into program or solution epics, and subsequently into features and Capabilities that are then prioritized in the respective Kanban systems. The epic remains in the implementation stage until the MVP is achieved and when other potential features for the epic cannot compete on value with features from other sources; at that point, it is considered to be done.

LEARN MORE

[1] Leffingwell, Dean. *Agile Software Requirements: Lean Requirements Practices for Teams, Programs, and the Enterprise.* Addison-Wesley, 2011.

Portfolio Kanban

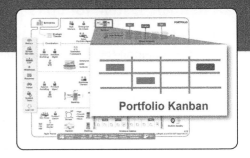

I urge everyone—no matter how big their portfolio—to truly understand every suggestion they're given before acting.

—Suze Orman

The *Portfolio Kanban* is a method used to visualize, manage, and analyze the prioritization and flow of portfolio Epics from ideation to implementation and completion.

SAFe describes the development and implementation of Kanban systems throughout the Framework, at the Portfolio, Solution, Program, and Team levels. The portfolio Kanban visualizes the flow of new strategic initiatives, known as epics, controlling much of the economics of the portfolio.

Implementation and management of the portfolio Kanban system occur with the support of Lean Portfolio Management (LPM). Implementing the Kanban system requires an understanding of Lean and Agile development as it applies to portfolio-level practices. It also requires understanding of the capacity for each Agile Release Train (ART) and the portions of that capacity available for new development, business-as-usual maintenance, and support activities. When these issues are well understood, the Enterprise can evaluate portfolio-level initiatives logically and pragmatically, knowing the initial feasibility and forecasted timing for implementation. The portfolio Kanban system is explicitly designed for this purpose.

Details

The portfolio Kanban system is used primarily to address the flow of epics, those large, crosscutting initiatives that affect the course of action for the ARTs and Solution Trains that realize them. This makes the capture, analysis, approval, and release of epics essential activities. Their implementation requires the participation of some key stakeholders, including LPM and representation from the affected trains.

The portfolio Kanban system provides many benefits:

- It makes the most significant business initiatives visible.
- It brings structure to analysis and decision-making for epics.
- Work in Process (WIP) limits ensure that the teams responsibly analyze epics.
- It prevents unrealistic expectations.

- It drives collaboration among the key stakeholders.

- It provides a transparent and quantitative basis for economic decision-making.

A Kanban System for Epics

The portfolio Kanban system describes the process states (steps) that an epic passes through on its way to implementation (or rejection) and the collaboration needed for each state (Figure 1). Each state of the Kanban is described next.

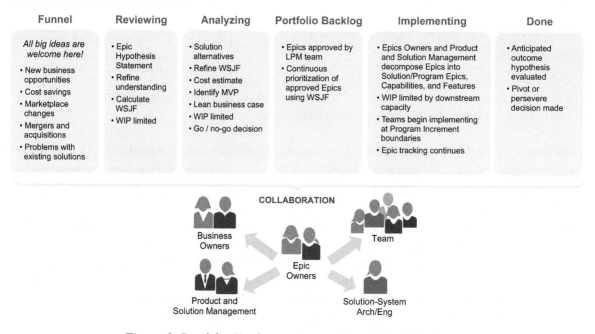

Funnel	Reviewing	Analyzing	Portfolio Backlog	Implementing	Done
All big ideas are welcome here! • New business opportunities • Cost savings • Marketplace changes • Mergers and acquisitions • Problems with existing solutions	• Epic Hypothesis Statement • Refine understanding • Calculate WSJF • WIP limited	• Solution alternatives • Refine WSJF • Cost estimate • Identify MVP • Lean business case • WIP limited • Go / no-go decision	• Epics approved by LPM team • Continuous prioritization of approved Epics using WSJF	• Epics Owners and Product and Solution Management decompose Epics into Solution/Program Epics, Capabilities, and Features • WIP limited by downstream capacity • Teams begin implementing at Program Increment boundaries • Epic tracking continues	• Anticipated outcome hypothesis evaluated • Pivot or persevere decision made

Figure 1. Portfolio Kanban system and typical collaborators

Funnel

The *funnel* is used to capture all new big ideas. Epics can come from any source and may be business or technical initiatives (enablers). These large initiatives are often the result of the following drivers:

- Portfolio strategic themes

- Unanticipated changes in the marketplace, business acquisitions, mergers, and response to competitors

- Improving the efficiency or cost of a solution or its operation

- Problems with existing solutions that hinder business or technical performance

Epics are typically described using a short phrase on a Kanban card, such as 'self-service for all auto loans.' After all, the investment in funnel epics should be minimal, until they are discussed on a periodic cadence established by LPM. Epics that meet the decision criteria are then moved to the next state, *reviewing*. There is no WIP limit for this step since it's just used for intake of potential new epics.

Reviewing

Epics that reach the reviewing state warrant some further time and effort. In this state, they are roughly sized and an estimate of their value is developed. Time investment is limited to the discussion level, with perhaps some preliminary investigation. Next, the epic will be elaborated in the epic hypothesis statement format (see the Epic chapter). Since the investment of time is now increasing, a WIP limit is applied to restrict the number of epics being reviewed. Sources of business benefit are identified, and epics are prioritized using the Weighted Shortest Job First (WSJF) model. Epics that rise to the top are pulled into the next state, *analyzing*, as soon as space is available in the Kanban.

Analyzing

Epics that make it to the analyzing step merit more rigorous analysis and require further investment. Epic Owners take responsibility for this ongoing work. They establish an active collaboration among Enterprise Architects, System and Solution Architects, Agile Teams, and Product and Solution Management. Other key stakeholders in the potentially involved ARTs and Solution Trains may also be included. Alternatives are explored for the solution and its design and implementation. A Lean business case (with a 'go/no-go' recommendation) is developed, and options for internal development and outsourcing are considered.

Most importantly, a Minimum Viable Product (MVP) is developed after the Lean Startup Cycle. It includes the smallest portion of the epic needed to understand whether the 'epic hypothesis statement' is validated. This MVP will be the part of the epic flowing through the rest of the portfolio Kanban system. (See the Epic chapter for more information about developing the MVP and the Lean Startup Cycle.)

Since epics in the analyzing step use scarce resources and, more importantly, imply a substantial upcoming investment, a WIP limit is applied here. The approval of epics is a critical economic decision for the enterprise. These decisions can be made only by the appropriate authority, based on the developed business case. Epics that meet the 'go' criteria are usually approved by a subset of LPM and are moved to the *portfolio backlog* state.

Portfolio Backlog

The portfolio backlog holds epics that have been approved by LPM. These epics are reviewed and prioritized on a periodic basis using WSJF. When sufficient capacity from one or more ARTs is available, the epic advances to the *implementing* state.

Implementing

As capacity becomes available, epics are pulled into the relevant Solution or Program Kanban, where they usually undergo further analysis. For example, the epics are split into Capabilities and Features, and acceptance criteria are established. When ready, these new capabilities and features are presented at the relevant Program Increment (PI) boundaries (PI Planning), including Pre-PI Planning events in Solution Trains. The development teams then begin their implementation. The solution is developed during regular PIs, and the PI Milestones provide the objective evaluation of progress. Epics can be tracked to completion via appropriate Metrics.

While responsibility for implementation rests with the development teams, Epic Owners remain available on a pull basis to share responsibility until the teams have attained a sufficient understanding of the work.

Done

Once its anticipated outcome has been evaluated, the epic is considered done. If the hypothesis is proven, more work will be done by features, capabilities, or epics. Conversely, if the hypothesis is not proven, the portfolio may pivot to another approach or drop the initiative altogether. Due to the scope of epics, completion to original intent is not always the desired case. Instead, some identified capabilities and features may eventually be discarded. In either case, the epic advances to done, and this marks the completion of work item for the Cumulative Flow Diagram (CFD), if applied at this level.

The portfolio Kanban states detailed here represent an example of the process. After the initial steps are taken and new learning occurs, the design of the Kanban should evolve to reflect improvements in the process. For example, the enterprise may adjust the WIP limits, split or combine states, or add classes of service to optimize the flow and priority of epics. It's also important to note that the Kanban system works in tandem with additional SAFe mechanisms, such as capacity allocation, which is used to balance the development of business epics versus enabler epics.

Driving the Portfolio Workflow with the PI Cadence

In the Kanban system, an epic review and specification workshop is often useful to advance epics from left to right in the process depicted in Figure 1. Such workshops typically involve portfolio stakeholders and content and technical authorities from the Solution Trains or ARTs. During these workshops, the following types of activities may take place:

- As WSJF and other data recommend, epics are validated against strategic themes and moved from 'funnel' to 'reviewing,' and from 'reviewing' to 'analyzing.'

- Solution strategies are discussed.

- Lightweight business case and go/no-go decisions are developed.

- Ways to split epics are identified. They may be split into program and solution epics, capabilities, or features.

These workshops may or may not occur on a cadence, but a cadence is preferred. However, the timing of implementation is driven by the cadence of the particular ARTs and Solution Trains, so these workshops must take place frequently enough to be able to provide input ahead of their target PI planning processes.

LEARN MORE

[1] Leffingwell, Dean. *Agile Software Requirements: Lean Requirements Practices for Teams, Programs, and the Enterprise.* Addison-Wesley, 2011.

[2] Anderson, David. *Kanban: Successful Evolutionary Change for Your Technology Business.* Blue Hole Press, 2010.

Value Stream Coordination

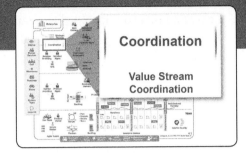

All it takes to play baseball is a strong arm, good speed, and the coordination to hit the ball. That's it.

—Ryne Sandberg

Value Stream Coordination provides guidance to manage dependencies and exploit the opportunities in a portfolio.

Value Streams are a fundamental organizational construct in SAFe. They establish the focus that allows a Lean-Agile enterprise to comprehend the flow of value from concept to delivery. As a business better understands its work streams, it can organize attention and resources around them, optimizing them by reducing waste, unnecessary steps, and delays. In this way, it can achieve and continuously reduce the lead time for value delivery.

Although it's sensible for value streams to be organized to be as independent as possible, some coordination of dependencies among value streams is necessary. More importantly, thoughtful coordination can create a differentiated and unmatchable Solution offering. To this end, Lean-Agile Leaders understand the challenges and opportunities that their value streams provide. They make them as independent as possible, while simultaneously interconnecting and coordinating them with the enterprise's larger purpose.

Decentralized and mainly independent value streams result in fast and free-flowing value delivery, which is substantially enhanced by exploiting opportunities that exist only in the interconnections.

Details

By their very nature, value streams are long-lived and often independent of each other. For example, a systems or software company may sell many products and services, with those outputs being largely decoupled from each other in terms of technology. The more likely case, however, is that they have some interdependencies. While we typically think of dependencies in a negative sense, systems thinking informs us that value flows through these dependencies. Yes, there are challenges to be addressed, but there are also valuable opportunities to exploit.

Most importantly, this additional value is often unique and differentiated. Indeed, an enterprise may offer a set of solutions via those very dependencies that cannot be matched by companies that do not provide an equivalent set. Or perhaps the competitor has not developed mastery in surfacing the unique and emerging capabilities that these coordinated value streams can provide—the enterprise can take advantage of its own, more well-developed abilities in this area.

Achieving this additional value requires the ability to coordinate value streams within a portfolio, as illustrated in Figure 1 and described in the sections that follow.

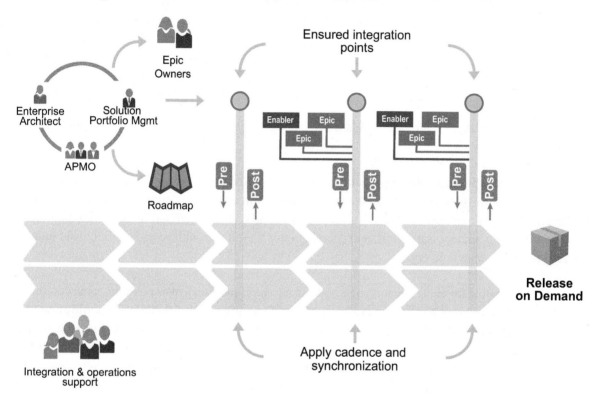

Figure 1. Cross–value stream coordination

Portfolio Coordination Trio

Smart observers of the SAFe are probably aware that each level is anchored by people in three primary roles, each with a parallel and consistent set of responsibilities, and each a repeating pattern of the one below it:

- **Responsibility for what gets built** – Product Owner > Product Management > Solution Management

- **Responsibility for how it gets built** – Agile Team > System Architect/Engineering > Solution Architect/Engineering

- **Responsibility for servant leadership–based operation and execution** – Scrum Master > Release Train Engineer (RTE) > Solution Train Engineer (STE)

Thus, whenever a significant degree of coordination is required, it isn't surprising to see similar roles and responsibilities appear in large portfolios. As shown in Figure 1, these roles are filled by the following entities:

- **Solution Portfolio Management** – Has the overall responsibility for guiding a portfolio to a set of integrated solutions.

- **Portfolio Architect/Engineering** – Provides technical guidance for the long-term evolution of the technologies and platforms and the larger Nonfunctional Requirements (security, Compliance, performance, and more) for the portfolio solution set.

- **Agile Program Management Office (APMO)** – Along with the STEs and RTEs, the APMO is typically responsible for supporting decentralized, but efficient, program execution. The APMO provides support for standard reporting patterns, shared best practices, and growth and dissemination of institutional knowledge.

Cadence and Synchronization

Figure 1 also illustrates how the principles of cadence and synchronization apply to the Portfolio Level just as they do to large solutions. The merits are the same:

- It makes routine that which can be routine, thereby lowering the transaction costs associated with change (e.g., SAFe events and meetings).

- It allows for synchronizing of the various aspects of multi-value stream solution development.

Shared cadence also provides the opportunity and the mandate for the portfolio-level solution (via business Epics) to move forward in sync with defined planning and integration points. Each creates the occasion to evaluate the solution set under development objectively.

These points are the only accurate measure of portfolio velocity. The more frequently the points are reached, the more rapidly we learn.

Injection of New Portfolio-Level Work

Figure 1 illustrates another vital concept: The portfolio cadence determines the rate and timing at which new portfolio-level work can be added into the system. During each Program Increment (PI), the Agile Release Trains (ARTs) and Solution Trains are focused on the committed PI Objectives. If new work is injected into the system in the interim, it causes substantial interruptions, task switching, realignment, and movement of people to new objectives. The portfolio cadence provides a reliable rhythm for introducing new portfolio work since teams sometimes cannot meet prior commitments *and* mix in significant unplanned work. It helps the programs achieve the predictability on which the enterprise depends.

Through the Portfolio Kanban system, this cadence also establishes conventional mechanisms for Epic Owners, Enterprise Architects, and other roles managing epics. Any epic that's not ready for PI Planning must wait for the next PI, even though resources may have been available to begin it. Time-boxing the cadence also limits Work in Process (WIP) for the new and substantial work that will be introduced into the system.

Portfolio Roadmap

Clearly, at this level of the portfolio, a plan of intent must be evident. As Figure 1 illustrates, a portfolio Roadmap is a useful artifact that highlights how new content, primarily in the form of epics, contributes to the plan of intent. This higher-level view also provides the opportunity to integrate aspects of the lower-level roadmaps, and their associated Milestones, into a more comprehensive view, communicating the larger picture to the enterprise stakeholders.

Deployment and Release

Due to the nature of the value streams and dependencies, deploying integrated value may also depend on effective DevOps capabilities. In some cases, ARTs provide all the DevOps capability that's needed. In others, additional considerations may exist, even requiring dedicated or Shared Services and System Teams that help integrate the solution into a portfolio-level release.

Part 9

Advanced Topics

scaledagileframework.com/**guidance**

Agile Architecture

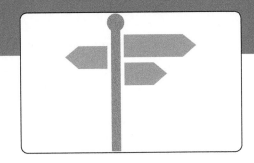

While we must acknowledge emergence in design and system development, a little planning can avoid much waste.

—*James O. Coplien, Lean Architecture*

Agile Architecture is a set of values and practices that support the active evolution of the design and architecture of a system while implementing new system capabilities.

This approach allows the architecture of a system (even a Large Solution) to evolve over time, while simultaneously supporting the needs of current users. This avoids the overhead and delays associated with the start–stop–start nature and redesign inherent in phase-gate methods. With Agile architecture, the system always runs, supporting a more continuous flow of value.

The Agile architecture principles support Lean-Agile development through collaboration, emergent design, intentional architecture, and design simplicity, as well as designing for testability, deployability, and releasability. It is further supported by rapid prototyping, domain modeling, and decentralized innovation.

Details

Agile architecture enables incremental value delivery by balancing emergent design and intentional architecture:

- **Emergent design** – This provides the technical basis for a fully evolutionary and incremental implementation approach. This helps designers respond to immediate user needs, allowing the design to emerge as the system is built and deployed.

- **Intentional architecture** – This is a set of purposeful, planned architectural initiatives, which enhance solution design, performance, and usability and provide guidance for design and implementation synchronization across teams.

By balancing emergent design and intentionality, Agile architecture is a Lean-Agile approach to addressing the complexity of building enterprise Solutions. In turn, this approach supports the needs of current users while simultaneously evolving the system to meet near-term future needs. Used together, emergent design and intentionality continuously build and extend the Architectural Runway that provides the technical foundation for future development of business value.

Agile architecture is applicable to all levels of SAFe and is supported by the following principles:

1. Design emerges; architecture is a collaboration.
2. The bigger the system, the longer the runway.
3. Build the simplest architecture that can possibly work.
4. When in doubt, code or model it out.
5. They build it; they test it.
6. There is no monopoly on innovation.
7. Implement architectural flow.

#1 – Design Emerges; Architecture Is a Collaboration

Traditional, phase-gate development methodologies often use Big Design Up-Front (BDUF) to create a roadmap and the architectural infrastructure required to fully address the needs of the future system. The belief is that a one-time effort can capture requirements and architectural plans sufficiently to support the system for years to come.

However, the future-proofing approach of BDUF comes with many challenges. One is the delay in starting implementation. A second arises when the planned architecture—a large set of speculative, forward-looking designs—meets the real world. Soon enough, the designs become brittle and hard to change, and eventually a big-branch-and-merge to a new set of speculative assumptions becomes the routine course of action. SAFe addresses this by combining emergent design and intentional architecture, driven by collaboration.

Emergent Design

Principle 11 of the Agile Manifesto is the primary driver behind the concept of emergent design: "The best architectures, requirements, and designs emerge from self-organizing teams" [2]. This principle has the following implications:

- The design is grown incrementally by those who are closest to it.
- The design evolves hand-in-hand with business functionality. It is constantly tested and enabled by Continuous Exploration, Refactoring, Test-First, Continuous Integration, and Continuous Deployment.
- Teams rapidly evolve the design in accordance with the currently known requirements. The design is extended only as necessary to implement and validate the next increment of functionality.

This new practice of emergent design is effective at the Team Level. However, emergent design alone is insufficient when developing large systems. For example:

- It can cause excessive redesign for things that could have been anticipated. In turn, that drives bad economics and slows time-to-market.

- Teams are not always able to synchronize with each other, which creates untested assumptions and inconsistent technical architectures.

- Teams may not even be aware of some of the larger, upcoming business needs; factors outside their scope of knowledge drive the need for future architectural redesign.

- A common technical architecture—which can enhance the usability, extensibility, performance, and maintainability of the larger system of systems—is lacking.

- New, crosscutting user patterns affect the future fitness of purpose.

- Planning and design for testing, deployment, and releasing are lacking.

- Mergers and acquisitions drive integrations and the need for commonality of infrastructure.

Intentional Architecture

Organizations must respond simultaneously to new business challenges with larger-scale architectural initiatives that require some intentionality and planning. Therefore, there comes a point at which emergent design is insufficient for large-scale system development. Simply put, it's not possible for teams to anticipate changes that may well occur outside their environment, nor can individual teams fully understand the entire system and thereby avoid producing redundant and/or conflicting code and designs. For this reason, some intentional architecture is needed to enhance solution design, performance, and usability and to provide guidance for cross-team design and implementation synchronization.

Architecture Is a Collaboration

Clearly, it's best to have both fast, local control of emergent design and application of systems thinking to provide a global view of intentional architecture. This combination provides the guidance needed to ensure that the system as a whole has conceptual integrity and produces the intended result. Figure 1 illustrates how to achieve the right balance of emergent design and intentional architecture.

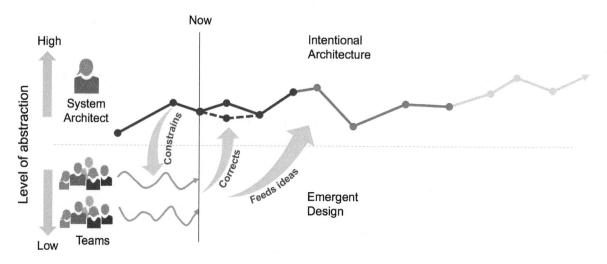

Figure 1. Intentional architecture, emergent design, and collaboration support system evolution

Figure 1 also illustrates how intentional architecture constrains the emergent design, but at a high enough level of abstraction to allow the teams to effectively adapt the intentional part to their specific context. At the same time, emergent design influences and corrects intentional architecture and surfaces new ideas for future, centralized, intentional effort.

Such a deep reciprocity between emergent design and intentional architecture can occur only as a result of collaboration between Agile Teams, System and Solution Architects, Enterprise Architects, and Product and Solution Management to create an environment that encourages this collaboration.

#2 – The Bigger the System, the Longer the Runway

An Architectural Runway exists when the enterprise's platforms have sufficient technical infrastructure to support the implementation of the highest-priority Features and Capabilities in the backlog without excessive redesign and delays. To achieve this runway to at least some degree, the enterprise must continually invest in extending existing platforms as well as building and deploying the new platforms needed for evolving business requirements.

In the Lean enterprise, architectural initiatives are incrementally developed and committed to the main code base. Doing so means that architectural initiatives must be split into Enabler Features, which build the runway needed to host the new business features (Figure 2).

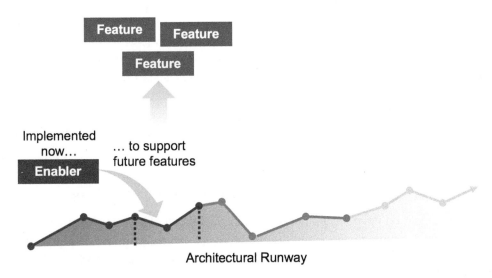

Figure 2. The Architectural Runway continuously evolves to support future functionality

Each enabler feature must be completed within a Program Increment (PI) such that the system always runs, at least at the PI boundaries. In some cases, this means that new architectural initiatives are implemented incrementally and may not even be exposed to the users in the PI in which they are implemented. In this way, the runway can be implemented and tested behind the scenes, allowing continuous deployment and then release to users when a sufficient feature or capability exists in the next PI or so.

The runway built by intentional architecture and emergent design effectively complement each other at scale: Intentional, high-level ideas in support of future functionality are adapted and implemented by Agile teams; they are empowered to figure out the optimal emergent design.

#3 – Build the Simplest Architecture That Can Possibly Work

"We welcome changing requirements even late in development" [2]. Yes, we do, but surely enabling change is facilitated by systems that have understandable designs. As Kent Beck notes, "If simplicity is good, we'll always leave the system with the simplest design that supports its current functionality" [3]. Indeed, at scale, design simplicity is not a luxury, but rather a survival mechanism. Many considerations help accomplish this:

- Use a simple, common language to describe the system.
- Keep the solution model as close to the problem domain as possible.
- Refactor continuously.
- Ensure that object/component interfaces clearly express their intent.
- Follow good, old design principles [4, 5].

Domain-driven design [6], design patterns [4], and application of a system metaphor [3] simplify both the design and the communication between the teams. This social aspect of design simplicity is critical, as it enables collective code ownership, which in turn fosters a feature—rather than component—orientation [7]. The dominant approach to evolving maintainable and extendable solutions is to consider the system as a set of collaborating entities. This prevents typical design flaws such as concentrating too much logic at the database layer, creating a thick user interface (UI), or ending up with large and unmanageable code classes. Maintaining simplicity requires design skill and knowledge. Communities of Practice help develop and spread these best practices.

#4 – When in Doubt, Code or Model It Out

Coming to agreement on good design decisions can be difficult. There are legitimate differences of opinion about which solution is best, and often there is no one right answer. While Agile teams and programs don't mind refactoring, they surely want to avoid unnecessary rework.

To decide on the best design, Agile teams can typically just code it out, using Technical or Functional Spikes and even rapid prototyping. Iterations are short and spikes are small; the result is fast feedback with objective evidence, which can then be subject to A/B testing by the teams, designers, and architects—or even end users.

Modeling is a useful technique to understand the potential impact of significant scope changes prior to implementation, especially where spikes and prototypes do not provide the necessary learning to avoid excessive redesign. As illustrated in Figure 3, Domain Modeling and use-case modeling are two relatively lightweight Agile modeling techniques that are particularly valuable.

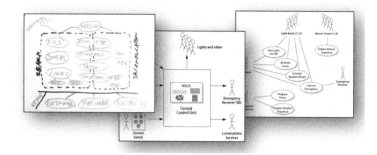

Figure 3. A domain model and a use-case model, supported by a system context diagram

Record Models in the Solution Intent

Of course, the models aren't useful if no one can find them. Therefore, models, technical knowledge, and even various design decisions are recorded in the Solution Intent, which provides a central point of communication. In practice, however, technical information is represented in many forms, from documents to spreadsheets to the models described previously. While documents and spreadsheets are easy for an author to create, they do not necessarily encourage the knowledge transfer or the continuous collaboration required for Lean systems engineering.

A better approach is Model-Based Systems Engineering (MBSE), in which the solution intent contains many different kinds of models, with many options for organizing and linking information. System and Solution Architects/Engineers are typically responsible for tasks ranging from specifying the model information and organization to ensuring its quality. Agile teams populate the model(s) with their respective knowledge and information.

#5 – They Build It; They Test It

The responsibility for knowing whether a design actually works rests with those who collaborate on designing the architecture. Testing system architecture involves testing the system's ability to meet its larger-scale functional and nonfunctional operational, performance, and reliability requirements. To do this, teams must also build the testing infrastructure and automate tests wherever possible to enable ongoing system-level testing. Moreover, as the architecture evolves, the testing approaches, testing frameworks, and test suites must evolve with it. Therefore, architects, engineers, Agile teams, and the System Team actively collaborate to continuously Design for Testability.

#6 – There Is No Monopoly on Innovation

Optimization of architecture is a collaborative effort of Agile teams, architects, engineers, and stakeholders. It can help create a culture of innovation, whereby innovation can come from anyone and anywhere.

Though such ideas come from anyone, capturing and knowledge requires some centralization via communication and recording in solution intent. One of the responsibilities of the Enterprise Architect is to foster an environment where innovative ideas and technology improvements that emerge at the team level can be synthesized into the building blocks of the Architectural Runway. Given that Agile can foster the 'tyranny of the urgent iteration,' time for innovation should also be built into Innovation and Planning Iterations.

#7 – Implement Architectural Flow

Enterprise-scale architectural initiatives require coordination across trains and Value Streams. Effective flow of these architectural initiatives is made visible via the Portfolio Kanban. In addition, the 'pull' nature of the Kanban system allows programs to establish capacity management based on Work in Process (WIP) limits. This helps avoid overloading the system.

Together with the portfolio Kanban, the Program and Solution Kanban systems provide a SAFe enterprise content governance model, which forms portions of the Economic Framework and helps Decentralize decision-making, both of which are vital to a fast, sustainable flow of value. In the Kanban systems, enabler features and capabilities follow a common workflow pattern of exploration, refinement, analysis, prioritization, and implementation.

LEARN MORE

[1] Leffingwell, Dean. *Agile Software Requirements: Lean Requirements Practices for Teams, Programs, and the Enterprise.* Addison-Wesley, 2011.

[2] Manifesto for Agile Software Development. http://agilemanifesto.org/.

[3] Beck, Kent. *Extreme Programming Explained: Embrace Change.* Addison-Wesley, 2000.

[4] Bain, Scott. *Emergent Design: The Evolutionary Nature of Professional Software Development.* Addison-Wesley, 2008.

[5] Shalloway, Alan, et al. *Essential Skills for the Agile Developer: A Guide to Better Programming and Design.* Addison-Wesley, 2011.

[6] Evans, Eric. *Domain-Driven Design: Tackling Complexity in the Heart of Software.* Addison-Wesley, 2003.

[7] Larman, Craig, and Bas Vodde. *Practices for Scaling Lean and Agile Development: Large, Multisite, and Offshore Product Development with Large-Scale Scrum.* Addison-Wesley, 2010.

[8] Coplien, James, and Gertrud Bjørnvig. *Lean Architecture for Agile Software Development.* Wiley and Sons, 2010.

Agile Contracts

. . . select a winning contractor and then expect them to deliver on the requirements within the specified time frame and budget. However, this traditional approach almost always led to failures— each a spectacular waste of taxpayer dollars.

—Jason Bloomberg, "Fixing Scheduling with Agile at the VA," Forbes

Builders of large-scale systems must continually align what's being built with the wants and needs of customers and other stakeholders. Moreover, they often must do so in the midst of continuous changes driven by development discoveries, evolving customer needs, changing technologies, and competitor innovations.

Traditionally, requirements and design decisions were made up-front with the goal of ensuring customers were getting what they wanted. That was the basis of the contract with the systems provider. Unfortunately, these early requirements and design decisions constrained teams, reducing their ability to adapt to emerging data that could have informed a Solution that could have delivered better economic and competitive value. In short, the contract held them back. Thus, attempts to manage risk by requiring early specificity often backfired, to the detriment of all stakeholders.

To avoid this, other contract approaches evolved, characterized by more shared risk and reward. In many cases, they worked better. Even then, however, the conventional thinking of fixed requirements tended to influence agreements and expectations.

What is truly needed is a more Agile approach to contracts, one that benefits both parties in the near and long terms. This chapter describes the current state and then provides guidance for an Agile Contract approach, the 'SAFe Managed-Investment Contract.'

Details

Traditional Approaches to Systems Purchasing Contracts

Buyers often outsource complex systems development to suppliers who have the ability to build the kinds of systems that buyers need to run their business. There's a continuum of approaches to contracting, ranging from firm fixed price to time and materials, and almost every point in between. Figure 1 characterizes these various approaches and highlights the means by which the parties share risk.

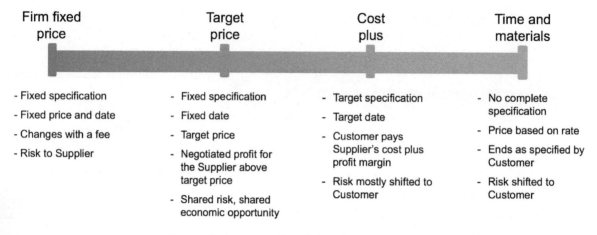

Figure 1. A range of traditional contract types

Clearly, a wide range of approaches to contracting exist. In general, however, most everyone understands that neither extreme delivers the best overall economic value, as discussed in the following subsections.

Firm Fixed-Price Contracts

On the left end of the scale in Figure 1 are firm-fixed-price contracts, which are quite common in the industry today. The convenience of this approach derives from the assumption that buyers will get exactly what they want and are willing to pay for, as Figure 2 illustrates.

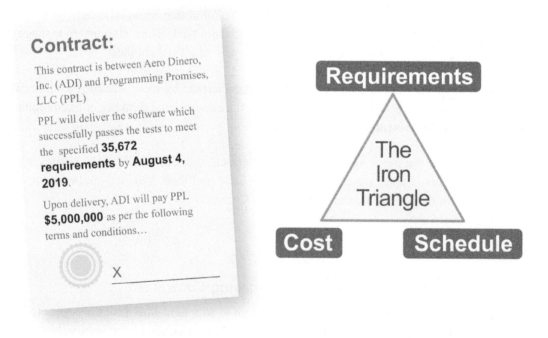

Figure 2. Firm-fixed-price contracts create the 'iron triangle'

On the surface, this contracting approach makes sense. It also provides an opportunity for competitive bidding, which may be required in many cases. In theory, competitive bidding can potentially provide economic advantages, as the winner of the bid will be the supplier with the lowest cost.

However, there are many downsides to this approach:

- It assumes that the buyer's needs are well understood, far in advance of implementation.
- The buyer's needs must be reflected in requirements specifications and early design details. This triggers Big Design Up-Front (BDUF), waterfall-based development, and waterfall-based contracts.
- The contract is typically awarded to the lowest-cost bidder, who may not provide the optimal long-term economic value for the buyer.

Moreover, to get a fixed bid, critical decisions are made far too early, when the least amount of knowledge about the solution is known (see Principle #3: Assume variability; preserve options). The parties have entered into the 'iron triangle' of fixed scope, schedule, and cost, as illustrated in Figure 2. If facts subsequently change, both the buyer's and the supplier's hands are tied to the contract, which may now define something no one wants to build or buy exactly as was stated when written. Much of the rest of the time is spent negotiating contract changes, with significant waste in the process.

Worst of all, once the agreement is entered, each party has an opposing economic interest:

- It's in the buyer's best short-term interest to get as much out of the supplier as possible, for as little money as possible
- It's in the supplier's best short-term interest to deliver the minimum value necessary to meet the contractual obligations and maximize its own profits.

The net result is that this type of contract often sets up a win–lose scenario, which thereafter influences the entire business relationship between the parties, typically to the detriment of both.

Time and Materials Contracts

It's clear why many would want to move to the right of the spectrum of approaches shown in Figure 1. But the time and materials agreements on the far right—which might appear to be extremely Agile on the surface—have their challenges as well. The buyer has only trust to count on. Trust is a precious commodity, indeed, and we depend on it in Lean organizations. But misunderstandings, changes in the market or technical conditions, and changes in buyer or supplier economic models can force trust to take a back seat to other concerns. After all, it's in the supplier's economic interest to continue getting paid for as long as possible. This can drag contracts out for longer than necessary. Coupling this approach with a phase-gate process, whereby real progress can be known only at the end, compounds the problem.

Challenges can exist on the buyer's side as well. For example, when interviewed during a project postmortem, Stephen W. Warren, executive in charge and CIO of the Department of Veterans Affairs Office of Information and Technology, noted that according to the project manager, "the project was never in crisis" since they were spending the entire budget every year, and thus were able to renew their funding for the next year. The measure of success at the time was whether the project would continue to get funding, rather than whether it was able to deliver the necessary functionality [1].

A Collaborative Approach to Agile Contracts

Since neither endpoint on Figure 1 provides much assurance, perhaps the range in the middle is the sweet spot? Possibly, but even then, the biases of traditional contracts—whether from the left or the right end of the scale—will likely creep into these agreements and expectations. What's needed, then, is a different approach—one that trusts but verifies that the suppliers are building the right thing, in the right way. Ideally, it provides regular and objective governance for the buyer, yet allows suppliers to have confidence in their customers, as well as in implied future economic commitments.

Characteristics of such an Agile contract would include the ability to:

- Optimize the economic value for all parties in both the short and long terms
- Exploit variability via adaptive responses to requirements as new knowledge emerges
- Provide complete and continuous visibility and objective evidence of solution fitness
- Provide a measured approach to investment that can vary over time and stop when sufficient value has been achieved
- Offer the supplier near-term confidence in funding and sufficient notice when funding winds down or stops
- Motivate all parties to build the best solution possible within agreed-to economic boundaries

SAFe Managed-Investment Contracts

Clearly, the industry would benefit by moving toward an Agile contracts approach, where the economics benefit both the buyer and the supplier. The SAFe managed-investment contract represents one such approach.

Pre-commitment

Prior to engaging in any significant investment contract for developing a complex system with many unknowns, some due diligence is required. In this case, the Customer and the Supplier work together to come to terms on the basis of the contract. This is the pre-commitment phase, illustrated in Figure 3.

During pre-commitment, the customer has specific responsibilities, including understanding the basic constructs and obligations of this form of Agile contract, and defining and communicating the larger program mission statement to the potential supplier(s).

 Customer responsibility	Shared responsibilities	 Supplier responsibility
• Training in SAFe • Commit to the contract model • Define program mission	• Establish initial vision and roadmap • Define fixed and variable solution intent • Establish economic framework • Establish responsibilities and contract boundaries • Prioritize P1 planning backlog • Determine Minimum Viable Product (MVP)	• Commit to contract model • Define preliminary scope and feasibility • Establish resource availability

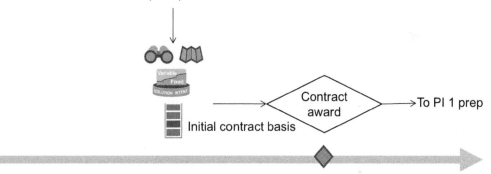

Figure 3. SAFe managed-investment contract pre-commitment phase

The supplier does its initial homework as well. This often includes the first analysis of potential feasibility and alignment of the buyer's solution needs with the supplier's core competence. It also demands some understanding of the potential resources that will be required over the initial contract periods and a rough cost estimate.

The shared responsibilities, illustrated in Figure 3, start the customer and supplier toward a more measured investment, supported by continuous objective evidence of fitness for use. These responsibilities include:

- Establishing the initial Vision and Roadmap

- Identifying the Minimum Viable Product (MVP) and additional Program Increment (PI) potential Features

- Defining the initial fixed and variable Solution Intent

- Prioritizing the initial Program Backlog for PI Planning

- Establishing execution responsibilities

- Establishing the Economic Framework, including economic trade-off parameters, the PI funding commitment (number of PIs committed), initial funding levels, and other contractual terms

In some cases, the supplier may need to provide a preliminary estimate to secure the PI funding commitment for completion. In other cases, a pay-as-you-go approach may be suitable. Based on the terms, the customer will agree to fund the supplier for the early PIs. The length of this initial commitment period depends on context, but two PIs or so (20 weeks) may be a reasonable starting point.

Depending on the context, the customer may have discussions with multiple potential suppliers. If technical feasibility is a significant question, it can often be addressed under some form of feasibility contract, whereby each potential supplier is compensated for the efforts to get to commitment. Alternatively, it may be simply business as usual for the supplier, with these pre-commitment investments occurring as a normal part of presale activities.

At some point, however, the customer can move on to award the contract.

Contract Execution

After the contract is awarded, development begins, as illustrated in Figure 4.

A description of the activity timeline follows:

- **PI preparation** – Both supplier and customer invest some time and effort in preparing content and logistics for the first PI planning session. Note that in some cases, the first PI planning might actually be part of the pre-commitment phase, though this route clearly requires significant investment by both parties.

- **PI planning** – The first PI planning event influences the entire program. During this event, customer and supplier stakeholders plan the first PI in iteration-level detail.

- **PI execution** – Depending on the context, customers participate at various levels in iteration execution. At a minimum, direct customer engagement is usually required for each System Demo. For large solutions, the multiplicity of system demos may be replaced by a more fully integrated Solution Demo, which can occur more frequently than at PI boundaries.

- **PI evaluation** – Thereafter, each PI marks a critical Milestone for both the customer and the supplier. At each milestone, the solution demo is held, and the solution is evaluated. Agreed-to metrics are compiled and analyzed, and decisions are made for the next PI. Solution progress and program improvements are assessed during the Inspect and Adapt (I&A) event. At this point, the customer may decide to increase, decrease, or maintain funding levels, or even begin to wind down the initiative based on whether sufficient value has or has not been achieved. Thereafter, the next PI planning commences, with the scope based on the outcome of that decision.

Customer decision:
Increase, steady, decrease, stop?

?

PI evaluation

- Evaluate solution and metrics
- Provide feedback
- Participate in Inspect and Adapt
- Update Vision, Roadmap, Solution Intent, backlog

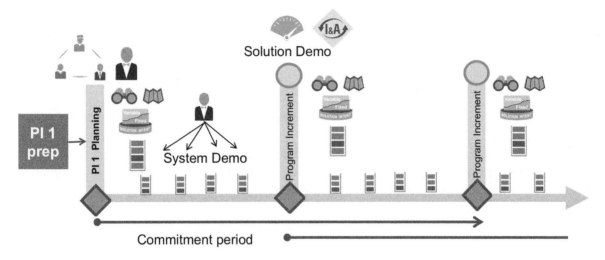

Figure 4. SAFe managed-investment contract execution phase

Managing Risk with the Lean Startup Approach

The Lean Startup Cycle (shown in Figure 5) is also used to manage major product development investments while ensuring sound, Lean economics. This model decreases time-to-market and helps prevent the system from becoming bloated with unnecessary features that may never be used. It also enforces the 'hypothesize–build–measure–learn' cycle described in the Epic and Continuous Delivery Pipeline chapters.

The implication is that Agile contract language is modified to reflect a combination of fixed and variable components. The MVP identified at the pre-commitment stage can establish a high-level definition of fixed scope to be delivered over a proposed number of PIs. Beyond the delivery of the MVP, the contract can specify the number of option periods consisting of one or more PIs. The goal is to optimize the delivery of prioritized features within each PI.

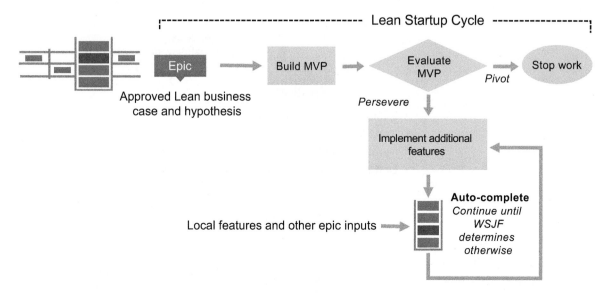

Figure 5. The Lean Startup cycle for managing large product development investments

This process continues until the solution has delivered the value that the customer requires. At this point, the customer stops exercising additional option periods and starts winding down funding commitments in accordance with the agreement. This provides the best of both worlds to customers:

- Better predictability of estimates associated with a far smaller MVP than the full list of all requirements

- Total control over the spending required for additional incremental features based on economic outcomes

Clearly, such an approach provides the greatest economic benefit to both parties, which will help create stable, long-term relationships.

LEARN MORE

[1] Bloomberg, Jason. "Fixing Scheduling with Agile at the VA." *Forbes*. October 23, 2014.

[2] Jemilo, Drew. *Agile Contracts: Blast Off to a Zone of Collaborative Systems Building.* Agile 2015. https://www.slideshare.net/JEMILOD/agile-contracts-by-drew-jemilo-agile2015.

Agile HR with SAFe

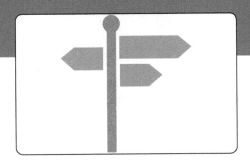

Bringing People Operations into the 21st Century with Lean-Agile Values and Principles

Fabiola Eyholzer, CEO, Just Leading Solutions LLC
with Dean Leffingwell, Co-founder and Chief Methodologist, Scaled Agile, Inc.

To win in the marketplace, you must first win in the workplace.

　—Doug Conant, American businessman and former CEO, Campbell Soup Company

Introduction

The digital transformation is affecting virtually every enterprise across the globe. Competing requires a level of competence and ability in the development and deployment of software and systems unlike that which brought the successful Enterprise to this point. Such new competencies can no longer be mastered through Industrial Age structures and practice.

Responsive enterprises act by (1) acknowledging talent, knowledge, and leadership as the new currency for competitiveness and (2) embracing Lean-Agile values, principles, and practices.

The Scaled Agile Framework (SAFe) has emerged as the leading framework for addressing this challenge at the enterprise scale. In addition to extensive practice guidance, SAFe promotes and describes a comprehensive set of values and principles—that is, a Lean-Agile Mindset leaders can use to foster the transformation and continue the journey to enhanced competitiveness in software and systems building. Figure 1 characterizes the SAFe approach.

This new mindset challenges human resources (HR) organizations to realign their people approach with this new way of working. It imposes a far-reaching transformation to bring HR into the 21st century by shifting from a process-oriented HR management to an empowering Lean-Agile people operations. It changes the face and significance of HR forever.

SAFe House of Lean

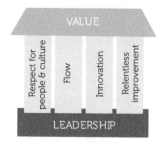

Agile Manifessto

Individuals and interactions over processes and tools

Working software over comprehensive documentation

Customer collaboration over contract negotiation

Responding to change over following a plan

SAFe Principles

#1 – Take an economic view

#2 – Apply systems thinking

#3 – Assume variability: preserve options

#4 – Build incrementally with fast, integrated learning cycles

#5 – Base milestones on objective evaluation of working systems

#6 – Visualize and limit WIP, reduce batch sizes, and manage queue lengths

#7 – Apply cadence, synchronize with cross-domain planning

#8 – Unlock the intrinsic motivation of knowledge workers

Figure 1. The SAFe Lean-Agile mindset

In this chapter, we will describe *six basic themes* that can guide leaders and their HR partners in addressing various aspects of more contemporary Lean-Agile people solutions in the Lean-Agile enterprise:

#1 – Embrace the new talent contract.

#2 – Foster continuous engagement.

#3 – Hire for attitude and cultural fit.

#4 – Move to iterative performance flow.

#5 – Take the issue of money off the table.

#6 – Support Impactful learning and growth.

#1 – Embrace the New Talent Contract

Today is the age of digital disruption, and enterprises must respond to the new realities by fundamentally reinventing their mindsets, behavior, leadership, and ways of working. The driving force behind the Lean-Agile organizations is knowledge workers—the fastest-growing and most critical workforce sector. Drucker defines knowledge workers "as people who know more about the work they perform than their bosses." Their jobs consist of converting information into knowledge and instantiating that knowledge in systems and solutions. It is their ideas, experiences, and interpretations that keep businesses moving forward. The results of their intermediate work are often intangible and require improvisation; the use of judgment in ambiguous situations, as well as interactions with others, is continuously required. As such, knowledge work defies traditional, task-based management.

Knowledge workers thrive on this kind of challenging work. It motivates their very being. At the same time, they also seek meaning and purpose in their careers, as well as appreciation and respect. They want to take responsibility and be actively involved. To innovate and contribute, they must be allowed to manage themselves with significant autonomy and empowerment.

This forms the basis for creating and honoring the new talent contract. It is about not only understanding the drive of knowledge workers, but also recognizing the power shift that comes with it. In SAFe, this goes hand in hand with a move away from task management and a command-and-control orientation and toward inspiring leadership. Two of the SAFe Lean-Agile Principles specifically address this transformation:

- Principle #8: Unlock the intrinsic motivation of knowledge workers
- Principle #9: Decentralize decision-making

Inevitably, this transformation also affects the way HR interacts and engages with both management and the workforce. Employees will claim a voice in shaping the way their organization takes care of them—not only when it comes to their career development, but across the whole HR value chain.

Like management practices, *people operations* must become less prescriptive and more flexible, empowering, and accommodating. HR solutions must become co-created and evolve constantly. This is an integral part of building places of work that are full of inspiration and engagement.

#2 – Foster Continuous Engagement

Tapping into the intrinsic motivation of people—keeping them deeply engaged in the enterprise's purpose—has never been more important. Yet while enterprises with engaged employees have much higher returns, the vast majority of employees worldwide are dissatisfied, disillusioned, and disengaged.

Agile understands the power of bringing intrinsically motivated people together to form collaborative empowered teams. In addition, SAFe then puts them onto an Agile Release Train (ART), where they are engaged with others on a common mission and collaborate via face-to-face planning. Anyone who has ever participated in a Program Increment (PI) Planning event has firsthand experience of the enthusiasm and energy in the room. Unsurprisingly, SAFe teams are more passionate and involved.

Simply put, engagement—perhaps sometimes dismissed as an idealistic HR notion—translates directly into better business performance and success when an enterprise adopts SAFe. Figure 2 illustrates the realities of disengagement and the benefits of high employee engagement [1].

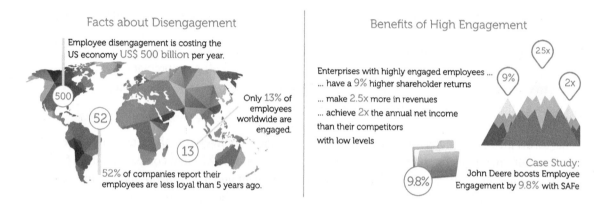

Figure 2. Employee engagement

Engagement fosters retention. The best way to lower turnover is to invest in people. The concept of improving the market value of employees and making them more attractive to competitors might seem counterintuitive, but actively developing people takes away their need to switch jobs to improve and advance.

Agile practices allow people to evolve through challenging work, powerful collaboration, constant reflections, continuous feedback, and relentless improvement—all deeply embedded into the workflow. In other words, Agile does not distinguish between learning and working: Working equals learning, and knowledge workers are learning workers.

Hence, the goal of Agile enterprises is not simply to retain talent, but to let those talented individual grow and thrive, and to develop a flourishing talent pool.

#3 – Hire for Attitude and Cultural Fit

Building a vigorous workforce starts with identifying, attracting, and hiring the right people. Finding top talent is becoming increasingly difficult. When it comes to Talent Acquisition, Agile enterprises get a competitive edge by focusing on the following considerations:

Build a strong employer brand. Agile is a magnet for talented people. Enterprises can—and should—build on their commitment to Agile excellence and use it to help build a strong employer brand.

Proactively attract and engage knowledge worker talent. It's a competitive market for top digital talent. Recruitment starts long before a new vacancy opens up. The talent acquisition team must continuously reach out and connect with interesting technical people to pull them into the talent pipeline.

Employ for attitude and cultural fit. Agile is a team sport. Technical expertise is important, but Agile teams prosper when they hire candidates with the right attitude and cultural fit. The tendency toward heroism and over-specialization must be avoided. After all, success depends on the collective and collaborative skills of the team. Figure 3 shows some interview questions that can be used to address candidates' ability to thrive in a team setting [2].

Interview questions to assess Candidate Agility:

- Were you able to flex your behavior when you realized the path you were on was not working and how reflective have you been?
- How successful have you been at partnering with others to generate creative solutions and plan collaborative strategies for success?
- What have you learned from successes and failure in your career?
- How did you course-correct when encountering roadblocks?

Figure 3. Interview questions

Inspire candidates with a larger sense of purpose. Knowledge workers need a sense of purpose in their lives. Something beyond the bits and bytes, and even beyond their local team environment, is required. Helping candidates understand the larger purpose of the organization is the best way to inspire them. Strengthen this understanding by being genuine and dependable throughout the whole process.

Make a solid, team-based decision. Talent acquisition is a shared responsibility, and no hiring decision should be made without the backing of the team. After all, no employee can thrive without team support. Therefore, the team must be actively included in the hiring process.

Excel at onboarding. Agile has fairly well-defined team practices and roles and is unbeatable in getting new people up to speed once on board. Prior to that, however, pre-integration activities, interactions, and access to information can enhance the onboarding experience. Post onboarding support requires communication and touch points with the individual to assure that the employee is happy in the role and that management is content with the employee's performance.

A high-quality recruitment process reduces the risk of bad hires and subsequent disruptions to the flow and performance of the team(s).

#4 – Move to Iterative Performance Flow

Performance management is undoubtedly the most criticized HR process today. Despite a long list of complaints, however, many organizations continue to invest large amounts of money in a broken performance appraisal practice. The facts are undeniable, though: Traditional performance appraisals don't work.

Performance management was initially envisioned as a way to align goals and foster joint efforts. It has since evolved into a pivotal point for an entire set of HR practices, especially compensation and talent management.

No wonder, then, that annual performance reviews have turned into a tense time for everyone involved. Managers tend to batch feedback, both negative and positive, into the annual feedback dump, depriving employees of the timely feedback they need to actually improve when it matters. For their part, employees are nervous about their appraisal because it affects their upcoming compensation and promotional chances.

Review tools are in place to help guide the discussion and 'force' managers to rank their people. As a consequence, many companies excel at calculating ratings—but that skill comes at a high cost to the morale and motivation of people. The tides are now turning, however, and organizations of all shapes and sizes are eliminating employee appraisals in an effort to respond to the challenges and interfaces to HR instruments. Figure 4 shows some key facts and trends for traditional performance management systems [3].

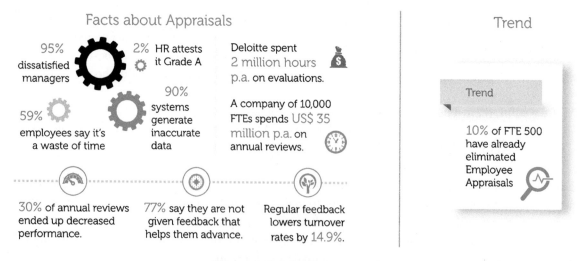

Figure 4. Employee appraisals

In particular, capitalizing some of the costs of software development can have a material effect on financial reporting. That is the topic of the remainder of this chapter.

Accounting for Software Development Costs

Rules for capitalization of software assets vary by country and industry. In the United States, the U.S. Financial Accounting Standards Board provides guidance for Generally Accepted Accounting Principles for U.S. companies that report financial data in the public interest. This includes those that report publicly under U.S. Securities and Exchange Commission regulations. Similar organizations exist in other countries. For example, the U.K. Financial Reporting Council (FRC) provides policies that are largely similar to those of FASB. In addition, the U.S. federal government has different standards under the Federal Accounting Standards Advisory Board.

For U.S. companies operating in the private and public reporting sectors, U.S. FASB 86 provides accounting guidelines for the costs of computer software to be sold, leased, or otherwise marketed [1]. FASB 86 states that costs incurred internally in creating a computer software product must be expensed when incurred as research and development until technological feasibility has been established. Thereafter, software production costs may be capitalized and subsequently reported at the lower of either the unamortized cost or the net realizable value. Capitalized costs are amortized based on current and future revenue for each product, with an annual minimum equal to the straight-line amortization over the remaining estimated economic life of the product. For these purposes, a software product is defined as either a new product or a new initiative that changes the functionality of an existing one.

Software Classifications under FASB 86

There are three primary classifications of software development under FASB 86:

- **Software for sale** – Software developed for sale as a stand-alone or integrated product, typically by independent software vendors (ISVs)

- **Software for internal use** – Software developed solely for internal purposes or in support of business processes within an enterprise, which is further described in Statement of Position (SOP) 98-1 (also FASB Accounting Standards Update 350-40 for fees paid in Cloud Computing)

- **Embedded software** – Software as a component of a tangible product needed to enable that product's essential functionality

Capitalization standards are treated differently within these categories, so the relevant guidelines must be taken into consideration.

Capitalization versus Expense Criteria

In general, FASB 86 requires that a product must meet the following criteria to capitalize ongoing development costs:

- The product has achieved technical feasibility.

- Management has provided written approval to fund the development effort.

- Management has committed the resources to development.

- Management is confident that the product will be successfully developed and delivered.

Before software can be capitalized, finance departments typically require documented evidence that these specific activities have been completed. Once these criteria are met, further development costs may be subject to capitalization, as described in Table 1.

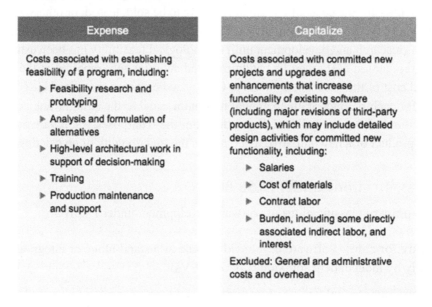

Table 1. Categories of expensed and potentially capitalized costs

Capitalization Triggers in Waterfall Development

Historically, capitalization has been applied in the context of waterfall/phase-gate development. Waterfall development has a well-defined up-front phase, during which requirements are developed, the design is produced, and feasibility is established. For those projects that receive further approval, the requirements and design milestones often serve as stage gates for starting capitalization, as shown in Figure 1.

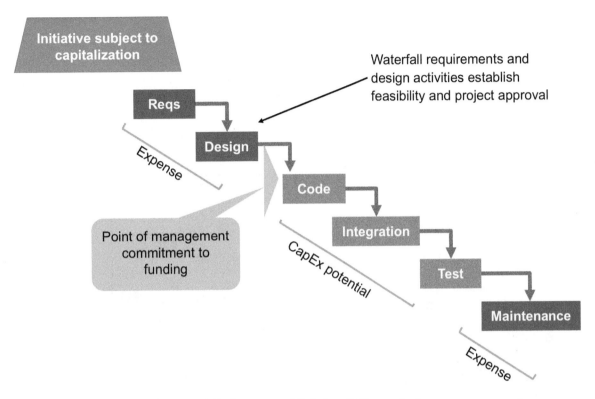

Figure 1. Early waterfall phases establish feasibility and trigger management commitment to funding

Agile Development Capitalization Strategies in SAFe

In Agile, requirements and design emerge continuously, so there's no formal phase gate to serve as an official starting point for capitalization. That does not mean that projects fund themselves. Instead, the SAFe enterprise organizes around long-lived flows of value in value streams. The personnel and other resources of an Agile Release Train (ART), operating on a fixed Program Increment (PI) cadence, implement them.

The majority of the work of most ARTs is typically focused on building and extending software assets that are past the point of feasibility analysis. They generally do this by developing new Features for the solution. Since features increase the functionality of existing software, the User Stories associated with those features constitute much of the work of the ART personnel. Therefore, this labor may be subject to potential capitalization.

The ARTs also help establish the business and technical feasibility of the various portfolio initiatives (Epics) that work their way through the Portfolio Kanban. This feasibility work is somewhat analogous to the early stages of waterfall development and is typically expensed up until the 'go' recommendation, at which point new feature development would begin.

Thus, both types of work are typically present in any PI—and, by extension, any relevant accounting period. Much of this is new feature work that increases the functionality of the existing software. Other work includes innovation and exploration efforts. These may be initiated from the portfolio Kanban, as part of the research and feasibility for potential new portfolio-level epics, or they may arise locally. In addition, maintenance and infrastructure work occurs during the period. Figure 2 illustrates these concepts.

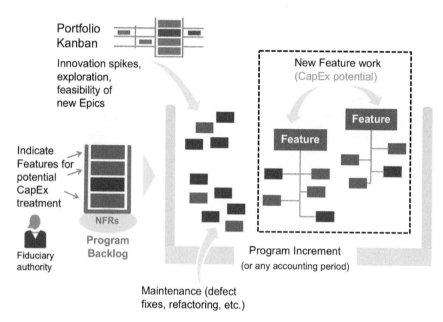

Figure 2. Many types of work occur within a given PI timebox

Categorization of Features for OpEx and CapEx

Creating new features for the solution is part of implementing new projects and enhancing existing products. By their very definition, features provide enhanced functionality.

Features can be easily identified and tracked for potential CapEx treatment. To do so, accounting fiduciaries work with Product Management to identify them in the Program Backlog. The selected features are 'typed' (flagged) for potential CapEx treatment, which creates the basic tracking mechanism. Thereafter, teams associate new stories with those features and perform the essential work of realizing the behavior of the features by implementing stories in the new code base.

Applying Stories to CapEx and OpEx Treatment

Most stories contribute directly to new functionality of the feature; the effort for those stories may be subject to CapEx treatment. Others—such as Enabler stories for infrastructure, exploration, defects, refactoring, and any other work—may not be treated as CapEx projects. Agile Life-Cycle Management (ALM) tooling can support the definition, capture, and work associated with implementing stories.

By associating stories with features when applicable in the tooling (typically called 'parenting' or 'linking'), the work related to feature development can be identified for potential CapEx treatment. Various query functions in the ALM tool can help automate the needed summary calculations. Table 2 indicates three of the possible mechanisms for calculating the percentage of work that may be a candidate for CapEx treatment.

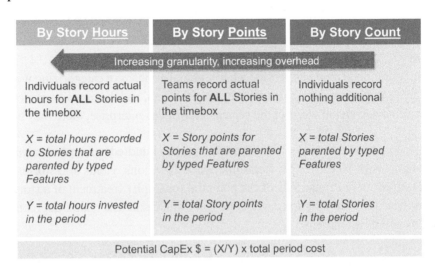

By Story Hours	By Story Points	By Story Count
Increasing granularity, increasing overhead		
Individuals record actual hours for **ALL** Stories in the timebox	Teams record actual points for **ALL** Stories in the timebox	Individuals record nothing additional
X = total hours recorded to Stories that are parented by typed Features	*X = Story points for Stories that are parented by typed Features*	*X = total Stories parented by typed Features*
Y = total hours invested in the period	*Y = total Story points in the period*	*Y = total Stories in the period*
Potential CapEx $ = (X/Y) x total period cost		

Table 2. Possible mechanisms for tracking effort associated with CapEx stories

By Story Hours

The most granular means of capturing the labor effort is to have team members record their hours against each story. Although some overhead is present, many teams do this anyway because of traditional time-tracking requirements for job costing, billing, estimating, and other needs. However, this should not be the default mode for CapEx, as it incurs overhead and, therefore, reduces value delivery velocity. The rest of the calculation is straightforward: The CapEx potential percentage is simply the percentage of hours recorded for CapEx features divided by the total of all hours invested in any period. After converting hours worked to cost, the enterprise can assess the total cost that may be subject to CapEx treatment.

During planning, some Agile Teams break stories into tasks and estimate and update task hours accordingly. The 'by story hours' method requires only that actual total team hours are recorded for the story; tasking is not mandatory.

By Story Points

Story points are the common currency of Scrum. Scrum teams estimate stories in points and update their estimates when actual data are available so as to help improve future estimates. Although story points are relative (not absolute) units of measure, they're all that's necessary. The enterprise simply needs to know the percentage of story points allocated to stories that have CapEx potential, relative to the total story points delivered in any accounting period. Conversion to actual costs is handled in the same way as for the preceding example.

This low-friction, low-overhead method generally does not create any additional burden on teams, other than the need to be sure to update estimates to actual data for each story completed. Again, ALM tooling typically supports the recording and automated calculation of such measures.

To compensate for the relative nature of story points, which can vary from team to team, SAFe suggests a means for normalizing story point estimating across teams as part of the common economic underpinnings for an ART.

By Story Count

The two previously described methods provide a fairly granular means of categorizing work to be capitalized. But then there's the labor of entering and capturing the data, and that extra work does not, by itself, deliver end-user value. Given the scope of the typical ART in the enterprise, there may be an easier way.

In a single PI, it's not unusual for an ART to implement many hundreds of stories, in various types and sizes (e.g., 10 teams, with 10 stories per Iteration, over 4 iterations, yields 400 stories per PI). Sizing a story is not biased by an understanding of the potential for CapEx treatment of a story, so story sizes will average out over time. In addition, over time the CapEx and associated depreciation schedules resolve to expense all development.

Thus, near-term perfection is not necessarily the goal, as it's probably false precision that may come at too high a cost. Instead, simply counting stories by type is a fair proxy for the amount of effort devoted to potential CapEx stories. In a manner similar to the first two methods described, this percentage can then be used to determine the CapEx potential in a given accounting period. Some Agilists have reported that this percentage approach is being applied to new Lean-Agile development initiatives, sometimes based on just the initial capacity allocation (see the Program Backlog chapter). While subject, appropriately, to occasional audits, this method provides a fairly friction-free approach that allows teams to focus exclusively on value delivery.

Which Labor Is Subject to CapEx Treatment?

There is one final aspect left to discuss: Which labor elements may be applied to CapEx treatment? Again, the answer is highly specific to the actual enterprise. However, within the Agile development world, the following guidelines are often applied:

- The salaries of Agile team members who are directly involved in refining, implementing, and testing stories may be subject to CapEx, as is largely consistent with existing waterfall practices. This may include software developers and testers and User Experience (UX) and other subject-matter experts.

- Product Owners (POs) and Scrum Masters are part of the Agile team and directly contribute to story definition and implementation. This indirect labor is directly associated with new value delivery and, therefore, may be appropriate for CapEx treatment. This can be accomplished by including an additional average cost burden on a CapEx story.

- Not all work for a feature is performed solely by Agile team members: System Architects, System Teams, and IT Operations also contribute to the features under development. Some portion of their cost may be subject to CapEx as well.

- Additional roles in the Solution Train may contribute to value creation via Pre- and Post-PI Planning, creation and maintenance of the Solution Intent, and the Solution Demo. While further removed from the specific implementation tasks, all of these activities and roles provide value. Thus, they may potentially be candidates for CapEx treatment, at the discretion of the enterprise.

LEARN MORE

[1] FASB 86 summary, fasb.org/summary/stsum86.shtml.

[2] Reed, Pat, and Walt Wyckoff. "Accounting for Capitalization of Agile Labor Costs." Agile Alliance, February 2016.

[3] Greening, Dan. "Why Should Agilists Care about Capitalization?" *InfoQ*, January 29, 2013.

[4] Connor, Catherine. "Top 10 Pitfalls of Agile Capitalization." *CA*, February 2016.

[5] Footnote from a U.S. public reporting software company's Form 10-K filing, highlighting a policy of not capitalizing software development expense: "Research and development expenses primarily consist of personnel and related costs of our research and development staff, including salaries, benefits, bonuses, payroll taxes, stock-based compensation, and costs of certain third-party contractors, as well as allocated overhead. Research and development costs related to the development of our software products are generally expensed as incurred. Development costs that have qualified for capitalization are not significant."

Iteration 2

- Roadmap epics into features (Enterprise Architects/System Architects)
- Identify enablers

Iteration 3

- Feature refinement
- Enablers refined

Iteration 4

- Top x features vetted with Business Owners
- Prepare Executive Briefing for PI planning
- Feature refinement
- Top x features discussed with System Architects
- Enabler versus feature capacity allocation agreed
- Prepare product vision and roadmap
- Prepare architecture vision

IP Iteration 5

- Top x features socialized with teams
- High-level starter stories created
- Finalize presentations
- Train and prep new ART members, Business Owners, and other Lean-Agile Leaders

Large Solution Level

As with the Program Level, we need to ensure that all large solution–level PI preparation activities don't occur at the eleventh hour. Here, too, we must coordinate and refine the artifacts that support the next PI planning event. Although the Solution Train Engineer (STE) remains the key facilitator for ceremonies at the large solution level, the primary responsibility falls to Solution Management to conduct the capability backlog refinement sessions with the affected ARTs and Suppliers. Solution Management also participates in epic refinement, which is conducted by the Epic Owner. (Keep in mind that epics can exist at the portfolio, large solution, and program levels).

Figure 4 depicts a parallel, large solution–level track of PI execution and preparation activities based on weeks within the PI. The remainder of this section consists of a typical PI Planning preparation timeline in a checklist format that identifies checkpoints for STEs, RTEs, Scrum Master, Product Managers, and others as they work with their Solution Trains/ARTs to prepare for the next PI. These checkpoints serve as guideposts for Solution Train leaders so that they do not fall too far behind. Effective readiness requires coordination with others to ensure alignment and "no surprises" at the Pre-PI and Post-PI Planning events of the Solution Train.

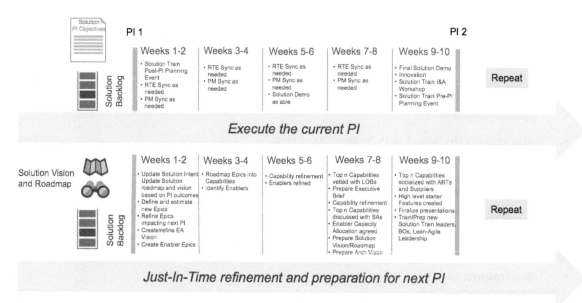

Figure 4. Parallel execution and preparation activities at the large solution level

Executing the Current PI: Large Solution

- Post-PI planning event, 'RTE Sync' as needed, 'PM Sync' as needed, Solution Demos, Innovation, I&A workshop, pre-PI planning event

Preparing for the Next PI: Large Solution
Iteration 1

- Update Solution Intent

- Update Solution roadmap and vision based on PI outcomes

- Define and estimate new Epics

- Refine Epics impacting next PI

- Create and refine the Enterprise Architecture vision

- Create enabler epics

Iteration 2
- Roadmap epics into capabilities
- Identify enablers

Iteration 3
- Capability refinement
- Enablers refined

Iteration 4
- Top x capabilities vetted with Business Owners
- Prepare Executive Brief
- Capability refinement
- Top x capabilities discussed with SAs
- Enabler Capacity Allocation agreed
- Prepare Solution Vision/Roadmap
- Prepare Architecture Vision

IP Iteration 5
- Top x capabilities socialized with ARTs and suppliers
- High-level starter features created
- Finalize presentations
- Train and prep new Solution Train roles, Business Owners, and Lean-Agile Leadership

Portfolio Level

To enable the flow of strategic initiatives at the Portfolio Level, Lean Portfolio Management (LPM), Epic Owners, and Enterprise Architects need to keep the vision and roadmap current, refining associated epics so that they're ready for the trains. This includes Business Epics and Enabler Epics. Also, the epics need to align with Strategic Themes from the Enterprise, and the strategic vision needs to be kept up-to-date. This provides executives with access to information that informs the Solution Trains/ARTs on key strategic initiatives that affect them as they proceed through the pre-PI, PI, and post-PI planning events.

Summary

"It does not happen all at once. There is no instant pudding."

   —Deming

SAFe provides a framework that helps enterprises deliver value in manageable chunks using a flow-based, systematic approach. To enable consistent flow at various levels, the enterprise backlog structure needs to be understood. Even in the face of changing strategic priorities, the responsible roles need to drive their backlogs continuously to keep them in a ready state. Staying ahead of PI preparation will enable a consistent flow, with the PI timebox as the heartbeat of program execution. Using a Just-in-Time (JIT) approach, parallel execution, and PI preparation activities at the portfolio, large solution, program, and team levels allows sufficient lead time for ART leaders and the rest of the enterprise to prepare. Attention needs to be paid to ensure we truly enable JIT decomposition as close as possible to delivery, without doing too much decomposition early in the PI (a big form of waste). This will facilitate the collaborative discovery, discussions, and alignment that PI planning fosters.

Essential SAFe

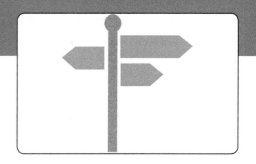

Simplicity—the art of maximizing the amount of work not done—is essential.

   —Agile Manifesto

The *Essential SAFe* configuration is the most basic configuration of SAFe. It provides a starting point for implementing SAFe and describes the most critical elements needed to realize the majority of the framework's benefits. It consists of the Team and Program levels, along with the Foundation, as illustrated in Figure 1.

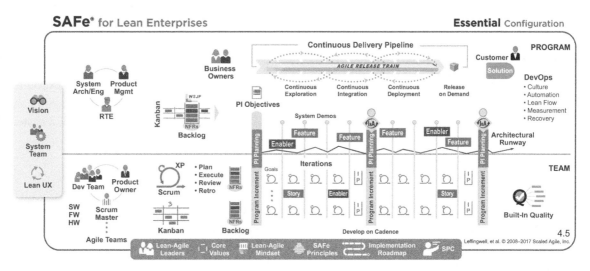

Figure 1. Essential SAFe configuration

SAFe has a proven ability to scale in all situations, from complex software and systems development, to bond trading and medical devices, to memory chips and fighter aircraft. But, with such a robust framework, a question arises: How closely does an organization need to follow various SAFe practices to get the desired result?

Also, we've observed that not every implementation realizes the full business benefits that others achieve. When diagnosing SAFe implementation problems, we've discovered that these enterprises have skipped some of the essential practices. It's easy to see how that can happen. After all, it's a big framework, how would an enterprise know what's most important?

The Ten Essential Elements

#1 – Lean-Agile Principles

SAFe practices are grounded in fundamental principles. That's why you can be confident that they apply well in your case. And if the practices don't directly apply, the underlying principles can guide you to make sure that your organization is moving on a continuous path to the 'shortest sustainable lead time, with best quality and value to people and society.'

#2 – Real Agile Teams and Trains

Real Agile Teams and Agile Release Trains (ARTs) are fully cross-functional: They have everything, and everyone, necessary to produce a working, tested increment of the solution. They are self-organizing and self-managing, which enables value to flow more quickly, with a minimum of overhead. Product Management, System Architect/Engineers, and Release Train Engineers provide content and technical authority, along with an effective development process. Product Owners and Scrum Masters help the Dev teams meet their PI Objectives. The Agile teams should engage the customer throughout the development process.

#3 – Cadence and Synchronization

Cadence provides a rhythmic pattern, a steady heartbeat for the development process. It makes routine those things that can be routine. Synchronization allows multiple perspectives to be understood and resolved at the same time. For example, synchronization is used to pull the various assets of a system together to assess solution-level viability.

#4 – PI Planning

No event is more powerful in SAFe than PI Increment (PI) planning. It's the cornerstone of the PI, which provides the rhythm for the ART. When 100 or so people work together toward a common mission, Vision, and purpose, it's amazing how much alignment and energy that collaboration creates. Gaining that alignment in just two days can save months of delays.

#5 – DevOps and Releasability

DevOps provides the culture, automation, Lean flow, measurement, and recovery capabilities to enable an enterprise to bridge the gap between development and operations. Releasability focuses on the enterprise's ability to deliver value to its Customers more often and according to the demands of the market. Together, these principles and practices allow an organization to achieve better economic results by having more frequent releases and faster validation of hypotheses.

#6 – System Demo

The primary measure of the ART's progress is the objective evidence provided by a working solution in the System Demo. Every two weeks, the full system—the integrated work of all teams on the train for that iteration—is demoed to the train's stakeholders. Stakeholders provide the feedback the train needs to stay on course and take corrective action.

#7 – Inspect and Adapt

The Inspect and Adapt (I&A) workshop is a significant event held every PI. A regular time to reflect, collect data, and solve problems, the I&A event assembles teams and stakeholders to assess the solution and define and take action on the improvements needed to increase the velocity, quality, and reliability of the next PI.

#8 – IP Iteration

The Innovation and Planning Iteration occurs every PI and serves multiple purposes. It acts as an estimating buffer for meeting PI objectives and provides dedicated time for innovation, continuing education, and PI planning and I&A events. It's like extra fuel in the tank: Without it, the train may start straining under the 'tyranny of the urgent' iteration.

#9 – Architectural Runway

The Architectural Runway consists of the existing code, components, and technical infrastructure necessary to support the implementation of high-priority, near-term features, without excessive delay and redesign. Without enough investment in the Architectural Runway, the train will slow down, with redesign needed for each new Feature.

#10 – Lean-Agile Leadership

For SAFe to be effective, the enterprise's leaders and managers must take responsibility for Lean-Agile adoption and success. They must become leaders who are trained—and become trainers in—these leaner ways of thinking and operating. Without leadership taking responsibility for the implementation, the transformation will likely fail to achieve the full benefits.

Features and Components

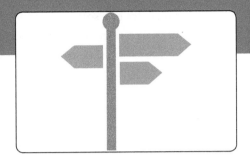

Innovation comes from the producer, not the customer.

—W. Edwards Deming

Features and Components include two key abstractions we use to build software and systems:

- *Features* are those behaviors of the system that directly fulfill some user need.

- *Components* are distinguishable system parts that provide and encapsulate common functions needed to implement features.

The Agile model's value delivery focus emphasizes *features* (and constituent *stories*) that solve user needs and differentiate solutions. However, resilient large-scale systems are built out of *components* that provide for separation of concerns, foster logic reuse, and improve testability. These properties provide a foundation for fast system evolution.

Both abstractions exist and may be commonly recognized in an Enterprise. Particularly in the context of enterprise agility, some interesting discussions can arise about how to organize teams—around features, around components, or around some mix of the two. Getting the organization of the enterprise right drives innovation on scalable systems that can grow as your knowledge grows. Getting it wrong leads to one of two suboptimal outcomes:

- Brittle systems that are unmaintainable and rapidly obsolescent (all features, all the time)

- Brilliantly designed systems with inherent future user value to keep the enterprise competitive (all components, all the time)

This chapter describes features and components in the context of large-scale Agile systems development and provides some organizational guidance to continually evolve the Agile organization to optimize velocity and accelerate value delivery.

Details

Components and Features

The architecture of a software system can be described, in part, in terms of its component structure and its features. The components interact to deliver the consistent user-facing behaviors that constitute the features. Teams build systems out of components to provide scalability, flexibility, common functions reuse, and maintainability.

The creation of a specific component can be driven by a number of motivations:

- Implementation/isolation of a specific technology (e.g., PHP-based user interface, Java-based business logic)

- Reuse of logic (e.g., transaction processing module)

- Protective isolation for purposes of controlling security, compliance, safety, and so on

- Support for an anticipated high rate of changing requirements (e.g., bridge/adapter modules, proxy objects)

The word 'component' is a pretty broad term. In SAFe, it can refer to any of the following:

- A system layer (such as the UI, Application, or Data layer)

- A software module or package

- An application library

- A subsystem

Component Teams

A *component team* is a Define–Build–Test Team whose primary area of concern is restricted to a specific component, or a set of components, of the system. Accordingly, the team backlog typically consists of Technical Stories (as opposed to User Stories), as well as Refactors and Spikes. It can make sense to create a component team when a component has the following characteristics:

- Can be used by other entities, business units, or subsystems

- Would otherwise appear in many places in the code base, complicating maintenance and testability

- Can be uniquely responsible for functionality related to compliance, safety, security, or regulation

- Contains unique or legacy technology

- Provides algorithms or logic that require specific, deep technical and/or theoretical expertise

- Operates on large data sets, performs highly intensive computations, or has to satisfy some critical nonfunctional requirements, such as availability or throughput

Prior to the Agile development movement, most large-scale systems development programs were typically organized around components and subsystems (the old mantra: Organization follows architecture). Therefore in an Agile transformation, sometimes the simplest first step is to create Agile Teams that follow the existing, component-based organizational pattern (Figure 1).

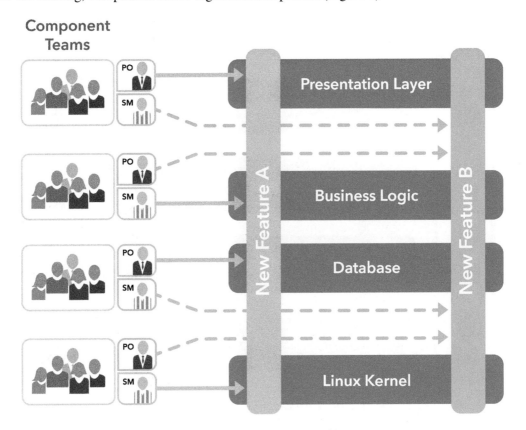

Figure 1. An Agile program consisting of component teams

Feature Teams

The disadvantages of the previously described model are obvious: *Most new features create dependencies that require cooperation between these teams.* This is a continuing drag on velocity, as the teams spend much of their time discussing dependencies *between* teams and testing behavior *across* components rather than being able to deliver end-user value. We certainly don't need components or component teams in the following situations:

- Most new user stories require unique changes to specific parts of the code base.
- The code of interest has no higher criticality than any other component in the system.

- The code does not require unique, rare, or different skills and technologies.
- The code will be not heavily used by other code, components, or systems.

In these cases, it is best to create feature teams that are organized around user-centered functionality. Each team, or small team of teams, is capable of delivering end-to-end user value (Figure 2). Feature teams operate primarily with user stories, refactors, and spikes. In addition, technical stories may occasionally occur in their backlog.

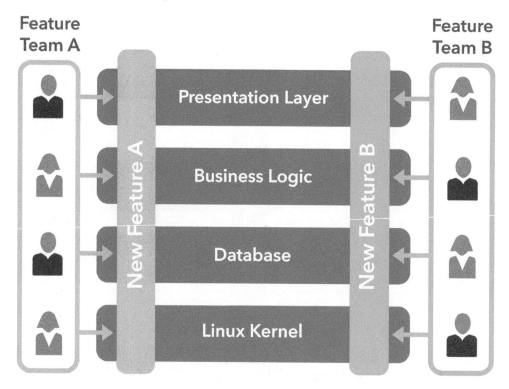

Figure 2. An example of feature teams

Even then, though they are called feature teams, it is not always true that such a team can complete a feature by itself. Features can be too big to be consumed by one Agile team and so may be split up into multiple user stories. These, in turn, are implemented by other feature teams. In addition, the very notion of a feature *or* component team is a bit simplistic, as many effective teams have responsibility for a number of both features and components. Nevertheless, the following guideline applies:

> To ensure the highest feature throughput, SAFe generally recommends a mix of perhaps 75 to 80 percent feature teams and 20 to 25 percent component teams.

Given that a mix is most likely to be appropriate, two main factors drive it:

- The practical limitation of the degree of specialization required

- The economics of potential reuse

Figure 3 illustrates these parameters and a curve that can be used to choose one organization over other options.

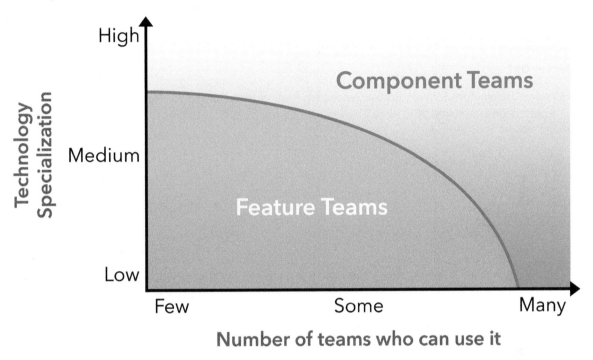

Figure 3. The feature and component teams power curve

This 'mixed model' emphasizes additional capabilities needed to drive program velocity:

- **System-level, Continuous Integration (CI) infrastructure** – Feature teams must be able to integrate the entire system at any desirable point.

- **Test automation** – Broad, automated regression test suites must be built and available.

- **The System Team** – This special team is engaged in actively improving and supporting the CI systems and processes used by the feature and component teams.

- **Communities of Practice** – These communities can be organized to share component-related knowledge across feature teams.

- **Strong emphasis on endemic code quality** – Along with refactoring skills, this perspective is mandatory for scaling.

Summary

This chapter described the issues of organizing Agile programs around feature teams versus component teams. Evolution to a mix of these teams, although one biased toward feature teams, appears to produce the highest velocity and efficacy of larger-scale Agile development. In general, dependencies are fewer and easier to manage, and value throughout is higher with feature teams. Even then, however, we recognize that features and components are both abstractions, such that one person's feature may be another's component. To that end, Agile programs must continually inspect and adapt, and indeed reorganize, as necessary to follow the value that is driving the market.

LEARN MORE

[1] Leffingwell, Dean. *Agile Software Requirements: Lean Requirements Practices for Teams, Programs, and the Enterprise.* Addison-Wesley, 2011.

Invitation-Based SAFe Implementation

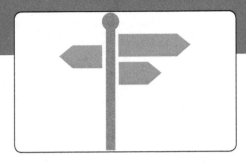

By Yuval Yeret, SPCT, Chief Technology Officer, AgileSparks

Introduction

Implementing any kind of organizational change, such as adopting SAFe, is hard and raises several key concerns:

- How do we convince people to adopt the new ways of working?

- How do we get the organization moving in the new direction?

- How do we make decisions about how to implement SAFe in the enterprise?

SAFe recommends decentralizing control, while providing vision and gaining alignment. It also emphasizes respecting people and culture and maintaining effective flow. In this guidance chapter, we discuss ways to 'walk that talk' in the way we run a SAFe implementation.

The default approach for implementing organizational change is the 'mandate' or 'push' approach. This may appear to be the fast and easy way, where a central group of change agents decides when people will 'board' the Agile Release Train (ART) as well as how the train should operate.

It may seem easy because the change is mandated and there is little or no discussion about whether the change should occur. It also appears to reduce the risk of a shallow SAFe adoption that doesn't even cover the essentials, due to bad implementation decisions by people who have limited or no experience. The problem with this classic approach is mainly that people don't like to be changed; that is, instead of being passive targets of change, they prefer to be involved in making the decision to change as well as in designing the change.

The Vision – Implementing SAFe Using Invitations

Martin Fowler, one of the Agile Manifesto signatories, wrote an article in 2006 called "The Agile Imposition." In the article, Fowler says, "Imposing an agile process from the outside strips the team of … self-determination, which is at the heart of agile thinking." But what if we can't wait for people to self-determine that they should go agile? Should the organization wait? Even if it kills the business?

SAFe's Principle #9: Decentralize decision-making provides some guidance here. The decision whether to go Agile and which approach to take is *infrequent*, is *long lasting*, and *provides a significant economy of scale*. Based on these characteristics, it is a classic strategic decision to centralize.

But once that central decision to go SAFe has been made, the Agile Manifesto says, "Build projects around motivated individuals. Give them the environment and support they need, and trust them to get the job done." Also, "The best architectures, requirements, and designs emerge from self-organizing teams." If we apply these two principles to SAFe implementation, it would mean the best plans for implementing SAFe will emerge from self-organizing teams (or teams of teams) of the people adopting SAFe. Implementing SAFe using a leaner and more Agile approach will send a message about the strength of management's commitment to the Lean-Agile mindset described in SAFe. Can you think of a better way to signal 'respect for people and culture'?

During the Program Increment (PI) Planning event, Business Owners and Product Management present the business context—that is, the vision. The planning context and structure of PI Planning is a 'container' in which the ART self-organizes to figure out how and how much the train members can do to further the vision.

Similarly, Invitation-Based SAFe implementation needs to set the context and provide the right structure for the group to figure out how much of SAFe they can achieve in their first implementation PI. A flow of an invitation-based implementation can be seen in Figure 1, with the blue boxes showing the places where invitations might be extended to leaders and practitioners.

Figure 1. Invitation-based SAFe implementation flow

Using the SAFe Implementation Workshop to Invite the Enterprise to Consider SAFe

Leadership is charged with making these types of [strategic] decisions, supported by the input of those impacted by the decisions.

—SAFe Principle #9

One approach that my company, AgileSparks, has discovered works well when teaching leading SAFe is to accompany pure training mode with a SAFe Implementation Workshop. In this workshop, whose agenda is shown in Figure 2, a group of leaders discuss the following topics:

- The reasons for considering SAFe

- How good of a fit SAFe seems to be

- Identifying Value Streams and designing ARTs

- Guidelines for determining how roles in SAFe are chosen or assigned to people

- Implementation risks and organizational impediments

Figure 2. Implementation workshop sample agenda

Through this interactive collaborative process, members of this group will become the initial 'guiding coalition,' a term popularized by Kotter. They consider options, make decisions, and commit to work together toward the shared vision.

As shown in Figure 1, this workshop format is useful when considering SAFe with a group of leaders across an enterprise (or division) as well as later on when preparing to launch a specific value stream or ART. Another way to look at it is as a different variant of how to run the SAFe value stream workshop, which is frequently used following up an Implementing SAFe/Leading SAFe class to help identify value streams and ARTs for actual implementation of SAFe in the organization.

Spreading SAFe through an Invitation to Leaders

The outcome of the enterprise-level implementation workshop is an invitation to potential value streams and ARTs to consider what SAFe would mean in their context and to figure out when and how to start their SAFe journey.

In most cases, the potential ART and value stream leaders (think vice president–level leaders) will have participated in the initial Leading SAFe + Implementation workshop and are now ready to consider bringing SAFe to their group. By comparison, in larger enterprises, there might be a need for further Leading SAFe and Implementation workshops to expose more potential ART/value stream leaders to SAFe. In the 'invitations' spirit, you can invite leaders to participate in such a class or bring SAFe into their organization, rather than force or mandate these actions. The first leaders to accept the invitation are ideal 'prospects' (innovators or early adopters) for starting the SAFe journey and should be where SAFe Program Consultants (SPCs) should initially spend most of their time.

Using the SAFe Implementation Workshop to Launch a Program/Value Stream

Once leaders decide that the timing is right to consider SAFe in their area, they should again repeat the same pattern—that is, Leading SAFe combined with a SAFe Implementation workshop to figure out how to go SAFe. This time the audience is Lean-Agile leaders for the ART and value stream, as well as ART and value stream roles such as the Release Train Engineer (RTE), Product Management, and System Architect.

Typically the Product Owners and Scrum Masters don't participate in this workshop. Instead, this workshop is often where the leadership team figures out the mapping between the Product Owner (PO), Scrum Master, and Product Management roles and determines which roles and people will be included in the group.

As the POs, Scrum Masters, and Product Management are identified, they get trained in PO/Product Management and SAFe Scrum Master workshops. When using the 'SAFe Invitations' implementation approach, these workshops should include vignettes from the implementation workshop, such as starting with a pains/why session and then gauging confidence level and ROAMing implementation risks toward the end of the training. This approach will help POs, Scrum Masters, and Product Management connect to the vision and feel more involved in designing the implementation approach and will rally them to join the 'guiding coalition' of the group.

Invitation-Based ART Launch

Once leaders of a certain area are on board and have identified an ART or value stream on which to focus, and after the ART stakeholders and roles have been trained and brought on board, it is time get the team-of-teams rolling. A combination approach—training everyone using 'SAFe for Teams' at the same time, plus planning the initial PI and getting a real feel for how SAFe will look like—works better than just sticking to theory, training exercises, and games.

Bringing an invitation approach into the ART launch means decentralizing some decisions about how to operate SAFe to the people on the ART themselves. Program board structure, Definition of Done (DoD) policies, ready policies, engineering practices, Agile testing strategies, and some other aspects are great candidates for having breakout sessions, followed by integration discussions, as part of the SAFe for Teams training. Additionally, you may want to allow teams to make other local decisions about how they use SAFe, as long as they're aligned with the SAFe principles and it does not cause problems for the other teams on the train or the ART as a whole (Figure 3).

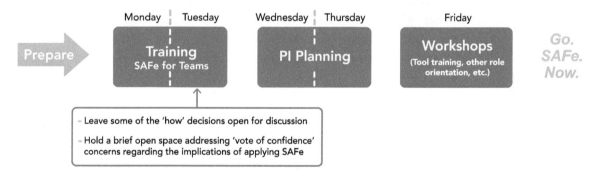

Figure 3. Invitation-based ART Quick Start

As a blueprint of how the ART will work starts to emerge, it's time to gauge people's level of confidence for how the implementation of SAFe will work and to surface risks. You can use a 'fist of five' confidence vote (similar to what we do in PI planning) to gather this feedback, as well as proactively invite people to share their concerns.

Follow up with pertinent questions: 'Based on what we just learned so far, are there any significant concerns that would prevent us from starting to use SAFe?' The responses from the teams can be used as seed topics for a brief problem-solving workshop or 'open space' session, where people can raise their concerns, and then join or lead a breakout session to identify solutions to that problem.

Another approach is to ROAM each risk and issue, like we do in PI planning. The use of the facilitation techniques, such as ROAMing risks, confidence votes, and open space, all demonstrate a 'servant leadership' style. As leaders, we are not just telling people what to do, but rather engaging them in figuring out the 'how' and serving them by owning resolution of key systemic risks to the change. This same technique can be applied during the PI planning confidence vote and ROAMing of the risks.

Another interesting practice that invites people on the ART to participate in figuring out implementation details is team self-selection. In this practice, the ART leaders provide guidelines and constraints and let the people on the ART figure out what at the actual teams should look like [8–10].

Be careful when allowing customization at this point. There's a risk of either removing too much from the SAFe model or adding too much overhead with additional process. There's tremendous value in trying out the SAFe framework more or less 'as is,' or with careful configuration (or customization) with the help of a seasoned SAFe program consultant, and only then seeking to remove, add, or change practices. For a view on the essentials that shouldn't be changed, see the Essential SAFe chapter.

Summary

In essence, the approach described in this chapter uses Lean-Agile practices and principles to drive the adoption of SAFe. In essence, it's using SAFe to adopt SAFe. We're asking leaders to set the vision and direction for implementing SAFe and inviting their people to come on board and to participate in designing this change that will have so much positive impact on how work will be performed in the future.

Decentralizing control and engaging as many people as possible in figuring out how to use SAFe tends to improve the quality of SAFe implementation because of the 'wisdom of the crowd' effect and the higher motivation that people have when they're invited to be involved. This applies to leaders at various levels using the SAFe Implementation Workshop that complements Leading SAFe training as well as to teams and ART stakeholders using vignettes such as identifying pain points and vision mapping, implementation confidence votes, and risk ROAMing in each and every SAFe training used to prepare and launch SAFe in ARTs and value streams.

LEARN MORE

[1] https://www.linkedin.com/pulse/openspace-agility-right-you-daniel-sloan.

[2] Kotter, John. *Leading Change*. Harvard Business Press, December 30, 2013.

[3] http://openspaceagility.com/big-picture/.

[4] http://yuvalyeret.com.

[5] http://www.infoq.com/news/2014/10/kickstart-agile-kanban.

[6] http://www.infoq.com/interviews/lkfr14-yeret-kanban-agile.

[7] https://management30.com/practice/delegation-board/.

[8] https://www.linkedin.com/pulse/large-scale-self-selection-australia-post-interview-andy-sandy-mamoli.

[9] https://www.amazon.com/Creating-Great-Teams-Self-Selection-People-ebook/dp/B019EKWG6M/.

[10] https://www.scrumalliance.org/community/articles/2013/2013-april/how-to-form-teams-in-large-scale-scrum-a-story-of.

[11] http://www.agilesparks.com/safe-implementation-strategy-leadership-focusing-workshop/.

Refactoring

You just have to have the guidance to lead you in the direction until you can do it yourself. It is the neglect of timely repair that makes rebuilding necessary.

—Richard Whately

Refactoring is the activity of improving the internal structure or operation of a code or component without changing its external behavior.

The goal of software development is the continuous delivery of business value to users and stakeholders. Constantly changing technology, coupled with the evolution of business objectives and changing user paradigms, makes it difficult to maintain and constantly increase business value. Two paths to the future exist:

- Keep adding new functionality to an existing code base toward an eventually unmaintainable 'throw-away' state
- Continuously modify the system to provide a foundation for efficiently delivering not just the *current* business value but the *future* business value as well

The second choice, refactoring, is better. With continuous refactoring, the useful life of an Enterprise's investment in software assets can be extended as long as possible, and users can continue to experience a flow of value for years to come. Refactors are a special type of Enabler story in SAFe and, like any other Story, they must be estimable, demonstrable, and evaluable, as well as accepted by the Product Owner.

Details

Figure 1 illustrates the essence of *refactoring*, which is the modification of any software entity—a module, method, or program—to improve its structure or viability, without changing the external functionality. For example, refactors may accomplish such things as increasing processing speed, sourcing different internal data, or improving security concerns. Another type of refactoring involves streamlining some aspect of the code to make it more efficient, more maintainable, or more readable.

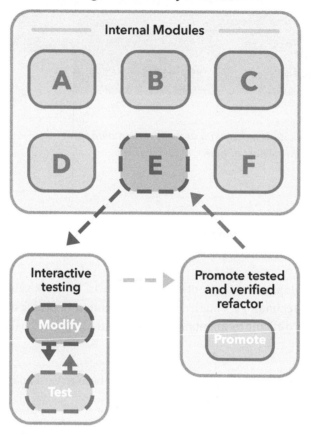

Figure 1. Refactoring in an isolated environment for change within a larger entity

Refactoring mandates that each change is tested immediately to verify the accomplishment of the desired goal. A refactor may be broken into a series of sequential micro-refactors so as to accomplish a larger goal; each small refactor must be tested to ensure correctness. This iterative process preserves the integrity of the software at any stage.

SAFe emphasizes the importance of keeping all work visible, including refactoring. Like user value work, it must be planned for, estimated, and prioritized at all levels of the Solution.

Sources of Refactors

Refactors arise from various sources, as illustrated in Figure 2. For example, a refactor can be insti-gated by a business Feature or can be a part of larger refactoring initiative required by some new archi-tectural enabler. New user stories may also require some refactoring of code. Accumulated technical debt may drive the team to refactor certain components. Some refactors may be necessitated by new Nonfunctional Requirements.

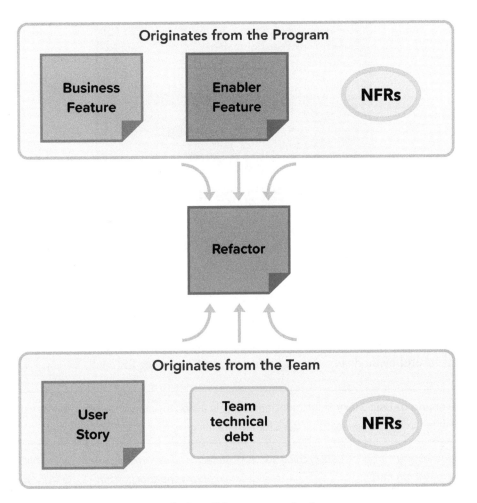

Figure 2. Possible sources of refactors

Not all the team's refactoring effort comes in the form of specific story refactoring. Much of it should be 'in-line' clean-up work, done while implementing user stories. Such work should be factored into the estimate of the corresponding story (see the continuous refactoring techniques described in [1–3]). Specific refactors, however, represent larger pieces of redesign that need to be planned and tracked as separate backlog items.

Specifying Refactors

It is important to understand what value will be achieved once the refactoring effort is completed. Teams may wish to use the ' . . . so that . . . ' portion of the user story voice form to foster shared understanding of purpose and value, as illustrated in Figure 3.

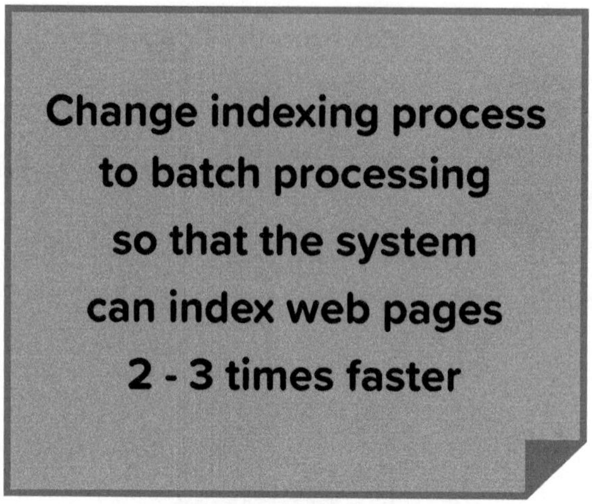

**Change indexing process
to batch processing
so that the system
can index web pages
2 - 3 times faster**

Figure 3. Refactor example

Splitting Refactors

As with user stories, splitting refactors is important, as it helps sustain better development flow. Table 1 provides some useful methods for splitting refactors, and examples for each.

1. By User Scenario or User Story Refactor incrementally in a story-by-story or scenario-by-scenario mode, or otherwise identify the functional areas as a basis for incrementing.	
*Improve DB queries and introduce data caching **so that** the system will run faster*	*. . . Refactor all user management functionality . . . Catalog browsing functionality . . . Check functionality*
2. By Component First, refactor everything related to a single component, then move to the next.	
*Change indexing process to batch processing **so that** the process is at least 2–3 times faster for an average web page*	*. . . For parsing (parser component) . . . For entity extraction (analyzer component) . . . For storing in the index (index component)*
3. Interface / Implementation First, create new interfaces and wrap in the old functionality, then refactor the functionality itself.	
*Extract all parsing parameters into an xml configuration file **so that** that the process can be tuned easily without changing the code*	*. . . Install PINGID Protocol server and test with mock identity provider . . . Read configurations from file in any format . . . Refactor configuration functionality to support certain structure and schema validation*

4. Strangle Component Incrementally move the functionality of the component to other components; once everything is moved, delete the old code.	
*Replace database with custom search index **so that** indexing and search performance improves 10–20 times*	*. . . Move index data to custom search index first . . . Move entity dictionaries*
5. Inline Refactoring / Extraction Refactor the functionality in-line where it currently is, but then extract it and encapsulate into a component, class, or method / function.	
*Replace current ad hoc parsing with grammar-based functionality **so that** changing parsing rules would become easy and without need for coding*	*. . . Refactor the code (as is) to use grammar notation . . . Extract all grammar-related functionality into a grammar engine*

Table 1. Methods of splitting refactors

Establishing Acceptance Criteria

As with user stories, defining acceptance criteria for refactors helps resolve ambiguities. Figure 4 illustrates the additional specificity that comes with an established acceptance criteria.

Change indexing process to batch processing so that the system can index web pages 2 - 3 times faster

- Batch size is configurable
- Debug logs capture full batches
- Entity dictionary is queried only once per batch
- Items in batch are processed asynchronously

Figure 4. Example of acceptance criteria for a refactor story

Acceptance criteria can often be used as a natural basis for splitting. For example, the first step in Figure 4 might be to '. . . make synchronous nonconfigurable batch processing with a single query to dictionary, but without the debug logging.' Then '. . . add capability to read batch size from the file.' Step 3 would be '. . . process items asynchronously,' and finally '. . . add debug logging functionality.'

Demonstrating Refactors

Even though refactoring focuses on the internal working of the code, as with any other story, teams demonstrate the results. With the example in Figure 4, the teams might demonstrate the following outcomes and artifacts:

1. Reduced processing time on a few web pages, compared to the previous benchmark

2. Dependency of processing time on the size of the batch, which can be configured from the file

3. A code snippet for asynchronous processing

4. The debug log file that captures all the operations

5. The number of queries to dictionaries per batch (from the log file)

Adopting the Culture

Refactoring is a mandatory skill for Agile Teams. Refactors should routinely appear on the Team Backlog and be included—along with in-line refactoring—in story estimates. A Design Community of Practice (CoP) can foster awareness and attention to refactoring techniques. Scrum Masters can help their teams learn efficient approaches to specifying, estimating, and splitting refactors. Finally, Product Owners should embrace refactoring by prioritizing the work and by helping to define acceptance criteria.

LEARN MORE

[1] Fowler, Martin, et al. *Refactoring: Improving the Design of Existing Code*. Addison-Wesley, 1999.

[2] Martin, Robert. *Clean Code: A Handbook of Agile Software Craftsmanship*. Prentice Hall, 2008.

[3] Wake, William. *Refactoring Workbook*. Addison-Wesley, 2003.

SAFe Requirements Model

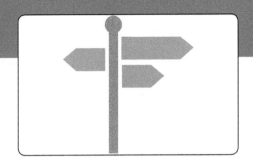

Essentially, all models are wrong, but some are useful.
   —George E. P. Box

To support bringing the benefits of Lean and Agile development to larger enterprises—or to smaller businesses building more complex systems—SAFe provides a scalable requirements model that demonstrates a way to express system behaviors: Epics, Capabilities, Features, Stories, Nonfunctional Requirements (NFRs), and more. As shown in Figure 1, each of these work items is expressed in different ways. For example, a feature is described by a phrase, benefit hypothesis, and acceptance criteria; a story is elaborated by a user-voice statement and acceptance criteria.

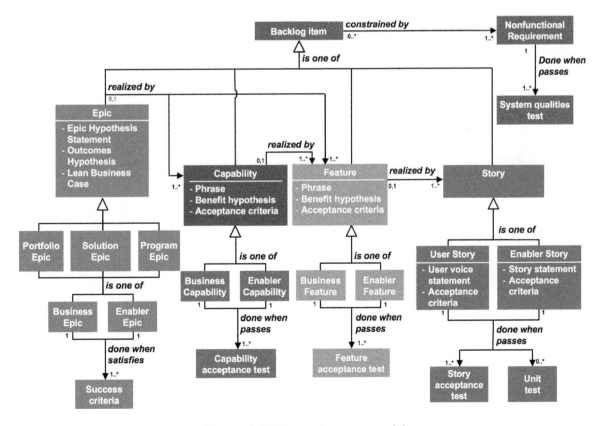

Figure 1. SAFe requirements model

These artifacts mostly replace the traditional system and requirements specifications with new paradigms based on Lean-Agile development. These examples are also intended to help teams avoid focusing on a point solution too early and avoid picking specific requirements and designs at the beginning of the learning process. Instead, they encourage teams to leave room for an emerging understanding based on intent, not specificity.

In addition, patterns and relationships for attributes, acceptance guidelines, and testing are included to support the NFRs that are also imposed on the world's most important systems.

Taken together, it's a comprehensive model, as Figure 1 suggests.

Most practitioners need only a portion of these items. For example, Agile Teams primarily employ user stories, story acceptance tests, and NFRs. However, each element is designed to provide the right amount of expression of behavior and testing at the various levels of SAFe.

This guidance chapter is intended for those consultants and SAFe experts who need to know how everything works together as a system—and for those who provide tooling around SAFe, where the semantics must be unambiguous.

If the model appears complex, that's because contemporary software and systems development at scale is complicated, even with Agile methods. If an element is not needed, then it need not be used. However, teams and programs that are building world-class enterprise solutions of the highest possible quality can probably apply most of these elements.

LEARN MORE

[1] http://www.goodreads.com/quotes/680161-essentially-all-models-are-wrong-but-some-are-useful.

Six SAFe Practices for S-Sized Teams

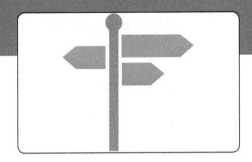

By Juha-Markus Aalto, Director Product Development,
Qentinel Group

SAFe has been designed to tackle the challenges of 'M to XXL' (medium to extra, extra large-sized) programs. Such programs consist of several Agile teams with approximately 50–100 people, or even as many as hundreds or thousands of practitioners.

Are Scrum and Kanban Enough?

But what about 'S-sized' (small) development organizations with just one or a few teams? Is there anything in SAFe for them—or are Scrum and Kanban just enough? The answer, of course, is it depends. Read on to find out what those things are.

If a pure software team mainly works on short programs, Scrum or Kanban would seem to be the way to go. However, while a full-scale use of SAFe practices, roles, and events wouldn't make sense for an S-sized project, a small team can certainly benefit from selected SAFe practices, at least in one of the following situations:

- **Strategic software product with a long lifespan** – The longer the lifespan of the software product, the more important it is to link software development explicitly to the strategy of the enterprise. Scrum provides little support for linking such development to the longer-than-sprint time span of strategic goals.

- **Dependencies with multiple non-software development teams** – It's common for a company that has a relatively small software team to develop solutions for other teams for integration. For example, software teams face this situation in a hardware or services company that has a decent portfolio of products but has just a moderate amount of software assets. Software companies whose products are heavily tailored for each customer, through delivery, have this multi-project challenge, too; all the dependent teams need to sync and agree on priorities and plans.

- **Necessity to invest in long-term capabilities such as DevOps** – Intense focus on delivering the next set of user stories, sprint by sprint, may result in great products, but it's all too easy to forget about investments in the team's own capabilities. We can all probably agree that investing in DevOps capabilities is worthwhile to achieve higher quality and faster time-to-market. However, becoming a true DevOps team doesn't happen overnight. It requires planning and executing, as you would do for any project. Changing the development technologies or modernizing the software architecture are other examples of long-term capability investments that are, in fact, true projects.

- **Expectation to scale from S to M size** – If a startup (a new business or internal business unit) expects strong growth in the near future, it makes sense to prepare for it up-front and use Agile approaches that scale when needed. Unless the foundational capabilities have been built from the ground up, however, scaling can be painfully slow, difficult, and challenging.

Applying Six SAFe Practices for S-Sized Teams

There are several ways to handle these four cases with pure Scrum or Kanban, but experience suggests that it's better to apply the following six practices of SAFe to deal with them more effectively (Figure 1):

1. Strategic themes shortlist the portfolio's strategic priorities and help the team align with them.

2. Program epics define the valuable key initiatives that the team needs to focus on so that the team can meaningfully prioritize their backlog.

3. The program Kanban shows the priorities and status of epics for the stakeholders.

4. Features elaborate epics, thereby providing a common language for the team and its stakeholders. Features are sized so that each fits in a single PI.

5. PI planning happens on a cadence, building a shared understanding of priorities and goals for the next 8–12 weeks (depending on the chosen cadence).

6. The innovation and planning iteration held at the end of each PI gives the team a well-deserved break from the urgent and allows it to spend some time on innovating and developing its capabilities.

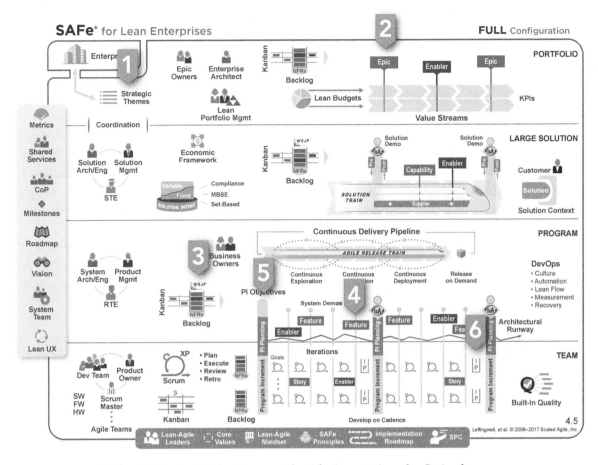

Figure 1. Scaled Agile Framework with six practices for S-sized teams

1. Strategic Themes

Companies big and small need a strategy to be successful. It's crucial to understand how a company's products create value—how they affect processes and the concrete benefits that customers gain. Product quality and user experience are equally important for long-term success. In addition to product strategy, a software development team needs to have an idea of how to continuously improve its engineering capabilities so as to increase its productivity and competitiveness.

While SAFe does not offer explicit tools to identify and build the strategy, it does have Strategic Themes. These themes are the business objectives that connect the team's portfolio to the strategy of the enterprise.

I've successfully used strategic themes during sprint (Iteration) planning to help ensure that the team works on strategically relevant items. Some tools, such as Visual Studio Team Services (VSTS), allow the tagging of work items with theme keywords, which further helps match backlog items with strategy. If a strategy exists, the extra step to identify the strategic themes requires minimal effort.

2. Program Epics

Scrum teams typically interpret epics just as really big user stories that don't fit in one sprint. SAFe defines epics as "initiatives significant enough to require analysis, using a lightweight business case and financial approval before implementation." The requirement to prepare a business case is not the point here. Rather, the important point is the need to ensure that an epic creates significant value and is feasible.

SAFe contains a rich hierarchy of epics to ensure sufficient scaling: Portfolio Epics, Large Solution Epics, and Program Epics. Portfolio and large solution epics are not relevant for small-scale development, but program epics are. Moreover, when a team works on a program epic linked to a strategic theme, the team's efforts contribute to something valuable and are aligned with the company's strategy.

Epics are useful for an S-sized team. They describe the ongoing key initiatives, those proposed by stakeholders for such an initiative, or those invented by the team itself. Software teams should also have some enabler epics in their backlog, in addition to business epics, to improve architecture or DevOps capabilities.

As 'significant-enough' initiatives tend to require significant investments of people, development of a lightweight business case is recommended for each epic before determining its approval for implementation or rejection. This process is particularly useful when the team has several stakeholders, and each initiative's priority and capacity need to be understood to make trade-off discussions meaningful.

3. Program Kanban

SAFe uses Kanban systems to manage initiatives at the portfolio, value stream, and program levels. The program level is sufficient for an S-sized team, and it's particularly useful if the team has several stakeholders offering their own epic proposals for implementation.

SAFe Program Kanban provides a simple and transparent process for capturing, analyzing, approving, and tracking epics. Completed epics will have passed through six states during this process: funnel, review, analysis, backlog, implementing, and done. For an S-sized team, the process to study epics can be extremely lightweight. Even so, these logical steps should definitely be present, so the Product Owner will know that the team can create the most value for the next time. Managing the key initiatives as epics in the program Kanban requires only moderate effort but offers transparency into the team's priorities at the program and portfolio levels.

4. Features

A Feature is not really a part of the core definition of Scrum; there are just product backlog items. Many Scrum teams borrow 'user stories' from Extreme Programming (XP), however; they label big stories as 'epics' and bunch related stories together as themes.

SAFe defines a feature as "a service provided by the system that addresses one or more user needs." Features elaborate epics and are defined by their benefits and acceptance criteria. Features are exactly what they sound like—the main functional characteristics of the proposed product. It can be difficult to explain the team's plan and progress to customers, members of dependent projects, or management through user stories alone. In contrast, features, as defined in SAFe, serve that purpose well. Their size is suitable and understandable, whereas user stories tend to become too small and numerous.

What makes features particularly useful is that they're sized to fit in one Program Increment (PI). As a result, they are concrete deliverables, facilitating clear communication with stakeholders.

5. PI Planning

Traditional Scrum teams work in a sprint cycle, which is where the planning and execution of work occur, with two weeks being the most popular duration for a sprint. More often than not, Scrum teams provide true visibility into their plan for just the next sprint, along with the backlog, which hints at the order in which the user stories might be implemented. Different variations of PowerPoint and Excel roadmaps are typically used to address the need for longer-than-the-next-sprint visibility. Backlog tools can help plan stories for future sprints, and some provide forecasts based on the team's velocity and the order of the backlog items.

In contrast, a program increment in SAFe is "a cadence-based interval for building and validating a full system increment, demonstrating value, and getting fast feedback." The duration of a PI is typically 8–12 weeks, or four to six sprints of 2 weeks. The last sprint of the PI is the Innovation and Planning (IP) Iteration, which is discussed in the next section.

Just as there is sprint planning in Scrum, so SAFe provides a planning practice for these super-sized iterations, known as PI Planning. In my own experience, I have facilitated SAFe PI planning, more or less by the book, for S-sized teams. The planning horizon of 8–12 weeks is short enough for useful planning and long enough for a team to achieve something really valuable: a set of potentially releasable features.

The PI planning event is a good use of time for all participants. The team gets an update of the bigger picture from the business, which includes the vision and priorities and develops an Agile plan. The stakeholders can contribute to planning directly. They also get an overview of all the work that the teams will do during the PI. For an S-sized team, the PI planning event can be condensed into one long day so that the investment of time is commensurate with the benefits.

6. Innovation and Planning Iteration

Thomas Edison described his innovation approach as "1 percent inspiration and 99 percent perspiration." In other words, innovations require time and hard work, not just a creative mind. In 'never-ending' continuous product development, there's a risk that a team just executes sprint after sprint without taking a break and becomes exhausted. Sprints tend to be hectic, and for an S-sized team, it's likely to be harder to find time to work on some more risky, seemingly lower-priority, yet innovative ideas.

SAFe doesn't have any silver-bullet solutions to magically free up lots of time for developers to innovate like Edison. Even so, its IP iteration, which occurs at the end of each PI, is something that teams should appreciate. No stories are planned for this iteration. Instead, teams have an opportunity to do some final system integration and testing activities, such as performance or security testing. The program-level retrospective, known as the Inspect and Adapt (I&A) event, is also held during the IP iteration. During the I&A workshop, the achievements of the PI are demoed to stakeholders, with this demo followed by a retrospective and problem-solving workshop. The IP iteration is also where we plan our next PI.

More importantly, as the name suggests, the IP iteration is the time for innovation. During this iteration, some teams do a hackathon or work on innovations or improvements in infrastructure, refactor code, or improve architecture. Last but definitely not least, the team gets a break from the hectic pace of software deliveries. Part of the break can be used for competence development, as an example.

Conclusion

Scrum and Kanban by themselves can be just enough for S-sized teams. However, in at least four circumstances, using select SAFe practices, along with Scrum or Kanban, is clearly more effective:

- Strategic software product with a long lifespan

- Dependencies with multiple non-software development teams

- Necessity to invest in long-term capabilities like DevOps

- Expectation to scale from S to M size

There are ways to handle these four cases with pure Scrum or Kanban, but experience suggests that it's better to apply the six practices of SAFe described here to deal with them more effectively.

Spikes

If we knew what we were doing, it wouldn't be called research.
—Albert Einstein

Spikes are a type of exploration Enabler Story in SAFe. Defined initially in Extreme Programming (XP), they represent activities such as research, design, investigation, exploration, and prototyping. Their purpose is to gain the knowledge necessary to reduce the risk of a technical approach, better understand a requirement, or increase the reliability of a story estimate.

Details

The Agile and Lean approaches value facts over speculation. When faced with a question, risk, or uncertainty, Agile Teams conduct small experiments before moving to implementation, rather than speculate about the outcome or jump to a Solution. Teams may use spikes in a variety of situations:

- Estimate new Features and Capabilities to analyze the implied behavior, providing insight into the approach used to split them into smaller, quantifiable pieces

- Perform feasibility analysis and other activities that help determine the viability of epics

- Conduct basic research to familiarize the team with a new technology or domain

- Gain confidence in a technical or functional approach, thereby reducing risk and uncertainty

Spikes involve creating a small program, research activity, or test that demonstrates some aspect of new functionality.

Technical and Functional Spikes

Like other stories, spikes are estimated and then demonstrated at the end of the Iteration. They also provide an agreed-upon protocol and workflow that Agile Release Trains (ARTs) use to help determine the viability of Epics. Spikes primarily come in two forms: technical and functional.

Functional spikes are used to analyze overall solution behavior and determine:

- How to break it down
- How to organize the work
- Where risk and complexity exist
- How to use insights to influence implementation decisions

Technical spikes are used to research various approaches in the solution domain. For example:

- Determine a build-versus-buy decision
- Evaluate the potential performance or load impact of a new user story
- Evaluate specific technical implementation approaches
- Develop confidence in the desired solution path

Some features and user stories may require both types of spikes. Here's an example:

"As a consumer, I want to see my daily energy use in a histogram so that I can quickly understand my past, current, and projected energy consumption."

In this case, a team might create both types of spikes:

- ***Technical* spike** – Research how long it takes to update a customer display to current usage, determining communication requirements, bandwidth, and whether to push or pull the data.
- ***Functional* spike** – Prototype a histogram in the web portal and get some user feedback on presentation size, style, and charting.

Guidelines for Spikes

Since spikes do not directly deliver user value, use them sparingly. The following guidelines apply.

Quantifiable, Demonstrable, and Acceptable

Like other stories, spikes are put in the Team Backlog, estimated, and sized to fit in an iteration. Spike results differ from a story in that spikes typically produce information rather than working code. They should develop only the data necessary to identify and size the stories that drive the results confidently.

The output of a spike is demonstrable, both to the team and to any other stakeholders. It shines a light into the research and architectural efforts and helps build collective ownership and shared responsibility for decision-making. The Product Owner accepts spikes that have been demoed and meet its acceptance criteria.

Timing of Spikes

Since they represent uncertainty in one or more potential stories, planning for both the spike and the resulting stories in the same iteration is sometimes risky. However, if the effort is small and straightforward, and if a quick solution is likely to be found, then it can be quite efficient to do both in the same iteration.

The Exception, Not the Rule

Every user story has uncertainty and risk—that's the nature of Agile development. The team discovers the right solution through discussion, collaboration, experimentation, and negotiation. Thus, in one sense, every user story contains spike-like activities to identify the technical and functional risks. The goal of an Agile team is to learn how to address the uncertainty inherent in each iteration. Spikes are critical when high uncertainty exists and when there are many unknowns.

LEARN MORE

[1] Leffingwell, Dean. *Agile Software Requirements: Lean Requirements Practices for Teams, Programs, and the Enterprise.* Addison Wesley, 2011.

Test-First

We never have enough time for testing, so let's just write the test first.

—Kent Beck

Test-First is a Built-In Quality practice derived from Extreme Programming (XP) that recommends building tests before writing code to improve delivery by focusing on the intended results.

Agile testing differs from the big-bang, deferred testing approach of traditional development. Instead, the code is developed and tested in small increments, often with the development of the test done ahead of writing the code. This way, tests help elaborate and better define the intended system behavior even before the system is coded. Quality is built in from the beginning. This just-in-time approach to the elaboration of the proposed system behavior also mitigates the need for the overly detailed requirement specifications and sign-offs that are often used in traditional software development to control quality. Even better, these tests, unlike conventionally written requirements, are automated wherever possible. Even if they're not automated, they still provide a definitive statement of what the system does, rather than a statement of early thoughts about what it was supposed to do.

Details

Agile testing is a continuous process that's integral to Lean and built-in quality. In other words, Agile Teams and Agile Release Trains (ARTs) can't go fast without high quality, and they can't achieve that goal without continuous testing and, wherever possible, testing first.

The Agile Testing Matrix

Brian Marick, an XP proponent and one of the authors of the Agile Manifesto, helped pioneer Agile testing by describing a matrix that guides the reasoning behind such tests. This approach was further developed in *Agile Testing* and extended for the scaling Agile paradigm in *Agile Software Requirements* [1, 2]. Figure 1 describes and extends Marick's original matrix with guidance on what to test and when.

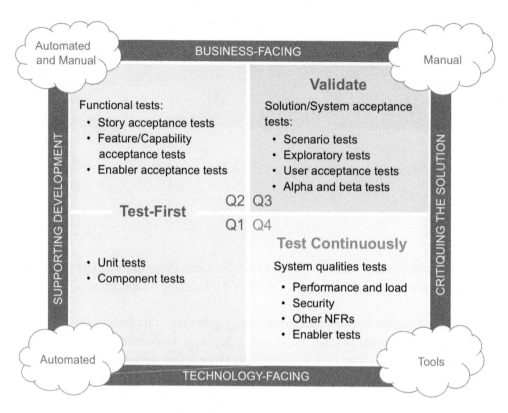

Figure 1. Agile testing matrix

The horizontal axis of the matrix contains business- or technology-facing tests. Business-facing tests are understandable by the user and written using business terminology. Technology-facing tests are written in the language of the developer and are used to evaluate whether the code delivers the behaviors the developer intended.

The vertical axis contains tests supporting development (evaluating internal code) or critiquing the solution (evaluating the system against the user's requirements).

Classification into the four quadrants (Q1–Q4) of the Agile testing matrix enables a comprehensive testing strategy that helps ensure quality:

- **Q1** – Contains unit and component tests. Tests are written to run before and after code changes to confirm that the system works as intended.

- **Q2** – Contains functional tests (user acceptance tests) for Stories, Features, and Capabilities to validate that they work the way the Product Owner (or Customer/user) intended. Feature- and capability-level acceptance tests confirm the aggregate behavior of many user stories. Teams automate these tests whenever possible and use manual ones only when there is no other choice.

- **Q3** – Contains system-level acceptance tests to validate that the behavior of the whole system meets the usability and functionality requirements, including scenarios that are often encountered in actual system use. These tests may include exploratory tests, user acceptance test, scenario-based tests, and final usability tests. Because they involve users and testers engaged in real or simulated deployment scenarios, the Q3 tests are often manual. They're frequently the final system validation before delivery of the system to the end user.

- **Q4** – Contains system qualities testing to verify the system meets its Nonfunctional Requirements (NFRs), as exhibited in part by Enabler tests. These tests are typically supported by a suite of automated testing tools, such as those examining load and performance, designed specifically for this purpose. Since any system changes can violate conformance with NFRs, they must be run continuously, or at least whenever it's practical.

Quadrants 1 and 2 in Figure 1 define the functionality of the system. Test-first practices include both Test-Driven Development (TDD) and Acceptance Test–Driven Development (ATDD). Both involve creating the test before developing the code, and both use test automation to support continuous integration, team velocity, and development effectiveness. The next section describes Q1 and Q2. The companion chapters, Release on Demand and Nonfunctional Requirements, describe Q3 and Q4, respectively.

Test-Driven (Test-First) Development

Beck and others have defined a set of XP practices under the umbrella label of TDD [3]:

- Write the test first, which ensures that the developer understands the required behavior.

- Run the test and watch it fail. Because there is no code yet, this might seem silly initially, but it accomplishes two useful objectives: It verifies that the test works, including its harnesses, and it demonstrates how the system will behave if the code is incorrect.

- Write the minimum amount of code needed to pass the test. If it fails, rework the code or the test until it routinely passes.

In XP, this practice was designed primarily to operate in the context of unit tests, which are developer-written tests (and code) that evaluate the classes and methods used. Unit tests are considered a form of 'white-box testing,' because they test the internal workings of the system and the various code paths. In pair work, two people collaborate to develop the code and tests simultaneously; this practice provides a built-in peer review, which helps assure high quality. Even when not developed through pair work, the tests ensure that another set of eyes review the code. Developers often refactor the code to pass the test as simply and elegantly as possible, which is one of the main reasons that SAFe relies on TDD.

Unit Tests

Most TDD involves unit testing, which prevents quality assurance (QA) and test personnel from spending most of their time finding and reporting on code-level bugs. Instead, these personnel can focus on system-level testing challenges, where more complex behaviors are identified based on the interactions between unit code modules. The open source community has built unit testing frameworks to cover most languages, including Java, C, C#, C++, XML, HTTP, and Python. In fact, unit-testing frameworks are available for most coding constructs a developer is most likely to encounter. They provide a harness for the development and maintenance of unit tests and for automatically executing them against the system.

Because unit tests are written before or concurrently with the code, and their frameworks include test execution automation, unit testing can occur within the same Iteration. Moreover, the unit test frameworks hold and manage the accumulated unit tests. As a result, regression testing automation for unit tests is mostly free for the team. Unit testing is a cornerstone of software agility, and any investment made in comprehensive unit testing usually improves the organization's quality and productivity.

Component Tests

Similarly, teams use tests to evaluate larger-scale components of the system. Many of these components extend into multiple architectural layers, where they provide services needed by features or other modules. Testing tools and practices for implementing component tests vary. For example, testing frameworks can hold complicated unit tests written in the framework's language (e.g., Java, C, C#). As a result, many teams use their unit testing frameworks to build component tests. They may not even think of them as separate functions, as they are merely part of the testing strategy. In other cases, developers may incorporate other testing tools or write entirely customized tests in any language or environment that supports testing of the broader system behaviors. These tests, which are automated, serve as a primary defense against unanticipated consequences of refactoring and new code.

Acceptance Test–Driven Development

Quadrant 2 of the Agile testing matrix shows that the test-first philosophy applies to testing of stories, features, and capabilities just as it does to unit testing—an approach called Acceptance Test–Driven Development (ATDD). Whether ATDD is adopted formally or informally, many teams find it more efficient to write the acceptance test first, before developing the code. After all, the goal is to have the whole system work as intended.

Ken Pugh notes that the emphasis with this approach is more on expressing requirements in unambiguous terms than on focusing on the test per se [4]. He further observes that there are three alternative labels for this detailing process: ATDD, Specification by Example (SBE), and Behavior-Driven Design (BDD). Although these approaches actually have some slight differences, they all emphasize understanding requirements before implementation. In particular, SBE suggests that Product Owners should provide realistic examples instead of abstract statements, as they often do not write the acceptance tests themselves.

Whether ATDD is viewed as a form of requirements expression or as a test, the understanding is that the result is the same. Acceptance tests serve to record the decisions made in the conversation between the team and the Product Owner so that the team understands the specifics of the intended behavior the story represents. (See the 3Cs in the "Writing Good Stories" section of the Story chapter, referring to the card, conversation, and confirmation.)

Functional Tests
Story acceptance tests confirm that each new user story implemented delivers its intended behavior during the iteration. If these stories work as intended, then it's likely that each increment of software will ultimately satisfy the needs of the users.

During a Program Increment (PI), feature and capability acceptance testing are performed, using similar tests. The difference is that capability tests operate at the next level of abstraction, typically showing how several stories work together to deliver a more significant amount of value to the user. Of course, multiple feature acceptance tests can be associated with a more complex feature. The same goes for stories, with tests being needed to verify that the system works as intended for all levels of abstraction.

The following are characteristics of functional tests:

- Written in the language of the business

- Developed in a conversation between developers, testers, and the Product Owner

- 'Black-box tested' to verify only the outputs of the system meet its conditions of satisfaction, without concern for the internal workings of the system

- Run in the same iteration as the code development

Although everyone can write tests, the Product Owner as Business Owner/customer proxy is responsible for the efficacy of the tests. If a story does not pass its test, the teams get no credit for that story, and it's carried over into the next iteration to fix either the test or the code.

Features, capabilities, and stories must pass one or more acceptance tests to meet their Definition of Done. Stories realize the intended features and capabilities, and multiple tests may be associated with a particular work item.

Automating Acceptance Testing
Because acceptance tests run at a level above the code, a variety of approaches have been proposed for executing them, including handling them as manual tests. Manual tests tend to pile up very quickly: The faster you go, the faster they grow, and then the slower you go. Eventually, the amount of manual work required to run regression testing slows down the team and causes delays in value delivery.

To avoid this pattern, teams must automate most of their acceptance tests. They can use a variety of tools for this purpose, including the target programming language (e.g., Perl, PHP, Python, Java) or natural language as supported by specific testing frameworks, such as Cucumber. Alternatively, they may use table formats such as the *Framework for Integrated Testing* (FIT). The preferred approach is to use a higher level of abstraction that works against the business logic of the application, which prevents the presentation layer or other implementation details from blocking testing.

Acceptance Test Template/Checklist

An ATDD checklist can help the team consider a simple list of things to do, review, and discuss each time a new story appears. *Agile Software Requirements* provides an example of a story acceptance-testing checklist [2].

LEARN MORE

[1] Crispin, Lisa, and Janet Gregory. *Agile Testing: A Practical Guide for Testers and Agile Teams.* Addison-Wesley, 2009.

[2] Leffingwell, Dean. *Agile Software Requirements: Lean Requirements Practices for Teams, Programs, and the Enterprise.* Addison-Wesley, 2011.

[3] Beck, Kent. *Test-Driven Development.* Addison-Wesley, 2003.

[4] Pugh, Ken. *Lean-Agile Acceptance Test-Driven Development: Better Software Through Collaboration.* Addison-Wesley, 2011.

The Role of PI Objectives

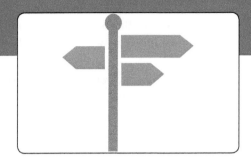

By Eric Willeke, SAFe Fellow

Introduction

The role of PI Objectives is often misunderstood by teams new to PI Planning. They struggle at first to understand the difference between Team PI objectives and Features. SAFe does not provide a lot of guidance on the intent behind the usage of PI objectives, and they are often misunderstood or misinterpreted. In my field practice, I've come to really value them, so I wanted to take the time to document my perspective in this guidance chapter.

PI objectives support development in the following ways:

- Validate understanding of intent

- Focus alignment on outcomes rather than process

- Summarize data into meaningful and steerable information

Without an appreciation of these qualities, it's quite easy to view PI objectives as nothing more than a shorthand list of features to be delivered.

Validate Understanding of Intent

Two of SAFe's four core values are Program Execution and Alignment, and one of the key Lean principles underlying SAFe is decentralized decision-making. Most of the PI planning event agenda focuses on supporting these values by conveying a clear understanding of the desired goals and outcomes for the Agile Release Train (ART), then getting out of the way and allowing practitioners to achieve these goals effectively. We place governing structures and other feedback loops into play through the Product Management and Product Owner roles, but we generally support the teams' ownership of the details in pursuit of the larger business outcomes.

One of the key risks that has plagued every software development approach is ensuring that the initial intent (scope) was clearly understood and articulated by the stakeholders, transmitted effectively to the development team, and interpreted by all parties involved in the same way. In SAFe, this path also includes the extra steps of translating information from the end users to the Business Owner (who requires this capability), then onward to Product Management (for the release train implementing the capability.)

SAFe's use of PI objectives provides a unique tool to create an immediate feedback loop from the teams back to the Business Owners, allowing a quick validation of the teams' grasp of the desired outcomes. In short, we pose the following challenge to the teams:

> Can you concisely convey, in words that the Business Owner understands, the essence of the value sought by implementing this set of features?

If a team cannot do this in a clear way by the end of planning, are we comfortable investing more than $100,000 to pursue these goals over the next 10 weeks? By forcing the teams to summarize the intent and the outcomes they believe the Business Owner wants to achieve, we close the loop of understanding and drive crucial conversations that expose these misunderstandings. This, in turn, enables a much tighter form of alignment that transcends the written language of the feature and is amplified by the tacit understanding gained between the team and the Business Owner.

Focus on Outcomes Rather Than Process

The second hidden value of PI objectives is that they help the team shift the focus away from the feature language and onto the desired business outcomes. Features and acceptance criteria are amazing tools to help understand, capture, and collaborate around the work that needs to be done to iterate the Solution to the next level, but it's all too easy to get caught up in 'finishing the features' and miss the overall goals hidden inside them. The core question becomes:

> Is our goal to complete the listed features, or is our goal to provide the outcomes desired by those features? In other words, if we could provide the same value with half the amount of work and without building all of the features, would that be acceptable?

My experience shows that the language of features frequently steers the team into overlooking creative, valid, and architecturally sound solutions because someone outside the team already provided a preconceived notion of how that value should be provided. The closer understanding of the intent illuminated through direct conversations with the Business Owner occasionally results in the teams offering new perspectives to the architects and product managers and quickly finding ways to apply their expertise more effectively.

Summarize Data into Steerable Information

Finally, there's a simple 'comprehension' aspect to PI objectives that can prove particularly valuable. In my own work, I've come to accept that no large group will reliably read every item in a list if that list exceeds 5–7 items. Given that I see small trains with only four teams consistently take on 10 features per PI, while large trains may take on as many as 40 features per PI, it's likely that no one except the product manager reads every single feature carefully—and certainly no one outside the train has read every feature. In the face of this reality, I deeply value the summary of intent that the Program PI objectives provide, and the subsequent use of those objectives as a key for providing clear evidence of progress both within and beyond the train.

Ideally, teams should fully and transparently share the features they intend to complete and their progress against them using a percentage of complete mindset. Nevertheless, it can be valuable to summarize the 5–7 key objectives per train and report on progress against them. This is especially the case when four or more trains are working with the same value stream, aggregating their work in a shared System Demo to a senior executive audience every two weeks. Quite simply, you need a more compact way to convey the same information to augment the quantitative reporting.

A Bit of Philosophy

As I captured these thoughts, I was reminded of a key difference between release trains, and it strongly impacts the degree of value placed on the 'focus on outcomes.' I tend to see release trains fall to one of two extremes: Either they drive the vast majority of their work (85 to 95 percent) through portfolio epics, thereby reducing the autonomy of the trains, or they drive the vast majority of their work as features, reserving epics for the 5 to 10 percent of work that truly cuts across trains. While neither of these approaches is fundamentally wrong, a majority of companies solving the big 'system of systems' engineering problems, which strongly favor an epic-driven approach, will find that SAFe for Lean Software and Systems Engineering will be a more effective approach.

At the same time, the mindset of epic-driven development is serving the same role for steering at scale that 'waterfalling iterations' served for teams. Namely, it provides a way for organizations to avoid learning those crucial lessons about how to work together in ways we never had to in the past.

Part 10
Glossary

scaledagileframework.com/**glossary**

SAFe Glossary

A

Agile Architecture

Agile Architecture is a set of values and practices that support the active evolution of the design and architecture of a system while implementing new system capabilities.

Agile Release Train (ART)

The Agile Release Train is a long-lived team of Agile teams, which, along with other stakeholders, develops and delivers solutions incrementally, using a series of fixed-length Iterations within a Program Increment (PI) timebox. The ART aligns teams to a common business and technology mission.

Agile Team

The SAFe Agile Team is a cross-functional group of 5 to 11 people who have the responsibility to define, build, test, and where applicable deploy some element of Solution value—all in a short Iteration timebox. Specifically, the SAFe Agile Team incorporates the Dev Team, Scrum Master, and Product Owner roles.

Architectural Runway

The Architectural Runway consists of the existing code, components, and technical infrastructure needed to implement near-term features without excessive redesign and delay.

B

Built-In Quality

Built-In Quality practices ensure that each Solution element, at every increment, meets appropriate quality standards throughout development.

Business Owner

Business Owners are a small group of stakeholders who have the primary business and technical responsibility for governance, compliance, and return on investment (ROI) for a Solution developed by an Agile Release Train (ART). They are key stakeholders on the ART who must evaluate fitness for use and actively participate in certain ART events.

C

Capability

A Capability is a higher-level solution behavior that typically spans multiple ARTs. Capabilities are sized and split into multiple features to facilitate their implementation in a single PI.

CapEx and OpEx

Capital Expenses (CapEx) and Operating Expenses (OpEx) describe Lean-Agile financial accounting practices in a Value Stream budget. In some cases, CapEx may include capitalized labor associated with the development of intangible assets—such as software, intellectual property, and patents.

Communities of Practice (CoPs)

Communities of Practice are organized groups of people who have a common interest in a specific technical or business domain. They collaborate regularly to share information, improve their skills, and actively work on advancing the general knowledge of the domain.

Compliance

Compliance refers to a strategy and a set of activities and artifacts that allow teams to apply Lean-Agile development methods to build systems that have the highest possible quality, while simultaneously assuring they meet any regulatory, industry, or other relevant standards.

Continuous Delivery Pipeline

The Continuous Delivery (CD) Pipeline (also referred to as the 'pipeline') represents the workflows, activities, and automation needed to provide a continuous release of value to the end user.

Continuous Deployment (CD)

Continuous Deployment is the process that takes validated Features from Continuous Integration and deploys them into the production environment, where they are tested and readied for release. It is the third element in the four-part Continuous Delivery Pipeline of Continuous Exploration (CE), Continuous Integration (CI), Continuous Deployment, and Release on Demand.

Continuous Exploration (CE)

Continuous Exploration is the process of continually exploring the market and user needs and defining a Vision, Roadmap, and set of Features that address those needs. It is the first element in the four-part Continuous Delivery Pipeline, preceding Continuous Integration (CI) Continuous Deployment (CD), and Release on Demand.

Continuous Integration (CI)

Continuous Integration is the process of taking features from the Program Backlog and developing, testing, integrating, and validating them in a staging environment where they are ready for deployment and release.

Core Values

The four Core Values of alignment, built-in quality, transparency, and program execution represent the fundamental beliefs that are key to SAFe's effectiveness. These guiding principles help dictate behavior and action for everyone who participates in a SAFe portfolio.

Customer

Customers are the ultimate buyer of every Solution. They are an integral part of the Lean-Agile development process and Value Stream and have specific responsibilities in SAFe.

D

Dev Team

The Dev Team is a subset of the Agile Team. It consists of the dedicated professionals who can develop and test a Story, Feature, or component. The Dev Team typically includes software developers and testers, engineers, and other dedicated specialists required to complete a vertical slice of functionality.

DevOps

DevOps is a mindset, a culture, and a set of technical practices. It provides communication, integration, automation, and close cooperation among all the people needed to plan, develop, test, deploy, release, and maintain a Solution.

Develop on Cadence

Develop on Cadence is an essential method for managing the inherent variability of systems development in a flow-based system, by making sure important events and activities occur on a regular, predictable schedule.

E

Economic Framework

The Economic Framework is a set of decision rules that align everyone to the financial objectives of the Solution and guide the economic decision-making process. It contains four primary constructs: Lean Budgets, Epic funding and governance, decentralized decision-making, and job sequencing based on the Cost of Delay (CoD).

Enabler

Enablers support the activities needed to extend the Architectural Runway to provide future business functionality. These include exploration, infrastructure, compliance, and architecture development. Enablers are captured in the various backlogs and occur at all levels of the Framework.

Enterprise

The Enterprise represents the business entity to which each SAFe portfolio belongs.

Enterprise Architect

The Enterprise Architect promotes adaptive design and engineering practices and drives architectural initiatives for the portfolio. The Enterprise Architect also facilitates the reuse of ideas, components, services, and proven patterns across various solutions in a portfolio.

Epic

An Epic is a container for a Solution development initiative large enough to require analysis, the definition of a Minimum Viable Product (MVP), and financial approval prior to implementation. Implementation occurs over multiple Program Increments (PIs) and follows the Lean Startup 'build–measure–learn' cycle.

Epic Owner

Epic Owners are responsible for coordinating portfolio Epics through the Portfolio Kanban system. They define the epic, its Minimum Viable Product (MVP), and Lean business case, and, when approved, facilitate the epic's implementation.

Essential SAFe

The Essential SAFe configuration is the heart of the Framework and is the simplest starting point for implementation. The basic building block for all other SAFe configurations, it describes the most critical elements needed to realize the majority of the Framework's benefits.

F

Feature

A Feature is a service that fulfills a stakeholder need. Each feature includes a benefit hypothesis and acceptance criteria and is sized or split as necessary to be delivered by a single Agile Release Train (ART) in a Program Increment (PI).

Foundation

The Foundation contains the supporting principles, values, mindset, implementation guidance, and leadership roles needed to deliver value successfully at scale.

Full SAFe

The Full SAFe configuration is the most comprehensive version of the Framework. It supports enterprises that build and maintain large integrated solutions, which require hundreds of people or more, and includes all levels of SAFe: Team, Program, Large Solution, and Portfolio. In the largest enterprises, multiple instances of various SAFe configurations may be required.

GHI

Innovation and Planning Iteration

The Innovation and Planning (IP) Iteration occurs every Program Increment (PI) and serves multiple purposes. It acts as an estimating buffer for meeting PI Objectives and provides dedicated time for innovation, continuing education, PI Planning, and Inspect and Adapt (I&A) events.

Inspect and Adapt (I&A)

The Inspect and Adapt event is held at the end of each Program Increment (PI). During this significant event, the current state of the Solution is demonstrated and evaluated by the train. Teams then reflect and identify improvement backlog items via a structured, problem-solving workshop.

Iteration

Iterations are the basic building block of Agile development. Each iteration is a standard, fixed-length timebox, during which Agile Teams deliver incremental value in the form of working, tested software and systems. The recommended duration of the timebox is two weeks. However, one to four weeks is acceptable, depending on the business context.

Iteration Execution

Iteration Execution is how Agile Teams manage their work throughout the Iteration timebox, resulting in a high-quality, working, tested system increment.

Iteration Goal

Iteration Goals are a high-level summary of the business and technical goals that the Agile Team agrees to accomplish in an Iteration. They are vital to coordinating an Agile Release Train (ART) as a self-organizing, self-managing team of teams.

Iteration Planning

Iteration Planning is an event in which all team members determine how much of the Team Backlog they can commit to delivering during an upcoming Iteration. The team summarizes the work as a set of committed Iteration Goals.

Iteration Retrospective

The Iteration Retrospective is a regular meeting where Agile Team members discuss the results of the Iteration, review their practices, and identify ways to improve.

Iteration Review

The Iteration Review is a cadence-based event, where each team inspects the increment at the end of every Iteration to assess progress and then adjusts its backlog for the next iteration.

JKL

Large Solution Level

The Large Solution Level contains the roles, artifacts, and processes needed to build large and complex solutions. This includes a stronger focus on capturing requirements in the Solution Intent, the coordination of multiple Agile Release Trains (ARTs) and Suppliers, and the need to ensure compliance with regulations and standards.

Large Solution SAFe

The Large Solution SAFe configuration is appropriate for developing the largest and most complex Solutions that typically require multiple Agile Release Trains and Suppliers, but do not require Portfolio-Level considerations. It is commonly used in industries like aerospace and defense, automotive, and government, where the large solution—not portfolio governance—is the primary concern.

Lean-Agile Leaders

Lean-Agile Leaders are lifelong learners who are responsible for the successful adoption of SAFe and the results it delivers. They empower and help teams build better systems by learning, exhibiting, teaching, and coaching SAFe's Lean-Agile principles and practices.

Lean-Agile Mindset

The Lean-Agile Mindset is the combination of beliefs, assumptions, and actions of SAFe leaders and practitioners who embrace the concepts of the Agile Manifesto and Lean thinking. It serves as the personal, intellectual, and leadership foundation for adopting and applying SAFe principles and practices.

Lean and Agile Principles

SAFe is based on nine immutable, underlying Lean and Agile Principles. These tenets and economic concepts inspire and inform the roles and practices of SAFe.

Lean Budgets

Lean Budgets is a set of practices that minimize overhead by funding and empowering Value Streams rather than projects while maintaining financial and fitness-for-use governance. This is achieved through objective evaluation of working systems, active management of Epic investments, and dynamic budget adjustments.

Lean Portfolio Management (LPM)

The Lean Portfolio Management function has the highest level of decision-making and financial accountability for the products and Solutions in a SAFe portfolio.

Lean User Experience (Lean UX)

Lean User Experience design is a mindset, a culture, and a process that embraces Lean-Agile methods. It implements functionality in minimum viable increments and determines success by measuring results against a benefit hypothesis.

M

Metric

Metrics are agreed-upon measures used to evaluate how well the organization is progressing toward the Portfolio, Large Solution, Program, and Team's business and technical objectives.

Milestone

Milestones are used to track progress toward a specific goal or event. There are three types of SAFe milestones: Program Increment (PI), fixed-date, and learning milestones.

Model-Based Systems Engineering (MBSE)

Model-Based Systems Engineering is the practice of developing a set of related system models that help define, design, and document a system under development. These models provide an efficient way to explore, update, and communicate system aspects to stakeholders, while significantly reducing or eliminating dependence on traditional documents.

N

Nonfunctional Requirements (NFRs)

Nonfunctional Requirements define system attributes such as security, reliability, performance, maintainability, scalability, and usability. They serve as constraints or restrictions on the design of the system across the different backlogs.

OP

Portfolio Backlog

The Portfolio Backlog is the highest-level backlog in SAFe. It provides a holding area for upcoming business and enabler Epics intended to create a comprehensive set of Solutions, which provides the competitive differentiation and operational improvements needed to address the Strategic Themes and facilitate business success.

Portfolio Kanban

The Portfolio Kanban is a method used to visualize, manage, and analyze the prioritization and flow of portfolio Epics from ideation to implementation and completion.

Portfolio Level

The Portfolio Level contains the principles, practices, and roles needed to initiate and govern a set of development Value Streams. It is where strategy and investment funding are defined for value streams and their Solutions. This level also provides Agile portfolio operations and Lean governance for the people and resources needed to deliver solutions.

Portfolio SAFe

The Portfolio SAFe configuration helps align portfolio execution to the enterprise strategy, by organizing Agile development around the flow of value, through one or more Value Streams. It provides business agility through principles and practices for portfolio strategy and investment funding, Agile portfolio operations, and Lean governance.

Pre-and Post-PI Planning

Pre- and Post–Program Increment (PI) Planning events are used to prepare for, and follow up after, PI Planning for Agile Release Trains (ARTs) and Suppliers in a Solution Train.

Product Management

Product Management has content authority for the Program Backlog. These managers are responsible for identifying Customer needs, prioritizing Features, guiding the work through the Program Kanban, and developing the program's Vision and Roadmap.

Product Owner (PO)

The Product Owner is a member of the Agile Team responsible for defining Stories and prioritizing the Team Backlog to streamline the execution of program priorities while maintaining the conceptual and technical integrity of the Features or components for the team.

Program Backlog

The Program Backlog is the holding area for upcoming Features, which are intended to address user needs and deliver business benefits for a single Agile Release Train (ART). It also contains the enabler features necessary to build the Architectural Runway.

Program Increment (PI)

A Program Increment is a timebox during which an Agile Release Train (ART) delivers incremental value in the form of working, tested software and systems. PIs are typically 8–12 weeks long. The most common pattern for a PI is four development Iterations, followed by one Innovation and Planning (IP) Iteration.

Program Increment (PI) Planning

Program Increment Planning is a cadence-based, face-to-face event that serves as the heartbeat of the Agile Release Train (ART), aligning all the teams on the ART to a shared mission and Vision.

Program Kanban

The Program and Solution Kanban systems are a method to visualize and manage the flow of Features and Capabilities from ideation to analysis, implementation, and release through the Continuous Delivery Pipeline.

Program Level

The Program Level contains the roles and activities needed to continuously deliver solutions via an Agile Release Train (ART).

QR

Refactoring

Refactoring is the activity of improving the internal structure or operation of a code or component without changing its external behavior.

Release on Demand

Release on Demand is the process by which Features deployed into production are released incrementally or immediately to Customers based on market demand.

Release Train Engineer (RTE)

The Release Train Engineer is a servant leader and coach for the Agile Release Train (ART). The RTE's major responsibilities are to facilitate the ART events and processes and to assist the teams in delivering value. RTEs communicate with stakeholders, escalate impediments, help manage risk, and drive relentless improvement.

Roadmap

The Roadmap is a schedule of events and Milestones that communicate planned Solution deliverables over a timeline. It includes commitments for the planned, upcoming Program Increment (PI) and offers visibility into the deliverables forecasted for the next few PIs.

S

SAFe Implementation Roadmap

The SAFe Implementation Roadmap consists of an overview graphic and a 12-article series that describes a strategy and an ordered set of activities that have proved effective in successfully implementing SAFe.

SAFe Program Consultant (SPC)

SAFe Program Consultants are change agents who combine their technical knowledge of SAFe with an intrinsic motivation to improve the company's software and systems development processes. They play a critical role in successfully implementing SAFe. SPCs come from numerous internal or external roles, including business and technology leaders, portfolio/program/project managers, process leads, architects, analysts, and consultants.

Scrum Master

Scrum Masters are servant leaders and coaches for an Agile Team. They help educate the team in Scrum, Extreme Programming (XP), Kanban, and SAFe, ensuring that the agreed Agile process is being followed. They also help remove impediments and foster an environment for high-performing team dynamics, continuous flow, and relentless improvement.

ScrumXP

ScrumXP is a lightweight process to deliver value for cross-functional, self-organized teams within SAFe. It combines the power of Scrum project management practices with Extreme Programming (XP) practices.

Set-Based Design (SBD)

Set-Based Design is a practice that keeps requirements and design options flexible for as long as possible during the development process. Instead of choosing a single point solution up-front, SBD identifies and simultaneously explores multiple options, eliminating poorer choices over time. It enhances flexibility in the design process by committing to technical solutions only after validating assumptions, which produces better economic results.

Shared Services

Shared Services represents the specialty roles, people, and services that are necessary for the success of an Agile Release Train (ART) or Solution Train but that cannot be dedicated to the train on a full-time basis.

Solution

Solutions are the products, services, or systems delivered to the Customer, whether internal or external to the Enterprise; they are produced by Value Streams.

Solution Architect/Engineer

The Solution Architect/Engineering role represents an individual or small team that defines a shared technical and architectural vision for the Solution under development. Working closely with the Agile Release Train (ARTs) and Solution Train, this role participates in determining the system, subsystems, and interfaces; validates technology assumptions; and evaluates alternatives.

Solution Backlog

The Solution Backlog is the holding area for upcoming Capabilities and Enablers, each of which can span multiple ARTs and is intended to advance the Solution and build its Architectural Runway.

Solution Context

The Solution Context identifies critical aspects of the operational environment for a Solution. It provides an essential understanding of requirements, usage, installation, operation, and support of the solution itself. Solution context heavily influences opportunities and constraints for releasing on demand.

Solution Demo

The Solution Demo is the event in which the results of development efforts from the Solution Train are integrated, evaluated, and made visible to Customers and other stakeholders.

Solution Management

Solution Management has content authority for the Solution Backlog. These managers work with customers to understand their needs, prioritize Capabilities, create the Solution Vision and Roadmap, define requirements, and guide work through the Solution Kanban.

Solution Train

The Solution Train is the organizational construct used to build large and complex Solutions that require the coordination of multiple Agile Release Trains (ARTs), as well as the contributions of Suppliers. It aligns ARTs with a shared business and technology mission using the solution Vision, Backlog, and Roadmap, and an aligned Program Increment (PI).

Spanning Palette

The Spanning Palette contains various roles and artifacts that may be applicable to a specific team, program, large solution, or portfolio context. A key element of SAFe's flexibility and configurability, the spanning palette permits organizations to apply only the elements needed for their configuration.

Spike

Spikes are a type of exploration Enabler Story in SAFe. Defined initially in Extreme Programming (XP), they represent activities such as research, design, investigation, exploration, and prototyping. Their purpose is to gain the knowledge necessary to reduce the risk of a technical approach, better understand a requirement, or increase the reliability of a story estimate.

Story

Stories are short descriptions of a small piece of desired functionality, written in the user's language. Agile Teams implement small, vertical slices of system functionality and are sized so they can be completed in a single Iteration.

Supplier

A Supplier is an internal or external organization that develops and delivers components, subsystems, or services that help Solution Trains provide Solutions to their Customers.

System Demo

The System Demo is a significant event that provides an integrated view of new Features for the most recent Iteration delivered by all the teams in the Agile Release Train (ART). Each demo gives ART stakeholders an objective measure of progress during a Program Increment (PI).

System Team

The System Team is a specialized Agile Team that assists in building and using the Agile development environment, including Continuous Integration, test automation, and Continuous Deployment. The System Team supports the integration of assets from Agile teams, performs end-to-end Solution testing where necessary, and assists with deployment and release.

T

Team Backlog

The Team Backlog contains user and Enabler Stories that originate from the Program Backlog, as well as stories that arise locally from the team's local context. It may include other work items as well, representing all the things a team needs to do to advance its portion of the system.

Team Kanban

Team Kanban is a method that helps teams facilitate the flow of value by visualizing workflow, establishing Work in Process (WIP) limits, measuring throughput, and continuously improving their process.

Team Level

The Team Level contains the roles, activities, events, and processes that Agile Teams build and deliver value in the context of the Agile Release Train (ART).

Test-First

Test-First is a Built-In Quality practice derived from Extreme Programming (XP) that recommends building tests before writing code to improve delivery by focusing on the intended results.

UV

Value Stream

Value Streams represent the series of steps that an organization uses to build Solutions that provide a continuous flow of value to a Customer. SAFe value streams are used to define and realize Portfolio-Level business objectives and organize Agile Release Trains (ARTs) to deliver value more rapidly.

Value Stream Coordination

Value Stream Coordination provides guidance to manage dependencies and exploit the opportunities in a portfolio.

Vision

The Vision is a description of the future state of the Solution under development. It reflects Customer and stakeholder needs, as well as the Feature and Capabilities proposed to meet those needs.

WXYZ

Weighted Shortest Job First (WSJF)

Weighted Shortest Job First (WSJF) is a prioritization model used to sequence jobs (e.g., Features, Capabilities, and Epics) to produce maximum economic benefit. In SAFe, WSJF is estimated as the Cost of Delay (CoD) divided by job size.

Bibliography

- Anderson, David. *Kanban: Successful Evolutionary Change for Your Technology Business.* Blue Hole Press, 2010.

- Aoki, Katsuki, and Thomas Taro Lennerfors. "New, Improved Keiretsu." *Harvard Business Review.* September 2013.

- "Backlog." Merriam Webster. https://www.merriam-webster.com/dictionary/backlog.

- Bain, Scott. *Emergent Design: The Evolutionary Nature of Professional Software Development.* Addison-Wesley, 2008.

- Beck, Kent. *Extreme Programming Explained: Embrace Change.* Addison-Wesley, 2000.

- Beck, Kent. *Test-Driven Development.* Addison-Wesley, 2003.

- Beck, Kent, and Cynthia Andres. *Extreme Programming Explained: Embrace Change* (2nd ed.). Addison-Wesley, 2004.

- Bloomberg, Jason. "Fixing Scheduling with Agile at the VA." *Forbes.* October 23, 2014.

- Bloomberg, Jason. *The Agile Architecture Revolution.* Wiley, 2013.

- Bradford, David L., and Allen Cohen. *Managing for Excellence: The Leadership Guide to Developing High Performance in Contemporary Organizations.* John Wiley and Sons, 1997.

- Bucking, Marcus, and Ashley Goodall. "Reinventing Performance Management." *Harvard Business Review,* April 2015.

- Carter, B. "Gallup via Employee Engagement and Loyalty Statistics." 2014.

- Cockburn, Alistair. "Using Both Incremental and Iterative Development." *STSC CrossTalk* 21, 2008.

- Cohn, Mike. *Agile Estimating and Planning.* Robert C. Martin Series. Prentice Hall, 2005.

- Cohn, Mike. *Succeeding with Agile: Software Development Using Scrum.* Addison-Wesley, 2009.

- Cohn, Mike. *User Stories Applied: For Agile Software Development.* Addison-Wesley, 2004.

- Collins, Jim, and William Lazier. *Beyond Entrepreneurship: Turning Your Business into a Great and Enduring Company.* Prentice Hall, 1992.

- Connor, Catherine. "Top 10 Pitfalls of Agile Capitalization." *CA,* February 2016.

- Coplien, James, and Gertrud Bjørnvig. *Lean Architecture for Agile Software Development.* Wiley, 2010.

- Crispin, Lisa, and Janet Gregory. *Agile Testing: A Practical Guide for Testers and Agile Teams*. Addison-Wesley, 2009.

- Cunningham, Lillian. "In Big Move, Accenture Will Get Rid of Annual Performance Reviews and Rankings." *The Washington Post*, July 21, 2015.

- Deming, W. Edwards. *Out of the Crisis*. MIT Center for Advanced Educational Services, 1982.

- Deming, W. Edwards. *The New Economics*. MIT Press, 1994.

- Dent, Millie. "Why Employee Performance Reviews Are So Old School." *The Fiscal Times*, July 2015.

- Derby, Esther, and Diana Larson. *Agile Retrospectives: Making Good Teams Great*. Pragmatic Bookshelf, 2006.

- Drucker, Peter F. *The Essential Drucker*. Harper-Collins, 2001.

- Evans, Eric. *Domain-Driven Design: Tackling Complexity in the Heart of Software*. Addison-Wesley, 2003.

- Fowler, Martin. *Refactoring: Improving the Design of Existing Code*. Addison-Wesley Professional, 1999.

- Fowler, Martin. Strangler Application. http://martinfowler.com/bliki/StranglerApplication.html.

- Gallup via Employee Engagement & Loyalty Statistics 2014 by B. Carter, Office Vibe "13 Disturbing Facts About Employee Engagement," November-2014.

- Gladwell, Malcolm. *The Tipping Point: How Little Things Can Make a Big Difference*. Little, Brown and Company, Kindle Edition.

- Gothelf, Jeff, and Josh Seiden. *Lean UX: Designing Great Products with Agile Teams*. O'Reilly Media, 2016.

- Greening, Dan. "Why Should Agilists Care about Capitalization?" *InfoQ*, January 29, 2013.

- Gregory, Janet, and Lisa Crispin. *More Agile Testing: Learning Journeys for the Whole Team*. Addison-Wesley, 2015.

- Heath, Chip, and Dan Heath. *Switch: How to Change Things When Change Is Hard*. Crown Publishing Group, Kindle Edition.

- Humble, Jez, and David Farley. *Continuous Delivery: Reliable Software Releases through Build, Test, and Deployment Automation*. Addison-Wesley, 2010.

- Iansiti, Marco. "Shooting the Rapids: Managing Product Development in Turbulent Environments." *California Management Review, 38*. 1995.

- Infographic "11 Eye-Opening Statistics on the Importance of Employee Feedback", Officevibe 2015 – Why Employee Performance Reviews Are So Old School, Millie Dent, The Fiscal Times, Jul-2015.

- International Council on Systems Engineering. "What Is Systems Engineering?" http://www.incose.org/AboutSE/WhatIsSE.

- Jemilo, Drew. *Agile Contracts: Blast Off to a Zone of Collaborative Systems Building*. Agile 2015. https://www.slideshare.net/JEMILOD/agile-contracts-by-drew-jemilo-agile2015.

- Kennedy, Michael. *Product Development for the Lean Enterprise*. Oaklea Press, 2003.

- Kim, Gene, Jez Humble, Patrick Debois, and John Willis. *The DevOps Handbook: How to Create World-Class Agility, Reliability, and Security in Technology Organizations*. IT Revolution Press, 2016.

- Kim, Gene, et al. *The Phoenix Project: A Novel about IT, DevOps, and Helping Your Business Win*. IT Revolution Press, 2013.

- Knaster, Richard, and Dean Leffingwell. *SAFe Distilled: Applying the Scaled Agile Framework for Lean Software and Systems Engineering*. Addison-Wesley, 2017.

- Kniberg, Henrik. *Lean from the Trenches: Managing Large-Scale Projects with Kanban*. Pragmatic Programmers, 2012.

- Kniberg, Henrik. *Scrum and XP from the Trenches*. lulu.com, 2015.

- Kotter, John P. *Accelerate: Building Strategic Agility for a Faster-Moving World*. 2014.

- Kotter, John P. *Leading Change*. Harvard Business Review Press, 1996.

- Kotter, John. *Leading Change*. Harvard Business Press, December 30, 2013.

- Labovitz, George H., and Victor Rosansky. *The Power of Alignment: How Great Companies Stay Centered and Accomplish Extraordinary Things*. Wiley, 1997.

- Larman, Craig, and Ahmad Fahmy. "How to Form Teams in Large-Scale Scrum? A Story of Self-Designing Teams." Scrum Alliance, April 5, 2013. https://www.scrumalliance.org/community/articles/2013/2013-april/how-to-form-teams-in-large-scale-scrum-a-story-of.

- Larman, Craig, and Bas Vodde. *Practices for Scaling Lean and Agile Development: Large, Multisite, and Offshore Product Development with Large-Scale Scrum*. Addison-Wesley, 2010.

- Leffingwell, Dean. *Agile Software Requirements: Lean Requirements Practices for Teams, Programs, and the Enterprise*. Addison-Wesley, 2011.

- Leffingwell, Dean. *Scaling Software Agility: Best Practices for Large Enterprises*. Addison-Wesley, 2007.

- Leffingwell, Dean, and Don Widrig. *Managing Software Requirements*. Addison-Wesley, 2001.

- Leffingwell, Dean, and Don Widrig. *Managing Software Requirements: A Use Case Approach* (2nd ed.). Addison-Wesley, 2003.

- Leith, Carson. "Co.Tribute: A Performance Review That Actually Means Something." March 2016.

- Lencioni, Patrick. *The Five Dysfunctions of a Team: A Leadership Fable*. Jossey-Bass, 2002.

- Liker, Jeffrey, and Thomas Y. Choi. "Building Deep Supplier Relationships." *Harvard Business Review*. December 2004.

- Liker, Jeffrey, and Gary L. Convis. *The Toyota Way to Lean Leadership: Achieving and Sustaining Excellence through Leadership Development*. McGraw-Hill, 2011.

- Linders, Ben. "Kickstart Agile the Kanban Way." *InfoQ*, October 2, 2014. http://www.infoq.com/news/2014/10/kickstart-agile-kanban.

- Mamoli, Sandy. *Creating Great Teams: How Self-Selection Lets People Excel*. Pragmatic Bookshelf. Kindle Edition.

- Mamoli, Sandy. "Large Scale Self-selection at Australia Post: Interview with Andy Kelk." March 4, 2015. https://www.linkedin.com/pulse/large-scale-self-selection-australia-post-interview-andy-sandy-mamoli.

- Martin, Karen, and Mike Osterling. *Value Stream Mapping*. McGraw-Hill, 2014.

- Martin, Robert. *Clean Code: A Handbook of Agile Software Craftsmanship*. Prentice Hall, 2008.

- Maurya, Ash. *Running Lean: Iterate from Plan A to a Plan That Works*. O'Reilly Media, 2012.

- Moore, Geoffrey. *Crossing the Chasm*. Harper Business Essentials, 1991, 2014.

- Moore, Geoffrey. *Escape Velocity*. Harper Business Essentials, 2011.

- Moore, Geoffrey. *Inside the Tornado*. Harper Business Essentials, 1995, 2004.

- Nokia New Recognition Framework. HR Tech World Congress, 2015.

- Oosterwal, Dantar P. *The Lean Machine: How Harley-Davidson Drove Top-Line Growth and Profitability with Revolutionary Lean Product Development*. Amacom, 2010.

- Pink, Daniel. *Drive: The Surprising Truth About What Motivates Us*. Riverhead Books, 2011.

- Poppendieck, Mary, and Tom Poppendieck. *Implementing Lean Software Development: From Concept to Cash*. Addison-Wesley, 2006.

- Pugh, Ken. *Lean-Agile Acceptance Test-Driven Development: Better Software Through Collaboration*. Addison-Wesley, 2011.

- Reed, Pat, and Walt Wyckoff. "Accounting for Capitalization of Agile Labor Costs." Agile Alliance, February 2016.

- Reinertsen, Donald G. *The Principles of Product Development Flow: Second Generation Lean Product Development*. Celeritas, 2009.

- Ries, Eric. *The Lean Startup: How Today's Entrepreneurs Use Continuous Innovation to Create Radically Successful Businesses*. Crown Business, 2011.

- Rother, Mike. *Toyota Kata: Managing People for Improvement, Adaptiveness, and Superior Results*. McGraw-Hill, 2009.

- Rubin, Ken. "Agile in a Hardware / Firmware Environment – Draw the Cost of Change Curve." Innolution. www.innolution.com/blog/agile-in-a-hardware-firmware-environment-draw-the-cost-of-change-curve.

- Shalloway, Alan, et al. *Essential Skills for the Agile Developer: A Guide to Better Programming and Design*. Addison-Wesley, 2011.

- SHRM Survey. "HR Professionals' Perceptions about PM Effectiveness." October 21, 2014.

- Sloan, Dan. "Is OpenSpace Agility a Fit For Your Agile Transformation?" November 1, 2015. https://www.linkedin.com/pulse/openspace-agility-right-you-daniel-sloan.

- Takeuchi, Hirotaka, and Ikurijo Nonaka. "The New New Product Development Game." *Harvard Business Review,* January 1986.

- Talent Management, "Discovery Education." May 2012.

- The Distance Consulting Company. *Community of Practice Start-Up Kit*. 2000.

- "Toyota Supplier CSR Guidelines." 2012. http://www.toyota-global.com/sustainability/society/partners/supplier_csr_en.pdf.

- Trompenaars, Fons, and Ed Voerman. *Servant-Leadership across Cultures: Harnessing the Strengths of the World's Most Powerful Management Philosophy*. McGraw-Hill, 2009.

- Wake, William. *Refactoring Workbook*. Addison-Wesley, 2003.

- Ward, Allen. *Lean Product and Process Development*. Lean Enterprise Institute, 2004.

- Ward, Allen, and Durward Sobeck. *Lean Product and Process Development*. Lean Enterprise Institute, 2014.

- Wenger, Etienne. *Communities of Practice: Learning, Meaning, and Identity.* Cambridge University Press, 1999.

- Womack, Jim. *Gemba Walks: Expanded 2nd Edition*. Lean Enterprise Institute.

- Womack, James P., Daniel T. Jones, and Daniel Roos. *The Machine That Changed the World: The Story of Lean Production—Toyota's Secret Weapon in the Global Car Wars That Is Revolutionizing World Industry.* Free Press, 2007.

- Yeret, Yuval. "Yuval Yeret on Using Kanban for Agile Adoption." *InfoQ*, January 12. 2015. http://www.infoq.com/interviews/lkfr14-yeret-kanban-agile.

Other Resources

- 2015 State of DevOps Report: https://puppet.com/resources/whitepaper/2015-state-devops-report?link=blog.

- "Achieving Regulatory and Industry Standards Compliance with SAFe" [Webinar]: https://www.youtube.com/watch?v=-7rVOWTHZEw&feature=youtu.be.

- "Achieving Regulatory and Industry Standards Compliance with SAFe" [White paper]. http://scaledagileframework.com/achieving-regulatory-and-industry-standards-compliance-with-safe/.

- "Adventures in Scaling Agile": www.prettyagile.com/2017/01/facilitating-team-self-selection-safe-art.html.

- Agile Retrospective Resource Wiki: www.retrospectivewiki.org.

- Agile Sparks: http://www.agilesparks.com/safe-implementation-strategy-leadership-focusing-workshop/.

- Ambler, Scott. "Agile Architecture: Strategies for Scaling Agile Development." Agile Modeling, 2012. http://agilemodeling.com/essays/agileArchitecture.htm.

- "Continuous Delivery": https://www.youtube.com/watch?v=VOjPpeBh40s.

- Extreme Programming: www.extremeprogramming.org/rules/collective.html.

- FASB 86 summary: fasb.org/summary/stsum86.shtml.

- Fun Retrospectives: www.funretrospectives.com.

- George E. P. Box quote: http://www.goodreads.com/quotes/680161-essentially-all-models-are-wrong-but-some-are-useful.

- Innovation Games: http://www.innovationgames.com.

- Lean Budgets (white paper by Rami Sirkia and Maarit Laanti): http://pearson.scaledagileframework.com/original-whitepaper-lean-agile-financial-planning-with-safe/.

- Lean Enterprise Institute: https://www.lean.org/Workshops/WorkshopDescription.cfm?WorkshopId=20.

- Management 3.0: https://management30.com/practice/delegation-board/.

- Manifesto for Agile Software Development: http://agilemanifesto.org/.

- "Non-functional Requirement": https://en.wikipedia.org/wiki/Non-functional_requirement.

- OpenSpace Agility: http://openspaceagility.com/big-picture/.

- Scaled Agile, Inc.: http://scaledagileframework.com/about.

- Scrum Alliance: https://www.scrumalliance.org/.

- Scrum Guides (Jeff Sutherland and Ken Schwaber): http://scrumguides.org/.

- "Servant Leadership": http://en.wikipedia.org/wiki/Servant_leadership.

- TastyCupcakes.org: http://tastycupcakes.org/tag/retrospective/.

- "T-Shaped Skill": https://en.wikipedia.org/wiki/T-shaped_skill.

- Yuval Yeret on Lean/Agile/Flow: http://yuvalyeret.com.

Index

team size, 268

velocity, 266

ARTs (Agile Release Trains), preparing for launch

assessing launch readiness, 94

component teams, 92

defining the ART, 90–91

establishing a cadence, 91

evolving launch readiness, 94

features teams, 92

first planning session, 103

organizing Agile Teams, 92

PDCA (Plan-Do-Check-Adjust) cycle, 94

preparing the Program Backlog, 96–97

Quickstart approach, 102–103

readiness checklist, 95–96

setting launch date, 91

setting program calendar, 91

summary of activities, 89. *See also specific activities.*

training, 91–92

Assuming variability (SAFe Principle #3)

description, 37, 145

preserving options, 145

SBCE (Set-Based Concurrent Engineering), 145–146

SBD (Set-Based Design), 145–146

ATDD (Acceptance Test-Driven Development). *See also* Test-First.

acceptance test-driven development, 730–732

acceptance testing template/checklist, 732

automating acceptance testing, 731–732

Built-In Quality, 198

functional tests, 731

PO (Product Owner), 188

template/checklist, 732

Automated testing

acceptance testing, 421, 422–423, 430, 731–732

Iteration Execution, 237

System Team, 489

testing, 421, 422–423, 430

Automating

CD (Continuous Deployment), 430–431

deployment, 430

DevOps build, 402

everything in DevOps, 399–400

Autonomy, motivating knowledge workers, 164–165

B

Backlog refinement

Team Level, 175

WSJF (Weighted Shortest Job First) prioritization, 299

Backlogs. *See also* Enterprise backlogs; Portfolio Backlog; Program Backlog; Solution Backlog; Team Backlog.

improving, 390

Little's law, 301

NFRs as constraints, 319

prioritizing. *See* Backlog refinement.

Program Level, 263

queues, 301–303

tracking with Program Kanban, 393

wait time, 301–303

Banking institution, Value Stream example, 74–76, 81

Batch sizes, reducing. *See* Reducing, batch sizes (SAFe Principle #6).

BDUF (Big Design Upfront) approach, 293–294

Benefit hypotheses, 306–307, 452

Beyond Entrepreneurship, 582

Big Picture

alignment, 21

Built-In Quality, 21

Core Values, 21

Essential SAFe, 2–4

Full SAFe, 8

Large Solution SAFe, 6

Portfolio SAFe, 5

program execution, 21

Roadmap, 40

SAFe foundation, 10

SAFe House of Lean, 28

transparency, 21

website, 1

Books and publications. *See also* Classes and workshops.

Agile Software Requirements, 215

Agile Software Requirements: Lean Requirements Practices for Teams, Programs, and the Enterprise, 446

Waterfall development. *See* Phase-gate (waterfall) development.

Weighted Shortest Job First (WSJF). *See* WSJF (Weighted Shortest Job First).

WIP (work in progress), managing
DevOps, 402–403
Iteration Execution, 236
managing (SAFe Principle #6), 38
PI (Program Increment) Objectives, 378
Team Kanban, 254–255
visualizing and limiting (SAFe Principle #6), 155–156. *See also* Kanban.

Workshops. *See* Classes and workshops.

WSJF (Weighted Shortest Job First)
backlog refinement, 299
calculating, 327–328
Cost of Delay, 326
definition, 325, 748
formula for, 281, 299
job duration, 327
job size as proxy for duration, 328
prioritization, 596
Program Backlog, 297
Solution Backlog, 297

Credits

Chapter/Section	Selection Description	Attribution
01-01	"It's not enough that management commit themselves to quality and productivity, they must know what it is they must do. Such a responsibility cannot be delegated"	W. Edwards Deming
01-02	"Find people who share your values, and you'll conquer the world together."	John Ratzenberger
01-02	"Inspection does not improve the quality, nor guarantee quality. Inspection is too late. The quality, good or bad, is already in the product. Quality cannot be inspected into a product or service; it must be built into it."	W. Edwards Deming
01-02	"Continuous attention to technical excellence and good design enhances agility"	http://AgileManifesto.org
01-03	Values of the Agile Manifesto	Manifesto for Agile Software Development. http://agilemanifesto.org/
01-03	Principles of the Agile Manifesto	Manifesto for Agile Software Development. http://agilemanifesto.org/
01-04	"The impression that 'our problems are different' is a common disease that afflicts management the world over. They are different, to be sure, but the principles that will help to improve the quality of product and service are universal in nature."	W. Edwards Deming
01-05	Many leaders pride themselves on setting the high-level direction … you need to script the critical moves.	Dan and Chip Heath, Switch: How to Change Things When Change Is Hard
01-06	"The people who are crazy enough to think they can change the world are the ones who do."	Steve Jobs
01-06	"sufficiently powerful guiding coalition"	John P. Kotter. Leading Change. Harvard Business Review Press, 1996.
02-01	"While you may ignore economics, it won't ignore you."	Reinertsen, Donald. The Principles of Product Development Flow: Second Generation Lean Product Development. Celeritas Publishing, 2009.
02-02	A system must be managed. It will not manage itself. Left to themselves, components become selfish, competitive, independent profit centers, and thus destroy the system. The secret is cooperation between components toward the aim of the organization.	Deming, W. Edwards. The New Economics. MIT Press, 1994.
02-02	Everyone is already doing their best; the problems are with the system … only management can change the system.	Deming, W. Edwards. The New Economics. MIT Press, 1994.
02-03	Generate alternative system-level designs and subsystem concepts. Rather than try to pick an early winner, aggressively eliminate alternatives. The designs that survive are your most robust alternatives.	Ward, Allan C. and Durward Sobek. Lean Product and Process Development. Lean Enterprise Institute Inc., 2014.
02-04	The epiphany of integration points is that they control product development and are the leverage points to improve the system. When timing of integration points slips, the project is in trouble.	Oosterwal, Dantar P. The Lean Machine: How Harley-Davidson Drove Top-Line Growth and Profitability with Revolutionary Lean Product Development. Amacom, 2010.

02-05	There was in fact no correlation between exiting phase gates on time and project success...the data suggested the inverse might be true.	Oosterwal, Dantar P. The Lean Machine: How Harley-Davidson Drove Top-Line Growth and Profitability with Revolutionary Lean Product Development. Amacom, 2010.
02-06	Operating a product development process near full utilization is an economic disaster.	Reinertsen, Donald. The Principles of Product Development Flow: Second Generation Lean Product Development. Celeritas Publishing, 2009.
02-07	"Cadence and synchronization limit the accumulation of variance."	Reinertsen, Donald. The Principles of Product Development Flow: Second Generation Lean Product Development. Celeritas Publishing, 2009.
02-08	It appears that the performance of the task provides its own intrinsic reward...this drive...may be as basic as the others...	Pink, Daniel. Drive: The Surprising Truth About What Motivates Us. Riverhead Books, 2011.
02-08	"Knowledge workers are individuals who know more about the work that they perform than their bosses".	Drucker, Peter F. The Essential Drucker. Harper-Collins, 2001.
02-08	Many organizations still operate from assumptions about human potential and individual performance that are outdated, rooted more in folklore than in science. They continue to pursue practices such as short-term incentive plans and pay-for-performance schemes in the face of mounting evidence that such measures usually don't work and often do harm.	Pink, Daniel. Drive: The Surprising Truth About What Motivates Us. Riverhead Books, 2011.
02-08	"To effectively lead, the workers must be heard and respected"	Drucker, Peter F. The Essential Drucker. Harper-Collins, 2001.
02-09	"Knowledge workers themselves are best placed to make decisions about how to perform their work."	Peter F. Drucker
03-01	The success of any kind of social epidemic is heavily dependent on the involvement of people with a particular and rare set of social skills	Gladwell, Malcolm. The Tipping Point: How Little Things Can Make a Big Difference. Little, Brown and Company, Kindle Edition
03-01	"vision for change"	Kotter, John P. Leading Change. Harvard Business Review Press, Kindle Edition.
03-02	A strong guiding coalition is always needed. One with the right composition, level of trust, and shared objective.	Kotter, John P. Leading Change. Harvard Business Review Press, Kindle Edition.
03-02	i. Establishing a sense of urgency ... new approaches in the culture	Kotter, John P. Leading Change. Harvard Business Review Press, Kindle Edition.
03-02	"In a rapidly moving world, individuals ... effective under these circumstances."	Kotter, John P. Leading Change. Harvard Business Review Press, Kindle Edition.
03-03	The questions is 'Does the group include enough proven leaders to be able to drive the change process?'	Kotter, John P. Leading Change. Harvard Business Review Press, Kindle Edition.
03-03	"The moment you stop learning is also the one in which you will stop leading."	Bill Gates
03-03	"It is not enough that management commit themselves to quality and productivity, they must know what it is they must do."	William Edwards Deming
03-04	A guiding coalition that operates as an effective team can process more information, more quickly. It can also speed the implementation of new approaches because powerful people are truly informed and committed to key decisions	Kotter, John P. Leading Change. Harvard Business Review Press, Kindle Edition.
03-04	"The size of an effective coalition seems ... or in small units of larger firms."	Kotter, John P. Leading Change. Harvard Business Review Press, Kindle Edition.

03-05	Break down barriers between departments.	William Edwards Deming,Out of the Crisis. Cambridge University Press, (1986)
03-06	The more detailed we made our plans, the longer our cycle times became.	Don Reinertsen,The principles of product development flow: second generation(2009)
03-07	Short-term wins help build necessary momentum.	Kotter, John P. Leading Change. Harvard Business Review Press, Kindle Edition.
03-08	We often don't think through carefully enough what new behavior, skills, and attitudes will be needed when major changes are initiated. As a result, we don't recognize the kind and amount of training that will be required to help people learn those new be	William Edwards Deming,Out of the Crisis. Cambridge University Press, (1986)
03-08	"shape the path"	Heath, Chip and Dan Heath. Switch: How to Change Things When Change Is Hard. Crown Publishing Group, Kindle Edition.
03-09	Whenever you let up before the job is done, critical momentum can be lost and regression may follow.	Kotter, John P. Leading Change. Harvard Business Review Press, Kindle Edition.
03-10	Consolidate gains and produce more change	Kotter, John P. Leading Change. Harvard Business Review Press, Kindle Edition.
03-10	"shape the path"	How to Change Things When Change Is Hard
03-11	Anchor new approaches in the culture	Kotter, John P. Leading Change. Harvard Business Review Press, Kindle Edition.
03-12	Excellent firms don't believe in excellence—only in constant improvement and constant change.	Tom Peter
03-12	There is constant sense of danger	Koki Konishi-Toyota
03-12	"What's measured improves."	Peter Drucker
04-04	"Business people … throughout the project"	Agile Manifesto
04-05	Good leaders must first become good servants.	Robert K. Greenleaf
04-06	Inspection does not … be built into it."	W. Edwards Deming
04-06	"Continuous attention … design enhances agility."	Manifesto for Agile Software Development. www.AgileManifesto.org
04-06	"disciplined technique for … its external behavior."	Martin Fowler, Refactoring: Improving the Design of Existing Code, Addison-Wesley Professional, 1999.
04-06	"Any developer can … improve designs, or refactor."	Don Wells
04-07	a holistic or 'rugby' approach... today's competitive requirements.	Nonaka and Takeuchi, "The New New Product Development Game"
04-07	Scrum Master, Product Owner (PO), and Development Team	Sutherland, Jeff and Ken Schwaber. Scrumguides.org.
04-08	Stories act as … work together effectively	Bill Wake, co-inventor of Extreme Programming
04-08	The 3Cs: Card, Conversation, Confirmation	Ron Jeffries, one of the inventors of XP, is credited with describing the 3Cs
04-09	"None of my inventions... trial until it comes"	Thomas Alva Edison
04-10	Stay committed to your decisions, but stay flexible in your approach.	Tom Robbins

04-11	Clarity adorns profound thoughts.	Luc de Clapiers
04-12	Vision without execution is hallucination	Thomas Alva Edison
04-14	At regular intervals, the team reflects … adjusts its behavior accordingly.	Agile Manifesto
04-16	"The only way … having excess manpower"	Goldratt, E. M., Cox, J., & Goldratt, E. M. (2016). The goal: A process of ongoing improvement.
05-01	"A system must be managed…aim of the organization"	W. Edwards Deming
05-02	The more alignment … the one enables the other.	Stephen Bungay
05-03	"It is hard to imagine a more stupid … people who pay no price for being wrong."	Thomas Sowell
05-05	"It is a misuse of our… belong to others"	Peter Block
05-06	"Engineering is a great profession. … This is the engineer's high privilege"	Herbert Hoover
05-06	"an interdisciplinary approach and … meets the user needs."	International Council on Systems Engineering. "What Is Systems Engineering?" http://www.incose.org/AboutSE/WhatIsSE
05-07	The emphasis should be on why we do a job.	W. Edwards Deming
05-08	There's innovation in Linux. There are some really good technical features that I'm proud of. There are capabilities in Linux that aren't in other operating systems.	Linus Torvalds
05-09	Luck is what happens when preparation meets opportunity.	Seneca
05-10	"[4]: • Using virtualized hardware… Creating similar environments"	Larman, Craig and Bas Vodde. Practices for Scaling Lean & Agile Development: Large, Multisite, and Offshore Product Development with Large-Scale Scrum. Addison-Wesley, 2010.
05-11	If you only quantify one thing, quantify the Cost of Delay.	Don Reinertsen
05-11	impact of correctly applying WSJF	Reinertsen, Don. Principles of Product Development Flow: Second Generation Lean Product Development. Celeritas Publishing, 2009
05-12	Doing is a quantum leap from imagining.	Barbara Sher
05-12	"integration points control product development"	Barbara Sher
05-13	Inertia is the residue of past innovation efforts. Left unmanaged, it consumes the resources required to fund next-generation innovation	Geoffrey Moore
05-13	"100 percent utilization drives unpredictable results"	Don Reinertsen
05-14	Control flow under uncertainty	Don Reinertsen
05-14	SAFe Practices	Reinertsen, Don. Principles of Product Development Flow: Second Generation Lean Product Development. Celeritas Publishing, 2009.
05-16	While we must acknowledge emergence in design and system development, a little planning can avoid much waste	James Coplien and Gertrud Bjørnvig, Lean Architecture: for Agile Software Development
05-16	"the best architectures, requirements, and designs emerge from self-organizing teams."	Jim Highsmith

05-17	"Future product development … . and react to the end results."	Michael Kennedy
05-17	"The most efficient and effective method of conveying information to and within a development team is a face-to-face conversation."	Jim Highsmith
05-18	"Making and meeting small commitments ... with its own intentions"	Nonaka
05-20	"Kaizen is about changing the ... kaizen. So change something!"	Taiichi Ohno
05-20	"a problem well stated is a problem half solved."	American inventor Charles Kettering
05-20	"At regular intervals, the team reflects on how to become more effective, then tunes and adjusts its behavior accordingly."	Jim Highsmith
05-21	"It is said that improvement is eternal ... become fixed at any stage."	Taiichi Ohno
05-22	Imagine a world where product ... reliability, availability, and security.	The DevOps Handbook
05-22	"high-performing IT organizations deploy 30x more frequently with 200x shorter lead times. ... 60x fewer failures and recover 168x faster."	Kim, Gene and Jez Humble, Patrick Debois, John Willis. The DevOps Handbook: How to Create World-Class Agility, Reliability, and Security in Technology Organizations. IT Revolution Press
05-23	Our highest priority is to satisfy the customer through early and continuous delivery of valuable software.	Jim Highsmith
05-24	Specifically, you can take the time ... year's operating plan.	Geoffrey Moore, Escape Velocity
05-25	"The epiphany of integration points is that they control product development. They are the leverage points to improve the system. When timing of integration points slip, the project is in trouble"	Oosterwal, Dantar P. The Lean Machine: How Harley-Davidson Drove Top-Line Growth and Profitability with Revolutionary Lean Product Development. Kindle Edition.
05-25	"integration points control product development."	Oosterwal, Dantar P. The Lean Machine: How Harley-Davidson Drove Top-Line Growth and Profitability with Revolutionary Lean Product Development. Kindle Edition.
05-26	In order for you to...entirely on demand.	Kim, Gene, et al. The Phoenix Project: A Novel About IT, DevOps, and Helping Your Business Win. IT Revolution Press, 2013.
06-01	"The most important things.. measured in advance"	W. Edwards Deming
06-01	"Working software is the primary measure of progress"	Agile Manifesto
06-02	"A specialist is .. less and less"	William J. Mayo
06-03	"It's said that ... from others' successes"	Zen proverb adapted by John C. Maxwell
06-03	"Domain – An area..regular interactions"	Wenger, Etienne. Communities of Practice: Learning, Meaning, and Identity. Cambridge University Press, 1999.
06-05	"Prediction is very difficult, especially if it is about the future"	Niels Bohr
06-05	"Responding to change over following a plan"	Agile Manifesto
06-06	"People at work .. to a larger whole"	Daniel Pink
06-07	"The whole is greater than the sum of its parts"	Aristotle
06-08	"What if we... and on budget?"	Eric Ries
06-08	"Lean UX literally has ..of the process."	Gothelf, Jeff and Josh Seiden. Lean UX: Designing Great Products with Agile Teams. O'Reilly Media. 2016.

07-01	Everything must be made as simple as possible. But not simpler.	Albert Einstein
07-02	Principle of Alignment: There is more value created with overall alignment than with local excellence	Don Reinertsen
07-03	Even when they don't yet know it … you many such examples.	Jeff Bezos
07-04	A long-term relationship between purchaser and supplier is necessary for best economy	W. Edwards Deming
07-04	Contracts governing … and nonbinding targets	Aoki, Katsuki and Thomas Taro Lennerfors. "New, Improved Keiretsu." Harvard Business Review. September 2013
07-04	At the Toyota Technical Center … same project	Liker, Jeffrey and Thomas Y. Choi. "Building Deep Supplier Relationships." Harvard Business Review. December 2004
07-04	Honda tells the suppliers … . coming years	Liker, Jeffrey and Thomas Y. Choi. "Building Deep Supplier Relationships." Harvard Business Review. December 2004
07-04	Toyota uses the term genchi genbutsu or gemba …how suppliers work	Liker, Jeffrey and Thomas Y. Choi. "Building Deep Supplier Relationships." Harvard Business Review. December 2004
07-04	Automobile manufacturing … matters of importance	Toyota Supplier CSR Guidelines." 2012. http://www.toyota-global.com/sustainability/society/partners/supplier_csr_en.pdf
07-04	While other automakers …cost savings with Honda	Liker, Jeffrey and Thomas Y. Choi. "Building Deep Supplier Relationships." Harvard Business Review. December 2004
07-04	There is a bear trap … ..will double the cost of the items	Deming, W. Edwards. Out of the Crisis. MIT Center for Advanced Educational Services. 1982
07-07	The objective of the … . with the objective to physically demonstrate it	Oosterwal, Dantar P. The Lean Machine: How Harley-Davidson Drove Top-Line Growth and Profitability with Revolutionary Lean Product Development. Amacom, 2010
07-08	Click. Boom. Amazing!	Steve Jobs
07-09	Context is the key—from that comes the understanding of everything	Kenneth Noland
07-10	working software over comprehensive documentation	Agile Manifesto
07-10	Favoring models over documents … . contractual obligations.	Ambler, Scott.
07-10	Quality begins with the intent	W. Edwards Deming
07-11	Trust, but verify	Ronald Reagan
07-11	Inspection is too late. The quality good, or bad, is already in the product	William Edwards Deming
07-12	All models are wrong, but some are useful	George E. P. Box
08-01	To succeed in the long term, focus on the middle term	Geoffrey Moore
08-10	Innovation comes from the producer, not the customer	W. Edwards Deming
08-11	I urge everyone—no matter … .given before acting	Suze Orman
08-12	All it takes to play baseball.... That's it	Ryne Sandberg
08-02	A strategic inflection point … make a radical shift or die.	Andy Grove, Only the Paranoid Survive

08-04	Innovation distinguishes between a leader and a follower	Steve Jobs
08-05	Agile software development and traditional cost accounting don't match	Rami Sirkia and Maarit Laanti
08-06	What if we found ourselves... .and on budget?	Eric Ries
08-07	To be in hell is to drift; to be in heaven is to steer	George Bernard Shaw
08-08	All men can see these tactics ... ..victory is evolved	Sun Tzu
08-09	Most strategy dialogues ... . on issues this abstract.	Geoffrey Moore, Escape Velocity
08-09	By documenting the current ...never-ending process	Lean Enterprise Institute
09-01	"While we must acknowledge emergence in design and system development, a little planning can avoid much waste"	Coplien, James and Gertrud Bjørnvig. Lean Architecture for Agile Software Development. Wiley and Sons, 2010.
09-01	"The best architectures, requirements, and designs emerge from self-organizing teams"	Jim Highsmith
09-01	"We welcome changing requirements even late in development"	Jim Highsmith
09-01	"If simplicity is good, we'll always leave the system with the simplest design that supports its current functionality."	Beck, Kent. Extreme Programming Explained: Embrace Change. Addison-Wesley, 2000.
09-02	"select a winning contractor and then expect them to deliver on the requirements within the specified time frame and budget. However, this traditional approach almost always led to failures— each a spectacular waste of taxpayer dollars".	Forbesindia.com
09-03	"To win in the marketplace you must first win in the workplace"	Doug Conant, American businessman and former CEO, Campbell Soup Company
09-03	"as people who know more about the work they perform than their bosses."	Peter drucker
09-03	Employee Appraisals	Adapted from Nokia New Recognition Framework, HR Tech World Congress 2015
09-03	Examples of role-based career paths	Just Leading Solutions, 2016
09-03	Interview Questions	Just Leading Solutions, 2016
09-05	"It does not happen all at once. There is no instant pudding."	W. Edwards Deming
09-06	Simplicity — the art of maximizing the amount of work not done — is essential.	Jim Highsmith
09-07	Innovation comes from the producer, not the customer.	W. Edwards Deming
09-08	"Build projects around motivated individuals. Give them the environment and support they need, and trust them to get the job done." And "The best architectures, requirements, and designs emerge from self-organizing teams."	Jim Highsmith
09-08	"Imposing an agile process from the outside, strips the team of the self-determination, which is at the heart of agile thinking."	Martin Fowler
09-09	You just have to have the guidance to lead you in the direction until you can do it yourself. It is the neglect of timely repair that makes rebuilding necessary	Richard Whately
09-10	Essentially, all models are wrong, but some are useful.	George E. P. Box
09-11	"one percent inspiration and 99 percent perspiration."	Thomas Alva Edison
09-12	If we knew what we were doing, it wouldn't be called research.	Albert Einstein
09-13	We never have enough time for testing, so let's just write the test first	Beck, Kent. Test-Driven Development. Addison-Wesley, 2003.